OLIVIER

BY THE SAME AUTHOR

NON-FICTION

The Railway Navvies: a history of the men who made the railways
Providence & Mr Hardy (with Lois Deacon)
Passage to America: a history of emigration from Great Britain and Ireland
The Liners: a history of the North Atlantic crossing
Thatcher's Britain: a journey through the promised lands
Nelson: the man and the legend

FICTION

A Girl for the Afternoons
Southern Cross: a novel of early Australia
Thanksgiving: a novel in praise of America
Empire: a novel of the Texas Republic

COLLECTED JOURNALISM

The Only True History
The Scented Brawl
Movers & Shakers: collected interviews

AS EDITOR

An Indiscretion in the Life of an Heiress: Hardy's unpublished first novel

OLIVIER
The Authorised Biography

TERRY COLEMAN

BLOOMSBURY

First published 2005

Copyright © 2005 by Terry Coleman

The moral right of the author
has been asserted

Bloomsbury Publishing Plc, 36 Soho Square,
London W1D 3QY

A CIP catalogue record for this book
is available from the British Library

Hardback ISBN 0 7475 7798 6
Hardback ISBN-13 97807475 77980
10 9 8 7 6 5 4 3 2 1

Trade paperback ISBN 0 7475 8350 1
Trade paperback ISBN-13 97807475 83509
10 9 8 7 6 5 4 3 2 1

Export paperback ISBN 0 7475 8306 4
Export paperback ISBN-13 97807475 83066
10 9 8 7 6 5 4 3 2 1

Typeset in Bell MT by Palimpsest Book Production Ltd,
Polmont, Stirlingshire
Printed by Clays Ltd, St Ives plc

The paper this book is printed on is certified by the © Forest Stewardship Council 1996
A.C. (FSC). FSC products with percentage claims meet environmental requirements to be
ancient forest friendly. The printer holds FSC chain of custody SGS-COC-2061.

FSC
Mixed Sources
Product group from well-managed
forests and other controlled sources
Cert no. SGS-COC-2061
www.fsc.org
© 1996 Forest Stewardship Council

www.bloomsbury.com/terrycoleman

For VIVIEN
and for Eliza and Jack, learned friends

CONTENTS

ACKNOWLEDGEMENTS

I owe great debts to many people, without whom this book could not have been written, and whose generosity with their help was extraordinary. First to the family, to Dame Joan Plowright (Lady Olivier) and to the Hon. Richard Olivier, for allowing access to the archive in the British Library and to other papers in their own possession, for giving long interviews, for permission to quote from their own books, and for their most kind help in other ways. Also to the Hon. Tamsin Olivier, the Hon. Julie-Kate Olivier, and David Plowright, CBE. Then to Suzanne Farrington, for her kindness in allowing me to explore the splendid and unexpectedly rich collection of the papers of Vivien Leigh, her mother. And to Hester St John-Ives, the widow of Olivier's brother Dickie, for ready help with family papers, and for helping me to a better understanding of the last years together of Olivier and Vivien Leigh.

Then to Olivier's executors and friends of many years, G. Laurence Harbottle and Peter Hiley, for their deep knowledge, priceless guidance, and generous advice. They knew Olivier, in many ways, better than anyone else now does, and could not have been more helpful.

Hugo Vickers, whose impeccably researched biography of Vivien Leigh is by a mile the best study of the woman who obsessed Olivier for twenty years, magnanimously placed at my disposal the transcripts of many interviews he made in the late 1980s with men and women since dead, and suggested other lines of inquiry. Mark Amory, Olivier's collaborator in his autobiography, *The Confessions of An Actor*, searched for and let me have transcripts of his many hours of conversation with Olivier in 1980–81. Gawn Grainger, Olivier's young colleague who ghosted his second book, *On Acting*, gave me his recollections of that and of his other times with Olivier.

I am also grateful to the following persons and institutions: Kathryn Johnson, curator of the Modern Theatre Archives at the

British Library, who produced for me anything I asked for from the vast Olivier archive while it was still in the process of being catalogued. Richard Mangan, administrator of the Mander & Mitchenson Theatre Collection at Greenwich and editor of John Gielgud's letters, for frequent kindnesses. Kathy Beilby, of Harbottle & Lewis, London, who gave me plentiful copies from that firm's archives. Sophie Bridges, curator of the Churchill Archives Centre at Churchill College, Cambridge, for showing me the Olivier papers in the Chandos archive there. Eliza Louizeau-Hutchinson, for copies of Olivier's letters to her mother, Dame Peggy Ashcroft. The Hyman Kreitman research Centre at the Tate Gallery, London, for Kenneth Clark's correspondence with Olivier and Lord Chandos. Sir John Mills. Sir Peter Hall. Sir Michael Gambon. Sir Richard Eyre. Michael Blakemore. Sarah Bolt, for long conversations and allowing me to quote from her memoirs. Kent Barker, son of Felix Barker, for showing me his father's notes and collection of photographs, and generously allowing me to use some. Christopher Fry. Pieter Rogers. Michael Korda. Trader Faulkner. John and Suzanne Goodwin. Lyn Haill. Mr and Mrs Allan D. Woods of Rowayton, Connecticut, for showing me Sneden's Landing and many other kindnesses. Lynne Kirwin. Deborah Granville. Sofka Zinovieff. Sheridan Morley. John Lahr. Sir Tom Stoppard, OM. Matthew Tynan and Tracy Tynan, for permission to quote from their father Kenneth Tynan's letters and diaries respectively. Stephen Fay. The Rev. Canon Peter Burch. Mrs Danny, formerly of Notley. Denise Silvester-Carr. Gavin Clark, archivist of the Royal National Theatre. Dr Christopher Rawll, archivist, All Saints, Margaret Street. The London Library. Stewart Darby and Kathryn de Belle, of Granada Television. The Theatre Museum, London. Kate Hughes, curatorial officer, The National Archives: Historical Manuscripts Commission. The New York Public Library. The Museum of Television and Radio, New York. The New Haven Public Library, Connecticut. The Hartford Public Library, Connecticut, Hartford Collection. The library at Sneden's Landing, New York. The Very Rev. Michael Mayne, KCVO, formerly Dean of Westminster. David Christie, Warden of St Edward's School, Oxford; Karen Garvey, school archivist; and Tricia Cook. The late Rev. Stephan Hopkinson and his daughter, Selina Thistleton-Smith. Dr

Michael Stansfield of Durham University Library. Julian Reid, Merton College, Oxford. The letters from John Gielgud to Laurence Olivier and Joan Plowright are quoted by kind permission of the Executors of the John Gielgud Charitable Trust. Extracts from the Noël Coward Diaries and from Noël Coward's letters to Laurence Olivier are published by kind permission of NC Aventales AG, copyright agent Alan Brodie Representation Ltd, Fairgate House, 78 New Oxford Street, London WC1A 1HB, info@alanbrodie.com.

I thank Caroline Dawnay, sweet woman, of Peters, Fraser & Dunlop, without whom I should never have written this book. The idea was hers, over lunch, out of the blue. And I thank Michael Sissons in London and Peter Matson in New York, who negotiated the deal. And Maria Dawson for tactful advice in time of need. At Bloomsbury, I thank my editor, Rosemary Davidson, Mary Tomlinson, and Mary Davis.

This book is based firmly on the papers of Laurence Olivier, of course assisted by the recollections of those who knew him. I ought perhaps to indicate the limits of my own slight acquaintance with Olivier. I knew him as a journalist knows the director of the National Theatre. From the mid-1960s, when I was for some years arts correspondent of the *Guardian*, I saw his stage performances and met him regularly, sometimes formally and sometimes informally. This gave me some small understanding of the man. Once, when by chance I arrived early and unnoticed for a press conference at the workmens' huts which were then the offices of the National Theatre, I discovered him pacing up and down rehearsing the spontaneous off-the-cuff remarks which he would deliver half an hour later to the assembled reporters; so I know that little he ever did was unrehearsed. On another occasion, after I had known him for some years, I covered a trial at which he gave evidence in support of the English Stage Company at the Royal Court Theatre, when it was prosecuted for staging a play which the Director of Public Prosecutions considered indecent. I looked for him in court but did not see him. When, after an hour or so, he was called to give evidence, one of the solicitors sitting at the side of the court rose and went to the witness box; so I had firsthand evidence of his astounding ability to make himself invisible. He told me, as he must have told many others, that he feared dying and leaving his young family penniless. He spoke with eloquence about his early days in Hollywood and about planting trees and flowers. He told me an anecdote about girls pleasuring themselves with the fruit of medlars, so I knew his penchant for such tales. I was at the royal opening of the new National Theatre in 1976 and heard his speech, and therefore know as a truth that it was magical, and that he had the gift of magic. I last saw him at the National's gala performance of *Happy Birthday, Sir Larry*, when he was eighty.

LIST OF ILLUSTRATIONS

FIGURES IN THE TEXT

PICTURE CREDITS

1

As the Olive Tree Flourishes

LAURENCE OLIVIER WAS THE greatest English actor and man of
the theatre of the twentieth century, and he was this because of his
devouring will, and his magic, and his genius. But genius was a
word he deeply disliked and distrusted. He said so again and again.
He thought genius was too unreal, and that the theatre was for the
practicable, 'with no room for flashes of genius or anything like
that'. Early in his career, in 1933, Garbo rejected him as her leading
man. He remembered this and tried to make light of it all his life.
In spite of her rejection of him, or perhaps because of it, he retained
the greatest respect for her which he expressed by saying she was
'a master of her trade'. He intended this as the highest compliment.
Later on, in 1951 when he was near the height of his powers and
directing *A Streetcar Named Desire*, which his entire instinct told
him to cut but which the playwright did not wish to see cut, he
told a friend that he wished that 'real geniuses' like Tennessee
Williams would listen to 'practical old craftsmen'.[1] Olivier was
calling himself the craftsman. This suits his name well. This great
man of the English theatre and cinema was, by descent, in large
part French. Olivier may sound an exotic name – American audiences of the 1930s were told by studio publicists how to pronounce
it: 'O-live-ee-ay' – but in French it means olive tree or, by extension, a man who tends olive trees. It is a trade name. The English
would be Oliver.

Famous men attract genealogists. The Thomas Arundell Society, which exists to celebrate the lineage of Arundell, an English soldier of fortune who in 1595 was created a count of the Holy Roman Empire for services against the Turks, announced on the world wide web in 1997 that Olivier was descended from Arundell through the barons Baltimore and Charlotte Fitzroy, a natural daughter of Charles II. For Olivier to have had royal blood in his veins would have been good box office, but a necessary link was one Emma Park, who flourished about 1827. The whole chain fell apart when other genealogists showed that she was not Olivier's grandmother at all, but merely the wife of a great uncle.[2]

The Oliviers themselves have traced their descent back to 1520, but this invites caution. Few families, unless they are royal or noble, can convincingly show a line which goes further back than the eighteenth century. When Margaret Thatcher became prime minister in 1979, and the best genealogists in England put their minds to exploring her heritage, they could not get further back than 1750. So what we have is the Olivier family tradition, and this says that they come from the village of Nay, south of Pau in the furthest south-western part of France, a few miles from Spain across the Pyrenees, and that they were Huguenots, Protestants in a Catholic country. The earliest surmised Olivier is Laurent, born 1520 at Nay, and the family stayed in that region for three generations until Louis XIV, in 1685, forced the Huguenots to abjure their Protestantism or emigrate. One Huguenot pastor who emigrated, to the Netherlands, was Jerome Olivier. Some of this family tradition is not old at all but seems to date from as late as 1947, when Laurence Olivier was knighted and the interest in genealogy was stirred. It was then that the family motto, though probably an old one, was resurrected. It is SICUT OLIVA VIRENS LAETOR IN AEDE DEI: 'As the Olive Tree Flourishes I Rejoice in the House of God.' It was then too that the tradition was discovered that the Oliviers or de Oliviers of Nay were of the minor nobility, and that Jerome Olivier came to England from the Netherlands in 1688 as chaplain of William of Orange, who became King William III.[3] There is another tradition that the first substantial Olivier in England was clerk to Sir Robert Walpole, when he was paymaster general to the army in 1714, and that the family fortunes were founded through that connection.[4] This is the Walpole who became, in effect, the first prime minister of Britain. That his clerk should have become rich has the ring of probability about it.

However all that may be, the first undoubted and traceable member of the family is Daniel Josias Olivier, born 1722, a diamond merchant in the City of London. He married Susannah, believed to be a daughter of Jean-Baptiste Massé, a court painter to Louis XV. Some of Massé's miniatures were still possessed by one of Laurence Olivier's uncles until the 1980s. Daniel Josias Olivier had a son, Daniel Stephen Olivier, who became Rector of Clifton in Bedfordshire, the first English clergyman in the family. His son Henry Stephen Olivier, born 1796, married the daughter of Vice Admiral Sir Richard Dacres, became a lieutenant colonel in the army, a banker, High Sheriff of Wiltshire, and raised a cavalry militia known as Olivier's Horse to put down riots before the 1830 Reform Bill.[5]

Henry Stephen Olivier, this banker and High Sheriff, had three sons. All of them became clergymen, and the pattern of the family was established. Laurence Olivier, when he was famous, liked to emphasise the poverty of his early life, but he came from a family of solid country gentry. The new money, which soon became old money, came from Daniel Josias the diamond merchant, from Henry Stephen the banker, and perhaps from the corrupt Walpole's corrupt clerk. They were the grandees of the family. The others mostly went into the army or into the church. But the soldiers rose to command their regiments, and the clergymen were not poor parsons. Henry Arnold Olivier, the banker's eldest son, born 1826 and Laurence Olivier's grandfather, was a man who created no stir in his long life of eighty-six years, but he was at Rugby under the great Dr Arnold, then at Balliol College, Oxford, and then married the daughter of the Deputy Lieutenant of Berkshire, Queen Victoria's ceremonial representative in that county. He held comfortable livings in Wiltshire and Surrey, and took himself off in the winters to be chaplain at Nice or at Alassio on the Genoese riviera. He had six daughters and four sons, the youngest of whom was Laurence Olivier's father.[6]

These four sons were a disparate lot. The eldest, Henry Dacres, born 1850, came from the old, solid breed. He passed halfway up the list of cadets into the Royal Engineers, served in the little Victorian wars of the British Empire in Afghanistan and the Sudan, was mentioned in despatches and rose to lieutenant colonel. The second, Sydney, born 1859, had the brilliance of the diamond merchant and the banker, did well at Oxford, came first in the entrance examinations to the colonial service, became a socialist and friend of Bernard Shaw and H.G. Wells, and did great and unexpected things; we shall hear much more of him. The third, Herbert Arnould, born 1861, became an artist but not of the bohemian sort. He toured Kashmir with the Duke of Connaught, Queen Victoria's third son, had the honour of showing some of his Indian sketches to the Queen herself, and became a fashionable portrait painter. The fourth, Gerard Kerr, was born in 1869, eight years after his nearest brother and nineteen years after the eldest. All had gone to good public schools. He went to Winchester, which was academically the best of all, and then on to Merton College, Oxford. Little went right for him thereafter. He was the father about whom Laurence Olivier seldom had a good word to say.

Gerard went up to Merton in October 1888 and was soon in trouble. In March 1889 he and two others were warned that the college expected them to be less 'noisy and disorderly in their rooms and in the quadrangles'. He also missed chapel, and was warned that his work was unsatisfactory. At the end of his first year he asked to be allowed to remain out of residence for a year; this was permitted, provided he sat collections, the college examinations, in March 1889. These were formal and undemanding, distinct from the university examinations. Olivier did take them and was adjudged 'on the whole satisfactory'. But he never returned to Merton, and thus completed only one of the three years necessary before he could have taken his degree. The reasons given in the family for his having come down were that he had driven a coach and four down the High Street, or that he had pelted the Warden of Merton with snowballs, or that his reading of Plato caused him to lose his faith and his desire to take Holy Orders. We do not know why, but he had somehow made himself unwelcome at Merton. If he had simply wanted a degree it would have been easier, if he could, to return to Merton after his year away, do a little work, and complete his second and third years. And he did want a degree, because in October 1890 he matriculated at Durham University. This was a comedown after Oxford, but at Durham a man could take a Bachelor's degree after only two years' residence of six months each year. To complete this two-year course took him five years, however, until 1895, when he at last graduated with a BA in Classical and General Literature, and then only in the fourth class. Three years later, in 1898, probably without further examination, he took his Master's degree.[7]

It was not a brilliant start. By that time his brother Henry was a lieutenant colonel; Herbert had exhibited his work at the Royal Academy in London and in Boston, Massachusetts; and Sydney was a bright star of the colonial service. He had already been Colonial Secretary of British Honduras, effectively second in command after the governor, had been Auditor General of the Leeward Islands, and in 1898 was in Washington D.C. to negotiate a trade agreement between the West Indies and the United States. That year he was made a Companion of the Order of St Michael and St George, one step down from a knighthood, and wrote to his mother saying he had been given this honour some years younger than anyone else he knew of. He was a man of various talents. He was, with Bernard Shaw, a founder of the socialist Fabian Society and also wrote three plays, one of which was performed by the semi-professional Stage Society, though only for one night. Shaw described him as extraordinarily attractive and handsome, looking like a Spanish grandee, and strongly sexed. This last quality showed itself in his single performed play, *Mrs Maxwell's Marriage*, which had an autobiographical element to it. The hero was a merchant and planter who, like Sydney, had been awarded the CMG. The heroine was the fast and loose Mrs Maxwell, who had affairs in a semi-tropical colony called Mangrovia. Sydney wrote in his stage directions: 'If you'd ever lived in a country like Mangrovia, where the sun draws passion up out of the earth like a vapour, and sex is the most insistent thing in life, you wouldn't need to wonder how any particular man comes to fall in love with any particular woman, no matter what their antecedents might be.'[8]

As for poor Gerard Olivier, he had little talent of any sort, and the predominant impression is that he also had little common sense. By the age of thirty he had done little but accumulate around himself a few small myths. He was said to have been told, on a tour of Italy when he was sixteen, that his voice was good enough for him to train for the opera; we know he and his brothers and sisters were taken on long holidays to Italy and Switzerland, but that is all. He was also said to have attended the University of Heidelberg, but there is nothing to show he ever did. He was firmly believed to have played county cricket for Hampshire, which would have been a distinction equivalent to playing major league baseball. Laurence Olivier believed this of his father all his life, but it was not true. First-class cricket is the best documented of games, and the Hampshire records show that two Oliviers played for the county. One was a South African and the other was Sidney Richard Olivier, a cousin of Gerard's, who played once in 1895 and made a duck. Gerard *was* a member of M.C.C., the oldest cricket club in the country, founded in 1787, which in his lifetime governed cricket in England and still sets the laws of cricket worldwide. But a man did not need to be an exceptional cricketer to be a member. Gerard was a good club cricketer and no more. Very little is known for sure about his early life except that, like many others with mediocre degrees in Classics, he taught at a preparatory school, near Guildford. Indeed he had already been teaching there while he was still trying to graduate from Durham. There he met the sister of the head-master's wife and, on 30 April 1898, his twenty-ninth birthday, he married the handsome and brown-eyed Agnes Crookenden. She became the beloved and idolised mother of Laurence Olivier, and she brought more French blood into the family. Agnes came mostly from Dutch stock, but had a French great-grandmother named Villeroi who had fled to England from the French Revolution.[9]

Before Laurence there were two other children. Sybille was born in 1901, and Gerard Dacres (ever after known first as Bobo and then as Dickie) in 1904. Laurence Kerr Olivier was born three years later, christened Laurence, he believed, after the Laurent Olivier of 1520. The middle name of Kerr − pronounced, as he later explained, 'Carr in England, Cairrh in Scotland, and Cur in the rest of the world' – was, like Dacres, a favourite in the Olivier family. There had at least been a Dacres, the admiral who as a captain had once served with Nelson and whose daughter had married into the family in 1823, but of a Kerr there is no trace. As a boy Olivier wore a kilt of the Kerr tartan; his father was supposed to be related to the clan, though he was not. It was another one of his myths. This did not stop well-meaning correspondents from suggesting Kerr ancestors to Olivier when he became famous, including one Kerr who was transported to Tasmania for forgery. Nor did it later prevent Olivier from assuming the name of Andrew Kerr when he wished to check into a hotel with a woman not his wife.[10]

But to return to the newly married Gerard Olivier and his wife Agnes. Gerard had hoped to succeed to the headmastership of his brother-in-law's school, but when this proved unlikely he started a school of his own in Dorking. With the help of his wife's family he managed to live in a large house with a view and to support a household with indoor and outdoor servants and, when Sybille was born, a nanny. But the school did not prosper and Gerard Olivier felt a revival of the vocation he had lost at Oxford. He took holy orders, was ordained as a priest in the same year as Dickie was born, and became an assistant priest at St Martin's, Dorking. The stipend was small; they could afford to keep only the nanny, and had to move to a much smaller house in the town. There, at 26 Wathen Road, Laurence Olivier was born on 22 May 1907.[11]

The story goes that Gerard was frying sausages downstairs when the doctor appeared with the new infant in his arms, as yet unwashed and smeared with blood. He took the child with a sense of slight disgust and, after a decent enough pause, handed it back and continued with the sausages; then, only at the doctor's suggestion and with hesitation, he visited his exhausted wife upstairs, gave a little tender stroke to her damp forehead and returned to the sausages. That is Laurence Olivier's account, written seventy-five years later in his autobiography. He says his father told him.[12] It has the characteristic tone of an Olivier anecdote. Most of what we know about his youth and his mother and father comes from this autobiography, which has naturally been relied on by anyone who has written about Olivier. It is best to say straight away that it must always be taken with a large pinch of salt. There is not only the great passage of years between the event and the telling, during which his memory must have faded. There is not only the undoubted fact that Olivier wrote when he had been gravely ill for many years, and that his illness coloured his recollection. There is also the whole nature of Olivier to be considered. If his father was given to the creation of little myths, the son was a magnificent maker of great ones. His life's work was in the theatre and cinema, which encourage and nurture myths. He also persistently called himself a liar, writing that it was a compulsion in him to invent a story and tell it so convincingly that it was believed at first without doubt or suspicion. He would mischievously inquire, 'What is acting but lying?' The probability is that he did not so much consciously lie as instinctively improve the truth. As an acute reporter from the *Christian Science Monitor* remarked in 1939, when he interviewed him in New York after the triumph of *Wuthering Heights*, 'Mr Olivier's idea of storytelling is to give it everything credulity will bear.'[13] He certainly did that and more. In his late memoirs he elaborately invented an attempt to murder him. We shall come to that. The story of the birth, with its detail of the sausages, is typical Olivier. Such circumstantial detail, meant to give verisimilitude, comes to be recognised as the sign of pure invention, as is discovered when such stories can be checked. In piecing together the story of his childhood it is best to use first whatever direct evidence there is, for instance occasional letters and reports, and then the account of his sister Sybille. She was six years older and would have seen more of their early years. In early middle age she wrote a long and lively but unpublished memoir. When they were both in old age they reminisced together. We have fragments of their tape-recorded conversations, in which she would sometimes soften and correct what he said. So when the only evidence of some early event is Olivier's own account this is made clear, to put the reader on his guard.[14]

The young Laurence adored his mother and detested his father. His first memory, as he insisted later to Sybille and others, was an erotic one of his mother's breasts 'in a black lace sort of thing', having embrocation rubbed into her shoulders so that would it would come out as milk. Sybille remembered nothing of the sort. He recalled vividly that his mother spanked him frequently, which gave her more pain than it did him. Sybille remembered no such thing. The small Olivier was at first called Baby by his mother and nanny, and then, because he roared with rage, Paddy. He disliked this name and, when he was about three, his mother proposed he should become Larry. His father reluctantly agreed, but every time he pronounced the name he did so with an emphasis, 'so that mummy had to suffer a little'. That is Olivier's account. Sybille went so far as to recall their father's irritation at Larry's deliberate way of eating, and how he would glare at the child who would tumble from his chair and get out of the room as quickly as he could. Olivier went further; he was convinced that his father saw no point in his younger son's existence, and remembered him principally for his uncertain temper and his parsimony. The first two pages of his autobiography are devoted to his father's meanness: his wafer-thin carving of meat, his thimblefuls of whisky and his insistence that his two sons should share their father's bath water, one after the other.[15]

By 1910 the Rev. Gerard Olivier had decided that his real vocation would best be practised not in a pleasant country town like Dorking but in the slums of west London. So they moved to Notting Hill. As Olivier remembered it, he gave up a decent, ordered gentleman's life to go lower socially and higher spiritually. Not that they lived in the slums. Sybille made it clear they never did. Though their father ministered at a tin shack called St Gabriel's they lived about a mile away in a solid Victorian house in Elgin Crescent, an elegant and spacious district. He adopted High Church, Anglo-Catholic practices, wearing a long cassock, liking to be called Father by his congregation and using incense in the services. Then in 1912 he became curate at St Saviour's, Pimlico. Many of his parishioners may have been poor, but the church was a huge and extravagant Victorian pile at the head of a prosperous square and the curate's house, nearly opposite, had six solid storeys and was within walking distance of Westminster Abbey and the Houses of Parliament. The High Church rituals continued. By this time Laurence was generally known as Kim in the family, not after Rudyard Kipling's *Kim*, as has been suggested, but as an abbreviation of Larry-kin. Theirs was a family given to nicknames. Sybille was Baba or Bar, Kim's elder brother was Dickie or Bobo, and their father was Fahv. Fahv was not flourishing in his profession. His brother Sydney, having been Governor of Jamaica since 1907 and received the regulation knighthood conferred on this appointment, was about to return to England to become Permanent Secretary at the Board of Agriculture and Fisheries, the most senior civil servant of a department of state. But Fahv was not poor. He was certainly not having to scrape by on the 'lowest imaginable income' that Olivier remembered so tenaciously. It is true that his stipend was less than £100 a year. But when the Rev. Gerard Olivier's father died in 1912 he had left a considerable fortune to be shared among his children. Gerard's share was £4,679, which was placed in trust for him. That was probably worth, in today's money, about £400,000, of which Gerard had the use and the income. There was also a Crookenden Trust, brought to him by his wife, which would pay for their childrens' education. Larry went to three preparatory schools, the last of which was Francis Holland School in Chelsea, a Church of England school for girls which also took very small boys. In 1916, when he was nine, he went to the choir school at All Saints, Margaret Street, near Oxford Circus, where Dickie was already a pupil. This was an extraordinary school, and important in forming the character and career of Olivier.[16]

2

Sweet Singing and 'Whispering'

ALL SAINTS MAY BE in a backstreet, but it is one of the most important Anglo-Catholic churches of the nineteenth century. The foundation stone was laid in 1850 by Pusey who, with Newman and
Keble, led the High Church movement which held that there was
an essential continuity between the Roman Catholic and English
churches. The single spire was built to resemble that of the
Marienkirche at Lübeck in north Germany and is higher than any
point of Westminster Abbey. The walls, floor, and roof are tiled,
marbled, banded, painted, stained, gilded and otherwise sumptu-
ously decorated; the organ is splendid enough for a cathedral, and
the whole is a theatrical High Church demanding chants, vestments
and incense. The choir school was small but as good as any cathedral's, and its boys had sung at Victoria's jubilees and at the coro-
nations of Edward VII and George V. There the young Olivier
received a magnificent and rigorous musical education in Mozart,
Handel, Bach, Beethoven, Schubert, Mendelssohn, Gounod, Dvořák,
Palestrina and Tallis. He sang masses, evensongs, anthems and
requiems. He firmly believed, later on, that it was the finest choir
in England. There is no doubt it was among the finest, and musically more adventurous than most.[1] He was also given a decent
academic education in Latin, French, English, history, and mathematics. His first report, when he was nine, showed that his Latin
was good, his French fair, his English bad, his Old Testament
knowledge bad, but that he had made a very good start indeed in

the choir. By the time he was a month away from his twelfth birthday his Latin, French and English were all good; as for his choir work: 'His voice has improved tremendously. . . Just wants to use a little more brain.' His conduct varied over the years. The report for the Christmas term 1920, when he was thirteen and a half, is typical: 'Rather careless and unreliable, but well disposi-tioned.' It was then that his voice began to break. He was always a good chorister, of 'splendid strength', and when he left the head-master's comment on his last report was that he was a nice boy and would be greatly missed.[2]

The services and the singing were theatre in themselves, but All Saints also gave Olivier his first taste of the London stage, and then of Shakespeare. The Duke of Newcastle was a churchwarden of All Saints and patron of the choir school, and at Christmas 1916 he took a party of boys to see the Drury Lane pantomime, *Babes in the Wood*. The choirboys also put on plays of their own. The vicar, Father Henry Mackay, had a passion for the theatre. Father Geoffrey Heald, himself a talented amateur actor, produced *Julius Caesar* at Christmas 1917, in Olivier's second year. He was given the part of First Citizen but rehearsed so well that he was promoted to Brutus. The Rev. Gerard Olivier was a friend of Canon A. J. Thorndike, the father of Sybil Thorndike, and they brought other theatre people to the All Saints performances. One was the celebrated Ellen Terry, who is reputed to have written of the boy Olivier, in her diary: 'Already a great actor.' It may sound apocryphal, but this excerpt from her diary was first published in 1933, when Olivier was no more than very promising. Sir Johnston Forbes-Robertson, the actor-manager, surpassed even Ellen Terry in hyperbole and is reported to have exclaimed to Olivier's father, 'My dear man, your boy does not play Brutus; he *is* Brutus.' Olivier himself never believed that, but he always remembered his performance and recalled it in an American television advertisement he made in 1972, saying it was the first time he had known that there was something wonderful about being on stage.[3]

In 1918 the Rev. Gerard Olivier became Rector of St Michael's, Letchworth, which was thirty miles north of London and the first of the new garden cities, built in 1903. It was a big step up for him.

The stipend was a comfortable £400 a year and the rectory was a handsome Queen Anne house in the old village, near a twelfth-century church. Because of the distance from London, Laurence had to board at All Saints. Then, when he was twelve, catastrophe came. His beloved mother died of a brain tumour at the age of forty-eight. He was told not by his own father but by Father Heald, the priest who was closest to him. Sixty years later he described how he took the news: 'She was my entire world. And I cried just at first, but never again. I felt it appallingly deeply but I bore it. I remember the priest said, "Look, do you still want to sing your solo?" And I said yes, and it was a Benedictus. Of course I thought it was mother doing it with me, you see, so I sang like a bloody angel. Never sang so well, before or since.'

He sang at the funeral service too, and the beauty of his singing was remembered in the family. In the churchyard after the service Sybille, who was then nineteen, took her place in the slow and dreadful procession taking the coffin to the open grave and was suddenly overcome by the thought of how her mother would have giggled at all the solemnity. She turned round and gave her brother a broad grin. 'This,' she said, 'was met with the most appalling glare and heavy frown from Larry, whose sense of ceremonial was bitterly upset by this lapse.' She also observed of her father that, though he suffered acutely over the loss of his wife, 'at the same time some part of him enjoyed the drama of it'. Fahv had eccentrically insisted that the funeral should take place at Church Crookham, in Hampshire, miles from where they lived or ever went, because it was there, twenty years before, after they had taken early communion together, that his new wife had finally assented to his wish to leave schoolmastering and take orders. It was typical of him that he wanted to erect a great stone Calvary over her grave but on consideration found he could not afford it, put up a simple wooden cross instead, and then procrastinated and did no more.[4]

When Gerard returned to Letchworth he sold the old rectory two or three miles outside the new town and moved to a new and smaller one, to be near the new and bigger church in the new town. His desire to preach to the masses was sincere, and his sermons were dramatic. Larry mourned his mother and later said, often, that he had been tempted to throw himself off Chelsea Bridge into the Thames. Sybille had taken her place as the woman of the family. As Larry saw it, she had *become* his mother, and he much admired her complete fearlessness of Fahv. 'She would oppose him directly, her brilliant, strong eyes straight in his. Her feeble brothers would lend no support – just weakly deprecating "O, I say Baba, that's a bit . . ."' Sybille was the first member of the family to wish to go on the professional stage, and in 1920 she went off to London to study at the Central School of Dramatic Art. Dickie had already gone to his public school, Radley College. There was a family trip to Guernsey, where Larry was coached in Latin and mathematics by his aunt Mab, his late mother's sister. Then in August 1921 Fahv rented a houseboat on the Ouse at St Neots, in Cambridgeshire. It was half on shore, half on piles in the river and was called *White Wings*. The young Oliviers made friends with a party of cockneys on a neighbouring boat, the *Water Lily*, and envied them their gramophone on which they played the popular foxtrot, 'Whispering', half the night. 'Beastly noise,' said Fahv. Another evening one of the *Water Lily* girls played her cello. The holiday remained in Olivier's memory. Nearly thirty years later, reminded of it, he wrote to Sybille: 'In love for the first time – Bertha her name was – I felt her tits in the punt and rode endless merry-go-rounds with her – "Whispering" still v. nostalgic for me.'[5]

At about this time there was trouble with Sybille. Either when she was still at drama school or when she was making one her first appearances on the provincial stage, she made a hasty marriage with an actor, at a register office. Though Larry was still only a boy, she confided in him. When the marriage collapsed after only a year and Fahv got to know, he was merciless with Larry, making him feel guilty for not having informed on his sister. As Olivier later put it, 'She was drifting, a bit derelict in fashion, from a first disastrous marriage, for which there was no reason; stage folk did plenty of living temporarily together, in those days. None of the family knew anything of that occurrence until she tripped none too daintily from that marriage into the next.' It was a story persistently told by Olivier that Fahv then, from his own pulpit, condemned his own daughter for adultery. Larry never forgave him. Neither

Sybille's account nor Larry's gives exact dates, but Sybille's first marriage had to have taken place within a year of their mother's death. It was not a happy family.[6]

Meantime Larry had returned for his last year at All Saints. In his final Christmas play he took the part of Katharina in *The Taming of the Shrew*, earning more praise from Ellen Terry, who said he gave an idea of what the boy players in Shakespeare's time had been like and that she had never seen the part played better by any women except Ada Rehan, a great American actress who was famous for that role. This was gratifying, but the greatest influence on the young Olivier was the ritual and the numinousness of All Saints itself, with 'the sweet singing and the merry organ and the feeling of a show'. And of course he had acquired a Christian faith. It would have been an insensible boy, in that church and that school, who did not.[7]

It was time for him, like any boy of his class, to go to his public school. The Oliviers had been promiscuous in their choice of school. Fahv had been at Winchester, his brother Sydney at Tonbridge, their father at Rugby, and Dickie was at Radley. Larry preferred Harrow and believed his mother had wished that too. But Fahv's choice fell on St Edward's, Oxford, which specialised in educating the sons of gentlemen clergy. The fees were only £114 a year as against £210 at Radley, but Fahv may have chosen it not only for that reason but because it had been founded, in 1863, by a leader of the same Oxford Movement which had built All Saints, Margaret Street, and to which Fahv had devoted the years of his ministry. The High Church was good on incense, slums, and stark schools. St Edward's was stark. There were two compulsory services every weekday and four on Sundays, to which the boys wore surplices. Prefects could beat their juniors, or give up to two hundred lines as punishment, to be copied from the works of Virgil. Small boys had to fag for big ones, making toast, polishing shoes, running errands. Breakfast was porridge, bread, and margarine. Lunch was dished out in platefuls by skivvies known collectively as 'John' or 'Annie,' according to their sex. Supper, after evensong, was bread, margarine, and metallic tea from tin urns, though boys could buy eggs and baked beans from the school shop with their own money.

The school was divided into forms named after parts of the British Empire – Ceylon, Canada, New Zealand, Natal, and Jamaica, in ascending order of precedence. Olivier never rose higher than New Zealand. There were small privileges. In the first year jackets had to be buttoned with their tails pushed in front of the wearer's hands. A year later the jackets were still buttoned, but the tails could be behind the hands. In the third year jackets could be worn unbuttoned. It was a normal English education, though the young Olivier had it soft since the Warden in his time had abandoned Swedish drill and was a keen musician.[8]

There was one loose end from All Saints to be tied up. The choir school had been selected to take part in the 1922 Shakespeare birthday festival in April at Stratford-upon-Avon, and had revived its Christmas performance of *The Taming of the Shrew*. Olivier was given leave for two days from St Edward's and returned to the All Saints company. What followed was his introduction to public life and to the public theatre. The Great Western Railway put on a special first-class saloon to carry the Duke of Newcastle, the All Saints' clergy, and the choristers from London to Stratford. At Stratford the choristers, in white surplices and rose-coloured caps, cassocks, and socks, and wearing patent shoes with silver buckles, walked in procession to the parish church where Shakespeare's tomb lay. The young Olivier led this procession, carrying a wreath of bays bound with Roman purple, which he knelt and laid beside a wreath sent by King George V himself while the choir sang a dirge, *De Profundis*. After lunch with *fraises Melba* the boys were introduced to James Hackett, the celebrated American actor who was playing Othello at the Stratford Memorial Theatre; they then saw some of his rehearsal that afternoon. Next day, a Friday, the boys presented the *Shrew* at a matinée at that theatre. There Olivier played Katharina again. The boy players were not named in the programme and in those days the theatre critics of the *Daily Telegraph* and *The Times* were anonymous as well. The *Telegraph* critic said that the boy who took the part of Kate made a fine, bold, black-eyed hussy, badly in need of taming, and that he could not remember seeing any actress in the part who looked it better. From *The Times* Olivier received a notice which was as good as any he received in his life.

The reviewer wondered at lines so clearly spoken and said one boy's performance as Katharina had a fire of its own. Then he wrote: 'You felt that if an apple were thrown to this Katharina she would instinctively try to catch it in her lap, and if apples give her pleasure we hope with all gratitude that someone will make the experiment.' A greater compliment to instinct refined by technique, and so early on, is difficult to imagine. In the evening the boys were back at the Memorial Theatre as members of the audience at that night's performance, and when they took their seats in the stalls they received a standing ovation. At the matinée, and in the evening, Olivier had heard the public applause which became his life's music. Next morning the triumphant adventure continued when the choristers were taken to see the famous novelist Marie Corelli at her house in the town, where they sang to her in her music room.[9]

Olivier told no one at St Edward's about Stratford. That would have invited mockery. He always insisted he was unhappy at the school. At All Saints he had been a star. At St Edward's, which he liked to call St Edward's the Martyr, he was not even good at cricket, rowing, or rugby. He was of course put in the school choir and was soon the soloist, which did nothing for his popularity. He did moderately well at his work. Exercise books still exist in which he listed British naval bases: in the East were Gibraltar, Malta, Port Said, Aden, Bombay, Madras and Calcutta; in the Atlantic were Cape Town, St John's, Halifax, Trinidad, Barbados and Quebec. He recalled that he once had a hand in unjustly beating a smaller boy, Bader, who was uppity and terribly good at games, and who had incidentally bowled Olivier out in a house cricket match. Olivier was jealous and had him hauled up before the president of his form room for cheek: 'And I think I had the luxury, because I had made the complaint, of delivering two of the blows, and I simply loathed myself.' The boy was Douglas Bader, who later became nationally famous as an RAF fighter ace in the Battle of Britain. As for a best friend, Olivier did not have one, though his friendship was sought. Nearly sixty years later he remembered one incident in which a letter from another boy fell out of his pocket and a passing master saw it. Years later, Olivier recalled what happened.

'What have you got there, Olivier?'

'Nothing, sir.'

'I should still like to see it.'

Olivier handed it over.

'And the master read it: "Apollo, how I long to see you more than I am able to. Can you meet me for tea somewhere in Oxford?" Or something like that. And I only know, his name was – poor darling fellow – his name was Gosling, and he was an awfully nice fellow, but I'm afraid the poor fellow made the mistake of falling for me, and the incredible mistake of writing notes. . . After that term I never saw him again, so I'm afraid I was responsible for his demise.'[10]

The school was not, as one of Olivier's contemporaries recalled in a memoir, markedly homosexual. It was a matter of crushes, and did not go further than the accepted right of prefects and other seniors to have favourites whom they rewarded with tuck.[11]

Olivier was regarded as a flirt. He called himself one in a school essay which has survived. It was written in his last term but one, in March 1924, and was ostensibly on the subject of soap. He pictured a boy lying in a bath washing his hair. As a little boy, he wrote, he had thought soap disgusting stuff, but now he saw it forming 'swans' around him on the surface of the water. Then he described the boy in the bath as an 'excellently brought up, strong and silent, handsome, upright, not to say strapping, young gentleman. And that particular personage,' he continued, 'is me!!. . . I am beginning to think that I am a most fickle young man, that I am a flirt!! and that one day the life of many a fair maid will be ruined by the faithlessness of my heart.'[12]

This was written soon after he enjoyed his one success at St Edward's. He was told, and there was no argument about it, that he was to play Puck in the school production of *A Midsummer Night's Dream*. He had dreaded this 'dismally wretched' part but said to himself, right, he would 'knock their bloody eyes out with it somehow'. And so he did. Puck was a success throughout the show, dancing among the audience, darting up and down the aisles making surprise appearances, his face lit from underneath by two torch lamps fixed to a harness round his chest. He learned there and then that Shakespeare could look after himself, and look after the actor who trusted him.[13] That, at any rate, is what he said many years later. It is more likely that what he noticed at the time was that his performance had done wonders for his popularity, and that next day an undreamed of number of boys wanted to walk round the quad with him, arm in arm.

He was just over seventeen. It had earlier been assumed that he would become a parson. He had toyed with the idea of going into the merchant navy, because of the uniform, or into forestry. St Edward's would have fitted him for any of these careers. Of those who entered the school in the same year as he did, four eventually went into the Church and nine into the army or navy; four became doctors; ten went into other professions as engineers, surveyors, accountants, and architects; and nine went to farm in or govern the countries of the empire – Canada, Australia, Burma, Southern Rhodesia, Tanganyika, and Ceylon. Olivier, in later life, regretted that he had not been to a university. This is strange, since nor had the greatest of his contemporaries – not John Gielgud, Ralph Richardson or Alec Guinness. Nor would many boys of his class and from his school have expected to do so in the 1920s. Of the fifty-five boys in his year at St Edward's only seven went on to university, all to Oxford or Cambridge. It depended on their parents' means. Most boys went into the world, or began training for their professions, at seventeen or eighteen. The young Olivier had the typical education of a gentleman, and it had changed little since Victorian times. It was thorough. To add to his splendid knowledge of music, he had had eight years of Latin, translating into and out of that dead language until he had at least a competent knowledge. He could hardly have avoided it. He also had eight years of French. This did not necessarily mean he could speak much more than was necessary to order dinner in a restaurant, but he had enough to read a letter or a newspaper in that language, and enough to write risqué little anecdotes in French for his own amusement, which he later did. He also had at least a smattering of German. He could write English correctly and eloquently, though his spelling remained at times eccentric. And he could name the ports of the British Empire. All in all, he was much more literate than most present-day graduates of most English and American universities.[14]

This was in 1924, which was a momentous year in the Olivier

family. Sybille had already been on the stage for two years, though with no success. In January Dickie had left Radley and set off, with a gift of £60 from the remaining assets of his late mother's trust, for the life of a tea planter in India. That same month Ramsay MacDonald had become Prime Minister and formed the first Labour government in Britain. Having a Cabinet to fill but no one to choose with any experience in government, he appointed Sydney Olivier, who was a known socialist and had at least been Governor of Jamaica, to be no less than Secretary of State for India, one of the great offices of State. This was at a time when the King of Great Britain was also Emperor of India. Since a Cabinet Minister had to be a member of either the Commons or the Lords, since it was much easier to create a peer than to engineer a by-election to get him into the Commons, and since, as George Bernard Shaw put it, Sydney was 'eminently presentable and much more aristocratic-looking than most of the hereditary nobles', he was created Baron Olivier and made a member of the Privy Council. Fahv went off on a church mission to Jamaica, met Isobel Buchanan Ronaldson, and married her on his return to England. The ceremony was not in his own church but at All Souls, Langham Place, London, and among the guests were the new Lord Olivier and his nephew Laurence. It was Olivier's recollection that Fahv was in trouble with his parish. High Church priests were expected to be celibate. If they were already married that was overlooked, but for a widower to remarry was not done. That had indeed been the view of Fahv himself. At St Saviour's, Pimlico, he had condemned a priest for just such a remarriage and now he was acting hypocritically in doing so himself. That was the story as Olivier later told it. For whatever reason, Fahv left his Letchworth living, was unable to find another for six months, and began his new marriage unhappily. He had no stipend, the funds of the Crookenden Trust had been exhausted by the education of Sybille, Dickie, and Larry, and he had used up half the capital of his inheritance, selling off shares at a loss. He was not poor. He never was. But he had less than he was used to. So what was to become of Larry?[15]

The classic story is that when Fahv and Larry returned from London that January, having seen Dickie off to India, Larry lay in his father's leftover bath water and expressed a wish to follow his brother as soon as he left school that summer. Whereupon his father promptly replied, 'Don't be a fool. You are going on the stage.' This version first appeared in 1953, in a joint biography of Olivier and Vivien Leigh which was written with Olivier's approval and was faithful to the information he provided, and Olivier repeated it in his autobiography. But the story of how the decision was taken had appeared before, in a different form. This was in August 1939, in an American magazine interview with Olivier, at a time when he had become suddenly famous in America for *Wuthering Heights*, was about to film *Rebecca*, and was giving many uninhibited interviews. The story appeared under the headline:

HE SAID NO IN THE BATHROOM

It then continued: '[Olivier] decided early that he did not wish to follow his father's footsteps up the pulpit. Later [in the bathroom] he said 'No' to following his brother's footsteps on an Indian tea plantation. His father, on learning this, came forth with an alternative. He said, "Why not try the stage?"'[16]

There is a choice here between the two versions. Father and son had never been close or sympathetic to each other. In the classic version Fahv shows an enthusiasm for Larry which he had previously reserved for the Church. In the other, earlier one, he shows the indifference with which he had generally treated his son. The version given in the biography, of course, is the better story.

3

An Unanswered Wish to be Liked

SO OLIVIER WENT OFF to the Central School of Dramatic Art at the Albert Hall in London for an audition. It is an amphitheatre which can seat 5,000, and when he first looked in he had a moment of terror that he would have to perform on that stage to that vast space. But the school was housed off one of the side porches of the hall and its auditorium was no more than six rows deep. There he met the principal, Elsie Fogerty, who had acted in London and Paris, produced Greek plays and written manuals of speech-craft, and was then in her late fifties. Her eyes were dark, her voice a rich baritone, and she commanded respect. She came to feel a sense of adulation for Olivier. For his part he said that, though she was often kind to him, he never felt drawn to her by any kind of affection.[1]

On that first occasion he recited Jacques' speech on the Seven Ages of Man from *As You Like It.* She remarked that it was not necessary to make fencing passes when he described the soldier, the man of the fourth age, as being 'sudden and quick in quarrel', and then offered him a scholarship which paid the fees of £50 for the year. Laurence asked about the bursary as well, which Fahv had told him was necessary if he was to embark on an acting career. Miss Fogerty then acted mystically. This is Olivier's account. She leaned towards him, placed the tip of her little finger on his forehead, against the base of his hair-line, slid it down to rest at the top of his nose and said, 'You have a weakness . . . *here.*' He thought this a 'penetrating foray into the hazardous area of an actor's psychological weakness', and was immediately convinced. It was a weakness which, if it existed, thousands in the theatre and a million members of cinema audiences never noticed at all, but what matters is that Olivier was ready to believe it. He embarked on decades of false noses, not only and most famously as Richard III but also as Romeo and in any other part that gave any such opportunity. What was true was that in 1924, and for some years after, Olivier's brow-line was low and his bushy eyebrows almost met in the middle. Having made her observation, Miss Fogerty also gave him the bursary of another £50. His sister Sybille had been at the Central School and had been one of her favourites. Miss Fogerty also needed promising male students. That year there were only five, compared with eighty girls. One of the girls was Peggy Ashcroft, in whose mind Olivier left an indelible picture – those eyebrows, the dark hair standing on end, and the eyes even then unlike anyone else's.[2]

As a student Olivier was not prosperous, but not that poor either. He had the £50 bursary to live on, £15 from the remnants of his mother's trust money, and £1 a month from his father. In the Christmas and Easter holidays he earned some money appearing with a semi-professional cast at Letchworth, which was a try-out place for modest managements. At the Central School there were classes in movement, voice, diction, and theatre history. Miss Fogerty, having herself acted in Paris, persuaded Jacques Copeau – who had produced Shakespeare and Molière in Paris, New York, and London – to come and lecture at the school. He said something which was profoundly congenial to Olivier and which he always remembered: 'There is only one way to begin to do a thing, and that is to do it.' At seventeen he was already, and above all, practical. He was impatient with his classes, and wanted to get on with the acting. He did win the school's gold medal with Peggy Ashcroft at the end of his year, playing a scene as Shylock to her Portia. The judge was Athene Seyler, already a famous comedienne.[3]

Then he had to find work. There is some disagreement about his first stage appearance. It was perhaps at Letchworth on 1 January 1925 in a forgotten play called *Through the Crack*. Olivier's diary for that year does not survive, but in his 1927 diary he wrote: 'Anniversary 1st Night on Stage.' But that seems to have been as assistant stage manager. When he was asked by one of his father's former housekeepers what he did, he is said to have replied that when she heard the interval bell ringing to call the audience back to their seats she would know it was his finger on the bell. The first time he appeared on a stage as an actor, in public, was at the Brighton Hippodrome at a charity gala at the beginning of August 1925. It was in music-hall and he fell flat on his face. It was an all-star bill – Gertie Gitana, Harry Lauder, George Robey. Olivier was in the one straight act of the evening, a short, curtain-raising sketch called *The Unfailing Instinct*. The sets for this had a high sill, over which an actor had to step to make his entrance. The stage door-keeper warned him of this. So did a fellow actor as they made up together. So did the call boy. So did the stage manager. So did a friendly stage-hand, whom Olivier waved away; then he made his entrance, did a shattering trip over the sill, sailed through the air, and landed flat on his face in the footlights. 'I have flattered myself,' he wrote in his autobiography, 'that I could generally fetch the size of laugh that I thought I, or the comic situation, merited, but I have sighed in vain; never, never in my life have I heard a sound so explosively loud as the joyous clamour made by that audience.' Next day he was off with the company on a tour of Manchester, Birmingham, Eastbourne (on the pier), Aberdeen, Glasgow, and Brixton, to play as cast for £4 a week, appearing in his sketch and in *The Ghost Train*, a spooky hit of the moment. But in this he had only a walk-on part as a policeman, with not a line to speak. It was a twelve-week tour, but with gaps. The standard contract was 'no play, no pay', so only six of those twelve weeks were paid.[4]

There then followed a month with the Lena Ashwell Players, whom Olivier renamed the Lavatory Players. He remembered the company playing one-night stands in such unthought-of parts of London as Deptford, Ilford, Islington, and Shoreditch, playing in boarded-over swimming pools and changing in the lavatories. But Miss Ashwell was not negligible. She had made a name as an actress in England and America, had entertained the troops in France during World War I and then, seduced by the idea of public service, had decided to take Shakespeare to the masses. Olivier played small parts in *The Tempest* and *Julius Caesar*. But he was a joker. In *Julius*

Caesar he found that if he tore the backcloth it would expose the naked bottoms of the women of the cast changing behind it. And then one night, after the underpants of one member of the cast fell down under his toga, Olivier abandoned him and walked off the stage, quaking hysterically. He was fired by Miss Ashwell the next morning. They had not got on. He complained that he had been reduced to 'near starvation', but he was paid £3 a week and was, besides, receiving £2 a week from his new stepmother. At first he had resented her, but she was always tender towards him and he soon gave her the family nickname of Ibo, after the initials of her name, Isobel Buchanan Olivier.[5]

By late 1926 Fahv, whatever his own failings, had two children on the stage who were not doing well. Larry had little love for his father, and recalled some nasty moments when he was 'faced with the most appalling prospect' of having to return to his rectory. He did face that prospect when he was out of work after Miss Ashwell dismissed him. As for Sybille, she had had what her brother called 'all sorts of variegated romantic lives' and was barely clinging on to her profession. After the Central School, and then a dancing school, she had gone to Dobell's Irish Company for £3 a week. She toured Ireland and the English provinces, mostly third-rate tours in melodrama, and only once came to London. That was in July 1926 when she was at Fulham, Croydon, Wimbledon, and the Shepherd's Bush Empire. She thought it was her big chance. Olivier went to see her with Lewis Casson, Sybil Thorndike's husband and a friend of the family. Both found it embarrassing. 'I'm afraid,' said Casson, 'that you shouldn't have any hopes for your sister in the theatre. You'll be perfectly all right, but I think your sister has no hope.' Olivier agreed. He knew Sybille thought that she had a great future, but she was appalling; to save her life she could not be convincing on stage.[6]

It was to Lewis Casson that Olivier next turned for a job. Sybil Thorndike had just had a great triumph in Shaw's *St Joan*, and he was now producing her in *Henry VIII* at the old Empire Theatre in Leicester Square. It was the last season there before it was elaborately converted by Metro Goldwyn Mayer into a cinema. 'All right,' said Casson, 'spear, halberd, and standard bearer, all the understudies you can undertake without looking ridiculous, and second assistant stage manager.' This gave Olivier four months' work and in *Henry VIII*, and in Shelley's *Cenci* which followed, he made a small success and gained the cachet of having been a member of Sybil Thorndike's company.[7]

Then came his break. An entry in his diary for 8 March 1927 reads, 'Barry Jackson? Phone.' Sybil Thorndike had suggested he should. Sir Barry Jackson, as he had just become, was a stage-struck millionaire who had made his money from a chain of dairies and spent it on building and running a theatre in Birmingham, which put on anything from pantomimes to Shakespeare and Shaw. It was then the best repertory theatre in England. He was not asking Olivier to join his company, but he was casting for the London production of a medieval French mystery play on the life of St Bernard. It was a typical rich man's indulgence. He had translated and adapted the play himself. Olivier auditioned for the name part of the saint, but had to be content with the lesser part of a minstrel. The run was interrupted by the General Strike of 1926, which paralysed the country for ten days, during which Olivier worked as a gateman on the London Underground. He was paid £5 a week for this, barely less than he was getting in St Bernard. The play folded soon after the strike, but it had run for seventy-six performances. Olivier was still having trouble with his name. At Brighton he had been called Mr Oliver, his first name was consistently spelled Lawrence with a 'w', and in the St Bernard programme his surname was printed as Ollivier, with two 'l's. But he had his foot in the door, and for twenty weeks from July 1926, for £8 a week and with the undertaking that he would also understudy in any other play required of him, he toured the provinces as the lead in *The Farmer's Wife*. This was a wholesome, drawing-room comedy of the 'love among the teapots' sort, by Eden Phillpotts, which had been running on and off since 1916 and had seen more than 1,300 performances. At one time Jackson was running it in three separate tours with three casts. Olivier was in the number one tour, which took in Manchester, Glasgow and Edinburgh, along with Wimbledon and Southend.[8]

This was one of the bread-and-butter plays which subsidised

Barry Jackson's more ambitious ventures, but the members of the cast took themselves seriously and read Stanislavsky's book, *My Life in Art*, which had recently been published. Stanislavsky was the co-founder of the Moscow Arts Theatre, the first director of Checkhov, and an enemy of mannerism who insisted that an actor should *be* the character he played; and there he was being read by rep actors in the English provinces, among the teapots. Olivier remembered the book's effect on his fellow players: 'After a while some young scallywag of a character actor who would just, just, get to the theatre when they were calling five minutes, who would sort of slap his make-up on, sort of change, forget about his boots, that sort of thing, and just scrape on to the stage to catch his cue – after a while he'd suddenly start arriving two hours early, and wandering about the stage touching the scenery, and giving himself a sense of ownership, then we'd know he'd got to such and such a chapter.' At the time Olivier took his turn reading Stanislavsky too, even if he did later say an actor should work on a building site rather than enter a Method studio.[9]

Then in 1927 he joined the Birmingham Repertory Theatre proper. It would have been difficult to find a better training ground for a young actor. He spent all year in that city. His contract was to play as cast. He appeared in fifteen plays, almost all now forgotten, but among them were *Uncle Vanya*, in which at the age of nineteen he played the name part, and *She Stoops to Conquer*, in which he was Tony Lumpkin. He appeared with an even younger Peggy Ashcroft in *Bird in Hand*, a comedy by John Drinkwater which was to have an important influence on his life for the next three years. The critics began to toss him scraps of praise. Jackson invited him to join the London company which he took to the Royal Court for the first five months of 1928. The season opened with *The Adding Machine*, a play by the American Elmer Rice, which satirised, rather as Charlie Chaplin did in *Modern Times*, the increasing regimentation of man in the machine age. For this Olivier required a New York accent of the sort spoken on the Lower East Side. It was before the time of the talkies, so he had never heard the like. He set about acquiring it in the thorough manner which later became so familiar, seeking an introduction to the American actress Clare Eames who was then playing in London. She coached him. The critics were impressed. So was Miss Eames, who became most conscious of her young pupil's power. 'Larry looks down at me,' she said, 'with the eyes of a conqueror.' As the season progressed, Olivier moved from Malcolm in a modern-dress *Macbeth* to a small part in Shaw's *Back to Methuselah*, and then to the name part in *Harold*, an unactable epic by Tennyson. Even Irving had declared it impossible. Olivier played the lead, was paid £20 a week for it, vastly more than he had ever earned before, but he had to speak such lines as 'Oh Tostig, Tostig, what art thou doing here?' The critics described his perform-ance as sincere.[10]

Olivier was not quite twenty-one. He was already established in a modest way, and Miss Eames had seen something in him which was more than modest. He had made three important friendships. One was with Ralph Richardson. The two men had not at first been easy with each other, perhaps because Olivier flirted with Richardson's wife, but after playing together in two of that season's productions they were warily amiable. The second friendship was with Peggy Ashcroft, and the third with Denys Blakelock.

Olivier and Ashcroft had always been sympathetic. She remem-bered his scrawny figure and threadbare cuffs at the Central School. This scrawniness is strange, since in 1926 Olivier weighed 147 lbs, which was the same as in 1939. When they were at Birmingham in *Bird in Hand* they both went to Stratford with the author, John Drinkwater, to see *Antony and Cleopatra*. She also remembered this: 'Many years later Larry told me that when they went to tea with a member of the Rep. Co. in his digs in Birmingham and our host had retired to the lavatory, the sudden pulling of the chain prevented him from proposing. The company dispersed – the opportunity never recurred!'[11] That was a sad mischance.

Olivier's relationship with Denys Blakelock was more complex. Both were sons of clergymen and both were actors. They had met in 1926 when Olivier first auditioned for St Bernard with Barry Jackson's company. Olivier did later say of him that he was the first human being he could really think of as a friend. 'Having lived through my earliest days with a desperate wish to be liked unanswered, I embraced this unaccustomed happiness with an innocent young gratitude that I often think must have given Denys, who was a few years my senior, some embarrassment in those early days.' Blakelock seems not to have been embarrassed but rather to have returned these feelings, saying Olivier was his greatest friend; that he had first seen him, years before, at his performance as Katharina at All Saints; that they were both deeply religious; and that from the time they met they saw a great deal of each other. Olivier visited Blakelock's father's rectory. Blakelock was often at Fahv's, and saw Larry serving for his father, acting as his acolyte at a weekday service in a church which was otherwise empty except for Ibo. Larry had given him something which he thought of as a relic, a little Christmas card on the back of which he had written 'a very special prayer'.[12] He also stayed with Olivier at the family cottage at Dymchurch, next to one called 'St Joan' which belonged to Sybil Thorndike. He and Larry often shared a minute bedroom there.[13] Blakelock also went into detail about Olivier's appearance. When they first met, he took him home to meet his parents, who said afterwards; 'He's very nice, your friend Mr Olivier. (Pause). He's a very *plain* young man, isn't he?' Which, said Blakelock, enraged him, though he could not say it was untrue.[14]

He said that Olivier did not dress well at all. He wore suits which were castoffs from a step-uncle [a brother of Ibo's], but that under those unbecoming suits were the 'square shoulders and long straight legs that were to stand him in such good stead as a romantic actor in the days ahead'. He was pale, with an unmanageable mass of thick, black hair, and a gap between his two front teeth. Later, when he came to London for the Birmingham Repertory's Royal Court season, he looked completely different. 'He had somehow got his hair to part at last; he had had the gaps between his teeth filled in, his eyebrows trimmed and straightened, and he was beautifully and rather gaily dressed.'[15]

In the summer of 1928, after the Royal Court season, this gaily dressed young man who had just turned twenty-one was offered the lead in another of Barry Jackson's London ventures. This time it was in a play guaranteed to run for months, Drinkwater's *Bird in Hand*, which he had already played in Birmingham. His leading lady this time was not Peggy Ashcroft – who by then had gone on to better things and was playing Desdemona to Paul Robeson's Othello – but Jill Esmond. She came from a theatre family. Her father was H.V. Esmond, an actor-manager-writer who had written thirty sentimental comedies and made a fortune. Her mother was Eva Moore, who had appeared in many of these plays. Miss Esmond was no Peggy Ashcroft, but she was slim, pretty, and lively. Her father had by then died of drink in Paris, and she lived with her widowed mother in a lavish house on a Berkshire hill with a distant view of the Thames at Marlow. Olivier visited Jill at home and saw that she lived with an ease he had never known. In the play their roles were rather reversed. Olivier was the squire's son who wooed the innkeeper's daughter. One of the high points was his sentimental kissing of the door of his sweetheart's room. It ran for months, but Olivier was aspiring to higher things.[16]

The theatre talk of the moment was that Basil Dean – who was to the London theatre what Sam Goldwyn was to Hollywood movies – was about to produce *Beau Geste*, an extravaganza of the French Foreign Legion with a cast of thousands, and he was searching for a leading man. Olivier did a read-through of the part at an audition but heard nothing. He was then offered the lead in *Journey's End*, a play to be performed only twice, at a theatre club on a Sunday evening and a Monday afternoon, so that it would not interfere with its cast's professional engagements. The play was written by R.C. Sherriff, an insurance clerk no one had heard of, and was set in the trenches of World War I, where the author had himself served as an officer. Olivier had no hopes for it but did it for £5 and another chance to bring himself to Mr Dean's attention. Sherriff went to a rehearsal in a freezing room over a shop, and there he saw his leading man. 'He was sitting over the small, bleak fire trying to warm himself . . . He looked slighter and paler than he had appeared on the stage [in *Bird in Hand*]: not at all like the tough drink-sodden company commander that I had visualised. He looked bored and restless. I got a feeling that he was wishing he hadn't come.' There was no money for costumes, so he lent Olivier his own uniform tunic and Sam Browne belt.[17]

No play of the sort had been produced since the war. It caught the spirit of the time. Erich Maria Remarque's *All Quiet on the*

Western Front was filmed in the following year. In the play there are no heroics; all is fear and futility. The trench caves in and in the final scene a young subaltern dies in his company commander's arms. The notices were wonderful. Mr Dean saw a performance and promptly offered Olivier the lead in *Beau Geste*, which he accepted. *Beau Geste* was not about reality, except that it had a real Maxim gun, real battles, and both a crucifixion and a real funeral pyre on stage. It was above all the part he wanted. 'Christ,' he said, 'I was the envy of all London, of all the young actors there were.' It was exactly as he saw himself. *Beau Geste* had been a famous silent film, with Ronald Colman in the lead; the ultimate dashing, smooth Englishman, with a pencil-thin moustache. 'He,' said Olivier, 'was the subject of my intense study and shameless copy. I was always a copycat, copied absolutely shamelessly, and nobody ever recognises that you're actually copying. I went so far as to grow the same moustache and have my hair done the same way.'[18]

The rehearsals did not go well. 'I remember Basil Dean screaming at me, I mean directions that were impossible for anyone to follow. "For Christ's sake show us some charm, boy." "Oh, thank you Mr Dean, yes I'll do that." I mean, how can you "show us some charm"?'[19] But Olivier did not at first regret taking the part. How could he? He was being paid £30 a week for rehearsing what was expected to be the great hit of the season. He bought himself a camel hair overcoat and moved to a better apartment. Then *Beau Geste* opened. The grand spectacle appeared ludicrous: its battles filled the theatre with choking smoke, its extravagant performances dragged on till nearly midnight, its audiences were exhausted, and it folded after five weeks.

The play Olivier had left, *Journey's End*, had trouble in finding a producer even after the raves it had received, and that producer was so pushed for money he had to paint the set himself. But then, with Colin Clive playing the part Olivier had created and could have kept, it ran for two years in the West End, transferred to New York and Chicago, and was played all over the world throughout the 1930s. Sherriff became one of the most successful screenwriters in Hollywood.[20]

Mr Dean, wanting to make it up to Olivier, offered him the lead in his next extravaganza, *Circle of Chalk*, and even increased his pay to £45 a week. Olivier, despite Dean's impossible demands in *Beau Geste*, accepted. The play was said to be adapted from the ancient Chinese. Olivier's leading lady, Anna May Wong, was half-Chinese herself and she was a star, but of the silent screen. When she opened her mouth the play closed. As one critic put it, 'Her face is a lotus flower of Pekin; her voice is the nasal pipe of Broadway.' There followed two other short-lived West End openings and closings.[21]

For Olivier, who was outwardly cocksure but inwardly wanted to be liked, it was a dreadful run. But he had been chosen as leading man in four West End plays in less than a year. Whatever the failings of the plays, his credit as an actor was still good. In August he was offered a part in New York, again in a play that promised sure success. He leapt at it, not only for its own sake but also because Jill Esmond, his partner of the year before in *Bird in Hand*, had gone with that play to New York, where it again promised to run and run. This was a time when Olivier was, as he put it, unremittingly obsessed by the thought of sex and was dying to get married so that he might, with the blessing of God, enjoy that pleasure. At the Birmingham Rep he had flirted with Angela Baddeley, who happened to be married, and with Muriel Hewitt, who happened to be not only married but married to Ralph Richardson. His heart had 'throbbed with the pangs of despised love' for another actress, Jane Welsh. He had failed to propose to Peggy Ashcroft. But he proposed to Jill Esmond, thinking that with her antecedents in the theatre, though she was not *dazzlingly* attractive, she would most certainly 'do excellent well for a wife'. That is how he coldly put it when, as an old man, he came to write his autobiography. At the time it was more than that, and also less simple. For both of them the notions of God, sex, guilt and marriage were all tangled together. When he had proposed she had temporised and then gone to America. So when Olivier was offered the part on Broadway he reflected that 'in the west his pleasure lay' – the words are his – and on 10 August 1929, the day of his patron saint, St Laurence, he sailed for New York on the Cunard liner *Aquitania*.[22]

4

Our Particular Pet Devil, or What?

'I WAS NEVER,' SAID Olivier, 'so excited in my life as when I got on the boat to go to New York, and when we got there it was so thrilling. I'll never forget the sort of late night parties and the light of dawn in New York.' On the day of his arrival, with what he called his pitifully irresistible inclination to dramatise everything, he did not announce his presence to Jill until after her performance, though she knew he was coming, and then went to her dressing room.[1]

It was a time when English actors with English voices were far more likely to succeed on Broadway than they are now. At least three English plays were doing well. Olivier hoped his play, a thriller called *Murder on the Second Floor*, would become a fourth. It had already done well in London. He and Jill should have had a high old time, young and in New York in the boom days of 1929, just before the crash. She was in *Bird in Hand*, a hit which refused to stop running, and he had a guarantee of ten weeks at $500 a week. But her play's determined success depressed Jill. She had already played the same part in it for almost a year in London, then for another four months, since April, in New York. She was bored with it, and lonely. From the start it had not been a fortunate visit. Her ship had crawled into New York harbour hours late, in a fog. She found her hotel room overlooked the elevated railway on Sixth Avenue. She could not sleep for the racket and was so hot she walked up and down naked till five in the morning.[2]

When Olivier arrived they went to Tiffany's and bought an

engagement ring. There were the late night parties. His producer put him in the Warwick, which he thought a rather grand hotel, and he lived in 'careless extravagance'. Then Olivier's play closed after six weeks. It was his fifth flop in a row. He stayed on, collecting his guaranteed $500 each week, and they fought it out – Jill, Larry and God. He left for England in mid-November, not this time in the *Aquitania* but in the smaller, slower and cheaper *Lancastria*. He wrote to her on board ship, saying he had been standing on the top deck watching the sea, which was calm, like black glass.[3]

'Lovely just standing there with no one but God and you and the sea in the bright moonlight . . . I suppose our *happiest* moment has just the faintest shadow lurking somewhere near it, some doubt, or fear – fear perhaps of hurting some ideal, God perhaps, or the moment itself, and then I suppose our really happy moments are when we don't know they're there, and we look back and say 'I was happy then.' Being conscious of happiness always rather makes one step out of the picture and watch oneself being happy. . . But one must go on, eliminating the fears and doubts and feelings of safety and love, until one can be fully conscious of being happy. . . Yet I used to be *like* that – a little while ago. I must have strayed a little from God I suppose. I have been frightfully slack about religion since I've been in America. You must keep me up to that, Jill, it's my only hope of being of use to God and the world and I think everybody should try to be that. Goodnight darling. I kiss you.'

Jill, back in New York, was glad he had come to America and felt they had grown much closer and that theirs was a quiet and steady love. She wondered what Karl would think of her.[4] Karl was the Rev. Karl Ludwig Tiedemann, an American priest who had been in London the previous year and had acted as Olivier's confessor, but who by then had returned to America and had a temporary post at a school in Connecticut.[5]

Jill's mother was possessive. She came out to New York and stayed for a month, which was supposed to cheer Jill up, but she and Larry continued to agonise. She wrote from New York that she wished she could say she loved him perfectly and for always, but she couldn't: perhaps she would be able to after they were married. It seemed years since she had seen him and held his body close to hers.[6]

Olivier, back in England, had been obliged to stay with his father at his rectory at Buckinghamshire. By then he was on easy terms with his stepmother, and found her more congenial than he did his father. She was Ibo to him, he was Kim to her, and he thought her an absolute angel. This was also the time when his elder brother Dickie returned home on long leave from his Indian tea plantation. Then Larry fell on his feet again, and again had the leading part in a show that looked as if it was likely to last. This was *The Last Enemy*, in which he played a mentally wrecked airman who came back from the dead. His performance attracted a wonderful notice from Ivor Brown of the *Observer*, one of the London critics whose views mattered. He wrote that Olivier had given a series of brilliant performances in consistently ill-fated plays. 'May this one break the unlucky series. At any rate, his time will come.' Olivier, though, was overcome by guilt, writing to Jill from a club full of out-of-work actors playing poker that he felt a swine to be happy in his play while she was sick to death of *Bird in Hand*. 'Oh I'm a lucky boy. . . I'm loving you Jilli darling much better now, and the mental battles are getting less frequent. I should think so too. I'm a bloody fool ever to have them, but they just happen like a very well laid plan before I know where I am. . . Why can't I write to you properly – I've got one of those fear things – You seem snatched away from me and I can't say anything I want to say, as if you were all closed up.' He sent his love to her mother and to Karl, his confessor, whom Jill had by then met.[7]

By mid-December Jill's mother had gone home and her play had transferred to Chicago. She arrived in a snowstorm and compared the city to Sheffield, which was uncomplimentary and unjust and reflected her unhappy state of mind. She was wearing Larry's engagement ring but still dithering about marriage.[8]

Then a more immediate crisis arose at home. Larry's sister Sybille gave every sign of having gone mad. She had given up the stage, married a schoolmaster and writer, Gerald Day, and had a baby daughter. Then she had a nervous breakdown and lost all interest in the child. Day was concerned. Larry came to visit and swore his sister was no more mad than her husband. Then she screamed in the night. She tried to give her baby away to passing nuns. Larry

was shaken, and Sybille was taken to a mental hospital in north
London where she was allowed to dance in the garden. Larry of
course wrote to Jill in Chicago, who was apprehensive and curiously unsympathetic.[9]

She first sent a cable saying it was his problem and not hers, and
then wrote that she knew he wanted to do all he could to help his
sister, but that he should not do so at the cost of his own health.
She said he was 'Theatre of the Theatre', that there was a great
deal of the artist in him, off stage as well as on, and that this business was going to play the devil with him mentally. He shouldn't
do anything that would affect him later in life.[10] Jill was prescient
to see that early that Olivier was 'Theatre of the Theatre', but it is
not clear how helping his sister could have hurt him. She was
evidently wary of his being associated with his Sybille's condition.

It was Prohibition time. Jill was taken to parties in speakeasies.
On New Year's Eve the theatre's head property man gave her two
bottles of whiskey. His name was Red Gallagan, he called her 'girlie',
and she thought he was a bootlegger, a gangster and a senator.[11]

In the early hours of New Year's Day Jill sat up until half past
four to receive a telephone call from Larry. Those were the days
when long-distance calls were costly and had to be reserved in
advance. This was probably the first of the thousand transatlantic
calls with which Olivier enriched telephone companies throughout
his life. She sobbed to hear his voice and feared that their love was
going to have a hard fight to live, and that they would both be lost
souls without it.[12]

That was how 1930 began. On 19 January Jill wrote from Chicago
that she was coming home almost at once. She did not. She went
back to New York and at the end of January left on a holiday to
Florida and the Bahamas. Only then did she return, arriving home
just before Olivier's run in *The Last Enemy* ended in mid-March.
Then began the longest period of unemployment in the theatre that
he ever suffered in peacetime. It lasted five months. He did however
make his first film, in Berlin. It was a crime thriller whose working
title was *Hocus Pocus*, later changed to *The Temporary Widow*, and
was shot in two versions with separate English and German casts.
Olivier was paid £80 a week for five weeks and had to supply his

own clothes. Jill saw him off at Croydon Airport on 15 April and had a shock when she saw an evening paper placard saying 'Croydon–Berlin Plane Down', but that was an earlier flight. He had planned to return for two days during the shooting but the day after he left she cabled not to come home but to save money to marry. Then she havered over whether to fly out herself to see him but discovered it would cost £30 for four days, and this was too much. He had only £50 left from the £1,000 he had earned in America, and a large car to pay for, and tax not paid, and Jill's own holiday to the Bahamas had cost a small fortune.[13] She constantly worried about money. He hardly gave it a thought.

Jill wrote to him constantly. She asked him to be a master to her, and to undress her and put her to bed. She also told him she had seen Henry Ainley's Hamlet. He was one of the principal romantic actors of the day. She said it was beautiful, the way the speeches rippled from his tongue. She thought Larry would be perfect as Hamlet, just as good as Ainley, and better because of his youth.[14]

In Berlin, Olivier went frequently to the opera; ten times during his stay. In his first ten days he saw performances of operas by Gluck, Verdi, Bizet, Mascagni and Puccini. Back in London, Jill pined. The night he went to *Carmen*, she was writing that she hadn't even looked for a job. She was afflicted by doubts and did not know what he saw in her. But, recalling one recent night, she said he had looked lovely with nothing on, but that he had to put on weight.[15]

She entirely lacked confidence in herself. When she failed to get a part in a play she was convinced she was a flop. By the time Olivier had progressed to Wagner, to *Mastersingers* and *Tannhauser*, Jill had become despondent. They had spoken on the telephone and again it had ended badly. She begged him to tell her what the trouble was. Was it their imp? Was it the dancing instructress or what she called their bigger devil, their particular pet devil, or what?[16]

What is all this talk of imps and bigger devils and pet devils, and of a dancing instructress? Larry and Jill had spent ten weeks together in New York, and she writes of his undressing her and of her seeing him naked. There may have been just that and no more, and their tormented religious scruples make this likely. Was Olivier, at the age of twenty-two, still virginal? He appears to say so, in the most convoluted fashion, in his autobiography. But everything he wrote there should be construed with as much care as if it had been drafted by Treasury Counsel, with what is not said every bit as significant as what is said, and he might equally have been saying no more than that his 'religious convictions and practices' remained intact until his marriage. On the other hand he did say to a friend a few years later – and this was a friend who kept a detailed diary whose narrative is reliable – that he had been 'alarmingly loose before he married Jill'. But then, even if Olivier did say that, what did he mean by loose?[17]

What then of the dancing instructress? It may have been a girl in Berlin, or it may have been Fabia Drake, an actress and dancer who had taught Larry as long ago as the time he was at All Saints. She was three years older than him. Throughout their lives they remained close, and she always wrote to him and of him with love.

If that were so it would be the straightforward explanation, but the straightforward is unlikely with Olivier. More importantly, and more obscurely, what about the imps and devils? There is no doubt that Jill later, ten years later, lived with women partners, and that she was bisexual. Had she felt an early and harmless attraction to other women and was this what so worried her? And what of Olivier? What did she fear he had not revealed to her? His close friend Denys Blakelock was later known to be homosexual, and his affection for the young Olivier is plain. They were often together. Olivier returned this affection but it may, at least at first, have been no more than an idea coloured by incense. Later on Blakelock took to writing books which made much of his early friendship with Olivier, who even wrote a short preface to one. But Blakelock complained that Olivier did not even acknowledge that he had received the inscribed copy of his last book, which he sent him when it was published in 1967. Perhaps this trading on an early friendship had by then become tedious, but when there was no response Blakelock did remonstrate with Olivier, fearing he may have 'done the wrong thing' but saying he had written about him 'with the utmost discretion'. There was *something* to be discreet about, as we shall see, but it has to be borne in mind that Olivier throughout his life was devoted to guilt. It took very little to convince him, even after he lost his religious faith, that he had strayed from his only hope of being of use to God and the world.[18]

In early 1930 he still had his faith and his confessor. Karl had written saying that Jill had told him about her difficulty and that he had told her not to worry or be afraid but just to love Larry a lot more. He would say no more than that he trusted and honoured them both utterly, and that all problems were solved if they loved the Lord.[19]

Back in London on 17 May, Olivier embarked on his second film, a four-day quickie called *Too Many Crooks*, in which a stately home is burgled simultaneously by a playboy, a real crook and a pretty girl. He was the playboy. It earned him £60 towards his marriage, which had been fixed for 25 July. Jill then wrote, or rather gave her name to, an article entitled 'What I Think of Marriage', which appeared – with a large photograph of her – on the leader page of the *Daily Herald*, which had a circulation of more than one million. She had evidently forgotten how she had pleaded with Olivier, only a month before, to master her. Wives, she now wrote, were partners not playthings. She did not expect marriage to be one long romantic dream. In the conventional view of marriage, there were supposed to be no secrets between husband and wife, and no friends that the other did not know, but she did not agree with this. She would certainly have secrets and friends unknown to a husband of hers, and would have a holiday from him as well as from work. 'That perverted form of communism whereby a wife is expected to sink her independence, even to her separate bank account, throws a dreadful strain upon married happiness. . . Marriage, if it is to be any better than slavery, must mean perfect freedom of thought and action for both parties. . .'[20]

This happened to appear on Olivier's birthday. But nowhere in a long article, the most prominent in that day's paper, did Jill mention the name of the man she was going to marry.

Then Olivier was offered a play. In his diary for 18 June 1930 is the entry 'Noel Coward 10.' Coward was sitting up in bed in Japanese silk pyjamas, finishing his breakfast. He called Olivier 'Larry', so Larry called him 'Noel', often. Coward was already a great man of the theatre, as an actor and as a writer. In 1925 he had had five plays running in London at once. He was offering Olivier the part of Victor Prynne, one of the two secondary roles in his new comedy, *Private Lives*, in which he and Gertrude Lawrence would play the leads. It was not the leading part Olivier was by then used to, but it paid £50 a week and would enable him to marry knowing that he had a job to go to.[21] It has been often suggested that the Esmonds helped Olivier's career. But by 1930 H.V. Esmond, the actor-manager-playwright, had been dead for eight years, Eva Moore was doing little and Jill was having a hard time finding work for herself. Olivier's own connections to Sybil Thorndike and, through her, to Barry Jackson, had served him much better. But Jill had, as early as 1925, appeared in Coward's *Hay Fever*. If Olivier owed his introduction to Coward to her, as is likely, then he owed her a great debt.

Eva had wanted Jill to marry at the Chapel Royal of the Savoy, where she had herself been married. Olivier asked Fahv to marry them there. He refused, saying that he would not enter the place since divorced people were able to be married there as they were not, in those days, in most English churches. So the ceremony was arranged to take place neither at the Savoy nor with Fahv officiating. It was to be at Larry's old church, All Saints, Margaret Street, where it would be much grander.[22]

The night before the wedding, Olivier's pet devil showed itself. He told a colleague about it thirty years later, in these circumstances. He had been on the wagon for a year, and celebrated coming off it by getting drunk with the administrator of a theatre which he directed. This colleague, being homosexual, was naturally curious about Noel Coward and after many drinks said, come on, there must have been something between Coward and Olivier. To which Olivier replied that he had known about Coward's attraction to him but had said no, thank you. He said the closest he ever got to that sort of thing was the night before his wedding to Jill, when his best man climbed into his bed. This was Denys Blakelock. Blakelock's hands strayed. Olivier decided he couldn't do it, and that was that. That Olivier should have given this account does not make it the gospel truth, particularly after so many years, but it may go some way towards identifying the bigger devil.[23]

The day before the wedding, Ibo wrote a sweetly innocent letter to her stepson:[24]

'Kim darling – Just a little word on your wedding morning. I wish I could come and wake you up and sit on your bed and have a little talk – but that can't be, so I must send it on paper. It is such a big day for you and Jillie, there will be other big days in your lives, but nothing can be quite like this one.

'You said the other day, that you were both feeling such strangers to one another – that is just how it is – you *are* strangers until that wonderful service – afterwards you are just a complete one! Larry darling it's just beautiful and every day you will, please God, find that oneness becoming bigger and bigger.

'Be very gentle with her, darling, but be the leader.'

She then went on to write about Larry's late mother, who had died ten years before:

'*She* knows darling, that I have never tried, nor wanted, to take her place, only to carry on and so help her, in what she would have done – She will be very close to you tomorrow – nearer than any of us. God bless you and Jillie and keep you close to one another and close to Him – I love you very much darling. Your Ibo.'

At the service All Saints gave Olivier the whole choir as a present, something which, as he remarked, was a distinction not usually enjoyed except by the high, mighty, or rich. Denys Blakelock stood as Olivier's best man. Eva gave a reception in the garden of her Georgian house in Chelsea. Olivier made a speech, bride and groom changed into their going-away clothes and then, in the Chrysler he could not afford, they started the long journey to Lulworth Cove in Dorset, where a friend of Eva's had lent them a seaside house for the honeymoon. It was a drive of a 150 miles; too long.

The kind lender of the house had strangely left her two grown-up unmarried daughters to act as hostesses. They served the married couple an embarrassed supper. What happened then was described by Olivier fifty years later. He and Jill went to their room. 'After some hesitant efforts to accomplish something we hoped would pass for foreplay – my own efforts, I knew, would not pass muster in a third-floor back room in Lisle Street, and all that would rest in my bride's memory would be an endurance test – at last we turned away from each other. I remember going to sleep with the dazzlingly selfish sulk, "My wife doesn't suit me", as if to some club friend. . . It really did look like a pretty crass mistake. I had insisted on getting married from a pathetic mixture of religious and animal promptings. . . The indications were that my dreams of high sexuality were not to be realised, which was depressing and soon became oppressive. I was just not imaginative enough to find what might be the key to Jill's responsiveness.'[25] Lisle Street is on the southern fringes of Soho. If he knew his efforts would not pass muster with a girl there, then he can not have been entirely without experience.

The day after his wedding night he wrote to his mother-in-law, calling her 'darling Mum', thanking her for making everything perfect for them and saying it *had* been perfect. The weather, though, had not been kind and he had a cold, and that morning there was a tragedy when by accident he shaved off half his moustache. He drew her a little sketch of it and hoped it would grow again before he came back to London. 'O Mum darling, I think only you can imagine what Jill is like down here, climbing over rocks and being a pirate and pointing at imaginary fishes and things in the water – life is perfect and I think she's fairly happy – O she's grand. . . "O Shenandoah I love your daughter."'[26]

Olivier's diary entry for his wedding day reads 'Jilli & Larry', in ink rather than the usual pencil, and with emphasis. And there his diary for that year ends. There are no further entries. He made a point of this in his autobiography, saying he kept no diary again for ten years and did not pursue his religious practices ever again. Having gone to the trouble of making this point he then wrote that there was 'nothing in the scrappiest bit revelatory' about it.[27]

He had work to return to. Rehearsals for *Private Lives* started soon. In August the play opened its pre-London run with a week in Edinburgh. While he was away Jill was depressed. She could not get a part in a play, was testing for a film and was gloomy about her prospects there. She asked him not to gamble as they owed so much. She felt lost without him and lonely in bed.[28]

From Edinburgh *Private Lives* went on to Birmingham and then Manchester, where Olivier gave a newspaper interview.[29] The anonymous reporter, who seems to have been a woman, wrote that he was irresistible and called him a virile youth, but remarked that he knew everything and seemed to be pessimistic, almost cynical, about everything. 'Only fools are happy,' he said. 'I suppose it is because they don't really know what they want in life, and so every little pleasure that comes along they regard as a promise of happiness. I somehow can't get that way. I always examine things so very closely that immediate pleasures are dwarfed by my insistence on ultimate benefits.'

It was very like the Olivier who looked out over a black sea from the *Lancastria* on his passage home from New York and wrote black thoughts. The reporter tried to cheer him up by telling him he was well on the way to fame, but he replied that with few exceptions he had always had parts he had not liked, and that he hated the part he was playing then. The reporter persisted. Through the stage, had he not found himself a most charming wife? No reply was recorded.

The play's London opening was brilliant. 'I experienced for the first time the incredible sense of being in a West End smash success – the thronged stage door and the parties every night. One of the advantages of being in a tiny cast was that "those other two" seldom got left out of an invitation. Well, it was exciting then, before blasé sophistication had set in.' *Private Lives* played to full houses for three months and could have run for a year, but Coward was determined to take it off and transfer to Broadway. When the play was in the last month of its London run Olivier was filming in the daytime at Elstree. The film was *Potiphar's Wife* – later in America retitled *Her Strange Desire* – and Olivier was the chauffeur whose employer, Lady Diana Bradford, fails to seduce him and then out of pique accuses him of attempting to rape her. It was made in three weeks and was remarkable for three things. The first was that in the trial scene, when the seductress's case collapsed, Olivier commanded attention though he hardly had a word to say: there, already, was a screen presence. The second thing was that by paying him £60 a week the film more than doubled his earnings, and the third was that his contract, for the first time, stipulated that no other male actor should have better billing. But his main business was the theatre and *Private Lives* and its forthcoming transfer to New York. It happened that the actress who had been playing the other half of 'the other two' was pregnant, and so Jill was offered the part.[30] In January 1931 Mr and Mrs Laurence Olivier sailed back to New York.

5

The Lick of Luxury of Those Lush Valleys

COWARD RAN *PRIVATE LIVES* in New York for his stipulated three months, no more, and to even greater applause than in London. Unemployed men sold apples in the streets but the Depression had not yet hit the theatre and there were parties every night after the show. Larry and Jill met Charlie Chaplin, Lynne Fontanne, and Alfred Lunt, and in the day time they did film tests. Jill's were better than Larry's. This was not the natural order of things. His salary in *Private Lives* was $500 a week against her $250. She had offers from Paramount, Fox and RKO Radio – the last seeming to think she was the eighth wonder of the world. Larry had no offers and was even more discouraged when Jill was described by the *New York Journal and American* as 'the wife of Mr Olivia'. Jill believed that Hollywood was a God-forsaken place and hated the idea of going, particularly if Larry did not go too. But Fox were offering her $875 a week for a year.[1]

This was tempting because she had been on the London stage for seven years and considered she had done nothing really worthwhile. Her last London salary had been £8 a week [$40 at the time]. Even if Hollywood threw her out at the end of the year she thought she would have done three or four pictures and made a great deal of money. But she was not a bit excited about Hollywood itself, and would probably be on her own as Larry was not keen to go because he had a bigger career in the theatre. But she couldn't give up the film offer while he leapt ahead.[2]

When *Private Lives* still had a month to run Olivier discussed his future with Coward. What should he do? Should he go? He later said Coward sneered at him: 'Hahlleewood'. But the two of them talked till four in the morning, and Coward's advice was that he should go with Jill anyway. He hesitated. Then he got offers after all, to do two pictures for RKO at $1,000 a week and an option for two more at $1,400. He still hesitated, changing his mind from day to day. On Coward's advice, Jill made up his mind for him. They would go together.[3]

So they were both ready to leave for Hollywood. Then something happened which showed why marriage had proved, for both of them, such a disappointment. Jill had been feeling slightly unwell for some time and thought she had a grumbling appendix. That was not it at all. Coward had persuaded her to see his doctor in New York, who found an ovarian cyst the size of an apple. 'Which,' wrote Olivier in a letter to her mother, 'was probably the cause of all the trouble and other little troubles she'd been having lately. So Bertie [the surgeon] planned to take this away, and the appendix at the same time, and also to enable another alteration lower down – thereby killing three birds with one stone – and making the most tremendous difference to her enjoyment of life.'

It is a long and detailed letter, of eighteen pages, which he illustrated with drawings of the cyst and the appendix. It is the first evidence of Olivier's lifelong and sometimes macabre fascination with the workings of the body. His description makes it sound as if poor Jill had been suffering from a prolapsed uterus. 'The little alteration low down took a long time, which he did first of all, then he made the incision and removed the cyst.' Then, as a routine precaution, the appendix was removed.

When Larry went to see Jill afterwards she vomited and the nurse pushed him out of the room. 'Funny,' he wrote, 'how when someone one loves is suffering one always wants to torture oneself and suffer too. I did – so I listened outside the door.' Next day he returned, stroked Jill's head for a bit, and then went downstairs to watch her surgeon perform another operation.

'And I was so interested that I stayed for a second one. It was awfully funny Mum, I'm not really a bit squeamish and I stood for two hours watching Bertie sawing peoples' insides about – without turning a hair.' There are more and lengthy details of Jill's sufferings, of catheters inserted into her and of her painful inability to urinate. Four days after the operation Olivier was going to leave Jill in hospital and go ahead to Hollywood on his own. He went to see his wife before he caught his train from New York. 'Just before I left. . . Victory of Victories, after trying all day long – through hours of concentration, she performed the glorious act by herself! (wee wee).' Having observed all this he wrote his long letter to Eva between New York and Chicago, headed it 'On the train to California' and signed himself, 'Your Jilli's loving Larry.'[4]

Olivier's gynaecological details go some way to explaining why their marriage had not been a delight. They do not, however, explain the earlier concerns about imps and devils. If Jill's troubles were physical there would have been no point in Olivier consulting his confessor, as he did.

Jill stayed in hospital another two weeks to recover and then made the four-day train journey west. The house in Los Angeles that Olivier, or the studio, had found seemed wonderful to her. She had lived in some style at her mother's house in the gentle Buckinghamshire countryside, with views stretching down to the Thames, but the vistas from 8945 Appian Way, at Lookout Mountain Crest, had an altogether American grandeur. The views west extended eight miles over the sprawling city and down to the Pacific Ocean. To the north rose the Santa Monica mountains. Fig and mimosa flourished in their garden. The house came with balconies all round, automatic hot air heating, a Steinway baby grand piano, and a German couple who kept house and acted as maid and valet. They bought two cars. They became friends with P. G. Wodehouse, Joan Crawford, and Douglas Fairbanks Jnr. Fairbanks was the closest of these friends. They went fishing down the Mexican coast, drank vodka and learned to sing lusty songs in different languages. 'It was a time,' said Fairbanks, 'when Hollywood producers referred to Olivier loftily, whenever they did refer to him at all, as that "rather nice Englishman with a French name who looks like a young Ronald Colman", but that was about it.' Larry and Jill bathed off the Pacific coast beaches, became bronzed all over, and in the evening went to symphony concerts at the Hollywood Bowl or entertained, giving dinner parties with six courses and different wines all served by a butler. Olivier found other peoples' parties, particularly the grand ones, 'unbelievably true to their reputation, a sheer joy if you were in the mocking vein. Those glorious creatures, with their entrances and their descents down the the staircase, were quite magnificent in their grace and stateliness and their confident composure – so soon to disappear without trace. After a couple of bootleg shots, and in as many minutes, all that majesty was sprawling and rolling about unable to utter a sentence that could be understood.'[5] He was never short of an acerbic remark about the Hollywood movie people among whom he worked.

By the end of June, Jill had turned down the part of a tough American gangster's moll, having persuaded the studio she was not right for it. Her illness had put her back six weeks, she had done no work since she arrived, and she had been paid £360 for sitting in the sun. Larry had finished his first film, *Friends and Lovers*, with Adolphe Menjou and Erich von Stroheim. He later said that the cast, apart from its eminence, was wretchedly ill-assorted and that the film died the death of a dog, but at the time he was elated. The studio head had told him he would be a star in a year, and he was so pleased with himself that he had decided to do another two or three pictures and make a name in Hollywood.[6]

When they were offered their old stage parts in the film of *Private Lives*, with Norma Shearer and Robert Montgomery, they were confident enough of better offers to smile and say no. Jill thought she was wanted for the lead in the first film adaptation of Mary Shelley's novel, *Frankenstein*, the film in which Boris Karloff made his name, but she did not get it.[7] Larry was due to star opposite the silent star Pola Negri in a melodrama where his part would be that of the last Serbian king, whose defenestration ended the dynasty. He had admired Negri's films but in the studio found her to be a ham actress and rather fat, and he complained that she killed him with passion.[8] He then contracted the first of his many illnesses. He suffered from jaundice, found himself unable to swallow water, spent four days in hospital and did not complete the film. He then did another melodrama, this time set in Czarist Russia, called *The*

Yellow Ticket, with Elissa Landi and Lionel Barrymore. Jill had still done nothing. In her whole time in Hollywood she played only two supporting parts. Larry did eventually make a third film, *Westward Passage*, and this time was pleased with it. He took a great shine to the leading lady, Ann Harding. She was a beautiful woman, a natural blonde who was generous to her inexperienced leading man, and he felt 'the stir of optimism'. He remembered her with pleasure. When a friend asked him, years later, how he knew she was a natural blonde, he replied, 'Because I asked her. I said, "Ann, is your blonde hair really natural?" And she said, "Yes. I could prove it to you if I knew you better."'[9]

The film lost $250,000. The depression had caught up with Hollywood. The young David O. Selznick, who was all of twenty-nine years of age, was brought in to rescue RKO, which he did by cutting the number of films made and halving salaries. How Olivier and his wife came to leave Hollywood is a matter of dispute. Olivier's story is that he was bored and went home. Selznick's is that he was going to fire Olivier anyway. All this is complicated by Jill's position. In spite of all the easy living she was unhappy.[10]

But Jill did, in spite of everything, have the chance, no more than a chance, of the principal role in *A Bill of Divorcement*, a film which looked set to make a star of its leading lady. Again she was due to be disappointed in her hopes. Olivier's version is that he had an appointment with Selznick, who was late, and that while he was waiting he looked round Selznick's desk and there found a draft contract to engage Miss Katharine Hepburn, an unknown, at $1,500 a week for the first year, rising to $2,000 and $2,500 in the second and third. He knew that Jill's salary had been cut to $750. It was obvious to him that Miss Hepburn would not be paid these sums if she were not destined for stardom. The studio's version is that this was the meeting at which Olivier was fired, and that the document he says he saw did not exist since Miss Hepburn had already been engaged at $1,250 a week, and with only a three-week guarantee.[11]

At any rate, Jill wanted to stay but Olivier was going; he suggested they should separate for a while. Jill had not proved to be the eighth wonder of the world and whether she could have had the part is doubtful, but it would have been decided one way or the other in a month or two. Olivier could have waited to find out. Eventually the part went to Miss Hepburn and was the start of her splendid career. Olivier, in his last years, spoke more generously about Jill than he had done before. 'I don't think, honestly, in the final analysis, she would have got it, but she was up for it and she was promised it, but they were looking like mad for something a bit better. Poor old Jill. And they found this strange little creature who had this absolutely awful voice, and the big shots decided there was something about her. Mark you, every studio was looking for its Garbo. Garbo was MGM's and that was theirs.'[12] Jill went home with her husband. Selznick made sure the incident came back to haunt Larry. But then there was never any love lost between those two men.

For Olivier his two Hollywood years were mixed. He did not become a star, but there were moments of elation. As the mood took him, he could later talk about the 'wasteland' of his early years or he could say, looking back; 'I needed the lick of luxury of those lush valleys'. One factor which must not be overlooked is that he instinctively feared the leisure which Jill so enjoyed. Their home movies show him diving athletically and naked into pleasant swimming pools, but all his life he needed and craved work. Three films in two years was not enough.[13]

Mr and Mrs Olivier returned home by way of San Francisco, the World's Fair in Chicago, and New York. It was not even as if he were hastening home to his beloved theatre. His first two jobs in England were both films. Gloria Swanson, a great of the silent screen, was choosing to make a comeback at Ealing Studios in a film to be distributed in America. She continued to make such comebacks until *Sunset Boulevard* in 1950. She told Noel Coward she wanted a Ronald Colman type. He told her Olivier was better than that. *Perfect Understanding*, the film they made together, was, according to Olivier, nothing of the sort. It was a disaster. The lightness of Coward was all the rage, but it needed Coward to write it. Larry's next film, *No Funny Business*, had even more Coward ingredients: quarrelling couples, reconciliation, trains traversing France, art-deco hotels on the Riviera, and even three members of the cast of *Private Lives* – Gertrude Lawrence, Olivier and Jill Esmond – but that too failed. The *New York Times* said it deserved some kind of booby prize for its success in reaching such a devastating level of mediocrity with such a cast. It was the only film Olivier made with Jill, and he never mentioned it.[14]

At last he found a play in the West End, and a good one, with the unglamorous title of *The Rats of Norway*. It is set in a boys' preparatory school in Newcastle, its themes are those of loyalty and nostalgia for times past, and it earned for Olivier one of the best notices he had ever received. Harold Hobson, then drama critic of the *Christian Science Monitor* and later famous as a critic for the London *Sunday Times*, said Olivier's performance was heartbreaking and later listed it as one of the seven occasions in the theatre when he had felt himself in the presence of greatness. Olivier also seems, in this play, to have found himself a congenial mistress in his leading lady, Helen Spencer. 'I think this handkerchief is yours,' she says in one note, sending it back to him. She often wrote to him playfully. Later on, she was the only one of his women friends to chivvy him openly about Vivien Leigh, and to warn him against her. They remained friends for another thirty years. Joan Plowright, Olivier's third wife, seeing them together in the 1960s, sensed even then that there had been something between them. About this time there was also Annie Rooney, another actress, who wrote to say she had seen Larry's performance and was sorry she couldn't come round afterwards, but added, 'If a mistress can send love to a wife, give yours my love!'[15]

Olivier, who had previously lived in a modest house, now found one which was not so much grand as grandiose, and moved in that June. It was on Chelsea Embankment, where the painters J.M.W. Turner and James MacNeill Whistler had lived. He took Whistler's old studio, looking south over the Thames. Its windows were twenty-five feet high, requiring white silk curtains of that length and thirty feet across. The main doors were bronze, as on an ocean liner. A firm of decorators fashionable in theatre society was employed to attend to the subtler details and the walls were painted duck-egg blue. Larry and Jill's bed was seven-feet wide. In the main room a bar of pickled oak was erected, something which was not done in decent English society. For a man who had turned his back on Hollywood it was strangely like Hollywood-on-Thames.[16]

But he had not turned his back on Hollywood. Midway through

the run of his new play MGM offered him $1,000 a week for a year. He declined, not wishing to commit himself for so long. Then his Hollywood agent cabled with a much more attractive offer.

HAVE ONE PICTURE PROPOSITION LEADING MAN OPPOSITE GARBO
GREAT PART STARTING IN TWO WEEKS ANSWER IMMEDIATELY

Garbo was unquestionably the greatest film actress and the greatest film legend of the day. Playing opposite her could make Olivier. It was an offer he could not refuse. But he could stall and he could haggle. Cables went back and forth. He did not know when he could get out of his play and, if he could, he wanted not less than $1,500 a week and first-class transportation both ways; and he wanted to be back by autumn. How long would the picture take to shoot? And would his agent look out for a picture for Jill, who might accompany him? And would his moustache be required?

MGM agreed the $1,500 and, after a further exchange of cables, offered Olivier the option of doing a substitute picture if the Garbo was cancelled. Olivier agreed this only if his salary was paid from the date of his arrival and continued to be paid whether the Garbo film was made or not. He agreed to the substitute picture only if he had script approval. MGM told him to let his moustache grow in case it was needed and requested his measurements, in order to make the costumes in advance. He cabled in reply that he was five-feet ten-inches tall, thirty-eight chest, thirty waist, thirty-eight hips, and ended, MOUSTACHE BEING WORKED ON SAILING EUROPA SATURDAY.[17]

He had cabled earlier to ask what the picture would be about but had received no direct reply. He first learned from the newspapers that Garbo would play Queen Christina of Sweden (1626–89) and he would be Don Antonio, a Spanish envoy with whom she fell in love while he was at the Swedish court asking her hand in marriage for his master, the King of Spain. Not until he reached Hollywood did he learn that Garbo's contract gave her the right to choose her leading man, and that she had had old films run through for her and had liked what she saw when she viewed Olivier in *Westward Passage*.

That an English actor should be given the part was extraordinary, and the publicity immense. As Olivier described it: 'The news hit the front page of the *Daily Express* [then Britain's biggest-selling daily paper]. My photographs were splashed all over the various organs of the press, and I felt quite a little hero. I sailed across the Atlantic in great style, with all the attendant publicity hounds at every dock and at every stop of the train to Los Angeles. I had all my clothes made and was posed with Miss Garbo, and worked with her for a fortnight on the film, with every conceivable kind of attendant bally-hoo. At the end of this fortnight I was found wanting.'[18]

There are two accounts of just what happened. The first is Olivier's own, written almost fifty years later when he had been trying to make light of the matter for most of his life. 'I realised in the first two weeks,' he said, 'with an ever increasing apprehension, that I was not by any means making the best of myself; something was stopping me. I was too nervous and scared of my leading lady. I knew I was lightweight for her and nowhere near her stature, and began to feel more and more certain that I was for the chop. I made up my mind that I must make a big effort to get along with her and find some way to get on friendlier terms.

'Before work had started one morning, I found her sitting on an old chest on the set. I went boldly up to her and said the three or four sentences that I had made up and practised: but no utterance came from her. I began to flounder and grab at anything that came into my head: some saying of Will Rogers, of Noel — anybody — anything at all, until I came to a wretched end and stopped, pale and panting. After a breathless pause, she slid herself off the chest sideways and said, "Oh vell, life'sh a pain, anyway." I knew then that the end was not far off.'[19]

There is a second version, from 'the MGM crowd' on the set. It has the advantage of being more nearly contemporary, having been related by a *Collier's Magazine* reporter only six years after the event. The MGM crowd were not sympathetic to the uppity Englishman among them, but on the whole the two versions do corroborate each other.

What the MGM crowd said was that Larry had been tossed out on his neck. This is how they described the famous meeting on the set:

'Olivier gave her the old British charm. He turned it on till it gushed out of his pores. No response from Garbo. Then he dazzled her with English wit, the Noel Coward stuff, epigrams popping all over the place. No response. Then the he-man approach. Big swear words. Swagger. From G, nothing. Then he tried the pathetic angle. Put his finger in his mouth and pouted, pathetic as hell. At the pathetic approach, G finally arose from her seat, looked up at Olivier tragically and said, "Life is a pain." And walked away. From which Olivier deduced that he was through and he wasn't wrong.'[20]

Olivier's story is that Walter Wanger, the producer, sent for him the next day and said, 'Larry, I want you to know something. We are crazy about you here at MGM and want to put you under contract. But it's just that in this particular part. . .' Olivier let Wanger struggle on for a bit and then told him he was not bothered, provided he got his money.

'Why of course. Glad to get on to money terms, so much easier than other things.'

He had another two weeks' pay to come, at $1,500 a week. As a face saver it was put about that Garbo had not found him tall enough.

It was the first great failure of his career. He was not yet the master of his trade that Garbo was. More than that, it was greatest rebuff of his entire career. He never again says, nor does anyone else even hint, that he found himself on a stage or a film set with an actor or actress beyond his stature.

Collier's says he left Hollywood in high dudgeon, drawing room E, car 198, vowing that never again would he be dragged across the wastes of Kansas for the likes of these. Nor was he. The next time he flew. And also, before taking the train east in 1933, he and Jill, yet again spending money while they had it, took a holiday in Hololulu. There, at the Royal Hawaiian Hotel, they received a cable from Larry's Hollywood agent.

WOULD YOU BE INTERESTED IN METRO CONTRACT FIFTEEN HUNDRED WEEKLY FORTY WEEKS IN ONE YEAR GUARANTEE REGARDS.[21]

The cable survives. It was sent and received. The classic story is that Olivier told the telegraph boy, 'No reply'.

6

Matinée Idol to Roaring Italian Boy

OLIVIER'S 'NO REPLY' TO MGM may have been in part a grand gesture of hurt pride. He had already turned down the substitute role his agent had negotiated in case the Garbo film fell through, declining to play Romeo to Norma Shearer's Juliet and giving as his reason that Shakespeare would never work in the cinema. But there was another reason why he did not want a long-term contract of any sort. He and Jill had already agreed to appear in a play opening in New York that October.

This was *The Green Bay Tree*. They had been seduced into it before they left London by the Broadway producer Jed Harris, who had 'charmed the daylights' out of them. Olivier's fee was $800 a week, more than he had earned in any play. In New York, however, the charming Mr Harris – who also directed – transformed himself, as Olivier put it, into a hurtful, arrogant, venomous little fiend. Olivier admitted the play was brilliantly done, but found it a poisoning experience. He did later have his own back on Mr Harris, when he based his own poisonous portrait of Richard III on him, in the play and in the film. Walt Disney was also said to have taken his cartoon Big Bad Wolf straight from the features of Jed Harris. That December of 1933, from New York, Olivier wrote to his sister Sybille: 'It's a terrible thing for an actor to say, isn't it, because we do need the money and have no prospects in England, but I've never hated playing any part so much before.'[1]

The trouble may not have been entirely Mr Harris, though Olivier did say he was never so near to losing his self-control and walking out on a director.[2] It may also have been the play. The story is that of a young man, played by Olivier, who is introduced by a rich homosexual to a life of leisure and pleasure but then falls in love with a girl and wants to escape, and fails. Reminiscing in his old age Olivier said that the play was his first big success in New York. Then he said. 'I mean, it was a play that was intensely brave on its own, and the performances in it had to be equally brave, and I was playing the old man's young man, trying to get out of it because I had fallen in love with a girl, and I wanted to found in my nature now a desire to be a normal sort of person, which of course set the old man in a thorough fighting fettle. No need to tell you he won, and that was a wonderful thing for me, because I certainly did make a great enormous success in it.'[3] He did get marvellous notices. The *New York Times* said that he gave an extraordinary study in the decomposition of a character. The *Pittsburgh Press* was even better: 'In the horrifying scene where he is beaten into slavish submission by his benefactor's abnormal attraction for him, his acting becomes not *acting*, but an exhibition of emotional collapse so painful to witness that the eyes of the audience are torn away; the spectacle of his ignominy actually becomes too terrible to bear.' This is penetrating. It was the first time a critic ever saw and remarked on that most Olivier-like characteristic, that he did not merely act a character but, through the means of his acting, *became* that character.

In spite of what he had told Sybille, he did have prospects in London, where he went straight into *Biography*, a Sam Behrman comedy directed by Noel Coward. It was a lovely play with a splendid director, but it folded in five weeks. Then he had two great pieces of luck. The first was in an historical play, *Mary Queen of Scots*, where he played Bothwell, the queen's lover. He got the opportunity only because Ralph Richardson, who had been rehearsing the part, took such a dislike to its romantic excesses that he asked to be released. Olivier, who replaced him only eight days before the first night, cannot have avoided all the excesses, since the critic of the London *Evening News* wrote that he did not believe any Scottish nobleman of the time could have so many of the Hollywood mannerisms of Clark Gable. The play ran happily for three months but its principal interest for Olivier was that it introduced him to so many people who were important to his later career. There were the three Motley girls, designers with whom he often worked; Bronson Albery, the theatre manager with whom he was later associated at the Old Vic company; and most of all, and at a critical point in Olivier's career, John Gielgud, who was the play's director. There was one other thing about this play that delighted Olivier. An American actress, Francine Langmore, was in London. She had happened to see *The Green Bay Tree* in New York. Noel Coward brought her to see Olivier as Bothwell and she refused to believe it was the same actor she had seen before. Coward brought her to Olivier's dressing room to meet him after the show, and still she did not believe it.

'Oh purr purr purr,' said Olivier, remembering this, 'Bliss, bliss.'[4] Once again, on stage, he had been not himself but the man he was playing. Once again he had achieved the grand act of making himself invisible and becoming someone else.

Then came the most archetypical of all Olivier's matinée idol plays, which he somehow fails even to mention in his autobiography. It was a take-off, almost a lampoon, of the Barrymores, one of the greatest of all American theatrical families. In America it had already had great success as *The Royal Family*, but that was hardly a title which could be used in 1930s England, where it would have seemed lèse-majesty. It was changed for its British performances to *Theatre Royal*. The producer was Noel Coward and in the cast was Marie Tempest, aged seventy, a grande dame of the theatre who had toured the world. It was the first play in which Olivier's contract stipu-lated that his name should appear above the title.[5] He played the part of Anthony Cavendish, the thinly disguised John Barrymore, who had played a magnificent Hamlet in New York and London and then starred in Hollywood movies. In 1925, when he was eighteen, Olivier had seen and much admired his Hamlet, saying that when he was on stage the sun came out.[6] He had later met him in Hollywood. *Theatre Royal* was one long swashbuckle with twirling moustaches, a duel fought on stage and a Fairbanks-style leap from a balcony. This was the first of many athletic and dangerous stunts for which Olivier became notorious. The press loved it. As the London

Daily Telegraph put it, Mr Olivier, playing a wild screen-lover with all the women in the world at his feet, gave the best performance of his career.

In one such performance he nearly damaged poor Marie Tempest. In the duel his rapier flew from his hand and struck her ample bosom. This brought the following rhyming telegram from Noel Coward:

> LARRY YOUR PRODUCER BEGS DO NOT BREAK YOUR PADDED LEGS
> DARLING DO NOT OVERACT TRY TO LEAVE THE SET INTACT
> DO NOT TIE YOURSELF IN COILS KEEP THE BUTTONS ON THE FOILS
> THOUGH YOU SHOW EACH MANLY CURVE KEEP A LITTLE IN RESERVE
> AND REMEMBER LARRY SWEET MARIE TEMPEST NEEDS HER FEET.[7]

Larry took precious little notice, continued to play the part up to the hilt and, after a run of three months, in the famous leap from the balcony, broke not his leg but his ankle. It was at the end of the second act and an understudy had to take over. The London papers gave this grave event full coverage. The *Daily Mirror* carried a picture of Larry in bed, with Jill perched solicitously on the edge. The *Daily Sketch*, a rival tabloid, also sent a reporter who commented on the famous cocktail bar in the lofty studio, revealing that Larry, from his bed, could see the view which had inspired Whistler to paint his famous 'nocturne' of Battersea Bridge, and added the information that Jill had not been surprised to hear of the broken ankle because she had dreamed a premonitory dream. Larry's former mistress, Helen Spencer, wrote saying there must have been panic when he couldn't go on for the last act, enquiring whether he had enough to read and ending, 'I suppose you are surrounded by ministering blondes'.[8]

One of Olivier's entourage at Cheyne Walk – though not ministering to him in Helen Spencer's sense – was the exotic Sofka Zinovieff, a White Russian refugee, who came as his secretary first two mornings a week, then five, and then full-time. She had been born Princess Sophia Dolgorouky and was descended on her father's side from the princely family that founded Moscow and on her mother's side from an illegitimate son of Catherine the Great. As a girl she had played with the last Tsarevich of Russia. In 1919, after the Bolshevik revolution, she was brought out of the Crimea on the same British warship as the Dowager Empress, to whom her grandmother was lady-in-waiting. She spoke Russian, English, French, competent German and Italian, and later even some Czech. In England in the 1930s she had to earn a living as a secretary and came to Olivier through an agency called Universal Aunts. She asked for 17s 6d a week and remembered Jill calling downstairs to Larry, 'Give her thirty bob.' She liked Jill and thought of her as 'one of the very rare unequivocally nice people [she] had ever met.' For £1.50 a week, then £7, she managed Olivier's fan mail and looked after his pet ring-tailed lemur, Tony, who leapt round the studio, sometimes encouraged by the sips of alcohol he was allowed. She stayed with Olivier for six years until the outbreak of war.[9]

In November 1934, in the middle of the run of *Theatre Royal*, Olivier gave one performance, at a gala for an ex-servicemen's charity, of Stanhope in *Journey's End*. He appeared by special request of Princess Alice, granddaughter of Queen Victoria and the president of many such charities. The play was by then world-famous. Colin Clive, who had taken the part Olivier had abandoned, was in Hollywood starring in films like *The Bride of Frankenstein* and drinking hard. Olivier received wonderful notices. The *Morning Post* wrote that he managed to suggest, better than any of his predecessors, that Stanhope was still a magnetic and sympathetic officer, and that this made the pathos of his maddened and drunken outbursts only the more poignantly appealing. The *Daily Telegraph* said that though Clive's Stanhope had more leadership, Olivier's had more humanity.[10]

After *Theatre Royal* Olivier appeared briefly in *Ringmaster*, a play which required him to act from a wheelchair. He played the part of a formerly fashionable actor, now crippled, who ran a Devonshire hotel and dominated the lives of the residents. The director was Raymond Massey and the strong cast included Cathleen Nesbitt, Dame May Whitty, Nigel Patrick, and Jill Esmond. *Country Life* did

not like it, saying it would do Olivier no end of good to play a part
in which he had no opportunities for sulking or snarling. Helen
Spencer again wrote to Larry, saying she now had children but
would like another smell of the stage. 'So,' she said, 'if you want a
dirty mind in one of your theatres in the future, you might think
of this old sod.'[11] But *Ringmaster*, in spite of its cast, lasted only
eight days; it was Olivier's shortest run in the West End.

He then made his first venture into production. For the first time
the words 'Laurence Olivier presents' appeared on a poster. The
play was *Golden Arrow*, Olivier played an ambitious politician and,
as his mistress, a young Irish girl called Enid Garson made her
first appearance, adopting the stage name of Greer Garson. Jill
believed she also became Olivier's mistress in real life. However
that may be, she was the first of his many discoveries and was
always grateful to him for it. She went on to play Mrs Miniver and
many other Hollywood leads.[12]

Another member of the cast was Denys Blakelock, the religiously
enthusiastic friend of Olivier's youth. He required an American
accent, and imitated that of Karl Tiedemann, the American priest
who was his old friend and who had, in the late 1920s, been Olivier's
confessor. Olivier produced, acted the lead, and directed. And
inevitably he lost money. Blakelock said that Olivier at that time
was at his most smart and sophisticated, dressing immaculately,
having a small moustache, and still taking pleasure in his resem-
blance to Ronald Colman. This is Olivier described by a friend
whom he was outgrowing. They never appeared in another play
together. Perhaps Blakelock realised that he was being shaken off
and perhaps there is an edge to his remark, made at the same time,
that Olivier the conqueror had arrived and that the building of his
empire was about to begin.[13]

In the two years since his rejection by Garbo and his return to
the stage, Olivier had demonstrated a great range and great virtuosity. He had come from *The Green Bay Tree* – which sounds, from
all accounts, as if it required him to demonstrate the psychological
and technical gifts of his maturity – to the glorious and wilful
larking of *Theatre Royal*, to the humanity of that one performance
of *Journey's End*. He had then presented a production of his own,

taking his first steps as an actor-manager. He was a great actor and man of the theatre unfolding. But it is important to realise that no one could have mistaken him at that time for a great classical actor in the making, for a Richardson or a Gielgud. It is astonishing but, by the time he was twenty-eight, he had never played the lead in a single play by Shakespeare. Indeed he had not played any part in any Shakespeare play in the previous six years. As he put it himself, looking back, 'Somehow in the wasteland of my early days Shakespeare had got lost.'[14]

To call those early days a wasteland is, to put it mildly, an overstatement. But in 1935 the state of his mind was uncertain. His marriage was unsteady. On 17 June of that year, two days after *Golden Arrow* folded, Olivier found himself at three in the morning in a Lyons Corner House on the Strand, an all-night restaurant, telling Emlyn Williams – actor, playwright, and old acquaintance – 'I'm all washed up. I'll never make it.'[15] He again harked back to his rejection by Garbo and was, says Williams, sad, sardonic, and without hope. A man may be forgiven a little despair at three in the morning, but at the time Olivier was erratic in the accounts he gave of himself. A month before, in an interview he gave at Oxford during the pre-London tour of *Golden Arrow*, when he was asked about films, he replied, 'Films? I try not to think of them. I've played in some, but I don't intend to do so again if I can help it.'[16] This is all very well, but he had just been offered a contract by Alexander Korda, the Hungarian who for years ran a large part of the British film industry. And a week after his dismal conversation with Williams he began filming *Natasha* – later retitled *Moscow Nights* – a romantic spy-thriller set in Russia during World War I. What he had lost on his play he needed a film to recoup. His diary for the time shows he dined again with Helen Spencer, that he was discussing theatre projects with Ralph Richardson and J.B. Priestley, and that he was beginning to take flying lessons. He did also gain in reputation from *Moscow Nights*. A man could hardly persist in thinking himself washed up when *Film Pictorial*, then an influential magazine, said of his performance, 'With this film is born a new English star.'[17]

Then came an offer which changed his life. John Gielgud had already made his reputation in Shakespeare. He had twice played

Hamlet, once in 1929 and more recently in 1934. While Olivier was in *Theatre Royal*, failing to prevent his sword from striking Marie Tempest and breaking his own ankle, Gielgud had for six months been performing Hamlet in the West End to great applause. Only Henry Irving, back in 1874, had achieved a longer run in that play. He wished to follow this with *Romeo and Juliet*, in which he and another actor would alternate the roles of Romeo and Mercutio. Gielgud himself would direct. He approached Robert Donat, but Donat, hinting that he had been planning a production of his own, declined. Then, remembering how Olivier had replaced Richardson at short notice in his production of *Mary Queen of Scots*, Gielgud proposed the parts to him.

Olivier accepted, but not before hinting that he too had been planning his own production, with Jill as Juliet.[18] There is no evidence that he was really thinking of anything of the sort. Nor is there of the statement in his autobiography that he had always seen himself vividly as the one and only Romeo.[19] He had made no attempt for years to do any Shakespeare on stage, and he had declined MGM's proposal that he should play Romeo opposite Moira Shearer. However, he accepted – 'grabbed it', he said – and for £70 a week. It was agreed that on advertisements and play-bills the names of the players should appear in the following order:

John Gielgud	Edith Evans
and	and
Laurence Olivier	Peggy Ashcroft

Edith Evans was the nurse, and Peggy Ashcroft was Juliet.[20]

In rehearsal it became plain, as both Olivier and Gielgud must have known before, that there was a chasm between the different ways they spoke the verse. Gielgud was lyrical. Olivier was real. Gielgud was always the soul of tact and courtesy with Olivier. Olivier, on the other hand, was often sarcastic with Gielgud, and seldom tender of the other man's feelings. This remained so throughout their long careers. So it is no surprise to hear Olivier saying, 'I really was convinced, that I was better in Shakespeare than John Gielgud because I didn't sing it, and my form of self praise was to pat myself on the back because I didn't *have* to sing it, because I spoke Shakespeare naturally. I spoke Shakespeare as if that was the way I spoke, so I despised people who sang it, and of course those two schools couldn't have been more opposite.'[21]

According to the way his mood took him, he could put it more gently or more brutally than that. More gently when he said that was the way things were *done* then, that people wanted the verse sung. 'So I was the upstart and John was the jewel, and a shining one too, deservedly so. . .but I felt in those days he allowed it [his voice] to dominate his performances, and, if he was lost but for a moment, he would dive straight back into its honey.'[22] He put it more brutally when he said that even Gielgud's then boyfriend had made it known that he preferred Olivier because he was more real. 'And John was affronted because he didn't believe in being real in Shakespeare. I mean, he was all "The honey of thy breath," and all that. Always sang. And I absolutely refused to sing it, and I played it real. . . They [the audience] are always going to go for the guy that makes them believe he's alive and breathing and doing it to Juliet.'[23]

Gielgud, when he remembered their performances, was typically self-effacing. 'I was very busy enunciating all the poetry very beautifully, but I was very cold aesthetically compared with him. And I was struck then, as we all have been since, by his [Olivier's] extraordinary power and originality, and the way he dashes with a part, and really wrings its neck without self-consciousness. . . He doesn't act with the sort of caution and fear that some of the rest of us have.'[24]

The run was meant to last six weeks. Gielgud let Olivier play Romeo for the first three. The critics hit hard with what Olivier called the 'sledge hammer of opprobrium'[25]. The London *Evening Standard*'s reviewer wrote that Olivier's blank verse was the blankest he had ever heard, and *The Times*'s that he was a ranting, writhing Romeo. Some members of the audience were kinder. Esmond Knight, a colleague, wrote that he had brought to life a living, roaring, Italian boy. Another told him, 'This, one feels, is what the young Keats should have been.' Cecil Beaton wrote that he was deeply moved. 'You are so lovelorn, so young, earnest, helpless, and victimised, and the effect is so genuine, as against being theatrical.' He ended by hoping they could manage to take some photographs. Olivier's diary shows that an appointment was made.[26] His truest admirer was Fabia Drake, once his dance instructress, who came to the dress rehearsal. 'I can still hear you saying, "My dear" under the balcony, when it became the most moving line in the play.' She also took St John Ervine of the *Observer* to a performance, a man whose good opinion could sell tickets, and he wrote that Shakespeare's eyes would have shone if he could have seen this Romeo, young and ardent and full of clumsy grace.[27]

For whatever reason, perhaps because the production offered this extraordinary contrast of Olivier's virile reality and Gielgud's epicene grace, *Romeo and Juliet* ran not for six weeks but six months; for 186 performances, twenty-five more than Irving's version of 1882. It was the longest run of the play since it had been written.[28] This was Olivier's real start as a Shakespearean actor. He owed a great debt to Gielgud but never afterwards acknowledged it. Perhaps he simply did not see it that way.

Jill Esmond believed that Olivier and Peggy Ashcroft were lovers during the run of the play. So did Gielgud.[29] Olivier half-admits it in one of the oblique and gratuitous asides in his autobiography, where he says:

'The theatre is replete with emotional legends; it is not surprising that those playing Romeo and Juliet are supposed to present a more stirring partnership if they develop the same passion between themselves as that which they are emulating; some believe that Shakespeare's magic depends on it. After long reflection, I must point out that this is a dangerous notion. It would imply that actual death is necessary to the feigning of it, or at least that physical pain is necessary to give a successful impression of it. Such an idea robs the work of its artfulness as well as its artistry. It is a tempting belief, but a bad principle.'[30]

Olivier did not have to write this passage, which only invites questions that might not otherwise have been asked. There are two late letters which cast some light on the matter. In late 1981 or early 1982, when he was finishing his autobiography, Olivier wrote to Peggy Ashcroft, evidently asking whether she objected to his using some material concerning her. This letter does not survive. Her reply does. She wrote:

'*Well!* Of course your very sweet letter gave me much to think about; and I will a admit my first reaction was to say, 'Please, no!' You know I'm a rather reticent character and shun publicity like poison. But I have thought about it carefully and I think I understand why you want to write as you do – and am very touched by that. I *don't* feel I could say "yes" – such as it stands – but you very sweetly suggest my editing. I feel I *could* do that but need to know how you lead into the passage you sent me. . .'

Some seven weeks later Olivier wrote to her: 'Darling, I have decided not to mention us at all in that context.'[31]

What we are left with is another long letter of hers to Larry which we shall meet in its place in the next chapter, and an affectionate and undated scrap apparently written during the run of *Romeo and Juliet*: 'Darling Larry. . . I wish you every every everything tonight. It's so lovely doing it with you – hell! Let's enjoy ourselves tonight. Love, Peggy.'[32]

Olivier's success as Romeo led quite directly to his first appearance in a film of Shakespeare. In Hollywood he had said Shakespeare would not work on film. Two years later he accepted an offer to play Orlando in *As You Like It*. He may have done so because of what Ralph Richardson called 'the artistic satisfaction of £600 a week' – a sum which was then worth $3,000, twice what Hollywood had last offered him. Or he may have consented because he was asked by no less an actress than Elisabeth Bergner, who had seen his Romeo on stage and been impressed. Miss Bergner was not Garbo, but she was a big name. Her recent *Catherine the Great* had been a huge success and she had the advantage that her husband, Paul Czinner, had directed that film and would direct *As You Like It*. So for two months, from late December 1935 to the end of February 1936, he played Romeo or Mercutio in the evenings and Orlando, against Miss Bergner's Rosalind, in the daytime. The venerable Sir James Barrie, author of *Peter Pan*, had adapted the play for the screen, which was thought to guarantee the sanctity of Shakespeare's text. It did not quite work. Mis Bergner was Austrian and her accent was too thick. The settings were resolutely pastoral, with real animals all over the place. As the young Graham Greene put it – he was then earning part of his living as a film critic – 'how the ubiquitous livestock, sheep and cows and hens and rabbits, weary us before the end.' Or as Olivier said, 'The director's flocks of sheep ran away with the film.'[33]

Olivier had done it before, but this time he felt the strain of filming and appearing on the stage in the same day. He would sometimes arrive back in London so late that he had to go on stage wearing the same boots, the same make-up, and the same padding for his calves that he had worn all day. After the play Olivier and his friends Glen Byam Shaw and George Devine would chew over the cinematic events of the day in the half-amused way that was then typical in the theatre, where the cinema was considered hardly an art. Both later became directors and played important parts in his life, but both were then playing small parts in *Romeo and Juliet.*

Olivier had one story about Henry Ainley, who was playing the old exiled duke in the film. Ainley was a bit of a legend who had made his first appearance on the London stage as far back as 1900. He had acted in Paris and New York, had managed the St James' Theatre in London for two years, and had played a celebrated *Macbeth* in 1926 with Sybil Thorndike's company. He had a great fund of stories, which he had been telling in slack moments at the film studios. One was of Sir Johnston Forbes-Robertson, a leading man famous for his voice. Ainley had seen him in a play where he appeared as a general watching a march-past of his men, when he had exclaimed, 'My men, my men, my wonderful men.'

'Well,' Olivier told his listeners, 'you know what a magnificent voice old Ainley has. When he came to show me how Forbes-Robertson had delivered that line, he made all the make-up jars on his dressing table *vibrate.*' At which Byam Shaw and Devine challenged Olivier to do the same. They lined up some jars on his dressing table at the theatre and invited him to demonstrate. 'My men, my men, my wonderful men,' he shouted. The jars remained unmoved. All three then tried together, but no jars vibrated.[34]

Ainley did indeed have a magnificent voice and he had, as we shall see, made a great impression on the young Olivier. When *As*

You Like It appeared the *Daily Telegraph* critic wrote that, as he had said before, Olivier seemed to him to be one of the most brilliant actors in the world. The long run of *Romeo and Juliet* came to a triumphant end and Olivier gave regular sittings to Harold Knight for his portrait in the character of Romeo. It was his first portrait and always remained his favourite. He dined with Korda to discuss more films. He continued his flying lessons: 'Six landings, all bad.' And on 27 January 1936 he wrote in his diary: 'Vivien Leigh lunch'.[35]

Vivling and Dark Destruction

THE CHILD WHO GREW up to become Vivien Leigh was born in 1913 on the properly dramatic date of 5 November, Guy Fawkes Night, and in the properly dramatic setting of the foothills of the Himalayas, at Darjeeling in north-east India. It was a hill town, at an altitude of 7,500 feet, where the British who ruled the Raj took refuge from the heat. It commands one of the most splendid vistas in the world. The peak of Kanchenjunga is forty miles directly north, and on a clear day you can see Mount Everest.

Her father, Ernest Hartley, came from a family of Yorkshire gentlemen, and was a junior partner in a firm of Calcutta exchange brokers. Her mother had been born Gertude Yackjee in Darjeeling and may have had some Armenian or Parsee blood in her veins, though she was fair-skinned. Their daughter was christened Vivian Mary, Vivian with an 'a'. There is no truth in the legend much put about by Hollywood that the portrayer of Scarlett O'Hara was half-French and half-Irish, just like the character she played.

Hartley in due course became a senior partner. In 1920, when the family went home on leave, Vivian, whose mother was a Roman Catholic, was sent to board at the Convent of the Sacred Heart at Roehampton in south-west London. She stayed there for eight years, being brought up as a good Roman Catholic, praying four times a day and acquiring the civilised accomplishments of a young lady – drawing, dancing, speaking French, and learning to play the piano and violin. In the summer holidays she accompanied her parents, who came home on leave, to Biarritz, Paris, Cannes, Monte Carlo, Lugano, Salzburg, and Zurich. When she was fourteen she was sent for a year to a convent at San Remo, on the Italian Riviera. She was briefly at a school in Dinard. Then she spent six months each at schools in Paris and Biarritz. Her finishing school was at Bad Reichenhall in the Bavarian Alps, where she spent a year at the establishment of the Baron and Baroness von Roeder. At the age of eighteen she had an easy command of spoken French, German, and Italian.

Back in England she decided she would become an actress and, like many well-brought up girls of her time, went to the Royal Academy of Dramatic Art in London. One of her contemporaries there was Rachel Kempson, who married Michael Redgrave and became the mother of Vanessa. Vivian then met, at the South Devon Hunt Ball, a young barrister called Leigh Holman. He was thirty-two. She married him when she was nineteen, in a Catholic church, and gave birth to a daughter before she was twenty. Next summer she was presented at court to Queen Mary and George V. The Holmans lived in a small house in Mayfair, but Vivian was not content to be a mother and a trophy wife. She was single-minded about becoming an actress and poor Holman had to tolerate it. When he took her on a Baltic yachting holiday she insisted on leaving him and returning to England when, at Copenhagen, she received a telegram telling her there was the chance of a walk-on part in a film. Holman was indulgent and did not complain; he carried on yachting alone and saw her off on the train. 'Adorable little Vivling,' he wrote to her, 'you looked so angelic steaming away . . .' He was calling her Vivling long before Olivier adopted that name for her. She did get a part. It had one line, which was cut in the final version.[1]

She found an agent, John Gliddon, who found her a part at five guineas a day in a 'quota quickie' at Elstree – one of the shorts made to fulfil the quota of British films which exhibitors were obliged by Act of Parliament to show. She now needed a stage name, having decided that neither Vivian Hartley nor Vivian Holman would do.[2] April Morn was suggested. For a while she favoured the modified form of Averill Maugham, but then she adopted her husband's first name of Leigh and became Vivian Leigh. She made her first stage appearance, as a flirtatious wife, in a play called *The Green Sash* at the small Q Theatre, which lasted two weeks. Then came a small part, playing the daughter of a tycoon, in *Look Up and Laugh*, a film written by no less a man than J.B. Priestley and starring Gracie Fields, a Lancashire girl famous for her north country songs, who was then the highest paid film actress in England. She was nervous on the set and sometimes nearly in tears. According to Gliddon, Gracie Fields was kind and told him Vivian would go far but would need careful handling.[3] She got her first mention in *Film Pictorial*, which said, 'Vivian Leigh has spent a great deal of her life in France so she can "parlez-voo" without difficulty. In fact she has appeared at the Comédie Française in Paris.'[4] She had not, but this invention was often afterwards picked up and reprinted by other publications. Its only basis in fact was that, at her finishing school in Paris, when she was sixteen, an actress from the Comédie Française had visited to teach the girls deportment.

Vivian got her first chance in the West End in May 1937, playing the lead in *The Mask of Virtue*, a play adapted from an idea by the eighteenth-century French philosopher and playwright Denis Diderot. It was set in the days of Louis XV and she played the part of a courtesan masquerading as an innocent virgin. The producer was Sydney Carroll, who had wanted Peggy Ashcroft, Anna Neagle, or Diana Churchill but could have none of them. He took Vivian Leigh for her beauty and because she let him read her palm. He believed in palmistry.[5] Carroll afterwards claimed to have made her. He certainly created the name by which she was known, telling her that Vivien with an 'e' looked more feminine than Vivian. She appeared as Vivien Leigh on the playbills then and ever afterwards.

It was one of those first nights that newspapers love. She was acclaimed as a star. She must have shown talent because *The Times* said that she showed 'a demure repose and a lively understanding', and James Agate in the *Sunday Times* wrote that she had 'incisiveness, *retenue* [restraint], and obvious intelligence', though if she wanted to become an actress as distinct from a film star she should improve her 'overtone'. But it was mostly a popular paper story of an unknown who had become a star overnight.[6] Early next morning the reporters and photographers were at the Holmans' house. Vivien, who had not gone to bed until she had seen the notices in the late editions, at about 4 a.m., was woken early and photographed in shorts playing a banjo and, in her role as wife and mother, with her eighteen-month-old daughter Suzanne in her arms. Pictures of her carrying Suzanne appeared in six London papers.

For the *Daily Mirror* she rather embroidered the busy time she had filming by day and acting by night. She had after all done very little filming and only one play of consequence. 'I had to leave the house by six or seven every morning when I was filming, and part of the time I was rehearsing and playing at the theatre as well. I had to run the house by a sort of correspondence course with my housekeeper – I'd leave her a note last thing at night about the baby and the next day's meals – but I'd be gone before she got up in the morning. Then she'd leave me notes before she went to bed which I'd get when I got home late at night. There simply wasn't any leisure, and my husband and I hardly saw each other at all. That was rather awful, of course . . .'[7]

She told the *Daily Express* that she would like to be like Elisabeth Bergner [Olivier's leading lady in the film of *As You Like It*] and would like to play Ophelia. Then the reporter noticed something: 'A lightning change came over her face, and she ended: "But I feel now as if I am floating down a stream. I think I'll really have a lie down. I still have to listen to details of a contract."' It took a good reporter to see this; it is the first public mention of the sudden changes of mood which were characteristic of her.[8]

One member of the first-night audience was Alexander Korda, and he put Vivien Leigh, as he had put several other actresses, under contract. The terms, as haggled over by Gliddon and Korda, were that she should receive £1,300 for the first year, with an option for the second and further options at rising fees for a total period of five years, with £18,000 for the fifth year if it were ever reached. If all these sums, definite and speculative, were added up the result – pleasing to Korda, Gliddon, and Vivien Leigh – was that the newspapers could at a stretch run headlines saying: £50,000 FILM CONTRACT FOR VIVIEN LEIGH.[9]

In the London *Evening Standard* a story appeared under the

headline, MULTI-LINGUAL DEBUTANTE TAKES A FILM LEAD. It was written by John Betjeman, later Poet Laureate and always susceptible to fetching young women, who described Miss Leigh as 'the essence of English girlhood'.[10] After its opening success *The Mask of Virtue* did not do that well, and ran for only twelve weeks in the West End. But Vivien Leigh was now a name and was much seen about London, dining at the Ivy and the Savoy Grill, often with men who were not her husband. Among her escorts were Oswald Frewen, a distant cousin of Winston Churchill and a barrister and friend of Leigh Holman; Hamish Hamilton, later a publisher of great distinction; John Fremantle, who as Lord Cottesloe later played a big part in the building of the National Theatre; and John Buckmaster, son of Gladys Cooper and a great sportsman. She was often with Buckmaster. A picture of them together appeared in the *Sketch*, the society magazine. She later said he had been the first man with whom she had an affair after her marriage.[11]

This was the Vivien Leigh whom Olivier took to lunch on 27 January 1936. In his autobiography, looking back forty-five years, he wrote:

'I first set eyes on the possessor of this wondrous imagined beauty . . . in *The Mask of Virtue*, in which she had attracted considerable attention – though not, at this time, chiefly on account of her promise as an actress. Apart from her looks, which were magical, she possessed beautiful poise; her neck looked almost too fragile to support her head and bore it with a sense of surprise, and something of the pride of the master juggler who can make a brilliant manoeuvre appear almost accidental. She also had something else: an attraction of the most perturbing nature I had ever encountered. It may have been the strangely touching spark of dignity in her that enslaved the ardent legion of her admirers.'[12]

In calling her a master juggler Olivier is attributing to her a gift he treasured in himself. He goes on to say that he and Jill once ran across her in the Savoy Grill lobby, and that later she popped into his dressing room when he was making up for a matinée of *Romeo and Juliet*, ostensibly to invite him and Jill to something or other. 'She stayed only a couple of minutes, and then she gave me a soft little kiss on the shoulder and was gone.'[13]

If she went to see him when he was in *Romeo and Juliet* it had to be before 28 March 1936, when the play came off. It may have been in January, before he asked her to lunch. But his diaries show that it was not until the end of 1936 that he and Jill began to see much of the Holmans; it was only then that she could have come ostensibly to invite them to something or other. Where Vivien is concerned, his autobiography tends to make everything happen earlier than it could have done. He makes much, in his confessional mode, of their 'two years of furtive life, lying life' when he felt 'a worm-like adulterer, slipping in between another man's sheets', before they rewarded themselves with the 'selfish relief of confession'.[14] Jill and Leigh Holman were eventually told in early June 1937. If there had been two worm-like years they would have to have started in June 1935, when he had glimpsed Vivien only once, in *The Mask of Virtue.*

Everything suggests that their affair began much later than has been assumed; certainly not in 1935, and probably quite late in 1936. Olivier did lunch with her in early 1936, but at that time he twice met Ann Todd, a young film actress then rather better known than Vivien Leigh. In March Vivien toured Manchester and Southport in *The Happy Hypocrite* – a play adapted from a story by Max Beerbohm and set in the Regency period – which came into London in April for a short run. In May Olivier lost more money on his second venture into management, in a play called *Bees on the Boatdeck* by J.B. Priestley. 'This couldn't go wrong,' he said. 'Priestley had never had a failure and we had Ralph Richardson in the cast. It was an absolute cinch.'[15] But it was a satire on contemporary England, a subject which audiences did not warm to, so a play presented by Priestley, Olivier, and Richardson lasted only a month. They shared losses of £2,000. Olivier comforted himself with flying lessons; during the short run he flew on nine days and, soon after, wrote in his diary, 'SOLO'.[16] He could fly. Olivier's portrait by Harold Knight was shown in the Royal Academy's summer exhibition, and so was Vivien Leigh's by T. C. Dugdale. That was in May, by which time Olivier's wife Jill was five months pregnant.

It was an eventful year. But despite Olivier's lyrical later description of Vivien's wondrous, unimagined beauty, it is probable that at the time she rather than he was the pursuer, if only in her mind. One of the cast of *The Happy Hypocrite* was Carl Harbord, who seems on reasonable authority to have had an affair with Vivien during the run. He later complained, 'Even when she was sleeping with *me*, she was thinking of Olivier.'[17]

Then Olivier and Leigh were brought together in the great romantic costume drama which Korda had been longing to make since his great success with *The Private Life of Henry VIII* three years earlier. It was *Fire Over England*, in which Flora Robson, as Queen Elizabeth I, repelled Philip of Spain, played by Raymond Massey, and the Spanish Armada. It had a cast of thousands – which included Leslie Banks, James Mason, and Robert Newton – and was of course meant to be Miss Robson's film, but it was stolen by Olivier as the young sea officer who courts and wins one of her ladies-in-waiting, played by Vivien Leigh, and incidentally saves England by his heroic exploits at sea. Filming started at the new Denham Studios on 15 July. By then the Holmans did know the Oliviers, though only slightly. Vivien wrote to her husband, who was off sailing once more, describing their studio on the Thames and mentioning that Jill had started to have her baby but that the pains had then stopped.[18] The child, Simon Tarquin, was eventually born at 11.30 a.m. on 21 August. A few days later Vivien wrote to Holman in a casual, chatty letter that Larry was already reciting Shakespeare to his son and that they had drunk the child's health at the studio. As Olivier's sister Sybille put it, 'Laurence was reasonably proud of Tark, as the baby soon began to be called, but by this time his intense desire to have a family had faded, and he was immersed in other things.'[19]

These other things were supposed by most to be *Fire Over England* and Vivien Leigh. Those who later knew Olivier and Leigh as lovers, and who had seen them together during the filming, naturally assumed that they had seen them at the time when they became lovers. Vivien herself was said to have admitted to Korda then that they had fallen in love and were going to be married, but that depends on Korda's hearsay account, reported years later.[20] There is no knowing whether they were lovers by then. Ten days after Tarquin's birth, while Jill was in the country and Leigh Holman was still yachting in the Baltic, Olivier took Vivien to the ballet; she wrote and told her husband so.[21] About the same time Frewen, paying a visit in Holman's absence, found Vivien with a sore throat and Olivier in attendance. Frewen kept a detailed diary and at this point it becomes important. That evening he noted with amusement that Olivier could not make out what he was doing in the house, did everything he could to ensure that Frewen left the house at the same time as he did, failed, and was not pleased.[22]

The filming ended after three months and on 16 October Olivier and Jill went on holiday together to Capri. Eight days later, with her husband's knowledge and escorted by Frewen, Vivien went off to Rome and Sicily and then chose to return by way of Capri. There, at the Hotel Quisisana, they found the Oliviers. They took three adjoining rooms – Vivien, the Oliviers, and then Frewen. Frewen wrote: 'Nobody ever knocked to enter and we used all three rooms at will and Viv confided to me that she thought that was all right and that we were not unwelcome. It was a great surprise. . .' From Capri she wrote telling Holman that they had been boating, that her handbag had fallen into the sea and that Larry had dived in to retrieve it. She said Larry and Jill were thrilled to see them since they hadn't spoken English to anyone for two weeks.[23] Frewen took a photograph of Larry with Jill on his right and Vivien on his left; his arm is round Jill's waist but he is closer to Vivien. After a few days they crossed to Naples, where Vivien and Frewen got on the train and the Oliviers waved goodbye to them. Frewen recorded in his diary that Vivien was upset in Rome when Larry telephoned her from Naples. By then he knew there was something between them. 'I begged her to give herself time,' he wrote, 'not to do anything impetuous.'[24]

She returned to England to make another film for Korda. Her leading man was Rex Harrison, who fell for her but gazed on her face with unhopeful ardour since, he said, 'all she wanted to do was to talk about Larry'.[25] That November and December the Oliviers and the Holmans saw a lot of each other. They had dinner together three times in November and met at a party. On 7 December Olivier wrote in his diary, with emphasis, CHRISTENING. There is a photograph taken after the ceremony at Chelsea Old Church with Jill

serene and holding the swaddled Tarquin, and Eva Moore apparently scowling at her son-in-law, as if she were aware that everything was not right. Jill Esmond, serene though she looked, was
later said to have believed that Larry came to the christening with
the scent of Vivien's perfume on him.[26] If there was another woman's
scent, it may not have been Vivien's. The day of the christening,
and the day before, the name of Ann Todd appears again in his
diary. Later that month the Oliviers again spent an evening with
the Holmans and also went to the theatre with them. Olivier said
that at first Holman struck him as a dull man, cerebral, without
sparkle – intelligent, clever, but not exciting or outwardly romantic.[27]
Then in late December Vivien and her husband went on a skiing
holiday.[28]

Olivier was in some turmoil. He had a new baby but his marriage
was on the rocks. Vivien was in love with him – they were by then
probably lovers – and he and his wife were regularly meeting Vivien
and her husband socially. He was continuing to meet Ann Todd.
Also, his driving licence had been suspended in the police court.[29]
He was about to start a Shakespeare season with the Old Vic and
was rehearsing the first play, which was *Hamlet*. At this time, apparently while Vivien was away skiing with her husband, there is some
evidence that he had a homosexual fling.*

As we have seen, there is no doubt that as a young man Olivier
worried a great deal about the *idea* of homosexuality, which seems
to have been entangled with his doubts about religion. We know
that Jill Esmond, writing to him two months before their marriage
in 1930, and knowing he was troubled, asked him about 'the bigger
devil, our particular pet devil'. Whatever it was, and it may very
well have been Blakelock, Olivier wrote to the priest who was his
former confessor, who replied that the matter was too delicate for
a letter and advised him to trust in God.

Fifty years later, when he was writing *Confessions of An Actor* in
1980–82, Olivier wrote an involved passage on homosexuality.[30] He
did not need to do this, but obviously wanted to. It was a passage

---

* For the views of Joan Plowright in this matter, see Author's Note, 'The
Androgynous Actor', on page 505.

that he worked and reworked as he wrote. In the three typescripts
of his autobiography, now at the British Library, there are 157 pages
typed by himself: this is evidently the original typescript from which
the book as it was published was adapted. In the original the passage
is longer and more strongly worded. Here is part of it. Where he
took out words or sentences or replaced them with a weaker version,
the words he first wrote are set here in italics.

I had got over like a spendthrift sigh my so nearly passionate
involvement with the one male for whom some sexual dalliance
had not been loathsome to contemplate. I had felt it desperately
necessary to warn that, *tiresome and* dustily old-fashioned as *I was
sure* it must seem, I had ideals which, though overtenderly sensitive, must not be trodden underfoot and destroyed or I could not
answer for the consequences, and neither would he *be able to do so.*
It must be exceedingly difficult to believe that with my history of
the pampered choir-boy . . . *in truth* the homosexual act *was* [in
the book, 'would be'] darkly destructive to my soul, and that I
was firm in my conviction that heterosexuality was romantically
beautiful, promoting of justice, *dissolving in pleasure,* rewarding in
contentment. It is surprising that this faith should withstand an
onslaught of such passionate interest that had come upon me, or
that this, *in conspiracy* with the disillusionment presented by the
initial experiences of my early life did not *combine to* throw me off
course or even *stagger me on it* [in the book, 'make me waver'] –
well perhaps I must admit I did *go that far* [in the book, 'do that'].
*Perhaps there existed in my subconscious a strong suspicion that that
element was all my fault. In the study of humanity I don't believe there
can be found anything conclusively definite; there must, I am satisfied
there must always be, no matter how faintly drawn, a question mark
attached to any found solution regarding human behaviour.*[31]

The 'one male' of the first sentence of that passage has always been
assumed to be Noel Coward. This is probably what Olivier intended,
since the previous two pages are about Coward and the rehearsals
for the 1931 production of *Private Lives.* In the book the account
of *Private Lives* is followed by three asterisks, then follows the 'one

male' passage and the reader is led to make the assumption. Later, in 1984, when Olivier was talking to Gawn Grainger, the friend who ghosted his second book, *On Acting*, he spoke again about Coward, in a manner in which he both suggested and denied any such relationship. He said, 'He was fond of me anyhow, and he was very fond of me as an actor. And he realised that my acting was more important to me than having an affair with him. And he sort of understood that, because I wouldn't fall for those plays at all. Simply refused. And Noel could be pretty persuasive . . . I had a great love for him, but not of the right kind that suited him. Because I never went that way. And if you didn't go for Noel you were sure ablutionised from that trouble because you couldn't – Noel was very attractive and very, very, very winning . . . You know. Devastatingly. Almost irresistible. And I had to pull out my strongest stock of masculinity that I could find . . .'[32]

But I believe the 'one male' was not Coward but Henry Ainley. It was he who staggered Olivier. He was the actor whose Hamlet Jill had thought beautiful in 1930, telling Larry that the speeches had just rippled from his tongue.[33] He was also the actor who had played the Duke in Olivier's film of *As You Like It* in 1935. He was the man whose magnificent voice had made the jars vibrate on Olivier's dressing table.[34] Ainley was as well-known for his charm and stage presence as for his voice, and was one of the most able actors of his generation, but since 1932 he had hardly appeared on the stage because of illness. At the end of 1936 he was fifty-seven, nearly twice Olivier's age. He was married and had a son, Richard, who was also an actor.[35]

Olivier preserved among his papers fifteen letters from Ainley. There is also a telegram and a card.[36] Nine of the letters are explicitly homosexual. The more explicit are not quoted here. What seems to be the first is undated and is on the writing paper of a private hotel in Broadstairs, Kent. It says, in part:

Larry darling.
My pretty. Please. This is very serious: – who told you I was one of those? Have you seen my Osric? Haven't you? O. Dear old boy, I really must pull myself together. How are you? I

have been tossing (now now) about at night thinking of you.
No dammit, *really*, I am serious. I would like to hear from you
if you are well and happy. How Jill must hate me, taking you
away from her! I've fallen for a very nice curate down here.
He is very High Church. . . I should like to run my fingers
through your hair. *Yes I am a Psod.* And what is more, *so are
you* . . .
Your sweet little kitten, Henrietta.

On the first night of *Hamlet* at the Old Vic, 5 January 1937, there
is a telegram from Ainley saying THE READINESS IS ALL, a line of
Hamlet's from the last scene of the play. Then, on the same date,
he wrote from Broadstairs:

Larry Kin Mine.
To you, and yours, my love and affectionate thoughts. If only
you could act − Ah! Oh! I would give you a life contract, and
£10,000 a year. Have you got that? Well, now you know
what you can do. All my love to Jill, and none to you. . .
Harry kin thine.

He wrote again on 11 January, also from Broadstairs.

Darling
Christ! You are a lousy pansy. Don't you ever dare write to
me again. The Brute who is keeping me found your letters,
and beat me unmercifully. O I did enjoy it! You, my sweet, are
my Mecca, my Bourne from which no Hollingsworth returns.
Pay no heed to the critics, they do not know. *You are playing
Hamlet, therefore you are a king.* The critics are yeasty buggers.
They have to show off. Let them be. You rank, now, among
the *great.* I am proud of you, so is *Jill.* 'The readiness is all.'
And you have fulfilled your destiny. BRAVO.
Your affectionate and loving Harry.

[In the left hand margin is written: 'I am very proud to be
your friend. H.A.']

There is one more letter from Henry Ainley in early 1937, which he signs Diana. Then there are eleven others, dating from late 1937 to early 1939, some expressing good wishes, some mock indignation, some love, but all looking back. Ainley's letters show that Olivier did write to him as late as August 1938, but their probable fling was obviously brief; in late December 1936 and early January 1937. In a way Ainley knew Olivier well, well enough to call him Larrikin, which was a family nickname of his youth. He also knew Jill, but not that she had as good as lost Larry. As his later letters show, he had at the time no notion about Vivien Leigh.

8

Hamlet and Mr and Mrs Andrew Kerr

IN 1936 OLIVIER DECIDED to become a Shakespearean actor. It was a cool decision. As he said, he was determined to be a great actor and he knew that unless he could make a reputation in the classics he could not achieve that. 'My ambition required it. I required it of myself. I knew it wouldn't happen unless I crashed that market. So I had to go on with the critics giving me bad notices, saying I couldn't speak the verse to save my life and all that, and I just went on and on, and after about a year the Press referred to me as "that Shakespearean actor." Then I knew it had been done.'[1]

He had played Romeo in the West End. But in those days the only place where a man could do a whole season of Shakespeare was the Old Vic, which was not in the West End at all but south of the Thames, across Waterloo Bridge. It had opened in 1818 as the Royal Coburg Theatre and offered mostly melodrama, with occasional ballet. Edmund Kean played there once, but for five nights only. In 1833 it was renamed the Victoria because Princess Victoria, later the Queen, visited it once. The Victoria soon became popularly known as the Old Vic. In 1871 it became a music hall, and then in 1880 it was transformed by the philanthropic Emma Cons into a temperance hall and coffee tavern. Her niece, Lilian Baylis, made it into a theatre for the people, putting on opera, then silent films and then, in 1914, Shakespeare. By 1923, under her management, it had presented the entire canon of his thirty-seven plays. By 1936 Miss Baylis was sixty-two and a power in the London theatre, a people's impresario who was said to pray, 'Oh God, send me a good actor – and cheap.'[2]

Olivier gave two accounts of how he came to do his first Shakespeare season there. The first was this: 'In those days if one was a leading West End actor one phoned up Lilian and said, "I'd like to come." Sure, and they were thirsty for you. You only cost £25 a week and you were welcome. I mean, you know, the smell of a leading man to Lilian was like oats to a racehorse.'[3]

The second and more likely version was that in September 1936, soon after the birth of his son, he and Jill invited Tyrone Guthrie, who was Miss Baylis' director for the season, down to Jill's mother's house in the country. 'And after dinner we talked, and I remember him saying, "You think you should open with *Hamlet*?" "Yes, agreed." And after that I said, "Well then, let's see. I'll stay the season and we'll pick up parts as we go along, shall we?". . . I knew, I would have been dumb not to know, that I was quite a snip, for Lilian and for Tony.'[4]

To reassure himself Olivier phoned up Ralph Richardson, who was playing Mercutio to Katharine Cornell's Juliet in New York, and said, 'Ralphie, shall I go to the Old Vic?'

'Think it's a very good idea,' said Richardson.

'Thanks, goodbye.'[5]

That settled the matter.

In this second version, after the agreement was made with Guthrie, Olivier met Lilian Baylis in her small office at the back of the theatre, after he had been rehearsing *Hamlet* for four weeks. He was giving up £500 a week in films for £25 at the Old Vic, and she knew it. He entered a room with faded photographs on the walls and her pet dog snarling at his ankles on the floor. He could not remember what she said, except that she ended by remarking, 'Of course you really oughtn't to come here at all when you can get so much money elsewhere but still it's your business. Goodbye.'[6] Olivier warmed to her. 'She was very friendly,' he said. 'She loved me. Well, she was thrilled because I was naturally the biggest name up to then. And she knew I'd pull them in so she loved me. I brought this great socking movie public into her theatre.'[7]

It was a fair bargain. Olivier would get his season of Shakespeare.

The Old Vic would get its leading man. 'They had to have a so-called star to whom they need pay only £25 a week. They'd had Maurice Evans, they'd had Gielgud, they'd had Ralph. . .but I'd done these films, you see, and I had a fantastic name for them. I'd said we should start quite boldly with *Hamlet*, and Guthrie swallowed that. . . I had something John Gielgud never had, which was extreme athleticism, and I really founded my Hamlet on John Barrymore. Nobody recognised that, but I was a very physical Hamlet, which they had never seen. We had to be real people. We don't necessarily do that at the expense of the verse . . . Find reality through the verse, and if the verse is a sort of veil in front of reality you go through that veil and take a little bit of the veil with you.'[8]

These two accounts are from Olivier's recollections in his seventies, when he could speak more candidly than he had before. But it may also be that he was not, in 1936 and 1937, quite as brash as he remembered himself to have been. He was a catch for the Old Vic but he would not have been, at the time, the biggest star to have appeared there. Gielgud had famously played there, and in 1934 Charles Laughton had played seven leading roles in a season, including Hamlet.

Olivier and Guthrie's *Hamlet* was to be played uncut, and it adopted the Freudian thesis of a recently published book by Dr Ernest Jones that Hamlet had an Oedipus complex and was almost incestuously in love with his mother. At first the Ophelia was to be Peggy Ashcroft and she, Olivier, and Guthrie went to see the doctor to hear him expound his theory. 'He said Hamlet offered an impressive array of symptoms: spectacular mood swings, cruel treatment of his love, and above all a hopeless inability to pursue the course required of him.' From that meeting Olivier believed in that reading of *Hamlet*. 'Audience after audience for nearly 500 years have watched it with infinite patience trying to make it out because it's so interesting. A man in black is always interesting, and I think you've got to realise, as an actor, that the only thing is to try and make the audience follow the journey from mood to mood, and you can work out quite easily that when he was fucking Ophelia, which unquestionably he was, that that simply represented his nymph and shepherd period: the mood took hold of him. Everything he does is a mood taking hold of him: the man of action is a mood, and he can ginger himself up to giving a great performance of that.'9

This Oedipal treatment of the play, though faithfully followed, went almost unnoticed by the audience and critics. Even Hamlet's lascivious kissing of his mother was little remarked. The play opened on 5 January, when Ainley sent his congratulations. The reviews conceded the virility of the performance but lamented its lack of Gielgudian pathos. Dr Jones himself was sniffy, writing to Guthrie: 'You will not, of course, expect me, who have known Hamlet himself, to be content with any human substitute. Mr Olivier played well and understandingly the scenes with the queen. But temperamentally he is not cast for Hamlet. He is personally what we call "manic" and so finds it hard to play a melancholic part.'10

In March Olivier continued his Shakespeare season as Sir Toby Belch in *Twelfth Night*, in which Jill, as Olivia, appeared with him for the last time. But the great event of that time was the opening on 24 February of *Fire Over England* at the Leicester Square cinema.11 This was attended by a vast crowd including nine admirals, the First Sea Lord, the Duke and Duchess of Norfolk, the French and Portuguese ambassadors, H. G. Wells, author of *The War of the Worlds*, A.A. Milne, creator of Pooh Bear, and Lady Diana Cooper, wife of the Secretary for War. Olivier and Vivien Leigh commanded full pages of pictures in no fewer than three society magazines – *Harper's Bazaar*, the *Sketch* and the *Bystander*. The film strangely became one of Hitler's favourites. He liked it better than James Agate in the *Tatler*, who wrote that it had cost £75,000 to make and found it 'melancholy to think how far this sum could have gone towards a National Theatre'.12

Olivier, only a few days before, had made another of his deprecating remarks about the cinema. In a curtain speech after a Saturday matinée of *Hamlet* he told the audience: 'It makes me very happy that you have come here today instead, perhaps, of going to some pantomime or movie, which might seem a more amusing way of spending the afternoon.' The film correspondent of the *Observer*, thinking it careless of Olivier to compliment people on staying away from the cinema when *Fire Over England* was about to open in London, and when his *As You Like It* with Elisabeth Bergner was being shown in the provinces, went to see him at Cheyne Walk. A baby's pram occupied the hall. In one corner stood a toy theatre. Olivier came in carrying his six-month-old son.

'That,' said the reporter, 'was a villainous speech you made, Larry.'

'Was I tactless?'

'Very.'

'Oh heavens, I'm sorry. I'm always saying the wrong thing. Actors really shouldn't talk; they always make fools of themselves. I only wanted to cheer up those kids who had been dragged to *Hamlet* by their teachers, and sat so patiently through four and a half hours of it. I didn't mean it as an insult to the movies. It was a compliment really. Curtain speeches are all blah-blah, anyhow.'

Could he play *Hamlet* for the cinema?

'Never. I don't really like Shakespeare on the screen at all – the shot is too big for the cannon. The later plays, like *Lear*, are too big even for the theatre. But the real trouble with *Hamlet* is that I could never play it again in a cut version.'[13]

About this time Peggy Ashcroft, who had been going to play Ophelia to Olivier's Hamlet but who had instead, at Gielgud's suggestion, gone off to Broadway, wrote to Olivier from New York. It is a long and intimate letter. She was playing a ghost in a play she hated (*High Tor*), was lonely living in an apartment block at the bottom of Fifth Avenue near Washington Square, and was miserably awaiting a divorce after her very brief second marriage to the Russian director Fedor Komisarjevsky, whom she called Komis. She was delighted at Olivier's success in *Hamlet* and glad about Sir Toby too. 'Hell, how I wish I were playing Viola.' Olivier had obviously asked to see her again soon, to which she said yes. She wrote that she was trying to get over Komis. 'Perhaps that doesn't happen until something new takes its place. But I feel now that much as I long to love and be loved I don't want to take something impermanent or transitory if I can possibly help it, though God knows I'm not very strong willed. I think you will be very good as Henry V and I don't think he's a chit at all. I can't tell you how glad I am the Vic is such a success for you. I feel very excited. I am sleepy now darling so goodnight. Give my love to

Jilly and Tarquin – much he cares. Be happy. God bless you always. Very much love always, Peggy.'[14]

Miss Ashcroft, well though she knew Olivier, and though they had recently been preparing to do *Hamlet* together, seems to have known nothing of Vivien Leigh at a time when Olivier was seeking happiness every which way, but principally with her. The proprieties were still observed. He was careful to show himself carrying his son. He and Jill together had dinner with the Holmans at least three times, but he was having supper alone with Vivien at the Moulin d'Or. Vivien had by then read the novel *Gone With the Wind*, as had nearly everyone else, and asked her agent to put forward her name to the film's producer, the same David Selznick with whom Olivier had fallen out in 1931. He replied that he had no enthusiam for her, never having seen even a photograph of her, but would be seeing *Fire Over England*.[15] In March Korda signed Olivier and Vivien to star together in a film called *Twenty One Days*. Oswald Frewen, seeing more of the game from the sidelines, talked with Vivien until 2.30 one morning and begged her not to run away with Larry, 'anyway for a year'.[16] At about the same time, one night after dinner, Frewen also talked to Olivier.

'Later Larry discussed it with me (between the Old Vic and the Moulin d'Or) – he was deceiving himself, I felt, with arguments that it was for Viv's benefit that she should live with one who shared her artistry and her life, and not with Leigh. . . I made all the obvious demurrers, and Larry accepted them as all true, but he also said he had been alarmingly loose before he married Jill, that with his terrific temperament he was afraid of fetching loose again, and that the only partner in the world who could keep him steady was Viv. I said 'If she *should* fail (and statistics are against you) you will have wrecked *her*, and that is a very serious matter." He said if this *did* crash he would despair of himself and let himself go to the devil, and then, on the other side, said that Viv anyhow could never continue living with Leigh, so unsuited were their tastes and temperaments, and if it was not him it would be someone else: the one a selfish and the other a cynical statement, but he did not realise it. As a last shot I told him frankly that I didn't expect the passions of two people of his age and Viv's to endure, and begged him to give themselves at least a year before doing anything irrevocable, and indeed he said he would. . .'[17]

Olivier and Vivien were together whenever they could be, making 'darting, sporadic little hops' to odd and unexpected places to reduce the likelihood of detection by the gossip columnists. They registered at hotels as Mr and Mrs Andrew Kerr. One visit to Stamford in Lincolnshire remained clear in his memory all his life.[18] He wrote to her: '*Now I'll show you how I do it.* I shall never forget you saying that to me at Stamford as you got out of the first bath we ever had together at Stamford to dry yourself.'[19]

1937 was coronation year. In 1936 Edward VIII had agonised over Mrs Simpson and then abdicated and became the Duke of Windsor. His brother the Duke of York was to be crowned George VI on 12 May 1937. The Old Vic needed a coronation play and the choice fell on *Henry V*. Olivier, as Peggy Ashcroft's letter to him shows, did not feel happy in the part. There is the double irony of a man later famous for his film of *Hamlet* saying it could not be filmed, and of the man later famous for his patriotic film of *Henry V* at first disliking the play for its declamatory heroism. Ralph Richardson again helped him. 'I know he's a boring old scout-master on the face of it, but being Shakespeare he's the exaltation of all scout-masters. He's the cold bath king and you'll have to glory in it.' At first Olivier could not bring himself to glory in it enough. His Crispin speech, which he later ended in the film with a rising howl of 'Cry God for Harry, England, and St George,' fell flat in rehearsals at the Vic. He insisted on taking it gravely and quietly until Guthrie told him he was taking all the thrill out of the play which, for goodness sake, he said, was all it had.[20] *Henry V* was a success too. Olivier was most effectively crashing into his market. Among those to congratulate him were Anthony Bushell, an English friend from the Hollywood days of 1931, and his mistress, Consuelo. She wrote to tell Larry, 'We saw that you had pulled another trick out of the hat with Henry. You will be Lord Cheyne Walk and Baron Embankment before you can turn round.'[21]

The double life went on. During the run of the play Olivier and Jill, and Vivien and Holman, actually visited Frewen together and stayed at Rye in the same hotel. Olivier was intriguing with Jill,

Vivien, and Holman; playing *Henry V* at night and filming *Twenty One Days* in the daytime; and incidentally planning to take the Old Vic company to Denmark to perform *Hamlet* at Elsinore. His father, who did not know the half of it, congratulated Larry on his wonderful success but warned him against overstraining himself. Fahv had not had a parish since 1930, when he had retired from Addington, though he was still licensed to preach and did take services. He had officiated at Tarquin's christening. He and Ibo had lived at Tunbridge Wells but in early 1937 they were preparing to move to a small flat in Worthing and asked Larry which of their old furniture he would like. They found the move a wrench.

Fahv wrote wishing Larry all success and acclamation provided it did not entail too great a strain on his health and strength. 'I do – we both – hate your being so continually tired and overstrained. Of course I know that you know and have so completely shown, that you cannot achieve real success without work, and work, *and* work. It's the only *real* way, old son. . . In that you are a true Olivier. Some of us have gone on and on without intermission without apparent harm; but sooner or later there has come a sudden "flop".'[22]

By then Larry had flown to Elsinore, seen the mayor and corporation, arranged everything, and flown back. By 7 May, two days after his return and three weeks before the whole company was due leave for Denmark, he had determined to leave Jill for Vivien. 'Durham ready,' he wrote in his diary for that day. This was Durham Cottage in Chelsea, where he and Vivien were to live. But as yet he made no move. When the Old Vic company sailed for Denmark on 27 May, Olivier was accompanied by both Jill and Vivien. Jill was a spectator. Vivien, though she had not appeared in the production at the Old Vic, was to play Ophelia. How Vivien came by the part is not clear. Probably Olivier insisted. Guthrie was severe at rehearsals, telling her, 'Much too pretty! Much too dainty!' perhaps thinking her a 'jumped up little film star who had no right to be attempting Ophelia'.[23] But she and Larry were a properly carnal Hamlet and Ophelia. 'We could not keep from touching each other', he wrote in his autobiography, 'almost making love within Jill's vision. This welding closeness tripped the obvious decision, and two marriages were severed.'[24]

They gave six performances. All were to be in the open air at
Kronborg, Hamlet's castle. On the first night it rained in ropes, but
it was impossible to cancel what was to be a gala performance for
the Crown Prince of Denmark. So the company and the audience
moved to the Marienlyst Hotel, where 800 chairs were hastily
arranged in the ballroom. The exits and entrances had to be recast.
Guthrie left it to Olivier. '"Fix it for me, Larry". . . He left all that
lovely invention to me, I was thrilled to do it, and of course I
enjoyed myself wildly.'[25]

The other performances were in the open air, though one had to
be called off after two acts. This was seen by the young John
Steinbeck, who years later reminded Olivier of the event. 'It was
on a scaffold in the courtyard,' he said. 'I and three thousand [others]
sat on wooden trestles. The rain poured down and your black tights
grew blacker with the moisture. Finally, to save your lives, you, a
wet and melancholy Dane and your prematurely damp Ophelia,
called the non-existent curtain down.'[26]

Olivier, Jill and Vivien flew back together on Tuesday, 8 June.
The events of the next few days are recorded in his diary. On the
Thursday Leigh Holman was told, presumably by Vivien, that she
was leaving him. On the Friday, Larry told Jill. Next Monday Jill
went to see Vivien. Nothing came of this visit, and next day Jill
left Cheyne Walk and went to her mother's house in the country.
Then, on Wednesday, 16 June, Olivier's diary reads: 'Vivien leaves
Little Stanhope Street [the Holmans' London address] just after
midnight. Stay Tony and Consuelo.[27] Tarquin was left with Jill, and
Suzanne with Holman. While he went to tell Fahv and Ibo, Larry
left Vivien with Sybille and her husband Gerald. Sybille remembered it as her 'first sight of this lovely young girl'.[28]

'This thing,' Olivier said, 'was as fatefully irresistible as for any
couple from Siegmund and Sieglinde to Windsor and Simpson. It
sometimes felt almost like an illness, but the remedy was unthinkable; only an early Christian martyr could have faced it. Virtue
seemed to work upside down: love was like an angel, guilt was a
dark fiend. At its every surge *Macbeth* would haunt me: "Then comes
my fit again." It sounds like a Novello musical – "Rapturous
Torment"!'[29]

Frewen saw things less grandly and with no thought of Christian martyrs. He wrote in his diary for 28 June: 'It must be nearly a year, or even the full year, since they first fell in love, and they have fought against themselves, *each* of them, *hard*. . . But the disaster is none the less there, and I'm terribly afraid that he is inconstant and unballasted and that it won't last ten years – perhaps not five. Once cast loose from steady old Leigh's helmsmanship I have awful doubts for *her* too. She says in a letter, 'It was a week of nightmares for us and torture for the others. . .' She has heart and a brain, but no ethical upbringing and instead an overdose of temperament. Can she remain unsubmerged?'[30] Frewen also wrote a note to Jill, trying to comfort her by telling her Larry and Vivien *had* tried. 'She said flatly that they hadn't, and didn't answer me! So there it is, very very sad; and I think Leigh and I are the only two people who look upon it without just cold disdain or cynicism.' He was pleased that Suzanne had been put in charge of an efficient nursery governess.[31]

Olivier and Vivien completed the filming of *Twenty One Days*, from which Korda had given them leave to go to Denmark. It was based on a story by John Galsworthy and the screenplay was by Graham Greene, but it is dire. Olivier's character shows flashes of power, but Vivien is wooden. The film's greatest point of interest is that the principal male character is called Larry, so that throughout its length Vivien calls him 'Larry' in the tones she must have used to him in real life. Reports of Vivien's determination to get the part of Scarlett O'Hara in *Gone With the Wind* date from this time. On the set of *Twenty One Days* a reporter from the London *Evening News* asked what she read. '*Gone With the Wind*,' she said. 'I've cast myself as Scarlett O'Hara. What do you think?' The reporter wrote that in reply he 'muttered something inaudible'.[32]

Here was a little-known English film actress saying what many film actresses were saying and hoping at the time. It was almost a stock response, which would have been expected from any girl under contract to Korda. It would help to publicise his name too. Selznick had made a great thing of his public search for the right girl, had invited anyone to come forward and had auditioned hundreds. After the event, when everyone knew Vivien Leigh had been Scarlett, many claimed to have forseen that she would be or, at any rate, that they had heard her express a repeated desire for the part. Several of the sequences in *Twenty One Days* were set on a paddle-boat trip from the Tower of London to Southend. A few reporters were on board, among them C.A. Lejeune, who was film critic of the *Observer* at the time. In 1964, when she was famous, she wrote a book of reminiscences in which she reported the talk on board that paddle-steamer. Paulette Goddard, Bette Davis, and Barbara Stanwyck were suggested for Scarlett. Someone told Olivier he would be a marvellous Rhett Butler and he laughed it off. Discussion of the casting went on in desultory fashion, wrote Miss Lejeune, until the new girl, Vivien Leigh, brought it to a sudden stop. 'She drew herself up on the rainswept deck, all five-feet nothing of her, pulled a coat snug around her shoulders, and stunned us all with the sybilline utterance, "Larry won't play Rhett Butler, but I shall play Scarlett O'Hara. Wait and see."'[33] Here is the full-grown legend. But in an article she wrote in February 1939, although Vivien was by then known to have the part, Miss Lejeune was less emphatic. She then recalled that there had been a mention of *Gone With the Wind*, she thought by Olivier, and they had argued whether Bette Davis or Margaret Sullavan would make the better Scarlett, and then: 'Suddenly Vivien looked up, and said in a surprised sort of way, "Do you know who could play Scarlett O'Hara? Don't laugh, but I believe I could." We did laugh, and teased her about it, but the idea went on growing.' But in an article she wrote at the time of the trip to Southend in July 1937 Miss Lejeune, even though she had two pages to herself, did not mention *Gone With the Wind* at all.[34]

This river trip, whatever was or was not said that day, took place just after Olivier and Vivien had begun to live together. This was the time when Olivier made a handwritten will.[35] He named Ralph Richardson and Anthony Bushell as his executors. To Jill he left any insurances which would fall due at his death, any property at Cheyne Walk, and a wish that she should provide for the welfare of his son, Simon Tarquin. To Vivien he left all other moneys he had in stocks, shares, security or cash. He then finished with a preposterous passage which deserves to be quoted in full:

It is my most earnest wish that my wife and Mrs Holman shall live in friendliness and harmony of spirit both forgiving and forgetting any possible bitterness that may perhaps be between them.

My dearest love, in the proportions that they know they own it, be with them, and my family, my son and my good friends for ever.

Where souls do couch on flowers we'll hand in hand
and with our sprightly port make the ghosts gaze.
Dido and her Aeneas shall want troops
and all the haunt be ours –

[*Signed*] Laurence Olivier.

Olivier does not identify the lines. They are spoken by Antony in *Antony and Cleopatra*, act IV, scene 15, lines 51–3, just before he stabs himself. They do not quite fit the case, since Olivier did not fall on his sword but promptly took Vivien off, the next day, on a continental holiday. They crossed to Calais and took the Orient Express to Venice, where they stayed on the Lido and dined at the Danieli, near St Mark's Square, crossing the lagoon by gondola. After three days they went north to Cortina in the Italian Dolomites, walking by the lake in the light of the full moon. They drove to Salzburg in Austria, crossed Europe by train by way of Munich and Frankfurt, and then flew home from Brussels. They had been away ten days.

It was quite fitting that Olivier's melodramatic will had been witnessed by his secretary Sofka, an émigré Russian princess, and by her lover, Grey Skipwith, the heir to an ancient English baronetcy, one of whose ancestors had been knighted by Henry V. Sofka's life at the time was as complicated as Olivier's. Her marriage to another Russian émigré, Leo Zinovieff, had been in trouble for some time, and she was in love with Grey. To give the marriage a chance she decided to have a second child by her husband, but then, while still pregnant, decided that when she gave birth she would ask for a divorce after all and marry her lover. This she did. After Olivier had gone to live with Vivien, Sofka remembered that Jill had asked her to come round one morning. Larry had left no address; nor had he left Jill the money for living expenses. But he had been used to leaving Sofka with a couple of blank cheques for general expenses. She had always liked Jill, so she used these cheques and contrived an arrangement with Olivier's bank manager which allowed her to overdraw, which she did for some months. As for Vivien, she thought her beautiful and supreme in a 'slightly larger than life company where "darling" was the ordinary form of address and four letter words flicked unnoticed through conversations'. After the parting neither Jill not Larry wanted to live at Cheyne Walk, and Sofka moved in with Grey for a while. Olivier had given her as a wedding present a vast bed, six-and-a-half-foot square, a king-size bed at a time when such things were unknown in England. It is not clear whether he was giving away his and Jill's marital bed.[36]

When Olivier and Vivien returned from their European holiday both went into films. Olivier played opposite Merle Oberon in *The Divorce of Lady X*. Vivien had a small part – for which Korda had lent her to MGM – in *A Yank at Oxford*, in which she played the flighty wife of an Oxford bookseller. They lived at Iver, which was convenient for the film studios, until they could move into Durham Cottage in November. Anthony Bushell wrote to them: 'Darling Vivien and Filthy Laurence – The Press boys have been uncommon forbearing – I cannot understand it but am none the less relieved. God bless you both and long and happily may you live in your beautiful house.'[37]

At the film studios Vivien was already gaining a reputation for being difficult. She wanted time off to watch Olivier rehearse at the Old Vic, which would have been unprofessional conduct in a star and was downright perverse in her. She then made an inordinate fuss about the cost of five pairs of shoes she had bought for the film. Her contract required her to find her own shoes. MGM would not budge and Vivien insisted that her agent, John Gliddon, should take up this trivial matter with Korda's lawyer. The correspondence dragged on until the people in Korda's front office became irritated and told Gliddon that if Vivien did not behave herself in future her option might not be renewed. When he went to see Vivien to pass this on she demanded to know just who had said it. He, protecting his professional contacts, could not tell her, at which she flew at him. Her voice became hard and contemptuous, the look in her eyes changed and she told him to get out of her house. It was frightening. Something of the same sort had happened at Elsinore. She had been lucky to get the part of Ophelia. Before one performance her behaviour had been so erratic that the cast had doubted whether she would be able to go on. She veered from silence one moment to yelling the next. Olivier said 'something about Viv having gone bonkers, having attacked him, having had a fit of some kind'. Then she appeared saying not a word to anyone, just staring blankly into space. However, she made herself up and the performance went ahead. Olivier was concerned and went to her dressing room afterwards. There was no explanation, and the next day she was perfectly all right.[38]

After *The Divorce of Lady X* Olivier went into *Macbeth* at the Old Vic. Michel Saint-Denis, the director, brought over the Australian-born American actress Judith Anderson as Lady Macbeth. Olivier's make-up was exaggerated, almost that of a Mongol emperor. 'You hear Macbeth's first line,' said Vivien, 'then Larry's make-up comes on, then Banquo comes on, then Larry comes on.' It was not a fortunate production. First it was not ready, so the opening had to be postponed from a Tuesday to the Friday, on the pretext that Olivier had lost his voice. Then Lilian Baylis suffered a heart attack and, on Thursday, died. Should the show go on, or be postponed again? Her companion, Miss Prevost, who had been at her bedside, reported that among her last questions had been, 'Is everything all right at the Old Vic?' The play opened on Friday with Miss Baylis's chair in her box left empty. The audience stood in her honour before the play began.[39]

Macbeth played to the best houses the Old Vic had ever known and was a triumph for Olivier. James Agate, one of the most powerful of the critics, said that the last act was the best of any *Macbeth* he had seen. 'Mr Olivier, who has made enough noise, and some people think too much now gives the part the finest edge of his brain. "Liar and slave" is uttered with a cold Irving-esque malignity. If the voice. . .still cannot accomplish a cello, it achieves a noble viola.'[40] But the opinion of even the most esteemed critic is worth less than that of Elizabeth Bowen, a novelist of high distinction, who wrote: 'Played as it is at the Old Vic, *Macbeth* might be called, first of all, a play about a marriage, the instinctive complicity of these two people, their powerful natural tie, the hypnosis they exercise over each other, is palpable the whole time. . . As for Mr Olivier, he has that gift, above price for a Shakespearean actor, of speaking every majestic, well-known line as though it sprang, only now, direct from his own heart.'[41]

Olivier did not see his parents that Christmas, as he had not the previous year either, but he did send them a Christmas hamper, for which Fahv thanked him. 'An absolute giraffe of a turkey,' he wrote, 'and the glory-be ham, and the Stilton (glumptious, I'm sure) and the plum pudding, and the Carlsbad plums (Ibo's favourites). . . and the wines including my beloved Pol Roger.'[42] This does not sound like the parsimonious, thin-slicing father that Olivier described in his later memoirs. He was also sending money to his sister Sybille, who wrote saying she did not know what she would do without his help. Her husband Gerald Day had been ill in the summer and, after Jill had left for the country, they had stayed at Cheyne Walk while he had an operation. 'My darling Bro.,' she wrote, 'G up to ears in book and lyric writing . . . (no fucking allowed for weeks) and nothing to do but to keep cheeeeer-full.' She had three young children. Gerald's second book of light verse, *Outrageous Rhapsodies*, had been completed and appeared later in 1938, with cartoons by Vicky, who became probably the best political cartoonist of his time. One of the lyrics was a skit entitled 'The pathetic film star.' Here are two stanzas:

O, pity the Hollywood star!
How she hates all this horrid publicity;
She longs for a cat and a sweet wee brat
And the pleasures of domesticity.

O, weep for the Hollywood star!
The Goddess of Salebility,
Whose priests exalt in the ludicrous cult
Of glamorous imbecility.

In her letter of thanks Sybille asked Larry to 'Kiss sweet Viv for me.' It was as well the film star lyric was then written but not yet published, or it might have been too near the bone for Vivien's liking.

Henry Ainley, after a gap of some nine months, had twice written to Olivier in November 1937 from Manchester, where he was living, addressing him as Lorenzo, wishing him well in *Macbeth* and saying, 'And now you come, like a snake in the grass, a hidden asp to give me my quietus.' Then, having evidently heard about Vivien, he wrote again on 10 January 1938: 'You call me names but I do *love* you. . . I am a stale! A wanton! I would to God I were. I would wear fur undies, and I *would* be a tease! And now, please, may I be serious just for a tick. Allow an old friend just a word. *Both* of you. Be happy. Let not a second of your united lives be thrown away, and wasted on the *past*. You have both been so *brave*, and done the right thing. Forget what has been, and thank God for what is, and what will come. Guard your happiness with both your hearts. Fret not, neither regret. . . I have a few more years; from which lonely height I see so clearly. Fate ordained that you and Vivien should possess this beauty. Let not the past mar by thought your well won peace and glory. *Shine*. Like the angels you both are. Be happy. I am proud to be your friend, and always at your service. For ever my LOVE, Harry.' Then, in the left margin: 'Your hard and successful work has put you in the centre of the Front Rank. Bravo. All love. H.A. Bastard!'[43]

Olivier then played Iago to Richardson's Othello. Without telling Richardson he and Guthrie went back to see the Freudian Dr Jones, who was again as ready with advice as he had been for Hamlet. His reading was that Iago was jealous not because he envied Othello his position or his wife, but because he possessed a subconscious homosexual affection for the Moor.[44] 'In a reckless moment during rehearsals,' said Olivier, 'I threw my arms round Ralph and kissed him full on the lips. He coolly disengaged himself from my embrace, patted me gently on the back of the neck and, more in sorrow than in anger, murmured, "There, there now; dear boy, *good* boy. . ." I had one more trick up my sleeve; Ralph had to fall to the ground when Othello, frenzied by Iago's goadings, is helpless in the clutches

of a paroxysm. I would fall beside him and simulate an orgasm –
terr*if*ically daring, wasn't it? But when the wonderful Athene Seyler
came round after a matinée she said, "I'm sure I have no idea what
you were up to when you threw yourself on the ground beside
Ralph." So that was the end of that stroke of genius and out it came.
No more shenanigans now. . .'[45]

Vivien had also appeared at the Old Vic, as Titania in a Victorian
Midsummer Night's Dream, with Robert Helpmann as Oberon, sets
and swathes of gauzy costumes by Oliver Messel, and choreography
by Ninette de Valois. The young princesses Elizabeth (later to be
queen) and Margaret were brought to see this as their first taste
of the theatre. Vivien also appeared as a cockney street girl, with
Charles Laughton and Rex Harrison, in a film called *St Martin's
Lane*. C.A. Lejeune called her a 'hard little heroine'.[46]

Olivier went from strength to strength at the Old Vic. *The King
of Nowhere*, a modern play by James Bridie, in which Olivier played
a mad actor who becomes leader of a party of the far Right, got
bad notices. But then he returned to Shakespeare, with *Coriolanus*.
The death scene was as spectacular as had come to be expected
from him, and much admired. 'He throws himself down a staircase
in a complete somersault which shakes the stage, then rolls over
three times on his side, and crashes dead at the footlights.' *John
O'London's Weekly* declared that he was 'the only sign of a great
actor in the making in England today.'[47] He had played six of
Shakespeare's great roles in sixteen months. His gamble of making
a name as a Shakespearean leading man – and it had been a gamble
– had paid off triumphantly.

Then he and Vivien went on holiday through France. Olivier
lived for his work, disliked holidays and would never drag himself
away for more than a few days except in his first year with Vivien.
His holiday with her in 1938 was one he remembered all his life,
though he remembered it as having taken place in 1937, the wrong
year. But 1938 it was, and for two whole months. They drove in
her old Ford V8 from Boulogne, down the *route gastronomique* which
had been mapped out for them by Charles Laughton, past Paris to
Avalon, Dijon, Beaune, Macon, Vienne, Montelimar and then east
to the hill town of Vence in the foothills of the Alps, a few miles

north of Nice. They met John Gielgud, Peggy Ashcroft, and Glen Byam Shaw, who were staying on the Riviera, and then drove west to the village of Agay on the rocky coast between Cannes and St Raphael, where they stayed in a hotel called the Calanque d'Or [Golden Creek]. The proprietor owned eighteen Siamese cats, one of which Vivien took back with her to London.[48] The film star had her cat.

While they were at Agay a cable arrived: ARE YOU INTERESTED GOLDWYN IDEA FOR SEPTEMBER FIRST FOR VIVIEN YOURSELF AND OBERON IN WUTHERING HEIGHTS. Olivier sent a temporising answer. A week later, to help convince him, a script arrived, by Ben Hecht and Charles MacArthur. He could not have asked for better writers but still he was wary of Hollywood. It also emerged that Vivien was being offered not the principal part of Cathy but that of Isabella. Merle Oberon would play Cathy. Olivier and Vivien continued their trip westward to the Pyrenéen village of Nay, from where his Huguenot ancestors had come, and then they set off north. In the Loire another message reached them. William Wyler, who was to direct *Wuthering Heights*, was in France, at Juan les Pins. Could Olivier meet him? Juan les Pins was by then two hundred and fifty miles away by road, to the south-west, so he could not.

But Olivier was being pursued. Wyler visited him twice on his return to London. Still the difficulty was Vivien's wish for the part of Cathy, which was not on offer, and which she could not reasonably have expected. Wyler gently suggested that for a first part in Hollywood, Isabella was as good as she would get. Olivier once again telephoned Ralph Richardson to ask for advice. Should he do *Wuthering Heights*? 'Yes. Bit of fame. Good,' said Richardson.[49]

This was a tense time in Europe. Hitler was making territorial demands. The Royal Navy was mobilised and Frewen was sent out to Gibraltar as a sub-lieutenant. Air-raid shelters were dug in London parks. Vivien and her friend Ursula Jeans considered joining up as ambulance drivers.[50] War was in the air, though the tension eased when, at Munich, Britain agreed to Germany's annexing of the German-speaking parts of Czechoslovakia and the prime minister, Neville Chamberlain, returned waving a piece of paper signed by Hitler and declaring it was 'peace for our time'.

Ainley continued to write to Olivier from Manchester, calling him 'Lorenzo Mio' and 'My Blessed and Most Dear Larry', asking him not to upbraid him for writing and at least to get his secretary to keep him informed of how he was.[51] Vivien had given up for the moment any hope of the role of Cathy in *Wuthering Heights*, and resigned herself to staying in England to do *A Midsummer Night's Dream* again as the Christmas show at the Old Vic. Olivier took Richardson's advice and left for Hollywood but not before he gave another tactless interview, this time to *Film Weekly*. 'One just drifts,' he said, 'and tries to enjoy the financial rewards.'[52]

He sailed on the *Normandie* from Southampton on 5 November, Vivien's twenty-fifth birthday. In the morning they drove to Waterloo station and she saw him off on the boat train. On the way to Southampton, 'blind with misery' at the parting, he wrote her two letters. 'I'm still feeling numb from parting from you my dearest dearest love. Your darling face driving away. I do worship you my love. . . In the car was like a Noel Coward sketch, it was so brave!' Nearer Southampton he wrote again saying Durham Cottage, when she returned to it, would only *seem* empty because it would be filled with his thoughts and love. She was his heart's blood. Would she plant the daffodils in the lawn, about three clumps of ten to twelve? 'Also order about four doz. anemone bulbs and plant in fairly large clumps so that they make what is known as a "brave" show which is what you have been doing all day my splendid girl.' He gave the letters to a Western Union boy on the quay to post, with 'diligent tippings' so that he would not forget. The boy was not diligent: the letters were not postmarked until late the next day.[53]

9

The Making of *Wuthering Heights*

'THAT,' SAID OLIVIER, 'WAS a star-maker without any question. It was just lucky, terribly lucky.'[1] He was speaking of *Wuthering Heights*. In a season at the Old Vic, in 1937–38, he had established himself as a Shakespearean actor. In late 1938 he set off to film *Wuthering Heights*, and then *Rebecca* and *Pride and Prejudice*, and these established him as a Hollywood star. He set off cocksure of himself, confident that he understood the character of Heathcliff and later saying he had done his homework, having learned from Garbo, who had known everything there was to know about Queen Christina.[2] That is how he remembered it, but in truth he had not done his homework. He had seen the screenplay but he had not even read Emily Brontë's novel. He took it with him on the *Normandie* but lost it after three days, bought another copy in New York, and was still finishing it on his two-day flight from New York to Los Angeles.[3]

The director was William Wyler, who was only thirty-six at the time but had made twenty-seven silent Westerns and then fifteen talkies, the last of which had been the splendid *Jezebel* with Bette Davis. Olivier came to think him a genius, but when they first rehearsed they hated each other. Olivier was obsessed with his appearance and had himself heavily made up as Heathcliff ages throughout the film, first aged seventeen, then at twenty, then at thirty and then at fifty. Wyler scoffed. Then they fell out over how to act the part. Olivier wrote to Vivien in detail telling her what had happened.

Olivier's sketch in a letter to Vivien, showing her how he made himself up for Heathcliff

'He said on the screen you must be *right* for a part, and everybody thinks *you're* right for Heathcliff, so you must just play it as yourself. Well, really, I stayed as patient as I could and explained that an actor's job is pretending to be someone *else*, at least that is my reading of an actor's job, and it always has been and always will be. I have trained myself to search for *other* people than myself in the parts I have played, and except for Hamlet and one or two others, I have not tried to find them in myself, and I certainly didn't intend to find *Heathcliff* there, and that if he asked me to do that I would be utterly LOST and he would really be better off with almost anybody else. We argued and argued, and I must say he didn't argue very brilliantly. . . I suspect he must have good instinct with no brains.'[4]

Here Olivier is stating the essence of his art or trade, and here he had to be right, though the exception he makes for Hamlet is arresting. Which of Hamlet's moods and characteristics did he see in himself? But for the rest Wyler was right, as Olivier came to see and later admit. 'He thought he knew more about films, and he was damn well right.'

But that was not Olivier's opinion then, and he and Wyler had spitting arguments.

Wyler: 'For Christ sake what are you doing now? Come off the clouds. Come down to earth.'

Olivier: 'I suppose this anaemic little medium can't stand anything great in size like that.'

Wyler: 'If you wouldn't mind pausing to think of the best effect you can create in such an anaemic little medium, I would ask you to turn left and march out of the door.'

But, said Olivier, though he had done nothing to deserve it, Wyler had a liking for him – perhaps a sense that he was 'a mite more civilised than most of the other people he might talk to in that great big city' – so he invited Olivier home to dinner. There he said, 'I want to talk to you. Now I want you to be patient about this and I want you to understand something. You are quite wrong to take this patronising attitude about this medium. Let me tell you something I believe in with my whole heart and soul – this is the greatest medium ever invented, there's nothing to touch it. Don't you sneer at me that nobody could do Shakespeare and that you've tried in that damn stupid Bergner picture. There's nothing in literature – Greek tragedy, anything you want, the most primitive, anything in the world – that you can't do successfully in this medium. All you've got to do is find out how.'[5]

Then Sam Goldwyn, who was producing, came and told Olivier he was ugly, bawled Wyler out, and stalked off. Olivier thought him a disgraceful sort of a man, but recognised that he had a great feeling for what would work and what would not. After he'd gone Wyler said, 'I'm sorry, but he's right. All he says about you is right. You are hammy, you are stagey, it won't do, and you'll have to do it all again.'[6]

Nor did Olivier get on easily with his leading lady, Merle Oberon, who was perceptive and generous enough to see that he'd rather have been acting with Vivien. Wyler saw this too and told him to *think* of Vivien and *act* with Merle; as for Merle, she'd have to act with Olivier and think of Alex Korda, whom she married the following year.[7] Still they did not get on. They had filmed together before, and amicably, but in *Wuthering Heights*, in the close-ups, she accused him of spitting at her. 'Daggers drawn . . . We spat at each other, we hated each other, and after one appalling row in which we were both trembling and tears were streaming down, and we were absolutely trembling with rage, Willy said "Roll them," and it was the most heavy-making love scene we'd done and we did it hating each other, but it was one of the top love scenes in the film as it turned out. That was Willy, very bright, very clever.' Then there was trouble with the heather. It was meant to be Yorkshire heather, eight inches high, but in the California rain and sun it grew to three feet.[8]

In such a way was the film made that it established Olivier's film reputation. When it was released the posters of Olivier as Heathcliff read: THE MARK OF HELL WAS IN HIS EYES.[9]

But we must return to Vivien Leigh. Just before Olivier left for America she had asked Holman to give her a divorce and he had declined.[10] Before Olivier had left she had told Holman there was a chance she might have to go Hollywood for a film, and this seems to have been so. Olivier, on board the *Normandie*, started writing to her, day by day, during the five days of the crossing. By the time he reached New York the letter stretched to thirty-two pages. On the first morning out he told her he had changed his cabin because it had only a shower, not a bath. 'You,' he wrote, 'were to have had the bath, if you remember.'[11] From this letter and from those he wrote later it becomes plain that she had promised Wyler she would take the part of Isabella, and that she very nearly kept this promise.

Among Olivier's fellow passengers on the *Normandie* were Noel Coward, Leslie Howard, Herbert Wilcox and Anna Neagle. He told Vivien there had been good luck cables from, among others, Sybille – 'Extravagant bitch on my money.' He was depressed. He kept weeping, calling himself Vivien's 'worshipping seducer'. When he changed cabins he was he was offered number sixty-nine, which he declined, thinking she might not have liked that. He was offered one on the southern, sunny side of the ship but chose one on the starboard, northern side to be facing her way. He drank hard. Before lunch on the second day out he had three vodkas and four champagne cocktails, with more champagne afterwards. He telephoned her each day and they shouted each other hoarse for what he called 'three heart-breaking minutes'. He swam in the *Normandie*'s great pool and drew a picture of himself looking like a frogman. 'They've invented some wonderful rubber *fins* that you attach to your feet which make you swim terribly fast – very enjoyable but a bit tiring. I love thinking of you when water is rushing past my face. I always used to find a cold sponge very soothing at Capri – do you remember? Great comfort in thoughts of you while in water. I must have a pre-natal wish, somewhere, to be your child. DARLING.' His mother fixation was showing itself even to his mistress.

The *Normandie* docked in New York at midday on 11 November and he went to the Gotham on Fifth Avenue at 55th Street. There he took a phone call from her in which she 'sounded so terribly miserable and hurt'.[12] Next day they talked again. 'O my darling little lovling I adore you so. You're so original. The way you make absolutely *no* attempt to hide your darling feelings is so a*dor*able! I hope you've noticed what a healthy regard I have for your anger! I've spent thousands of pounds in the last few minutes assuring myself that you're not displeased with me. Oh my sweet that sounds ungracious . . . The girls just phoned up and told me the last phone call cost $105! And more yesterday I think. It really would be cheaper to come out my dove. After all nearly fifty quid for two days, half hour each day, of *des*perate gabbling – when we could *H———ave* each other for less than that!'[13]

As he was writing this letter Sam Goldwyn telephoned. 'FLASH!' wrote Olivier when he resumed the letter and reported Sam as having asked whether Vivien was with him, saying he was crazy about that girl, tremendously impressed with her last picture, and that she had a great future. When Olivier asked him whether he was after her for Isabella, Goldwyn asked whether she would she play the part. 'I said I don't think so. He – "Would she play Cathy?" Me – "*What?* YES", but he only laughed, and said "Anyway I'm sorry she's not with you." Weeell, something may transpire. I don't know . . . I fear it's only a catch for Isabella.'[14]

On his second day in New York Olivier went to see the English actor Maurice Evans in *Hamlet*. It was one of the successes of the season. Evans was a great singer of verse and Olivier loathed it. 'No reality, character, truth, imagination whatever. He can't act at all.'

He also met Charles MacArthur, joint scriptwriter of *Wuthering Heights*, and suggested Vivien for a part in his new play which would be opening almost at once. He wrote again, as he had on his arrival, that he didn't know whether Vivien should come out.[15] Next day, flying to Los Angeles on an American Airlines DC3, he wrote again, in a letter posted at Nashville, that he was still reading *Wuthering Heights* but was looking with dumb misery into the future. Next they landed at Tucson to refuel, at sunrise. When they were airborne again he drew for her the view from his seat, showing the plane's wing and, down below, mountains near the Colorado river.[16]

In Los Angeles he stayed at the Beverly Hills Hotel. He had been spending a small fortune on telephone calls but took a room for eight dollars a day rather than a suite for twelve. He soon learned from his agent why Goldwyn had telephoned him in New York. Sam had asked Merle Oberon to play Cathy for nothing, she had refused, and he was holding Vivien out as a pretext to force her to consent. He saw Goldwyn, who reiterated how crazy he was about Vivien and how there was trouble with Merle, but insisted that he owed a lot to Merle. Then he repeated that he would like to have Vivien, but again there was his loyalty to Merle, and wouldn't Vivien come out on the off chance? If she didn't play Cathy he would guarantee Isabella. Olivier said no. Then, said Sam, would she do it for $15,000 if it was only a question of money? Olivier said, 'Maybe, probably not, perhaps'.

'I was going *mad!*' he wrote. 'Then I had lunch with Wyler, who is furious you broke your promise to play Isabella – do you remember you wrote him a letter saying . . . you *would* do Isabella? I'd forgotten that too. Then a long interview with the publicity, whose main anxiety was how did I wish my *ro*mance angle to be treated?! They all felt very strongly that if you came over different addresses would be the thing etc.'[17]

If Merle Oberon did not settle with Goldwyn then there would at least be the prospect of Vivien's coming out to test for Cathy. Meanwhile Olivier had devised another plan. Shooting on *Wuthering Heights* was unlikely to start before the beginning of December, so if he went to New York Vivien could take the *Normandie* and come and meet him there on 24 November, and they could have eight days together in that city. Wyler squashed this immediately, saying Olivier should act professionally and not even think of going away, that he wanted him for costume, make-up and rehearsals, and that even if Sam Goldwyn agreed he would not. Olivier wrote a pitiful letter to Vivien. 'I couldn't explain or make him understand that I was never able to believe that I would ever really come, even the day I left I couldn't believe it; but I'm beginning to believe it now alright – always in my mind there's been the sort of hope, the self-deceiving "telling myself" that I would see you again soon, that *some*how you would come out here, *some*how I would get to New York – even if we had to meet in space, we would and could do it. But now I really am in Hell my love – the valley of the shadow. . . I keep crying.'[18] That day he heard that Goldwyn had settled with Merle. He told Vivien and then came up with another idea, proposing and then rejecting as impracticable the notion that she should come out to him in Hollywood. He then ended a letter of 2,500 words with this passage:

'Darling please tell me when your pains come, and everything that you do, whether you are at all naughty – playing with yourself or *any*thing, and I promise to do the same, but I'm de*ter*mined not to do *any*thing till I see you again. I suppose I will do *that* one day if I *have* to, thinking of you, only thinking of you my beloved.'[19]

At home Vivien's daughter, Suzanne, was being brought up by her grandmother and a governess, but Leigh Holman had allowed Vivien to see her daughter and take her out. On the weekend of 19 and 20 November she took Suzanne to see Helen Spencer and her husband, Tully Grigg. Helen, writing with the freedom of a former mistress, and with some irony, told Olivier about the visit. 'Most enlightening. She doesn't care a bugger about that child, only corrects its manners, and shows it *no* affection whatever. She spent the whole time simply torn with the anxiety of whether she could go to you or not, or whether you were fucking someone else or not! You!! One cannot help feeling that Vivien has a rather shallow outlook on that question! I suppose that when a girl has fucked a bit herself she finds it difficult to understand constancy. One of your great qualities I should have thought. We did our best to convince her anyway. Darling, is it Hell out there? Or will the film be fun?

Do hurry home.' They had, she said, gone to a film ball with Vivien, which had been torture, with awful people fighting for autographs. 'Bobby Helpmann there, a *dear* little man, understands Vivien awfully well, and so attractively unmasculine.'[20]

In Hollywood Olivier was by then in a fever of longing. 'My dearest little darling passionate supreme love – I am with you, and round you, and *in* you all the time, my treasure.' He made no secret of his wish that she were there. Wyler knew, Merle Oberon knew, the studio publicity men knew, and he told any acquaintances he met about Vivien. 'The conversation,' he told her, '[is] so firmly clamped on to you and me, then on you, then me, then you and me.' He confided in a couple he and Jill had known in 1933 when they did *The Green Bay Tree* in New York. They recommended that Vivien should come over at once and he then wrote to her, 'O how can I support it, this purgatory, it's like living without a soul.' Then, in the same letter, while he was in his room waiting for her phone call, he conceived another and quite different idea. 'We really *ought* to be together, and yet I've got it fixed somehow in my idiotic soul that it would be a wonderfully great thing to us, if we managed to stick it out, as a sort of *task* for each other. Poor Jacob had four-teen years before he got his Rachel.[21] If only we could bear the *prospect* of it with a little more fortitude.' Olivier, as a clergyman's son, knew his Bible but quite lacked Jacob's patience. He was barely able to stand a separation of less than three weeks. 'I shall have to alter very considerably,' he wrote, 'or I shall be in a loony bin.'

He spent hours writing to Vivien. This same letter, twenty-one pages of it, extended into the next day. They had spoken again, he had slept, and then he wrote, 'About two hours after our phoning I woke up absolutely raging with desire for you my love, it was so strong I think you must have been having it too. O dear God I did want you – perhaps you were stroking your darling self my dear sweet. I know that you must have been wanting me.' Even Merle Oberon was now being sweet to him, suggesting not only that Vivien should come out but that she should stay with her. When he told Vivien that he wrote, 'Stop spitting and gnashing your teeth darling.'

He hired a car, a Pontiac convertible, and drew a sketch of it for

Vivien. He went to a motor show and to a Bach concert on the harpsichord. He played poker and, with his bad memory for cards, lost $50. 'If I'm not careful I shall have to borrow some money off Jill when I get back. (Our beloved phone call cost £30!)'

Then his whole mood lifted and he wrote; 'Oh my DARLING – how THRILLING. Your darling wire has just come. . . Oh my lamb. I AM SO GLORIOUSLY HAPPY.'[22] Vivien's cable to him has not survived, but she had evidently told him she was coming out. At much the same time she told Holman that as there was nothing happening in the way of work at the moment she 'might as well go'.[23] Larry replied: 'HOW GLORIOUS...WILL MAKE ARRANGEMENTS FOR EIGHT HEAVENLY DAYS WHAT HAS HAPPENED LONDON COMMITMENTS I AM SO HAPPY SHOULD DIE WITHOUT YOU ANY LONGER DELICIOUS LOVE.'[24]

He cabled two days later telling her not to bring a trunk but to buy light aeroplane luggage from Asprey and to bring two sports dresses, evening dresses, and fur coats.[25] She sailed from Southampton in the *Queen Mary* on 27 November, arrived in New York on 1 December, and flew on to Los Angeles. A fellow passenger of Vivien's on the *Queen Mary* was Hamish Hamilton. She told him he would love Larry. He said no, he hated him for robbing his best friend, Holman, of his wife. She said, 'You won't.' When he asked her why she was going she said, 'Partly because Larry's there, and partly because I intend to get the part of Scarlett O'Hara.'[26] This was Hamilton's recollection in an interview he gave forty-eight years later, when the Scarlett legend was unbreakable and very likely coloured his recollection. But even if Vivien did say that, it was almost certainly just an expected throwaway line with no substance to it. In all the thousands of words Olivier wrote to her during their separation, letters in which he made this and that proposal for their meeting and in which he repeatedly went over what they had said to each other in their frequent telephone calls, *Gone With the Wind* is never once mentioned, even in an aside.

In New York he had tried to get her work in a play. In New York and Hollywood he had done his utmost to press her claims to play Cathy. *Gone With the Wind* was not in her mind or his. She went to Hollywood for love and lust of Larry.

10

Gone With the Wind

WHEN VIVIEN ARRIVED IN New York on 1 December 1938 she was greeted by three cables from Olivier. He sent one to the *Queen Mary* in which he said, quoting from both *Macbeth* and *Romeo and Juliet*, 'Time and the hour runs through the roughest day but so slowly through this one. Cable safe arrival. I die till you come.' He sent a second to the Cunard dock on West 42nd Street saying, 'Welcome my heart', and a third to the American Airlines office, saying, 'Good morning O my darling.' All were addressed to Mrs V. M. Holman.[1] She flew straight on to Los Angeles. The legend, assisted by Olivier in his biography, is that he waited for her there, at Clover Field, crouched in the back of a car a few feet beyond the airport entrance.[2]

Olivier's agent in Hollywood was Myron Selznick, the brother of David O. Selznick, who was producing *Gone With the Wind*, and Olivier had told Myron of Vivien's arrival. In early December there was no finished screenplay and casting was far from complete. In a splendid farrago of a publicity campaign Talullah Bankhead, Paulette Goddard, Bette Davis, Katharine Hepburn, Jean Arthur, and Joan Bennett had all been tipped for Scarlett. Selznick then announced that he was convinced the public needed a 'new girl' in the part.[3] On 10 December a start was at last made by burning old sets to simulate the sacking of Atlanta, and doubles of Rhett and Scarlett were filmed driving in a horse and buggy through the flames. These scenes are among the most famous in the history of American cinema. Against such a backdrop Vivien Leigh met David

O. Selznick. It is the very stuff of myth, embroidered ever since, and the only way to get near the truth is to look at what was written at the time. Two days later Selznick wrote to his wife Irene: 'Myron rolled in just exactly too late, arriving about a minute and a half after the last building had fallen and burned and after the shots were completed. With him were Larry Olivier and Vivien Leigh. Shhhhh: she's the Scarlett dark horse, and looks damned good. (Not for anyone's ears but your own: it's narrowed down to Paulette [Goddard], Jean Arthur, Joan Bennett, and Vivien Leigh.'[4]

Three years later Selznick's memory had improved and sharpened, and he then wrote: 'When he [Myron] introduced me to her, the flames were lighting up her face and Myron said: "I want you to meet Scarlett O'Hara." I took one look and knew that she was right. . . I'll never recover from that first look.'[5]

As for Olivier, by 1948 he was recalling that as they approached the blaze he saw Vivien's hair streaming in the breeze and her eyes alive in the reflection from the flames, and that he took Myron's arm and said, 'Just look at Vivien tonight. If David doesn't fall for that I'll be very surprised.'[6] By 1982, in his autobiography, his recollection was as follows: 'David peered very intently at Vivien; Myron made a vague gesture towards me. David threw a "Hello, Larry," into the air, roughly in my direction. Myron and I were left together, eye to eye and ho to hum. David had drawn Vivien a little way apart from the crowd and was fixing up an immediate test with her.' Olivier also remembered that he saw the roof of a barn fall in a flaming crash, which he could not have done if, as Selznick said, he arrived with Myron and Vivien after the last building had fallen.[7]

It is a lovely story, but there was nothing inevitable about it. Myron Selznick's office papers show that Vivien had already been taken by one of his employees to meet the people at United Artists, and then to meet the director William Wellman, who was casting for his new film, *The Light That Failed*. According to these same papers she had already decided to get out of the Old Vic's production of *A Midsummer Night's Dream*.[8]

At any rate, six days after her meeting with Selznick, Vivien wrote to Holman: 'You will never guess what has happened and no one is more surprised than me. You know that I only came out here for a week. Well just two days before I was due to leave, the people who are making *Gone With the Wind* saw me and said would I make a test – so what could I *do* and so now I am working frantically hard and rehearsing and studying a Southern accent . . . I don't know what I think or what I hope – I am so afraid it will mean me staying here (IF I get it) for a long time, and that I know I don't want to do.'9

She had by then secured her release from the Old Vic production. She did her tests for Selznick and on Christmas Day was told the part was hers.10 She and Larry were living in different places for the sake of appearance. On New Year's Day 1939 he wrote her a note from the Beverly Hills Hotel and drew the stamp on the envelope as an image of her head, writing underneath 'Queen Scarlett'.11 Tony Bushell, Consuelo, Tully Grigg, and Helen Spencer (who had lately been so scathing about her) sent a joint telegram saying: LOVE AND CONGRATULATIONS WE TOLD YOU SO.12

Vivien had her star part, Selznick had his 'new girl' and he had got her cheaply. She did not make a fortune from her most famous film. She was paid a flat fee, with no royalties, of $1250 a week, and in all earned $25,000. Selznick insisted on putting her under contract for seven years, the longest period allowed by law. Since she was already under contract to Korda, the agreement was that she should work six months of each year for Selznick and then six months for Korda. Selznick later claimed that Olivier was possessed by pure jealousy, tried in every way to kill the casting of Vivien as Scarlett, and advanced every possible argument against it. Two things have to be remembered. First, Selznick made this statement in 1944, in the context of a dispute between him and the Oliviers over his contract with Vivien.13 And secondly, he and Olivier had, to say the least of it, been cool to each other since 1932, when Selznick fired Olivier and as good as accused him of depriving Jill of her chance in *Bill of Divorcement*. The story is that in early 1939, when Olivier questioned Vivien's contract, Selznick told him, 'Larry, don't be a shit twice.' Olivier may not have been delighted at Vivien's success, forseeing further long separations. On the other hand, he may just have been trying to improve the terms of her contract. She did receive only a fifth of what was paid to Clark Gable.

She wrote again to Holman, who at the time had not given up

hope of getting her back, but whom she treated like a brother. 'As you well realise,' she said, 'I loathe Hollywood, and for no other part would I have dreamt of signing a contract. . .the more I see of Hollywood the less possible it becomes. . . In fact I do not think there is anything nice about America except the football, and the politeness of men in garages.'[14] She told her mother much the same, saying that if Larry were not there she would go mad.[15] On the same day as she wrote that letter, 26 January 1939, shooting started. She was by then living at 520 North Crescent Drive, Beverly Hills, with Sunny Alexander, a Texan girl from Myron's office, as her secretary and companion. There was a staff of a maid, butler, cook and gardener. The house was guarded day and night to keep pests and reporters away. Olivier stayed at his hotel.[16]

In January *Wuthering Heights* was finished and Vivien knew that, though she might go mad without him, she could not expect Larry to spend all his time in Hollywood.[17] Olivier again put things more bluntly. 'It was better not to smudge the career image by hanging around, hoping for a job. *Wuthering Heights* wouldn't make its effect yet awhile, and I was against just continuing to dance attendance, "announcing her guests and walking the Pekingese"; the best thing career-wise would be to get myself a good appearance in the New York theatre.'[18] In February he signed a contract to play opposite Katharine Cornell, the first lady of the American theatre, in *No Time for Comedy* by Sam Behrman. His salary was $1,000 a week and ten per cent of the gross above $15,000 a week. He had the part of Gaylord, a young playwright who feels himself misunderstood by his actress wife and seeks consolation with the wife of a banker, who almost inspires him to run off to Spain to fight in the civil war. So by early in March Olivier, who had so recently found a month's separation to be intolerable, had again left Vivien. As he saw it, she had forced the separation.[19] He wrote to Vivien's mother Gertrude as confidingly as he had once written to Jill's, saying it had been an agonising decision for them both, but a wise one. Vivien wrote to her mother saying it was the only thing to do, and that Larry had engaged himself for a play in America so that he could telephone her and fly back to her, and he would be lonely too.[20]

Sunny Alexander also wrote confidingly to Olivier. She took his letters on set to Vivien and observed how radiantly she received them. 'Do keep it up because she absolutely thrives on these thrills that come only from your letters and phone calls.'[21] *Gone With the Wind* was not going smoothly. Two directors had come and gone. 'My heart ached for little Vivien,' Sunny told Olivier, 'as she cried last night after talking to you – in fact most every night and Sunday mornings are awful without you.' But they were going to see a preview of *Wuthering Heights*.[22]

The American opening of this film, in Hollywood, was a triumph for Olivier. Eleanor Roosevelt, Marlene Dietrich, Douglas Fairbanks Jnr, Paulette Goddard, Merle Oberon, and the David Selznicks were there. Louella Parsons wrote that the film buried for ever any idea that he resembled Ronald Colman; he was a personality entirely on his own and his performance as the sulky stable boy was magnificent. The *Los Angeles News* said the Hollywood mob took one look and wished it had shown better judgment in appreciating his talents while he was in town before – a reference to the Garbo fiasco. The *New York Times* said, 'Mr Olivier is one of those once in a lifetime things, a case of a player physically and emotionally ordained for a role.'[23] Hedda Hopper, the gossip columnist whose good opinion was gold dust, wrote: 'When Laurence Olivier says, "Come here, you're mine," how gladly you'd go.' But by this time Vivien was exhausted and hysterical, and Olivier was summoned by Selznick to go to her.[24] He was released from dress rehearsals of his play. There followed the familiar adventures of night flights, telegrams, clandestine meetings, and joyous letters. They were again doing what they did best. He took the midnight plane from New York, cabling: ARRIVE BURBANK FOUR TWENTY JEALOUS EVERY MINUTE REVIVALIST WORSHIP – ANDREW.

Then, about halfway through the long, transcontinental flight he cabled again from Amarillo, Texas, telling her not actually to meet the plane but to be somewhere near because of 'slightly embarrassing company', presumably fellow passengers.[25] They had two days and two nights together. Then he flew away again, not to New York but directly to Indianapolis where *No Time For Comedy* was starting its pre-New York run. 'O what a joyous little respite our darling little flying visit was my angel – the joy of it will last for weeks. My life is *perched* on your darling love.' He posted this during a refuelling stop at Albuquerque. The flight back took fourteen hours.

He had no sooner played the first night in Indianapolis, in what can only have been an exhausted condition, than he received the news that his father had died at Worthing, just before his seventieth birthday. Fahv had suffered a stroke and was found on the floor by Ibo when she returned from shopping. He died on a Thursday. The funeral was the following Monday in his old parish of Addington. It would have been impossible for Olivier to return in less than seven or eight days, even if he could have left his play. Ibo wrote telling him about the funeral, saying she was grateful to Jill for coming. 'She and I had a long talk afterwards and she told me of your letter to her asking her to take out divorce proceedings – which she said she would be starting on – Oh Larry *must* it be – she loves you so much and I can't believe that your love for her is completely dead.'[26]

Sybille wrote in quite a different tone. She said Worthing had been plastered with posters saying, 'Father of Famous Actor Dies.' He would have no idea how Fahv had treated Ibo in the last year: fuss, fuss, fuss, wouldn't be left, hated her going out. Did Larry remember how they'd gone for a walk and he'd asked her how long he thought the old man might last, and she'd replied gloomily that he might taggle on for twenty years? All she could feel now was acute relief. At the funeral they'd played 'Then Praise My Soul', which was the favourite hymn of her 'best beloved of the moment'. Wasn't it odd, she asked, that when you were crazily happy loving someone you wanted to cry? Did Vivien affect him like that? Then she turned to Jill. At the funeral, she'd never seen her look prettier. 'She still kids herself like Hell of course. Says portentously that *you* are not at all happy. . . It's odd, you know Kim, but I believe that if you and Jill hadn't married, maybe she and I would one day have had a thundering love affair!'[27]

Olivier had offered both Ibo and Sybille a trip to New York and a holiday. Both declined. Sybille couldn't at the moment, but would love a cruise later. Ibo had Fahv's estate to settle and, deep though their love was, did not think she and Sybille would be happy travelling companions.[28]

Henry Ainley wrote to Larry for the last time. 'My love to you in your great loss. I miss *my* father even today, and I am a grandfather. Affectionate sympathy to you both. Harry.'[29]

Vivien, in Hollywood, was not happy in her work and was comforted by letters from two English friends. Ursula Jeans, the actress with whom both she and Larry had stayed, pointed out the advantages of being where she was. 'Darling, I hear you loathe the place – which I knew you would – isn't it an idiotic little suburb? – but it offers such opportunities with a terrific amount of hard cash into the bargain. What can one do?' Tony Bushell's mistress, Consuelo, who was keen on astral planes and spiritualism, offered Vivien advice on how to ease her loneliness. 'If you exerted yourself – and when going to bed concentrated on Larry with all your force and love, making it your last conscious thought, you will, in your astral body, go to Larry (in N.Y.) and be able to look down on him!'[30]

One night on the tour of his play, in Baltimore, Olivier dined too well, drank too much of a good Burgundy, then started on mint juleps, and was not in his room when Vivien's telephone call came through. Next day he wrote her a letter of remorse and maudlin religiosity. 'I was too miserable even to cry. I was dying to ring up and say, "O Vivling my darling forgive me, please forgive me. I'm so sorry Mummy darling."' He had been to see a musical, *Broadway Parade*, and at sentimental moments howled into his handkerchief and said 'O Pussey, O Pussey'. He sang *very* loudly to her when the organist made them all sing 'Easter Parade'. 'My throat does ache so for you my beloved darling Vivien child, Mary child, O how I reverence you, wrap you in mental cotton wool and put you on the mantelpiece and burn *candles* to you.' He enclosed six newspaper cuttings. One praised his ease and his completely natural stage presence. A second described him as 'a more bounding Gerald du Maurier'. Another said that, offstage, he was dark and silent like Heathcliff, seldom speaking until spoken to and not always then, and mercurial in his moods, shifting quickly from gaiety to a sombreness that bordered on the morose.[31]

No Time for Comedy opened in New York to excellent notices. The headlines were all for Katharine Cornell but Olivier was much praised. Brooks Atkinson of the *New York Times* said he had a hundred ways to express as an actor what the author had put into the play. The

Daily News said there was about him a haunting memory of Alfred Lunt or maybe of Noel Coward. Only the *Post* dissented, calling him a 'sort of indifferent understudy for Alfred Lunt'.[32] At the same time, posters of him as Heathcliff were all over the city and cardboard cut-outs of Olivier stood outside cinemas. One evening a taxi driver, not recognising him but making conversation, told him what a good film he thought *Wuthering Heights* was. 'I thought I'd say "I'm in that," and then followed a lot of "Who yes kiddin?" stuff – but I went on and said "Yes really, look *that's* me, *there* (pointing to a huge cardboard thing)," then he said "Gwaan, take yer hat off" and I did – and he nearly died – it was quite fun, he was so pleased and said "You sure showed who was boss, yessir, gimme a stong man!!" He seemed very sure that men were the stronger sex.'[33]

It was one thing to kid taxi drivers, but quite another to give consistently tactless interviews. The man from the *Christian Science Monitor* wrote: 'He is whacky. When Mr Olivier opens his mouth his press agent shudders. Mr O's idea of story telling is to give it everything credulity will bear. How does it feel to be New York's newest matinée idol? "Nothing I didn't expect. . . I always knew I had it in me. I was a matinée idol at the Old Vic. I was the matinée idol of the acolytes as a boy. I expect I've always been a matinée idol." By this time the press agent gazes at Mr Olivier with the appearance of a cornered deer.'[34]

He certainly did give his press agents a hard time. He told the *World Telegram* that *Wuthering Heights* was the only good film he ever made, but then could not resist adding, 'But there were parts that you just had to – slide through. Really, some of the lines were most embarrassing.'[35] On the page in his cuttings book in which such pieces were stuck he wrote, 'Je déteste les films. HURRAH, Ha-ha.'[36]

What with *Wuthering Heights* and such notices for his play, Olivier was in demand for his autograph, and the fans were bolder than he was used to in London. He was, as his sister Sybille put it, 'swept by the winds of aggressive adulation'.[37] Sometimes he basked in this adulation; at other times, when the mood took him, he went to extremes to shun his fans and mightily offended them. His theatre was built back to back with another, as was common on Broadway. One night he climbed down a fire escape, entered through a dressing room window in the adjacent theatre, and got out unnoticed that way. As he told Vivien, 'I wanted to hurry home and not bugger about with all that stage door balony.'[38] He was being thus temperamental at a time when everything was going right for him in the theatre and cinema, except perhaps that Maurice Evans, in *Hamlet*, was voted by the New York critics to have given the best performance of the 1938–39 season. Olivier came equal sixth with Katharine Hepburn in *Philadelphia Story*.[39]

He wrote to Vivien flattering her performance in *Gone With the Wind*, seeking to illustrate the way she was imposing her views on the producer. 'David O. S. comes in to your room and explains that Melanie is dying and that you must consequently look very sad. . . and you look in wrapt attention and all the time are thinking what you're really going to do.'[40]

She was often jealous and showed it in their phone calls. 'I really thought,' he wrote after one call, 'that I was going off my head with wanting you – and you wasting all that *precious* time saying I must *have* somebody. O how could you? I'm simply in *prison* here without you, success and all.' He wore a carnation in his underpants during performances, and then sent the flower to her. She sent him a pair of her knickers. 'NO – ahah. . .' he wrote, 'absolutely doused in scent and quite discoloured! Aaaaaah my darling – *what* am I supposed to do with them hey? You know how susceptible I am!' He slept with them. 'O my love this morning I beat you to it! I woke up at 7 am my time (3 am yours) aaah my sweet I'm afraid you didn't feel me loving you then – 'cos you were asleep hey?' Later he added to the letter: 'Oooh your panties are awfully hard to bear in the mornings – I kissed them and kissed them this morning – and thought of your mummy kissing them perhaps when you were a little girl asleep.'[41]

At about this time he wrote to Karl Tiedemann and sent a copy to Vivien, saying he'd written because the priest used to be his confessor. He hoped she didn't mind. He couldn't face seeing Karl because it would be a terrible meeting, but had told him what he needed to know.

Back in London, Jill had been in two plays. Each lasted only two weeks, the first having earned her £6 and the second £10. She wrote telling Olivier that Fahv's funeral had been simple and dignified. It was impossible for her to describe Tarquin to Larry, as he didn't know the boy at all, but he did look like Larry at times. She had gone to see *Wuthering Heights* with their friend Mercia Relph and they wept buckets. She had never thought Larry a really first-class film actor before, but she did now. If he wanted to be a film star he could be one of the biggest of the lot, but she hoped he did not want to be, at least not at the expense of his stage career.

Then she turned to what she called their jolly little divorce. She had seen the lawyers and would go and see Holman to find out if he would go ahead at the same time. Would Larry tell her truthfully whether he wanted a divorce straight away with Vivien named as co-respondent or whether he preferred to wait a year and be divorced for desertion. It didn't matter to her whether she waited or not. Without their being together she could not feel she was his wife. She sent all her love, hoped he would be back in July, and was longing for him to see Tarquin again.[42]

Olivier sent Jill's letter to Vivien, hoping that its tone would not annoy her too much. And this, more than anything else, shows the depth of his enthralment to her, because the tone of Jill's letter was self-evidently decent, civil, and affectionate, even loving. He went on to tell Vivien he had lost $40 on the racecourse that day, backing names or jockeys' colours that seemed to have anything to do with her – horses called Fighting Fox, Ballinderry, and Thorn Apple, and a jockey in pale blue with a scarlet cap. Then he seems to have found her knickers again, because he writes 'WELL!!!', rings a yellowish stain on the writing paper and goes on, 'Aaah aaah LOVE, a sort of finger print! O my writing isn't very good now. Oh dear how funny – how adorable – how wonderful you are my sweet heaven I do worship you so.'[43]

Vivien wrote telling Holman of Jill's letter, asking again for a divorce, and asking him also to divorce her from his mind and not cling on to a hope. On the set she was muttering and moaning, saying the dialogue was silly, particularly when it differed from the novel's. She was not easy to direct. By mid-May they were taking dawn shots and she was writing that she was exhausted and miserable.[44]

Olivier wrote to her nearly every day. He recalled bathing with her off Sark in the Channel Islands, in shallow blue water. He called her his country, his tree, his blossom, his lovely break o'day actress, his mistress of such gracious parts, such graces and such arts.[45] Anyone's love letters can become repetitive. His letter of Thursday, 18 May, can stand for most of the others. It is probably the most revealing. He had moved from the Barclay Hotel on East 48th Street to the New York Athletic Club on Central Park South. He started writing to her at 1.45 in the early hours of Thursday; at 2 a.m. they spoke on the telephone, and then he resumed: '2.25. O God how dreadful – half an hour of absolute madness again. I really don't know what to do. What is happening to us darling pussey? Hey? Something's gone so wrong and it only becomes apparent on the phone. O darling dear I am so sorry we're getting so horribly spoilt. It's just insanity, that's all. . . I'm always reproached with having a gay time and I'm not having any such thing. . . On the phone when it costs a fortune – you *wilfully misunderstand* and distort what I've said and construe it all in the best way to keep up the quarrel longest.'

They had apparently quarrelled that night about his having agreed
to stay longer in the play than she had expected. He explained that
it was not for the salary but because he felt it his duty to the company.
'O Baby we are getting so depressed we must *try* not to. . . It feels
that I have learned to expect "trouble" somehow, and I find myself
rising from my cave, with smoke coming from my nostrils before
my cue. So please forgive me my dear one. [Here he drew a dragon
in a cave on the left confronting a hissing, arch-backed cat on the
right.] We *mustn't* let misunderstandings heap up – dear darling O
please forgive me – the truth is we've been so miserable and frustrated and tired and aching and bored for so long that we've
temporarily lost our senses of humour.' He wrote on for more than
another two hours, telling her the news about their friend Tony
Bushell in England and drawing for her a minutely correct map,
street by street, of Manhattan between Central Park South and 47th
Street, showing her where his theatre was, the hotel he had moved
from, and the Athletic Club. He stopped at 4.40 a.m., writing that
he was going to take her in his arms, and went to bed.

He was soon woken by a call from Sunny. Vivien had taken an
overdose. Sunny had found her staggering round naked and trip-
ping over the furniture. She managed to make her way to the shower
where she turned one cold splash and then fell into Sunny's arms.
How Sunny managed after that is not clear. Vivien did recover after
a long sleep.[46]

It was alarming but in the event not serious. At lunch-time on
Thursday Olivier, having dealt with this crisis from a distance of
3,000 miles, resumed his letter to her. 'Darling baby oh sweet little
tiny baby girl, I do so love you. O how terribly touching you are.
I do adore you Vivien my darling little girl. O but I ought to be
soooooo cross with you. Urrrrrrggh! Urrrrrrgh! How *dare* you take
four pills like that you hysterical little *ninny* (and I know perfectly
well you knew people would get alarmed and ring me up and put
the fear of God into your poor old Larry at five in the morning).
Urrgh! Bend over – Yes, take your drawers down – no, lift your
skirt up – *now* then: – Smack! Smack! Smack! –! –! –! –! –! –! –! –!*!!!
Yes – *Eleven! Naughty pooossey.* Now you come here and I'll kiss it
and make it better – Ooooh but Vivling. What did your poor three

friends *think*, hey?. . . Poor Sunny was de*men*ted. I'm afraid you lead
your loving ones one hell of a dance and that's *terribly* naughty.
You're awfully spoilt yes you are, and all because you're so pretty.
Aaaaaah poooor pussey that's enough isn't it? Hey? Oh my dear
dear true love I do adore you and love you so put on a *brave front*
my own, like this [here he drew an elegant cat holding an umbrella].
True blood, stout hearts and grey herrings and preeety pussies and
Larry's carnations, and beloved, O beloved Vivlings, don't give way
in front of the common herd like this!!!'[47]

Sunny wrote to him the next day saying Vivien was much better.
She did not think she realised what she had done or that the seda-
tives she had taken were so strong. She would make sure she got
no more. Vivien had been a perfect angel for the past twenty-four
hours and was very sorry for doing such a stupid thing. She, Sunny,
had telephoned the studio and said Vivien was ill. She ended: 'Try
to keep happily in love. I get so upset when things aren't right –
and Vivien is impossible – or need I tell you?'[48]

Larry was making preparations for her to come to New York
when filming was completed. He had talked to the sympathetic
manager of the Barclay Hotel who said the only thing would be to
register as Mr and Mrs Smith. He knew it was different in Europe,
but American hotels had to preserve family values. Olivier decided
they should take an apartment and live there as Mr and Mrs Kerr.
He would keep a room at the club and Vivien would register at the
Waldorf, where Sunny could take phone calls for her. For the weekends they would take a house at Sneden's Landing on the Hudson,
a few miles north of Manhattan.[49]

When he expected her within two weeks he wrote to her. 'I do
not think there is a solitary second when my mind is not *completely*
buried in you. You are really on my brain – I am like a mad thing.
I suppose if you happened to represent something dangerous I
should be locked up – but no it's not quite like that. I am not *always*
thinking sweetly of you. I am thinking angrily or indignantly or
sulkily, quite often, but I am *never* not thinking of you. More often
than not I am just *worried* about you, concerned and distressed about
my baby lamb being tired or unhappy – and of course *often* it is with
mad, mad passion and sometimes it is naughty, sometimes only

sometimes it is dirty or even sadistic. . . You are all over me, in
sorrow or in joy, all of the time – O yes in drunkenness too, in
conversation, in work, with every breath and heart-beat.' After he
wrote this, in the early morning, his breakfast arrived and he was
off to the theatre to practise his voice by yelling into the empty auditorium, 'Once more unto the breach'.[50] At such a moment *Henry V*
came back to him.

On 16 June, the second anniversary of the day Vivien had left
Holman to live with him, he sent her a long telegram. He addressed
it, in an attempt at discretion, to Mary Holman – Mary being her
second Christian name – and did not sign it.

```
TO BRING YOU MY MOST JOYOUS GRATEFUL LOVE TODAY MY TWO YEARS
GLORY TWO YEARS FROM ETERNITY THE MEREST SALTED ALMOND MY
ETERNAL FEAST MAY YOUR DEAR LIFE BE SWEETENED WITH THE
RICHNESS YOU HAVE GIVEN MINE MY HEART AND MY SOUL ADORE
AND REJOICE IN YOU TODAY AND FOREVER BELOVED WONDERFUL
LITTLE PUSSCAT=
            (NO SIG).
```

From Beverly Hills Sunny reported that every night Vivien scratched
off another day and yelled 'Whoopee', but the poor little thing was
awfully tired, working day and night. It had been the most God-
awful picture. She had never heard of a studio doing business in
such a screwy way. 'And poor little Vivien with her heart in New
York and trying to put her mind on this – it's been awful. Several
times I thought she really was going mad. She warned me once
that some day she would and I was beginning to believe that time
had come. But there's been a great improvement the last week –
she's wearing a beautiful smile all the time and seems to have herself
under control. God, how I hope it lasts.'[51]

By this time there was nothing secret about Olivier and Vivien's affair. The *Syracuse Herald,* in New York State, ran a detailed and substantially accurate story under the headline, VIVIEN LEIGH'S ROMANCE GIVES JITTERS TO GONE WITH THE WIND DIRECTORS'. It said that Sam Goldwyn, Olivier's boss in *Wuthering Heights,* had been dismayed when Vivien Leigh had showed up. It had been said, and she had later confirmed it, that she came to be near Larry. Gossip had it that while they were together in Hollywood two divorce suits would be filed in England. Their devotion had won Hollywood's wistful admiration. Everyone in the *Gone With the Wind* company knew that they exchanged letters and gifts every day and telephoned frequently. For his birthday on 22 May she had sent him a personally iced caked by airmail. She lived with a secretary and a couple of servants in Beverly Hills. Other newspapers ran hinting stories and full-page advertisements for *Wuthering Heights* were appearing in magazines, featuring Olivier's head and the caption: 'I am Heathcliff. I love a woman who belongs to another by law. . .'[52]

The filming of *Gone With the Wind* ended on 27 June and Vivien flew to Olivier in New York. 'Just so happy to be back with Laurence Olivier and who could blame her?' wrote Hedda Hopper. 'Wouldn't we all like the chance?' Louella Parsons reported that Vivien had spent her 'first American Fourth of July in New York with the boy friend', and later spotted the two of them at Sneden's Landing. She also gave the news that Olivier had signed to play Max de Winter in *Rebecca* and continued, 'Apparently, all Vivien Leigh's brave plans to return to England for a stage play will go a-glimmering. . .for she is now mentioned for the role of wife opposite her very good friend Laurence.'[53]

Olivier and Vivien did return to England at the end of July. The English press was less direct in its reporting; it simply mentioned the two in the same paragraph and let readers deduce what they would. 'Vivien Leigh sneaked home in the *Ile de France,*' said the *Daily Express.* 'Her name wasn't on the passenger list. Nor was Laurence Olivier's, though he was on the boat too.' The *Daily Sketch* reported that Vivien's luggage did not bear her name but was labelled with an 'X'.[54]

It had been an exhausting year for them both. She had played the role of her life and would for ever afterwards be Scarlett, like it or not. He, having established himself as a Shakespearean actor, had with Heathcliff become a Hollywood star of the first rank. They were in thrall to each other and quarrelled viciously. He thought of her often with passion, sometimes sadistically, sometimes as Mummy. He thought of her as 'Mary child' and burned candles to her. She feared she might go mad one day. He had asked himself whether she happened to represent something dangerous and had then decided no, it was not quite like that, but that she was all over him.

11

Not Sceeered, Just Proud

THEIR RETURN TO ENGLAND on 28 July 1939 was no more than a short holiday, since both had to be in Hollywood that autumn: she to finish off any necessary retakes for *Gone With the Wind* and he to play Maxim de Winter in the film adaptation of Daphne du Maurier's novel *Rebecca*. During this holiday there was the matter of the divorces to be agreed. Jill had moved out of Cheyne Walk to a smaller house in St John's Wood in north London, and then to a cottage in Pulborough in Sussex. Both Olivier and Vivien wanted to marry as soon as possible, and Jill and Holman both agreed to bring petitions for divorce on the grounds of adultery. There was also the matter of Fahv's estate, which had been diminished by his nine years without a parish or a stipend. His flat in Worthing went to Ibo. Olivier received £6 6s 7d as his third of the cash Fahv had left, and shared with his brother and sister the remains of his beloved mother's marriage settlement. The same trust which had paid the young Olivier's school fees now paid to Olivier the film star the sum of £265 and some pence.[1]

Only one tangible piece of evidence remains of Olivier and Vivien's brief visit – a bill for £8 3s 10d from the Royal Hop Pole Hotel in Tewkesbury, Gloucestershire, for the night of 8–9 August, for dinner and beds for 'Mr and Mrs Andrew Kerr and Miss Consuelo and Friend'.[2] The political situation was tense, but no more so than at the same time the previous year. War seemed no more inevitable than it had then.

They were in England only nineteen days and sailed for New York on 17 August in the *Ile de France*. Olivier had confidently planned on Vivien's playing opposite him in *Rebecca*.[3] Vivien had counted on it too and had tested for it before she left for England. She was of course wrong for the part. She was Scarlett, and Scarlett could not have become the sweet and diffident girl the film required as Maxim's new wife. On the second day out Selznick sent two long cables to the liner, one to Vivien and one to Larry, telling them so.

Vivien was about to become the biggest female property in Hollywood, and Selznick's cable reflects this. He went on for three hundred words, assuring her that the same care, patience and stubbornness about accurate casting that had put her in 'the most talked-of role of all time in what everyone who has seen it agrees is the greatest picture ever made', made it necessary for him to tell that she would be as wrong for the role in *Rebecca* as the role would be wrong for her. It would have been very simple to cast Bette Davis as Scarlett and it would have saved a great deal of expense and agony. In the same way it would be easy to cast Vivien in *Rebecca* but her career, which was off to such a splendid start, would be materially damaged. And so on – 'Affectionately, David.'

To Olivier he was polite but briefer and more to the point. 'I know you must be disappointed, but Vivien's anxiety to play the role has in my opinion been largely if not entirely due to her desire to do a picture with you.' She hadn't been interested until she knew he was playing Maxim, and they would after all both be working in Hollywood – 'Cordially, David.'[4]

They did not stop over in New York but flew straight on to Los Angeles. Vivien did the retakes for *Gone With the Wind*. Olivier prepared for *Rebecca*. They spent the Labour Day weekend of 2–3 September, the official end of summer, sailing with Douglas Fairbanks Jnr in a chartered yacht off Santa Catalina, an island sixty miles from the coast of California. There they found the English actors David Niven and Nigel Bruce. On the radio they heard the news of Hitler's lightning invasion of Poland and Neville Chamberlain's broadcast that Britain was at war with Germany. As Olivier remembered, 'We felt blighted right through: careers, lives, hopes. Shortly reaction set in. Doug knew what drink existed for and a consequent hysteria began. . .'⁵ Olivier careered round in a speedboat, in and out between the other yachts, declaiming, 'You are finished all of you, you are relics.' He was taken for Ronald Colman, who got the blame for these antics.

England was at war but the show went on. How could it not? The United States was still at peace. Olivier finished *Rebecca* and he and Vivien spent hours planning a stage production of *Romeo and Juliet* for the following year in New York, which he would produce and direct himself. They had a happy time, very quiet. Olivier was composing music for Romeo's entrance, was proud of it, and signed it. Vivien was having voice lessons in preparation for Juliet.⁶ And in December the grand opening of *Gone With the Wind* was upon them, with five days of celebrations in Atlanta. Producer, director, and stars flew in from Hollywood, bouquets of roses were thrust upon them at the airport, and the cars in which they travelled into the city 'moved at the pace of a coronation procession through three miles of cheering people.'⁷ Vivien Leigh was now a bigger name than Laurence Olivier.

Then there was more frustration. They had expected to film *Pride and Prejudice* together, but Greer Garson was preferred to Vivien and Larry was unhappy. They had expected to do *Waterloo Bridge* together, a romantic tragedy in which Vivien played a good girl turned prostitute, but Robert Taylor was preferred for her leading man; Vivien was convinced the part was written for Larry, and was discontented. She was afraid it would be a dreary job for her and so concentrated on preparing for their *Romeo and Juliet*. And now at last they had the prospect of marriage. In January and February 1940 both Jill and Holman brought undefended petitions in London, and both were granted decrees nisi. After another six months the decrees would be absolute and the parties could remarry. Jill was given custody of Tarquin, and Holman of Suzanne.⁸

At the end of February came the Oscar ceremony, otherwise known as the annual banquet of the Academy of Motion Picture Arts. Vivien received an Oscar for Scarlett. Olivier, who was nominated for Heathcliff, did not. He lost to James Stewart in *Philadelphia Story*. One still photograph of Vivien and Larry together at the ceremony shows her radiant and him impassive, and this has been put forward as evidence of his jealousy. It is not convincing evidence of any such thing. A thousand pictures were taken of them that night and he could have been caught with any expression on his face. The ceremony started at 9.30 in the evening and Vivien was not given her Oscar until 1.15 the next morning. Perhaps Olivier was just caught in a moment of boredom. However that may be he did not, in his published work, or in any of the surviving transcripts of his recollections, ever mention that night. Nor did he ever mention an event in England at the same time, which he must surely have remembered.

This is what happened. That February, two weeks before her divorce, Jill had faced an ordeal.[9] It had started with Tarquin being feverish. He had an awful Friday night, not sleeping. He asked for water, but when she lifted his head for him to drink he screamed. Her mother was with her for the weekend, so she stayed with the boy while Jill went to get a doctor, walking half a mile through eight inches of snow to where she kept her car. All the doctors were in the army but eventually she found one who would come. Tarquin kept whimpering. When the doctor came he said nothing but gave her a prescription for a sleeping draught. She drove through the snow to Pulborough to get the medicine but then her mother dropped the bottle as she was unwrapping it, so Jill had to go all the way back again. Tarquin could not move his head and kept licking his lips. A specialist came from London and was convinced it was meningitis. Jill's car broke down. She had to hire another to take her son to hospital in Petworth, and he screamed with pain when he was moved. Then the car got stuck in a snowdrift and Jill had to put branches under the wheels to get it moving again. By now a retired specialist had been found, who said if it wasn't meningitis it must be infantile paralysis and that he didn't see much chance of Tarquin moving again. She called that day Black Tuesday.

Then on the Wednesday Tarquin sat up. Next day he ate some jelly, his first food in six days. He still could not move his head. At the weekend he got up but his legs were so weak he couldn't stand. The following Tuesday she brought him back home. The doctors called it mystery meningitis. She thought Tarquin's recovery was a miracle.

It was a miserable time for her. Her last play, called of all things *Judgment Day*, had run for ten weeks but made her only £50. Then, during her divorce hearing, London had never seen so much snow. The court was like a poor stage set. She was handed a photo of Larry to identify, and it was a horrible film still of a man who looked like a movie co-respondent. The judge glanced at it and gave her a decree nisi straight away. To make things worse, her brother Jack was off to France, going to the war. But she was filled with a great thankfulness because Tarquin was well. She wrote and told Olivier all this, and sent her love.

It is a tale of fear and terror in an English winter landscape, in wartime. Olivier's Hollywood, which of course Jill knew well, could not have been more distant in every way.

At the outbreak of war some of the Hollywood colony of British actors had come home. The first was David Niven, who had made *Pride and Prejudice* with Olivier. But Niven was a Sandhurst man who had held a commission in the regular army before he took up acting; most were advised by the British consul in Los Angeles to stay put.[10] They would be more useful where they were, and most were above service age. Olivier, at thirty-two, would certainly not have been called up but his brother Dickie, who was four years older, was already in the navy. Holman, though also older than Olivier, volunteered for the navy. Olivier had no instant urge to return. As he wrote to the solicitor who was managing Fahv's estate, who happened to be an uncle of his on his mother's side, 'I feel that the money we may be able to earn here is probably more useful than the redundant services we might be able to tender at home just yet.'[11]

That was in February 1940 when, as he told his uncle, he was filming in the daytime and preparing for his stage production of *Romeo and Juliet* in the evenings. He had been planning this for the best part of a year. In May 1939 – when he was in *No Time for Comedy* in New York, and was newly famous for *Wuthering Heights* – he wrote to Vivien that he had noticed that outside a cinema showing *Fire Over England* his name was spelled Luarance Olivier. Irritated by this, he had gone to see Lillian Hellman's *Little Foxes*, a good and successful play, which he considered 'a pointless, meretricious melodrama which I'd think four times about doing in Scunthorpe'. He then continued, 'I think the theatre here is worse than at home. If you give a play a good enough set, and spend enough *money* on the show costumes, lighting etc (so that it is *obvious* that a lot has been spent) this bloody public will feel sufficiently reassured to swallow anything.' He went on to outline to her his rough idea for *Romeo*, making three sketches of an elaborate revolve which displayed, at different parts of its circumference, the Capulets' hall, Juliet's bedroom, a street in Verona, Friar Lawrence's cell, and the orchard.[12]

George Cukor, first director of *Gone With the Wind* and a great friend of Vivien's, encouraged the project; Olivier's heart quickened to the idea of making a splash and perhaps a great deal of money, and he assembled an English cast, brought the Motley sisters as stage designers over from England, and everything looked splendid. The opening was in San Francisco. Years later he used to wake up in the night and relive it. He had directed and rehearsed the play, nursed everything through, relit the performance himself after the dress rehearsal, working through the night, then rehearsed the company all next day and, at the opening performance, was more dead than alive. In the balcony scene he was supposed to leap up a wall but when the time came he didn't have the strength and was left in mid-air, hanging on by his fingers, kicking and scratching. The curtain was brought down. One thing he was sure of, that it would be all over Hollywood the next morning.[13]

'Didn't I have augury enough?' he wrote later. 'Oh, no! I swung on into Chicago where the reception was ominously mild.' The theatre there was a concert hall that held 3,500. Olivier always believed that you could not mesmerise more than a thousand people, and he was proved right. But he pushed on, reasoning that all the production needed was a New York reception and intelligent, intellectual criticism. A commercial management might have pulled the show in San Francisco or Chicago, but that was impossible for Olivier. He could not admit to himself that an actor who had conquered London in Shakespeare could not conquer New York, and he was dead set on demonstrating that Vivien was as good a stage actress as a film star. They both wanted 'a little extra acclaim as Shakespeareans, not just film actors'. There was also the small matter of revenge on Maurice Evans, whose New York *Hamlet* of the season before Olivier had so much despised, but which had been so much praised.[14]

So, as producer, director, and leading actor, he put on *Romeo and Juliet* on Broadway, in a vast cinema which he renamed the 51st Street Theatre for the occasion. *My Fair Lady* eventually ran and ran at that theatre, but Olivier's *Romeo* was the first straight play to be staged there. *Gone With the Wind* was showing nearby, so was *Wuthering Heights*, and so was *Twenty One Days*, the film Olivier and Leigh had made in 1937. This last film was, as Olivier said, a shameful shocker which got a showing only because its leading players were now famous. The lights outside said, 'See the first time they kissed.' Not that the publicity for *Romeo* was much better: 'See real lovers make love in public.'[15] It was a disaster. The notices were terrible. Brooks Atkinson of the *New York Times* dismissed the production as lamentable and overblown, said Shakespeare's two hours' traffic of our stage had lengthened to more than three, and remarked that as his own director Olivier had never heard himself in the play, which was just as well, because he would have been astonished if he had.

The *Herald Tribune* called Olivier and Leigh 'celebrated visitors from another medium, if not another planet', and the *Sun*, which thought that both Olivier and Leigh boggled the verse badly, concluded that *Romeo and Juliet* was not 'something to be tossed off between films'. John Mason Brown in the *Post* wrote that a heavy fog had descended on almost all the beauties of the play, that Olivier gulped down most of his lines as if they were bad oysters, that both he and his Juliet were tone-deaf and that the play seemed twice as endless as *Gone With the Wind*. Olivier was wounded. 'The whole production,' he said, 'was bitched and absolutely dismissed in outraged dignity by the critics who only found in it an excuse to capitalise on our world-famous vulgar romance.'[16] Perhaps so but Olivier – with his too elaborate set and his money too ostentatiously spent – was committing the same errors he had condemned in the New York theatre the year before, and was finding to his cost that the bloody public would not swallow anything. Vivien came out of it better than Olivier. The *Herald Tribune* said that, bad though Olivier was in his acting and directing, the play was worth seeing for Miss Leigh's lovely Juliet.[17] Others said she was inaudible. Olivier and Leigh were rejected.

At this moment their chauffeur, John, turned up, having driven Olivier's Packard across America from Los Angeles. They had little use for him now, checked out of their Manhattan hotel, sent back the celebration champagne, and retreated to live more frugally at Sneden's Landing. When there were queues round the block at the theatre Olivier asked why. He was told that the advance bookings had been prodigious and that people had come to demand their money back. He said give it to them. His sister Sybille, when she came to write her memoir of him, gave a dramatic explanation for Larry's generosity. 'Gangsterism was rife in New York,' she wrote. 'It was unsafe to risk offending a large section of the populace, especially if you were British. If the management had refused to take back the tickets the theatre might have been burned down over their heads.' Olivier, seeing this, replied, 'Steady! Oh no no no. It was only for the first two weeks of the run that we handed their money back at the rate of $1,000 per day, but after two weeks I stopped it as pride was becoming too expensive. It wasn't that we was sceeered. It was that we was PROUD.'[18]

As Olivier remembered it, New York did not like failure. Friends no longer called. But the Lunts remained faithful, inviting Olivier and Vivien to dinner and talking ceaselessly about every subject in the world except the play. He had never known such a 'supreme example of good manners'. *Romeo and Juliet* was kept going by curiosity but closed after thirty-five performances. Olivier and Vivien lost $96,000 they had saved out of their earnings from *Gone With the Wind*, *Wuthering Heights*, *Rebecca*, and *Pride and Prejudice*.[19]

In Europe the war had gone badly. By the beginning of June, as *Romeo* was limping to the end of its run, Holland and Belgium had fallen, France was rapidly collapsing, and the bulk of the British Army in France had been evacuated from the beaches of Dunkirk. Olivier and Vivien had arranged with their former spouses for Tarquin and Suzanne to come to spend the war in North America. This was at a time when thousands of British children were making the same journey. Olivier resumed the flying lessons he had started in England in 1936. Across the Hudson from Sneden's Landing, twenty miles north of New York City, there was a flying school at Dobbs Ferry. He flew landplanes and floatplanes, starting on 20 June in a little Piper Cub. A week later, after eight hours' flying, the instructor wrote in Olivier's log, 'Solo – Perfect (2 landings)'. Throughout July he flew two or three hours a day, making trips to Stamford Yacht Club and to Port Washington on Long Island. He flew five types of plane, all more modern than the Tiger Moths he had flown in England. The largest was a Fairchild 24, which could take three passengers. By 20 July he had an American pilot's licence, which said he weighed 150 lbs, was five-feet ten inches tall, and described his eyes as dark grey.[20]

In early July Tarquin and Jill, and Suzanne with her grand-mother Gertrude, arrived in Halifax on the Cunarder *Sythia*, having by chance crossed in the same ship. It is Tarquin's recollection that his mother had been through a bad time, that a rash had developed on her face, that her hair had turned white and that she then dyed it auburn. This was not at all what Sybille had seen when she met her in May 1939, almost two years after the separation. Perhaps Jill's worst time was in the first winter of the war, when she was earning little and Tarquin was so ill.[21] At any rate, when Jill arrived in Canada Olivier's first proposal was that she should settle there. They did look for a farm near Toronto, but she and Tarquin stayed first in Connecticut and then in New York City in an apartment on West 72nd Street. Jill thought Larry quite the film star, terrified of being recognised and distrusting everybody, sometimes charming but at other times bad tempered. He got on very well with Tarquin but never asked about his illness.[22] When Jill visited Larry in New York she met Vivien. She thought her more beautiful than ever, but described her face as just a mask and her eyes as hard and cruel.[23]

Olivier's recollection was that he went so far as to telephone Duff Cooper, Minister of Information in Churchill's government, to ask whether there might be a job for him in England. In reply he received a cable saying: THINK BETTER WHERE YOU ARE KORDA GOING THERE. Korda was a Hungarian but an adopted and passionate Englishman who had some connections with British Intelligence.

He came to America to make, in effect, propaganda films dressed up so as to be acceptable to a neutral United States. He hit on the idea of a film about Nelson, the greatest of English naval heroes. Nelson's England fighting against Napoleon and, in 1805, in fear of invasion provided a parallel with Churchill's England standing alone against Hitler and also, in 1940, in fear of invasion.

Here is Olivier's account of what happened. A few days after the cable Alex Korda's voice came on the phone. 'Larry, you know Lady Hamilton?'

'Lady Hamilton? She was the tart who fucked Nelson?'

'Yes, it's a very good story.'

Olivier said he thought it the tiredest, oldest story in the world.[24]

But Korda was right. Olivier and Vivien, having lost so much on *Romeo*, jumped at the chance to earn some money, and back they went to Hollywood. Olivier leased a house in Beverly Hills, on San Ysidro Drive, next to one occupied by Danny Kaye. He was a comedian and actor from Brooklyn who had made his reputation playing the 'borscht circuit' resorts in the Catskill mountains of New York. He and Olivier found each other immediately congenial. It was the start of a long friendship.

By then six months had passed since Olivier and Vivien's decrees nisi, and they could marry. Ronald Colman advised them not to hold the ceremony in Los Angeles, where the press would attend in hordes, but to go eighty miles north to Santa Barbara where all they needed to do was give three days' notice. There things could be managed more quietly. So as not to arouse suspicion Olivier did not buy the ring himself. This was done by Colman's wife, Benita. Larry and Vivien registered in Santa Barbara and then, three days later, on 30 August, made the three-hour drive back there with their two witnesses, Katharine Hepburn and the director Garson Kanin. According to Kanin, they quarrelled all the way there. Then it was discovered that their three days' notice did not expire until midnight so they, and the judge, had a good few drinks while they waited for midnight. At five minutes past twelve on a moonlit night, at Montecito in the county of Santa Barbara – standing to face eastwards because that way they were looking towards England – Laurence Kerr Olivier, native of England, 'resident in the London county of Chelsea', colour white, and Vivian Mary Holman, native of India, colour white, were married by Fred Marsh, police court judge, who ended the ceremony by crying 'Bingo'.[25] The Colmans had not attended the ceremony but were waiting with their schooner at San Pedro. It was between three and four in the early hours when the newly married Oliviers arrived, and they set sail for Santa Catalina. Olivier had done everything to prevent publicity of the wedding but was surprised when there was no mention of it on the radio news at two and four the next afternoon, miffed when there was nothing on the six and nine o'clock bulletins in the evening, and relieved when the news was at last reported at ten. Colman understood. 'After all,' he said, 'there's not much point in having a secret the other fellow doesn't want to know.'[26]

They began shooting *Lady Hamilton* in a small studio right in the middle of Hollywood called General Services, because it was cheap. Korda himself directed. It was a happy film. Olivier and Korda liked the showman in each other and shared a taste for extravagance. Olivier admired Korda's way with expensive hotels – move in, spend money lavishly, and get someone else to pay for it. 'What I like,' he said, 'is this tip of his, which says, don't pay your bill but keep tipping liberally. Pay your bill and don't tip, you'll never get served. Marvellous bit of philosophy.'[27]

Lady Hamilton – shown in America as *That Hamilton Woman* – is hokum but glorious hokum, and the work of a director of high talent. The principal characters are Emma Hamilton, a blacksmith's daughter who rose to be first the mistress and then the wife of Sir William Hamilton, British ambassador to Naples in the 1790s. There she met and became the mistress of Horatio Nelson, first a captain and then an admiral, who later died during the greatest of his victories at Trafalgar, which scotched Napoleon's plans for an invasion of England. Nelson was a paramount genius as a ruthless sea officer, but he was small, with a high-pitched voice, and none too lovable a character. Olivier played him as a romantic hero. Lady Hamilton had once been a great beauty, but by the time she became Nelson's mistress she was a huge, blowsy and much caricatured figure. She was played by the slim and porcelain Vivien Leigh. It was all absurd, but done with great dash. The scene in which Vivien, as Emma, is told that Nelson has arrived at Naples and runs to meet him – across a palatial room and through the columns of a wide terrace, with the Bay of Naples in the background – could have come from *Gone With the Wind*. And Nelson's death scene, as played by Olivier, touches the heart. It became Churchill's favourite film. He showed it again and again to his guests and was always much moved. It was shot in six weeks because Korda had no money for longer. Olivier came to like it in spite of his early misgivings: 'A damn good film, actually. It stands up.'[28] Even Vivien, who was not the easiest actress to work with, got on well with Korda and loved his Hungarian English. He had, she said, been known to say such things as, 'Print both three.'[29]

It is far and away the best film Olivier and Leigh ever made together. It was also the last.

Olivier continued his flying lessons in California and flew throughout the shooting of *Lady Hamilton*, something Korda could not conceivably have insured against. From Clover Field he flew to Santa Barbara, San Diego, Monterey, and San Francisco. He flew right up until 22 December, when he left for New York on his way home. That year he completed 246 flying hours.[30] Now that he and Vivien had earned enough to support themselves and to give some help to their exiled children, he was determined to get back to England and join the Royal Air Force. Reports from England were dismal. The blitz was at its height: 4,558 British civilians were killed by German bombing that November. Olivier became aggressively opposed to those members of the English colony in Hollywood, like Charles Laughton, Cedric Hardwicke, and Herbert Wilcox, who had plans to play cricket matches for war charities and other 'bloody nonsense', though it is difficult to see what of greater use those three could have been in England.[31]

Gertrude had taken Suzanne, now aged seven, to Vancouver, where Vivien visited them that December. Jill and Tarquin, aged four, were still in New York. Olivier visited Jill to say goodbye on 26 December. He was charming, quite his old self. She did not go to the docks to see him and Vivien off two days later, wanting to avoid pictures of Larry with his first and second wives.[32] The ship on which they sailed was the *Excambion*, an American freight and passenger liner one eighth the tonnage of the *Queen Mary* or the *Normandie*. They were nervous of the German sympathies of the crew. The captain, though an American citizen, was German born and on New Year's Eve gave the toast 'Deutschland Uber Alles'. Their fears later seemed over-dramatic to Olivier, but at the time they were apprehensive of being taken prisoner by some marauding U-boat. They docked at Lisbon early in the new year and then begged two seats on a plane home. Halfway through the flight one of the crew rushed into the passenger cabin for a fire extinguisher. The second pilot, firing a recognition signal, had forgotten to open a window and the cockpit was in flames. They landed at Bristol in the middle of an air raid.[33]

12

Not Ever Having Been an Actor

OLIVIER HAD LEFT AMERICA telling reporters that he was going to join the Royal Air Force. Vivien had just as clear an ambition, if a more unlikely one, which was to be a nurse in Epypt.[1] But in England nobody for the moment wanted their services. They were offered only a variety show to be broadcast for the forces. Then Olivier was cast in another propaganda film, *The Forty Ninth Parallel*, in which a German U-boat crew land in Canada and make their way, murdering as they go, towards the American border. One of those murdered was Olivier, who gave another virtuoso performance as a French-Canadian trapper. It lasted only ten minutes but was much praised. *Variety* said it was 'a bit, but the best thing he has ever done'. Even Olivier asked himself, 'Had I learned something about the economy and directness of film acting from my days in Hollywood?'[2]

He had volunteered to fly not in the RAF but in the Fleet Air Arm, the flying branch of the navy, probably because Ralph Richardson was already a lieutenant in that service. He was at first rejected by the Admiralty on medical grounds because of some defect of the inner ear, but was reprieved and given a flight test in February. He flew a Magister trainer for thirty minutes, was given a temporary commission, and told to report to HMS *Daedalus* at Lee on Solent in April. The commanding officer there happened to be the man who, back in 1936, had taught him and Ralph Richardson to fly. Elsie Fogerty, his old teacher at the Central School, gave him a four-leafed shamrock on the day he joined the navy.[3] At Lee on Solent he started a ten-day training course, during which he flew seven types of aircraft – Osprey, Magister, Tiger Moth, Gipsy Moth, Hawker Hart, Proctor and Shark – almost all of them obsolete and all but two of them biplanes. The Hart was a biplane fighter, canvas over a wooden frame, which dated from 1929 and had seen its only active service against rebellious Afghan tribesmen on the North West Frontier.

During his training in the Solent Olivier was as conscientious as he was always was with everything he did. In his course book he wrote notes on airmanship, cockpit drill and attitude of mind – 'Never give up.' Two passages in his handwriting read: '*The Strength of gentleness* (women driving). . . It takes a good head to navigate a craft to its destination but a better one to lead it to its destination after losing the way. Only by continuous self-badgering can one achieve proper attitude of alertness for flying.' And: '*Reverence for machine.* Gentle handling, train to be *un*careless – aim for expert touch.' But still, he was no ordinary trainee pilot. On one page headed 'Elementary Flying Drill' he scribbled in pencil, 'Phone Ritz.'[4]

In late April he was posted to 755 Squadron at Worthy Down, four miles north of Winchester, to an airfield that had been abandoned by the RAF in 1920. It was set on a large sloping hill so that, he said, only a skilful pilot could make a three-point landing by putting the machine into a double stall at the last moment. This sounds a tall story, as does the tale, put about by himself, that he once taxied his plane into another, writing both off. The tale improved in the telling, and the number of damaged aircraft later became three. One of those who remembered Olivier's own stories of this glamorous trail of wreckage was John Mills, one of his closest friends then and afterwards. But then, as Mills says, 'You never knew what was made up with Larry.'[5] There is no mention of any such incident in his service record or in his commanding officer's report, where he was assessed as an average pilot. In the same way, his recollection that he was 'confined to four hours flying a day except in the long, light days of summer when one could get permission for aerobatic practice' must have been enhanced by the passage of years; from the time he joined until the end of 1941 he flew only 250 hours, just four more than he had flown at his own expense in America the year before.[6] Aerobatics seem unlikely too. The job of 755 Squadron was to train air gunners. Its pilots ferried gunners round the skies as they learned to shoot at towed targets. It was not Olivier's fault that he had no chance of seeing active service or that his squadron was equipped, like the training squadron at Lee on Solent, with a mixed bag of aircraft nobody else wanted. A predominant memory was of 'sitting in the ante-room trying to refuse another gin or kicking my heels in the pilots' room gazing impotently at other aircraft taking off or at the surrounding ceiling zero'.[7]

Olivier found a bungalow a few miles from the station and lived there with Vivien. She brought down from London some Indian rugs, two Sickerts and a Boudin. She already had a taste for paintings and from the start her choice was excellent.[8] Coward at this time thought that Olivier was unhappy and that it was a great mistake for him not to live at the station and mess there.[9] It probably did not help him with his fellow officers. As an actor Olivier had often wanted to be with what he thought of as 'real' people; now he was with real people he found them ordinary. But he did his best to become a naval officer, as he might have become a person in a play. 'I've always thought,' he said, 'that my performance as a naval officer was the best bit of character work I've ever done. If they didn't catch my name they would never have known that I wasn't a regular navy boy.'[10] Ralph Richardson thought the same of him and noticed that his uniform was perfect for the part. 'It looked as though it had been worn long on arduous service but had kept its cut. The gold wings on his sleeve had no distasteful glitter; only the shoes shone. The hair under his cap had a touch of debonair cheek, being perhaps a quarter of an inch longer than the dead correct. His manner was quiet, alert, businesslike. . .'[11]

But he was touchy about rank. Having been commissioned as a sub-lieutenant he was soon promoted to lieutenant, the equivalent of a captain in the army. As such he wore two broad bands of gold braid on his sleeves. Richardson, having been in the navy longer, was promoted to lieutenant commander, which gave him another half-stripe, a narrow band of braid worn between the two broad ones. 'That,' said Olivier, 'almost killed our relationship. I didn't want one particularly [an extra half-stripe] and I wouldn't have cared at all if it hadn't been for Ralph having one, but it made him unbearably pompous with me, I shall never forget it, and I thought, "My God, when the war is over I'm going to give it to you."'[12]

It was not true that only Richardson's promotion upset him. He brooded about the differences and difficulties of rank for years afterwards, and in 1967 gave an American television interviewer an exact image of how it affected him. 'If you are sitting at a dining table and an arm comes over your shoulder, if your conditioning, if you like, makes you form the habit of looking at the sleeve to see how many stripes there are before you look up at the face, to adjust your expression accordingly, these circumstances create pettinesses in human nature.' So, he said, he had not found it necessary for him, later on, to find any psychological reason for Iago's villainy. 'Because I became a villain myself, and I certainly wanted to kill more than one person.'[13] One such man whom Olivier loathed had a charming wife, and Olivier wondered if he could hurt him through her, by turning to her one evening when the wives were present and, by the merest slip of the tongue, in front of her husband, calling her 'darling'. He would have become Iago.[14]

These hates went beyond all reason. When one of his fellow lieutenants was promoted and wrote to tell Olivier, he replied with fulsome irony, congratulating him on his 'most magnificent half-stripe, the most deserved in the entire service, much the thickest, much the richest gold. . . I can see it in my mind and it puts a glow into my heart. I presume the job is with the Chief of Staff and guess probably has some title like S.O. [staff officer] 2, or even 1.'[15]

By mid-1941 Jill had moved from New York to Hollywood, where she had friends and the hope of a film part. Tarquin spoke American at school and English at home. He went to Barbara Hutton's house where he and the young Hutton boy, Lance, were given swimming lessons by a Captain Nast, formerly of the Imperial Russian Army. He also learned ice-skating. She was having trouble finding work, but had done some radio.[16] On Tarquin's fifth birthday, 21 August 1941, Larry sent a cable, signing it 'Lieut Olivier.'[17]

Vivien Leigh did not become a nurse, but continued her career. She and Olivier had been to see Tyrone Guthrie at Burnley, where the Old Vic had moved for the war, but Guthrie thought of her as a film star and not a good enough stage actress, so nothing came of it.[18] So she went into a production of Shaw's *The Doctor's Dilemma* which, starting in September, toured in Manchester, Liverpool, Leeds, Blackpool, Leicester, Glasgow, and Edinburgh, where Cecil Beaton saw her. He wrote in his diary that she was as sweet and lovely as ever but older and more tired. She told him how exhausting the theatre was, everyone prematurely old, and how each time they assembled at the station for the next journey they looked smaller and tireder than before.[19]

She came to spend the Christmas of 1941 with Larry. With her working in the Midlands and the North, and with Olivier serving in the south, they continued the life of comings and goings, separations and reunions, on which they both thrived. It was as if they were once again living one on each side of a continent, as they had for much of 1939 in America, before their marriage. Sometimes he could go to her. There is a bill for Lieut. Olivier from the North British Hotel in Edinburgh which shows that in austere wartime Britain, where food and clothes and fuel were rationed, Georges Goulet champagne, 1928, could still be had for £2 4s a bottle. More often she went to him. He remembered into his old age how he would drive to Winchester station to meet her on Sunday mornings, when they could be briefly together. Vivien, travelling great distances by slow wartime trains to see him, took to reading Dickens and read all his novels.[20]

At Worthy Down, Olivier added more ancient planes and misfits – Albacore, Hornet, Leopard Moth, Fulmar and Swordfish – to the great number of types he flew. The single Leopard Moth the squadron possessed had been commandeered from its pre-war civilian owner. The Fulmar was a modern fighter which had failed to come up to expectations and of which few were made. It was the only modern plane, and the fastest, that Lieut. Olivier ever flew. Then his duties became even more mundane. He underwent a course in parachute packing and passed in Class A. He was put in charge of demonstration flights for local air cadets, teenage boys who wanted to join the RAF.[21]

He descended into depression. At about this time he wrote a memo to himself, which was placed in his papers along with the handwritten will he had made in 1937. It read:

> Should the situation change or allow of any changes, and Government and Admiralty attitudes alter publicly enough, there might be done all sorts of things: but as things are, I feel it expedient simply not to look upon myself as ever having been an actor while political disinterest in entertainment, or rather the preoccupation that creates it, allows that any departure from the service should cause genuine dissatisfaction among one's comrades in arms, to whom one feels in these days first consideration is due.[22]

This was not the Olivier who had agitated to return to England to do his bit. But then, he had been given only humdrum things to do.

Jill continued to write to him, sending him a sweater she had knitted and photographs of Tarquin. His best friend was Fred Astaire Jnr, who was six months older. He had played a small part in *Eagle Squadron*, a Hollywood film about American airmen who volunteered to join the RAF.[23]

When Olivier did write to Jill, much of his disillusionment with his part in the war showed through. 'Life is just the same and therefore a bit harder to cope with all the time – slightly stiffer restrictions, all very necessary – slightly less of this (nice), slightly more of that (nasty).' He said people abroad didn't seem to grasp the *cumulative* effect of what was going on. It was like a dentist's drill. Suddenly it hit a nerve and there was bleeding agony for a bit. Then the terrible part stopped and there was no particular pain, but the drill went on and on just the same. It was the way chaps stood that monotony which he thought so marvellous, even more remarkable than during the heavy dramatic stuff when there was a strong sense of gallantry to keep them going. He had an affectionate admiration for his men, though he didn't think much of some of the officers. 'Sometimes,' he wrote, 'I have to go outside and make "Warship weeks" speeches etc. Last week I was at the Albert Hall – "crystallising the fighting spirit of the Empire" or something' – or maybe it was "epitomising" something – anyway *The Daily Express* knew what it was.'[24]

He was disenchanted, and no wonder. Film survives of an appearance he made at the Albert Hall, and it is very much a rant. He stands, in navy uniform, arms spread in Henry V mode, howling in ever-rising tones, 'We will attack. We will smite our foes. Our watchword will be urgency, speed, courage, and may God bless our cause.'[25] It was typical of what he was asked to do, though the Albert Hall was grander than most of the venues he played. At Winchester Guildhall Olivier, with a company of naval ratings and Wrens in the smaller roles, gave a scene from *Henry V* itself, and then sang a 'shanty fantasia'.[26] And one Daphne Jervois, Women's Voluntary Service organiser for Winchester, tried to recruit him for her salvage drive. She was going to drive round with a loud-speaker van and told him, 'I have got to find a man with a good voice (I don't mean musically) who would deliver impassioned appeals to villagers to bring forth their salvage. . . Perhaps you could help me in organising other stunts.'[27] Hamlet and Heathcliff had come to this.

The scene of his greatest disaster and greatest triumph of this time was the Garrison Theatre, Aldershot, in February 1942. Olivier as Henry V was on the bill again. The earlier acts, in a sort of variety show, were barracked by an audience of bolshy servicemen. When Olivier appeared in a hired suit of armour he was greeted with derision. When he drew his sword and flourished it the house rocked with laughter. He began the St Crispin's Day speech to cat calls and then in desperation came forward on the stage, turned his eyes upwards and sank to his knees. The audience paused, and in that pause he began Henry's prayer before the battle.

> O God of battles, steel my soldiers' hearts,
> Possess them not with fury. . .

It worked. The audience heard him out in silence and then broke into applause. That was the story as Olivier told it in 1952. If it is true it is magnificent. If it is not true it deserves to be.[28]

While Olivier fretted, Vivien's acting career prospered. In March 1942 *The Doctor's Dilemma*, after six months of provincial touring, came into London at the Haymarket. Here it had the advantage that those who had seen *Gone With the Wind*, which was still showing in Leicester Square, could then go to the Haymarket to see Scarlett in the flesh.

By the autumn of 1942 Olivier was coming to the end of his naval service. An entry in his log book for August shows that he spent a day practising 'low level and dive bombing', but practice was as far as any pilot from Worthy Down was going to get. He made his last flight on 9 October, when he flew a Lysander to Hastings and back. This was the fifteenth and last type of plane he flew in his military career. In all he had flown 456 hours in the navy.[29] He then accepted an invitation from the Ministry of Information to make another propaganda film, for which he was given leave. This was *The Demi-Paradise*, in which he played a Russian marine engineer who came to England and at first found the natives as strange as they found him. But after Russia had been attacked by Germany and become an ally of Britain, the engineer made many firm friends and thus helped to establish Russo–British solidarity. Olivier was as always fascinated by accents, and determined that he should sound as authentically Russian as possible. He learned that Soviet should be pronounced Suv*yett*, and found a Russian woman to teach him until he found his consonants 'becoming alarmingly, not to say suspiciously, effeminate'. He then turned to a male Russian, who immediately told him, 'Avreesink see hus tolld yoo iss alll wrongg', at which he decided he might do worse than invent his own Russian accent, which he did.[30] He was back on a film set, was no longer seen at Worthy Down, and Jill once again, as in 1939, had no address for him. When she sent him more photographs of Tarquin she had to send them to Lieutenant Olivier, care of the Admiralty, London, where someone pencilled on the envelope: 'c/o Miss Vivien Leigh, Haymarket Theatre, London W1'.[31]

Whatever his wishes, Olivier had never really been a full-time naval officer. Apart from the performances he was drafted into at the Albert Hall, Aldershot, and Winchester, he had made many broadcasts with patriotic themes and titles like 'Into Battle'. These broadcasts earned him £600 in 1941–2, as much as his navy pay, and meant frequent absences from his duties, which again cannot have made him popular with his colleagues. He seems never, then or afterwards, to have publicly mentioned the war record of his brother Dickie, who did see active service in motor launches in the North Sea and the English Channel and was awarded the Distinguished Service Medal. In February 1943, while Larry was filming *The Demi-Paradise*, Lieutenant G. D. Olivier was commanding a forty-foot A-class launch, laying mines on an exceptionally dark night in the Dunkirk Channel. He had laid all his mines when he ran into two German destroyers, who shot at him for four or five minutes before he managed to evade them and make it home.[32]

13

The Walrus and the Sceptred Isle

'AS I FLEW OVER the country in my Walrus,' said Olivier, 'I kept seeing it as Shakespeare's sceptred isle.'[1] This is splendid, but it is fantasy. The Walrus was made by the aircraft company that made the Spitfire, but did not look like even the most distant relation. It was an awkward, slow, helpless amphibious plane, with a pusher prop, which was designed to be carried on board battleships and large cruisers. It was catapulted off, did a reconnaissance of the surrounding seas, and then returned, landed on the sea alongside its mother ship, and was winched back up on deck. Olivier never flew one. He never flew any float plane. He had, sometime in 1942, asked to be transferred to Walruses because that would have got him away from the boredom of his training squadron, but the Walrus was an antique, was withdrawn from service, and Olivier went off to make *The Demi-Paradise*.[2]

What Olivier *had* done was fly from Worthy Down, in the ragtag aircraft of 757 Squadron, over the south coast of England. He had flown from Poole in Dorset, west to Teignmouth in Devon, and farther west to St Ives in Cornwall. His last flight was over Hastings in Sussex, so he had also seen the coast farther east. What he saw was a largely defenceless coast. 'I tell you,' he had said to an uncle of Vivien's, 'there's nothing there. Bloody well nothing. A few, very few strands of rusting barbed wire. Occasional hunks of concrete in a line of tank traps which could easily be driven round. I tell you honestly, there's nothing to stop them at all, nothing.'[3]

By the time he saw that, an invasion of England was next to impossible and the Allied forces were planning an invasion of Europe. But the notion of a sceptred isle would come naturally to a man who knew and had lived his Shakespeare, and after *The Demi-Paradise* he had been asked to make a film of *Henry V*. 'They wanted me,' he said, 'to make it in battledress, and I said "No, it's got to be beautiful", and so they said "All right".[4] The contract gave him an advance of £20,000, twenty per cent of the profits, and his name above the title.[5]

Henry V was not originally his idea. A BBC producer, Dallas Bower, had wanted to make a television version before the war and had written a script, but it was never made. He then produced a fifteen-minute radio programme in which Olivier gave Henry's speech at Harfleur. He had even adapted his old television script for a film. That is where Filippo del Giudice came in. He was an Italian who had been interned at the outbreak of war, but had been released and had made a most patriotic film, *In Which We Serve*, with Noel Coward. He was short, pot-bellied, cigar-smoking, optimistic, bon-vivant, instinctively extravagant and generous, and lived in a service flat in Park Lane. He was the money raiser and the encourager, and the man who convinced the Ministry of Information that 'every care would be taken to stress the propaganda angle of the subject'.[6] He proposed the idea to Olivier. From the start Olivier was determined to do everything. 'I had the advantage of knowing more about the medium than anybody else. I didn't want to argue with anybody about it. I wanted to cast it the way I could, and tell everybody, which I did at the beginning, that we must be real people.'[7] That is the way it seems to have been. First the idea of Bower as producer was abandoned, and then the idea of him as director. Olivier decided he would act the king and he would produce. Then he abandoned Bower's script and had an entirely new one written.[8] Olivier did make the gesture of asking William Wyler to direct, but it is not easy to see this as more than a gesture. He and Wyler had at first loathed each other on *Wuthering Heights*. Olivier came to admire him, and in 1943 he was in England with the American forces. For whatever reason he did not direct the film. Olivier then approached Terence

Young, but at the time Young had not directed anything of consequence, and he too can hardly have been a serious possibility. It
would be strange if he were, because Olivier wrote to him before
filming started, saying, 'I am really relieved, if I cannot get you,
to be doing it myself; the tortuous business of balancing one
second rate director against another and trying to decide which
would be worse was really too much. It really feels better for me
to be riding a terrible great horse myself than pretending to trust
somebody else whose riding I suspect. I'd rather land my own
horse in my own ditch than have some hack land it in his.'[9] William
Walton, who wrote the film music and became a great friend of
Olivier's, observed that Larry wanted the lot. As for Young, he
remarked generously to Del Giudice that it was a godsend he did
not direct, because Larry was going to startle the world. Dallas
Bower was given the role of associate producer and Olivier's thanks,
who said he would be grateful to him for the idea of the film till
he died.[10]

In England in 1943 it was impossible to film the battle sequences
of *Henry V*. Where were 650 able-bodied young men to be found
to act as archers, cavalrymen, and other extras? Where were 150
horses to be found, or nails for their shoes? It was Bower's idea to
film in southern Ireland, which was neutral. Men could be employed
there for £3 10s a week, with another £2 for those who brought
their own horses.

It happened that Vivien, whose long run in *The Doctor's Dilemma*
had just ended, was going off to tour North Africa with a concert
party to entertain the British and American forces there. She left
England before Olivier and was in Gibraltar by 20 May. He left for
Ireland nine days later, to film on the estate of Lord Powerscourt,
near Dublin. On the train Olivier travelled with John Betjeman,
who was then press attaché at the British embassy in Ireland. They
amused themselves by composing alternate lines of verse as they
went along:

Betjeman: *If I should die think only this of me*
Olivier: *I could not live without my Vivien Leigh.*[11]

He and Vivien wrote to each other constantly, and sent even more frequent cables. HENRY WILL CONQUER, she cabled, before he had even started.[12] He in return wrote letters which are of course love letters, but which also describe in detail how he went about the making of his film.

Stable boys, labourers and even a Dublin cab driver readily volunteered and, since they were paid from the time they started to grow beards, they already had a stiff, late-medieval stubble on their chins by the time Olivier arrived. He adopted as his own horse a grey gelding he named Blaunche Kynge, after one of Henry's own. His own helmet and gorget were bronze and his armour was metal. The men's could not be. Their chain mail was made from coarsely woven twine sprayed with aluminium paint.[13] Olivier immediately told them that he would expect them to do nothing he would not do himself, and then explained how simple it would be for a foot soldier to jump down from a tree to bring a French cavalryman off his horse. To which a pleasant Irishman replied, 'We'd like to see you do it first, Mr Oliver.' Olivier's name was again being simplified, by men who had never seen him on the screen. Some had never seen a film of any sort. Olivier did as he had promised. He leapt down from a high branch, fractured his ankle, gallantly hid the pain and called out, 'There you are. OK for you now, old chap?' He also sprained his back. Before he arrived he had already wrenched his elbow climbing a tree to rescue one of Vivien's kittens. He sustained a further injury whilst encouraging a French cavalryman brandishing a lighted torch to ride more directly and fearsomely at the camera. The young Irishman did ride straight into the camera, the horse sustained a twelve-inch gash on its flank and the camera viewfinder went straight through Olivier's gum, leaving him with a distinguishing mark which was listed on his passport for the rest of his life. He was concerned about the Technicolor camera, which was the only one they had.[14] When Vivien heard of this catalogue of injury she cabled: WHAT HAVE YOU HURT NOW VERY WORRIED BAB.[15]

After he had been there a week he described to her the antics of the Irish clouds, which were forever obscuring the bright light his Technicolor camera needed. 'The sun played lovely games with me all the afternoon – clouds changed their course quite deliberately from all directions and just got in front of the sun – perfectly blue everywhere else! [Here he drew two sketches of recalcitrant, revolving clouds.] Cloud sailing in this direction sees sun and says "Ah, Henry V, yes", and changes course and makes very slow circular movement.'

When finally these clouds did clear, they did so to reveal the sun still obscured by the only high cirrus in the sky. He then drew for her sketches of his caravan, with a sheep scratching itself outside, a diagram showing the English and French camps in the Irish landscape and a sketch of French cavalry advancing over a hill in V-formation.

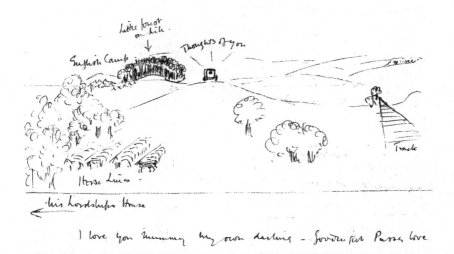

Henry V: A sketch of the English and French camps by Olivier sent in letter to Vivien.

He admitted that the filmed scene did not look as tidy as the sketch, since it would take about six months' cavalry training to make the riders keep in line. But his cameramen were really making 160 men and horses look more like 1,000.

Henry V: French cavalry advancing, as drawn in letter of Olivier to Vivien Leigh.

Blaunche Kynge was giving a little trouble. She didn't like the megaphone, wouldn't behave in front of the other horses, and wanted to rejoin them all the time. His letter, which extended itself over three days, ended by telling her that 500 men had come in the night before, so he now had his full complement. 'I love you Mummy my own darling – Goodnight pussy love.'[16]

On the day he posted that letter Vivien wrote from Algiers. 'Oh darling I do miss you so dreadfully. I think I will die with joooy when I see you. . . I call to you so many times in the day and night and I hope I hear you [saying] "Baba" to me too – Dearest most beloved love. I kiss and kiss you and surround you with my adoration. . . Your Vivling FOR EVER.' She was enjoying herself. Alec Guinness was serving in the navy near Algiers and she summoned him to meet her at the show. There was then some difficulty about his getting back to his ship. Vivien approached an admiral, caressed the lapels of his uniform and asked him what he was doing for the next few hours. Guinness described the scene. 'His eyes danced with excitement as he blushingly replied "Nothing." "Then," Vivien went on, "you won't be needing your car."' That way Guinness was able to rejoin his ship.[17]

'I hear,' wrote Olivier after ten days in Ireland, 'that they consider me a "plain" man which is considered a high compliment. Oh it is funny, they are so sweet, it's just that they [are] so natural, one feels quite a primeval sort of kinship with them. They always show exactly what they feel like children when one's working with them. If ever they're uncomfortable or depressed because they have to ride through the rain or something they shout and roar and moan with rage, or if ever I tell them they're good and that I'm pleased with them, they simply *yell* for joy – it's angelic.'[18]

On 15 June, the day before the anniversary of the day she left Holman for him, he wrote: 'I shall think of you so hard all tomorrow. Six years, it seems quite timeless altogether, just as it should. . . My Vivling I do thank you with all my heart for the undreamt of prize you have brought to me. You have sown such a harvest in my heart my beloved.' Then he told her about the shower of arrows in the air which is one of the most celebrated scenes of the film. They had to be dubbed in artificially, 'Because ours can only fly about twenty five yards and all in different directions – as the men aren't trained properly of course, and anyway there aren't nearly enough men or arrows as the sky should be black with them.' The clouds were still playing games. At one time he really had seen three groups of clouds approaching each other from three different directions.

And in another way there was trouble. He had wanted Vivien to play Catherine, the French princess in *Henry V*, but Selznick, who had her on contract, was being difficult. 'David O.S. is being a bastard and has refused the government a second time. I'll probably have to give David your tits, my balls, our three kittens, and all the takings.'[19]

That same day she wrote from Tunis that she was staying at the villa the German general had occupied before his retreat, and sleeping in the same bed. They'd performed at a vast theatre where the stagehands were French; it was nice to be speaking the language again. She wished she and Larry were living this together. And: 'Oh, I drove the plane we flew in yesterday for fifteen minutes! How I thought of you. . .my heart's blood I adore and love you.'[20]

Vivien's concert party was on an exhausting tour of North Africa that took them from Gibraltar westwards to Morocco, Algeria, Tunisia, Libya, and Egypt, and then back again to Gibraltar. They covered more than 3,000 miles, in great heat and sometimes without water to wash in. Olivier's mind went back to the time he had seen her worn out in 1939. 'My love, I hope you're not getting too madly tired. Do you remember when you came to New York after GWTW? Blimey we shall both be like that this time won't we?'[21]

By then he had filmed the charge of the French cavalry, one of the great set pieces of the film. Sequence by sequence, it went like this:

SCENES 172–180. FRENCH HORSES WALK, TROT, CANTER, GALLOP.
GALLOP GROUP.
GALLOP DISTANCE.
FRENCH HORSES INTO CHARGE.
187.   GENERAL HORSE CONFUSION. HORSES HIT.
190.   KICKING CONFUSION.
192.   HORSES START RETREAT.[22]

There remained the most difficult scene of the morass. His cameraman bet him it would take a week. It was a longish tracking shot, starting with an argument between a large party of retreating Frenchmen and a reinforcing party of horses who were trying to get past them. Then it tracked back to a troop of crossbowmen who came rushing in but were checked by a mass of dying and dead horses and men in a swamp. More French reinforcements came up and were pushed into the morass by the weight of numbers behind. It was very tough trying to get the horses to lie down in the water and pretend they were dead. The men had to jump in and hold their heads down. Having heard that you could lead Irishmen through hellfire but couldn't drive them, Olivier made them push him down into the mire first and then they took to it like ducks to water.[23]

On her long tour Vivien of course was Scarlett O'Hara, and appeared throughout in an Atlanta-style crinoline. At Algiers General Eisenhower and Harold Macmillan, the British minister in North Africa, were in the audience. At Hammamet she performed before King George VI and was later presented to him. In the Roman amphitheatre at Tripoli the company performed to an audience which included General Montogomery. They gave two performances at Suez, one in a ship and the other in the desert, where 6,000 men sat in the sand. After that the civilisation of Alexandria and Cairo was a great relief. They saw the Sphinx and the pyramids, and in Cairo stayed at Shepheard's Hotel. Vivien wrote to her mother that there the war did not exist, and that it was extraordinary to see huge tables spread with 'every sort of deliciousness and bowls of cream'.[24]

Back in Powerscourt Olivier was again writing to her that he did not know why, but this separation had been harder to bear than that of 1939 and *Gone With the Wind*.[25] But he was getting on splendidly with his Irishmen and Irish horses.

'A little while ago I couldn't understand why they couldn't get more spirit into something, as they were usually so good, and someone said, "Ah they like it when you talk to 'em Sor, that's what they like." They really are the most endearing people, so completely unselfish and simple and direct. . . I'm mad about them and I'll never forget how wonderful they've been – their gay peaty eager to please attitude, and I'll never forget these silent nights with just the rhythmical munching of the horses at their lines – it's most peculiar but they seem to keep time when they eat – it's funny, but all my harshly sublimated passions seem to have developed into a great fascination for these curious, nervous, shy, sweet and most beautiful beasts. I love them and can't keep my hands off them, I stroke their dear soft heads and think so hard of you and of their furry little chests that feel just like patting a little girl at San Remo's bottom.'[26]

All their letters to each other were opened, read, and resealed by the wartime censors, so they could not write as openly as they had in 1938 and 1939. Olivier was resorting to an allusion which would not have been apparent to the most diligent censor. Vivien had been a schoolgirl at San Remo.

Olivier, as a lieutenant in the Royal Naval Volunteer Reserve, was now commanding an army and doing so with panache and not without craft. In mid-July, when they were nearly finished, the Irish learned that extras in England were paid more than they were. They wanted a raise, and in particular demanded that those who jumped out of trees should get more than those who did not. 'Today I was faced with a sort of strike in the camp,' he told Vivien. 'I was asked to address them all right away. I was hustled into a marquee full of them, and furnished them with a dainty tissue of unfinished sentences. . . The camp commandant said he was pleased and they were satisfied.'[27] The Olivier charm had got its own way.

By the end of the third week in July the work was done. To shoot the Agincourt scenes had taken thirty-nine days, but fourteen of these were spent watching the rain come down. The Irish prime minister, Eamon de Valera, came to watch the filming, though why he should have done so is a mystery, since he had fought the English in the Easter rising of 1916 and never been a lover of anything English. The day he went to Powerscourt it rained. During the shooting the only injury to anyone except Olivier was to a cab horse, which lost an eye. It was a dun horse, pale buff with a black mane and tail, which was a favourite of Olivier's. He did not know how it lost its eye, since all spears were tipped with silver-painted leather wadding. The poor beast returned to drawing a Dublin cab and its owner was summoned for a petty traffic offence. When asked if he had anything to say, he told the magistrate, 'Sure and your honour wouldn't be taking it out on a poor old war-horse that lost his eye fightin' for the Irish at the battle of Ag'ncourt.' In the more or less contemporary version of this story the magistrate fined the man for contempt of court. In Olivier's own later version he doubled the fine.[28]

Vivien's tour was so successful that, much to her exasperation, it was extended. Many other members of the company were only too eager to stay for two weeks longer in the sun at Gibraltar on their return trip, rather than return to the privations of England in wartime. So Olivier got home before her, and told her by letter that Selznick had not relented. He would not permit his star to play the small part of Catherine in her husband's film. 'I am so heartbroken about Henry my dear Baba but I never would have felt quite guiltless about your doing it, as it would only have been for me that you had done it – so sweeeetly though Pussey. I think of you all the time in it. We've settled on Ascherson.'[29] This was Renée Ascherson, who joined a cast of Leslie Banks, Robert Newton, Leo Genn, Robert Helpmann, and the great comic George Robey as Falstaff. Olivier had originally wanted Stewart Granger and Bernard Miles as well.

The music was by William Walton. This was, as Olivier acknowledged, Bower's idea as well. Both Olivier and Walton had been choristers, Walton at Christ Church College, Oxford. He had written the music for the Elisabeth Bergner's *As You Like It* of 1936, but the two men did not know each other until 1943. Olivier said that the score for *Henry V* was the most wonderful he ever heard for a film.[30] He also said he never attempted to tell Walton what music to write. Walton always swore he did. His original guide track was never used, and he then had to fit the music to the edited action. Walton wrote to a friend: '*Henry V* is being more of a bloody nuisance than it is possible to believe. . . Ten minutes of charging horses. How *does* one distinguish between a crossbow and a longbow, musically speaking? The whole work was pretty grim, though I managed it.' It was, however, a notable success. Walton's story is that when Olivier heard the Passacaglia for the death of Falstaff he suddenly realised he had a great film on his hands because he found the music so moving and exactly right.[31] But the most memorable moments of sound in the entire film – the swishing of the forest of English arrows through the air towards the charging French cavalry – are not music at all. Phil Samuel, Olivier's production supervisor, took a sound crew into a field, cut off a long willow switch and swished it past a microphone a hundred times. This soundtrack was multiplied into a quick crescendo, then into a diminuendo, and then Walton's music took over again.[32]

When he first saw the rushes of the tracking shot of the cavalry charge, Del Giudice – now universally known as Del – had cabled Olivier that it was magnificent, without precedent, and that he was proud.[33] But he was already in deep financial trouble. The filming in Ireland would contribute fifteen minutes to the finished film of two hours, but had cost £80,000. He had raised £350,000 but it was plainly not going to be enough to complete the film. To raise more he had to go to J. Arthur Rank, who could hardly have been more antipathetic to him. Rank was a film financier and distributor from Hull, a man with no artistic flair or ambition, who had made his millions out of the family flour mills. He was a Methodist who liked to say he was in films to spread the Gospel. He provided the necessary money but in return acquired a controlling interest in Del Giudice's film company, Two Cities.

Vivien had returned by September. She had lost thirteen pounds in weight, more than so slight a woman could afford to lose. But she was soon busy preparing for a film of *Caesar and Cleopatra*. Olivier was finishing Henry in the studios at Denham. Blaunche Kynge and a selection of the best of the other horses, for the nobles, had been bought in Ireland and shipped over. *Henry V* was at last finished in July 1944. When he saw the complete version Del Giudice told Olivier that it had given him the greatest joy of his life. He wished he could write in English as well as he could in Italian, to express his true feelings. He did not do too badly in English. 'I was not exaggerating when I said this masterpiece will make film history and that millions will be talking about it for ages to come.' Olivier replied that he was touched, and that it had been a joy to work with Del.[34] Del then pressed Rank not to give the film a general release, but to keep it at the Carlton in London, where it had opened, for at least six months, and then show it in only a few cinemas. This would prolong the run and make the film a revenue gold-mine for the next twenty or thirty years. 'It is a timeless film, a classic and a triumph of art and beauty. It will interest every citizen of the world much more than *Gone With the Wind*.' He asked Olivier to write a memo to show to Rank. Olivier did, saying he was certain that *Gone With the Wind* would not have had a hope of taking more than a quarter of its $20 million if it had been released in the usual way. Theodore Carr, head of Eagle Lion distributors, having seen a preview, told Olivier that his film stood unequalled. 'One feels that one is seeing and hearing British dignity – and no other race of people have such a quality.' His patriotism sounds fulsome, but it was wartime.[35]

Rank did agree to show *Henry V* at selected cinemas in London

and the provinces, perhaps in the hope of recouping more of the
£474,888 which the film had eventually cost. This was well over
budget, but Del and Olivier were both insisting that they had a
masterpiece. One memo, apparently prepared for Olivier or by him
– which is not clear – states that Sir Kenneth Clark, then director
of the National Gallery, had recently written an article called 'Art
and Democracy', in which he suggested that true art was appreci-
ated by only one per cent of the people, but that this was enough
to maintain necessary progress in the world. Two Cities' primary
motive had been to make not a financially but an artistically
successful picture. 'In other words it is agreed that the picture might
not have a universal appeal, but that the appreciation of a few might
spread to a greater number of people. . . Our primary object must
be to give the minority pleasure, and the majority the possibility
of grasping that pleasure.'[36]

The majority did not always see it that way. Olivier admitted
that the film was very variously received in provinces. 'It even had
to be withdrawn in some places up North – this was because of bad
salesmanship – the audience being quite unprepared for the shock
coming between a [Betty] Grable and a [George] Raft.'[37] At
Portsmouth, where the film was shown not in separate, timed
programmes but continuously, there was such a coming and going
of people up and down the aisles, and such a flashing of the usherettes'
torches, that Henry's speeches were inaudible. A scout told Two
Cities that if this sort of thing were repeated in other towns, 'then
this great effort by such a great man as Larry will be completely
wasted'.[38] The film did, however, run for eleven months in London.

In America there was trouble with the censors, the Hays Office,
who objected to Shakespeare's frequent mentions of the Deity, even
when it was only Henry uttering such pieties as 'We charge you in
the name of God.' The scruples of Rank the Methodist were overcome by Rank the moneyman, who was happy to remove God,
saying that if they wanted to show films in America they would
have to 'play ball'.[39] Del protested that this would mean redubbing
fifteen of the sixteen reels, all to delete such innocent phrases as
'with God's help'. Olivier intervened, telling Rank that it might be
helpful to remind the censors that the film had been seen without

objection by the King, the Queen, the Archbishop of Canterbury, and President Roosevelt. 'We cannot believe,' he wrote, 'that there is aught in it to disturb the morals of the naughtiest little boy on the East coast or the wickedest little girl in the dust bowl.'[40] The Hays Office in the end insisted only on the deletion of the word 'bastard', a damn or two, and some womens' screams.

Then the American distributors wanted to reduce the running time. Del expressed his and Olivier's objections to this: 'They have chosen to take a classical picture and in doing so they have chosen to take the consequences. If they want a commercial picture, Larry will make one any time they like. . . The point of making classical pictures is the attempt to win the admiration of people who know what they are talking about, and if the American distributors are only worried about the great unwashed then we had best only make the sort of picture that the great unwashed are going to like, and leave it at that.'[41] In Los Angeles the distributors, apparently without asking, cut 1,500 feet of the comic scenes with Bardolph and Pistol, and the raillery with the Welsh captain, Fluellen, saying that that it would not be understood.

Del was distressed by these cuts and by Rank's dictatorial way of running what had once been his own company. All his cables had to be sent and all his telephone calls made through Rank's personal secretary, to whom he had to submit six copies of all his letters. He complained bitterly to Olivier, saying he would never sacrifice his conscience or his pride. To which Olivier, whose opinion of Rank was low, replied that he had eyes and ears, that his blood had boiled and frozen at odd intervals and he had had to stifle his impulse to break in and crack a few heads, but that it would be silly of him to pretend he could do what he could not.[42]

There were the usual brawls about the state in which the film was exhibited abroad. When cuts of forty minutes were reported from Cairo, Olivier said it was obvious to any child that Rank had gone behind his back and wrecked the picture.[43] When three different versions were shown in Italy he wrote in exasperation that he had explained to Rank that *Henry V* had been made for the good of his name, not his pocket, and that if he could not see that *Henry V* was better for his name than *The Wicked Lady* [a most successful Rank bodice-ripper] then 'however many millions they may have taken at the box-office, he and his organisation will have done no more for British films than bungalows have done for architecture'.[44]

The American opening was a triumph. *Time* magazine gave its cover to Olivier and wrote, 'The movies have produced one of their rare great works of art.'[45] The picture played in Boston for eight months and in New York for eleven. At the New York first night Olivier made a speech saying the film was made not by one person but by a team. But he insisted on singling out Del Giudice, who at his own wish had not figured in the film credits but who, said Olivier, had 'shouldered the entire burden of business responsibility'. When he later received his first Oscar for *Henry V* he gave it to Del.[46] This was generous, but it was not an Oscar that much pleased him. That, at least, is how he remembered it. 'A special award for rare artistry or something,' he said. 'After all, I produced it, directed it, and played the leading part in it, and the whole profession was terribly worried that I might get the Best Producer, the Best Director, the Best Actor, and they were worried sick about it. And the Academy, I think, sensed this terrible atmosphere that might be brewing for them and so they gave me this Special. Best Actor was still going. Best Director was still going. Best Producer was still going. This was my first absolute fob off, and I regarded it as such.'[47]

He did not make this plain at the time. He could have said that he was not only producer, director and actor, but also best writer of special notes to cinema projectionists. Olivier the perfectionist did write such a note to American projectionists.[48] 'This picture more than almost any other, I believe, depends on excellent projection manipulation and the delicacy and balance of the sound.' Here are his suggestions for modulations in volume in reel six:

Up one [in volume] towards the end of the Crispin speech ('And gentlemen in England now abed . . .').
Up one on trot.
Up one on charge.
Up one on arrows.
Then step down to one above normal and build up again as French cavalry charge into woods.

The film did last the twenty years Del had foreseen. It did not make a profit until August 1949.[49] Rank then chiselled Olivier's contracted twenty per cent of the profits down to ten and by 1961 he had received, on top of his advance of £20,000, the sum of £10,403.[50] Olivier was so proud of the film he twice tried to buy the copyright from Rank and Rank's successors, first in 1951 and then – together with *Hamlet* – in 1965. In 1965 he considered offering as much as £40,000, but was dissuaded by his agent that this was not sensible.[51]

Henry V changed Olivier's stature. For a start, no one had ever filmed Shakespeare successfully before. Few had so successfully promoted themselves before, and so widely. He was actor, producer, director, finder of horse-shoe nails; everything. He had done all this with complete single-mindedness, taking everything on himself and to himself. For the first time, as a man of the cinema and of the theatre, he stood head and shoulders over his contemporaries.

An American entrepreneur, wanting to handle Olivier's films in the United States, wrote to him with a proposition. 'You should get a unit of your own I think in this film game, *now*, the reason being *Henry V* will. . .have established you, and at that moment you will have the ball at your feet with dozens of offers. No young fellow ever had such a chance as you have now. Don't hesitate.'[52] He did not hesitate, but he did not go into films. He had another world to go to. When one of Two Cities' people – having told him in confidence that the film had taken an unprecedented £50,000 in two weeks at one West End cinema – asked him to help promote *Henry V*, Olivier replied that he could not because he was fully engaged at the Old Vic.[53] So he was. By the time *Henry V* was released he had become co-director of the Old Vic, which saw itself and was seen as a National Theatre in the making. He did not need to bother with films for a while because Two Cities, not wanting competition from their own star, had paid him £15,000 in consideration of his agreeing not to produce, direct, or act in a film, in Britain or America, for eighteen months.[54] He could safely and profitably return to the theatre.

While Olivier was planning *Henry V* in February 1943 his uncle Sydney, first Lord Olivier, former Governor of Jamaica and Secretary of State for India, died at the age of eighty-three. In its obituary *The Times* called him one of the foster parents of the Labour Party, and said he had the appearance of a distinguished Spanish hidalgo.[55] He was the only member of the family greatly to distinguish himself before Laurence. It is surprising that uncle and nephew should have met, so far as is known, only twice, particularly since Sydney was a lover of the theatre and had even written a passable play which did receive a performance, though only a single one. Years later Laurence, as the second Lord Olivier, making his maiden speech in the House of Lords, referred to his uncle as deserving, illustrious, and rich in service to his country.[56] And perhaps the nephew did inherit some of his uncle's strengths and much of his cast of mind. Sydney Olivier knew Bernard Shaw well. When a volume of Sydney's selected writings was published posthumously, in 1948, Shaw wrote a prologue. In it he said of Sydney, 'It was fortunate for mankind that he was a man of good intent and sensitive humanity; for he was a law to himself, and never dreamt of considering other people's feelings, nor could conceive their sensitiveness on points that were trivial to him. . . He had no apparent conscience, being on the whole too well disposed to need one; but when he had a whim that was flatly contrary to convention he gratified it openly and unscrupulously as a matter of course, dealing with any opposing prejudice by the method of. . .walking through it as if it wasn't there.'[57]

Was Laurence Olivier also a man of good intent and sensitive humanity? Or did he never dream of considering other people's feelings? Could he not conceive the sensitiveness of others? Had he – and this is the biggest question – no apparent conscience? Whatever the answer to these questions, there can be no doubt that some of the attributes of Sydney Olivier were among those of Laurence, who was a law unto himself when it came to the making of *Henry V*, and would be again and again.

14

Kean's Sword, and the Thrill

OLIVIER WAS STILL AT Denham working on *Henry V* – fine frame-cutting, sound-dubbing, and adding the last shades of colour – when Tyrone Guthrie and Ralph Richardson came to him suggesting that together they should revive the Old Vic company, not at the Old Vic Theatre, because the roof had been damaged by bombs, but at the New Theatre, in the West End. The danger of more bombing was, they thought, over. For the first time in England the government, to encourage the morale of the people and in a wartime spirit of collectivism, was offering money for the arts. It would guarantee half of any losses.[1] Olivier thought the scheme hair-brained but resigned his navy commission, being a little hurt that the Admiralty so readily accepted his resignation, and in his turn accepted Guthrie's offer. Considering that in the previous two years he had earned £3,517 for *The Demi-Paradise* and £20,000 for *Henry V*, the terms he accepted were miserable.[2] He became one of three directors of the Old Vic, the others being Richardson and John Burrell, from the BBC. Guthrie would be overall director of the whole Vic–Wells organisation, which included the ballet at Sadler's Wells. Olivier's salary as a co-director was £15 a week. In any week that he acted he should receive £40, but in such a week he would not draw any salary as director.[3]

The Lunts sent congratulations from New York, saying they rejoiced with him. Elsie Fogerty was delighted at his news. 'I had hoped, when you began, that by now there would have been a great National Theatre with you as its brightest star . . . If it is in your power to pour into your work all you have felt and suffered and done in the last few years you ought to stand where no modern actor has quite reached in the coming days.' She offered her services as an honorary voice coach but died not long afterwards.[4]

These were dramatic times. On 6 June the Allied forces invaded Normandy. A week later the Germans started sending V-1s, pilotless flying bombs, over London. The Old Vic company, rehearsing in the empty rooms of the National Gallery, from which all the paintings had been removed to safety, had to carry on while the V-1s flew over. If, as sometimes happened, one appeared to be headed straight for them, the actors lay on the floor and were ashamed how relieved they were when an explosion and the ensuing shattering of timbers and glass told them someone else had been hit.[5] At the same time as these perilous rehearsals, Vivien was at Denham beginning to film Gabriel Pascal's *Caesar and Cleopatra*, a notoriously extravagant picture which in the end cost nearly three times as much as *Henry V*, and failed.

The Old Vic started in Manchester with Ibsen's *Peer Gynt*, which was Richardson's play, in which Olivier had only a small part, and Shaw's *Arms and the Man*, in which the two men had equal roles. Olivier had not acted on the English stage for six years, since his 1938 *Coriolanus*, and not at all since the disastrous New York *Romeo and Juliet* of 1940. He did not much like the part of Sergius in *Arms and the Man*. When one Manchester notice read, 'Mr Richardson is brilliant; Mr Olivier on the other hand. . .' he thought the only thing was to go back to the navy. Then something happened which, Olivier believed, changed the course of his actor's thinking for the rest of his life. He was given what he called the richest pearl of advice he ever received. Guthrie came to Manchester to see the play.

'Why don't you like the part?' he asked Olivier.

'What?'

'Don't you love Sergius?'

'Love that stooge?. . . God, Tony, if you weren't so tall I'd hit you.'

'Well of course,' replied Guthrie, 'if you can't love him you'll never be any good in him will you?'

By the end of the week Olivier loved Sergius, for his faults, his showing-off, his absurdity and his bland doltishness.[6]

Guthrie's was of course a piece of advice entirely sympathetic to Olivier's instinctive conviction that he did not just play a character but became that character. If he became a character he would love him, because a man will always love himself. From then on the play flourished, and by the time the company reached London it was a hit.

But Olivier's biggest play of the season was *Richard III*. It had been Jill, of all people, who had first recommended the part to him. That must have been in the 1930s, most likely after he had played Romeo. She had said there was this wonderful scene where the evil king woos a woman who detests him, a woman whose husband he has killed, and he woos and wins her in five minutes. The woman wooed is Lady Anne, widow of a prince murdered by Richard. She was played by Margaret Leighton, and Olivier decided in rehearsal to let loose upon her the utmost libertinism he could imagine. 'When I looked at her she couldn't look at me, she had to look away. And when she looked away I would spend time devouring the region between her waist and upper thigh. Shocking maybe, but right, I felt. It was right for my Richard, and he was becoming my Richard by the minute.' He felt, 'like a stoat coming out of its hole and smelling the morning air', that he was on to something.[7]

But by then he had something else on his mind. By August, in the middle of her film and in the middle of his rehearsals, Vivien announced that she was pregnant. 'What do you suppose?' she told Holman. 'I'm going to have a baby. Everyone is *very, very* cross and keeps asking me how I suppose they are going to make me look like the sixteen-year-old Cleopatra and I keep saying I can't help it, that it's an act of God and that they're not to be mean to me in my condition!'[8] She was advised to rest but did not, and in the first week of September had a miscarriage. Olivier, always a man to notice such things, observed that it was perfect foetus, that it had a penis, and would have been a boy.[9]

The miscarriage may account for his despondency before the opening of *Richard III*, which was only a week afterwards. Despite his earlier confidence that he was becoming Richard, by the first night he was 'haunted by unaccountable fears' that he would fail in his first big role for so long. He saw fear in others too, and thought he had never opened a play with so despondent a company. 'I walked towards my fate,' he said, 'as to my grave.'[10]

Before the first night he telephoned John Mills and asked him to come and see him in his dressing room before the performance. 'Amazing thing,' says Mills. '*No* actor wants to see anyone before the show, ever. But I went round. There he was in his make-up. "Sit down," he said. "You are my best friend, so I don't ever try to fool you. I'm just telling you that you're in for a very poor evening. I'm lousy in the part, I don't know it, and I just want you to know that I know.' So I went and had two double brandies. The curtain went up, on came his lordship, and said, "Now is the winter of our discontent. . ." and the whole theatre froze. It was the performance of a lifetime.'[11] At the end he was cheered. Noel Coward considered it the best performance by a man that he had ever seen. Among the critics, James Agate of the *Sunday Times* wrote that the death scene was as tremendous as, judging from Hazlitt, he took Edmund Kean's to have been. Olivier also had read Hazlitt's description of that scene, and admitted he studied to emulate it, 'after a fashion'. It was the first time in his life, in twenty years on the stage, that he sensed that the public, the critics, and he himself, all together, *knew* that a performance of his had been right. He breathed in the sweet smell of success, which he described as like seaweed, or like oysters.[12]

That season there were only five theatres open in London. Gielgud was presenting *Love for Love* and *Hamlet* at the Haymarket. He too made the connection with Kean. Gielgud's maternal great-aunt was Ellen Terry, who had been Irving's leading lady. In 1939 his mother, Kate Terry, gave him the sword Kean had worn when he played Richard III in 1813. That had been his most brilliant role, in London and New York. The sword had then passed to the actor William Chippendale, who in turn had given it to Henry Irving when he played Richard III in 1877, and thence it had come into the Terry family. When Gielgud's mother gave him the sword he told her it would be 'a nice thing to be handed on again to another young hopeful', and after Olivier's Richard III, in an act of great symbolism and generosity, he gave him the sword.[13] It was Gielgud who had first brought Olivier into Shakespeare in his *Romeo and Juliet* of 1935. Now he was implying by his gift that his rival was in the great line of actors – Kean, Irving, and now Olivier. He had the sword inscribed to Olivier and suggested it should be carried to him on a tray like the severed head of St John the Baptist. It was carried from the Haymarket, past Irving's statue near the National Gallery, to the New Theatre in St Martin's Lane where it was presented to Olivier on the stage. He kept it under his bed for years.[14] During the play's run, the film of *Henry V* was released in London and Olivier's reputation stood higher than it ever had before.

But he was dog-tired. In December he wrote to Jill and told her so. 'Straight out of *Demi-Paradise* into *Henry*, and straight from that after eighteen months into this maelstrom of work. I'm really more exhausted than I have ever been before.' He said Vivien had lost her baby at three months and then told her, with little tact, that before that happened they were about to cable and ask if Tarquin's old pram was still in existence, and whether she'd mind if they borrowed it. Suzanne had already returned with Vivien's mother from Canada. Jill had told him she was planning to return from California with Tarquin, which she did six months later. He warned her that England was not comfortable and would not be for years to come. 'London is quite filthy and all the restrictions begin to get more and more on the poor old nerves.'[15]

Vivien was exhausted too, but rejected her doctor's advice to rest and prepared to appear in Thornton Wilder's play, *The Skin of Our Teeth*, a vast sprawl which its author called a 'comic strip of mankind'. It did, however, have a part of which Tallulah Bankhead had made a great success on Broadway, and which Olivier thought would show Vivien off to advantage. He, tired though he was, would direct. David O. Selznick nearly saved them both from this excess. Vivien was still on contract to him. Of course he wanted more films from her. He had let her play in the disastrous New York *Romeo* of 1940, although he believed it seriously damaged her film career. He had then given her three months' leave to return to England and she had stayed for four years. He now saw no reason why she should not return to Hollywood, and feared this new play proposed by Olivier would damage his property.[16] He asked the English courts for an injunction to prevent her. It was disingenuously pleaded on her behalf that if she did not act she might well be drafted into war work in a factory. This was wildly unlikely, but the injunction was not granted.

At about this time Olivier bought Notley Abbey, at Thame, halfway between London and Stratford-upon-Avon. It was both a grand house and a ruin, both a delight to him and an endless drain on his resources. The abbey had been founded in the twelfth century, later endowed by Henry V, and then ruined in the Reformation. By the time Olivier saw it the principal remains of the original abbey were a stone tower with a cantilevered spiral staircase, a few arches, and a refectory used as a barn. The house was set in fifty-six acres of grounds. The habitable parts of it dated largely from the nineteenth century. There were three grand rooms to entertain in, ten bedrooms, stabling, hunting, fishing in the River Thame, which ran through the estate, and hunting with the Bicester, South Oxford, and Waddon hunts.[17] The price was £18,000. It was a house which over the years Olivier possessed it made a fortune for the builders and interior decorators he employed. Vivien was at first doubtful; her tastes were more sybaritic. But Olivier set his heart on it, and it was his principal home during what he later thought of as his baronial period.[18]

The war in Europe ended on May 8, 1945 with the German surrender. On VE Day Olivier was on tour in Blackpool with the Old Vic company. Vivien had already opened in *The Skin of Our Teeth* and on 19 May Olivier departed on a victory tour of Europe with Ralph Richardson and the Old Vic. They went to Brussels, Antwerp, Belsen, Hamburg, and then Paris.

Most of all he remembered one performance of *Richard III* at Hamburg. In tragedy he thought it possible, even advantageous, to *use* exhaustion, which seemed to add some extra dimension, but he found himself beyond that.[19] 'I was frightfully tired, and there was this audience, the whole audience were men in khaki with Sten guns between their legs, and I was absolutely dreading the performance. I was so tired, didn't know how the hell I was going to get through it, and there was such a feeling from out there, expectation, expectancy, and feeling they were lucky to be there [to have survived the war], and saying, "If only you knew how we are with you boy. I hope we're making you feel all right." I mean there was that. It was so strong. I couldn't believe that I could have given a performance of such tremendous verve, and scaled the heights, feeling as I did when I walked straight on stage. I don't think I've ever done anything as good as that in my life. It's these boys, made me.'[20] At Hamburg a young officer who admired his performance took him into the ruins of the German war office and gave him a magnificent English Purdey shotgun and a Luftwaffe dagger. It was not seen as looting. Men were stealing Mercedes from their garages and pictures off the walls of houses. Olivier thought a victorious army could be villainous.[21]

In the six weeks of the tour he wrote thirty-six letters to Vivien. One began:

> GREETINGS
> To the
> Wondrously Beautiful
> Dearest Beloved
> Most Adorable
> MISTRESS OF NOTLEY

'My darling, I do hope this is the first letter you get at Notley.' It wasn't. It was redirected to Chelsea. In the next he told her: 'I spent a most fretful night – sighing and longing for my mummy.' He told her about the visit to Belsen where, in the German extermination camp, twenty people a day were still dying from typhus. From Hamburg, where they returned for a second visit, he told her, 'You do help me. 'The honour of the family' I always say just before I go on and cross myself with a "V".' And two days after that, when he first arrived in Paris, 'I cannot live without you and I don't intend to bloody well try to ever again. . . You are my inspiration, my hope, my whole hope, the oxygen in my blood. . .'[22]

Back in England Vivien had developed a cough, was often feverish, and had become even thinner. By the time Olivier was in Hamburg she had seen two doctors. One told her she should go to a Swiss or Scottish sanatorium, the other simply to stop work and rest. She had a tubercular spot on her lung. She had not told Olivier, and was still appearing in *The Skin of Our Teeth*. He was in Paris before he heard of her illness, and then only indirectly from a friend. He had supper with the Lunts, who had been in London and seen Vivien, and they confirmed the friend's account. When he and Vivien first talked on the telephone from Paris she still did not tell him the full story, and he wrote demanding to know exactly what the doctors had said and whether it was true that she had to go to live in a dry climate for some months, in Switzerland or Arizona. 'You know that whatever the dark thing is – that the slightest shadow across your life troubles me so much more than any harm to myself. You're the only person in the world who could make hideously selfish me love anyone more than I do myself. You know don't you my Vivien that if I try to save you disappointment or give you happiness it is only selfishness on my part really. Your sorrow is my worst fear. . .your life my life.'[23]

Two days later she did tell him and he said his mind was at comparative peace. 'I thank you for giving me the privilege of sharing trouble with you, for anything shared with you is a sacred joy and a noble glory.' He had been out that day buying stockings for her.[24] Paris had not been bombed as London had been bombed. There were no ruins. But Paris had been occupied and was still celebrating the end of the war. The Old Vic was playing at the Comédie Française; Olivier was fêted and had received a great many invitations – 'from various princesses, countesses, baronesses etc' – and accepted at least three invitations to lunch, none of which, he said, he would keep.[25]

'My genital life,' he wrote to Vivien, 'has made no manifestation whatever since I've been away – most peculiar? It knows who it belongs to, doesn't it, hey? Perhaps my fatigue has something to do with it. You don't think it's because I'm getting old, do you? Hey? Well I don't. It just can't rise without you, that's what.' That same day *Autant en Emporte Le Vent* [*Gone With the Wind*] opened in Paris and he told her she'd made a fabulous successs. 'Up the family,' he wrote.[26]

The most sensational event of the Paris visit, in Olivier legend, was that Ralph Richardson came near to murdering him. This was a tale which did not see the light of day until the publication in 1986 of Olivier's second book, *On Acting*. This was not so personal as his earlier autobiography, *Confessions of an Actor*, but was almost entirely about his life as an actor and his reflections on acting. The bones of the story are that, since Richardson had appeared in *Peer Gynt* on the opening night of the Old Vic's London season, in Paris it was Olivier's turn to appear first, in *Richard III*. It was an outstanding success. There had always been a jealousy and a rivalry, 'perhaps a little deadliness', as Olivier put it, between the two men. After the cheers and the wining and dining Olivier returned to his hotel room and began to write a letter to Vivien. He then saw that a drunken Richardson was climbing a drainpipe up to his window. He yelled to him, 'Do you want to kill yourself?' and went down-stairs to let him in. Richardson walked up the stairs to Olivier's room, lunged at him, picked him up, carried him across the room to the balcony, and held him over the edge. The hard cobbles were sixty feet below. Olivier knew that if he struggled Richardson would let him go, so he remained still and quietly suggested to Richardson that he should pull him back, which after a pause he slowly did. 'I saw in his eyes that if I'd done anything other than I had he'd have let me go. For a brief moment he'd wanted to kill me.'[27]

Now Olivier had written his earlier autobiography himself. *On Acting*, though only Olivier's name appears on the title page, was in fact written by Gawn Grainger, an actor, writer, and Olivier's friend. He taped ten long conversations with Olivier, which were apparently transcribed verbatim, and out of that material he wrote a coherent and attractive book. The conversation from which the murder story came took place in February 1985. The story as it appears in the transcript is substantially what was printed in the book – the letter, hearing Ralph on the drainpipe, letting him in, the jealousy and the little deadliness, the picking up and holding over the balcony. But there is a sense of hearing Olivier making it all up for effect as he goes along, and then, in what follows on the transcript but did not appear in the book, this becomes quite clear:

LO: But if I'd done anything other than that [stay still] I think he'd have let me crash on to the floor. I could have broken my back, my spine, hips, anything you like. He wanted to kill me. . . And then next morning I said, 'Ralphie, that was rather a near one last night, wasn't it?' He said 'Yeah.' He said 'Yes, we were both very foolish.' It was a double

> fault. He held me over the balcony and threatened to drop me on the fucking pavement – it was MY doing.'
> GG: Yes. 'Would you please hold me over there for a moment?'
> LO: Yes (laughing).
> GG: 'I'd like to experience . . .'
> LO: 'I'd like to know what the thrill is.'
> GG: Yes.
> LO: Boy, there are some thrills you can do without.
> GG: 'But I think you should experience everything in life and, um.'
> LO: (Laughter) 'I'd like to be thrilled.'
> GG: 'So throw me over the balcony.' O dear. Would you like a beer or something?
> LO: Or something.[28]

In Paris, Olivier wrote to Vivien every day and his letters survive. He wrote after the first night of *Richard III*, writing on as usual into the small hours, and wrote again the next day. He gave her the most detailed accounts of his doings. Nowhere is there any mention of the slightest altercation with Richardson. Besides which Olivier, in his account, was attributing to Richardson the murderous instincts he had himself felt at the mess in Worthy Down.

When Olivier returned from Paris Vivien spent some weeks in hospital, and then they went on holiday to Scotland together.[29] When they returned she was forced to rest and stayed in the inhabitable rooms of Notley. Olivier was in London on weekdays, rehearsing for the Old Vic's new season. He declined invitations for the weekend, saying, 'My Sundays. . .are always in the country, where I dash off like a gazelle to my girl.'[30]

In the Old Vic's second season Olivier played Hotspur in *Henry IV Part I*, Justice Shallow in *Part II*, and appeared in the extraordinary double bill of Sophocles' *Oedipus* and Sheridan's *The Critic*. *Oedipus*, in a version by W. B. Yeats, was Guthrie's idea. Olivier, with his Oedipal convictions which had already shown themselves in his pre-war *Hamlet* with Guthrie, was eager to play in this terrible story of a man fated to kill his father and unknowingly marry his mother. But he did not like Guthrie's plans for a 'pretty, dainty-coloured décor', was shocked by what he called Guthrie's 'subservience to originality' in this matter, and insisted on Michel Saint-Denis directing. This was the first open breach between the two men, who had come not to like each other. Guthrie had thought the film of *Henry V* vulgar and said so. In the matter of *Oedipus* he was over-ruled by Richardson and Burrell; Saint-Denis did direct and the result was a triumph for Olivier. Oedipus' cry when he learns what he has done, and his bloody tearing out of his eyes, were the most memorable moments of the Old Vic season. For the cry Olivier imagined the torment of an animal in a trap, of an ermine trapped by salt scattered on hard snow, which when it begins to lick is held fast by the tongue freezing to the ice as the animal tries to tear itself free. Olivier also imposed his will when he insisted that *Oedipus*, a short play, should be followed in a double bill by Sheridan's *The Critic.* Fifteen minutes after tearing out his eyes he was back on stage, gaily cavorting as the dandyish Mr Puff. It was an evening of wilful virtuosity but it worked. He even devised his final exit as Mr Puff, being flown offstage on a painted cloud. This was another piece of recklessness. One night, when he was inching himself from his cloud-seat to a rope ladder, to descend, the rope slipped and stranded him thirty feet above the stage with only a wire to hang on to. He was just rescued by the crew in the flies, but it was a moment of terror. Or another thrill. He continued with his ingenious exit, allowing it to remain 'a living dread' to him for the next six months.[31]

In its second season the Old Vic was already beginning to be seen as a National Theatre. There was already in being a notional body called 'The Joint Council of the National Theatre and the Old Vic'. All that really existed was the Old Vic company, and that was in fact performing at the New Theatre, but this new body did have a printed letterhead and a secretary who consulted Olivier and Richardson.[32] Much more convincing evidence of the prospects of anything like a National Theatre coming into existence was provided by Bronson Albery, a man of the commercial theatre who owned the New. Olivier went to see him and asked for more space in the theatre programmes for the company's literature, at the expense of some advertisements which would have to be turned away since paper was still rationed. Albery declined, saying the programme matter was his concern. He had been in business for a long time and hoped to stay there. He said he wasn't in it only for the money. He had recently turned down a large offer for his theatres. But he had known times when he made more from programme advertisements and catering than he took at the box office. He agreed that the Old Vic had been at the New Theatre for two seasons and might stay a third, but he knew that there was already talk of a National Theatre and there would come a time when it would not be at the New. He looked on the existing company as a transitory affair and was not prepared to alter his existing arrangements to please it.[33]

At the end of October 1945 Henry Ainley, Olivier's lover of 1937, died. He had not been on the stage since one gala-night appearance in December 1938, in a scene from Flecker's verse-play, *Hassan*, his most famous part. *The Times* gave him a glowing obituary. 'Beauty of face, of figure, and of voice can rarely have been combined as they were in "Harry" Ainley, and his all too reckless expenditure of vitality in a world all too ready to prey upon it could not cloud the essential beauty and simplicity of his nature nor (till his health failed) impair his powers of hard and faithful work. He warmed both hands at the fire of life and throve on the warmth.' He had also helped to drink himself to death, which *The Times* did not say. There is nothing to show whether he and Olivier had kept in touch during the war years, but Oliver read one of the lessons at his memorial service at St Martin-in-the-Fields on 13 November. The reading was from I Corinthians – 'O death, where is thy sting? O grave, where is thy victory?' It was a theatre occasion. Others present were Lewis Casson and Sybil Thorndike, Bronson Albery, Robert Morley, Ivor Novello, Emlyn Williams, Binkie Beamont, Athene Seyler, Edith Evans, John Drinkwater, and Cathleen Nesbitt. Miss Nesbitt had acted with Ainley in *Hassan* in his great days, and had fallen in love with him and then with Rupert Brook. Ainley's second wife, an American novelist, had once accused Nesbitt of being pregnant by Ainley, which she was not.[34]

By 1946 Olivier's salary at the Old Vic was £60 a week, when he acted. By court order he had to pay £3,500 a year in alimony to Jill, to maintain herself and Tarquin.[35] He had to look for ways to earn more, and in May Laurence Olivier Productions was formed, a limited company with the very broadest of purposes. In the United Kingdom and elsewhere it could provide any kind of entertainment and services – theatrical, cinematographic, television, or of any kind whatever. It could also engage in farming, market gardening, landscape gardening, livestock breeding, and poultry farming. It could act as financier, merchant, contractor, and broker. In the articles of association the only shareholders were named as Olivier, Laurence Kerr, actor and producer, and Olivier, Vivien, 'married woman'. Each had forty shares.[36] This great breadth of activity was so that the company could not only exploit the services of the actor and his married woman in the making of plays and films, but also farm the acres of Notley and thereby hope to subsidise the vast upkeep of the house. As for Durham Cottage, the Oliviers' Chelsea house, this was held to be necessary to the company when either Olivier or Vivien was working in London. All its expenses, including tradesmens' bills, were to be paid by LOP. The company also bought, for the use of its principals, a Rolls-Royce, ALB 911, for £1,183. Olivier's old Invicta, which he had driven throughout the war, was taken in part-exchange for £275.[37]

Throughout the autumn and winter of 1945–6 Vivien stayed at Notley, with a nurse. Esmond Knight, Olivier's contemporary, who had been in the navy and appeared with him in wartime shows and then in *Henry V*, visited them there and described them as wrapped up in each other. Knight knew Vivien was distressed at the very idea of having to go into a sanatorium, and Olivier had said very well, she should stay at Notley with all the windows open and the fires burning all day long, and there she would recover from the tuberculosis. 'Which,' said Knight, 'amazingly she did, amazingly. It was probably the actual bug – like a worm in the blood, as Viola [in *Twelfth Night*] says; it probably began to eat away something in her and this sort of extraordinary deterioration began in her.'[38]

In late April of 1946, when the Old Vic company flew to New York for a six-week season, Vivien was fit enough to go with Olivier; not as a member of the company but, as she put it, for the ride. They stayed, of course, at the St Regis, though they could not afford it. They found their room there looking rather like a tent at the Chelsea Flower Show, decked with red roses, hydrangeas, daffodils, and narcissi. They met old friends like the Lunts, Katharine Cornell, and George Cukor. Throughout, the company played to full houses at the Century Theatre. Richardson, as Falstaff in both parts of *Henry IV*, was greatly praised. Olivier, in *Oedipus* and *The Critic*, was fêted. John Mason Brown of the *Saturday Review* called it great, and said that in *Henry IV* and *Oedipus* he had seen the sun rise and refused to mistake it for the moon.[39]

But Olivier had overworked for years. He had kept the perilous exit on a cloud in *Oedipus* and had nightmares in which he was killed falling from the flies, or in a plane crash. He did not fall, but in his last performance as Mr Puff in New York he did put in a couple of gratuitous somersaults and tore an Achilles' tendon. The last show was on a Saturday. The next day he and Vivien flew to Boston and went on to Tufts College, at Medford, where he limped on to the platform, was lauded as 'the real interpreter of Shakespeare of our age' and was given his first honorary degree. Olivier was charmed by it all. 'Articulate scholars talked as if they knew by heart every single job you ever undertook, and admired each as if it had been the work of a combined master of philosophy, art, and engineering.'[40] He liked honorary degrees, accumulated five, and could have had more if he could have made the time to collect them. Apart from Tufts, he accepted degrees from Oxford, Edinburgh, London, and Manchester, but declined offers from Yale and Glasgow. Universities never understood that he could not skip a performance in London to attend their ceremonies. He and Thornton Wilder once had a heated conversation in a dressing room about whose honorary degrees were better; Wilder won on quantity, having nine.[41]

The Old Vic company returned at the weekend. Olivier stayed to attend the first public American showing of *Henry V*, at which he made his speech singling out Del Giudice for praise, and then he and Vivien prepared to fly back to England.

The episode that followed is one he could not conceivably have forgotten, but he did not so much as mention it in his autobiography and his earlier biographers have never given it more than a few lines. Tuesday, 19 June 1946 made his nightmares real, and was very nearly the last day of his life. It is well-known in civil aviation history because the events of that day grounded an entire fleet of planes.

Olivier and Vivien boarded the Pan American Clipper '*America*', which took off from La Guardia at 5 p.m. bound for Newfoundland, Shannon and London. The aircraft was a four-engined Lockheed Constellation, then the fastest airliner crossing the Atlantic. There were forty-two passengers and a crew of ten. At 5.35 p.m., half an hour into the flight, a shaft from one of the starboard engines to the cabin pressuriser broke and thrashed around, setting fire to the plane's hydraulic fluid. The engine caught fire and the plane's carbon dioxide extinguishers failed to put out the blaze. The pilot turned back. The flames melted the engine mounting and, over Plainfield, New Jersey, the flaming engine fell off the wing. Through an overcast sky the captain searched for a landing place and saw Windham Field at Willimantic, Connecticut. It was a small field and the Constellation was then the largest civil plane in service. The plane's hydraulics were useless, so he had to land with the wheels up. He brought the plane in at 6.10 p.m. She skidded for 3,100 feet, more than half a mile, down the concrete runway before coming to rest tipped on one wing. No plane of her size had ever landed there before, not even an intact one.[42]

The passengers scrambled out and sat on the grass. Police and press arrived. Olivier told a reporter from the *Hartford Times* what had happened: 'The outer starboard engine caught fire when we were about 15,000 feet in the air. It burned completely through, the metal flowing like water from the intense heat, then dropped off. It is very awkward flying around with a motor missing. The pilot brought us down quickly, showing a great deal of courage. He dropped down through the overcast and he saw a landing field. He circled the field once, then brought us down in the most magnificent piece of airmanship I've ever seen. His hydraulic system was burned out so he had to bring us in with a belly landing. When we reached the ground the passengers burst into spontaneous cheering. We must have cheered for two minutes.' He mentioned to another reporter that after the engine fell off the fuselage started to crack.[43]

The passengers were taken by bus to Hartford. A relief plane was flown up from New York and all but one of the passengers chose to continue their flight. They took off for London after midnight. After the emergency landing Olivier and Vivien had considered going back

by sea instead, but as he said, making light of things, they couldn't
have done because they had only $17 left between them.[44] His recur-
rent premonitions of disaster had been exorcised. What he had
feared had happened, and he and Vivien had survived.

Planes that lose blazing engines do not commonly survive. If the
Clipper had been half an hour further into the flight she would have
come down into the sea. The Constellation fleet was grounded after
an inquiry. Vivien said later that she had looked round at the others
in the plane and their faces had changed, making them look like
skeletons. Olivier's was the same. She raised her hands and found
hers was too.[45]

They had been lucky. A clergyman friend of Olivier's, who had
read that they intended to fly home, preferred to think of a higher
reason. 'The day you made the flight,' he wrote, 'I remembered you
both at Mass that you might be granted safety. It must have been
almost at that exact moment that you met with your accident and
came through without hurt. Odd, perhaps you may say, but I prefer
to think there was a link which helped you and I am thankful I was
the humble cause.'[46] The near-disaster and the escape made front-
page news in the *New York Times* and other New York and Hartford
daily papers. The London *Times* did not carry a word and what had
happened was little reported in England.

There was then the question of what Olivier was to do in the
1946–7 Old Vic season. He wanted to play Lear but had long known
that this was the one part in the Shakespearean canon that
Richardson longed to do; that, he reasoned, inhibited him from any
thoughts of the part for himself. But that summer, nursing the
thought that Richardson had a certain cunning way with him, Olivier
adopted a certain cunning way himself. When the three co-directors met to decide the season and who should play what, Burrell
began, 'Well, whose turn is it; Ralph's isn't it?' Ralph suggested
with scrupulous politeness that he might be allowed to attempt the
part of Cyrano de Bergerac. 'Fine,' said Burrell. 'Fine,' said Olivier,
'fine.' And what, asked Burrell, about Larry?

'I,' said Olivier, 'would like to play and produce *King Lear*.' At
which, by his own account, he was rewarded by a slight but percep-
tible start from Richardson, who, having had the first say, was obliged

in his turn to mutter, 'Fine, fine.' Olivier would be Lear and Alec Guinness would play his Fool.[47]

Olivier was thirty-nine, young for Lear, whom he played as by no means entirely senile. He made the first scene, that of Lear's abdication of his kingdom and the wilful sharing out of it among his daughters, almost mischievously comic, and in doing so made it almost believable. So much so that Somerset Maugham wrote saying it was the first time he had seen the difficult beginning made probable.[48] This was Olivier at his most practical. What would make sense? What would work? The production succeeded, the play transferred for a week to Paris, and the critics were kind. But the best appreciation of the play was given not by any professional critic but by the novelist Rosamond Lehmann. She saw the first night with her publisher, Hamish Hamilton, who encouraged her to write to Olivier. She was reluctant to bother him but after a month did write. 'You have that power which belongs only to the great actor – of appearing physically to shrink and then to swell before one's eyes. I think about it every day – seeing Lear as a dwindled mad old man, then swelling in majesty and spiritually illuminated like Blake's Jehovah . . . This is the time, the age, to take in Lear, isn't it? It seemed prophetic for our day – the gigantic moral anarchy – every word true. I remember those Belsen women [here she was comparing the female camp guards with Goneril and Regan] and Cordelia dead, like a raped and strangled creature thrown away on a concentration camp rubbish heap. And the Fool saying all that could be said, the world's eternal clown. Your loving compassion for him tore me up.'[49]

At the same time, Olivier was keeping an eye on his production of *The Skin of Our Teeth*, in which Vivien had returned to the West End, though her health was still precarious. Michael Denison, who had been an acquaintance of Vivien's for ten years, went backstage with his wife Dulcie Gray to see her after a performance of that play. 'She had in her dressing room two very beautiful Siamese cats and there were three pairs of the most beautiful eyes looking at us, Vivien's and the two cats'. I think she wasn't frightfully well at the time – she was certainly frightfully thin – and I think it was the first time we heard of the TB threat.'[50]

Vivien put on a great front for her public, for visitors to her dressing room. But she was far from well in any sense. Olivier was playing Lear, directing *The Skin of Our Teeth*, entangled in the administration of the Old Vic and apprehensive about Vivien – all this after an already exhausting year. An American author writing a book on the Old Vic's American season wrote asking for help, and received this reply. 'I am in an absolute maelstrom of business, work and worries just now . . . I realise from your letter that time is of the essence with you and only hasten to warn you that it is an essence that has completely evaporated from the bottle with me.'[51] Then Del Giudice wrote saying he intensely wanted to meet Olivier again but knew he was busy. He had been unable to get a ticket for *Lear* and would not mind standing. Could Olivier help? He ended: 'Is there any chance of seeing you and Vivien one night when you don't feel tired? Much light and honour came to me from your friendship.' The eternally busy Olivier did get his secretary to find Del tickets but then wrote – and this was to the man to whom he owed so much and whom he had so much praised at the New York opening of *Henry V* a few months before – 'I shall look forward to seeing you for a wee while afterwards. I am so sorry I cannot manage supper that night.'[52]

15

Buckingham Palace, 10.15

DEL GIUDICE DID FINALLY persuade Olivier to lunch with him in his Park Lane apartment in December, and there he did his best to persuade him to make another Shakespeare film. There had been tentative plans for Olivier and Vivien to make a Hollywood film of *Cyrano de Bergerac*, which would have been much more profitable, but on 1 January 1947 Olivier made up his mind, telephoned Del in Switzerland, and agreed to film *Hamlet*.[1] It was a big gesture, but it was a day on which he needed to make such a gesture. His friend and enemy Ralph Richardson had been knighted in the New Year's Honours for services to the theatre, and we have Olivier's own account of how he felt about that. 'You should have heard the screams when Ralph had got his knighthood before I had... Deeply fond of Ralph as I was, I was unable to stop the cracked record from grinding round in my head: I've done every bit as much as he has, look how I've carried the flag abroad, the American road, Hollywood pictures, and an even fuller record in the classics; *and* there was a little film called *Henry V*. If only we could have been done together, that would have been fine.'[2] Now there would be *Hamlet* as well as well as *Henry V*, and he would produce, direct, and play the prince.

One attraction of making a film in Hollywood had been the climate, which was mild in winter and kind to Vivien's health, which was still far from robust. Part of the understanding between Olivier and Del was that the early planning of *Hamlet* should take place on the

Italian Riviera, and there he rented a whole floor of a hotel at Santa Marguerita Ligure, a few miles south-east of Genoa. On their way Olivier and Vivien stayed with the Duff Coopers in Paris, at the British embassy. Olivier had known Cooper slightly before the war, and had approached him when he was trying to get back from America in 1940 when Cooper was Minister of Information. Vivien knew his wife, Lady Diana Cooper, rather better and was more at ease at the embassy than Olivier, who was unsure whether he should straighten up when the ambassador entered the room or ignore him; he ended up greeting him in an offhand way. Beaton was there at the same time, and Olivier expounded his conception of the film of *Hamlet* in schoolboy phrases which astonished him. 'With arms flailing he emulated with a big "whoosh" a great curtain falling down here – a pillar "pffutting" down there – "a hell of a lot of smoke and emptiness all over the place". . . Larry's imitations have about them something of the original clown or, at least, the essential entertainer, who can be found in some remote music hall or performing in the street outside a pub. This was the real Larry – the mummer, ale-drinking Thespian – not the rather overwhelmed and shy cypher with wrinkled forehead that goes into society.'[3]

After Paris Olivier and Vivien went south to Italy, travelling in cold trains by way of Milan. Genoa, when they reached it, was covered in snow, and Vivien was inclined to remind Del that there was no snow in southern California even in February; but only a few miles south, on the coast, the sun shone and the mimosa was starting to bloom. She and Larry were comforted by a suite of five rooms at the Hotel Miramare, and by the delivery from England of a newer and better Rolls-Royce, a Phantom III landaulette which cost Laurence Olivier Productions twice the price of the previous year's Rolls.[4] The company could afford it, since Olivier's salary for *Hamlet* was to be £1,000 a month for producing, £1,000 a month for directing, and £2,000 a month for acting. He was also to take three eighths of the profits. Del Giudice was generous with Rank's money, and Mr Rank had agreed to a budget of £500,000.[5]

What sort of *Hamlet* was it to be? For a start, no film could run for four and a half hours, so half the text had to go. To simplify the plot some characters had to go too. Rosencrantz and

Guildenstern were cut. So was Fortinbras, Prince of Norway. These changes were entirely Olivier's. He never let anyone else touch the text. Alan Dent was there as text editor. He was a croney, a drama critic who wrote unfailingly eulogistic notices of Olivier's work and had been with him, also as text editor, on *Henry V*. He called Vivien 'Viverina', and wrote Olivier memos which occasionally called him 'You cad, you sweetheart'. In *Hamlet* he was there, in Olivier's words, to get somebody else's name on the credits, but 'all the poor fellow was ever asked to do was nod vigorously in approval of everything.'[6] The very costumes were as Olivier wanted them. 'Claudius and Gertrude were dressed as the king and queen of universal playing cards, Hamlet in the timeless doublet and hose of a romantic young prince.' The music was by William Walton, as in *Henry V*. The sets, the halls and battlements of a lowering castle, were by Roger Furse, again as in *Henry V*.[7]

It was Olivier who chose to film in black and white. 'It wasn't because I saw the subject more as an etching than a painting – the fact is that I was having a blazing row with Technicolor. I wouldn't do another bloody film with them for anything. I would have got over my sulks with Technicolor if I really felt I should, but I thought it would be rather fun to do a black and white – I'd never done one – and really show them some things in the way of focus.'[8] With deep focus, which was impossible in colour, he could surround Hamlet with faces, all kept in focus, or show two characters far apart and yet both in focus. 'I could create distances between characters, giving an effect of alienation, or of yearning for past pleasure, as when Hamlet sees Ophelia. . .an eternity away down the long corridor, 150 feet actually, sitting on a solid wooden chair, in focus, with love clearly in her eyes.'[9] And why did he dye his hair blond for *Hamlet?* 'To be picked out from a distance. For Christ's sake, I wasn't going to play Hamlet and have a whole world audience not know which the hell I was in long shots: the only one allowed to be blond.'[10] All these deep-focused distances were splendid, but the New York critic John Mason Brown thought that as a result forty precious minutes were spent in travelogues up and down Furse's sets. 'To sacrifice great language, to have innuendo dispensed with, and to lose key characters, speeches, and scenes merely because so much time is wasted getting the actors from one part of the castle to another, is to be a *Hamlet* dislocated by being on location.'[11]

Although it was on film and not on the stage, and although it was little more than half the length, this *Hamlet* had a great deal in common with his Old Vic production of 1937. The relationship between Hamlet and Ophelia was clearly carnal – he knew, as Olivier put it, what was beneath her skirt. That was straightforward enough but Olivier again, as in 1937, made the relationship between Hamlet and his mother, Gertrude, central to the action. Here is a woman who is Hamlet's mother, a woman whose husband the old king has been murdered by his brother, whom she then marries within a month. It is her slipping with such dexterity between incestuous sheets, as much as his father's murder, that rouses Hamlet. Olivier clearly intended the relationship between Gertrude and Hamlet to be more complex than that common between mother and son, and such an idea is no surprise coming from a man who sometimes, in his letters to Vivien, called her 'Mummy', and had once even told her he wished he could have been her child.[12] The casting of both Ophelia and Gertrude was difficult. Vivien wanted to play Ophelia, and felt slighted when she was not asked. Either Olivier or Rank's backers would not have her, and the seventeen-year-old Jean Simmons was chosen. The casting of Gertrude took even longer.

When the right actress was eventually found, and after the first scenes had been shot, Olivier received a letter from an executive at Ealing Studios, who asked for what he called the 'de-Oedipusation' of the film. 'Chatting with Willie Walton and Walter Legge [a music impresario] the other evening. I learned that you play the bedroom scene as if there were some unnatural sex link between Hamlet and his mother. . . It seems clear to me that this idea will not only give offence, but is clearly refuted in the text.' Olivier told him not to worry, that there would be nothing complex, and that nothing Freudian would be forced on the text. 'Willie and Walter saw an extremely unfinished version of one scene, and for talking out of school should be whipped.'[13]

He was not being candid. He had auditioned several actresses for the part, and the principal difficulty was that whoever played it had to be young enough to be sexually glamorous and at the same time old enough to realistically appear on the screen as his mother. One of those he approached was Mercia Swinburne, the wife of his old friend George Relph. He wrote asking her to do a screen test for the queen.

'Darling Angel, Age of all kinds is almost impossible to disguise on the screen. I am forty and beginning to look it; therefore you, you lovely sweet, if you fail, it will probably be because you look too young. Now for the character. I see her more or less exactly like this; a perfectly respectable Queen, who has been a model fashionable queenly wife, and was seduced for the first time in her life into having one hell of an absolutely *gorgeous* time. For the first time in her life she has been sexually awakened; for the first time she has a highly agreeable companion over a jolly nice whisky and soda. This is to make it clear that she is not [of] a loose nature from the start, but is now; but of very recent date. Having been suddenly brought to life, as 'twere, her gratitude and joy in this new life is so great that it completely douses any suspicion she might normally feel she should have as to the mysterious rights and wrongs of how she has suddenly come by this happiness. Everything is wonderful for her now, except her darling son, on whom she dotes, who will be so moody and uncomfortable, and who makes her feel the guilt she is willing to forget. There is between many a wife and son an over-developed affection, that is commonly known as the "Oedipus complex". I think it is probably true to say that in most families that exist, either on the mother's part or the son's part. . .this not quite passion, but more than love, can be found. . . She must, in other words, be the most wonderfully glamorous mummy to Hamlet. Glamorous and mummy. *Very* difficult; very very hard to find, and almost impossible to cast in a film in view of the difficult situation wrought by their either being too old for the part or too young to me.'[14]

In the end Mercia Swinburne did not get the part, which went to Eileen Herlie. She was thirteen years younger than Olivier and a sexually alluring queen, but with the skilful use of make-up was made to look a credible mother. By special understanding with Olivier she was given second billing, her name appearing immediately after his.

As the shooting proceeded at Denham, Olivier cut yet more. With great reluctance he cut even the soliloquy, 'How all occasions do inform against me' – which he thought contained some of the most important lines in the play – because it held up the cinematic action. But all the time Rank was urging greater brevity on him and he resisted. When Rank craftily congratulated him on his efforts to get the length down from two hours twenty minutes to two hours, he made a rapid reply. 'Just so that there shall be no villainous sneaking up on me by gradual and most evilly cunning deductions of the true estimate of what I said about the timing of *Hamlet*. . . I will again repeat the reminder that on Tuesday, March 4, I tele-phoned you from Santa Marguerita and warned you that the length of *Hamlet* will be two hours and a half.' He then wrote that he had later agreed, in a garden at Pinewood, that it should be as near two hours as possible. But he had said then, and said again now, that it was beyond human endeavour to make an intelligible film of *Hamlet* confined to two hours, and that two hours twenty minutes was desirable. So he would make a great film out of it, rather than an entertainment which could be shown six times a day. 'Desperate attempts to please everybody at once will, I stake my life, result in pleasing nobody at all.'[15] The eventual running time was two hours thirty-five minutes.

Rank had by then done his best to lobby for Olivier in the matter of honours, and so had Lady Colefax, who had done much of the interior decoration at Notley and was a society hostess with influ-ence in the right places. According to Olivier she protested to Sir Stafford Cripps, the Chancellor of the Exchequer, who said, 'My dear, the chap has only been divorced three years, and you know the thinking in that regard.' 'It is *not* three years,' she screamed, 'it is seven years at least.'[16] Olivier's lobbyists succeeded. One day, during the shooting of the ghost scene, he received a letter from Downing Street telling him the King had it in mind to offer him a knighthood and inquiring whether he would accept it. Vivien was in Paris at the time, being fitted with dresses for a film of *Anna Karenina* she was about to do for Korda. She, eager for honours, said, 'You won't take it, of course?' He promptly sat down and replied that he would be honoured to accept. That at any rate was his account soon after the event. He later wrote that he found himself quite unable to accept without first writing to Noel Coward, 'as if it were asking his permission', since it was apparent that this honour had been withheld from Coward for quite the wrong reasons: his homosexuality. 'I asked him, though I knew it would be wrong for any theatre person to accept it before he had, would he, I wondered, be hurt with me beyond repair if I just had not got what it took to turn it down?' Coward, faced with this circuitous request, evidently replied that he would not be hurt beyond repair. Olivier also wrote to Gielgud, not asking permission but saying he was embarrassed to be recognised over him. Gielgud told his mother Larry was touchingly sincere.[17]

The investiture was on 8 July. In his diary for that day Olivier wrote, 'Buckingham Palace 10.15', and drew a tiny sketch of a sword. He was in the middle of filming, with his hair dyed blond for *Hamlet*. He did not possess a morning suit and had to borrow one. The waistcoat was Richardson's. He was just forty, the youngest actor ever to be knighted. At the palace he found himself among admirals and generals. The only other man he knew was Malcolm Sargent, the conductor, a frequent visitor to Notley who was also knighted that day. Korda gave Vivien the day off from filming and she accompanied Olivier dressed simply, in black, wearing no jewellery.[18]

She still had three more weeks of *Anna Karenina* to do at Shepperton. Richardson was a strong Karenin but Kieron Moore as Vronsky, Anna's lover, was all wrong. It was not a happy film. Cecil Beaton, who designed the costumes, saw that Vivien was fretting about her appearance, which she thought had deteriorated. When she complained that her gloves were too small he retorted that it was her hands that were too big, which did not help since that was something about which she had always been sensitive. He thought she was not of a contented frame of mind, and that she was a lucky girl to be getting 'so much expert attention (from Tolstoy downwards) and to be paid such a fabulous sum for doing it'. She was paid £35,000 for the film.[19] Beaton himself had a queenly waspishness and was hardly ever of a charitable disposition. But his opinion was less damning than that of Kenneth Clark, who was Vivien's friend, liked her, and was entertained by her conversation, but thought little of her as Anna. 'For some reason she couldn't convey the feeling of love. She could act it very skilfully, but one never felt it was really true. She was a passionate, but totally unsentimental character.'[20]

At Denham in August Olivier replaced Michael Godfrey, the actor playing Marcellus. It is a small part, that of a soldier, and the replacement was no less a man than the young Anthony Quayle. It was a blow for Godfrey, and Olivier wrote him a long letter telling him not to be disheartened. He said the same thing had often happened to him, and about the hardest to take had been the time he had been chosen as Garbo's leading man, had crossed the Atlantic, worked with her for a fortnight, had been found wanting and was, quite frankly, fired. 'Even in spite of that,' he continued, 'I can't help feeling I'm really getting along quite nicely, thank you.' It was kind of Olivier to write such a letter, but here was a man who was succeeding in everything he did and had just been knighted, harking back to an old disappointment which had stayed with him for years, and which he never forgot.[21]

The last scene to be filmed was Hamlet's leap from a balcony on to the king, when, crying 'Then, venom, to thy work', he runs him through with poisoned sword. There was no need for a leap at all. It was a piece of traditional Olivier recklessness. He hired two acrobats to demonstrate how best to do the leap, was dissatisfied with their timid antics, and resolved to do a swallow dive on to the king, fourteen feet below. He reckoned there were five possibilities: he could kill himself; damage himself for life; hurt himself badly enough to make recovery a lengthy business; hurt himself only slightly; or get away with it. The chances of each seemed about the same. He also wrote that he felt so strongly about the film being by far the most important thing he had done that he regarded the first five possibilities with an unworried steadiness that gave him a mild feeling of surprise. This is a tale he told many years later, however, and no doubt he told it with advantages. But whatever he felt at the time, he did do the dive. There were two obvious dangers. The king would be standing with his back to Hamlet. Olivier, in his flight, had to avoid catching the right side of the king's encrusted crown with his right eye, and at the same time his sword had to pass over the king's left shoulder avoiding the king's left eye. It didn't matter what happened after that, since the shot was entirely of his passage through the air. When these dangers became apparent to Basil Sydney, who was playing the king, he firmly said it would be better if he had a stand-in. A professional strong man called George Crawford was decked in the king's robes and Olivier made his flying leap. 'In the following second and a half everything worked like a dream – in fact like the dream I had so often rehearsed to myself. The landing was just right, my king fell back quite beautifully. . . The one brave moment of my life was over.' The strong man was knocked out, but Olivier got away unhurt. He was proud of the adventure. When he came to write his autobiography he devoted two thirds of his entire account of the film of *Hamlet* to this leap, which provided one and a half seconds of film.[22]

That final scene was filmed in November, and then the cutting and editing began. The total cost was £573,829, well over budget, and this at a time when Rank had not yet broken even on *Henry V*. Olivier earned £50,000 during the shooting. By 1950 the film was in profit, and by 1951 LOP had received another £120,701 as Olivier's share of those profits. The combined salaries of the rest of the cast amounted to £107,728.[23]

Hamlet took twice as much at the box office as *Henry V*, and much of this came from the United States. Anthony Bushell, Olivier's friend and a director of LOP, screened it for American buyers and told Olivier what happened. 'At Rank's order we showed the rough dubbed print to his Hollywood partners in crime. They were a choice lot – names of Benjamin, Seidleman, Blumberg and another. Their comments about the trailer were, "Not *Sir* Laurence?". . . They laughed uproariously at 'a fair thought to lie between maid's legs' but were otherwise silent; and at the end were quite touchingly enthusiastic. I gave them every sort of lead to criticism – asked what they would like to cut and tried all ways to get what might be the Hollywood commercial angle on it, but there was nothing but the most warm-hearted praise. Mr Blumberg got his crack in first, 'A knighthood is not enough!" They thought Wooland [as Horatio] a knockout, were very impressed with Herlie and lyrical about Simmons. We thought of taking a sound track of their comments and sending it to Rank and Davis [Rank's managing director] as an example of what to say after viewing distinguished pictures. Then a useful constructive criticism was that they could not understand the ghost narrative.' Bushell also showed the film to George Cukor, who 'quite independent from the other stiffs' said he found the ghost difficult too, so it was redubbed.[24]

In spite of the Americans' laughter, the Hays Office objected to Hamlet's line to Ophelia about lying between maid's legs as 'unacceptably blunt' for a US audience and it was deleted.[25] The New York takings were beyond the distributors' wildest dreams. 'This is a funny thing,' wrote Two Cities' US representative, '– in the Negro houses, particularly in Harlem, the business was best of all. No one could quite figure it out. The only answer we have had thus far is that the Negroes went and were astounded by the ghost, beyond all else. That is what the surveys seem to show.'[26]

The critics were not unanimous in their praise. The American James Agee, who wrote film scripts and novels as well as criticism, said that a man who could do for Shakespeare what Olivier was doing was among the more valuable men of his time. Eric Bentley, whose reputation was almost as high, thought on the other hand that the film had no style and was simply grandiose in the academic manner. But whatever else it might have been, the film was not academic. Olivier's principal concern was to make the story *clear*. And whatever anyone thought of it, the film introduced a whole generation to the play and to Shakespeare. For most it was the first, and for many the only, Shakespeare they ever saw.[27]

The film's English premiere in May 1947 was attended by the King and Queen and by Princess Elizabeth. Olivier was by then touring on the other side of the world but, as with *Henry V*, he made sure that the projectionists had their instructions. He got one of Two Cities' executives to tip them five pounds and to send a fake telegram of thanks purporting to come from him. They were flattered, thanked him for his generous gesture, said it had been an honour to project *Hamlet* in the presence of the Royal Family, and promised to continue giving his film a good showing.[28]

Olivier's mind was set on an Oscar, and while he was making

the film he insisted on being photographed in Hamlet's costume carrying the Oscar he had received for *Henry V.* That was before he gave it to Del. 'This,' he said, 'made everyone think that I had the Oscar for *Hamlet* and I seriously believe that when it came along it was because of this foregone conclusion in the atmosphere.[29] *Hamlet* did win four Oscars, one for Best Picture, one for Olivier as Best Actor, one for Roger Furse's sets, and another for Carmen Dillon's art direction. Rank wrote Olivier a letter of mercenary congratulation. He had listened to the Oscar presentations on the radio. 'While the envelope was being torn open I thought that if *Hamlet* is on the paper inside the envelope that means at least a million dollars to be shared between you and me.' For Christmas 1948 the grateful Rank sent him the gift of a desk diary, with his name stamped on the front in gilt lettering and misspelled as LAWRENCE OLIVIER.[30]

16

God and the Angel

AT ABOUT THE TIME the filming and editing of *Hamlet* was completed, Olivier and Richardson attended a meeting to arrange an engagement between the Old Vic company as it existed and the joint committee of the proposed but non-existent National Theatre. Not a penny of government money had yet been voted to build a National Theatre, but a Bill was due to be introduced into the House of Commons in November 1947.[1] The idea was that a notional committee would stand a better chance of screwing funds out of a reluctant government if it were betrothed to the real Old Vic which put on real plays. That was the view of Oliver Lyttelton, who had been a member of Churchill's war cabinet and was now chairman of the notional committee, and of Lord Esher, who was chairman of the Old Vic. Olivier and Richardson went along with it.

On the walk home afterwards they told each other how pleased Lilian Baylis would have been by what had just been accomplished when Richardson suddenly said, 'Of course, you know, don't you, that all very splendid as it is, it'll be the end of us. You do realise that?'

'Why?' asked Olivier.

'Well, I mean it won't be our dear, friendly, semi-amateurish Old Vic any more; it'll be of government interest now with some appointed intendant swell at the top, not our sweet old friendly governors eating out of our hands and doing what we tell them. They're not going to stand for a couple of actors bossing the place around any more. We shall be out, old cockie.'[2]

This was prescient. But for the moment it did not prevent Olivier
from dreaming up grand plans, telling Richardson they ought to
create two companies, so that one could be touring England and
the other playing at the Old Vic. 'And maybe we could breed finally
into three companies, and another one could be touring America,
and we could have a proper little empire. . . I'll get together a
company and I'll go to Australia for the best part of a year and I
promise you they will be a decent company by the time I come
back. It will be respectable and worthy of being called one of the
National Theatre companies, I promise you that.'[3]

This is one answer to the astonished question Sam Goldwyn is
reported to have asked Olivier: 'Why are you, the greatest actor
in the world, taking a touring company to Australia of all places?'
It does now seem strange that Olivier, Vivien Leigh, and the Old
Vic should have spent ten months in Australia. The tour was a
grand gesture of showing the flag in an empire which still just
existed. It was in part organised by the British Council, a quasi-
governmental organisation which promoted Britain abroad, and
was subsidised with quasi-governmental money. A tour of the
United States and Canada, in half the time, would have made more
sense and more money, but Australia it was. The tour had already
been delayed. It should have started in the late autumn of 1947.
Olivier's story is that, so soon after the war, shipping space was
still a problem and no boat could be found until February to take
the whole company. Guthrie maintained that Olivier had postponed
it because of delays over *Hamlet*.[4]

Throughout January 1947 the company rehearsed in London. All
was not well between Olivier and Vivien. Martin Battersby, who
was acting as assistant to Cecil Beaton with the costumes, observed
them coming into the rehearsal room looking daggers at each other,
obviously having argued like mad all through a meal. She was playing
Lady Anne in *Richard III*. He was directing and thought she should
fall off her chair at such and such a point; she said it was right out
of character. 'L.O. bore it for a while and then said through clenched
teeth, "The Lady Anne will fall off her chair if I have to bloody
well push her off myself."' Battersby thought that on the whole she
showed she was ideally cast as Scarlett O'Hara.[5]

Before he left Olivier received a letter from Gordon Craig, the seventy-five-year old son of Ellen Terry, then living in Paris. 'The company can count itself lucky and proud to be under you, and tell 'em so from me for they have a chance of a lifetime. I know all this is "the obvious" but one is so apt to overlook the obvious. I was under Irving, so I know. We hadn't the faintest realisation of what luck was ours – copying his few faults was all we could manage to do. You in your quiet way will say you are not Irving. That's true today – tomorrow you may equal him – the day after you may surpass him. It rests with you.'[6]

The company went by sea, from Liverpool. The night before the voyage the Oliviers threw a party at Durham Cottage for seventy friends, including Richardson and Danny Kaye, who was performing at the Palladium and whom they had known since 1939 in New York. They had a merry time. Richardson left very late without his overcoat but covered in whitewash from the garden wall. After only three hours' sleep they were called at eight, said goodbye to Vivien's Siamese cat New, which was named after the theatre, and went off to Euston. There they were seen off by the Australian High Commissioner and the stationmaster in a top hat. At Liverpool they boarded the liner *Corinthic*, to be greeted in their cabin by masses of flowers and a hundred telegrams.

A well-wisher had presented Olivier with a large leather-bound notebook with the words 'My Trip Abroad' on the cover. He did fill in his name, address, by whom he was accompanied, and the names of the places at which he and Vivien would call – Las Palmas, Cape Town, Fremantle, Adelaide and so on. It was done as diligently as he had listed the ports of the British Empire in his school books at St Edwards. Of the first night out he wrote, 'Restless night, hit rough weather in middle of night, heard later it was 2.30, apparently beginning of Atlantic off Cornish coast. Woke several times, Baba too, finally decided to wake 10.30 with ear badly bruised by pillow.'

He kept up the diary entries, for the most part in a curiously flat way, quite unlike his letters, but there are a few flashes of irritation. On the second night he slept, 'after some restless start-ups in dutiful response to Baba's groans'. And on the fourth night there is a hint of his exasperation at Vivien's habitual wish to stay up all

night and keep everyone else up with her. 'Tonight at dinner-at-
the-captain's-table Baba turned to me suddenly with an alarmingly
wild look and said, "Tonight I should like to play dominoes!" I have
left them up there playing Bingo. . . I console myself by going to
bed with the most beautiful stiff-neck in the world.'

He also suffered from a burning pain like a white-hot needle in
his right toe, which the doctor said was not gout though it later
turned out that it was. The passage was not a rest. He rehearsed
the company every day in a dining room. They saw the coast of
North Africa, the Cape Verde Islands, flying fish off Sierra Leone,
landed briefly at Madeira, stayed sightseeing at Cape Town for two
days, and arrived at Perth after two months' passage to find the
temperature was almost one hundred degrees.[7]

At a performance in the presence of the Lieutenant Governor of
Western Australia, Olivier decided to be very royal and play six
bars of 'God Save the King' at the beginning and have the company
sing the whole anthem at the end. The performance was in a cinema
and Olivier, making a speech, could not resist saying he was glad
of this; to bring a play there was like reclaiming land from the sea.
Olivier and Vivien got on well with the company, who called them
God and the Angel. But the tour, as it went on, became exhausting.
They gave 179 performances, many in vast cinemas, and often to
audiences who had rarely or never seen a stage play. The applause
was warm, but everywhere the hospitality was so kind as to be
oppressive. Olivier was expected to make speeches in support of a
Food for Britain appeal. Three years after the war food was still
rationed in England; even bread, which never had been in wartime.
He was obliged, in effect, to ask for food parcels, but was then riled
by reporters' questions which began, 'Now that England is finished,
Sir Laurence, what do you think about. . . ?'[8]

The Old Vic received its first cool reception in Melbourne, one
newspaper saying, 'We have better Richard III's here in Melbourne.'
As one of Olivier's duties was to talent-scout, he thought that
sounded very promising and made enquiries. He discovered that
there were no professional actors in the city. But he and Vivien
were treated everywhere as if they were on a royal visit and this
got too much at times. 'For grand balls and any big occasion a

speech was always expected, but even at small gatherings someone would toast the King in a cup of tea and one was on, replying to the toast apparently on behalf of the King.' By the time the tour was halfway through they were overtired.[9] He gave up making entries in the tour diary. There is not a word after Melbourne.

It was there that Olivier met Peter Hiley, who stayed with him for many years, virtually as his aide-de-camp, and is still one of his executors and a family trustee. His father had been general manager of New Zealand Railways and had advised on railways in India and Southern Rhodesia. The young Hiley was an Etonian who had gone on to Grenoble University and had served with the Intelligence Corps in the war. In 1948 he was with the British Council in Australia, looking after the social side of the Old Vic tour. He was twenty-six. He had seen Olivier's *Macbeth* and *Henry V* at the Old Vic in 1937. In Australia he fell for Olivier and Vivien's charm, thinking her the most beautiful woman he had ever met, and they in turn took to him and roped him into the family of the tour.

Olivier and Vivien had their ups and downs. Some of the ups were in Melbourne, at the Collins Hotel, where one note she left for him reads:

Sir Laurence Olivier MA Tufts
Now get on with your supper
Stop yer chatter
Don't get yerselves plastered
AND COME QUICK TO YER GIRL — LOVE
Red on mantelpiece — Chablis on ice.[10]

It was at Melbourne too that he learned that the marriage of the National Theatre and Old Vic had, against all reasonable expectation, proved fecund. The National Theatre Bill had passed into law, and the government had promised money, 'subject to such conditions as the Treasury may think fit'. He wrote to Esher, 'I wonder if you would accept a tiny note of warmth and appreciation from the southern hemisphere about the cool million that has miraculously descended on us all from governmental skies. . . Heartfelt personal congratulations upon it.' To which Esher modestly replied,

'I was delighted to receive your charming letter. I put a great many months of tact and tenacity into extracting from the Treasury the building necessary to crown your great profession, and I hope that everything will go well.' It took the Treasury fifteen years to think fit and produce the promised million, but that was not foreseen.[11] After Melbourne and Hobart the next stop was Sydney, where the company stayed for two months. Here Olivier gave a demonstration of charm and will which was witnessed by Trader Faulkner, an Australian whose mother had been with the Diaghilev ballet. He was engaged for a walk-on part in *Richard III* at the Tivoli, which was an old variety house. Olivier arrived in a Savile Row suit, before the first rehearsal, and was told there was trouble. There were painted backcloths which had to go up and come down rapidly for the scene changes and Mario, the chief technician, saying he didn't want to know these stuff-eyed Poms, had climbed into the flies and refused to come down. Olivier walked across the stage to the foot of the Jacob's ladder and called up, in a near-perfect Australian accent, 'Mario?'

'Yees.'

'I'm Larry. I'm your new boss. I want a word with you.'

Down came Mario, reluctantly. 'Sir Laurence?'

'No no, Larry'll do. Mario, I'm in trouble. They never got it right at the bloody New Theatre. Never got that scenery up and down on cue. Can you help me?'

'Oh yeah yeah, Sir Laurence – Larry.'

'Look, could we go and have a beer?'

'Yeah yeah, Larry.'

'*Richard III* is a real old melodrama. Speed is essential, the timing of those cloths. You're the expert up there.'

'Larry, you leave it to me, mate.'[12]

In Sydney, on a day when he had two performances of Richard to give, Olivier received a letter from Lord Esher telling him that the board had decided not to renew his contract, or Richardson's, or Burrell's, after the end of the 1948–9 season. The Old Vic could no longer be run 'by men, however able, who have other calls upon their time and talent'. They would be replaced by a full-time administrator.

The Oliviers: Kim, Mums, and Fahv

The Olivier family was much given to nicknames. Young Laurence was Kim before he insisted on being called Larry

1 LAURENCE with his mother Agnes in 1915, at the age of seven. He always said that no photograph revealed her true loveliness. She died aged forty-eight, when he was twelve, and he revered her memory

2 As MARIA (below) in *Twelfth Night*, aged eleven, at All Saints Choir School, famous for its singing and its Christmas plays

3 HIS FATHER, the Rev Gerard Olivier, a stern High Church clergyman called Father in his parish and Fahv by his family

Early days and school plays

4 AGED ELEVEN (below) at All Saints, Margaret Street choir school, dressed as a matador for a Christmas entertainment

5 AGED THIRTEEN, playing Katherina in *The Taming of the Shrew*, at All Saints. In 1922 he played this role again with the school at the Shakespeare birthday celebrations at Stratford-upon-Avon

6 SIR SYDNEY OLIVIER, Laurence's uncle, as Governor of Jamaica. In 1924 he became Secretary of State for India and was created the first Lord Olivier

Two seasons with the Birmingham Rep

In 1926-28 the young Olivier acted twenty-three parts with the Birmingham Repertory Company

7 AS HAROLD (left) in Tennyson's unactable play of that name, 1928

8 FRONT OF HOUSE picture (below) of the rising young actor

9 AS MATT SIMON (bottom) in *The Well of the Saints*, 1926, aged 19

10 PEGGY ASHCROFT and Olivier, aged 19, in *Bird in Hand*

Beau Geste, marriage, and first films

11 As Beau Geste (right), 1929, in a Basil Dean epic expected to run for ever but which folded after five weeks. To take it, Olivier gave up the lead in *Journey's End*, R C Sherriff's war play, which did run for years

12 Private Lives (below) Olivier's first play with Noël Coward. It gave him the money to marry. Here he is with Adrienne Allen, Coward, and Gertrude Lawrence. He went with the play to Broadway, where his new wife Jill Esmond took Miss Allen's part

13 Wedding to Jill Esmond, in July 1930. The best man is his close friend Denys Blakelock

14 Olivier's first film, *The Temporary Widow*, was made in 1930 in Berlin with English and German casts. Here (left) he shakes hands with his German counterpart

15 His first English film (above), was *Too Many Crooks*, a quota quickie

First time in Hollywood

OLIVIER SPENT most of 1931 and 1932 in Hollywood, enjoying 'the lick of luxury of those lush valleys' but making only three films in two years

16 IN HIS FIRST FILM, *Friends and Lovers*, a melodrama with Adolphe Menjou and Erich von Stroheim, he played an English officer in India (left) for $700 a week and was told he would be a star in a year. But the film died like a dog

17 HIS THIRD FILM was *Westward Passage* with Ann Harding, a star who was kind to the inexperienced Olivier. He admired her. In a hideous studio cut-out (above) he offers her a flower

18 OLIVIER'S STUDIO publicised him as an actor destined for 'he-man roles', and decided to build up his body. The original caption to this studio hand-out picture says that he added twenty pounds of muscle under the guidance of Carl Freemanson, coach to the Swedish Olympic team

Matinee idol
in London
and New York

19 OLIVIER SWASHBUCKLING for
West End audiences in *Theatre Royal*
in 1934, a satire on the Barrymores,
the most famous American theatrical
family. Olivier was so athletic that
his sword once flew from his hand
and struck his producer, Marie
Tempest, on the breast. At another
performance, leaping down the
staircase, he broke his ankle and was
obliged to retired hurt

20 WITH HIS WIFE JILL ESMOND on
Broadway in *The Green Bay Tree*,
1933. He played a man adopted by a
rich homosexual, and loathed the
play, but it brought him many
splendid notices

21 WITH HELEN SPENCER (above)
in *The Rats of Norway*, 1933. She
probably became his mistress, wrote
to him freely, warned him about
Vivien Leigh, and remained his
close friend for more than thirty
years

Romeo: first leading part in Shakespeare

22 OLIVIER had not acted in Shakespeare for seven years until Gielgud invited him to join his company in 1935, alternating with him the roles of Romeo and Mercutio. This portrait of Olivier as Romeo, by Harold Knight, remained his favourite and he left it to the National Theatre

23 HIS JULIET (below left) was Peggy Ashcroft, who wrote to him, 'It's lovely doing it with you – Hell! Let's enjoy ourselves tonight.'

24 HENRY AINLEY, a classical romantic actor with whom Olivier appeared in *As You Like It*, his first Shakespeare film, and whose splendid voice he greatly admired

Vivling and Larry

25 FIRE OVER ENGLAND (above) their first film together, in 1936, when those on the set believed they were lovers, but they were not

26 HAMLET AND OPHELIA at Elsinore in 1937, (right) when they had already planned to elope on their return to England

27 RIVER TRIP (below) to publicise their film *Twenty One Days*, when they were living together. On this trip Vivien announced that she was determined to play Scarlett O'Hara

Hollywood again

28 THE DIVORCE OF LADY X, advertised as 'slightly scandalous' and 'vaguely risqué', was Olivier's first colour film. It was made in English studios and released in November 1937, at the end of a year in which he had played *Hamlet* and *Henry V* at the Old Vic, eloped with Vivien Leigh, and was about to begin his second season at the Vic with *Macbeth* and *Coriolanus*

29 WUTHERING HEIGHTS, Olivier's second film with Merle Oberon, took him to Hollywood again and away from Vivien, who followed him after three weeks and, by chance and against long odds, was offered the part of Scarlett

The Star-Making Days

30 JAMES ABBE JR made this study of Olivier and Vivien on the set of *Gone With the Wind* early in 1939, after Olivier had finished *Wuthering Heights* and before he left Hollywood to play in *No Time For Comedy* on Broadway. It was the height of their absorption in each other, and Olivier wrote a long series of adoring letters to her during their separation (see opposite page, top)

Theatre. 10.5. Short interval

Darling sweet Its like me to forget to put in the carnation in this mornings letter isn't it?! but here it is — the one ... ... I am wearing it ... ... but I'll pop it in & Here is the ... ... (mine) (the Mores will arrive one day!) But I ...

31 CARNATION LETTERS. To remind himself of Vivien in Hollywood, Olivier wore carnations in his underwear throughout his Broadway run of *No Time For Comedy* in the spring and summer of 1939. Here, writing a hurried letter during a short interval, he sends her that day's flower

32 REBECCA. Olivier had wanted Vivien as his leading lady in Rebecca, shot late in 1939. Selznick decided that a women who had just played the spirited Scarlett in *Gone With the Wind* was wrong for the part of Max de Winter's timid second wife, and chose Joan Fontaine instead

Admiral Nelson and Lieutenant Olivier

33 IN 1940, still stuck in Hollywood but wanting to return to England, Olivier played Nelson to Vivien's Emma in a propaganda film, *Lady Hamilton*, produced by Alexander Korda (above). It was splendid hokum and became Churchill's favourite film

34 BACK IN ENGLAND in early 1941, Larry volunteered as a navy pilot and became Lieutenant Olivier of the Fleet Air Arm, but flew ancient planes and saw no action

Henry V and Richard III

35 HENRY V (above) was intended as another propaganda film, but it changed Olivier's life. He starred, produced, directed, procured nails for the horses' hooves, and commanded the army of actors and extras who shot the action scenes not in wartime England, which was impossible, but on an estate near Dublin, in neutral Ireland

36 GIVEN LEAVE to re-establish the Old Vic company in a bombed London, Olivier played Richard III (left) and breathed the sweet smell of success, which he said reminded him of seaweed, or oysters. It was a taste he never forgot

37 SPRING SUNSHINE. Olivier, Vivien, and her Siamese cat lie on a blanket in the open air in the late spring of 1945, a few days before the end of the war. She was exhausted but had defied her doctor's advice and was about to open in Thornton Wilder's *Skin of our Teeth*

38 VICTORY TOUR. Olivier and Ralph Richardson as honorary army lieutenants during a six-week tour of Europe with the Old Vic company in 1945. They played at Brussels, Belsen, Hamburg, and Paris, where Olivier learned from friends that Vivien had incipient tuberculosis

What Richardson had prophesied had rapidly come about. The same Lord Esher who had written to Olivier less than three months before about the new building which would crown his great profession was now dismissing him. 'It was so incredible a surprise,' wrote Olivier, 'that, as in a farce, laughter was a reflex action. At this precise time I tore a cartilage in my right knee; my limp in *Richard III*, in constantly fatigued conditions, had set up a weakness in the 'straight' leg, and one evening in the dance at the end of *School* it just went. Why is it that in troubled times one's body feels called upon to jump on the bandwagon?'[13] Hiley saw that Olivier was deeply wounded by Esher's letter, offended that anyone should do that to him and Richardson, and angry as well as hurt. This gave him a spurt of energy to fight back and he began sending telegrams in all directions.[14]

He cabled Richardson, who was in Hollywood filming *The Heiress* with Olivia de Havilland:

DEAR BOY PRIVATE AND CONFIDENTIAL COMMUNICATION FROM OLD VIC MAKES MANY CHANGES IN FUTURE OUTLOOK.[15]

To Burrell he cabled, O ME I SEE THE ENDING OF OUR HOUSE, which is a quotation from *Richard III*.[16] From London his friend and colleague George Devine wrote commiserating, condemning 'clandestine methods which have been borrowed from international politics, and are inexcusable'. The decision to get rid of Olivier and Richardson was known in theatrical London, but it was not publicly announced until the company returned to London, and that was another four months. Olivier saw his dismissal, while he was on active service in the colonies, as a betrayal. Guthrie saw it differently and did not bother to hide his opinion. 'In spite of enormous houses, no money had been saved. In less than two years it began to be apparent that the two stars must decide either to be actors, making films and radio appearances, going to America, Australia and so on, or else to be managers of the Old Vic. They tried, and failed, to have the cake and eat it.'[17] This was all very well, but it had always been understood that Olivier and Richardson were to have time off to film. The Old Vic could not have had them on any other terms. In 1947 Olivier did *Hamlet*. In 1948 it was Richardson's turn to go to Hollywood. As for going to Australia 'and so on', Olivier was there in the service of the Old Vic.

Before he left England, Olivier had authorised his sister Sybille to write his biography. As early as 1934, when he was in New York in *The Green Bay Tree*, he had received approaches from publishers, which he had always declined.[18] But in 1948 Sybille and her husband, Gerald Day, set to work and by July had written 59,000 words. At first it was intended that the book should appear as by G.W.L. Day, who had already published three books of light verse; a biography of Heath Robinson, the cartoonist and satirist of machinery; and a disguised account of Sybille's earlier madness. The publisher however preferred the name Olivier on the title page, and so Day's name was crossed out and that of Sybille Olivier substituted. The writing anyway was mostly hers. She knew her brother and her style is distinctive and more lively than her husband's. She dedicated the book 'to any future biographer'.

By 1 August the typescript was with Olivier in Sydney.[19] Its 229 pages bear many of his pencilled marginal comments. He corrected her title, which she had taken from *Hamlet*. *He Who Plays the King* became *He* That *Plays the King*. Where Sybille described Fahv turning on the infant Larry with a ferocious glare and a shout, he wrote, 'A bit tough?' She wrote that the Olivier children were hardly ever whipped, and he corrected her: 'I was quite often – always for lying.' When she described Fahv as distressed at their mother's funeral but at the same time enjoying the drama of it, he wrote, 'Steady!' When she said Larry at first found Jill 'exactly the person' he wanted, he amended this to 'just the girl'. She said that their bed at Cheyne Walk was six-feet wide, and he changed this to 'seven'. When Sybille wrote that he was at first reasonably proud of his son Tarquin but that his intense desire for a family had faded because he was immersed in other things, he let this pass without comment. When she wrote of Vivien in 1937 that no portrait showed her delicious vitality and happiness 'at this time', he commented, 'Sounds as if she was hatched-faced now.' He put a cross beside her mention that he and Vivien had got colitis from drinking the water at Nay in the Pyrennees, 'a village he had insisted on visiting to search for records of the Olivier family'. He corrected her notion that it was gangsters who scared him into giving ticket holders their money back after the New York *Romeo and Juliet.* When she wrote that he was not a good pilot, he scribbled at the side, 'Excellent pilot'.

Olivier's pencilled notes show he read the typescript carefully, but then he always did everything with care. He even added personal details. When Sybille mentioned the party of cockneys the young Oliviers had met on the houseboat, with a gramophone, he wrote in the margin that one girl's name was Bertha, that he felt her breasts in the punt, and that the tune 'Whispering' was still nostalgic for him. Then he decided he wanted nothing to do with the book. Perhaps the trouble was that Sybille wrote with a natural liveliness, was candid about her first and disastrous marriage, and gave too vivid a picture of Olivier's own childhood and youth. Four days after he received the typescript he cabled Cecil Tennant that he was very distressed by it. To Sybille he sent a long cable.

'Darling please forgive me but I must implore you not to publish biography as it is now. . . I will make up to you darling any financial sacrifice. Vivien myself and disinterested friend have read and feel most strongly though much of your writing has lovely original sparkle too much of it involving peoples feelings dangerously inaccurate and the balance of the work requires very careful reconsideration. I would feel very unhappy if brought out in present state and would feel bound dissociate myself from it in ways that would only hurt and discredit you. So dearly sorry darling if this distressing you and Gerald after so much work.'[20]

It is difficult to see how the book could have discredited Sybille, and if Olivier had dissociated himself from it this could only have attracted publicity. But it undoubtedly caused him anxiety and he cabled Tennant a second time, asking him to take Sybille to lunch and talk finance, since she was much out of pocket, and adding: SUGGEST FROM COMPANY'S VIEW GOOD AND PROPER BUY OFF UNFORTUNATE PUBLISHER. Things were not settled easily. The publisher, Herbert Joseph, was not sympathetic and Tennant, having met him, told Olivier, 'If we cannot get him to call off publication, we have to face the fact that we cannot prevent it. I think one would have a right of action if there was anything actionable in the book, but I do not imagine you want to engage in family litigation.'[21]

In the end Olivier had his way and the book did not appear. But in Sydney he was not a happy man. His dismissal had taken him quite by surprise. He was dog-tired and injured. His sister's book offended him. Vivien's cat, New, had been run over at Durham Cottage. She had suffered from bronchitis and was not fully recovered, but was still keeping Olivier awake into the small hours. At one hotel two members of the company, Terence Morgan and his wife, had a room next to the Oliviers and shared a balcony. 'Vivien,' said Morgan, 'never went to bed. She was out on the balcony drinking champagne. There was a huge terrace and the French windows opened on to the terrace. . .and they talked until three in the morning. We couldn't keep up. We wanted to go to sleep.'[22]

Olivier did have an apparent stroke of luck in Sydney. He now knew that the Old Vic company would no longer be his to direct after the end of the 1948–9 season in London, and was preparing to set up himself as actor-manager. He would have to assemble his own company. He was visited one day by a young man called Peter Finch, whom he had heard highly praised, and accepted an invitation to go and see him one lunchtime in a shortened version of Molière's *Imaginary Invalid*. The twenty-four-year-old Finch played Argan with panache; Olivier thought it a brilliant performance in as expert a production as could be imagined, and cabled Tennant to put him under contract.[23]

In September, having been in Australia six months, the company flew from Brisbane to New Zealand for the last five weeks of the tour. The two accounts of Vivien on this flight are apparently contradictory, but equally credible and very likely both true. She was like that. One account has her out of breath and needing to be given oxygen; the other has her bright as ever. One member of the company remembered: 'Ten hours sitting up all night after two performances. I was so ill. And in the morning at about six o'clock Vivien floated in and said "Oh, look at the sunrise." I didn't want to look at the sunrise, and I suddenly saw this vision coming down the aisle in a pale blue negligee. We were all creased. Everything was creased.'[24] From New Zealand Vivien wrote to Holman, with whom she remained on the friendliest of terms, telling him the quiet of the country was unearthly but that the New Zealanders were much more couth and better mannered than the Australians. She wrote on paper headed 'The Old Vic tour of Australia and New Zealand', crossed out 'Australia' and added a note: 'Over, God be praised.'[25]

They racketed around the North and South Islands – Auckland, Christchurch, Dunedin, Wellington – seeing nothing of the country, though Olivier did tell a reporter that they once flew low enough to see some Canterbury lambs 'quite distinctly'. It rained. One day with Vivien he told another reporter, 'You may not realise it, but you are looking at two walking corpses.' Then his knee, which he had injured in Sydney, gave out in Christchurch. He performed on crutches for a week and then went into hospital to have the cartilage removed.[26]

Still in hospital the day before their ship sailed, he dictated a long letter to Cecil Beaton about the costumes for *School for Scandal*, one of the tour plays with which he would finish off the last part of his last Old Vic season in London. He began by saying the production was his 'baby of all time' and that he desperately hoped it would be Beaton's too, and then demanded what amounted to a redesign. Lady Teazle's party dress, he said, looked like a telephone cover and her jewellery elderly and heavy; Lady Sneerwell's ball dress was like a dark brown tea cosy and her day dress, 'to be bestially frank', a bit common; Maria's outdoor costume, dear boy, was drab and her hat unbecoming; and Snake's costume was quite out of keeping with the rest, 'with some bad snakes painted in watercolour on dark green serge'. Having written quite enough to infuriate the touchy Beaton, he concluded, 'This letter has been written in great haste, and does not convey to you one thousandth part of the brilliant success that your work has been and how gloriously happy a little show the whole thing is. I am, dear fellow, so very thrilled with it, and long for us to work together on it just a tiny bit more to make it all quite perfect. You, Sheridan, Handel and me – quelle combination – particularly with little Puss to crown our cake. Vivien and Co. go on board tonight, and I am to be hoisted in my stretcher at dawn tomorrow, over the side, like Cleopatra and her carpet.'[27]

Just before seven the next morning an ambulance drove on to the quayside in the unceasing rain, Olivier was placed in a stretcher in a canvas sling while a girl from the crowd reverently held an umbrella over his head, and a crane swung him aboard. 'I soared into the sky, smoothly floating over the side of the ship and gently down, as delicately as if upon an angel's wing; I landed sweetly upon the topmost deck.' He made a good exit.[28]

Olivier was returning to England to sort out with the governors of the Old Vic what he called 'murder most foul, or, at least, problems most fraught'. The New Zealand surgeon had ordered him not to move without being carried for the first two weeks of the voyage. Vivien, seeking entertainment, openly flirted with Dan Cunningham, a young actor, until Olivier was driven to plead that she should not make her flirtation so obvious. He really couldn't see that it was justified that he should be so humiliated. 'To my great surprise, she took it all very calmly and sweetly; she saw that she had been thoughtless and assured me I wouldn't have cause for embarrassment any more. That was lovely as far as it went, how far was that, I wondered, though my confidence in the everlasting certainty of our passion was not for shaking yet.' His knee bled painfully and swelled under its heavy cast until the ship's doctor sliced the plaster off. The wounded Olivier then rehearsed the company relentlessly all the passage home.[29]

As they approached England, aware that Vivling would miss her cat, New, and anxious to console her with a replacement, he sent a ship's telegram to Cecil Tennant in London.

PLEASE IMPRESS WELFORD [LO'S SECRETARY] VITAL
IMPORTANCE SIAMESE KITTEN AT DURHAM STOP PLEASE MAKE
APPOINTMENT ROBERT BURNS ORTHOPAEDIC SURGEON DAY OF
ARRIVAL LOVE FROM BOTH.[30]

17

Living Like Royals

WHEN HE RETURNED FROM Australia Olivier, who had of course been dismissed, played out the agreed game of announcing that he was resigning from the co-directorship of the Old Vic at the end of the current season. Richardson and Burrell did the same. Then he got on with completing his last half-season, with *Richard III* again, with the redesigned *School for Scandal*, and with Sophocles' *Antigone*. He and Vivien had made three films together and had acted together in New York in the disastrous *Romeo and Juliet* of 1940, but that production of *School for Scandal* was the first time they had ever appeared together on the English stage. In London, in January 1949, their first night was a social triumph. They took six curtain calls. Later in the run the Princesses Elizabeth and Margaret and the Duke of Edinburgh came to the show and the Oliviers joined their party afterwards at the Café de Paris.[1] *Antigone*, which had been rehearsed on the boat coming back from Australia, was directed by Olivier and done at the suggestion if not the insistence of Vivien. He tried to dissuade her, but she wanted to play a tragic heroine. The critics on the whole thought she should not have done.[2]

Beaton and the Oliviers finally fell out over *School for Scandal*. Beaton was not too offended by Olivier's critical letter from New Zealand to go and see a performance at the New Theatre. He was mightily pleased with his own sets, his own costumes, and himself, and wrote in his diary that never before in the theatre had he so unrestrainedly enjoyed the fruits of his own work. He described

himself as wreathed in rapturous smiles. Afterwards he went round
to see Vivien and was met with a view of her back. 'She did not
turn round to greet me. I kept up a hollow form of flattery, filled
with green room jargon, in praise of her performance and appearance. Vivien's eyes of steel now stared at herself as she rubbed a
slime of dirty cold cream, a blending of rouge, eye black, and white
foundation over her face. Not one word did she say about my contribution to the evening.' Then he went to Olivier's dressing room
where he 'let forth an avalanche of praise' but received no word in
reply. The Oliviers were, said Beaton, out of his life for ever.[3] Except
that, ever afterwards, he never let go an opportunity to revile them.

Olivier's last three productions made a good end to his time with
the Old Vic, and he had besides brought back a profit of £40,000
from the Australian tour. Many were unhappy at his going just at the
time when the government, through the Arts Council, had started to
subsidise the Old Vic. If Olivier and Richardson had done wonders
without the £30,000 a year now promised, what could they not have
done with it?[4] There is a story, which surfaced only when Olivier
wrote it in his autobiography more than thirty years later, that Lord
Esher, having dismissed the three co-directors – and done it as unfeel-
ingly as he had, when one was in Australia and another in Hollywood
– had then asked Olivier to take over on his own. Olivier said he reeled
at the proposal, nearly fell backwards, and explained that he and his
partners just didn't do things like that to each other. There was not
a hint of this at the time and there is nothing in the surviving papers
to support it. If it had happened he could not have helped telling
Richardson, who never mentioned anything of the kind. What Olivier
suggests is inherently unlikely. Esher and his governors had said they
wanted a man who could devote his full time to the Old Vic, which
could never have been Olivier, and that they would appoint a director
for only a year at a time, which he would never have accepted. And
the man they did appoint to take over was an apparatchik from the
Arts Council, who was as unlike Olivier as they could have found.
Olivier's memory was surely misleading him.[5]

For the first time there was a certain weariness about him. An
impresario saying he spoke for the Egyptian government implored
him to visit Egypt, offering the use of the royal opera house in Cairo

at any time, a grant of £10,000, and the net proceeds. To which Olivier replied, 'We've had a terrible drubbing here with one thing and another; illness, Vivien very nearly killing herself falling downstairs, my old knee effusing, flu, and God knows what.' He said he and Vivien had been away for the better part of a year and were anxious not to stir again for a time because they got so homesick.[6]

Three weeks later he sent Jill a dispirited a letter. For the first time he was disenchanted with acting. He said he had been thinking about Tarquin, who was leaving his preparatory school and about to go to Eton.

'From a father's point of view in dreaming of his son's career I have always found myself greening up with envy of Bronnie [Bronson Albery] as he watches young Donald [his son] stalking about the New and slowly taking over responsibilities. To me there have always seemed few occupations more delightful than administering a theatre with imagination and dignity. I love acting of course terribly in my heart, but it's terribly exhausting, and if one just lacked that peculiar nervous energy necessary for success in the job, or if one just didn't come off for no apparent reason, I think I'd rather be Bronnie Albery than anyone.

'Anyhow I have determined to own a theatre before I die, with the vague idea that Tarkie might like to inherit it – a little shop, a nice little shop – all one's own with polished hand rails and professional staff going on behind the footlights. . . All jolly vague of course – just dreams – I haven't got a bloody theatre yet and probably never will have, but just LO Prods is building gently but surely (I think – hope?) in organisation – pity if it all fluffs out. . .

'The Old Vic was a fine dream you see for old Ralphie and me, as our work could go on, or we could think so. But we've been shaken up from that dream now. I don't know what old Ralphie will do – start his own shop perhaps, he thinks; he's just marking time and getting his breath now, like me.'[7]

Laurence Olivier Productions was certainly building up. There was already Tennant as managing director, and himself and Vivien. Now he recruited his friends Anthony Bushell, Roger Furse, and Alex Korda as directors. Peter Hiley, who had left the British Council and arrived from Australia in April, became company secretary. Peter Finch had come to England on his own initiative. Olivier had made him no promises but in March 1949 gave him a year's contract and put him into *Daphne Laureola*, a new play by James Bridie, opposite Dame Edith Evans.[8] For this Olivier had taken Wyndham's, which was conveniently back to back with the New, where the Old Vic was completing its season. LOP had existed since 1946. Now that Olivier had left the Old Vic it became much more active, exploiting the talents of its two principal assets, Olivier and Vivien Leigh, and taking over the business management of their lives. This was something they both needed. Their tax affairs, for one thing, were in a mess.

While Olivier was in Australia his accountant had received demands from the Inland Revenue for tax dating back to 1939, 1940, and 1941. No surtax had been paid for several years and at least £11,800 was owed for the years up to 1947. In June 1948 Vivien paid the Inland Revenue £6,300, which left £775 in her bank account; she hoped it would be the last large demand. Early in 1949 Olivier scribbled a note to Tennant: 'I got a demand for £10,637 yesterday!!!' Both the Oliviers had earned high fees in years of high taxation. In 1939 the standard rate of income tax was 22.75%. Then the war had to be paid for, and by 1940 the standard rate of income tax had risen to 35%, and by 1945 to 50%. Under the post-war socialist governments levelling became a matter of principle and income tax and surtax made a thorough job of it. Income tax on the first £2,000 earned was at 50%, but after that a surtax was added, making the highest rate payable an absurd 97.5%. This meant that as late as 1950 a person earning £20,000 would, one way and another, have to pay £15,688 of it in income tax.[9] Anyone personally earning a high salary or fees was, willy-nilly, making large donations to the State. But a person could legally arrange his or her affairs in such a manner as to pay the least tax. By 1949 Laurence Olivier or Vivien Leigh did not personally contract to appear in a play or make a film. Laurence Olivier Productions contracted to provide their services. LOP paid Olivier a salary of £7,000 a year and Vivien a salary of £5,000, which was of course much less than they earned for the company. On these salaries they paid income tax and surtax. The company paid tax too, but only on its profits. Great sums which might be lost on plays could be offset against greater sums made on films, and tax paid only on the small remaining profit. And in the conduct of its business LOP could lawfully look after its principal assets, Olivier and Leigh, by paying their justifiable expenses, which in practice meant pretty well the lot. LOP had already been paying the expenses of Durham Cottage, down to the grocer's bills. The company later assumed the running expenses of Notley Abbey and its attendant farm and market garden, and of course the professional expenses of its principals.

How it worked was well expressed by Tennant in one letter. 'Vivien dear,' he began, and then defined what LOP could reasonably pay for:

1) Manicures, hairdressing, and beauty treatments.
2) Massage, medical, and dental bills.
3) Any clothes purchased for parade purposes, that is to say, evening dresses for first nights, afternoon dresses for receptions, and hats and parasols and dresses for Ascot etc. 'Of course these must not be all the clothes you purchase during the year, there must be a reasonable balance left over which you have bought with your own money. Love.'[10]

The sums that Olivier had left for his personal use, after tax, surtax and alimony, were £1,626 in 1947, £1,984 in 1948 and £1,091 in 1949, not a great deal more than a bank manager's salary. But since his clothes, his wines, his motor cars, his travelling expenses, and the upkeep of his houses were all considered to be, in whole or in part, for 'parade purposes', and were paid for by the company, he and Vivien lived the life of royals. In 1949, when Olivier bought a new Bentley, the coachbuilders undertook to fit it with 'best quality twill upholstery covers to the four seats and squabs in the same materials as used for the Daimler cars we recently supplied to His Majesty.'[11]

All the Oliviers' entertainment expenses were paid by the company. In one three-month period forty-two bottles of champagne, sixty bottles of wine and twenty-one bottles of spirits were charged to LOP by Berry Bros, Justerini & Brooks, and Fortnum & Mason. Nor was it any old champagne. Taittinger and Krug 1943 were to the Oliviers' taste. Flowers from Constance Spry were a frequent expense. Many chits for petty cash were signed by Olivier and by Vivien. He would take £5 for tips and taxis, she £5 for tipping in the restaurant and cloakroom at the Dorchester.[12] Twelve yards of taffeta and satin found their way on to the same account. Her clothes were always lavish. When she went to Paris to be fitted at Balmain for costumes for *Anna Karenina* her luggage was lost on the Paris to Calais train and the contents were listed for the insurance claim of £1,061. She had been in France for a visit of two nights. In the lost suitcases were two Stiebel model evening dresses, one black evening dress, three afternoon dresses, two suits, three blouses, four pairs of shoes, and three handbags – and this does not take into account the clothes she was standing up in.[13] In 1949 Olivier possessed and insured fourteen watches, which included a Dresden watch of the eighteenth century, a topaz watch, a pearl ordered enamel watch, and two silver hunters.[14]

Olivier loved Notley's grounds. He planted hundreds of trees. 'Limes, whole avenues of limes. Oaks. Willows, cricket bat willows. Oh, divers flowering trees. I always wanted to: I don't know why. A complete walk, half lime, half nut. Poplars, the tall kind. An orchard of apple trees. My friends and I used to give each other trees. I gave some friends two umbrella pines from Ischia. When it gets known, people give you, oh, jasmine for Christmas.'[15] The avenue of limes and walnut was a third of a mile long. Vivien took a liking to a magnolia tree she had seen in a garden at East Acton on the drive out to Notley from London, and got Peter Hiley to write to the house-owner saying she would like to raise a similar tree, but from seeds rather than cuttings. Were there any pods she could have? She sent a spray of leaves she liked to Sheffield University's botany department, where it was identified as from *acer platanoides*, the Norway spruce. Lemon tree seeds were sent to her with the compliments of a Sydney nurseryman. Olivier tried to sell timber from some of his willows to a maker of cricket bats, but nothing came of it.[16]

More land had been bought to add to the original fifty-six acres at Notley, the orchard extended, and a dairy herd established. Olivier applied to join the Jersey Cattle Society, hoping to use the word Notley as a prefix to the names of his cows. Vivien knew them as

Sabina, Ophelia, Cordelia, Perpetua, and Octavia, and liked to go out and pat them. They were served by the bull Jericho Joshua of Jericho Farm, and produced calves. Hiley asked the Food Office at Aylesbury for a ration of sugar for the Notley beehives, so that they could produce honey. It was all meant to be self-sufficient and LOP, as its articles of association allowed, ran the farm as a business, at LOP's cost. Sir Laurence and Lady Olivier were formally sent small bills – seven shillings for one two-week period – for the fruit and vegetables from the estate which they personally consumed. If they ate with guests, that was business and allowable as a company expense.[17]

Inside the house Vivien decorated and redecorated, wanting a room blue one week and pink the next. For her new bathroom she wanted a canopy over the bath, blue prints on the cupboard doors, and the bath raised so that she could see out of the window while sitting in it. She was famously fastidious and wanted the lavatory pedestal masked from sight by an armchair which could be dropped over it.[18] A cinema for Notley was planned but never built, though rows of proper cinema seats were bought for it. The Post Office was asked what chance there was of the Oliviers acquiring a white telephone instead of an ordinary black one. Vivien continued to acquire an extraordinary collection of paintings. She may have had little left in her bank account after paying taxes but in 1947 she bought three Guardis, including a pair depicting islands near Venice, for £550. In 1949 she added Le Chat by Bonnard, bought for £250. These and works by Boudin, Degas, Veuillard, Sickert, Renoir, Morisot, Lautrec, and Cellini were hung at Durham Cottage and Notley.[19]

The Oliviers entertained, Vivien tirelessly so. Among the frequent guests were Sir Malcolm Sargent, the conductor, and Danny Kaye, Olivier's friend since 1940. He had made a great success with his film The Secret Life of Walter Mitty in 1947, and several times appeared in variety shows at the London Palladium. Another guest was Anne Norwich, daughter-in-law of Lady Diana Cooper, with whom the Oliviers had stayed at the Paris embassy. She later described a visit to Notley: 'Larry was there being very much the clergyman's son carving the roast and saying, you know, "My father always kept the keys to the cellar". . . I thought the house would have been much nicer if his rather more straightforward, stolid English side had been allowed to have more play. Vivien made it, in a way, at times too pretty.' And at Durham Cottage Lady Norwich had an awful feeling of Larry being rather like an unfortunate bull in a china shop. 'I could hardly move for Chelsea objects – it was an almost claustrophobic prettiness that Vivien surrounded herself with.' She said Vivien would talk all through dinner and she got the feeling, as so many others did, that Olivier would very much have liked to call it a day at 11.30 p.m. Of Vivien's beauty there was no doubt. 'She looked exquisite, like the beautiful feline little cat that she was, and she glittered and glowed. . . She had broken her wrist [in a fall on stage] and instead of just leaving the white cast she'd wound a marvellous piece of whispy scarf of the same colour as her dress round the cast and fastened it with a wonderful brooch so that it looked like something.'[20]

Michael Denison and his wife Dulcie Gray went to Notley only once, and never forgot it. 'Vivien was a wonderful hostess when she wasn't ill [but] in her own home she became very autocratic. I mean, you were not allowed to go to bed, however tired you as a guest were, until she was ready. . . We went down there and Viv drove us in the Bentley. She drove extremely well but very, very, very fast. Larry and Dulcie and I were on the back seat and I think her maid was beside her. So that was reasonably hair-raising. We then had a wonderful supper which was waiting for us and all that, then not allowed to go to bed until half past two or three or something like that.' Next morning they found Olivier wandering around, saying Vivien was ill and that he had sent for the doctor, who diagnosed pleurisy. There was a lunch party which included Danny Kaye. The guests went upstairs, had an audience with Vivien in her bedroom, and then quietly left the house. While she was sleeping, Olivier proposed a walk over the fields. The Denisons went with him and returned at dusk. As they came back to the house every light was blazing and there was a sort of hum. It sounded like the Duchess of Richmond's ball on the eve of Waterloo. And there Vivien was, in radiant form, having had a great telephoning marathon and invited all possible friends in for a party which went on until four the next morning. The Denisons woke at about noon the next day feeling twenty years older than the day before. 'How's Viv?' they asked, and Olivier said he thought she was all right. 'And there appeared,' said Denison, 'at the end of this gallery a girl of eighteen in the most beautiful narrow grey and white striped dress with an enormous thing of scarlet roses in her arms. I mean, all the fit people had been demolished and she was the belle of the ball. Pleurisy was forgotten.'[21]

This relentless entertainment continued. To show his guests the way there, Olivier commissioned the Royal Automobile Club to print 1,000 copies of a route map to Notley.[22]

One rare guest at Notley was Olivier's older brother Dickie. After his tea-planting venture in India had failed in the 1930s he had been forced to come home to live for a while with his father and Ibo and to borrow the odd hundred pounds from Larry. His best time was the war, when he distinguished himself in the navy and held the same rank as his brother, but then he fell on hard times. His first marriage had ended in divorce, his second was on the rocks, and he was quite unable to find a job. By 1949 he was obliged to ask for money again, but his letters were addressed not to Larry but to Tennant. He wanted to train at an agricultural college and asked for a loan of £150 to enable him to do this. LOP agreed to pay him £4 a week for the period of his training, in exchange for an option to employ him at a salary of £800 a year as farm manager at Notley. Olivier seems to have written to him only once in 1949, explaining that he had been too busy to answer the telephone when he called. Dickie then asked if he could come to spend Christmas at Notley, and wrote afterwards to say how he had loved it. 'Just like old times, bless you. Thank you so very much, Larry dear.' A few months later he had to ask his brother if he had any old clothes he didn't want, 'such as pyjamas, undies, socks etc. . . Everything is so hellishly expensive to buy.' It would not only have been the expense. Dickie had come out of the navy with little more than his demob suit; new clothes were rationed like everything else and could only be bought with clothing coupons. Olivier replied that he usually clung on to his old clothes while he could, as he found them more useful than new ones, but he sent a parcel. Dickie thanked him. 'Dear old lad . . . I shall enjoy wearing your things, which are always so very nice and of a quality way beyond the reach of my pocket.' When he completed his year's course there was no place for Dickie at Notley, but LOP allowed him £10 a week for three months while he found his feet, and he took a series of unhappy jobs as farm bailiff.[23]

Olivier's brother was struggling and his sister Sybille was back in a mental hospital at Netherne, near Coulsdon in Surrey. She wrote to Larry that she was excellently looked after by a brilliant Dr Freudenberg who, she said, had been one of the big shots in Vienna before the war. She had been given insulin treatment and was happy to stay there as long as they would have her. Her life had been dead wrong for twenty years, a sort of prison, and she swore she would never live with her husband again. Larry wasn't to listen to him, or even to Dickie, who had visited her: 'He was quite sweet when he came to see me though, and was quite relieved to find me peacefully in bed instead of dancing the can-can with straw in my hair.'[24]

In the summer of 1949, after the New Theatre season ended and Olivier was finished with the Old Vic, he and Vivien took a box for four days at Royal Ascot, for which LOP paid. As Olivier remembered it, he and Vivien then seized upon the rest of the year to refloat themselves on the London tide, 'almost violently embracing every kind of activity that profession or society could offer'. He describes in his autobiography what happened to promote this violent embrace.

Everything had seemed to be coming up roses, 'But – and please God let this be the most appallingly biggest "but" in this little life-time – one day early in spring "I heard a maid complaining". I think we must just have finished lunch; I know we were sitting at the table in the small winter-garden of a porch at Durham Cottage and that it was daylight. It came like a bolt from the blue, like a drop of water, I almost thought my ears had deceived me: "I don't love you any more."

'I must have looked as stricken as I felt, for she went on, "There's no one else or anything like that, I mean I still love you but in a different way, sort of, well, like a brother"; she actually used those words. I felt as if I had been told that I had been condemned to death. . . Some while later a close friend said that I should have kicked her out, or upped and outed myself; that I should never have endured in silence such humiliation apparently for the sake of appearances. The fact was I couldn't move; it would be some time before I could entirely take it in, grasp it, or wholly believe it. My recent knighthood, bestowed just before I set out of Australia, was sacred to me too; I just could not bring myself to offer people such crude disillusionment. I could only keep it bottled up in myself and, as Vivien had suggested, carry on as if nothing had happened. Brother and sister; ho, hum.

'Somewhat to my surprise, occasional acts of incest were not discouraged. I supposed I would learn to endure this coldly strange life, so long as I never looked to be happy again.'[25]

He was saying that Vivien was sacred to him, but so was his position in the public eye. One of the reasons he could only acquiesce in her suggestion, and accept the humiliation, was that he could not bear to disillusion those people, strangers to him after all, who thought of them as the first couple of the stage.

This 'I don't love you any more' is one of the crucial passages of his autobiography and of his life. Olivier's habitual style of storytelling is such that the very circumstantial details here – their being at table, after lunch, in the porch of Durham Cottage – tend to warn the reader that a tale is being told and embellished. And Olivier did not bottle his feelings up. He says in this passage that he told a close friend. He also told others, and in these retellings Vivien's words, 'I don't love you any more', were uttered variously in a taxi, or leaving a theatre in the evening; not at lunch and in daylight.[26] Nor can we be sure when. Was it 1949? Was it the spring? The autobiography is full of errors in time and sequence. But something of the sort happened. If it happened when Olivier said it did, then a couple of months later he and Vivien – either as man and wife and lovers, or as occasionally incestuous brother and sister – still went on a three-week holiday together at Opio, near Grasse, a few miles north of Cannes. They spent the time painting, having been inspired to this as a relaxation by Winston Churchill's book, *Painting as a Pastime*. It was, said Olivier, no honeymoon, but they still shared the same tastes in French food and wine.[27]

Then he returned to LOP. Finch and Edith Evans were doing well, indeed very well, at Wyndhams and Olivier had put Donald

Wolfit into the King's, Hammersmith for two weeks in *Julius Caesar*. But his big venture was to take a four-year lease on the St James' Theatre from November 1949, which happened to be the theatre at which he had first seen Vivien, in *The Mask of Virtue*, in 1935. He would open his season with a new play by Christopher Fry and would produce, direct, and play the principal role. Fry had made his reputation with a medieval verse drama called *The Lady's Not for Burning*, which Gielgud had commissioned and in which he had enjoyed long runs in London and on Broadway. Looking for the new and the fashionable, Olivier commissioned Fry's next play, *Venus Observed*, which was also in verse. After Gielgud's success it was hardly a rash choice. Fry was willing to take a royalty of five per cent, less than an author would usually get, in the hope that both Olivier and Leigh would play in it. From the start he was told there was no guarantee of Vivien, but he continued to hope. The draft of his first act was with Olivier in June, with instructions to 'Burn, inter, give to Boy-boy [Vivien's new Siamese], or otherwise dispose of.' But Olivier was enchanted. 'Great brains stirring,' he told Fry, 'wondrous thoughts flashing like lightning; the Muse beaming on you like a searchlight; mighty words being set down. . .' When Fry proposed to take a two-week holiday Olivier peremptorily told him to get on with the play instead. It was finished at the end of October. In December, acting clean contrary to all his instincts of professional diligence, Olivier interrupted rehearsals and flew to New York for two days, to read in Carnegie Hall the universal charter of human rights at the United Nation's celebration of its first anniversary. 'It seemed rather good that a British actor was asked to go,' he told Fry, 'so I'm going.' He said the same thing to Alfred Lunt, who replied; 'And not too bad for Laurence Olivier, eh?'[28]

Venus Observed opened in January 1950. Olivier played a duke who is also an astrologer cum astronomer. In his observatory, during an eclipse, he decides which of his former mistresses he will marry. Mighty words may have been set down but it was a flimsy piece. Still, it ran for seven months and would have run for even longer if Vivien had been in it as well. She was not because by then she was playing one of the most important and destructive roles of her life, Blanche DuBois in *A Streetcar Named Desire*.

18

Streetcar, Carrie, and the Cleos

TENNESSEE WILLIAMS' *A Streetcar Named Desire* is a great and frightening play. It is set in the semi-tropical summer of New Orleans and its principal character, Blanche DuBois, is a disintegrating woman who in the last scene is helplessly led off to the madhouse. Why then, in 1949, did Olivier direct his wife in such a play when he knew that her own sanity was none too sure? He did know this, and it was not only her recent erratic behaviour that told him. He had known for years. Ten years before, when she was filming *Gone With the Wind,* she had taken an overdose of sleeping pills and told her companion, Sunny Alexander, that she feared she would go mad. Sunny had told Olivier. So why did he do what he did?[1]

There are two answers. The first is that it was her own idea. She had seen the text before she and Olivier left on their Australian tour. She had been single-mindedly determined to play the part and had told Binkie Beaumont so. He was the producer who held the British rights and he had been prepared to wait a year until she returned to England. She had, as Olivier saw, 'fastened her hopes' on the play and the part.[2] The second answer is that Olivier was determined that Vivien should be seen not just as a beauty and a film star but as an actress in her own right. He said so in as many words. 'I thought, if her critics have one grain of fairness, they will give her credit now for being actress and not go on forever letting their judgements be distorted by her great beauty and her Hollywood stardom.'[3] When the *Observer* wrote, somewhat absurdly, that the play did not call for a star, he retorted that if it did not he would hate to tackle a play that did. 'And why this tremendous rebellion against the star?' he asked. 'It's too silly, this encouragement of "mediocracy"'.[4] His only hesitation over the play had nothing to do with Vivien; it was his not-quite-dead preoccupation with respectability'. Would it be wise for him to put on so pitiless a play? His friends George Devine and Michel Saint-Denis pointed out that it might be sensational, but so were *King Lear* and *Oedipus*.[5]

Soon after her return from Australia, while Olivier was working out his last few months with the Old Vic, Vivien agreed to do the play if Olivier directed. *Streetcar* had already been a great success on Broadway, where it had been produced by Irene Selznick, the former wife of David O. Selznick, with whom Olivier was never on easy terms. Olivier liked to describe *Streetcar* as a co-production between LOP and Binkie Beaumont. LOP negotiated the Oliviers' contracts directly with Irene Selznick, which accounts for the influence she tried to exert over the English production. The Oliviers asked for 17.5% of the gross takings. She bargained this down to 12.5%, with Vivien receiving £175 a week on top of this.[6]

The English censor required changes, the Lord Chamberlain demanding that the line in which Blanche says she had found her husband with an older man, with its implications of homosexuality, should be omitted; that the word 'Christ' should be replaced by 'God'; and that 'there must not be any suggestive business accompanying any undressing'.[7] So Vivien had to convey Blanche's distress at the wreck of her early marriage with a sentence which made nothing explicit but just broke off into tears. Blanche's rape by her brother-in-law remained, or at least its beginning.

In May, before the contracts were signed, Tennessee Williams and Irene Selznick came to London and saw Vivien in *School for Scandal* and *Antigone*. When Olivier conducted casting interviews he took over Beaumont's office while he and Irene Selznick waited outside, which led her to say, 'I didn't think anyone's position in the theatre was that high and mighty.' Her recollection was that in London Williams declined to allow cuts in the text. Olivier's was that during a visit to Notley they had come to an agreement so that, when Mrs Selznick protested at later cuts, Olivier could reply, 'Oh, the old boy won't mind.'[8] Olivier adopted the American sets and started work in September. 'We are hot in rehearsals of *Streetcar* now,' he wrote to his friend Garson Kanin, 'and are getting all steamed up under its foetid atmosphere. Vivien is going blond and is now in a pale pink stage; she's never quite got over how divine I looked during Hamlet.'[9]

Olivier allowed himself to be guided by Elia Kazan's direction of the play on Broadway, to the extent that he added to the English programme a note saying, 'After the American production'. But he thought it essential to cut, and he and Mrs Selznick fell out. She cabled Williams that it was a disaster, and not his play. Olivier then addressed himself directly to Williams. From Manchester, where the play opened, he wrote him a letter of thirty-two pages on Midland Hotel paper, a letter written far into the night.[10] He began by saying Williams must know *Streetcar* was a really great play, but that two scenes were 'dangerously loaded with length'. One was act II, scene 2, in which Mitch, Blanche's suitor in New Orleans, comes to her late at night having heard about her past. She says she wants not reality but magic. He turns the light full on her, brutally revealing her true age. She cries out and covers her face. When he accuses her, she tells him about her 'many intimacies with strangers', how panic drove her to a seventeen-year-old boy, and how her youth was suddenly gone. Mitch says he doesn't want to marry her any more, at which she tells him to go and screams, 'Get out of here quick before I start screaming fire. Fire! Fire!'

Here is part of what Olivier wrote:

'I have always felt that this almighty important Mitch–Blanche scene, *cut as we have it* now, is just about as tight as a drum, and *one more line* will burst it. Over the cup will flow, the audience will give way to its croup, gone will be their patience, gone will be the scene, gone will be Blanche's performance, and gone will be the true sympathy and tenderly nursed fascination with the whole piece. You simply dare not risk them finding Blanche tedious.

'I've known it, Oh God, so often, they will *only take so much*. I don't care what it is. They *will* not *remain* spellbound – the amount of hypnotism and magic with which they can be controlled is limited.

'There can hardly exist a more magnificently written scene than *Hamlet's* graveyard, packjammed with fascination, cleverness, wit, sweetness, observation, mood. There has never in history been an actor however resourceful who could play this in entirety without being drowned in coughing. *It's too* LONG.

'Now [back to the Mitch – Blanche scene] you can feel it – you can feel them [the audience] feeling that a long speech is upon them. You know it's getting near the point in a scene when the audience won't be rapt any more, they're just within a few inches of getting rebellious. Vivien is pretty bloody heavenly in it, and we are over the rapids. But *any* more, before that moment any one thing and I swear to you that they're beyond the stretch of your lassoo.

'This one of yours, like other masterpieces, will continue to live and be fortified by new readings. All the time.

'If Blanche goes on too long in one scene she has so to speak "lost a round" and with it the audience's confidence. She then has to exert much more pressure and hypnotising power to win them back for quite a time after that, and exhausts the energy that would be so valuable for the doing of her proper stuff for you in the mighty scenes later on. And every scrap of energy that is possible to conserve (and it's not possible to conserve much in this role) is essential for a great performance of a part like this.

'In other words apart from straining the audience – please be careful not to strain your actors – *too* much. I feel like a babe-in-arms preaching to God.

'Forgive me please. I am your servant but I wouldn't be keeping faith with you if I didn't tell you the things that I feel so strongly.'

Olivier appears not to have posted this letter but to have given it to Garson Kanin to deliver by hand to Williams. He cabled Kanin.

SO MANY THANKS DELIVERING LETTER TENNESSEE SO PROMPTLY AFRAID ALL NOT MUCH AVAIL IF ONLY REAL GENIUSES WOULD LISTEN PRACTICAL OLD CRAFTSMEN SOMETIMES THRILLED WITH DARLING PUSS IN STREETCAR.[11]

Olivier was rarely modest, but he was there. His letter to Williams is a splendid example of master-craftsmanship and sure knowledge which themselves amount to genius. And he did, in spite of everything, contrive to keep most of his cuts. Williams thought that if a man took the trouble to write him such a letter, then he had better go along with him.[12]

Kenneth Tynan, a critic much given to the sensational and a man who never lost an opportunity to give Vivien a bad notice, wrote that casting her in the part had been a mistake, that the play should have been retitled *A Vehicle Named Vivien*, that her Blanche was a bored nymphomaniac and a Hedda Gabler of the gin palaces, and that Olivier's error in casting had done what he would never have thought possible – made the whole action shallow and salacious. John Gielgud wrote in his diary, '*Streetcar* is an enormous success but the newspapers have written it up almost exclusively in its sex sensationalism, and Vivien says it is rather wretched, for the audiences who come and pack in are rather like apes.' Vivien wrote to Holman four days after the opening: 'I feel as if I'd been bulldozed and can't believe I have to "go through it" every night.' Christopher Fry, whose *Venus Observed* was in rehearsal, saw the play and told Olivier, 'Vivien battered us almost to pieces. . . I shall never forget how she went out at the last [to the madhouse] looking like a child.' She was shaking and white at the end of each performance.[13]

Streetcar was a play which Olivier vigorously defended against its critics. To one disappointed member of the audience he wrote at some length: 'You misapprehend the play. . . It is a tragedy; a tragedy in the purest sense of the word. The object of the theatre is not only one of entertainment, or even only one of uplift; the basic object of pure tragedy is to shock the soul, very much in the same way as violent exercise is meant to stir the liver. It is not even necessary for tears to be wept by the audience. I am not speaking of Shakespeare's romantic tragedies, but of earlier things, such as Greek tragedy which is designed to *upset* the audience, to beat, to harrow the mind so that it will spread and become familiar with new realms of thought. *A Streetcar Named Desire* is a fine piece of work. The fact that it can be accepted as a piece of salacious sensationalism is a reflection upon the audience, not upon the author.'[14]

He was less tolerant with J.B. Priestley, the novelist and playwright, whom he had known quite well since the 1930s when they had put on a play together. Priestley had given a BBC talk on show business in which Olivier took him to have dismissed *Streetcar* and to have likened Vivien to a bearded woman in a circus. If, as Olivier believed, he had not seen the play, then his offensive statement was without foundation; if he had, his judgment was unworthy of consideration. Priestley admitted he had not seen the play but tartly explained that he had said no such things, though he did have doubts about what he called Olivier's 'theatrical policy'. Olivier would not let it go at that, wrote back that Priestley had implied the play was 'show business' rather than serious theatre, and added that the *Streetcar* audiences were chiefly composed of men who more usually went to the Windmill [for the nude shows] and who sat squirming and giggling, waiting for the worst to happen. 'This has made Vivien's task, already cruelly arduous, almost impossible to bear. Whenever some priest, or puritanical peeress, or in fact any damned fool is ambitious for his speech to be reported, he has only to mention our play and he is certain of a headline.'[15]

LOP was being adventurous but not breaking even. *Venus Observed* ran for seven months at the St James's but did not show a profit. *Daphne Laureola*, with Peter Finch, ran for a year and did make money. Finch had besides become an asset to LOP, who could profitably hire him out to other managements. Mai Zetterling wept one entire weekend from Friday to Sunday until she learned he would play opposite her in *Point of Departure* at the Duke of York's; LOP took 7.5% of the gross.[16] But Olivier had one play which closed within a fortnight and another, with John Mills, which he pulled after its provincial tour, before it reached the West End. *Captain Carvallo*, another LOP production with Finch, had a good run at the St James's and helped Finch's reputation, but again it made no profit.[17] Olivier rejected many hopeless scripts and proposals submitted to him. He returned a confused adaptation of Dostoevsky's *Idiot* and declined the roles of Leonardo da Vinci, Manet, Shakespeare, and Lord Byron, all in new plays. He turned down an amateur dramatisation of the Book of Esther, with Vivien as Esther, and declined another play for which its author made the proud claim that it had no plot, no characters, and no story to tell. Even Mrs James N. Conboy of Utica, New York, who sent him a verse play which she said was 'the most perfectly conceived and beautifully written since Shakespeare', could not provide him with a commercial proposition. LOP's reader thought it pretentious and ludicrous.[18]

It was time to turn to Hollywood. Early in 1950 William Wyler asked Olivier to play Hurstwood in a Paramount film of Theodore Dreiser's *Carrie*, which he said was perhaps the finest novel written by an American. Olivier at first declined, but agreed when he learned that Warner Brothers wanted to film *Streetcar* with Vivien at the same time. They could be in Hollywood together. LOP's American agent was instructed to negotiate.[19]

That summer Vivien, who was exhausted after 326 performances of *Streetcar*, went on holiday in the Mediterranean on board Alex Korda's yacht *Elsewhere*. She charmed Korda's sixteen-year-old nephew Michael, letting him take her to the islands in the Bay of Cannes and drive her along the Croisette. But he observed that dinner with her could be a tense affair. After two or three drinks she was 'like a floating storm'. You never could be sure what she would throw, and what she would hit or damage. When she returned, the Oliviers put on their public face at Royal Ascot, where they again had a box.[20]

LOP's price for the Oliviers' services was high, $125,000 for Olivier and $100,000 for Vivien. Selznick at Paramount agreed to pay Olivier an extra $1,000 a week in expenses, to include a car, chauffeur, and maid. Warner stuck at $500 a week expenses for Vivien, but this made $1,500 a week between them.[21] To encourage Olivier to accept Paramount's offer Dreiser's widow, Helen, wrote to him calling him the greatest dramatic intellect of his time, praising his films of *Hamlet* and *Henry V*, and hoping he and Vivien would enjoy being in America this time. Olivier wrote thanking her for this 'sweet presentiment', and went on, 'We usually do, for some reason or another, but there is also usually a feeling of something not having been all right – probably our fault – and always an anxiety before one goes; it may be all homesick nonsense.'[22]

Olivier and Vivien accepted the terms offered. Wyler cabled Olivier that Jennifer Jones had been cast as Carrie and hoped he was as pleased with this as they all were. Olivier replied that he was delighted, which was just as well since she had just married David Selznick. He added that he had grown a fine moustache which, if Wyler liked, he would keep on his face for Hurstwood. He also, as requested, gave his measurements. His chest was forty-two and a half inches and his waist thirty-five and a half, as against the thirty-eight and thirty-three inches of his pre-war days. Selznick cabled that Jennifer was more elated than he had ever seen her before at the prospect of working with Olivier.[23]

The Oliviers did not fly to America together. Vivien went first so that she could spend a few days in Connecticut with her director, Elia Kazan. Cecil Tennant saw her off from Heathrow on the 9 p.m. flight to New York. It was a nineteen-hour flight in a Boeing Stratocruiser, in which the passengers' seats were made up into beds with proper sheets. The plane made refuelling stops at Scotland, Iceland, and Gander, Newfoundland. On board she wrote Olivier a serial letter.

'Oh sweet sweet Baba,' she began. 'If we were together this would seem quite exciting, but then that applies to everything in life.' After take-off she wondered whether she could see Notley if she looked down. By 11 p.m. she was at Prestwick, where she telephoned him. The plane took another two and a half hours to reach Iceland. 'They are going to make up the beds now. . . *In bed* – the berths are so very wide and it's just sheer waste you're not here beside me – I kiss you and miss you and love you so deeply and eternally – my love – my life – my friend – goodnight sweet sweet Larry.' During the refuelling stop at Gander she wrote to him from her warm berth that it was pouring with rain outside. At New York, having just talked to Olivier again on the telephone, she ended, 'Thank God we'll talk tomorrow.' She posted the letter at her New York hotel, the St Regis.[24]

They were back again in the routine they thrived on – separation, long letters, and long and frequent telephone calls. Olivier flew out ten days later, taking Vivien's seventeen-year-old daughter Suzanne with him. It was her first flight. Vivien had written affectionately on her flight out. When he met Garson Kanin, who had been present at their wedding in 1940, in New York, Olivier told him a different story. 'We never converse,' he said. 'We only confer.' In New York he bought the rights to Gian Carlo Menotti's opera, *The Consul*, which LOP would put on in London. Then he travelled on to Hollywood. The Oliviers' house in Hollywood on that visit was the same in which they had stayed when they made *Lady Hamilton*, ten years before. Looking back he said, 'Our love, which amounted to a religion, was still triumphant then, and confident in an eternal future.'[25] That was no longer true.

The Oliviers were stars returning to Hollywood after a long absence. She was the legend of *Gone With the Wind*, he the knighted Olivier of *Henry V* and *Hamlet*. He had to tell the studio not to use his title in his publicity and credits. They were lavishly welcomed back at a party given by Danny Kaye at the Beverly Hills Hotel. Anyone who was anyone was there – Groucho Marx, Errol Flynn, Ginger Rogers, Ronald Colman, Lana Turner, Louis B. Mayer, Marilyn Monroe, Humphrey Bogart, and Lauren Bacall. The young Suzanne was not taken to the party. She was taken to see Vivien and Olivier at the studios when they got down to work. Sunny Alexander acted as Vivien's secretary, as she had ten years before.

Carrie is a story in which Hurstwood sacrifices everything – his marriage, position, and good name – for the love of a younger woman, and ends up proud, outcast, and destitute. It is as much a tragedy as *Streetcar*. It is also, in everything, American and Olivier, as much a perfectionist as ever, wished to get it right. Before he arrived in Hollywood he cabled Wyler: 'Feel strongly my natural way of speaking quite wrong for Hurstwood who was probably born in Chicago if not points still farther from England. Please be kind and line up man you can trust to check my accent and intonations so I can feel in tune and happy about this.'[26]

Vivien started shooting at Warner with the young Marlon Brando. The first rehearsals were uneasy. When Kazan asked her to make a certain move she would say, 'When Larry and I did the play in London. . .' and go on to tell him what that was. As she spoke, Kazan became aware of the other actors looking at him. They knew, as he knew, that this was a moment he could not allow to pass unchallenged. 'Vivien,' he said, 'you're making it here, with us.' It took two weeks before director and star were at ease with each other. Then they became friends. 'In the end,' he said, 'I was full of admiration for the lady. She had a small talent, but the greatest determination to excel of any actress I've known. She'd have crawled over broken glass if she thought it would help her performance.'[27]

Vivien told the *Los Angeles Times* she found the role of Blanche more exacting than that of Scarlett, saying, 'I had nine months in the theatre of Blanche DuBois. Now she's in command of me in Hollywood.' And it was a ruthless piece of casting. She could look like a girl, but she was thirty-six and in her distracted moments appeared older than that. As Blanche she was herself, as she had been when she played Scarlett. Olivier *became* Hurstwood, however, which is a different thing. On the morning he began filming she sent him a scribbled note.

'My darling darling Hurstwood (alias Puuussy) – Good good luck to my adored one – my Baba – My Larrry.'[28]

Olivier became Hurstwood in his own way. Kazan happened to be living opposite him, and could see him rehearsing on his own. 'Some great actors imitate the outside and "work in" from there. Larry needs to know first of all how the person he's to play walks, stands, sits, dresses. . .concentrating on what might seem to us to be insignificant aspects of his characterisation. I remember pausing outside a window late one Sunday morning and, undetected, watching Larry go through the pantomime of offering a visitor a chair. He'd try it this way, then that, looking at the guest, then at the chair, doing it with a host's flourish, doing it with a graceless gesture, then thrusting it brusquely forward – more like Hurstwood that way? – never satisfied, always seeking what would be the most revealing way to do what would be a quickly passing bit of stage business for any other actor.'[29]

On the set at Paramount Olivier found Jennifer Jones not so much a delight as he had confidently asserted he would. Towards the end of *Streetcar* Vivien had to work on location in New Orleans for three weeks. Olivier saw her off on the train and then wrote to her. In one letter he said he had been rehearsing that morning while Jennifer was busy failing to understand Wyler. 'I'm doing the "Caerey downt DOWNT make me live through teoo much PAIN to get ut' sequence with Jennifer really being a cunt. "I guess I downt know" – I guess she bloody well fucking doesn't know *anything* about *anything*. No soul, like we always said about them, dumb animals with human brains.' Having had his ritual hack at Mr and Mrs David O. Selznick he signed himself, 'Your worshipping, welcoming, loving, and thinking-all-the-time Hermit-boy.'[30]

When he came to the sequences near the end when Hurstwood is down and out and starving, he really starved himself. He wrote to Vivien, 'I don't feel at all hungry – just as if I'm dying. It's very good for Hurstwood right now. . .don't worry my darling it's doing me good really I think – the diet I mean.' He said he had asked the Kayes that night for a quiet dinner, and the Colmans the next day, and ended: 'O my love I feel like a half cooked codfish thrown back into the sea when you're not with me. . . I love you so my heart's treasure – O O how I long for you and the sight of your lovely wonderful face – and not only that – for my sore boring eyes – Your boy.'[31]

Streetcar won Vivien an Oscar for best actress, her second. The Bank of England solemnly gave permission, in those days of nationalised austerity, for LOP to spend $400 on advertisements in the *Hollywood Reporter* and *Variety* thanking everybody.[32] *Carrie* won Olivier only praise. Helen Dreiser, saying she had never before in her life asked for an autograph, asked him to sign a copy of *Hamlet*.[33] She said *Carrie* was magnificent. 'I was actually startled by your natural American speech with no trace of English accent. However did you achieve this?. . . You conveyed so much that had happened to you but was not shown in that scene at the last. It was all shown in your facial expression – the fact that you had been ill in Bellevue [the New York municipal hospital] and so many other sufferings.'[34] Bert Allenberg of the William Morris agency in Beverly Hills wrote to him that Larry Olivier was the best goddamned actor in the world and Barney Balaban of Paramount, writing on paper headed 'From the office of the President', said he and his executives had been completely moved by his 'sensitive rendition of a man utterly rent asunder'. Mr Balaban was proud that *Carrie* bore the trademark of a Paramount Picture. To which Olivier replied mockingly, 'A letter from the Boss is something one very seldom gets in our business, and as a matter of fact yours is the first I have ever had in my career from the office of any President. . .'[35]

While they were in Hollywood Durham Cottage was redecorated, and there was a plentiful correspondence between Vivien and the

London decorators. She wrote that she *loathed* her existing bedroom, which had always been a crass mistake, and wanted white wallpaper with pink and red roses on it. A new bedhead of Louis XIV style was brought in, with couronne and hangings above. A soft-green marble fireplace was found, to match the carpet in the sitting room. Olivier wanted a sapphire-blue carpet for his bedroom but the decorator recommended a mustard carpet to bring more warmth and gaiety; dark yellow was settled on, to go with a folding sofa bed in French provincial style. All this awaited them on their return.[36]

Olivier made the mistake of coming back from California with Vivien the long way round. They were two of only five passengers on a French freighter which sailed by way of the Panama Canal. The passage took five weeks and was a dismal failure. Vivien may have been his heart's treasure, as he told her when she was away in New Orleans, but together they were bored. 'As I have already said, we were not exactly a honeymoon couple, and though we needed the rest, the stark reality of our own company plunged us both into deep depression. For the first time the idea of suicide had its attractions and I found myself more and more drawn to the ship's rail and the fascination of the foam sweeping by. We had never before been made to face the extent to which our lives together had been supported and bolstered up by the companionship of our friends and the glitter of our position.'[37]

It was not the first time suicide had crossed his mind. According to his own account he had, many years before, after the death of his mother, thought of jumping into the Thames. But for him to consider the glitter of his and Vivien's position in the public eye was not new. He had thought of it when a friend asked him why, when she said she no longer loved him, he had not kicked her out or left her.[38]

They landed at Tilbury on 18 November. Next morning in LOP's office Olivier went through the books and realised that the money he and Vivien had brought home was already spent. Things were worse than he foresaw, since the Menotti opera, which had been such a success in New York, struggled on for only six weeks in London and then closed. Next year was the Festival of Britain, the centenary of the first Great Exhibition of 1851 in London. It was a festival intended to be a tonic to the nation after the hardships and austerities of war, which still lingered on. LOP needed something spectacular, for the sake of the festival and to repair its own fortunes. Olivier seldom mentioned this later, but his first thought was to do *School for Scandal* yet again, this time with John Gielgud as well as Vivien, Richardson, and himself. Richardson was engaged elsewhere. Gielgud declined, saying that, much as he would adore to work with Olivier, he could not help feeling that a revival of something already done would be a confession of weakness. 'Although originally I thought it would be a good plan to have us all work together for the fun it would be, it is also true that too many stars in one play will not be a good plan, for nobody would be able to get in, and there would be one great attraction and a lot of second rate ones at the other theatres. Whereas if each of us who can command an audience (one hopes!) put on a new show at three or four theatres, it will make the festival more varied and divide the amount of work for the supporting actors to greater advantage.'[39] Gielgud did *A Winter's Tale* for the festival.

Olivier's thoughts then turned to Shaw's *Caesar and Cleopatra*, but that alone did not seem enough. At Roger Furse's suggestion, Shakespeare's *Antony and Cleopatra* was added. They would do both. Vivien looked scared. She had filmed the Shaw. The Shakespeare was quite another matter. Olivier told her – and it seems in not very complimentary terms – that one had to take risks, that the verse after all was so ravishing that anyone with half an ear would catch it, and the same went for the emotional content. It *would* click. He felt that there was no other choice, and she nervously agreed. Gielgud wrote to his mother: 'The Oliviers are surely biting off more than they can chew with the *two* Cleopatra plays. I fear Vivien has really too much control – she will never be able to touch the Shakespeare part, and he is not well cast for either play – the work alone of the two big productions is terrifying and I can't imagine how they can contemplate it, though I admit it makes a splashy announcement!'[40]

Olivier planned a five-month season with the two plays in London, then a short holiday, and then four months in New York. He was flogging Vivien. He admitted to himself that she would be pretty tired, but their finances demanded it. 'We depended on our separate command of high film salaries, which in turn depended on our box-office values, and these were checkable by producers. But together we could think of ourselves as pretty unassailable.'[41] Olivier may still have been infatuatedly in love with her, but at the same time he coolly reckoned on her financial value in their partnership. The challenge was Shakespeare's play. Vivien's notices were mixed. Ivor Brown in the *Observer* called her 'a lass unparalleled'. Tynan said she picked at the part with the daintiness of a debutante called upon to dismember a stag, with her little finger crooked.'[42]

But the gamble came off: the season was sold out, and Olivier's star rose higher. J.D. Salinger happened to be in London for the publication of the British edition of *The Catcher in the Rye*. He saw *Antony and Cleopatra* and wanted to write to Olivier but hesitated. His publisher, who happened to be Hamish Hamilton, encouraged him to do so, as he had some years before encouraged Rosamond Lehmann. This is what Salinger said: 'At risk of sounding terribly oracular, not to say presumptuous as hell, I'd like – in fact I'd love – to tell you what I personally think of your acting. . . I think you're the only actor in the world who plays in a Shakespeare play with a special, tender familiarity – as if you were keeping it in the family. Almost as if you were appearing in a play written by an older brother whom you understand completely and love to distraction. It's an almost insupportably beautiful thing to watch, and I certainly think you're the only actor who can bring it off. And I've seen you do it as long ago as 1938, when you played Iago at the Old Vic.' Other praise came from even higher quarters. On Olivier's birthday he and Vivien were given dinner by Winston Churchill, then Leader of the Opposition, who so took to them that he then asked them to his country house at Chartwell. When the women retired to leave the men at their port he expressed his approval of Vivien, calling her 'a clinker'. He presented her with one of his own paintings, one of the few he ever gave anyone.[43] Olivier was present when the Queen laid the foundation stone of the National Theatre in July. No matter that the theatre did not open for another twenty-five years, and then on another site. Olivier noticed – as he would, since he always loved flowers – that the bouquet given to the Queen was composed of flowers mentioned by Shakespeare. Apart from a rose, a daffodil, sprigs of rosemary and rue, sweetbriar, eglantine, and flower de luce, there was a leek, a docken leaf, dogweed, bogwort, darnel, hemlock, and rank fumitory. It smelled far from sweet and she held it at a delicate distance from her.[44] At much the same time Henry Irving's grandson, addressing Olivier as Laurentius Maximus and Magnifico, wrote asking him to open the gardens round Irving's statue opposite the Lyceum Theatre. Olivier, doing so, made a speech saying he was born two years after Irving's death, and yet was as conscious of him as if he had served as a member of his company.[45]

At the end of the London season he gave a river boat party for the company, with songs. One song, celebrating the success of *Antony and Cleopatra*, went:

> Now every story has an end
> And this one's full of pain
> For his lascivious wassails sent
> Poor Tony down the drain.

> 'Let's have another bawdy night'
> He cried, and then 'Oh Lord',
> He got so pissed he slipped and ripped
> His guts out on a sword.

> Poor Cleopatra wept, and cursed her fatal star,
> Then she borrowed a serpent
> And stuffed it down her bra.

> Now everybody here tonight,
> I think we ought to give
> A very liberal vote of thanks
> To Larry and to Viv
> For giving us this lovely spread
> Upon this burnished barge.

> So let's cheer the way
> To the USA
> Of Leigh and of Olivier.[46]

After the Cleopatras, Vivien went for another holiday on Korda's
yacht and this time Olivier went with her. They cruised in the Greek
islands, went on to Corsica and Rome, and then flew to Nice where
they were met by their chauffeur and their car, which he had driven
from England to take them back across France. He also brought
with him Vivien's mink coat and a pair of furs with which she had
not wished to overburden her luggage in Greece. An export licence
was required to take the furs out of England, which LOP obtained,
having to declare the value of the mink at £3,000 and undertake
that it and the furs would not be sold abroad.[47]

Their American tour began in December 1951. Olivier wanted
a hotel within walking distance of the Ziegfeld Theatre on 54th
Street. It had to be discreet so that they would not be pestered by
autograph hunters. Toby Rowland, a producer friend of his and
Vivien's, happened to be in New York and did some scouting for
them. He found the Hotel Dorset, which was full of old ladies with
Pekingese dogs. It recommended itself because, when Rowland
called, the manager had never even heard of Vivien Leigh or of
Olivier, and had indeed written his name down as Lawrence Olivia.
A suite to accommodate them, their butler, maid, and secretary
would be $455 a month. They did not take it in the end because
Gertrude Lawrence, with whom Olivier had appeared in *Private
Lives* in 1930, lent them her apartment as a Christmas present.
Hamish Hamilton, Vivien's friend of many years who knew her taste
in paintings, met her at a party before her departure and advised
her not at any cost to miss the Frick Museum on Fifth Avenue. She
said, what a funny name, at which he said, yes, neither one thing
nor the other, was it; she laughed inordinately.[48]

About a month before they left England Olivier noticed that
Vivien started to behave, almost imperceptibly at first, like a slightly
frightened daughter, leaning close to him and wanting her arms
round him. He knew this had little if anything to do with passion.
It was a funny, child-like, clinging need for protection, but for the
first time in three years she was giving him some sort of happiness
by making him feel strong and fatherly. He asked her if she was
nervous about New York and she gave vaguely troubled, non-
committal replies.[49] They opened on Broadway on 19 December in

front of an audience which included Margaret Truman, Sarah Churchill, Richard Rodgers, Marlene Dietrich, the David O. Selznicks, Tyrone Power, Hermione Gingold, Alfred Vanderbilt, and Lynne Fontanne. It was Christmas. On Christmas Day itself they had two shows. 'The season,' he wrote, 'carries enough glamour on its own, but together with the sudden blaze of new friends, the generous warmth of old ones, and the dazzling glitter of New York success, the reality of our situation was lost in a haze of northern lights.'[50]

The notices in New York were better than they had been in London. Brooks Atkinson, in the *New York Times*, said it was as if *Antony and Cleopatra* had never been played before. Everything glowed with vitality. Miss Leigh was superb. John Steinbeck saw the first night with his wife and wrote, 'I always know greatness because it makes me want to go gigantically to work. In the evening of the first opening there was in us a tone – hard to define – a singing that went on and on in us. We came home reluctant to sleep.' Thornton Wilder wrote to Olivier, 'Beautiful, beautiful, beautiful. And how you were playing last night. What flashing lives – what wondrous deaths. Do you blaze like that every night?'[51]

Olivier was never a man to do only two plays at once. While he was acting every night on Broadway in one or other of the Cleos, in the daytime he was taking the train to Philadelphia to rehearse *Venus Observed*, which LOP had transferred to America. To play the part of the Duke, which he had taken in London, he had asked Ronald Colman, who said he was flattered but declined. He then asked Robert Donat, who turned it down flat. The American producers then considered, in this order, Frederic March, Alfred Lunt, Rex Harrison, and John Gielgud. Rex Harrison took it, but only on condition his wife Lili Palmer played opposite him, and then only for sixteen weeks. Olivier supervised everything. The American producer was amazed, saying Olivier put his heart and soul into it, himself playing in two productions in New York but still coming early to rehearsal in Philadelphia. Even after the play opened he fretted that it was too long and cabled to Fry: 'Audiences leave overtired. Have I your authority to do what I think best?'[52]

He then wrote Fry a letter as long as that he had written to Tennessee Williams, asking him for cuts and to simplify the language. He said some of the cast had been accused of inaudibility, half on account of the huge theatre, half because the audience had difficulty in following the dialogue and *thought* they couldn't hear it. 'We [in New York] get "heard" in the Shaw, but not "heard" in the Shakespeare!' He said the play was verbally too rich. 'Please don't think I am being impertinent enough to preach at you, it is only my duty as a "theatrician" (which they call me here) and as a devoted friend, to offer you any conclusions that experience has brought to me. It cannot ever be right or desirable in the theatre that we should *lose our audience*. . . Their intellectual receptiveness gets tired as the evening wears on. W. S[hakespeare] was brilliantly conscious of this, and I think that is why he always manages to excite. All the tragedies show him gradually relaxing his call upon the intelligence as the evening progresses until he finally says, "Alright, you see it's quite easy now" and sometimes, "Here you are groundlings – here's a damn good fight." The *emotions* of the audience last the longest of the contributions that they bring to the theatre. *Intellect* wears out quickest. After all they have paid their money to enjoy themselves. Time and time again in *Venus* in London, I would have them in my hand like baby mice, and then out would come something *difficult* again, or obscure, or too clever, and it would suddenly be like playing in a hospital for croup – impatience had seized them and they were gone for a while. . . Be a bit easier on them cockie, will you?' Fry agreed, replying 'Cut if it must be.'[53]

Venus came into New York but made nothing for LOP and lost its American backers money. In New York the two Cleos played to full houses for eighteen weeks and made eight times what they had in London.[54] During their run Olivier received his first substantial approach from television. NBC wanted to broadcast at least part of the performances, and offered an audience of thirty million. 'I wish I could explain to you,' wrote a vice president of NBC, 'the revolution that is coming over this country through television, and show you that this would be the greatest triumph of your illustrious career, and the most important contribution to a better-informed, more alert American public made by anyone.' Olivier declined.[55]

Vivien was ill for one matinée and one evening performance, which cost $1650 in refunds.[56] It was surprising she did not miss more, because she was terrified and obsessed. The reality of her situation was desperate. Gertrude Lawrence's apartment oppressed her. The bedroom was hung in silk with dark grey walls and curtains; there was a grey satin cover for the bed and an even darker grey carpet. 'I would come home,' wrote Olivier, 'to find the sitting room empty; going into the bedroom I would find Vivien sitting on a corner of the bed, wringing her hands and sobbing, in a state of grave distress; I would naturally try desperately to give her some comfort; but for some time she would be inconsolable.'[57] He tried to persuade her to see a psychiatrist. She resisted, but then consented. They consulted Laurence S. Kubie, on East 81st Street. He was a celebrated psychiatrist whose work had been portrayed in the musical *Lady in the Dark*, which had played on Broadway for two years in 1941–2. It was about the editor of a fashion magazine and sought to dramatise the process of psychoanalysis. The lyrics were by Ira Gershwin, the music by Kurt Weill; the editor was played by Gertrude Lawrence and Danny Kaye was also in the cast. Dr Kubie, therefore, came well-introduced to Olivier by two close friends. He examined Vivien and was saddened by his and Olivier's failure to persuade her of the importance of accepting intensive treatment. He thought her condition explosive.[58] She was desperately anxious and uneasy, fearful of his keeping any record of her condition, and received suggestions for future appointments with such piteous dread that Olivier had not the heart to insist. He too was reluctant to return to Dr Kubie, feeling himself an irredeemable foreigner, 'a creature from another planet', unable to comprehend American psychiatry. To explain this feeling he said that the British and Americans were kindred in language only, and were otherwise as foreign to each other as the people of any other two nations.[59] This may be so, but Olivier by then had more than twenty years' experience of visiting the United States, and had lived there for two periods of two years each.

He had plenty of other things to worry about. *Venus* was coming into New York, the run of the Cleos was coming to an end and he had to make the arrangements to get his company back to England. The run was due to end on 12 April. The choice was to sacrifice a performance and sail on the *Franconia* – one of the smaller Cunarders – on that same date, or to wait for the *Mauretania* three days later.

The *Franconia* was cheaper, only £78 for the passage. Cunard agreed to delay the sailing time until midnight on the twelfth. The company members then objected that this would give them only half an hour to get from the theatre to the dock, at which Cunard, making history, agreed to put back the departure until 1 a.m. on the thirteenth. The Oliviers' own staterooms were reserved on the *Queen Mary*, for £562.[60] This booking was then cancelled, because Noel Coward insisted they should go to him in Jamaica before returning home.

'Now please please listen and be sensible,' he wrote to Olivier. 'You have been overworking to the point of madness. . . Just a couple more weeks in this place will set you up for the rest of the year. Oh hurry hurry hurry! Can't wait to see you. Do you like one double bed, two single beds or four hammocks? Do you like the sea, the sun, bananas and me? If you do you have nothing to fear.' They stayed nine days in Jamaica, where Olivier told Coward he feared Vivien was having quite a bad nervous breakdown. 'Nonsense,' said Coward. 'If anybody's having a nervous breakdown, you are.' 'Of course,' thought Olivier, 'Vivien had got in first. It was back to despair for me, and the well-worn teeth had to be clamped together again.'[61] They returned to England and to Notley, where they arrived on 23 April 1952, Shakespeare's birthday.

'I had,' he said later, 'a blessed sense of relief that Vivien's condition seemed to have righted itself. . . I am sure that they must have taken some pains to tell me what was wrong with my wife; that her disease was called manic depression and what that meant – a possibly permanent cyclical to-and-fro between the depths of depression and wild, uncontrollable mania. These changes of mood could be irregular, or regular, or increasing in frequency, this last the most dreaded as it invariably led to schizophrenia, which was so far regarded as being incurable. Whether the doctors didn't explain or I didn't understand matters not; the fact is I was quite unprepared for what was in store.'[62]

This is astonishing. Dr Kubie considered Vivien's condition explosive. That was the word he used in an emphatic letter not long after, in which he wrote about 'our failure' – his and Olivier's – to persuade her to accept treatment. It is difficult to believe he did not make himself clear at the time.[63]

19

Great God in Heaven, What Now?

WHILE HE WAS PLAYING the two Cleos, directing *Venus Observed*, and coping with Vivien's troubles, Olivier was also taking singing lessons two or three times a week in New York to prepare himself for a film of John Gay's *The Beggar's Opera*, in which he would play the highwayman Macheath. The voices of the other actors would be dubbed. He insisted on singing Macheath himself and made a recording which was sent to the composer Arthur Bliss, who considered his light baritone 'most musician-like'. Olivier the chorister, flattered by that, thought his life was about to undergo a sea change and that he was to become a 'miracle mixture of Caruso and Chaliapin'.[1]

From New York he wrote to his fifteen-year-old son, Tarquin, who was then at Eton, telling him about his plans for Macheath and saying he was trying to ring a little change in his career. The alimony he still had to pay Jill irritated him. She had shown no sign of remarrying and the cost of maintaining her and Tarquin was increasing. He complained to those around him that she was and had been a lesbian. Her alimony could not be paid by LOP and had to come out of his own pocket. Only the year before he had written to her, 'My God, how can Eton possibly send the fees up? They only have to send them up a little more and they'll have an empty school, won't they?' Jill's accountants had been pressing for an increase in her allowance. He offered another £450 a year on top of the £3,500 he already paid. He was eventually obliged by court order to make this an extra £750. Jill pointed out that Tarquin's living expenses alone were more than £800. She suggested putting him down for an army regiment; it was no good thinking of the navy since he was a bad sailor.[2]

Back at Notley Vivien was supposed to rest and regain her health, as she had rested there after her attack of tuberculosis in 1945. But she came to London and gave parties at Durham Cottage, filling the tiny house with guests. And she insisted on accompanying Olivier to Eton on the Glorious Fourth of June, the annual celebration of the birthday of George III, who had been a patron of the school. Jill had not thought it a good idea for Vivien to come, saying narrow-minded people might make dirty cracks if the three of them – she, Vivien and Olivier – were seen together.'[3]

On the day, Vivien was not understanding enough to stay away. Tarquin waited, dressed like the other boys in top hat, tails and rolled umbrella. Olivier was late. Tarquin slipped away from his mother and found him cruising in his Bentley with Vivien. In the back seat was Robert Helpmann, who was a not altogether benign presence at Notley and elsewhere. He amused Vivien. When she was for a moment insufficiently entertained she would cry, 'I want my Bobby.' That afternoon at Eton, Olivier had a word with Jill and then had to leave early. Tarquin wrote him an angry letter, and then an appeasing one, telling his father about the desires aroused in him by Virginia, a girl he admired.[4]

Olivier replied that he was dreadfully sorry but he couldn't get away to Henley Royal Regatta – to which Tarquin, who was a rowing man, had wanted to take him – and then addressed himself to the matter of the girl. 'You see, these wild horses that natural instincts are, are things that you must be sure to have control over. See that the reins are *firmly* in your hands. Don't let them take you where they will, because they don't know what's good for you, or care. Don't forget. Nature herself has only *one* interest, *one* concern throughout the entire gigantic realm of her animal and vegetable kingdom – procreation. Nothing, *nothing* else. She doesn't care how she gets it or who gets hurt in the process. Just recognise that all the romantic agonies, all the rosie reveries, the stopping of the heart when the phone rings, all the exciting and bewitching variations of

Love's sweet dreams that mankind is subject to, are basically, simply and solely Wicked old Nature's cold-blooded calculated *Bribe*, to bring children into the world. Simply that.'[5]

So Olivier may have believed. But that autumn, during the filming of *The Beggar's Opera*, he met Dorothy Tutin. She played the part of Polly Peachum. It was her first film; she was twenty-one, she was sweet, she was discreet, and she undoubtedly loved him. She was the first and most important of what he called his 'tender venturings into the blessed unction of sex' in the 1950s.[6] Trader Faulkner, the Australian who had a walk-on part in Olivier's *Richard III* in Sydney, had come to England, where he met and courted her. He went off to Bermuda to film in 1952, and the girl he said goodbye to was loving and gorgeous and warm. When he returned she was Olivier's and completely changed towards him. He believed Olivier was her first lover.[7] The film of *The Beggar's Opera* was a disaster. 'I hope and pray,' said Olivier, 'that my personal flop. . . will be the worst that I shall ever disenjoy.'[8]

Apart from his good fortune with Miss Tutin it was a time when everything was going badly. LOP had lost more money when it presented Orson Welles as Othello, and a comedy called *The Happy Time* had unhappily lasted only five weeks. Olivier's first biography had been written, with his help and Vivien's, and was due out early in 1953. It had started as a long series of feature articles by Felix Barker in the London *Evening News*, whose editor had assured Olivier he need have no fears about their dignity and good taste. He needed this assurance after his unhappy experience of Sybille's biography of 1948.[9] When in 1952 Barker put his articles together, and added to them to produce a joint biography of Olivier and Vivien, he saw Sybille's typescript – indeed Olivier himself asked her to show the author a copy – but used none of its entertaining indiscretions. Now Olivier had a biography due to come out at a time when he was obviously not doing well. He also stood to lose Notley. His accountants were telling him the house was costing too much, and that if he carried on running it he would face 'embarrassment of the most serious kind'. On the other hand there were no buyers.[10]

To his brother Dickie, Olivier wrote in December 1952, 'The news of Notley is that we still have it. I feel rather shame-faced about it, but the fact is that if you can't sell something it seems to me the only thing to do is keep it.' He also said, 'Vivien, you'll be pleased to know, is ever and ever so much better. Very suddenly she chirped up and came up just like new, two months ago.'[11]

Dickie was in Ireland by then, rather unhappily managing a farm in County Wicklow, but for the first time in years he had had a great stroke of good fortune. His divorce from his second wife had just been made absolute and he was hoping to get engaged to Hester Capel-Dunn, whom he had met on her stepfather's farm in Suffolk when he was an agricultural student. He wrote to Larry that he knew she was young enough to be his daughter, but she wasn't 'just a country girl'; she had done the London season, been to pretty well every deb dance and had already had two proposals of marriage. He had known her for four years and loved her for two. Miss Capel-Dunn was the daughter of Colonel Denis Capel-Dunn, who had been secretary to Churchill's joint intelligence committee and had been killed in the war. She was certainly young enough to be Dickie's daughter. He had met her when she was thirteen or four-teen. At the time of their engagement she was only seventeen and he was forty-eight, but he told Larry that marriages with even greater age gaps had been successful.[12]

Vivien, having chirped up, was happy to do an epic film for Paramount to be shot in Ceylon and Hollywood. It was called *Elephant Walk* because it was set on a tea plantation which was crossed by a traditional marching route of wild elephants. Vivien played the planter's wife, who was tempted to elope but remained faithful after many tribulations and a typhoid epidemic. The planter's part had been offered to Olivier but he could not do it as he was in the middle of editing and dubbing *The Beggar's Opera*. Clark Gable and Marlon Brando also declined the part. Vivien then suggested Peter Finch. He had done well since he came to England. He had been the only success of *The Happy Time* and since September had been leased out to the Old Vic, where he had played Mercutio in *Romeo and Juliet*, with Claire Bloom, and did it very well. The story is that Vivien took the script to Finch's flat in Victoria at two o'clock one morning. She was let in by Finch's wife Tamara, who had come with him from Australia, and set about talking him into it. Finch had played in six films – most notably as the Sheriff of Nottingham in *Robin Hood and His Merrie Men* and as a priest in Graham Greene's *The Heart of the Matter* – but he was unknown in Hollywood. However Irving Asher, the producer of *Elephant Walk*, had seen Finch as Mercutio and he too was talked into it.[13] So LOP leased two of its properties to Paramount, Finch for $24,000 for sixteen weeks, and Vivien for $175,000. She would also receive $1,000 a week expenses and another $200 a week for her maid, Ethel Helmsing. Finch and Tamara had been to Notley at weekends. He and Vivien were no more than friends at the time, though she had marked his birthday, January 11, in her diary.[14]

It was a time when Vivien was on one of her highs. Early in January she went on her own to Brighton for a late party given by Ralph Richardson, and called in on the way for dinner with Oswald Frewen at Brede. She arrived in her chauffeured Rolls-Royce at 6.30 p.m., drank gin and vermouth, red wine with dinner and brandy afterwards, then set off at 10.30 p.m. to drive the twenty miles to the Brighton party and then back to London that night. Frewen wrote, 'And that is the way she lives; sweet and plumb crazy. No *wonder* she had a breakdown. Told us she was off to Ceylon directly to be filmed with elephants, and then to Hollywood to complete the film. . . Trudgett [the chauffeur] looked a little anxious when she said she would drive, but they went off a'taunto [under full sail]. . .'[15]

She and Finch flew to Ceylon on 26 January 1953, by Comet – the first of the commercial jets – by way of Rome, Beirut, Bahrain, and Bombay. Olivier went to see them off and was allowed on to the tarmac at Heathrow Airport. As the plane began to move forward they both looked back at him through a window, Finch making an effort to look like a protective friend and she blowing a sad little kiss. He watched the plane for a moment or two as it moved off and then 'turned away and drove back to London in a state of nothingness, to pick up the relatively light cudgels of finishing off a picture'. Many years later, when he began to write about this episode in his autobiography he first wrote, and then omitted, these words: 'My God, what was going to happen? Great God in heaven, what was it to be now?'[16]

The day after she arrived, Vivien cabled Olivier to come and join her for a week, which she knew he could not do. She swam. She rode, fell off her horse, and had to stay in bed for a day. On her fourth day she sent Larry another cable: 'Have met no elephants yet but had a chat with a cobra. . . I just wish you'd bring yourself.' She filmed for three days in Colombo and Kandy, and among ruins. Then she became difficult. The director at first shot around her and then began shooting her scenes twice, once with her and once with only the other characters and the backgrounds. There was already a sense that she might not complete the film. Olivier at the time was in France. He had thought of bringing overseas companies to the St James' and was in Paris looking over the work of the Comédie Française and enjoying the congenial company of his friends Ginette Spanier, a directrice of Balmain, and her husband, both of whom he had first met there on the Old Vic's European tour of 1945. It was there that he received an urgent appeal from Irving Asher to come out to Ceylon and do something. Vivien was making the filming impossible. She cabled him too: 'Darling please bring white beaded evening dress top drawer right side dressing table and your dinner jacket tropical if possible.' He did not go back to London to find the dress. He flew out to Ceylon direct from Paris. It took twenty-four hours. The day he arrived she wrote in her diary, 'Woke (voices) 6.30. *Larry* [twice underlined].' She met him herself at Colombo Airport. She had got him out there after all. She wanted to stop at a rest house for 'a little drink and a relax'. When he suggested she had better be back at work in front of the cameras he was met with a blaze of rage. 'In the unhappy colloquy that followed,' he said, 'I thought ruefully of the wretched waste of time, effort and money that I had been a party to.'[17]

On location he found Peter Finch very much in charge, as the only person who had any influence over Vivien. He had sent her little notes. 'That crow outside your window is saying you're lonely. Are you?' And, 'Awake? Hope.' Vivien's maid Ethel told Olivier that Vivien and Finch had not been to bed but had lain all night in the open on the hillsides. As Olivier put it, 'I could find no blame in my heart for Peter – was he not simply doing what I had done to her first husband seventeen years ago? I found it pretty old fashioned to work up any extra feelings of outrage on account of my being his boss from which he had been able to glean a very nice career, thank you; besides, I had always liked him, and in the strangest of ways, just then the utter confusion of the mess in which we found ourselves seemed to dispel hostility.' He stayed only three days, during which Vivien went shopping for saris and bought four pictures, for which Olivier afterwards had to pay the gallery. Then he wished the unfortunate Asher all the luck he needed and went home, telling himself his mission had been 'as futile as any fool would have known that it would be'. On the day of Olivier's departure, in a busy entry in her diary, Vivien mentioned a lobster lunch but not that her husband – whom she had got out there by the exercise of her fickle will – had gone. Four days afterwards she and the film unit flew from Ceylon to Los Angeles by way of Paris and New York.[18]

Back in England Olivier quickly finished what he had to do with *The Beggar's Opera*. He gave some thought to Notley, writing in his diary: 'Girls out of orchard into New Acre. Harrow and lime orchard.' The girls were the cows of his dairy herd.[19] Then he went off to Ischia, in the Bay of Naples, for a holiday with his friends William and Susana Walton. He had only one day with them before news reached him that Vivien had broken down once more, this time in Hollywood. He set off on his travels again. He took the boat from Porto d'Ischia to Naples at 6.15 a.m. – I shall never forget the colour of the sky: blanketed all over with turbulent cloud, it was dark red; yes, it was ominous all right.' Then a train from Naples at 10 a.m., a Comet from Rome at 1.20 p.m. and then, having talked to Vivien's doctor in London, a 7 p.m. overnight flight to New York. Cecil Tennant went with him. They arrived at Idlewild Airport at 8.55 a.m. New York time, where they were met by Danny Kaye. Olivier's diary shows he went to the Sherry Netherland Hotel, where he had a massage and a sleep before returning to the airport at midnight to take the 12.30 a.m. 'Ambassador' flight to Los Angeles. He then made his second consecutive night flight before meeting the Nivens and Vivien's doctors next morning, 15 March, in Hollywood. 'Next was the encounter with Vivien, more dreadful than any other in my life. . . When I arrived at [her] house I was told I would find

her outside on an upstairs balcony; stepping gently on to this I saw
her. She was leaning with her elbows upon the railing and her face
in her hands. I called her softly and she looked up at me. It was as
if her eyes were misted over, all grey-green-blue; only the tiniest
pin-prick of a pupil was discernible. I said, "Hello, darling", and
when she spoke to me it was in the tone of halting dream-like
amazement that people in the theatre use for mad scenes when they
can't think of anything better. My instinctive reaction was that she
was putting it on. I took her very gently in my arms, not able for
the life of me to think of anything to ask beyond did she think
perhaps there was something the matter with her? She turned away
from the railing towards the wall and with the wonderment of a
first communion said, "I'm in love." I asked very gently, "who with,
darling?" Then – approaching the Most High – "Peter Fi-i-inch."
Where the hell was he by the way, I wondered.'[20] Olivier, seeing
Vivien's wonderment as that of a first communion and thinking,
however ironically, of Finch as the 'Most High', was seeing this
terrible meeting in religious terms.

Vivien had by then been behaving wildly for five days, and very
strangely for a week before that. After the events in Ceylon, Olivier
had with some reason been apprehensive about what might happen
in America, and before he went off to Italy he cabled Asher in
Hollywood asking if he could confidentially and tactfully find out
the name and address of Vivien's doctor and cable it to him. By
then Vivien had already refused to stay in the rooms reserved for
her at the Beverly Hills Hotel and insisted on staying at Spencer
Tracy's house in his absence.[21] She fluffed her lines on set, cancelled
an appointment for costume fittings, and began to call Finch 'Larry'.
She insisted on giving a party for Tamara Finch, who had come to
meet her husband in Hollywood. Seventy guests had been invited
including Niven and his wife and Stewart Granger and his wife,
and then at the last moment Vivien said she was ill and unhappy
and went to bed, leaving Tamara to act as hostess.[22]

What happened to Vivien in the next few days was later described
by both Niven and Granger in their memoirs.[23] Both of them were
good friends of Vivien and Olivier, having known them since before
the war. Both published their memoirs many years later – Niven in

1975 and Granger in 1981 – by which time their memories would have been less than sharp. There are many inconsistencies between the two versions. Perhaps out of tactfulness, Niven disguised his account by not naming Vivien, just referring to a film star called 'Missee'. Nor did he refer to the part Granger played, perhaps not wishing to implicate him. Granger's account, written later, named names and was more direct. Both obviously wrote in good faith. Niven's account is more brutal in its detail, and anyone in the theatre or pictures would have known that he was writing about Vivien, but it plainly did not offend Olivier since they remained firm friends after it was published. Here, compiled from the two accounts, is a summary of what probably happened, though what happened in what order is not clear.

After a party given by Vivien – perhaps the party for Tamara – Mae, the help at Vivien's house, telephoned Niven urgently asking him to come over quickly, which he did. Mae, saying Vivien was possessed, refused to stay in the house and left there and then. Niven took a key from her and let himself into the dark house. Suddenly all the lights came on and there was Vivien at the top of the stairs. Her hair was hanging down in straggly clumps, mascara and make-up formed a streaked mask down to her chin, one false eyelash was missing, her eyes were staring and wild, she was naked, and she looked 'quite, quite mad'. He tried to calm her down but she said she hated him and sat on the landing, alternately sobbing and snarling at him through the banisters. He coaxed her downstairs to watch television. At that time of night there were no programmes but she sat watching an empty screen, at times laughing and pointing at the set, at times shrinking back in horror. He put his arms round her naked body and found her icy cold. That, so far, is Niven's account. For whatever reason, he left out John Buckmaster, who figures in Granger's story. Granger wrote that Niven phoned him late at night, saying Vivien had had a nervous breakdown and that Buckmaster was in the house and refused to leave. Granger went round and found Buckmaster, dressed only in a towel, guarding Vivien's bedroom door and claiming he had been sent by a higher power to protect her. Now Buckmaster was the son of Gladys Cooper and an old lover of Vivien's from the 1930s, before Olivier. In 1952 he had been

convicted of assault in New York, having molested women in the
street and threatened his captors with knives, and was sent to a state
mental hospital.[24] He had somehow returned to Hollywood and
there found Vivien. One account says they wandered naked round
George Cukor's pool and tore up money together. At any rate, when
Granger found Buckmaster he told him he had been sent by an even
higher power and to get the hell out. This persuaded him to go.
Niven stayed to look after Vivien while Granger drove Buckmaster
home and then telephoned the studio doctor. He prescribed pills to
sedate Vivien, to be picked up from an all-night pharmacy, and
Granger returned to find her watching the blank television set. Then
followed a scene out of a farce. Granger mixed one pill with some
scrambled eggs and another with the coffee. Vivien became suspi-
cious and insisted Niven should eat and drink first. He did so and
fell into a drugged sleep, leaving Granger alone to cope with Vivien.
They had been friends for years and yet the strained, white-faced
woman facing him had nothing to do with the Vivien he knew. At
dawn she announced she would take a swim. 'Here I was,' wrote
Granger, 'at six in the morning sitting by a pool opposite a totally
nude and utterly deranged stranger.'

Niven woke and telephoned the head of the studio, who promised to send a doctor and to urge Olivier to come out. They agreed
it would take him at least three days to get there. Niven did eventually get Vivien to take some pills, stirring one into a glass of wine
and pounding another into some cottage cheese, but this only slowed
her down for a while. She then tried to entice him into bed with
her. He had become exhausted but she never showed any tiredness
and harried him endlessly to play hide and seek with her, flatter
her, comfort her, fight with her, or go to bed with her. 'I found,' he
said, 'that I had come to hate her.' When the doctor came with two
nurses she was terrified. Then she imperiously ordered them out
of the house. One nurse, trying to calm her, said, 'I know who you
are. You're Scarlett O'Hara, aren't you?' Vivien screamed back: 'I'm
not Scarlett O'Hara, I'm Blanche DuBois.' Granger, in his account,
took Vivien in his arms, whispered to her that everything was going
to be all right, pinned her underneath him, and yelled at the terrified nurse to stick the needle in. As she felt the point she looked

at him as if he had betrayed her. 'Oh Jimmy, how could you? I thought you were my friend.'

If there is no coherent account of those four mad days, and there is not, it is probably because nothing very coherent happened. Both Niven and Granger were shocked and exhausted. No fewer than three doctors attended Vivien and were in and out of the house. One was the Paramount studio doctor, Fraser McDonald, who was the first to see her and came every day. The second was Dr Ralph R. Greenson, a psychiatrist. It was after he first saw her on 12 March that Olivier was contacted on Ischia. He attended her for four days before Olivier arrived, spending on average eight hours a day with her. Then there was another psychiatrist. It was all confusion.[25]

The day after Olivier met Vivien he and Cecil Tennant went to see the Paramount people, who were generous and helpful. The film contract was at an end and Elizabeth Taylor would take over from Vivien, who would still keep the one third of her fee already paid to her. The more pressing concern was to get her home. If she remained in California the doctors would have to report her state and she was likely to be certified. After the meeting at the studio Olivier went back to see Vivien, who complained that in the night she had been strapped up and wrapped in sheets of cold water. He told the nurses they had some explaining to do. They said the most vitally important thing for Vivien in her condition was sleep, but she had the will-power to resist the strongest drugs. So, having sedated her all they dared, they had recourse to that crude way of inducing sleep. It did not take long for her body heat to warm the wet sheets and in the process sleep overcame her. They then removed the wet sheets, dried her, wrapped her in warm, dry bedclothes, and she slept the rest of the night.[26] Her will-power and her determination to protest were great. For four days she had written nothing whatever in her pocket diary, and her entry for that day was a scrawl of three illegible words, but she did manage to write in pencil, on a scrap of paper which still exists:

4 injections of sodium
Cold winding sheets
Left although called for help.[27]

The next day Olivier consulted the three doctors on how to get Vivien home. They decided to fly her back, by way of New York. Cecil Tennant had a more calming effect on her than Olivier did so it was Tennant, in his clothes, who held her in his arms all night before they took her to the airport on a stretcher. With the help of the Paramount people it went smoothly. Olivier called it 'the escape from Hollywood'. At one point on the flight someone hysterically reported, 'She's stopped breathing', but when they reached New York at midday Vivien walked down the steps of the plane and was whisked off to some friends of Danny Kaye's on Long Island, where no one would talk. That evening she refused to fly back to England, explaining that she had work to finish in Hollywood, and was carried on board the plane by Olivier and Kaye. She was first sedated. When she saw the syringe she tried desperately to escape. Olivier was horrified to see that the nurse was enjoying it but there was no time for anything: he and Kaye threw themselves on top of Vivien and held her down. 'Vivien fought us with the utmost ferocity as the needle went in, biting and scratching Danny and me, screaming appalling abuse at both of us, with particular attention to my erotic impulses; it seemed an eternity before she went limp and Danny and I were able to let go of her, both shattered and exhausted.'[28] At Heathrow she had recovered enough to walk down the steps of the plane herself and to write in her diary, though very shakily, in a large, sprawling hand, 'Larry and Drs Freudenberg and Child took me to Coolsden. Heathrow – Larry left me in Coolsden.'

Olivier wrote in his diary: '*Safe.*' It was 20 March, nearly five weeks since she had left for Ceylon. Dr Armando Child was Vivien's general practitioner, whom she trusted. Dr Rudolf Freudenburg was from the Surrey County Mental Hospital at Netherne, near Coulsden. Olivier went to Durham Cottage. '12 hours sleep,' he wrote in his diary. Next day he went to Notley – '14 hours sleep.'[29]

At Netherne, Vivien was induced into a sleep which, it was hoped, would last three weeks. Olivier had taken her there and entrusted her to Dr Freudenberg, because he had observed the treatment of his sister Sybille at his hands. Sybille had been his patient in 1949, and again in 1952. When she learned where Vivien was she wrote a letter to Olivier which may or may not have comforted him: 'Presumably Viv will be having "narcosis" treatment. Don't worry. When convalescent myself I have helped to give such patients their breakfast. . . Usually they were too sleepy to do more than take a few mouthfuls. They are kept heavily drugged, of course; but seem to make an amazing recovery once the treatment is over. . . I have seen some amazing cases. I remember one girl who had "milk fever" after a baby. My first sight of her brought to mind the lunatic in *Jane Eyre*. Three months later when I left the hospital I said goodbye to her as she sat peacefully knitting by a good fire in the lounge, looking well and contented and only waiting for her last insulin dose before she too was going home; an amusing, sane creature.'[30]

Olivier does seem to have been comforted by a letter which Jill wrote him, and replied with a warmth he did not often show her. 'You were right in guessing that I do most desperately feel the need of friends just now. It has been a very bad time. Getting her home was an incredible nightmare. As you may have gathered she set up the strongest resistance, and of course as naturally follows when things go wrong, I was to her, her worst enemy. She has suffered terribly and will be very ill for some time. But none of the horrors of the last ten days compare to the feeling of relief that somehow the mission was accomplished and that now she is safe in, I believe, the best hands in England. No one can see for a bit so I am taking the time to recharge the batteries a bit against whatever the future may hold.'[31]

By the time he wrote that letter he was back in Italy. There he also received news from Freudenberg and from Niven, who had come to England and was staying at Durham Cottage. Freudenberg said Vivien was sometimes sweet and charming, realising her illness, but at other times aggressive and hostile. She had however agreed to stay, 'so that no extension of the order was necessary'. There had, then, been an order to commit her. Niven wrote calling Vivien 'Whizzbang', and said she was sleeping a lot, but that during the little while she was awake she had told Dr Child three things – that she loved Larry, that she wanted to go back to Notley soon, and that Elizabeth Taylor was ridiculous casting. He said Freudenberg wanted to talk to him since it would be useful to him to know about the beginning of her collapse. The doctors were worried about her chest. Saliva tests showed no trace of tuberculosis but they thought that rest in Switzerland might be a godsend in disguise. 'Because obviously the trickiest time for her, and indeed for you, will be when she first comes home. It's going to be, or it might be, as hard as ever to get her to rest [so] if there is a worry about her chest she could go and rest in Switzerland and cure two birds with one stone.'[32]

Olivier had gone back to Italy straight after his two nights of long sleep. He caught an early morning plane to Rome, reached Ischia by the evening and again slept round the clock, from 11.30 at night until 11.30 the next morning. Before long the news of Vivien's illness and of Olivier's presence on Ischia was out. He was news because, as he put it, his wife was in a mental hospital and he was on the run. Journalists hung around outside the Waltons' house so they escaped to the mainland, smuggling Olivier out on the floor of their car underneath a blanket and crossing to Naples on a fishing boat. They then undertook not a leisurely tour but an 800-mile exploration of southernmost Italy. Olivier wanted to follow the route the Roman armies, and Antony, had taken on their way to Egypt. So they drove across Italy to the east coast at Bari and then travelled south to the very end of the Appian way at Brindisi. Then they crossed briefly to Sicily, before driving the long road north back to Naples. One Sunday Olivier and Walton, both former choristers, insisted on going to pontifical mass. Susana Walton thought they both regarded the ceremony as excellent theatre – altar boys swinging incense, the bishop and his acolytes gliding up and down the altar steps, all to the high-pitched sound of chanting. At Naples they saw *Götterdämerung* at the San Carlo opera and then returned to Ischia.[33]

A day later Olivier received a telegram saying, 'Awakening imminent. Come back quick.'[34] Freudenberg had succeeded in keeping Vivien asleep for only two weeks rather than three. Olivier returned immediately, but by the time he got back she had already been visited by Holman. Freudenberg, whom she called 'Rosenkavalier', had asked him to visit her and, in Olivier's absence, to persuade her to stay. Three more weeks of treatment were needed, but although she could not be left alone and needed three nurses he could not keep her there unless he certified her. Holman failed to persuade her. She was strong-willed as ever, would not stay, and had herself removed to University College Hospital in London. From there she summoned her maid Ethel, a beauty specialist and her leg-depilator, and telephoned Noel Coward, Alex Korda, and Victor Stiebel. She was back into her dizzy routine. When Olivier returned, which he did straight away, she found it impossible to understand why he had not been waiting at her bedside for her first stirring. Coward had placed by her bed, for her to see when she woke, flowers, Christian Dior perfume, toilet water, powder; the lot. She remembered that, and she remembered that Larry had not been there. 'I blamed myself,' he said, 'for not being more alive to my duties, no matter how painful or how mortally sick of them I was.' He knew that while she slept she had been given electric shock treatment, with a current sent from one temple to the other, and saw that there were changes in her. 'I can only describe them by saying she was not, now that she had been given the treatment, the same girl that I had fallen in love with. I have said that some four years before this her feelings for me had changed and that she had told me so; but now it was not so much a question of her feelings as my own. In so far as she was no longer the person I had loved, I loved her that much less. She was now more of a stranger to me than I could ever have imagined possible.'[35]

Vivien and Olivier were back at Notley together by 16 May.[36] It was two months since he had been summoned out to Ceylon to see what could be salvaged of his wife's film, and of her. Since then, travelling to exhaustion, he had done as much as anyone could have done. He was not, at the time, given much credit, and this is because very few people had any true idea of Vivien's condition. 'Throughout her possession by that uncannily evil monster, manic depression,' he said, 'she retained her own individual canniness – an ability to disguise her true mental condition from almost all except me, for whom she could hardly be expected to take the trouble.' The bitterness of that last phrase can be excused, because what he said was the truth.[37]

She did disguise her condition. Frewen, who had known her well for almost twenty years, called her poor pet and blamed Olivier for not staying at Coulsden – which he called a loony-bin – and for having gone off to Italy, 'address allegedly unknown'. When Olivier did appear, Frewen wrote that obviously his whereabouts had been known, and added, 'What a world of memory-losers and liars!' Yet Frewen meant well.

So most evidently did Peter Hiley. By then he had been for four years not only company secretary to LOP at the St James's and general overseer of the works at Notley and Durham Cottage; he had also acted as aide-de-camp to Olivier and to Vivien and held them both in the greatest affection. He knew she was demanding, difficult, and wayward, yet up to 1953 he had not foreseen any serious trouble. 'Larry, I think, afterwards, wanted to justify himself by saying, well, she was ill much further back.'[38] He could not have known, but she *had* been ill much further back. It is the saddest story, but she had been intermittently mad for years and the malaise went back at least to 1939. For him and other friends not to have known this in 1953 was the most natural thing in the world. For a biographer not to say so now would be grossly unfair to Olivier.

The events in Hollywood had also been closer-run than was ever publicly known in the lifetimes of either Vivien or Olivier. When the bills came in from the various doctors and nurses that of Doris B. Cotchefer, psychiatric nurse – who had attended Vivien in Hollywood and on the plane – came to $3,356.78. This was more than the combined bills of the three doctors. LOP challenged her bill. In the dispute she was supported by Paramount's doctor, who wrote to LOP strongly recommending she should be paid, and saying, 'On three or four occasions Mrs Cotchefer was aware that the life of the patient was at stake and "saved the day." This is the sort of service upon which it is difficult to put a tangible value.'[39]

One man who got close to an understanding of Olivier's state of mind at that time, if not Vivien's, was Noel Coward. After a talk with Olivier he wrote in his diary, 'Apparently things had been bad and getting worse since 1948 or thereabouts. It is really discouraging to reflect how needlessly unhappy people make themselves and each other. They are now going to start afresh down at Notley, which may work or may not. I shall be surprised if it does.'[40]

Notley was rescued for Olivier by a legal device. He could no

longer maintain it himself so LOP took a lease of the house, paying
him £250 a year rent, paying all outgoings and taxes, keeping the
house in good repair and allowing him and Vivien, as company
employees, to continue living there.[41] Finch was out of the way as
he had stayed on in Hollywood to complete *Elephant Walk* and had
then gone on holiday to Spain with his wife. Dickie and his new
bride Hester arrived at Notley in July. They had married in a
London register office while Vivien was in her first few wild days
in Hollywood. Dickie came as farm manager. Hester milked the
cows and gradually took over the running of the house. At the St
James's, because it was coronation year, LOP needed a coronation
play and chose a light confection called *The Sleeping Prince*. Vivien
was fit enough to start rehearsals in the autumn. She played a
chorus girl. Olivier played the crown prince of Carpathia. The royal
family of the English stage was back on public view again, apparently intact. The Queen, the Duke of Edinburgh, and Princess
Margaret attended one performance. Felix Barker's biography of
the Oliviers appeared with a jacket picture which showed a modestly
contented Vivien looking adoringly down at a smiling Olivier.

20

Richard III and the Ménage à Trois

IN MID-1953 OLIVIER FELT that his career as well as Vivien's had ground to a halt. *The Sleeping Prince* was a triviality, but such a successful triviality that it ran for 274 performances, until July 1954, and by then his spirits had revived. '*Richard III* is on,' he wrote to Tarquin. 'So you can imagine there is no spare moment for me now. It's OK. I intend enjoying it. I am sick of suffering under things and letting them make me unhappy.' He did write intimately to the son he had hardly known. Tarquin says he bullied him into it. 'I was determined to have a father, and he got into the habit of writing, sometimes most confidingly.'[1]

Olivier was going to make a film of what had probably been his most memorable role on the stage; for that he needed money, and this time there was no Del Giudice to raise it. After he lost Two Cities to Rank, whom he loathed, he had gone to Hollywood but failed to interest Louis B. Mayer and Selznick in art films. By 1951 he was planning to film in Florida, which he called a heavenly paradise. But he had been ill and lost an eye. In 1952, when Olivier was in New York with the Cleos, he wrote to Del saying a little bird told him he was 'almighty short of dough' and sending him a cheque, but also advising him that no one was going to lay out millions on artistic pictures. By 1954 Del had bounced back and was in Milan, where he was confident he would build a great studio. 'Here is the money! I am very happy.' But the money was not there, and *Richard III* was financed by Korda and by American money borrowed by LOP itself.[2]

Olivier directed again and co-produced with Korda. The casting
was grandiose. Gielgud and Richardson appeared, as did Cedric
Hardwicke; they with Olivier made four theatrical knights in one
film. Olivier approached every grand name in sight. He asked
Richard Burton to play Richmond, saying that to accept would be
'a charming gesture on the part of a bright, bright star to a blis-
tered old ember'; the star cabled regrets. Robert Donat 'loathed' to
decline a small part, saying the smallness had nothing to do with
it. Michael Redgrave at first agreed to play a part but then, as Cecil
Tennant put it, 'ratted'. John Mills and Richard Attenborough were
invited to play the first and second murderers, who had about five
lines each; Mills reluctantly decided this would be a bad thing for
the film since it might be regarded as a stunt, and Attenborough
bitterly regretted that a clash of dates made it impossible for him
to accept. Paul Scofield was considered but not approached. The
American backers wanted Vivien in the invented part of Jane Shore,
the old king's mistress; Olivier was tempted but was not certain it
would be good for her, so Pamela Browne was engaged. The seduced
Lady Anne, a most important part in Olivier's *Richard III*, was
played by Claire Bloom.[3]

Olivier, in his own handwriting, made a draft of what the film
set out to be. It was set in the Wars of the Roses, between the Red
Rose of the House of Lancaster and the White Rose of York. 'The
story of England is an unknown pattern of history and legend. The
history of the world, like letters without poetry, flowers without
perfume, or thought without imagination, would be a dry matter
indeed without legends, and many of these, whether scorned by
proof a hundred times, seem worth preserving for their own familiar
sakes.'[4] Among the legends, of course, were Richard's villainy and
crippled state.

The outside scenes were shot in Spain, with the help of the Spanish
Army. Spain later became a familiar location for films, but Olivier
believed that was the first time it was used by a foreign company.
During the shooting he sustained his usual injury. He insisted on
having his horse shot from under him realistically, so a real archer
shot a real arrow at a horse protected by real armour. The trouble
was that before it hit its mark it went through Olivier's unprotected

calf. The limp that ensued was dramatically right, since it was in the leg that the crippled Richard was already dragging. Olivier's death scene was spectacular. He modelled it on the death of a kitten he and Jill had in the early days of their marriage. He had been lying in his bath watching it playing with a ping-pong ball, and stretched out to push the door closed to keep the kitten inside. It darted out, and the door caught it and broke its neck. He leapt out of his bath and picked it up. The dying kitten's claws tore his bare chest.[5]

Then followed three months at Shepperton studios. Korda telephoned Olivier every night: 'Larry, you must cut, you know? You ruin me, you know.'[6] The location shots had been most difficult, particularly on a wide screen, with Olivier having to make do with 500 Spanish soldiers to represent two armies. He had opposed the use of Cinemascope, with its screen dimensions of 2.55:1. He had gone to see the new and spectacular *Three Coins in a Fountain* and said the thing was just a distraction, a gimmick to drag people away from their television sets. He settled for the 2:1 screen of Techicolor VistaVision, though Korda was irritable: 'They are all ecstatic about VistaVision. Of course they are equally ecstatic about every other damn thing.'[7]

Walton again wrote the music, as he had for *Henry V* and *Hamlet*. By 1954 he had come to feel that film music need not necessarily be good or bad, as long as it fitted, and that its great characteristic should be that it was not heard. He thought Shakespeare repeated himself, battle after battle, and that there was a limit to the number of ceremonial fanfares and battle charges he could manufacture for historical chronicles. On one score wrote the musical instruction, '*Con prosciutto, agnello, e confitura di fragiole* [with ham, lamb, and strawberry jam].' Ham or not, his coronation march from the film was later published separately, and so were another six items, as a Shakespeare Suite for orchestra.[8]

There were the usual agonisings over cutting the film for the American market. At one point an exasperated Olivier wrote, 'You can go on until you've got about four or five completely disjointed sequences; you'll have a short film all right, of which nobody will understand a solitary word any more than they would if the same treatment were applied to *Gone With the Wind*, *War and Peace*, *David*

Copperfield etc.'[9] In the United States the film was shown not in cinemas but on television, which Olivier bitterly opposed, but NBC's offer of $500,000 was too tempting to refuse. So a film made in colour and in VistaVision was shown in black and white on small television screens, with commercial breaks. The NBC publicity was not subtle: 'Yessirree! When do four good (k)nights equal three top TV hours?' Still, it was simultaneously broadcast by 146 stations coast to coast and watched by an estimated audience of fifteen-to-twenty million: more than had watched any one broadcast that was not on sport, and more than had seen the play in the 350 years since it was written.[10]

While Olivier was making *Richard III* Vivien was engaged on *The Deep Blue Sea*. She played a judge's wife who leaves a safe marriage for a young pilot and drives herself to attempted suicide. To ask Vivien to play an unstable woman was hardly helpful to her. Nor did it work to ask her to play a woman meant to be unattractive and therefore the more ready to fall for a young lover. It was Korda's film and he was taking a chance on her. Hers was not a safe history. In her time she had broken her contract with him as well as her contract with Selznick, and the disaster of *Elephant Walk* had made her difficult to insure. She was to be paid £65,000 and 20% of the net profit, but this sounds more than it was. For a start most films never show a net profit, and she was also to be paid in careful instalments. She would receive only £5,000 while the film was in production. The other £60,000 would be paid at the rate of 15% of Korda's net receipts. Only thereafter would she get a share of the profits, and as it happened there were none. She did however have the right to approve the other major casting, so it was surprising that she ended up with Kenneth More as the lover.[11] He did not like her at all. 'I could never really trust her and I suspected her almost overwhelming friendliness. I thought she was petulant, spoilt, overpraised and overloved. But I readily grant that she was a real woman, exceptionally intelligent (as actresses go) and a brilliant hostess.'[12] There is the opinion of one of the few people she did not charm.

She also had the right to retain her film costumes. There were twelve items, including a wool dress (£150), a silk suit (£150), an ocelot fur coat (£550), a pair of alligator shoes (£28 7s) and other things, which altogether had cost Korda £1,075. He sold them to LOP at half-cost, £537 10s. LOP then gave the lot to Vivien as parade clothes, requiring her to pay only £23 for articles deemed not essential to her work – one sweater and three bras. To arrive at present day values, these prices should be multiplied by at least twenty.[13]

By late 1954 Dickie and Hester had been at Notley for almost eighteen months. When Hester had first met Olivier in his crowded dressing room at the St James' three years before she had been struck by the theatricality of it all, by the exclamations of 'Darling' floating around, and he was smaller than she had imagined. She had no real impression of him until she went to Notley. There she saw him become the country gent. She and Dickie lived in the cottage but almost always had Sunday lunch with Larry and Vivien and saw a lot of them. There were endless games of canasta, into the small hours. Vivien liked playing charades. On Monday mornings Olivier, very much the squire, would walk round the place with Dickie and make plans for the farm. The two brothers were very much alike. Dickie was leaner, and more like Larry's photographs than Larry was himself. When they talked about their mother they practically gave her a halo. How much they really remembered or how much they just remembered remembering she did not know, but their mother was perfect. They told terrible stories about their father. When they talked about the war it was pure *Boys' Own Paper*. Both were almost Victorian in their view of women, wanting to put them on a pedestal, yet Olivier spoke unkindly of Jill, with a *lack* of feeling, as if he could not imagine why their marriage had ever happened. Hester also saw that he was ill at ease with Tarquin, and that the only real affection the boy got was from Vivien. 'She certainly had many faults, but she was a far more human person in her relationships. She was very kind, as well as very unkind, and she was kind *about* people.' Hester thought that in her manic phases Vivien looked awfully like the picture painted of her as Blanche DuBois, and heard her reciting Blanche's lines. She was terrified by her ECT treatment. Sybille was there occasionally and described her own treatment, but she was quite different, being intellectually interested in the treatment and the disease. 'Whereas Vivien was horrified and fastidiously repelled by the whole thing. I was very very fond of her.'[14]

At Christmas 1954 the Oliviers gave a house party at Notley. Among the guests were Rex Harrison and his wife Lili Palmer, the Waltons, and Peter Finch. He had by then been back in England for six months making films for Rank, but had tried to keep away from Vivien. Susana Walton had the distinct feeling that Larry, while he was setting off the fireworks, was pointing a rocket directly at Finch but changed his aim at the last minute and sent the rocket up into the evening air. She remembered Larry saying to her at the time that in Walton's music there was an inner vibrance. 'Not afraid of the brass, is he? An energy twin to sexual energy. . . I think it's very much the same thing; that exuberance, that spirit, that heart-quickening feeling, belongs in the same area of human nature. Certain types of actor have that quality; it has something to do with sex, but it has a lot more to do with love. It's a very vibrant sort of love; it's not a soft kind of love at all.' That, Lady Walton wrote later, was the quality she most remembered between Olivier and Vivien when she first met them, but after Vivien's illness that strong kind of love was there no more.[15]

Back in the summer of 1954 Olivier had agreed to lead the 1955 season at Stratford-upon-Avon. He would play Malvolio in *Twelfth Night* with Vivien as Viola, Macbeth to her Lady Macbeth, and Titus Andronicus with her as Lavinia. They would be paid £60 a week each, a trivial sum – less than Olivier had commanded as Romeo twenty years before – but a house would be placed at their disposal, free except for the wages of their own domestic staff. Rehearsals would begin on 14 March and the season would end on 26 November.[16] For Olivier this was a necessary thing to do. He had done nothing of consequence on the stage since the two Cleopatras three years before. But to commit an unfit Vivien to eight months of intensive repertory, and to expect her to play Lady Macbeth, was quite another matter. She had everything to lose and, if she cracked, so had he.

The Oliviers were received at Stratford with great ceremony. Every seat for the entire season was sold. They moved into the company house at Avoncliffe. The Earl of Warwick invited them to lunch at the castle and told them they would always be welcome there. Then work began. *Twelfth Night* was directed by John Gielgud, and the rehearsals did not go well. The two men had not worked together since their *Romeo* of 1935. Gielgud liked a play to develop in rehearsal. Olivier came with definite intentions from the first day. Besides that, he played Malvolio so broadly that Gielgud thought he resembled a Jewish hairdresser, and he would insist on falling backwards off a bench in the garden scene though Gielgud begged him not to.[17] He wrote a letter to Stark Young, an American friend, which sums up his view of Olivier and Vivien. Olivier, he wrote, was brilliant, but his gift for mimicry, as opposed to creative acting, stuck in the gizzard at times. 'His execution is so certain and skilled that it is difficult to convince him that he *can* be wrong in his own exuberance. . . The truth is he is a born autocrat, and must always be right. He has little respect for the critical sensitivity of others; on the other hand he is quite brilliant in his criticism of my directing methods and impatient with my hesitance and (I believe) necessary flexibility. He wants everything cut and dried at once, so that he may perfect with utter certainty of endless rehearsal and repetition – but he is good for me all the same, and perhaps I may still make a good thing of that divine play, especially if he will let me pull her little ladyship (who is brainier than he is but *not* a born actress) out of her timidity and safeness. He dares too confidently (and will always carry an undiscriminating audience with him) while she hardly dares at all and is terrified of overreaching her technique and doing anything that she has not killed the spontaneity of by over practice. It is an interesting problem, the pair of them – Lynn and Alfred, I suppose, *in parvo.*'[18]

This is a penetrating evaluation of one great actor by an another, and not an unkind appreciation of Vivien. Olivier, had he seen it, could not have welcomed the suggestion that his and Vivien's problem was that of the Lunts, in a small way. The letter makes plain why the two men could not see eye to eye, and with only a few days to go before the opening Olivier went so far as to ask Gielgud to leave the company to rehearse on their own, in effect under Olivier's direction. Gielgud consented to this request and on the opening day wrote Olivier a letter of great generosity, tempered perhaps by a light touch of irony.

> Dearest Larry
> I think you must know how deeply I have been touched and flattered to work with you on this play. . . Every suggestion you have made has been constructive, and you have been unfailing in your example, too, of throwing yourself into the rehearsals and encouraging the others. Don't hesitate now to bestride your own scenes with your own particular authority and relish and enjoy. . . the pleasure and response which I know will greet your every scene.
> Much love and gratitude, John.[19]

Then in June came *Macbeth*. Olivier was universally praised. Terence Rattigan told him his was the definitive Macbeth. Tynan wrote that on the opening night Olivier had shaken hands with greatness. But Tynan was a stranger to moderation of any sort: he wrote of Vivien that her Lady Macbeth was 'more niminy-piminy than thundery-blundery, more viper than anaconda, but still quite competent in its small way'. This was a blow to an actress who had already, in *Twelfth Night*, been said to have shown 'the qualities which distinguish an air-hostess' but no warmth. There was an extraordinary difference of opinion about her Lady Macbeth. The young Peter Hall, in his first season at Stratford, thought it competent but ordinary. Olivier himself thought her the best he had seen, and there may have been all sorts of reasons for that, but then so did Peggy Ashcroft, who was not inclined to trim her opinions to suit anyone and meant what she said. Maxine Audley, who played Lady Macduff, gave Vivien reasoned praise, saying she was wonderful because of her changes of mood. You believed that she and Macbeth had been in love and that it was beginning to crumble. 'Most Macbeths and Lady Macbeths don't seem to behave like a married couple. I never believe they actually lived together. But Larry and Vivien at the banquet scene, when he sees the ghost of Banquo and she's trying to keep control, they were like any married couple with awkward guests.' This is praise indeed, and the more convincing because Miss

Audley was also, about this time, one of Olivier's mistresses and she and Vivien were not always friends. The idea of Macbeth as a play in part about a married couple may have been in Olivier's mind; Elizabeth Bowen had said that of his Old Vic production in 1937. And Vivien was once more playing the part of a disintegrating woman, something she did well.[20]

The third play in which the Oliviers took part was *Titus Andronicus*, he in the title role of a Roman general, she as his daughter Lavinia. Peter Brook directed this early and almost unplayable piece of Shakespeare's, which includes five stabbings, a strangling, seven other murders, and the serving up to a mother of her sons baked in a pie. There are also sundry mutilations, from which Lavinia suffers most, having both hands and her tongue cut off. Philip Hope-Wallace, the *Manchester Guardian* critic, began his notice, 'Look! No hands!' The bloodiness was stylised. The stage was suffused with a red light, and Lavinia's lost hands were signified by red streamers flapping from her wrists and her wrenched-out tongue by red streamers flowing from her mouth. Olivier and Brook astonishingly made a success of all this.

During the rehearsals Vivien started to go a bit mad. Or, as Olivier put it, the crash came. He was trying to master an unknown part when the familiar trials and tribulations were renewed. She invited the younger members of the company back until three in the morning but would be up again by five. He could never allow her to wander too far from his sight. The River Thame ran through the bottom of the garden, and beyond that fast cars would blind down the road. He asked himself: 'With only two hours of sleep, how in God's name have I any hope of committing to memory the unfamiliar myriad of words in this huge part?' In desperation he took her to see Dr Freudenberg. She agreed to go but put on a convincing performance of a sane, normal woman: 'Poor Larry, he's over anxious, that's all; it's easy to understand when you think of all the terrible dances I have led him, but, you see, I've never really been or felt better.' To Olivier's horror Freudenberg did not think more treatment necessary. 'The only thing I could think of,' wrote Olivier, '— and it was not a very enlivening thought — was that I might get as mad as she and be taken away and locked up. As for

Vivien, she gave a really splendid party that night and I didn't even get my usual two hours. I was drained of everything.'[21]

Coward thought Vivien was on the verge of another breakdown, talking wildly at supper, her voice shrill and her eyes strange. Larry came and talked to him when she had gone out, and was distraught. 'Their life together is really hideous and here they are trapped by public acclaim, scrabbling about in the cold ashes of a physical passion that burnt itself out years ago. . . She, exacerbated by incipient TB, needs more and more physical satisfaction. They are eminent, successful, envied and adored, and most wretchedly unhappy.'[22]

When *Titus* opened Olivier thought she was fairly normal, 'like a spoilt woman a bit bored with things', and that she gave the impression that the part was beyond her. For the first time he felt bound to agree with Tynan when he wrote that, when she was raped over the body of her murdered husband, she expressed no feeling more vivid than that she would have preferred Dunlopillo. He survived by leaving her at Stratford and snatching nights at Notley, which was forty miles away, or by sleeping in his theatre dressing room, 'rather like some old actor who can't pay his rent'.[23]

Peter Finch was around again. Vivien had telephoned often, begging him to come. At Notley Hester had observed that when Vivien became manic and Olivier was exhausted, then – since his work mattered more to him than anything else – he 'tacitly almost encouraged Peter Finch, anything to mop up Vivien's spare energy'. She could remember him saying, 'It's so much easier when Puss has got someone to entertain her'.[24] At Stratford Vivien walked round the town openly holding hands with Finch. There is the famous story of the *ménage à trois* at Avoncliffe, of Olivier and Finch drinking in the library and of Vivien making an appearance and demanding, 'Which of you is coming to bed with me tonight?' It is told with variations. The wildest has Olivier summoning Finch to talk things over, Vivien saying it is up to them to decide which of them shall have her, and her leaving them alone in the library to thrash it out. There they act out a pantomime, Finch turning himself into a young aristocrat threatening to set the curtains on fire and Olivier into a senile family retainer trying to dissuade the young master from any such thing. The two actors give the performance of their lives until, at 3 a.m., Vivien appears like Lady Macbeth in her nightdress, demanding to know what they have decided and which is to come to bed with her. Then the three laugh till dawn. This was the account of Elaine Dundy, an American novelist who was Kenneth Tynan's first wife. She attributes it to an Australian poet, who told her he had it from Finch one heavy-drinking night in Rome many years after the event. That is what it sounds like. But there were certainly tales told around Stratford which cast Olivier in the part of a complaisant husband. Esmond Knight, who had known him for nearly thirty years and appeared with him in *Henry V, Hamlet,* and *Richard III,* said there were incredible stories. 'Laurence used ring up Peter Finch at night and say "For God's sake come round. Go up and see Vivien", and I suppose he quietly went up to see Vivien, made love to her and then came down, and they would spend the rest of the night getting absolutely pissed together.'[25] This is no evidence of what really happened, but it does give an idea of what was being said.

Olivier himself told the story, in its simplest form – 'Which of you is coming to bed with me tonight?' – to Joan Plowright, his third wife.[26] In essence, making allowances for Olivier's instinct to dramatise everything, it is likely to have been true.

But even that humiliation did not push him over the edge. He continued to bear with Vivien. Anthony Quayle said the season was nightmarish.[27] Two weeks after their supper together Coward saw her again and she was worse. Gielgud saw Olivier and Vivien together at much the same time. Their two accounts together give a fair idea of the state of affairs. Coward is downright, and Gielgud more perceptive. Coward had driven up to see the first night of *Titus* with Cecil Tennant, who was deeply perturbed and wanted to discuss the whole business. Coward thought Olivier wonderful in the play, and Vivien frankly not very good. 'Vivien was in a vile temper and perfectly idiotic. Larry was bowed down with grief and despair and altogether it was a gloomy little visit. Personally I think that if Larry had turned sharply on Vivien years ago and given her a clip in the chops, he would have been spared a mint of trouble. The seat of all this misery is our old friend, feminine ego. She is, and has been, thoroughly spoiled. She also has a sharp tongue and a bad temper. This, coupled. . .with an inner certainty that she can never be as good an artist as Larry, however much she tries, has bubbled up in her and driven her on to the borderline. Fond as I am of her and sorry as I feel for her, I would like to give her a good belting, although now I fear it might push her over the edge and be far, far too late.'[28]

Gielgud, when he saw the play, thought it Peter Brook's masterpiece, except for Vivien, who seemed in a bad way. 'She is utterly ineffective on the stage – like paper, only not so thick, no substance or power – and off stage she is avid, malicious, and insatiable, a bad look out for the future and for poor Larry who is saint-like with her and playing most beautifully as well.'[29]

Towards the end of November Vivien gave an even larger party than usual for the entire company and anyone else she could rope in. There were two hundred in all. When Hester got up in the morning to milk the cows some of the guests were still there, lying flat on their faces. It was the end of the Stratford season. Olivier was exhausted and ill. Over three days at the beginning of December he had blood tests, a barium meal and X-rays, a cardiograph, and a prostate massage.[30] He did have the premiere of *Richard III* to look forward to. It had not been chosen for the Royal Command Performance, that honour having gone to Hitchcock's *To Catch a Thief,* with Grace Kelly, but Olivier really did not seem to mind. *Richard III* had been suggested, but Oliver wrote to his friend Tim – Sir Terence Nugent, Comptroller of the Lord Chamberlain's office, with whom he had had dealings over the censorship of plays – that with command performances there was so much hullaballo and tutti-falla, with Hollywood stars having their frocks torn off in Leicester Square, that it was the worst atmosphere in which one's film could open. He also thought it was an evening to which the Queen must look forward with dread. Tim replied from St James' Palace that, thank God, he never had anything to do with that frolic. 'I have always been too backward to mingle in the crowd on the off chance of getting a handful of crêpe de chine from some film star's knickers.' He proposed a performance in aid of King George's pension fund for actors. This was held on 16 December 1955 in the presence of the Queen and the Duke of Edinburgh. Douglas

Fairbanks was there too, as were Jill, Sybille, Ibo, and Ginette Spanier. Tarquin had to decline. He had left Eton the year before, had been commissioned as an ensign in the Coldstream Guards, and posted to Germany.[31]

Olivier's tribulations with Vivien had not finished with the Stratford season. Towards Christmas she went on her own to Paris to stay with Ginette Spanier and her husband. Finch was due to arrive on the train at midnight. Ginette made it clear to Vivien that he could not stay in her house, saying she was a friend of Larry's. But after dinner Vivien left 'to meet a friend', and next morning Finch appeared wearing her dressing gown. The two of them then left for a villa near Hyères on the French Riviera, owned by a friend of Ginette's. Olivier followed from London. The game of distance and pursuit was on again. 'Night train Paris' he wrote in his diary. He spent a day with Ginette and then she, her husband, and Olivier travelled south. 'Train Toulon.' For two days all five of them stayed at the villa. Late at night Ginette and her husband heard raised voices, went downstairs and found Olivier yanking off his tie and exclaiming to Finch, 'Dear boy, I forgot to get you a Christmas present', while Vivien contentedly watched. Given the raised voices, Olivier's gesture with the tie may not have been friendly.[32] Finch withdrew, announcing that he would not, as had been planned, be joining Vivien in a new play by Coward. Vivien, so far as she was capable of resting, went for a rest cure in Bavaria, and Olivier to the Waltons in Ischia.[33]

Olivier had re-established himself as a great Shakespearean stage actor. His next plan was to film *Macbeth*, and Alex Korda was ready to finance it. Three days before Christmas 1955, while Olivier was in France pursuing Vivien and Finch, Tennant had already negotiated this on his behalf. Olivier, whose only refuge from Vivien was his work, had nevertheless insisted that she should play Lady Macbeth. She had other engagements for the coming year so he stipulated that the film should not be made until 1957. Korda agreed to these terms the same day.[34]

But a month later, on 23 January 1956, while Olivier was still abroad, Korda died of a heart attack. Olivier came home to give his funeral oration. *Macbeth* was, at least for the moment, dead.

21

The Prince and the Showgirl

LOOKING FOR ALL THINGS new, Olivier found Marilyn Monroe. She had a new film company, and somehow came by the idea that she would like to make a picture in which she would star with Olivier. Arthur Miller, the playwright, then her fiancé and later her husband, thought the very preposterousness of the pairing amused her. Whether *she* considered it at all preposterous is doubtful. When she made her whim known, such was its power that Olivier and Tennant flew to New York to attend on her. She kept them waiting for an hour, but when she did appear had them all at her feet in a second. Olivier had no memory of any word that was uttered, but a contract was signed. The film was to be of *The Sleeping Prince*, the play he had done with Vivien for coronation year, but for the screen it would be renamed *The Prince and the Showgirl*. Marilyn would be the show-girl and Olivier the prince. She would find the production money and he would direct. This was announced at a press conference in New York where she wore a low, backless dress, one of whose slender shoulder straps fortuitously broke in front of the cameras. *Time* magazine thought the whole thing prearranged.[1]

It was clear, thought Olivier, that he was going to fall most shatteringly in love with Marilyn. It was inescapable. She was so adorable, so witty, such incredible fun and more physically attractive than anyone he could have imagined. 'Wow!' he thought. 'For the first time now it threatened to be "poor Vivien"! (Almost thirty years before it had been "poor Jill!").' Vivien, he said, had taken being passed over for the role she had created very sweetly. Even though he told her clumsily, she had shrugged it off beautifully.[2]

That was his recollection. He may have thought Marilyn adorable, though when he returned from New York he told Holman she had the brains of a poussin.[3] He may have thought that it was the turn of 'poor Vivien' to be dispensed with, for she had given him every reason to think that way and to act accordingly. But having thought that, if he did, he then promptly overlooked the trials of the previous Stratford season – the *ménage à trois* at Notley and the attempted elopement of Vivien and Finch – and in the early months of 1956 began, as he put it, to 'try fucking our love back into existence'. He was taking the advice of his friend Lili Palmer who at the end of 1955 had asked why in God's name he had never tried giving Vivien a child. He thought his efforts went successfully, up to a point.[4] He comforted himself with the thought that Vivien was better and sweeter than for many years – and prayed to God that it would stay that way.'[5]

Olivier and Vivien had a new London house. Durham Cottage – which had for years been obviously too small – had been sold and, since the Waltons had decided to live permanently in Italy, their house in Lowndes Square, between Belgravia and Knightsbridge, had been taken.[6] It was a sort of new start. Olivier was on the up again. For the American opening of *Richard III* on television he went to Washington, which he had expected to be a groaning bore, but he was delighted when he was received at the White House by President Eisenhower himself. He said a great lump of pride came into his throat and he was moved to think that his picture had been seen by the Queen in London and the President in Washington.[7]

He also had a new source of income, from Olivier cigarettes, which were to be produced by Gallaghers, the makers of Benson & Hedges. He toured their factory in March; smoked a sample ciga-rette and found it agreeable; approved the royal blue packet with gold edges; and undertook to provide a silhouette of himself to appear on each packet. He was to receive twopence for every thou-sand cigarettes sold, and was given an advance of £2,500 against the first year's royalties. In addition to that Gallagher's would send him 500 packets of twenty every week, for his friends.[8] Vivien was

settling into her part in Coward's new play, *South Sea Bubble*, without
Finch, and was 'better and better in herself from the depressed state
in which she started the work'. He did not think much of the play.
'It is Noel at his lightest but it is I believe what the larger section
of the public enjoys. "Witty lines" and all that – piquantly relaxing
without the *slightest* danger of any exercise for the imagination or
intellect.'[9]

And there was the film with Marilyn to come in the summer. He
was rather teased about his association with her. Frewen went
round to Vivien's dressing room after a show, found Olivier there
looking rather fat and middle-aged, and asked, 'What are you doing
with Marilyn Monroe?' at which he made a gesture of annoyance.[10]
Preparations were being made for the big picture. A film crew was
assembled at Pinewood studios and a guarded house next to Windsor
Great Park, near the castle, was rented for Marilyn and Arthur
Miller, whom she had just married. Bernard Gilman, Olivier's chauffeur, arrived at LOP's London offices with crates of Olivier cigarettes. Olivier himself distributed them and told his new third
assistant director, Colin Clark, to be on hand at all times with the
cigarettes in case he wanted to smoke on the set, his own costume
having no pockets. Clark was well-connected. He was the younger
son of Sir Kenneth Clark, former director of the National Gallery
and a nominal director of a subsidiary company of LOP, and a
godson of William Walton. He had been found a job as a gopher
on account of this, and because of his father's long friendship with
Vivien. He was not as thrilled with the cigarettes as Olivier who,
when he saw this, remarked sharply that the same tobacco company
had previously named a cigarette after the famous actor Gerald du
Maurier. Clark preferred Woodbines.[11] Someone else not delighted
with the cigarettes was Ensign Tarquin Olivier, serving in Germany,
who wondered how to mitigate the contumely of his brother officers
and, rather than just saying nothing about the connection, stood
up at lunch in the officer's mess and announced it. They looked up
from their munching and regarded him mildly.[12]

Marilyn Monroe was due to arrive in London on 14 July to start
filming. Two days before that Vivien announced to the press that
she was pregnant, at the age of forty-two. The publicity this attracted

now seems incredible. She and Olivier were the pop stars of their day. The report and a picture covered practically the entire front page of the tabloid *Daily Sketch*. The *Daily Mail* gave half a page to the news. It was to be a baby for Christmas, expected to arrive on 22 December. Vivien, photographed sitting on a love seat, said they would prefer a girl and then looked up at Olivier, 'standing bashfully behind her', and said, 'Oh, you know men. They like to be comforted in their old age with a daughter.' Olivier was invited to kiss his wife and declined, saying 'We're too old for that.' That became the headline in the *Sketch*. Vivien had already chosen a nanny and was going to have a nursery at Notley painted yellow and white. When she was reminded that she had once been one of the youngest actresses to give birth to a child – that was Suzanne when she was nineteen – and would now be one of the oldest, she said, 'It's been so long. Much too long to remember what it's like to fondle your own baby.' Newspapers were more indulgent in those days. No reporter remarked that Suzanne had been abandoned when she was four and had been brought up almost entirely by her grand-mother. And how would Noel Coward feel about losing his leading lady? Vivien said he was delighted. Finally the reporters asked about Marilyn, who was due to arrive in two days. Vivien said she would not be one of the godparents.[13]

Coward was not delighted. His play had sold out because of Vivien and now he would have to find a replacement. He cabled loving congratulations but felt it was unforgivable of them. In his diary he consoled himself that Vivien had been far from ideal in the play anyway, charming but technically insecure; still, it was dismal to have to juggle with a capacity hit, and he'd hoped she would have carried on until at least Christmas. 'I also think, from Vivien's point of view, that it is a highly perilous enterprise. If anything goes wrong it will very possibly send her around the bend again; she is over forty, very, very small, and none too well balanced mentally. I am filled with forebodings and a curious sense of having been let down.'[14]

Coward, who was by then a tax exile in Jamaica, had at least been told a few days before the public announcement, but was angry that he had not been taken into the Oliviers' confidence earlier. He felt hurt and shut out. For many months there was bad blood between him and Olivier, until Coward eventually wrote apologising for what seems to have been a queenly outburst of anger. 'Please wipe from your mind for ever that I am contemptuous of the "crummy little human urge" to have children. It is one of the most important urges in human life, and whatever I may have roared in my unbecoming outburst was neither valid nor accurate.'[15]

Tarquin was not told at all and was offended. He read about Vivien's pregnancy in Germany, in the English tabloids, and felt poleaxed. He took the news badly and believed that Vivien never forgave him for this. Olivier, knowing his son would not like it at all, had 'rather funked' telling him, and telephoned him only on the evening after the news was out. Afterwards he wrote, 'You sounded very unhappy and I am awfully sorry. . . Believe me, I do understand your feelings. When my father threatened me with the same possibility I felt sick. Of course there was even a far greater difference in all of our ages than at the present time, and I could see myself landed with the responsibility for the thing in a few years, and there is reasonable hope that this will not bear the same problem. I do beg of you to try and feel happy about it, it is a thing that pleads for joyful feeling.'[16] Olivier here was referring to his father's second marriage, in 1924, to Ibo, when Larry was seventeen. For him to have feared, at that age, that he might later have to support 'the thing' was far-fetched. For him to have felt any such jealousy was self-indulgent; no wonder he understood that same jealousy in Tarquin.

The press conference at Heathrow Airport when Marilyn arrived was a circus far greater than Vivien had commanded two days before. There were at least 400 journalists and photographers and the whole mob was surrounded by a cordon of police. 'At one point,' said Miller, 'the camera flashes formed a solid wall of white light that seemed to last for almost half a minute, a veritable aureole, and the madness of it made even the photographers burst out laughing.'[17] The questions were searching:

'Miss Monroe, we have read several times that all you have on in bed is Chanel No. 5. Is this true, Miss Monroe? Are you sure you have nothing else – on?'

'Maybe the radio.'

The filming was a disaster almost from the beginning. Olivier should have expected trouble. He had asked William Wyler what she was like to work with and he had replied, 'Hitler.' She was never on time. Since it was her money this wasted, that was her business, but it undermined Olivier's authority as director. She could not remember the simplest lines. She was much taken by the Method theories of Lee Strasberg's Actors' Studio. Since Strasberg himself could not be there his wife Paula was, at Marilyn's insistence. She was paid a vast salary to be a coach and a nuisance. Olivier would explain a move to Marilyn, who would then turn to Paula and ask, 'Wasseee mean?' When he tried for one whole morning to inspire in Marilyn the wit and sparkle that was necessary to the first meeting of showgirl and prince at the start of the film, she made her inevitable way across to Paula, who said, 'Honey, just think of Coca Cola and Frank Sinatra.' Paula Strasberg knew nothing of the theatre or acting. Her only talent was for flattery. Colin Clark, driving with Marilyn and Paula in their limousine one day, observed Paula go down on her knees beside Marilyn in the back seat, saying, 'All my life, Marilyn, I have prayed on my knees for God to give me a great actress. And now he has given me you, and you are that great actress, Marilyn, you are. . .'[18]

On 11 August, when Olivier was three weeks into the film, Vivien left *South Sea Bubble* and gave a gay farewell party to the cast. There she met Colin Clark and asked him confidentially how Marilyn was working out. He rolled his eyes to heaven. She was delighted.[19] Late that night she drove down to Notley, and had a miscarriage the next day. There has often been speculation that hers was an imagined pregnancy and a phantom miscarriage, and that she did it all to distract attention from Marilyn. But it was real. Hester was at Notley and is certain of this. She remembers the GP calling a gynaecologist down from London in the middle of the night, and the doctor coming over and saying, 'I'm sorry, we couldn't save it. It was a girl.' 'And it had a tremendous effect on me. I was expecting my second child. It wasn't due for a couple of months and it tipped me into labour. I remember all this as if it were yesterday. And she gave me all her baby's clothes. We were all sitting up. I remember going to see her the next day. She was in tears. And I remember Larry coming to see me in hospital. He said, "What are you going to call your baby?" I said, "Catherine". He said "Please don't. That was our name."'[20]

Coward was unkind. 'What I, most irritably, expected has now happened. . . The miscarriage is about as about as inevitable as anything could be. Meanwhile a smash hit is destroyed, she is wretched and on her way round the bend again, Larry is wretched, a large number of people, including me, are inconvenienced, and all for nothing. . . *South Sea Bubble*, if only they had had the sense to see it, was a life-saver for Vivien. It gave her a glamorous success on her own, away from Larry's perpetual shadow.'[21]

In August an indignant protest was made to Olivier about his cigarettes.

'Sir,' wrote Lieutenant Colonel C.J. Barton-Innes of Kensington, 'had I not seen the enclosed advertisement in a London newspaper I would have regarded it as inconceivable that one who had received the honour of knighthood from his sovereign could so besmirch the dignity conferred upon him as to sell his name for such an igno-minious purpose as to boost a brand of cigarettes. It only serves to show that our forefathers were not altogether wrong in their clas-sification of actors and actresses.'

Olivier replied, from Pinewood Studios. 'The honour conferred upon me, to which you refer, can not in any way be associated with the fact that a cigarette has been named after me, a fact that should cause you no more distress than that the same tribute has in the past been paid to De Reske, Sir Gerald du Maurier, and even the Senior Service [the Royal Navy]. Whatever you may think concerning our forefathers' opinion of actors and actresses, I can hardly believe that they would have considered it justified such inso-lence as that expressed in your letter.'[22]

The Prince and the Showgirl continued its disastrous course. Miller saw that Marilyn verged on the belief that Olivier had cast her only because he needed the money her presence would bring. She had begun by idolising him: the Hollywood she knew was so vile that the legit-imate theatre could only be sublimely pure. But she increasingly came to perceive a menace in Olivier and to think that he was trying to draw the audience's attention away from her. Miller did not think this was so, and occasionally defended Olivier. This only made things worse because she then asked whose side her new husband was on. She could not bear any contradiction of her views and thought that if she was opposed she could not be loved. 'Olivier,' said Miller, 'was soon prepared to murder Paula outright, and from time to time I would not have minded joining him, for Marilyn, a natural comedienne, seemed distracted by half-digested spitballed imagery and pseudo-Stanislavkian parallelisms that left her unable to free her own native joyousness. . . As for Olivier, with all his limitations in directing Marilyn – an arch tongue too quick with the cutting joke, an irritating mechanical exactitude in positioning her and imposing his precon-ceived notions upon her – he could still have helped her far more than Paula with her puddings of acting philosophy. . .'[23]

At the end of October Marilyn and some other members of the cast were presented to the Queen at a film premiere in Leicester Square. To shake hands with the Queen, thought Clark, made Marilyn feel accepted as one of the great actresses of her time, not just as a sex symbol or a calendar girl. 'The Queen is not to know that the film is on the verge of falling apart because MM is always late and cannot remember her lines.' Olivier's opinion of his leading lady fell lower than ever. He told Holman at Notley that teaching her to act was like teaching Urdu to a marmoset, that she was inca-pable of learning five lines by heart, that she had once disapproved of the rushes and stayed away for three days, incurring losses of £6,000 to £7,000 – losses she bore but which meant nothing to her. Almost everyone on the set now disliked her. The electricians, the lighting men and the stagehands – who were kept hanging round by Marilyn's unpunctuality and her failure to remember anything – became impatient with her disdain and lack of profes-sionalism. When shooting ended on 19 November she did not even say goodbye. The next day the members of the company were shown a trestle table covered with identical packages, gifts from Marilyn: for the men identical bottles and for the women identical purses. One man picked up his bottle, walked across to a rubbish bin, stood there for a moment, and tossed it in. One of the women followed. Then everyone did the same.[24]

Through all this, Olivier had known that the camera loved Marilyn, that she was photogenic and that there was something between lens and screen which might come out perfect. He was right. The critics loved her.

During the making of this wretched film one of Olivier's consolations was Maxine Audley. They had met at Stratford the previous year when she had played Lady Macduff in his *Macbeth*. In the film she played Lady Sunningdale, an old girlfriend of the Grand Duke, played by Olivier. She was one of his 'tender venturings', a warm-hearted woman whose occasional gifts to him were what he later called 'acts of pure kindness'. He gave her a ring with a large, emerald-like semi-precious stone. They remained friends, as she did with Vivien, and they went on tour together the following year.[25]

In 1956, during the filming, Olivier and Arthur Miller twice went to the theatre together. On one occasion it was to *South Sea Bubble*. Miller, having been smuggled in with Marilyn through the stage door at the last moment to avoid the crowd, did not realise what the play was and had not been told. It seemed lifeless, and he had difficulty making out the very English dialogue. Every now and then there was a kind of Noel Coward line, but not often, and then he noticed that the leading lady, rushing to the right and left of the stage and then back again, was Vivien Leigh.

'Who's the author?' he asked Olivier.

'Noel Coward.'

'Really!'

'Quite.'[26]

The other and more successful visit was to the Royal Court Theatre to see *Look Back in Anger*. This was the Court's first season under George Devine, the beginning of the 'kitchen sink' era. To go to see *Look Back in Anger* was Miller's idea. Olivier had tried to dissuade him, saying he wouldn't want to bother with that and that it was 'just a travesty on England and a lot of bitter rattling on about conditions'. But Miller liked the title and persisted. They met at the theatre and Miller was struck by the very English, very un-American way in which Olivier was received by the theatre-goers. 'Entering the lobby, I saw for the first time how admirably adept the British were in their ability to notice a star like Olivier without intruding upon him by so much as a lingering stare. . . The English seemed able to accept Olivier with a certain prideful, looking-away warmth that did not imply they owned him.' It was a fine and gentle thing to experience for the first time, altogether different from the crowd aggressiveness and back home and its humiliating assumptions.'[27]

Olivier had seen the play before and disliked it. Miller thought it was wonderful and said so. There were hanging threads but who cared? It had real life, a rare achievement. Devine hurried over and asked if they would like to meet the author. They went upstairs to a bar. Miller, whose play *The Crucible* had just been put on at the Court, listened to Devine as he reported how it had been received by his young audience. '[Then] a few inches to my right I overheard, with some incredulity, Olivier asking the pallid Osborne – then a young guy with a shock of uncombed hair and a look in his face of having awakened twenty minutes earlier – "Do you suppose you could write something for me?" in his most smiling tones, which would have convinced you to buy a car with no wheels for twenty thousand dollars.' Miller was sure that Olivier represented for Osborne the bourgeois decadence of the English theatre, but he heard him say he would indeed write something.[28]

Towards the end of *The Prince and the Showgirl*, Olivier had got into the habit of staying behind at the end of a day's shooting to unwind over large whiskies and a chat. Colin Clark liked to think he was taken into his confidence. According to his recollections, Olivier complained that the film was killing him. He had hoped it would be a renaissance and that Marilyn would make him feel young again, but he looked dead in the rushes and he felt dead. Clark remarked that Olivier was obsessed with the fact that he was going to be fifty the following year, and saw this as a turning point. He constantly said he had had it, that Vivien was being difficult, that she had never liked the idea of the film, was jealous, and had started up the old round of house parties at Notley, which he hated. 'Fancy,' thought Clark, 'being tormented by both those women at once – Vivien Leigh and Marilyn Monroe. And I get the impression that he isn't having sex with either.'[29] Those are the recollections of a young man of twenty-three, just down from Oxford, who on that film was a glorified messenger boy, but Olivier often did impart confidences to the strangest people. And he did write of himself that at the time he was feeling frustrated by the boredom of his career, and that his personal life was a tiresome tease to him.[30]

An unusually long Christmas holiday of three weeks, which he took in southern Spain with Vivien and Ginette Spanier and her husband, did nothing to help. He and Vivien quarrelled most of the time. He spent most of Christmas Day and the whole of Boxing Day in bed with gout. Then Vivien took to her bed. His diary entries are terse. 'Party. Enjoyed all too much. Angry evening.' 'V not feeling well.' Then he had stomach trouble. 'Tum still N.G. . . No hot water. No light.' 'Trouble over seat at [Malaga] airport.' They toured Malaga, Ronda and the Alhambra; had one wonderful night in Cordoba; visited the Prado in Madrid; and then came home by way of Paris, returning to London by the middle of January 1957.[31] Vivien's mother rang her on the day she returned and said she sounded sweet and gay.

22

The King Comes to the Court

FIVE DAYS AFTER HIS return Olivier received a letter from Devine saying he expected the new Osborne play to be ready by the middle of February, and that if Olivier's plans for the autumn were not yet complete he might like to have a look at it. Olivier replied that he would look forward to seeing the play, but that he was off to New York. 'There is, I am afraid, only a faintish chance of my being able to do it. . .'[1]

And so there was. He had a European tour of *Titus Andronicus* with the Stratford company in May and June to prepare for, and the New York visit was to discuss a proposal by Kirk Douglas and Burt Lancaster to do a film of Shaw's *Devil's Disciple*. As it turned out they wanted him for the picture, but not yet. He agreed to a postponement until that autumn on condition that he was paid $100,000 immediately, which he was. Tarquin was by then up at Christ Church, Oxford, and Olivier went there on three days to watch him row in his college eight. He seemed proud of his son, recording in his diary, 'Ch Ch bump Merton' and 'Ch Ch bump Magdalen'.[2]

Then Osborne's play arrived. It was the story of Archie Rice, a seedy stand-up comic doing the rounds of dying music halls, and the whole thing was a metaphor – after the disaster of the British and French invasion of Suez the year before – for a seedy and collapsing England. Things moved fast. On 11 February Osborne was summoned to the Connaught Hotel, where he met both the

Oliviers. They were staying there while some works were carried out at Lowndes Square. 'Sir Laurence,' said Osborne, 'was suddenly "available" and eager, in the way of prized actors who come into season with occasional surprising suddenness and have to be accommodated while the bloodstock is raring. . . It is hard to convey what a royal impression those two had made on the press and public.'[3] And it was the two of them he met, Vivien for the first time, though Olivier, 'long regarded by all (including himself) as a bequest to the nation, seemed to be speaking for both of them'.

Olivier wanted the play. The faintish chance had become a certainty. It could be tucked in for a four or five-week run in April and early May before the *Titus* tour. They talked casting. Olivier suggested Vivien as Archie's wife, which astonished Osborne and Tony Richardson – the Court's assistant director – who accompanied him. Olivier craftily said he knew she was too young and too beautiful for the part, but suggested this could be overcome by her wearing a rubber mask. When this dutiful and unthinkable proposal was discarded – to Olivier's own evident relief, it being agreed by all that she was indeed too beautiful – Olivier suggested there was a little actress they might have heard of, Dorothy Tutin, who would do for his daughter. After they left the hotel and stepped into the cold air Osborne and Richardson cracked up with laughter at that rubber mask.[4]

The play was on. The king had come to the Court. It was a coup. Except that the board of the Royal Court then had cold feet. The play itself, with Suez at its centre, was controversial enough. With Archie played by so conspicuous a figure as Olivier it might become dangerously so. The board at first decided to drop the play. Then, on reconsideration, the casting vote of George Harewood – who happened to be not only a board member but also an earl and the Queen's cousin – saved it. Archie became one of Olivier's most famous parts, a part which every now and again he would say was his favourite. It was a part in a play which had survived only precariously, was suddenly put on, and did not at first even have a name. In the early correspondence with Olivier it was given none and the original typescript, with Olivier's emendations and cuts, bears only the title of 'A Play by John Osborne'. Still, it was called *The*

Entertainer by the time Olivier's contract was drawn up, on 7 March. He played Archie for £50 a week and a share of the gross.[5]

The Lord Chamberlain demanded no changes in the political content of the play. He did insist that 'shagged' should be omitted, and that 'rogered' should be replaced by 'had'. Olivier himself cut the text boldly, putting his pencil through a quarter of it. He took tap dancing lessons and Osborne took him round the few surviving music halls of London: the Chelsea Palace, the Met in Edgware Road, and Collins in Islington. He took Vivien too, feeling that it was important to engage her support. She took to it all, joining in, laughing at the dog acts, the ventriloquists, and the xylophone players. When rehearsals began on 12 March she joined in there too, dropping in without warning and sitting in the dress circle with her chauffeur Bernard, in chocolate-coloured uniform, sitting a row behind her. She sat there intent on Olivier. Osborne, who had only just met her but was from the start sensitive to her feelings, said he could only guess at her pain.[6] If Olivier was occasionally out of his depth at the Court, she was much more so. Osborne was intuitive. Olivier did not say then, though he did later, that the reasons for his haste in taking the part were not exactly pure: more and more his impulses were to 'create a condition of detachment' from his marriage, and a sharp change in the direction of his career might help.[7] Osborne had heard the rumours about 'early morning visits to girls on Thameside houseboats, recriminations and physical revenge'. He hoped they were not true, if only to protect his play from 'prurient interest in Britain's most famous and near-royal couple, which would surely divert attention from what was happening in the theatre itself'.[8]

He did not know it at the time, but the girl in the houseboat was Dorothy Tutin, whom Olivier had chosen to play his daughter and whom Vivien, from her seat in the dress circle, was watching rehearse.

By then Olivier and Dorothy Tutin had known each other for five years. All that time Trader Faulkner, from whom Olivier had taken her, had continued to hope. He lived in a houseboat called *Stella Maris* on the Thames at Chelsea Reach, almost opposite Cheyne Walk where the young Olivier had lived, and only a mile and a half from Lowndes Square. In the hope of establishing some hold over Dorothy, Faulkner had found her another houseboat and lent her the money for it. She paid him back at £10 a week. Hers was called *Undine*. He got to know the watchman at the moorings, who told him one night in January 1957 that Olivier had been visiting her. Trader hid himself in a dustbin near *Undine* and waited in the freezing cold: 'I had a bottle. I really was ready to clock him with it. I was going to crack him across the head. I thought, "You bastard."' At last, in the early morning, two figures appeared from *Undine*. One was Olivier, looking exhausted, vulnerable, pitiful, and unshaven. At the sight of the spectre of Trader rising from the dustbin Dorothy disappeared back into the houseboat. Olivier faced Trader, knowing what he was holding behind his back, and then raised his arms and held them wide apart.

'Baby, what are you doing here?'

'Oh, Larry, how lovely,' said Trader, his murderous intent having instantly vanished. 'How are you? I'm getting into character for a murderer I'm playing on TV.'

'Well, you are a very convincing murderer. You're going to be marvellous in the part, Baby.'

Then he kissed Trader on both cheeks, said his car was waiting, and left.

Trader – this is how he tells the story – knew he could have fractured Olivier's skull with his bottle, but was unmanned by Olivier's forgiving gesture of wide-open arms. He couldn't hit a man who did that. And the lie he had told, that he was getting into character for a murderer, gave Olivier the advantage. When he had gone another car pulled up on the Chelsea Embankment and out stepped a classy whore in a leopard-skin coat, who walked up and down for a bit and then left. Trader wondered what clients she could have hoped for there. Years later he told Vivien this story, and she said, 'Oh Trader, jealousy was eating both of us. The leopard-skin whore on the embankment was me.'[9]

That is the rumour Osborne had heard. It is a story told down the years, though with the names disguised until Dorothy Tutin died in 2001. The account given here is Faulkner's own, as recounted by him forty-six years after the event.

When he began rehearsals for *The Entertainer*, in March, Olivier started a rejuvenating treatment to combat his exhaustion. From then until August he received thirty regular injections of apiserum – Royal Jelly.[10] The rehearsals went well. Osborne, who had not at first been keen on Dorothy Tutin, found her a modest girl who liked a glass of Guinness. Olivier was revealing an astonishing skill at a comic's throw-away business. Then came a piece of virtuosity. Osborne saw it. 'One Saturday run-through, about midday, he sprang his first realised version of the scene in which Archie sings the blues and crumples slowly down the side of the proscenium arch. The spring sunshine and the noise of the Sloane Square traffic poured through the open door. A dozen of us watched, astounded. Vivien turned her head towards me. She was weeping. I immediately thought of the chill inflection in Olivier's Archie voice, "I wish women wouldn't cry. I wish they wouldn't. . ."'[11] Osborne saw only one brief example of Vivien's feared rage when, before the dress rehearsal, she summoned him, Tony Richardson, and George Devine to Olivier's dressing room and her fury erupted. Olivier was tired and said little. Osborne did not say what her fury was about, except that the production 'had perhaps become a vehicle containing all her sense of loss to come or already endured'.[12]

Before the first night, on 10 April, Olivier wrote to Osborne: 'Thank you for the thrilling and lovely play which will no doubt be in the same Reps Theatre drawer as *The Cherry Orchard* and *The School for Scandal* before the century is out. Thank you for the most deeply engaging part perhaps barring only Macbeth and Lear that I can remember – certainly the most enjoyable. . . Hope I don't fuck it up for you tonight.' Later that night Osborne – the great iconoclast of his time – replied, 'Whatever might become of me in the future, nothing could deprive me of your tremendous, overwhelming performance, nor the experience of working with such true greatness.'[13]

The notoriously mean management of the Court bought a few bottles of cheap wine for a celebration party. Stage-hands and actors drank and danced. Vivien sang, rather sweetly. Olivier was happy and went through his routines from the play, knowing, said Osborne, that he had created a remarkable memory for everyone.[14]

The congratulatory letters to Olivier were too many to mention. One stands apart. Gwen Ffrangcon-Davies wrote, 'Your tragic haunted little man with its mash of mirth, its ghastly courage, brought to my mind those inarticulate puppets of the *commedia dell' arte*. . . You may not have intended anything of the kind! But your Archie Rice had for me larger overtones than just his own pitiful life.'[15]

The play ends with Archie waiting for the police to arrest him for unpaid income tax. In the early hours after the first night party Osborne was dozing in the stalls when Olivier came over and put his arm round him. 'Whatever you do, dear heart, *don't* ever, ever, get in trouble with the income tax man.' He sounded like Archie, thought Osborne; he still *was* Archie. He probably was. He was also the Olivier who, in playing that part, had taken a quite calculated step and made no bones about it: 'Going to the Court was a great move. Far earlier than Gielgud or Richardson. It's most awfully funny because they followed me and they both offered themselves one after another to the Royal Court. Because they saw, a little later than me, that's all, *that* was the new theatre. . .as new as the Kean school once was. There was another newness and we've got to have it. Absolute bloody reality, and I was *always* for that.'[16]

It was a reality much noticed by the critics. Harold Hobson, in the *Sunday Times*, was struck by the same passage of the play which had so astonished Osborne when he saw it in rehearsal. 'There are ten minutes, from the moment when he begins telling his daughter, with a defiant, ashamed admiration, of a negress singing a spiritual in some low club, to his breakdown on hearing of his son's death, when he touches the extreme limits of pathos. You will not see more magnificent acting than this anywhere in the world.'

The Entertainer was a reincarnation for Olivier. It was the beginning of the end for Vivien. She did not let go easily, as her presence in and around the play showed. She was with Olivier when Osborne and Toby Richardson called on him at the Connaught, though what they had was a proposal for Olivier, not for her. After the nonsense of the rubber mask was tentatively suggested and then abandoned, and there was no part for her, she still came to rehearsals. Hers was an uneasy presence. She was a star in a mink coat with a chauffeur in a theatre whose cherished purpose was to be angry

at the Establishment and at the fashionable flimsiness she represented. She lived by fantasy, the Court by what it was quite certain
was reality. Before the dress rehearsal she harangued Devine and
Richardson in front of Olivier in his dressing room, when she had
no standing in the matter and no one cared what she thought. She
sang sweetly at the first night party. Osborne happened to think
gently of her. So did Tarquin, who had always found her more
congenial than he had his father. At Notley, one Sunday night after
dinner, he was there with other guests when they realised she was
no longer with them. Her mother, Gertrude, was afraid she might
have tried to drown herself in the Thame, at the end of the garden.[17]

The European tour that followed early that summer showed
Vivien at her worst. It had been agreed with the Shakespeare
Memorial Theatre when the contract for the 1955 Stratford season
was made. It was a joint venture by the SMT, LOP, and the British
Council. Stratford at first refused to pay the salaries and hotel and
other expenses of Olivier's secretary and chauffeur, but then gave
way. Both went, and Gilman proved most useful. The play chosen,
Titus Andronicus, had been a success at Stratford but it was a strange
choice to take on any tour. One of the play's least atrocious murders
and mutilations caused most spectators to faint. This was the chop-
ping off of Olivier's hand. The axe descended on wood, but the sound
heard was the crunch of a cabbage being cut in two backstage by
Colin Clark, who had continued as Olivier's assistant.[18]

Vivien Leigh was given top billing, her name appearing before
anyone's – including Olivier's – which was nonsense since she had
a part which allowed her to speak only a few lines, her tongue being
cut out a third the way through. The tour began in Paris, where
there were parties or dinners every night attended by the likes of
Sartre and Cocteau, Douglas Fairbanks and Charles Boyer. Olivier's
performance was a triumph. In one scene, when two of his sons
have been murdered and a third exiled, when his daughter has been
raped and mutilated, and his own hand has been hacked off, Titus
likens himself to an ocean overflowing with miseries and utters
these words: 'I am the sea.' Michael Blakemore, an Australian actor
– who later made a great name as a director at the National Theatre
– was in the company and said there was an explosion of applause

after this speech such as he had never known in the middle of a scene.[19] When that speech was over Olivier stood quite still. Blakemore, who had been a medical student before he went into acting, observed that the only sound on stage was that of his exhausted breathing and the only movement the rise and fall of his chest. 'At one performance I was amazed when at the end of the speech. . .his breath came in stops and starts, with moments in between in which he seemed to have stopped breathing altogether. Doctors are taught this is symptomatic of major shock. He had intuited it, perhaps hardly aware of what he was doing or how powerful it made the moment, because it was the only time it happened.' His performances were so audacious, characterised by moments in which there was always the possibility of humiliating misjudgments or even [as in *Coriolanus*, two years later] physical danger. 'He was,' says Blakemore, 'an actor of the greatest courage . . . As an actor-manager he led from the front, taking more risks than his subordinates, assuming a heavier workload and great responsibilities. These are Roman virtues, and his assumption of them added to his credibility when he played a general like Titus, or a warrior like Coriolanus.'

As to Vivien, Blakemore saw that though her part was small she was determined to be at the centre of the company's off-stage life. As several others on that tour recalled, she remembered everyone's birthday and gave cakes and presents. But she also exploited the company to indulge her own wilfulness. When Marie Bell, the former leading lady of the Comédie Française, offered a small party on board a Seine river boat Vivien insisted that all fifty-five members of the company should be invited or none. Then, when more food and wine was hastily brought in and Vivien had gained her point, she made a show of drinking with the company and neglecting her hostess. She did the same in a grander way to Paul-Louis Weiller, the richest man in France, who had arranged that she should receive the ribbon of a chevalier of the Légion d'Honneur, which she did, at a ceremony to which she summoned all the actors. They arrived half made-up, with towels round them. Weiller had also invited her and ten or twelve others to dinner. Again she insisted on the whole company, and he was obliged to go to the expense of fitting up his house to give an enormous banquet. Throughout her career almost everyone who knew Vivien, not only her hangers-on and sycophants, remarked on her social polish, but it was often a polish that did not give a damn for the convenience of others.

From Paris they took the train to Venice, where the show went badly and Vivien kept a party going till 5.30 a.m. Peter Brook, the director, assembled the company and told them the performance had been awful. Then they went on to Belgrade and Zagreb in Yugoslavia, to Vienna, and then to Warsaw, becoming the first English company to perform behind the Iron Curtain.

In Belgrade things got more difficult. Duff and Diana Cooper's son, John Julius Norwich, second Viscount Norwich, was third secretary at the British Embassy, which was expecting to lionise Olivier and Vivien but again found itself landed with the whole cast. Norwich's wife Anne thought that Olivier acted almost as a lady's maid to Vivien, anxiously inquiring whether she was wearing the right kind of frock. Vivien was enchanting but there was, said Lady Norwich, a great thing of 'Darling' and kissing between them that struck a false note. Vivien again wanted to stay up all night and invited the Norwiches back to their hotel, which infinitely embarrassed them since they knew Olivier wanted to sleep. She thought Vivien was 'slightly persecuting' him. At one dinner, when Lady Norwich sat next to Olivier and was, she recalled, 'beefing on about Nanny [her children's nanny] or whatever it was', he said, 'Oh well, dear Anne, if you don't like your life, change it.' She later wondered if he had been talking about himself, and what he intended to do.[20]

After Belgrade Vivien got worse. Her old illness returned. At one dinner, which Olivier did not attend, she was at the top table with Yugoslav academics who spoke no English. She got bored and beckoned to company members to come and fill empty spaces at her table. Wine was drunk, interminable speeches were made, understood by nobody, and then it was her turn to reply. David Conville, who played Second Goth, recounted what happened: 'There she was, wearing the Légion d'Honneur, and the same dress. Beautiful but mad. . . She got up with a charming little girl smile – I can't to this day believe it happened, but it did happen – she stood up with such charm and elegance and said, in English, "I think this is the most fucking boring evening I have ever had in my life. . ." It was the most awful language and it was terribly rude, in the most charming, wonderful way. And everyone went "Ya, ya". . . Even if they had spoken English her tone of voice was such, so flattering and charming. But to actually make a speech with some pretty vile words and to say "I've never been so bored in my life," and they were charmed.'21

In Yugoslavia one of the troubles was that, whereas few had heard of Olivier, Vivien was famous for *Gone With the Wind*. Crowds outside the theatres shouted for Scarlett. She refused to sleep and night after night kept the company up till dawn. She broke a window in her hotel room. In Zagreb she slipped her minder, stayed out all night, and the next day appeared somnambulistically drunk ten minutes before the curtain was due to rise on a children's matinée. Blakemore observed what followed. She never forgot her lines, but there was a dislocating pause before each speech. She did not forget her moves, but took an age to make them. Olivier came to his ocean speech, which had so roused the Paris audience: 'I am the sea'. At this moment, says Blakemore, 'Vivien had decided to make an observation of her own. Her words were not angry or loud – the tone was almost affectionate – but they had the piercing clarity of a child's voice. . . About this great moment of theatre she had given her verdict. To him, the entire cast and to a thousand Croatian children. "Silly cunt", she had said.' Members of the company bent double as they tried to smother their laughter. It was also, thought Blakemore, extremely sad. 'Olivier, invincible in Paris, had become ridiculous in Zagreb. He would never forgive her, though as a couple they had probably long been doomed.' After the last show in Zagreb David Conville remembered that she sat up all night with Gilman on a park bench, and it was her chauffeur who got her to the station in the morning. There she refused to get on the train. Olivier said, 'I can't stand it.' As the train began to move the police chief picked her up in his arms and put her on board, and she gave him a black eye. On the journey from Zagreb to Vienna the company manager, Paddy Donnell, had to keep Vivien away from Olivier. In the mountains the train stopped in a cutting with a sheer drop to one side. She got off the train to admire the view from this precipice; the train drew away, and had to return to pick her up. Maxine Audley was in the company and Vivien chased her through the train, throwing bread at her. At Vienna she was met by Cecil Tennant, who had once again been called out to look after her, as he had been in 1953. Doctors were summoned. The company was called together and told she had been given a heavy sedative and would not be playing in Vienna, and that no one was to accept any invitations from her if she did appear. She did appear, with a caravan of attendants, wine and picnic baskets. Then she collapsed.[22]

There was still Warsaw to come. There she organised a company picnic in the countryside and cut her foot on a broken bottle paddling in a lake. Blakemore cleaned the wound with vodka and bandaged her foot with a handkerchief, and she hobbled about for the rest of the day. 'It was impossible not to admire her pluck, though by this time we had grasped that it had an edge of craziness. She reminded me a little of some *principessa*, absolute in her whims, ruling over a small state in Renaissance Italy.' Olivier was exhausted. They flew back to London on 22 June. He wrote in his diary. 'Home.' Vivien's mother wrote in hers: 'Spent the day and night with Vivien. Very sad indeed. Got to bed at 4.30 a.m.' Noel Coward, having met Olivier who told him 'ghastly stories', thought the whole thing a nightmare.[23]

Titus still had another month to run at the Stoll in London. The St James's, which Olivier had run for five years, was about to be demolished to make way for offices. Vivien took up the cause. Olivier did not. He thought it a ludicrous farce and that her efforts were futile.[24] She led a few straggling protesters up Whitehall ringing a bell and no one took much notice. She complained that she couldn't go into a restaurant without people staring at her, but when she demonstrated nobody paid any attention. That evening, before the performance of *Titus*, she was on a high. Most of the company had gone on her march because they were frightened not to. Maxine Audley had not. Vivien demanded to know why not, and abused her. Maxine turned away, and as she did so Vivien deliberately put a foot on the hem of her dress, which ripped.[25]

She then rose from the public gallery during a House of Lords debate, throwing her voice, she said, as she would in a large theatre, and shouted her protest there too. Black Rod, the ceremonial usher who keeps order in the Lords, and who had been gulled into giving her tea beforehand, gently threw her out.[26]

At the end of the run she threw a spectacular party at Notley for the *Titus* company – cast, box office people, cleaners, everybody. 'It must have cost a hell of a lot of money,' said David Conville. 'But then of course she went a bit odd and we were all terrified at the end. . . She had this wonderful generosity and everyone adoring her and then she had a turn and life was difficult. The turns were quite common. . . Diana Cooper, I remember, appeared for some reason dressed in armour. Vivien kept changing clothes. She had got a bit manic by then and stood in the hall glaring and saying, "This is going to be the greatest party of all times. No one is to leave." And she wouldn't let anyone out. Some did have to go back to their children, and Larry pushed us all out through the kitchen.'[27] Gertrude wrote in her diary: 'Viv in great form.' The general manager at Stratford protested to LOP that the cost of the party was monstrous. He was sure it was beautifully done but he could have done it at half the price.[28]

Vivien was coming to the end, but she was about to despatch Dorothy Tutin. As Olivier later told it, he found himself 'wishing increasingly to form a union' with someone to whom he was attracted. This was Dorothy. He also said, to be misleading, that this attraction had been for some months, when it had been for some years. One day Vivien asked him sympathetically if he was in love with the girl; he admitted that he was and to his intense relief she said, 'How marvellous for you. How marvellous for her.' But two or three days later she was again sky-high, and was determined to allow him no sleep. One night, when he did doze off, she started slashing him across the eyes with a wet face-cloth. He evaded her by locking himself in another room, but she hammered on the door and was obviously prepared to keep it up all night. 'Something snapped in my brain – I know I must have read that phrase but it'll do fine. . . I threw open the door, grabbed her wrist, and pulled her along the passage, pushed open her door and with all my strength – it must be true that in an all-possessing rage it is doubled – hurled her half way across the room to the bed. Before hitting the bed she struck the outside corner of her eyebrow on the corner of her bedside table-top, opening up a wound half an inch from her temple and half an inch from her eye. I realised with horror that each of us was quite capable of murdering or causing death to the other. I must get out quickly. I had already taken a furnished room in a mews across the road as an escape hatch. I went to see Vivien early next morning to see how things were and found Mary Mills [wife of John Mills] already there dressing her wound. She looked up at me with horrified reproach. After six years of contending with the anguishes of this disease, my whole nature was in revolt against further voluntary torture. . . The break must be made.'[29]

From that moment the break was inevitable, but Dorothy Tutin would go first. She was, said Olivier, coming naturally and sensibly to the conclusion that the fruition of her love for him was altogether too mixed a blessing.[30] What he did not say was how this happened. Vivien had asked Dorothy to visit her. Dorothy did not want to meet her at all, but she was honest and well-meaning and eventually consented. When she did go to see Vivien, she found Vivien's mother there as well. Vivien said there was no future for Dorothy with Olivier unless she wanted to be known as a murderess, because she (Vivien) would kill herself. Gertrude said this was true, because there was no real control over Vivien in her manic phases. Dorothy was frightened. She went on seeing Olivier for a while, but then they parted and remained on the friendliest terms. He carried her last letter to him in his pocket until it became frayed from constant reading.[31]

The only good news for Olivier was that 415,865,980 of his cigarettes had sold in the previous year, earning him £3,465.[32] Vivien did not like them. On the tour the company manager had smuggled other brands in for her. There was also the film of *Macbeth* to prepare for. In August, Olivier left for Scotland with Tarquin, in the long vacation after his first year at Oxford. Their purpose was to search for locations. They put the Bentley on the train to Perth and then drove to the famous places of the play, to Dunsinane and Birnam Woods, to Glamis and Cawdor, photographing and painting in gouache. They spent more than two weeks on this reconnaissance.[33] *Macbeth* did seem to be taking shape. Rank had already tentatively proposed the same terms as for *Hamlet*. Lord Carnegie offered Dunnottar castle; Olivier declined, explaining that if the period of the play was taken to be 1000 AD then they would not want a castle that already looked a thousand years old, but would build new sets. Father and son returned to Notley for Tarquin's twenty-first birthday party on 21 August. Jill was there too.[34]

Vivien at the time was on holiday in Italy, where she had gone with Holman and their daughter Suzanne. Much was made in the newspapers of these separate holidays – Olivier with Tarquin in Scotland and Vivien with her first husband and their daughter in Italy. The etiquette of popular newspapers of the time has to be taken into account. The Oliviers were the royal family of the stage and as such they were pursued. It was evident that they were falling apart, but this was suggested and never stated. David Lewin, the show-business reporter of the *Daily Express*, had gone with the company on its European tour. He cannot have failed to see the antics which were obvious to everyone, but in a series of articles he did not hint at them. Show-business reporters tend to go native. In order to preserve future access and goodwill they do not openly offend the stars who are their daily bread. Nevertheless, Lewin and his colleagues would have seen what they saw, and their news editors would have got to know. So when Vivien marched down Whitehall, or when she shouted in the House of Lords, she made the front page lead in national papers, which also printed quotes from Olivier that could be read as showing that he was hardly wholehearted in supporting his wife.[35] When she went on holiday separately there were more headlines and more innuendo. In the same way, no newspaper ever said that Olivier and Tutin had been lovers: the practice was to juxtapose their photographs in the same apparently harmless piece, and that was enough. A classic example of this was the way the *Daily Mail* treated the tale of Olivier's night on the houseboat. The rumour was around. Osborne was not the only one to have heard it. The *Mail* sent a photographer who took a routine picture of Olivier and Tutin outside the theatre. This was printed across four columns. The story quoted Olivier as saying, probably in answer to a leading question, that he had been unable to sleep the night before the first rehearsal. The headline over the picture said, 'The Odd Case of the Sleepless Knight' and the caption beneath it read, 'Dorothy Tutin and Sir Laurence Olivier: "We are all very chummy."'³⁶

At the time of the separate holidays Holman hoped that Vivien and Olivier would simply agree to live apart for a while. She had talked about living alone but that, he thought, was only a variant on her theme of taking another husband. She had evidently talked about that too. But he did not think the marriage had irretrievably broken down.³⁷ He returned from Italy before Vivien, who took Suzanne to the south of France before they flew back on 30 August. Colin Clark went down with Olivier to Lydd Airport to meet them, and here occurred one of the most remarkable instances of Olivier's undoubted ability to make himself invisible. Because of the rumours of a parting, the local pub was full of reporters. Clark described what happened. 'They all saw me and they all recognised me as Olivier's assistant and said, "Oh Colin, what's going on? Is Larry coming?" I thought crikey, where's Larry? I daren't look around. And I said, "No, Larry's not coming, I've come down to meet Vivien". . . I thought: Where is he? Did he manage to back out or what? I turned round and Larry was standing right at my shoulder. Not one reporter, who were all there just to see if Larry turned up, could recognise him. His face dropped and sagged. He just turned into another person. They did not recognise him, nor could I hardly. And they said, "Who's this?" I said, "He's just someone come down with me to meet Vivien." Of course later on when we got to the airport they're all there again and they recognised him. They said, "Why didn't you tell us he was coming?" I said, "He was standing right with me." They couldn't believe me. They thought I was just kidding. But he was. That's really acting.'³⁸

As the next three years showed, the Oliviers' marriage was not yet at an end. She had, however, long been a liability and not an asset to LOP. There were still wrangles with the tax inspectors over whether it was an allowable expense to have forced her back from Hollywood when she broke down in 1953, against her will. Tennant had to explain to accountants that when he first went to Hollywood it had been intended that she should be allowed to recover, and then finish her film. But Paramount's doctors had said she would not recover within two weeks, so her contract ended, and with it her living expenses. The costs of keeping her in a nursing home there would have been astronomical, so it was best for the company to get her home as soon as possible. 'This course of action,' wrote Tennant, 'was of course not pleasing to Miss Leigh . . .' She objected strongly, had to be drugged and was got on board the plane at New York partly by force. 'I can state quite clearly,' Tennant ended, 'that Miss Leigh was brought back from California to London for the company's benefit.'[39] Before Olivier and Vivien went off for their separate holidays it had been arranged to transfer *The Entertainer* to the West End. It went into the Palace Theatre on 10 September for eight weeks, then on tour for another four, and then returned to the Palace.[40] Dorothy Tutin had withdrawn from the part of Archie's daughter and was replaced by Joan Plowright. Devine had asked her to take over. Miss Plowright was the daughter of a newspaper editor in Scunthorpe, Lincolnshire. She had trained at the Old Vic Theatre School, where she was taught by three remarkable men, all of whom happened to be Olivier's friends and colleagues. They were George Devine, Glen Byam Shaw and Michel Saint-Denis, who had directed Olivier in his pre-war *Macbeth* and in his famous *Oedipus* of 1945–6. This must be the only time three such distinguished, and practising, men of the theatre have run a drama school, and Miss Plowright flourished under their tuition. At one class, on A *Midsummer Night's Dream*, Devine told her she did by instinct what others had to learn. After drama school she played as the only girl in Orson Welles' version of *Moby Dick* and was in repertory at the Bristol Old Vic when, in 1956, Devine invited her to join his new company at the Royal Court. There she had a triumph in Arnold Wesker's *Roots*, where she played a country girl from Norfolk. She was very much the Court's rising star. When Olivier saw her in Wycherley's Restoration comedy, *The Country Wife*, he was entranced by her; her very name, he said, was enough to make him think thoughts of love.[41] On the other hand, he wrote, 'I went to the Palace season of *The Entertainer* determined that my philandering fit had best be called a halt for a breath.'[42]

When Olivier had first gone to the Court a year before he had sensed a hint of mockery, and he was right. Joan and her colleagues were young and rebellious, and he represented the West End. They also felt that he should have been doing better things than *The Sleeping Prince* and that he had become half of a showbiz couple rather than a great actor. But when Joan and Olivier began to rehearse *The Entertainer* for the Palace there was a rapport straight away. His determination not to philander did not prevent him from flirting. He pretended to have forgotten her name and called her Miss Wheelshare, saying that was equally agricultural. She was still living with her first husband, Roger Gage, though the marriage was in difficulties since the Court had so taken over her life that she was hardly ever at home. Olivier appeared to be living apart from Vivien most of the time. She knew the gossip about their troubles and she was, besides, a friend of Dorothy Tutin and knew she had been Olivier's mistress.[43]

She was spellbound by Olivier's flirtatious charm but also, and more dangerously, her heart was touched by the bleakness in his face when he wasn't acting or flirting. At the beginning, when she was in danger of being swept off her feet, she took a few steps backwards, suspecting that for him it was a routine flirtation. She was not a promiscuous girl and her pride was hurt by the thought that she might be just one of a long line singled out for such attention. So she became wary and made a point of disappearing during breaks in rehearsals, or sitting with other members of the cast.[44]

At the same time, Osborne and Vivien were spending evenings together. They were an unlikely couple. She would ring him up, ask what he was doing, then send round her Rolls, VLO 1, and they would go to the pictures. He asked himself if he was expected to seduce her but reflected that he was not Rhett Butler, Laurence Olivier, or even Peter Finch. After the film they would glide round to some restaurant for dinner, where she tactfully helped him with the wine and the menu, and once in his tussle with an unfamiliar artichoke. He liked her, and she him, and he gave a kind and gentle account of it. 'Vivien's virtue, always a prized one in my book, was enthusiasm, the physical expression of hope, the antidote to despair and that most deadly of sins, sloth.' On their return to Lowndes Square he was unsure whether to go in for a drink or not. He had no wish to be churlish, or to be caught in flagrante by Larry. This seemed to him a comic notion, but the events of the last few months had been so headlong that almost anything seemed possible. Taking Scarlett O'Hara out to supper might be only a starter. 'I felt a certain loyalty to Olivier. I was also racked by curiosity. In St Augustine's words, "A stiff prick hath no conscience." Maybe it was a Jacobean plot to damage *The Entertainer*? That seemed too vulgar a device. On the other hand. . . On the other hand what? On the other hand I wanted nothing to threaten the success of my play. Not for the first time, I fiercely regretted my indecision in such circumstances.'[45]

After the first weeks at the Palace *The Entertainer* went on tour to Glasgow, Edinburgh, Oxford, and Brighton. Scottish audiences were shocked. Olivier wrote to Tony Richardson that in Glasgow all his acts had been received in stoniest silence except for an occasional hiss, and that he had the uncomfortable feeling he was about to be booed. He received letters telling him he was plumbing the depths and prostituting his art. He took to writing long replies, defending the play as a modern tragedy. Here is one. '*The Entertainer* has observed human nature with as much cunning, though perhaps with not so much technical accomplishment, as Anton Chekhov, holding the people up to the public and saying, "Here we are; this is what we are like, how about it?" If you don't know that most of your brothers and sisters are [like this] then it is time that you did. You regret the fact that you were left without hope. Believe me, I very much appreciate this point but I suggest it is possible that eventually hope may be something that we must be strong enough to do without.'[46]

He saw the play as expressing his own feelings, and had no hope that he could any longer tolerate Vivien. When she came up to Glasgow for her birthday, on 5 November, she was not welcomed. The hotel had prepared a menu in her honour – *soupe Blanche DuBois* and *meringues Scarlett O'Hara* – which bored her. Colin Clark thought she knew Olivier and Joan were having an affair, that she had come up to see what was happening, and that her visit hastened things.[47] Vivien did not in fact know for some time.

When the company was at Oxford Olivier took Joan and the other members of the cast to Notley. She did not like it. 'It was a bit peculiar, very strained at the time. The Portuguese couple had

vanished the night before taking all the silver. You just felt it wasn't
a home. It was a place for show, and you needed a staff to run it,
and there weren't any.'[48] By then she had discovered that her evasive
tactics were not the slightest use. There was a kinship between her
and Olivier which had nothing to do with flirtation and they had
fallen in love.[49] He too thought of it as a kinship. 'By the end of
the four week tour. . .I was finding that in Joan "here every flower
was united". My relationship with her brought a new kind of headi-
ness in its rapture – nothing exotic, rather a strangely natural
kinship, and more powerful than anything I could remember. We
could foresee nothing; we had no notion of what might or could
happen.'[50]

They became lovers at Brighton on 28 November 1957. In his
diary he wrote in ink, instead of the usual pencil, 'With *Joanie.'*
They then returned to London to continue with an extended run
of *The Entertainer*.[51]

A week later Suzanne Holman got married. She had not been a
demanding daughter, as Tarquin was a demanding son. She had
been brought up by her father and her grandmother, whom she
adored. After school at Sherborne and a Swiss finishing school she
went to RADA, came out at a party for 600 guests, gave up acting
to work in her grandmother's beauty salon in Knightsbridge, and
then became engaged to Robin Farrington, a Lloyds broker. The
wedding invitations, from Leigh Holman and Lady Olivier, were
sent out from the Oliviers' new flat at 54 Eaton Square, to which
they had recently moved from Lowndes Square.[52] Again the press
coverage was great. The *Daily Mirror* splashed the story across two
pages. The *Mail* had a picture of Olivier's head mostly obscured by
a pillar and quoted him as saying it was not really his show. It also
reported that the cigarettes at the reception were Oliviers. To an
Express reporter Olivier unwisely said he felt like the uninvited
guest, and that became the headline. Every paper noticed that
Vivien left at the end with Holman.[53] Suzanne and her husband
went to live in Switzerland.

At about this time the idea of the *Macbeth* film, which seemed to
have died with Korda, revived. Filippo Del Giudice, having heard
of the project, wrote from Milan: 'I shall arrange everything in a

short time, especially the provision of pounds.' And Olivier had the consolation and encouragement of his new love. George Devine, knowing how matters stood with Joan, lent Olivier the key of a rented room he had in Walpole Street, Chelsea.[54]

23

Dropping the Legend

AT THE BEGINNING OF 1958 Joan Plowright was already in New York in the Ionesco double bill of *The Chairs* and *The Lesson*. When, in early February, Olivier opened on Broadway in the American transfer of *The Entertainer* she joined him in that. Every seat was already sold for three months. And there in New York, she remembers, their relationship grew deeper and more binding. Away from people about whom they felt guilty, they were happy together at the Algonquin. She still has the key to suite 808. They told each other everything. He confided in her that he had suggested a divorce to Vivien two years before, but that she had threatened to kill herself if he went ahead; she wanted the marriage and the legend to continue, though she conceded that each could enjoy other liaisons.[1] Olivier realised that on those terms a life of sorts might have seemed tolerable to a man who had, in his phrase, 'struck fifty'. He might, he felt, have determined not to be so 'goddamned spoilt', but, as he tortuously rationalised it, selfishness was almost like a gift to him. 'Artists must be selfish. It is in fact their duty. Ambition was not given to a man for nothing, it can be of service to mankind.'[2]

Back in London Vivien was opening in *Duel of Angels,* a French mixture of mythical tragedy and bedroom farce, and was having an affair with Peter Wyngarde, her leading man. He too had his difficulties with her. One night she ran round the gardens in Eaton Square with nothing on. He went after her with a blanket and found her with a policeman, who had recognised her as Scarlett O'Hara.

Another night at Notley, after a wonderful evening, he found her sobbing uncontrollably on the bathroom floor at four in the morning.[3]

Financially it was a good time for Olivier. *The Prince and the Showgirl* had brought in $250,000. *Roar Like a Dove*, an LOP production of the year before, had run for months. *Duel of Angels*, which was LOP's too, promised well. He would have another $100,000 to come from *The Devil's Disciple*. He had ten per cent of the profits from the American *Entertainer*, as well as $1,000 a week expenses to pay for suite 808, and that play did so well that its run was extended until mid-May.[4] When it did end Olivier gave a party on board a chartered yacht, *Knickerbocker VII*, on the Hudson. Douglas Fairbanks, Henry Fonda, Peter Ustinov, Elia Kazan, Greer Garson, John Osborne, John Steinbeck, and Joan Plowright were among the guests. It was a very English affair, with jellied eels, fish and chips, stout, and bottled Bass.[5]

In spite of everything Olivier and Joan were happy. She called it their New York idyll. He thought that in their time at the Algonquin they had discovered each other, but still feared there was no certainty as to their future. 'When we parted in New York to come separately home we had no notion of what might and could happen. She understood enough of my situation to recognise that we were both helpless, as if we were suddenly without our sight.'[6] As soon as he returned Glen Byam-Shaw, director of the Stratford Memorial Theatre, invited him to come back to Stratford in 1959 to play Lear and Othello. He was confident that the proposed film of *Macbeth* would be the greatest of all Olivier triumphs.[7] But Olivier had again met with constant disappointments when he tried to raise the money for the film. Rank had lost interest. Mike Todd had been prepared to back it so long as his wide-screen Todd-AO system was used, but he was killed in an air crash in March. The trouble was that although *Henry V* had eventually made a profit of £100,000 and *Hamlet* £300,000, *Richard III* was still not within £100,000 of recouping its production costs. Tennant was looking for £450,000 but only £150,000 was offered, by British Lion. Two German producers were tempted but then withdrew. Then Del Giudice bounced back yet again. He asserted that the film could make £600,000 in the American market alone. Olivier's advisers were brutal, telling him that Del was now a myth, that Rank declined even to see him, that the Home Office had refused him a work permit, and that it was idiotic to listen to his confident claims that God would prevail. They were probably right, since Del was unable to pay his London hotel bill and was grateful for £35 which Olivier sent him. Olivier told Tarquin, 'I have had a teasing time lately, money-chasing for *Macbeth*; it's not really my job and it's a bit humiliating, and I'm not sure I've done myself much good by it.'[8] In June he flew to Paris to see the Baron de Rothschild, and had lunch with another Rothschild in London, but the money was not forthcoming. Del never gave up. He wrote that he 'held certain moneys' in New York, and then pressed on Olivier the idea of playing the name role in *The Memoirs of Pontius Pilate*. He declined, saying he was not much given to biblical subjects. A woman from Port Elizabeth, South Africa, offered to bequeath her fortune to Olivier to help finance *Macbeth*; he wrote on her letter, 'Most touched'.[9]

The *Macbeth* film was abandoned. In July Olivier started the much delayed shooting of *The Devil's Disciple*, a drama of the American War of Independence in which he played the British General Burgoyne, with Burt Lancaster and Kirk Douglas playing American patriots. It is a lightweight, witty trifle which earned him unfailing good notices, but during the filming he was so confused by 'the heart-wrenchings, the guilt, the longing, the romantic joy, and the tortured conscience' of the previous few months that he even forgot names, and addressed Burt Lancaster as 'Kirk'. Each time he did this Lancaster looked at him 'straight and steely steady' and quietly said, 'Burt'.[10]

Vivien was living at Eaton Square or at Notley, where Peter Finch was once again a visitor. Olivier was living with friends or in rented rooms. 'My interests,' he said, 'were entirely preoccupied in the heart, soul, and lap of one I was proud to call "my Joan".' Yet he and Joan had been obliged to stay apart throughout the negotiations for *Macbeth*, in which Vivien, from whom he was estranged, had been cast as Lady Macbeth. Joan immersed herself in work, in more Ionesco at the Royal Court and then in the name part of Shaw's *Major Barbara*.[11] Olivier did his first English television work, in Ibsen's *John Gabriel Borkman*.

Then there was more trouble at Notley. Dickie was diagnosed

with leukaemia. Hester and Olivier did not at first tell him. In September the three of them were on holiday together in Spain when Vivien entered upon another crisis. Although Ken Tynan had never missed an opportunity to mock Vivien, he and his wife, Elaine Dundy, had twice dined with the Oliviers. When Olivier was in Spain Vivien invited the Tynans and others to Notley for the weekend. Vivien's mother and father were there, and so were Finch's mother and sister. At a picnic in the grounds Vivien became alarmed by a wasp and shrieked at it, becoming a Blanche DuBois figure. When Tynan went to take a nap she followed him upstairs and put on the suit of chain mail Sybil Thorndike had worn as Joan in Shaw's *Saint Joan*, and which she had bought. Then she insisted that Tynan should help her out of it and put it on himself. She became so distracted that a cable was sent to Olivier urging him to come home. He left his dying brother and Hester in Spain and returned. The other guests at Notley had the sense to leave but the Tynans did not. When Olivier appeared, in time for dinner, Tynan sat at dinner in the chain mail Vivien still insisted he should wear. Next morning Olivier asked him and his wife to leave. This is Elaine Dundy's story and is not to be taken as gospel, particularly when she adds that Tynan and Olivier talked long in his study about a National Theatre, and that thus was planted the seed which later grew into Tynan's presence as dramaturge at that theatre.[12] However that may be, it was the start of one of Vivien's highs that lasted almost four weeks. Two nurses and two psychiatrists were called in. After two weeks Vivien and her mother flew to Italy on holiday. Here are four abbreviated entries from Gertrude Hartley's diary:[13]

Oct 1. Happy day but unhappy night. V threw a glass of water in my face at 2 30 am.

Oct 2. We are asked to leave hotel. . .very unhappy night.

Oct 4. Viv told to leave hotel. Police sent for.

Oct 5. 2 am. Police affair. Viv bit two fingers of one of them.

Three days later they flew home, and the day after that Vivien returned to her part in *Duel of Angels*. A psychiatrist's report to Olivier read: 'She seems to be managing not too badly at the moment and we still hope that a major manic episode can be avoided. I am pretty sure that she will be more approachable when she gets depressed.'[14]

Olivier, who had taken refuge first in Ischia and then with friends in Paris, wrote Vivien a twenty-three page letter asking for a divorce. She replied from Holman's house in Wiltshire where she had retreated, as she often did. It was a letter which appeared to give him what he asked. 'You must,' she said, 'forgive the fact that I make quick decisions. I believe they are the only true and instinctively correct way for people such as I am to express their feelings. Because I have had a day almost entirely on my own – in bed – and able to think without interruption of our whole situation I have come to the conclusion – (a *fearfully* painful one) that a clean and *absolute* break is the only path to follow – So I intend to divorce you on the grounds of desertion – mental and physical – as soon as our present chores in the theatre and television are over – we are in any case separated. I did not want to do this until you had finished your work here but our telephone conversation tonight led me to think I was talking to a complete stranger – which is what you have chosen to become. . . Our lives will lie in quite different directions. I feel confident I should make my own life – and you have *always* made yours. . .'[15]

Three days after this was written, on her birthday, they had a quiet dinner together at which he promised her a new Rolls-Royce, apparently as a *douceur*. But their lives did not yet lie in different directions. Only two days after that quiet dinner they once again did something calculated to command columns of space in national newspapers. To Les Ambassadeurs, a nightclub, they invited 150 showbiz guests, including Lauren Bacall, Richard Burton, Kenneth More, Douglas Fairbanks, and the usual celebrities. The *Express* called it London's starriest party of the year. The usual glowing photographs appeared, across two pages.[16]

At Notley Dickie had taken a turn for the worst. Olivier and Hester discussed whether they should tell him the doctor's diagnosis. He wrote to Joan saying he did not know what to do. 'I think I should want to be told but I suspect my judgment in human matters is coloured by my sense of the dramatic and so, as often happens, I am deeply perplexed in my dealings with a really human matter. I think I would want to be told and I think I would rather be told by my brother. But, oh Lord, I can't really trust myself for true judgment. Hester, I think, wants me to tell him within the next dew days. I wish I could talk to you. I know that you would help me and that in your judgment I would always have faith, my darling, in human matters, indeed probably in all.'[17] Hester also seems to have suspected in Olivier this same instinct towards the dramatic and says that when he did eventually tell Dickie he did it with a hint of theatricality.[18] Having broken the news to his brother he went off to America for a television play of Maugham's *The Moon and Sixpence*, but was called back on his second day. Dickie had died. His best days had been in the navy, in the war, and he had asked to be buried at sea. Hester thought Olivier managed it all, but he got Peter Hiley, his 'fixer of fixers', to do it. He telephoned Harrods' funeral department, who told him you had to have stones in the coffin and bore holes to let the water in. 'Larry', says Hiley, 'liked to know about the holes and the stones. That was part of his black humour. He liked details of illness and death; quite a taste for the macabre. Once Dickie was dead it was, "How could I live without my brother?" Yet for years he went out of the back door if his brother came in at the front.'[19]

The Royal Navy provided a minesweeper, HMS *Shannon*, at Portsmouth. Hester, Olivier, his sister Sybille, and Vivien were on board. Olivier described the scene. 'The funeral (secret believers us all) was a splendid thing. . . His coffin was draped in the Union Jack, and the White Ensign flew at half mast astern of him. It was very moving, as we drew out from the dock, that all officers on watch and any hands on the decks of all the shops we passed, stood at the salute while his coffin on the port rail sailed by. I couldn't help thinking how pleased the darling old boy would, and I hope did, feel.'[20] He was equally observant at the committal. 'Poor Hester had to look quickly as the coffin bounced about in a distressingly grotesque way, before the holes let in enough water for it to find its dignity again.'[21] Hester noticed that Olivier wanted the chart afterwards. It showed the vessel's course from Portsmouth to St Helen's Road, south-east of Spithead, and the place of burial as 50° 42' 14" N, 1° 02' 61" W.[22]

That night they drove back to Notley. He and Vivien had not lived together for some time. As she had said in her letter to him, he had mentally and physically deserted her. He wrote in his published autobiography that, in order to avoid awkwardness, he left the three women at the house and went to sleep in Dickie's cottage nearby. It wasn't quite like that. In an earlier version he wrote that Vivien burst in on him demanding to be made love to, presumably in the main house. 'I suffered grievously for her being made to feel so horribly undignified and felt no end of a prig saying "No no no."'[23] His rejection of her left Vivien in a blaze of humiliation. Hester's recollection of that night corroborates Olivier's. 'By that time they were barely speaking to each other. I think, I don't know how I know this, because I was pretty low and didn't want to be close. . . I am conscious of there being a lot of raised voices. I think Vivien was probably trying to persuade him to stay. And he then rushed out and slammed the door and went to the cottage.'[24]

Next morning early, without stopping to ask if there was anything he could do for Hester, he left for London. He was evading Vivien, he was in his usual breakneck hurry to return to New York to complete his television work, and he wanted to see Joan before he left. From New York he was going straight on to Hollywood to make *Spartacus*. Joan would be remaining in England and there was little chance of their meeting for another six months. He did meet her and they went to his flat. Next day – which happened to be the day on which Suzanne had her first baby, a son, and made Vivien a grandmother – he flew off to New York. When he reached the Algonquin, this time alone, he wrote twenty-two letters, five to the navy people to thank them, and one to Hester, apologising for having dashed off 'in such a flurry' and thanking her for having given Dickie five years of happiness.[25]

Back in London on the same day Vivien, once more recovered, gave a party at the Savoy.[26] Olivier, as he had promised, ordered a new long-wheelbase Rolls-Royce Silver Cloud costing £8,400 for her, though it could not be delivered for some time. The dealer took Olivier's Bentley in part-exchange, and he traded down to a Jaguar. Vivien gave instructions to Hooper's the coachbuilders for purdah glass to be fitted to the rear-quarter windows of the new car, so that she could see out but be practically invisible to pedestrians.[27] She went to the theatre with Noel Coward, who thought she was in a bad way, drinking far too much and attacking everyone right and left. 'Larry has left her, and I for one don't blame him; she is certainly barmy up to a point, but she has been so spoilt and pampered for so many years that the barminess becomes ugly and dull. . . For all her beauty and charm and sweetness, she has let Larry down for years and really tormented him. If he can succeed in breaking away, good luck to him.'[28]

If Vivien was manic, so in his work was Olivier. In January 1959, completing the Maugham television play in New York, he has diary entries like, 'Finish 1 40am. Sleep in studio.' Even he said he had never known such wildly long hours. At one point he worked twenty-five hours at a stretch. His diary entry for 23 January 1959 reads: 'Finish 6 55am. Noon plane [from New York]. Arrive 6 [Los Angeles].' On that last day he only had time to dash from the Brooklyn studio to the Algonquin to pick up his clothes, and then straight out to the airport.[29] He was in Hollywood to do *Spartacus*, a Roman epic in which he played the patrician Roman general Crassus. There had been much haggling about his part, which he had insisted should be expanded in relation to those of Tony Curtis as his slave, Antoninus, and Kirk Douglas in the title role of the leader of the slave revolt. His fee was $250,000. The film cost $10 million, about ten times what he had failed to raise for *Macbeth*. He had asked Hester to come and keep house for him in California but she firmly declined. She thought Vivien would have been badly hurt if she had; not sexually jealous since they were brother and sister to her, but she did not wish to take sides between them. She remembers that Vivien, in spite of her own troubles, was a tower of strength to her after Dickie's death. She had two young children. The older, Louise, was three. Vivien would send round her chauffeur and take the little girl off to London to the ballet at Covent Garden. If she could sit still through only one act, Gilman would drive her round in the interval. Hester's firm recollection is that Vivien was very good to her. She could be most thoughtful. She had covered for Larry in many ways. Unless she had reminded him, his godchildren would never have got presents. Hester believes

Vivien did not know at the time that Olivier and Joan were lovers. 'There'd been others, so to speak. And Larry – extraordinary how they say these things – would say, "I haven't lived like a monk", or, conversely, "Well, actually, it doesn't mean that much to me."' She stayed at Notley, continuing to take the cream from the dairy herd up to the Ivy restaurant in London, which bought it, but looked for a flat in town. And she wrote regularly to Olivier telling him how Vivien was.[30]

In his replies he asserted again and again that he would not weaken in his resolve not to come back to Vivien. 'My heart aches for her, but I cannot let my mind follow it.' He said that the 'dear cows' at Notley would have to go. 'I do not think it is fair for you to go on crucifying yourself for the sake of Baba's sentimental attachment to those dear beasts which she must inevitably be parted from before long, and an occasional pat at the weekend does not justify things.' He suggested that they should be sold while Vivien was in London rehearsing. He calculated that her next crisis would be in June.[31] Vivien's friends continued to write to Olivier persuading him to return to Vivien, but he would not. As he told Hester, 'I feel the persuasion comes of sentiment, and I would feel an appalling duplicity and ghastly sense of burden which I just can't manage to cope with, knowing that when the time finally comes I've got to bash her in the face again.'[32]

Vivien, in spite of her determined letter about an absolute break, in spite of the apparent agreement during her birthday dinner with Olivier, and in spite of the new Rolls-Royce, had changed her mind. She had discovered that Peter Finch no longer wanted her. He did not return her telephone calls. His mother and sister had been present at the last disastrous house party at Notley, with the Tynans, so he probably knew what had happened then. As in 1953 in California, he was no longer there. He was pursuing a South African heiress and his wife was suing him for divorce.[33]

Olivier and Joan were going to be separated for many months. He would not be back until June when he would go to Stratford, not to play the Othello and Lear which had been asked of him, but Coriolanus. By the end of 1958 Joan was amicably separated from her husband. Before Olivier left she suggested they should allow themselves a

year's break, until the future became clearer. He had also thought of
something of the sort, as one of his first letters to her showed. He
wrote that if he really loved her he should 'cut the thing off'. But he
could not. 'I love you alright and I can't believe I could love you
more, but there is too much love of myself in my love for you for it
to be really a selfless love, it is. . .a communion of heart, spirit, and
body that is so beautiful that I am absorbed by it and live by it. You
can only turn your back upon something which is outside you. Already
by the time of NY *Entertainer* it was beyond that.'[34]

Joan did not write to him when he was in New York or at first
in Los Angeles. He thought she might be too miserable or paralysed to write. Then she did write to him, about moments when
she was overcome by feelings of awe and reverence. 'If you try to
hold on to that moment you can't – if you try to recapture the
feeling you can't. Understand? It is something "higher than man"
– but very rare and therefore completely undeveloped. And [I]
must confess that I believe it is only vouchsafed to those who are
suddenly illuminated by a deep and all-embracing love. Either love
of a human being or I suppose a true love of God. Mine has come
through love of you. . . This is a gift you have given me, my darling.
Though still small and struggling and not properly developed my
soul has really been awakened at last.'[35]

In March Suzanne wrote to Olivier about her mother. It took
him two months to reply. When he did, he said that he heard from
all that Vivien was so much better, and that people were saying,
'Come on, old boy, surely it's up to you now.' 'This,' he wrote,
'makes me feel desperate and panicky and want to run even further
across the Pacific and bury myself in the South Seas.' He did not
want to share his life with Vivien, who over the previous ten years
had become a different person from the one she so gloriously used
to be. Then he went further, saying that even if she were to be
exactly the same as she used to be, they had grown apart. Since
that had happened his natural survival instinct had caused him to
grow apart too, in his own way. It was something that just accrued,
like a shell round a sea creature. There was a gulf between them,
and even if they were to bridge it, it would only be for the sake
of a façade.[36] He had already written to Vivien telling her that he

was sure they could not go back to their old life, that it would be better if they did not see each other at all, and that when he returned in June he would go straight to Stratford. 'I think,' he wrote, 'that it is time now that we drop the legend which is being kept up for the press and the public.'[37] It was the first time he said in as many words that they were essentially a legend, and that what they presented to the world was a façade.

Victor Stiebel, Vivien's favourite couturier and – apart from Holman – probably her closest male friend, wrote to tell Olivier that if on his return there was no rapprochement Vivien might give up the treatment she had started. Would Olivier consider a normal home-coming on the understanding that she would press on with the treatment, and that at the first sign of trouble he would be free to leave immediately? This might, said Stiebel, sound like black-hearted blackmail, but Vivien, having come to face the reality of separation, would do anything to destroy the reason that had caused it. Olivier wrote telling Joan about this letter and then wrote, 'Now darling, I want to say this. When I read that my heart did not sink, my brain did not reel, I simply felt. . .a complete and solid cold determination even while reading it, and then felt lighter and lighter than for ages. Isn't that curious? Through the hell something has happened to me. . . I don't know what's going to happen except that that [a reconciliation] is not.'[38]

He wrote thousands of words to Suzanne and Hester alone. The message was always the same: he wanted a divorce and he had hardened his heart. At the same time he wrote to Vivien's doctors wanting to know how the treatment went on. Cecil Tennant went to see Joan and told her Vivien was in a worryingly self-destructive state. Joan went so far as to suggest to Olivier that when he returned to Stratford they should stay apart until they met for the filming of *The Entertainer* in October. The fear was that Vivien would do to Joan what she had done to Dorothy Tutin – threaten to kill herself and get rid of her rival in that way. Somehow the knowledge of Olivier's love affair with Joan was kept from Vivien, though many in New York and Hollywood knew of it and so did Joan's intimates at the Royal Court. 'Larry,' says Joan, 'was in terror of Vivien visiting me, and asked me not to weaken if such a visitation occurred.'[39]

The tone of Olivier's letters to Joan Plowright was quite different from that of his illicitly wanton letters to Vivien of 1938 and 1939. He was older, but that does not of itself alter the nature of a man. He was now looking for different qualities. The correspondence with Joan was as full of longing as that with Vivien, but on both sides it had at times an almost religious nature. She had written to him about a quality 'higher than man'. He wrote to her, after a telephone call that was not a bitter wrangle in the Vivien style but a conversation that left him with a serenity 'like a fresh moon', saying that their love was to him a purification. 'It is something we share – a communion that is transcendental, unexpressive [inexpressible?], a piercing of my hands into your flesh that hurts in order to give life, like the slap on a new born baby that makes it breathe. And the wish of God to inject life upon the earth. Your presence in the universe is a *wound* in my heart that sets the blood free, sets it free to fly back to you, to join with yours.'[40] He thought of his five months in America as an 'enforced romantic starvation' but believed there was no possibility of stifling the hopes that insistently sang in their hearts.[41] Vivien, though, was by then, as Coward noticed, calm, sane, heartbroken, counting the days until Olivier returned and refusing to envisage the possibility that he might leave her for ever.[42]

When he returned on 7 June Vivien did meet him at the airport, but he then went immediately to Stratford where he stayed in a hotel throughout his time in *Coriolanus*. Vivien was at Notley, which was being advertised for sale. She refused to accept that the marriage was at an end, and her doctors were so worried about her state that they asked Olivier to do nothing precipitate because of the utter hopelessness that any firm action on his part might cause in her. 'So I can see no relief from the difficulties that have beset my life,' he wrote to Hester. 'God, one keeps clinging on for some slight light. . .'[3] He resumed his course of Royal Jelly injections. He had given up drink for some months, was bronzed by the California sun and was fit, as his virile appearance in *Spartacus* clearly showed. He needed to be for the spectacular end of *Coriolanus*, where his death leap was a classical piece of Olivier bravado bordering on recklessness. At the end of the play, already bleeding from many stab wounds, he hurled himself from a platform twelve-feet high at his arch enemy, Aufidius, on the stage below. He launched himself into space, was grabbed by his ankles from above by four spear carriers and then spun round in the air so that the audience saw his dying face. It was the leap of the *Hamlet* film again, only more dangerous, and he was ten years older.

Michael Blakemore, who was understudying a Roman patrician, used to watch from the wings with the young Vanessa Redgrave, who had a small part. He knew that Olivier had in mind the igno-minious fate of the dead Mussolini, suspended upside down after having been riddled with bullets, and that he had practised the plunge over the end of a diving-board in Los Angeles while he was filming *Spartacus*. Sometimes one of spear carriers' hands would slip and latch at the last moment on to the strap of Olivier's sandal. Blakemore and Vanessa used to lay bets that this would be the night when the most famous actor in the world would be dropped on his head.

After the first night Olivier gave a party for the company at a grand hotel a mile or so outside Stratford. 'There he sat at his table,' says Blakemore, 'our host, this pleasant, greying man in a dinner jacket, surveying his guests through heavy, black-framed spectacles. He might have been a surgeon or a successful solicitor celebrating a wedding anniversary. This was his second performance of the evening in what might be described as an audacious double bill. Could this be the same man we had seen challenging the Roman mob, and was he taking surreptitious pleasure in provoking the question?' Vivien came to Stratford for the first night and sat beside him. It was the last time most of the company saw them together.[44]

It was a time of contrasts and deceptions. To the outside world, even to their old friend Douglas Fairbanks, Olivier and Vivien, when they were together, appeared their old selves; yet they were not. And Olivier, directed by Peter Hall, appeared happy with this young man who at the age of twenty-eight had just been appointed director designate of the Stratford theatre; yet he was instantly on his guard when Hall proposed to him grand plans which cut across his own ambitions for a National Theatre.[45] At the same time as he played *Coriolanus* in repertory, Olivier was filming *The Entertainer* with Joan. Some of the shooting was on location at Morecambe and he commuted back and forth in an ambulance, to get some sleep.[46] Vivien was appearing in an LOP production of *Look After Lulu*, a French farce directed by Coward, which opened at Nottingham and then transferred to the Royal Court, of all places, where she occupied the same dressing room Olivier had had for *The Entertainer*. John Osborne, then as always, was a sympathetic observer of Vivien. For whatever reason, they found each other congenial. He and Joan, for whatever reason, did not; he had not wanted her in the film of *The Entertainer*. But at any rate he was sensitive to Vivien and this is what he said of her: 'It must have seemed to Vivien that we, George [Devine], Tony [Richardson], even myself, were the instruments of her present misery and Larry's disavowal of the whole courtly progress of the legend surrounding their love and lives. However much one sympathised with Olivier's desperation to escape the destruction of her magic alchemy, it was impossible not to be affected. . .by the pain cascading over both of them.'[47] Early in December, after *Coriolanus* and *The Entertainer*, Olivier took a four-day holiday in France with Joan. He had by then, at last, told Vivien about her.[48] *Look After Lulu* was closing; Olivier would soon be off to America again, to direct Charlton Heston in a play on Broadway, and this time Vivien had no play which kept her in England, and therefore no plausible reason not to go with him. The secret was no longer secret anyway. A German magazine had reported that the marriage was ended and a fan from as far away as Christchurch, New Zealand, wrote to Olivier: 'In God's name don't let this happen. To us it's as tho' the Queen and Duke of Edinburgh were estranged.'[49] Vivien spent Christmas in Switzerland with Coward, desolate but gay and charming. Joan and Olivier were facing yet another separation. As he sailed to America aboard the liner *United States* he heard of the death of Vivien's father and wrote a letter of condolence to Gertrude, wishing her strength in her loss. 'I wish to God,' he wrote, 'that I could support that strength with the confident assurance of alrightness between V and me, but terrible sham it is, I do not honestly feel that I can do that.'[50]

He spent Christmas with Stewart Granger and his wife, Jean Simmons, and opened his heart to them too.[51] Then he was back in the familiar routine of rehearsals, Boston openings, New York openings, supper at Sardi's, and long letters to and fro. At 2.15 one morning he wrote to Joan from the Algonquin: 'How I long to be gazing raptly down at you from a few inches away. Occasionally giving your nose a little pinch and you will swallow and make a little grunt or two and start shifting your legs about. I have watched you so often when you are asleep. The dim light from the long narrow roof windows at Cheyne [Row] falling across your face, pale in the serene beauty of after love, and other times rolled up and gipsy dark witch-baby with the dolly's black hair. There are so many of you my darling girl. . . With what wealth of gratitude do all my memories of you fill my heart. My darling. My girl. My baby, infant, child of God. Wumpy, Scrumpy.' She replied, 'I feel so close to you, so much an integral part of you when you write those sort of intimate things about when I'm asleep and you're watching me. . . Sometimes you seem to know me better than I know myself. You say things to me occasionally which quite stun me for a moment with their perception, and very often I will deny them out of shyness or unease or simply rage that you know so much. And the knowledge that I will never be able really to hide anything from you, that you will probably always know exactly what I am feeling or thinking in any situation. It's rather wonderful in one way, and slightly irritating in another, but it is all part of this wondrous, mysterious experience of being wholly, devastatingly, shatteringly, deeply in love. You cannot surely be afraid that it could die?' And he replied, a week or so later, 'I need, I absolutely require my Joanie – you are essential to me like water and air.'[52]

While he was in New York Olivier was also arranging a Broadway transfer of *Duel of Angels*, in which Vivien was to star. At the beginning of March, a week before he came home, she telephoned him, ostensibly about this play. He made it clear to her that he wanted no more letters or phone calls except on business, and she seemed to accept this.[53] He came back to England, she left for New York, and once again they were safely on different sides of the Atlantic. Her friends, however, did not leave him alone. Rachel Kempson, wife of Michael Redgrave, wrote him what amounted to a threatening letter: 'She [Vivien] has told me that you have found someone else and who it is. . . I realise that this makes it even harder for you. I know how you have suffered from Viv: she knows it now and she has learnt her lesson. Viv would accept any terms at all I believe – I also believe that if you finally abandon her you will always feel defeated. How can you make someone else happy over Viv's unhappiness. . . ?'[54]

In New York, at the rehearsals for her play, Vivien met John Merivale. She had known him since 1937 – he had also had a part in the Oliviers' disastrous *Romeo and Juliet* of 1940 – and they had met occasionally since. In *Duel of Angels* he quickly became her protector. Then she went on another high. She bought a white Thunderbird with black leather upholstery, on impulse. She gave party after party. One evening she broke down before the play. Her mother, who had gone to her, wrote, 'I'm not happy about my pet.' When Vivien received a letter from Olivier formally asking for a divorce, she insisted on going shopping at Dunhill's and drinking at the St Regis and then, perhaps encouraged by the malign Robert Helpmann, talked to a reporter from the London *Daily Express*. She then sent a cable to Olivier reading: DARLING LARRY. . . I HAVE GIVEN A STATEMENT TO THE PRESS STATING THE FACTS.[55] Then she wept, had one shock treatment, and refused another.

The cable arrived on 22 May 1960, Olivier's fifty-third birthday. It was the first time Joan Plowright's name had been connected with Olivier's in public. She was woken early and spirited away to Tony Richardson's flat, to avoid the crush of reporters. She also withdrew from Ionesco's *Rhinoceros*, in which she was appearing with Olivier. He thought the cable was a black-hearted birthday present from Vivien. The statement she had made said, 'Lady Olivier wishes to say that Sir Laurence has asked for a divorce in order to marry Miss Joan Plowright. She will naturally do whatever he wishes.' The London papers carried the expected headlines.

SIR LARRY AND THE GIRL FROM SCUNTHORPE (*Daily Mail*)

A LEGEND CRUMBLES (*Star*)

Olivier declined to comment. The statement Vivien had made not only compromised Joan but also might have been an impediment to a divorce. It suggested collusion between Olivier and Vivien, which was then, strictly speaking, a bar to any proceedings. The legend was ended, but not as Olivier would have wished. Even Notley had at last been sold, with most of the furniture. The baronial period was at an end – house, farm, dairy herd, furniture and all.[56]

Vivien then came to London where she did consent to five electro-convulsive treatments from Dr Arthur Conachy of Harley Street, whom she trusted. In his report he described her as a charming, highly intelligent, determined, and ruthless woman, given to the sudden onset of manic phases during which she lost normal reserve, reasoning power, and insight, and was led by her increased libido into indiscriminate sexual activity. She drank too much but was in no sense an alcoholic. He remarked that she had a pathological and almost obsessional devotion to Olivier, and diagnosed her as suffering from a cyclic manic-depressive psychosis. He did not, however, think suicide 'a practical risk'. It is a pity that others did not know this. Olivier did not see the report at the time.[57]

Dr Conachy's report is terrible enough, but it is a more sympathetic portrait of Vivien than that given by Noel Coward, who wrote, 'Vivien has appeared in London and is busily employed in making a cracking ass of herself. She is right round the bend again, as I suspected, and looks ghastly. What has driven her round the bend again is the demon alcohol; this is what it has always been. I suspect there is far less genuine mental instability about it than most people seem to think. I went to see her "alone" and found the flat full of people. She arrived from Notley, where she had been insulting the new owners. She was almost inarticulate with drink and spitting vitriol about everyone and everything. . . Of course I am fond of her and of course I am sorry for her, but however upset she may be about Larry she should control herself and behave better.'[58]

Osborne, again, had the surest sense about her. He had seen her on television after her statement, looking pale and ill, and saw no reason to think that her grief was dissembled. He thought her 'rabid devotion' to Larry, however ruinous, was incontrovertible. And when he visited Olivier he thought that his 'glimpse of freedom from Vivien's mounting madness was blighted by the vulgar furore which enveloped his hubristic sense of National Dignity as much

as his hopes of deliverance from years of guilt and unhappiness.'
He saw Olivier's 'wild, terrible pain'.[59]

Ten days after she arrived in London Vivien flew back to America,
taking her Siamese cat Poo Jones with her, to embark on a tour
with *Duel of Angels*. During the flight she was once again rational
and wrote to Olivier: 'Pussy-cat my darling, Whatever may happen
let us be friends my dearest one. Conachy has done a very marvellous thing for me – and I am feeling as I have not felt for many
many years. Perhaps all the interim mistakes have made just too
much difference for our life together – I do not know – and you
must leave it to me to do what I think best for the future and in
my own time. It will take a little while to decide. . .one does not
let twenty five years go lightly. I feel very deeply in love with Jack
[Merivale] and very dearly grateful to him but it does not alter
the fact that I shall love you all my life and with a tenderness and
respect that is all embracing – I understand very well how difficult
– even impossible – it had become. . . Let us face that – Well, now
that is accomplished and I hope my life will prove a useful and good
one – to many people. . . Take care of your precious dearest self.
My love, dear dear heart – Vivling.'[60]

For his part, Olivier had already decided. The next day, before
he could have received that letter written on the plane, his solicitors wrote to Vivien's. Their client, at the persistent and urgent
requests of his wife, had met her before she left, and impressed upon
her that his decision not to return to her was irrevocable and that
he had no intention of resuming cohabitation with her. Their client
was concerned lest his wife should quite mistakenly believe that
there was a possibility of his returning to her, and trusted that she
would take steps in England to dissolve the marriage so that he
might remarry with the least possible delay.[61]

Olivier's solicitors also told him it was most important that he
should not write to Vivien, but he did. She had first written to him
suggesting that time was running out and asked if he didn't think
they should put their lives in order, to which he replied, 'Yes my
darling, I jolly well do.' She had also called Joan wretched, to which
he replied, 'My ('wretched') girl is better equipped than you could
possibly suppose and looks after me with what seems a special gift

for the things in life I really need.'[62] He wrote a second time, at length, saying her second cat – which she had left behind – was clawing up the Aubusson carpet, and would she please instruct her solicitors about the divorce.[63]

That was in mid-August. The day after he wrote it he received a letter from Jack Merivale saying that he and Vivien were wonderfully happy together and that she now agreed to co-operate in the divorce. Olivier replied with a lyrical and almost hysterical letter, saying he had broken down and sobbed with relief and gratitude and was filled with joy at their happiness. '[It] releases me from the from those barbs which have so tormented my own hopes and dogged the beauty which is within my reach. Oh God, to think we can all be happy at the same time. . .' Then, quite suddenly, he shifted the subject to Rolls-Royces. The one he had promised her could not be delivered until the following January, but he had seen a delicious left-hand drive Rolls drop-head in Ming blue which she could have straight away. Would she like it?[64]

It seems she did not. Another Rolls-Royce was found for her in sable, whereupon she insisted it should be resprayed grey. It was waiting for her when she returned from America in October. She sailed not to England but to France, to be fitted with costumes for a film. When she disembarked at Cherbourg from the *Queen Elizabeth*, along with Merivale and Poo Jones, they were met by Gilman and drove off to Paris in the brand new Rolls. She had to leave behind the Renoir she had also taken with her on her travels; the painting was impounded by French customs who said it was French and should stay in France. She said it was hers, that she liked to have something pretty to look at when she was on tour, and that she had taken it all over America. It was later restored to her. In Paris she had her fittings at Balmain, then cried and tore up the divorce papers which had been served on her and continued through France into Switzerland, to stay with Coward. He had modified his views since June and again found her gay and sweet, hankering after Larry but fond of Jack who was 'constantly fulfilling a long-felt want'.[65]

By then both Olivier and Joan were on Broadway again, she in *A Taste of Honey* and he in Anouilh's *Becket*. Both were great successes. They were still there when Vivien's divorce petition was heard in

London on 2 December. She was the petitioner and she cited Joan
as co-respondent, but in a discretion statement Vivien admitted her
own adultery in Ceylon, New York, and London. She was accompanied to the court by Cecil Tennant and Peter Hiley. Hiley remembers how she comported herself: 'She behaved impeccably. It was
rather like a scene from an early film, low key. She was very diminished by it, in a way, although she looked great. I've always felt that
she was expecting a telephone call from America the day before,
from Larry, saying "Call the divorce off." I think she was longing
for it. She knew in her good moments what a problem she caused
for other people. I think she loved him totally for the rest of her
life.' Newspaper reports said she wept in court. It is Hiley's recollection that she did not.[66]

The judge granted a decree nisi. No order for alimony was made.
In an affidavit of means Vivien stated that she had £9,500 in shares,
£21,124 in the bank, and jewellery, furs, and pictures worth
£45,000. She was also the beneficiary of £130,000 worth of insurance on the life of Olivier, which could give her a tax-free income
of £3,350 a year.[67]

Two days after the hearing, Olivier wrote to her from New York.
'Darling, This is awky to write you will understand. But I know
what horror it must have been for you, and I want to say thank
you for undergoing it all for my sake. You did nobly and bravely
and beautifully and I am very oh so sorry that it must have been
such hell to you, and I am dearly grateful to you for enduring it
and setting me free to enjoy what is infinitely happy for me. Oh
God Vivling how I do pray that you will find happiness and content-
ment now. I pray that I may take off from you some of your unhappiness on to myself and I must say it seems to work from this end
as your unhappiness is a torment to me; and the thought of it a
constant nightmare. Perhaps now it may be allowed to gently lift
off and blow softly away. That's all for now. . . Your L.'[68]

The year after the divorce Peter Hiley left Olivier's employment.
He was forty and thought that was too old to go on acting as aide-
de-camp. He and his wife had both inherited money and they had
a newborn son. He wanted a new start and went off to Australia.

Olivier was put out and regarded his leaving as a defection, but they parted amicably. Vivien gave him a generous leaving present. Olivier gave him nothing. He held them both in deep affection, indeed loved them both, and since he had worked for them closely for twelve years – at the St James' Theatre and at Notley – his impressions of them at that point are valuable.

'What I felt about Larry is that he was a giant in showbusiness, *the* giant. But as a man he was very light. Vivien was not light in that way at all. From one room to another he could switch his temperament. This is one of the actor's great talents. He treated serious things very lightly. He had a great sense of black humour. He was not a deep man. Vivien was a very strong woman, very intelligent, very streetwise, very generous. Larry was not really interested in people, you see. He would observe someone, thinking that would make a good something for Shylock, but he was picking up mannerisms; he wasn't wondering what that person was like. He was a very light, amusing man, and he was very patient. . . He hated being alone, and if he was going to eat in a restaurant someone was dragged along, and you could have a perfectly ordinary conversation as if he wasn't the greatest actor in the world.'

He remembers Olivier as a many-sided man. He could be snobbish, as he was when he chose the Board of the St James' Players, a virtual subsidiary of LOP formed in the early 1950s, whose purpose was to produce ostensibly educational plays in order to avoid the entertainment tax which was then levied on ticket sales. He selected the nominal directors of this company straight out of *Who's Who*. There was Sir Alex Korda, whom he did know well. There were Sir Malcolm Sargent and Sir Kenneth Clark, who were at least old acquaintances. But there was also Garrett Moore – then a courtesy viscount and later eleventh Earl of Drogheda – who was only a slight acquaintance, one of his houses having been rented to house Marilyn Monroe during her stay to film *The Prince and the Showgirl*. To attend Board meetings these men trudged up the stairs of the St James's Theatre to a room more squalid than they had probably ever seen, but their names looked impressive on the company's letterhead.

Hiley had seen clearly enough how single-minded Olivier could be in getting his own way, and ruthless in dropping an actor or a designer who was no longer of use to him, but he had also observed that he could be a warm man who inspired affection and love in his staff. There is ample evidence of this. From 1943 until near the end of his life he was served successively by three secretaries, who between them stayed with him for more than forty years – Dorothy Welford, Peggy Gilson and, later, Shirley Luke. All adored him. Mrs Welford would say how lucky she was to have been in the right place at the right time, and to have had the good fortune to work for him. He flattered them, describing Miss Gilson in a memo to the National Theatre company as a 'queen of heavenly receptiveness in the matter of personal trouble'. He was patient. When Miss Luke took to the bottle, gossiped, and left confidential letters hanging around and his office in disorder, he sent long handwritten letters to her, imploring her to sober up, but never dismissed her.[69]

He was less kind to his first wife. Hiley remembers that Olivier could speak vindictively about Jill and much resented her continuing alimony, saying he had worked out that she had cost him '£10,000 a go' and that there had been only seven such occasions during their marriage. But after his second divorce he was still often solicitous about Vivien. 'There were days,' says Hiley, 'when I saw them both. At Eaton Square she would say, "Have you heard from him this morning? Is he all right? Did he sleep well?" Then I went round to Larry, and he would ask, "Puss all right? Did she have enough breakfast?"'

Hiley returned from Australia sooner than he had expected. It was discovered that he still formally remained a director of LOP, and he was asked if he would mind signing company cheques. He did this. Olivier would then ask him for help, and so would Vivien, and he continued to help them unpaid during their lifetimes, and afterwards became an executor of their estates. As he says, he never escaped.[70]

24

New Wife, New National

BY THE END OF 1960 Olivier had no doubt that the central duty of his career was the creation of a National Theatre.[1] He was already its director-designate, though that was no more than being the director-designate of a notion, and he had other more pressing business to attend to. He had a new wife to marry and he was in the middle of the longest run he ever had on the American stage. He was also flattered to be asked to speak at the Inauguration Ball of John F. Kennedy in Washington in January 1961, even more delighted than he had been to be invited to the White House by Eisenhower five years before. He devoted quite a bit of space to this when he came to write his autobiography. JFK's father, who had been a disagreeable ambassador to the Court of St James in 1940, referred to him as 'Mr Olivier', and he was much gratified when the president-elect, correcting his father, said how pleased he was to see *Sir Laurence* there.[2]

His play, which ran for eight months in New York and on tour, was *Becket*, Anouilh's version of the story of Henry II and his turbulent and martyred archbishop, murdered in Canterbury cathedral. He first played the title role with Anthony Quinn as the king, and then, more successfully, took the role of the king himself. It was a typical Olivier play of the time. *The Entertainer* was his most outstanding venture into the new wave, but not the only one. In the summer of 1960 he had chosen to do *Rhinoceros*, by the Rumanian Ionesco, in which all the cast turn into animals. Then he elected to do not Christopher Fry's version of the Becket story, *Curtmantle* – which he had encouraged him to write – but that of the fashionable French playwright Anouilh.[3]

But first in his mind was Joan Plowright, and children. He wrote to Tarquin curiously saying he was touched that his son should 'condone and even bless' his wish for a family, and then went on to describe his wife-to-be. 'Joan is a very natural and splendidly earthy young woman (31), and if I am to make her happy and fulfilled she's simply got to have them, that's all, she's that type. She is very very beautiful to me, and wonderfully good and good for me.' He had bought a house in Brighton where they would live, using royalties from Olivier cigarettes to pay the deposit on it.[4]

Joan's divorce had come through too, and as soon as they could they married, on 17 March 1961, St Patrick's Day. To escape reporters the wedding was not in New York but in Connecticut. They first got the licence at Norwalk.

'Name?' asked a little old lady at city hall.

'Laurence Olivier.'

'Profession?'

'Actor.'

'Are you? How very nice.'

He and Joan then went to the small town of Wilton for the ceremony, where the judge did not recognise them either. They returned to New York the same day, appeared in that night's performances of their shows and then went on to a party thrown by Richard Burton, who was playing on Broadway in *Camelot*. Lauren Bacall gave them a three-tiered wedding cake and then the secret was out. But it was a matter of some patriotic pride to Olivier that, English clocks being five hours ahead of New York, the first report appeared in *The Times* of London.[5] Peggy Ashcroft wrote to him from Stratford: 'How *much* I wish you all the happiness and peace in the world with that darling Joan.'[6]

They wanted a child straight away. Olivier had his sperm tested by a doctor and phoned Joan with the results. 'Millions of the little buggers.' Then, as Joan describes it, he insisted on employing the old method of holding her upside down on the bed, by the ankles, so that none of the little creatures could escape. 'It would,' she says, 'have made a wonderful sketch. Like everything else, he did it with tremendous energy, jumping up and down on the bed.'[7]

Jill cabled to congratulate him on his marriage and he replied with a crashing lack of tact to 'Darling Jillikin', saying that he was beautifully and wonderfully happy, that he would soon be returning to 'Brighton and all that's joyous' and was 'bouncing about being "young" just this once more.'[8]

By May Joan knew she was pregnant. She had left the cast of *A Taste of Honey*, which had brought her a Tony for Best Actress on Broadway, and wrote to her parents that she 'had not yet noticed that extraordinary look of serenity and radiance which is supposed to transform the faces of pregnant ladies'. Larry's play was doing brilliantly, so they were happy on all scores. 'I'm extremely happy not to be acting for a bit I must admit, and love just being a *wife*.'[9]

For his last two months in America that year Olivier applied himself to making money to support his new family. *Becket* toured Boston, Detroit, and Toronto, where it played at the gigantic O'Keefe Centre which seated 3,500. He had always said an actor could not 'mesmerise more than a thousand', but was happy to be taking ten per cent of the gross at the O'Keefe. When the play returned for a final three-week run in New York he then, 'for a dollop of dough', played the Mexican whiskey priest in a CBS television play of Graham Greene's *The Power and the Glory*. It is a magnificent and almost unknown performance. The part was very much Olivier's, all guilt, masochism, and religious intensity. Looking like Heathcliff in *Wuthering Heights* he tells a kneeling crowd of ragged, hunted peasants, 'This is part of heaven, just as pain is part of happiness.' He thought he and the cast achieved a rare and spiritual communion. The shooting took everything from him and from them and, as in the televising of *The Moon and Sixpence*, he worked himself to exhaustion. Twice he worked through the night. On the last day he finished at ten in the morning, sailed on the *Queen Elizabeth* at 1.30 p.m. and then slept in his cabin for two days and two nights.[10] He did not then appear on the stage for a year. His first concerns were the National Theatre and the opening of a theatre in Chichester, which turned out to be a dry run for the National. There was nothing inevitable about the way he became director of the National. The appointment did afterwards seem so, but it emerged from an informal and very English understanding between people who had known each other for years, knew how to raise the money from powerful friends in high places, and knew how to see off powerful rivals in the theatre. This is not a history of the National, and will not attempt to follow in detail the complex haggling between Whitehall, the London County Council, and various competing theatre interests.[11] Most of the money had to come from the Treasury. There was already a joint council, of which both the Old Vic and the Shakespeare Memorial Theatre at Stratford were members. Its chairman was Lord Chandos, who, as Oliver Lyttelton, had been a member of Churchill's war cabinet and later Colonial Secretary. He wanted a National Theatre and had a minute knowledge of how government and the Treasury worked. Without him it could all have come to nothing. As far back as 1956 Chandos had asked Olivier to become a member of the council. Olivier had thought there must be some catch, as this gave him great power. He could be outvoted, but on the other hand if he violently disagreed with the other members on any decision, his public resignation could do them irreparable harm. He then realised that Chandos must believe that the idea would be a non-starter without him.[12] He also saw, after a while, that he and Chandos and Kenneth Rae, secretary of the joint council, were really running the whole thing themselves, between council meetings at which they just told the rest what was happening. Then, said Olivier, it became apparent one day at Notley that 'those two birds' were regarding him as the first director. He asked them if that was so.

'Yes. You surprised?'

'Do you realise what a cunt I am? Well, you'll find out now.'

That, he said, was how he received the news that he was to be director. For his part, he thought they needed his glamour and needed him as a figurehead.[13] That at any rate was his recollection many years later, though he did also say, on another occasion, that he could not imagine why they had not come to him on their hands and knees and begged him to run the National right from the beginning; but they hadn't.[14]

The invitation was probably as casual as he remembered it, but he never could recall *when* it was made, sometimes putting it as early as 1958.[15] It was almost certainly 1960. In December of that year Kenneth Clark, a council member and a friend, wrote to Olivier saying, 'I had sometimes thought about asking if you would consent to become the first director. . .but hardly dared to hope for it. No doubt at all that it would make all the difference, both to the public and to actors. Everyone has confidence in you, as well as admiring your genius.'[16]

But even then it was by no means a foregone conclusion that Olivier would be director of the National if and when it came to pass. Peter Hall at Stratford certainly did not think it was written in stone. In 1959, when he directed Olivier in *Coriolanus*, he was director-designate at Stratford – where the Memorial Theatre was about to change its name to the Royal Shakespeare Theatre – and he had plans to take over a London theatre as well. During and after *Coriolanus* he wrote letter after letter to Olivier. He said he knew how keen Olivier was on a National, and that he would of course be a leading member of it. 'But supposing,' the ambitious Hall went on, 'that it doesn't happen yet. Would you be prepared to help us to do it here in all but name? As a great classical actor, you could make a great theatre for us. . . I know it would be the making of my scheme.'[17] This, from a young man of twenty-eight who had not even taken over Stratford at the time, was a bit of a cool cheek. Olivier would obviously be more than simply 'a leading member' of the National, whatever form it took, and he would have no particular interest in any grand scheme of Hall's. But Hall persisted. Would Olivier become his leading actor, or become 'some kind of director' with him? Olivier, still more or less polite, would not. Hall then sent him Anouilh's *Becket* to read. Would he do that? If not that, would he do a *Lear*? Olivier telephoned from New York and told him he was doing *Becket* there, at which Hall came back with offers of Lopakhin in *The Cherry Orchard*, or Cyrano.[18] Early in April 1960, after Olivier returned from New York, he met Hall among the packing cases at Notley. It was Olivier's recollection that Hall agreed to act as his assistant at the future National. Hall remembers nothing of the kind and his letters, and in particular a letter he wrote the day after this meeting, bear out his version of events. He wrote that Olivier's was a bold and wonderful scheme and said he was flattered to be in the middle of it, but emphasised that Stratford was now committed to its London seasons. The nub of his letter was this: 'If you believe that the Stratford company could be the nucleus of the National Theatre, please give us a shove off. (This is blackmail). . .'[19] Olivier obviously thought that was just what it was. He repeated that the central duty of his career was the establishment of a National; he did not say *his* National but that is what he meant.[20]

In March 1961, just after Olivier's marriage, the government decided not to put up the cash for a National Theatre as such but to give more to existing companies. By July, thanks to an offer from the London County Council of a site and more than £1 million, Her Majesty's Government had changed its mind. There would be a National after all. But this had been envisaged as a coming-together of the Old Vic and Stratford, and it then emerged that if Olivier was to be director of the merged body, the governors of the Stratford theatre wanted nothing to do with it. Olivier, writing to Hall as 'My Dear Peterkin', was terse: 'The Nat. Th. seems to be at a complete impasse, tout *lasse*, tout *casse* and fuck me all dandy. I am in a bad way. I can't get a National Theatre. . . I can't get into my home [the Brighton house was still being refurbished], and Joanie's baby is *bursting* out. I can't wake up in the morning or go to sleep at night. I'm absolutely fucked.'[21]

Joan's first baby was born on 3 December, a boy. The house was ready in time after all. Olivier's son was christened Richard, after his brother Dickie, at Chichester cathedral. And in Chichester, the National having apparently stalled yet again, Olivier also had a brand new theatre being built for him to run.

This was the idea of Leslie Evershed-Martin, an optician and former mayor of the city. It was to be a theatre-in-the-round seating 1,400, the first of its kind in England, in the style of Stratford, Ontario. The invitation to become its founding director had come to Olivier that January in New York. He accepted it two months later. As soon as he returned home in June he went with Joan to Chichester to view the muddy site and was delighted with the promise of what he saw. Then they took a three-week holiday in the south of France. There was dinner with Prince Rainier and Princess Grace at Monaco, a party with Simone Signoret and Yves Montand at St Paul de Vence, and a stay with the Nivens at St Tropez.[22] Back home the new theatre rose rapidly. It was fortunate for Chichester that Olivier should at that moment have been looking for a theatre, and fortunate for him that it was only twenty miles along the coast from his new house at Brighton. He always publicly denied that he used it as a rehearsal for the National, but it did turn out that way.

While the Chichester theatre was being completed, and while he was planning its first season, his relations with Peter Hall grew worse. Olivier's claim to be director-designate of a putative National Theatre was settled, but it was Hall who was already the director of what was beginning to look like one in fact. He had Stratford; he had the Aldwych in London on a five-year lease; and he was planning to take the small Arts Theatre in London as well. He wrote to Olivier asking what Stratford's place might be in the ultimate plans for the National. The letter arrived while Olivier was making a film and putting together the Chichester season. He said in a long, irate and handwritten reply that the National was 'a safely locked away black cloud', and then he went for Hall's throat. 'The trouble as I see it (and have from the beginnings of your schemes) is that you have really set out to be a Nat. Th. yourself, or if you prefer it, for Stratford to develop a position for itself as heir to the throne, or else to make such a throne unnecessary. . . The trouble is that there has been for many years an organisation and machinery (no, not empowered) but recognised and dedicated to the construction of the thing. [He meant the joint council, Chandos, and himself.] And you can't kick them out. These boys have been working at it for years, long before Stratford ever thought of it. So Stratford must now (we think) join in to survive. . . You really musn't throw up words like "Empire" to me, not you with Stratford, Aldwych, and now the Arts, because here again you seem to be assuming N.T. responsibilities. . . Finally, the statement which, to me, represents the kernel of your feelings: − "otherwise the foundations I have fumblingly laid at Stratford might just as well not have happened"!

That's it, isn't it? And, my God, I understand it completely and I have apprehended it throughout. I realised all these implications when we first talked during *Coriolanus* rehearsals, naturally. The work you have done and the schemes you envisage belong in a N.T. set up. But the sad thing is, as things have worked out, that it is your governors not the N.T. who are responsible for your present impasse.' He finished with a description of the NT directorship as he saw it: 'At the moment it looks like the most tiresome, awkward, embarrassing, forever-compromised, never-right, thankless fucking post that anyone could possibly be fool enough to take on and the idea fills me with dread.'[23]

Olivier spent the next six months preparing the Chichester season, which he was running for £3,000 a year. To choose plays for his first season he read everything from P.G. Wodehouse's frolics to Webster's revenge tragedies. He asked Robert Bolt, Harold Pinter, and John Arden to write plays for him; Arden did.[24] The opening was on 3 July 1962. It was a festival theatre and he saw it as such. It was in a park, it had a restaurant, and people would drive the fifty miles down from London for a pleasant evening. He saw it as doing for the theatre what Glyndebourne did for the opera. It was strange then that he chose to include in the first three productions, all of which he directed himself, two forgotten seventeenth-century plays: *The Chances* by the Duke of Buckingham, and Ford's *Broken Heart*. His reasons for the second choice were astonishing. 'I did that of course out of sheer, frank, disgraceful gumming up to the critics, because I wanted Mr Tynan's high regard. I wanted, you know, people saying, "He doesn't just do *Peer Gynt* and *Charley's Aunt*."'[25] Why Olivier of all people should have been so apprehensive of *any* one critic, however acute, let alone one whose stock in trade was hyperbole, is a lasting mystery.

Olivier's position was made the more difficult when, two days before the opening, the news was leaked that he had at last been appointed director of the National Theatre. In the previous few months events had moved fast. Stratford had definitely dropped out; the Treasury had set up a National Theatre board and released the money to it; the Old Vic company was to be dissolved; and the new National would take over at the Old Vic theatre in the winter of

1963. Olivier was embarrassed and furious at the leak, thinking 'an enemy hath done this'. To his mind the enemy was Stratford; he was convinced the villain was Peter Hall.[26] The leak meant two things. People would think that once the National was launched he would not be bothered with Chichester. He was the more concerned at this since, as he later admitted, it was largely true.[27] It also meant that he feared he would be on trial, and that what he did at Chichester would show whether he was up to running the National.[28]

Socially, Chichester was a great success, but the first two plays were badly received by the critics. The Duke of Buckingham's play was dismissed as lightweight. Ford's *Broken Heart* did even worse. Tynan – who was meant to be impressed, and who, however he had abused Vivien Leigh, had always been fulsome in his praise of Olivier – condemned the production by saying a lot of vocal brandishing took place in a vacuum. In an open letter to Olivier in the *Observer* he asked: 'Does the fault lie in the play, in the theatre, or in you, its artistic director?. . . Within a fortnight you will have directed three plays and appeared in two leading parts. It is too much.'[29] Olivier did not expect the season to be rescued by his third play. Why he should have expected so little is a puzzle, since it was Chekhov's *Uncle Vanya*, with Olivier in one of his favourite roles as Astrov, Michael Redgrave, Joan Plowright, Joan Greenwood, Sybil Thorndike, and Lewis Casson. It was a great play with a magnificent cast. But he expected little and feared much. He feared it was a mad risk to put on Checkhov on an open stage. He feared it would be the end of Chichester, the nail in his coffin – 'utter extinction' for him – and that if it had failed he might have washed himself out of the National and would have to tell them to find someone else. So he believed, or so he said.[30]

Uncle Vanya was of course a triumph, and played at Chichester and then at the National for three years. Olivier was not extinct. His National Theatre agreement was drawn up after the Chichester season ended – £5,000 a year on a five-year contract, during which time he could take off not more than fifty weeks to work on films, television, or plays outside the National. He was the servant of the board, which did however state that it considered he 'had acted in a very public spirited way in accepting the financial terms, which were clearly far less generous than those he could command elsewhere.[31] So they were. The directorship of the National Theatre would pay him in a year one twentieth of what he had earned for a supporting role in *Spartacus*. He accepted because he regarded it as his destiny.[32]

It was part of the deal that there would be a new National Theatre building, but not yet. The company's first home was to be the Old Vic. In spite of Olivier's long connection with it, since 1937, he felt little affection for it, and once went so far as to say he hated the place. Kenneth Rae – who throughout the negotiations had kept Olivier, in America, up to date with what was happening – had lamented that taxpayers' money would be spent 'shoring up that moribund building in the Waterloo Road' and had forecast that the National would be kept in the 'crumbling Old Vic until such time as it falls down'.[33] The place was indeed shored up, redecorated, and re-upholstered at the then great cost of £93,000. A complicated revolve was put in which often failed to revolve. And Olivier set about bodging the auditorium. Influenced by the theatre-in-the-round at Chichester, he took out the first two rows of the stalls and built a new forestage which jutted out in front of the proscenium arch, making the Old Vic neither one thing nor the other. He was at the time disaffected with the idea of a proscenium theatre. 'As each and every family in Britain has a baby proscenium arch [he meant a television set] in their "through lounge" it would seem wise to offer them another sort of experience when they come to the theatre.'[34] He was very jolly about what he was doing to the Old Vic: 'We are rebuilding the stage again, bringing it yet more forward. We shall be playing in the foyer eventually, with the public in the new Cut.' The Cut is the name of the street outside.[35] His improvements had the unwanted effect of ruining the acoustics. People couldn't hear. 'I don't know what it is we did to the theatre when we did the rebuilding,' he told one friend, 'but we did something that changed a theatre remarkable for acoustics for 150 years into a constant cause of complaint.' He had, as he later cheerfully admitted, ruined the place.[36]

As his second in command Olivier had wanted his old friend George Devine, but he saw no reason to leave the Royal Court so as associate directors Olivier recruited two younger men from the Court, John Dexter and William Gaskill. Kenneth Rae remained company secretary. And Kenneth Tynan became literary manager, occasional inspirer, publicist for the National Theatre and for himself, and constant pest. He was a critic of whom, as we have seen, Olivier was in some extraordinary awe, but the manner of his appointment is still a puzzle. The well-attested legend is that Tynan, having slated Olivier at Chichester, then wrote offering his services as dramaturge at the new National Theatre. The word dramaturge was a German affectation. Tynan's letter has not survived, and this is strange. It is not in the Olivier archive. Joan Plowright thinks he may have destroyed it, but he kept everything down to laundry lists. It is even stranger that Tynan, a diligent preserver of his own legend and his own letters, did not keep a copy; it does not appear in his 597-page biography by his second wife Kathleen or in her even longer edition of his letters.[37] Olivier mentions the letter in both his books of memoirs, but the fullest account is the one he gave in 1979 in conversation with Mark Amory, the writer who was intended to ghost the first book.

He said he received the letter when he was 'at his boilingest in anger' against Tynan, and gave it to Joan saying, 'How shall I dismiss him so that he'll never know he was born?' And she said, 'Wait a minute. I mean, look what he's got to offer you – apart from how you may hate him personally. He will rid you of the accusation of being an old fashioned actor-manager. He will bring to you – he's the most modern influence in the English theatre today, and he will bring that to you.'

Olivier thought it was marvellous advice. 'And so,' he said, 'it was announced. Everybody was flabbergasted. It made just the right sort of sensation.'

Then, when Amory asked Olivier if Tynan was loyal to him, he replied, 'Yes. No. He hated me sometimes. There were times when he took a great hatred against me. But I never would get rid of him. I'd simply say, "Look, I've decided it shall be so. If you want to go you must go, but I'm not going to get rid of you."'[38]

There is another version of events, which is that the initiative was Olivier's, who had himself originally approached Tynan to join

the National, precisely in order to disarm him. The authority for
this is Virginia Fairweather, who had known Olivier for many years
and became a press officer at the National. He later dismissed her
and she wrote a book accusing him of disloyalty, so what she says
has to be considered with that in mind. But her recollection of how
Tynan came to the National is a neutral matter, so there may be
something in what she says. Olivier's diary does show that he had
previously lunched with Tynan.[39] They may have talked about such
an appointment, and the letter Joan saw may have been Tynan's
response. However that may be, Joan did then give Tynan her
strong support. She thought his proposal was brave.[40]

The result was that Olivier put Tynan up to the board for the
post of dramaturge, even using that word. It was the board which
changed the title to literary manager and defined his duties as being
to help plan the repertoire, look for new plays, and – dangerous
decision as it turned out – to act as the theatre's spokesman on
policy matters.[41] His salary was £2,750, substantially more than
he earned at the time as the *Observer*'s theatre critic. Olivier, with
this calculated decision, had neutralised a potentially damaging critic.
Tynan put it more bluntly: Olivier would rather have him inside
pissing out than outside pissing in.

Then Olivier held auditions for his company. His old friends
from the Old Vic and from his films were not chosen. He wanted
to move on. Esmond Knight, who had appeared in all three of
Olivier's Shakespeare films, offered himself and was offended to
be turned away. One of the newcomers was the young Michael
Gambon, later Sir Michael, who was at the time working as a
fitter on the floor of an engineering shop in Islington, and had
the splendid nerve to offer as his audition piece a speech of Richard
III's. 'God, you've got a bloody cheek,' said Olivier, but he heard
him out and then, when the young actor cut his hand on a pillar
he grasped for added effect, patched it up for him. Gambon remembers Olivier as a god – a god who wore his suits cut wide at the
shoulders and fitting at the waist, and wore his watch loose on
his wrist so that it hung on his hand, like a piece of jewellery; a
god who liked to be seen at times in the props room or in the
canteen as one of the boys, telling jokes. But when Gambon got

carried away one day and ventured a joke of his own, he got his head bitten off.[42]

A young Gambon was just right for Olivier, who noted him as 'to be renowned'.[43] For the new National he wanted all things new. He declined as 'fearsome clobber' an offer to the theatre of the bells from Henry Irving's famous play, *The Bells*, one of his earliest great successes. They were offered by Irving's grandson. 'Do we want reminders and mementos or a clean sheet and no ghosts?' asked Olivier, adding that theatrical memory was so short that the name of Henry Irving would soon mean precious little.[44]

For its first season the National's plays included *Uncle Vanya* and Shaw's *Saint Joan*, both transferred from Chichester. They had been the great successes of that festival theatre. *Vanya*, with its extraordinary cast, was a natural. So was the Shaw, in which Joan Plowright, directed by Dexter, had perhaps the greatest success of her young and distinguished career. Her Joan of Arc won her an *Evening Standard* award. Also among the National's first plays were *The Master Builder*, with Redgrave, and, later on, Olivier in *Othello*. The theatre opened on 22 October 1963 with a production of *Hamlet* with Peter O'Toole, then newly famous for David Lean's vast film of *Lawrence of Arabia*. Olivier explained this choice to Tyrone Guthrie, hardly a friend of his, who was then running a theatre in Minneapolis and had asked what the National would be doing. 'This is a special engagement,' Olivier wrote, 'and rather outside our general policy [which] concerns itself with a longed-for permanent ensemble (the old, old yearning), such an ensemble not to have its nose put out of joint by the invitation of outside stars except on very rare occasions, the sales talk being that, in the beautiful future, to be a National Theatre player is to be a star.'[45]

Olivier had a National Theatre and was determined to make it work. If it would help, he would bring in an old enemy in Tynan. He was an instinctive showman, always instinctively hostile to what he called 'mediocracy', and never a lover of the ensemble for its own sake. So, never mind the sales talk, he brought in the biggest star he could lay his hands on. As it happened, O'Toole was not a success. Olivier's two associate directors wanted nothing to do with him. Dexter did not like him. Gaskill was opposed on principle to any star. Olivier tried to win them round by explaining that people would always be asking, 'But who's in it?' and that a National without stars was next to impossible. Then, as he would have done anyway, he directed the play himself.[46]

O'Toole's hair was dyed blond, as Olivier's had been for his 1947 film, but there the director's absolute power ended. On the opening night O'Toole departed from Olivier's carefully plotted moves and pleased himself. 'It was tragic actually,' said Olivier. 'If O'Toole had given on the first night the performance he gave on the last dress rehearsal it would have been an absolute sensation. Somehow, when it came to performances, he either didn't do it, or he was being much too free and too brave in changing the pace of whole scenes. We'd mapped out the rhythms so carefully together, you know: "This scene has to go like lightning." The scene that follows the graveyard has to go like *lightning* to bring them forward in their seats again. And he'd be so sleepy in it that the audience that weren't asleep yet, were *now* fast asleep. And he wouldn't understand that he was absolutely fucking up his chances for the last scene of the play. He, I mean he would not understand that. He wouldn't. I couldn't talk to the dear fellow.'[47]

Still, the National Theatre of Great Britain was open at last.

By then Olivier and Joan had a second child, the daughter he had wanted, Tamsin Agnes Margaret, born on 10 January 1963. Fabia Drake wrote to him: 'You are clever, clever, clever – you and Joaney. . . It was quite a *don de Dieu* to get the girl, wasn't it, "get" being, clearly, the operative word.'[48] Olivier's children and the National were gifts from God, and they had changed the pattern of his life. Royal Crescent, Brighton, was pleasant but not at all on the scale of Notley. He did buy Joan a mink stole and an amethyst bracelet, but no more Rolls-Royces were acquired, only a Royale Pramette.[49] He commuted on the Brighton Belle to London, working fifteen or sixteen hours a day. The director's office was not at the theatre but in a row of workmens' wooden huts, of a style known in the trade as Terrapin 19, bought second-hand and erected at a cost of £6,200 on an old bomb-site a quarter of a mile away – ten minutes' squalid walk past a grim park infested by meths drinkers and through streets of crumbling terraces. The road in front of the huts was derelict and had to be resurfaced at a cost of £756.[50] Olivier did not only do the work of artistic director. He had an administrator but wanted to run everything himself. He insisted on being provided with a list of the names and nicknames of the stage-hands and electricians: the master carpenter was George and the head flyman Ted. He compiled lists of Christmas presents – hand-made shirts for John Dexter, a bottle of Rumeur Lanvin for a press officer, a bowl of flowers for Maureen in reception. He signed a chit to authorise the purchase of an electric stove for Annette in the huts, to give the actors one meal a day, and agreed in principle that a girl should be taken on to do the washing-up.[51] Then he could turn his attention to *Othello*.

25

Max Factor 2880 and Love of a Strange Strength

FAR AND AWAY THE most memorable production in the early years of the National was *Othello*, which was put on to celebrate the four hundredth anniversary of Shakespeare's birth in 1664. Olivier's performance in it was one of those that last in theatrical memory. The play stayed in the repertory over a period of nearly three years, and was given at the Old Vic, in Moscow and Berlin, in the English provinces, and at Chichester. And the matter of *Othello* at Chichester strained the already fragile association between that theatre and Olivier.

The Queen's visit to *Vanya* had gone well. The Duchess of Norfolk told Olivier that she and the Duke had to entertain the Queen at Arundel during the whole week of Goodwood races, and that he had no idea how were grateful they were to him for taking her off their hands for an evening.[1] But the Chichester board, composed largely of local businessmen, had been unhappy when Olivier's directorship of the National was announced, rightly suspecting it could no longer have his undivided attention. Evershed-Martin tried to put the best face on it, saying he could see nothing but good in the connection with the National but wanted to keep Chichester's independence. Olivier told him, before the second season opened there, that he could not see how it was possible to pursue the dream of the 'unique and separate' enterprise of which he spoke, and went on: 'Does it sound conceited of me if I say that you are not likely to do better with another choice, and are almost certain to do worse?' It was, he said, not very nice for the dignity of either party to suggest that it had all been 'put together for the convenience of Sir Laurence'.[2]

Things went from bad to worse. Evershed-Martin wanted to meet Olivier, who eventually agreed to half an hour, telling him this ought to be enough. This was a time when Olivier was busy being even busier than usual. The film director Joseph Losey, wanting to discuss a film project, was told to get his secretary to telephone Olivier's secretary in three months' time to fix an appointment; he replied that his secretary would never remember. Losey could afford to tell Olivier to get lost. Evershed-Martin could not. The members of the Chichester board were given only two tickets between them for the National's opening night, and were angry at Olivier's advice to hold a raffle to see who got them. 'Do forthcoming events cast their shadow before them?' asked one board member. 'Is this the kind of association we can expect in the future?' Olivier did not attend the Chichester Christmas concert. Evershed-Martin, whose own credit with the board was in danger, wrote to him saying that it would be a severe blow if he did not personally appear in the second season's productions. They particularly wanted to see him in *Othello*. 'Please Larry,' he wrote, 'this is terribly, terribly important for me.' Olivier replied that he did plan to appear there. Things might change but, he said, 'If the present looks good it is silly not to enjoy it for its own sake, isn't it?'[3] Olivier was being pretty cavalier with Chichester. 'I kept it running,' he said later. 'It was useful try-out.' Chichester asked for twenty-two performances of *Othello*; he pleaded voice strain and gave thirteen there, over four weeks.[4]

Olivier always insisted that he had to be persuaded into *Othello* and that he was reluctant for many reasons, particularly because his voice was a natural light baritone and Othello's was a dark, velvet bass. This is not quite true. In 1957 he had been asked by the London County Council to support an invitation to Paul Robeson to come to London to do *Othello*. 'I am afraid,' he replied, 'that I don't feel inclined to make this gesture, either for Mr Robeson's sake or for my own. . . There comes a time when one rather wants to have a bash oneself.' He said he might do it in the next year or two.[5]

In early 1964 he began to prepare himself. For *Lear*, he had once
bellowed at a herd of cows. For *Othello* he came in early to the huts
and yelled away there. He took voice lessons, roaring lower by the
semitone as each week went by, and then he had the voice of the
Moor.[6] Except that he had decided not to be a Moor at all, but a
full-blooded Black. Now Olivier was a great man for the text,
constantly asking what the text said, and the very title of the play
– as it appears in the First Folio of 1623 – is *The Tragedy of Othello,
the Moor of Venice*. He may, as he later wrote, have been rejecting
'the modern trend towards a pale coffee coloured compromise', but
it was not a modern trend. *Othello* is one of the most frequently
acted of Shakespeare's plays and that was the way the part had
traditionally been played. Olivier's decision to be firmly Black is
just as likely to have been another example of a determination he
first expressed in his first Shakespeare season at the Old Vic in
1937. 'I did make a study of being different. It was the only way I
could be memorable. . . That's how I see myself, yes. I like to be
different.'[7]

It took him two and half hours to make up. 'It was grease on
the face first of all, black grease on the face and round the neck
and then the rest was pancake, absolutely all over my body black
pancake. I remember the number, Max Factor 2880. And then when
that dried, which was a few minutes waiting about, a cigarette or
something, I applied a slightly lighter one called Negro No. 2, which
was browner, and so the application of a brown coat on top of a
black gave it that real mahogany, black mahogany colour – I mean
gave it a very rich ebony, sort of gold somehow. Then the great
trick was that glorious half yard of chiffon with which I polished
myself all over until it all shone.' He had himself lit with steel blue,
No. 18, which further accentuated his blackness.[8]

Then, working from the outside in, he visualised the character
of the man. He was dignified. 'But of course he has to be at first
so goddam innocent and so goddam cold blooded. I mean, he'd hardly
bring himself to have a fuck at all, let alone this charming creature
[Desdemona.] And of course that's one of the greatest parts. You
know the old sort of definition of Shakespeare's tragic theme, a
perfect statue with a fissure in it; shows how the fissure crumbles

the statue. . . There's an infinite world of self-deception in Othello. He makes himself out to be so cold to the senate, and it's only got to be strawberries on a handkerchief and a day and a half later he strangles her. And he's such a cold, well-judged individual, isn't he? And to think that up to the moment of his death he's the greatest exponent of self-deception there's ever been. He actually says, "Then you must speak of one who loved not wisely but too well, of one not easily jealous." Not easily jealous? When in twenty four hours after he's seen her handkerchief he kills the bloody bitch, and can honestly have the self-deception to describe himself as being not easily jealous? It's enough to kill you.'[9]

Olivier was undertaking this part, training his voice, weight-lifting to tune his muscles, managing the National, irritated by Chichester, delighted but also surrounded by a family with two babies, commuting to London and working fifteen hours a day when he suffered what appears, looking back, to be the first breakdown in his health. At the end of January 1964 he spent two days in bed with a viral infection, which became ten days. When his temperature had gone down he determined to get some sea air, put on a track suit and set off on a run along the front at Brighton. After a mile his legs gave out, and he sat helplessly and in tears at the side of the road until a tradesman recognised him and took him home in his van; he went back to bed.[10]

When Olivier returned to rehearsals Tynan was questioning the choice of Dexter as director. Dexter was probably the National's best director, and Olivier knew perfectly well what he required of himself. Tynan had never directed anything. This did not stop him addressing reams of notes to Olivier. After the last run through, the day before the first performance, he sent a memo with fifteen points, among which were that Maggie Smith as Desdemona should sound more tragic, and that Othello should brandish his knife more before he killed himself.[11] Joan Plowright was more specific, and a great deal more apt, when she reminded her husband that he had said of one actress that she tried to cry on stage, whereas in real life one tried to *stop* oneself crying, and continued, 'I think you are maybe trying to believe Cassio's kisses have been on her lips, instead of trying to *stop* yourself believing.'[12]

The critics varied in their opinions. Some did not like the idea of Othello as Black. All, one way or another, were astounded. The notice most worth quoting is that of a man who was instinctively moderate both in his opinions and in the tone of his writing, Philip Hope-Wallace of the *Guardian*. He said, 'In great tragic acting there is always a strong element of surprise. Othello, on the rack last night, was agonising in the sheer vehemence of his anguish, but it was the inventiveness of it above all, the sheer variety and range of the actor's art, which made it an experience in the theatre altogether unforgettable by anyone who saw it. . .the General self-broken, self-cashiered. "Othello's occupation's gone." We saw it go.'

Olivier as Othello. Sketch by Claude Marks, signed by Olivier.

Tynan believed he had inspired Olivier to do this *Othello*. Olivier himself said he believed Tynan's persuasion had been essential.[13] But in the previous year, since Tynan first arrived as literary manager, his advice had been treated with no great respect. He suggested the National should look for a resident playwright and should advertise for one in the posh papers. Olivier replied that he could not think of any such announcement that would not be slightly comic. 'Like a sort of poet laureate?' he asked. 'Well, we'd soon get sick of him, whoever it was.'[14] Then, for the benefit of an international drama conference at the Edinburgh Festival, Tynan submitted to Olivier a list of high-flown questions. He received derisive answers.

What elements in the theatre did he think most likely to damage its chances of survival? – Olivier: 'The theatre would seem to have been trying to kill itself for years and years, but does not seem to have found anything lethal enough yet.'

Which trends [a long question, this] in the contemporary playwriting would most influence the future course of the theatre? – Olivier: 'Sorry, love, have not the faintest idea.'[15]

When the National put on Max Frisch's *Andorra* the Lord Chamberlain cut a few lines. Tynan, as a protest against censorship, wanted to print them in the programme:

> . . . it's on the floor
> And shut the door
> And take your knickers off, girl

Olivier replied that he was in two minds about the value of the Lord Chamberlain's office, and that in any case he was quite against that sort of petulant attack. If Olivier had engaged Tynan for his intellect, as is the general opinion, then he sometimes mocked the utterings of that intellect.[16] Tynan then suggested a four-week tour of Paris, Cairo, Berlin, and Stockholm, without suggesting how this might be brought about. He once, and only once, addressed a memo to 'Dear Larry-Warry'. He also asked Olivier to ponder his [Tynan's] relationship with John Dexter, who, he said, would quite like to assassinate him, which was a pity. He inquired whether three directors at the theatre wasn't rather a lot, and then said, 'The function I'd hope to fulfil (apart from the obvious dramaturge chores) is that of a sort of built-in objective onlooker, able at times to see more of the game than the directorial participants.'[17] He also showed his desire, which he later made plain, to be not only literary manager but a director.

The National occupied most of Olivier's life, but there were echoes from the past. Filipo Del Giudice, who had retired to a monastery, died near Florence. In his memory, Olivier sent a contribution to the Italian Hospital in London, and at the same time asked about his Oscar for *Henry V* which he had given to Del. 'I should well understand if it vanished with the rest of the rubbish, but if by chance someone has it still who does not particularly require it, I would very much like to have it back as a memento. . . It is no exaggeration to say that my short-lived and sporadic, though to me intensely enjoyable, career as a film producer, owes itself to the courage and encouragement of Filipo del Giudice.' Del's son Emanuele, a lawyer in Rome, said he would bid for the Oscar at the auction of his father's effects, but Olivier heard no more of it.[18] Then there was Vivien. Since their divorce, enormous relief though it had been, he had not forgotten her, or she him. In July 1961 she had gone off on a year's tour of Australia and South America with Jack Merivale; then in 1963, on her own, had played the lead in *Tovarich*, a musical, in New York and on an American tour. Even before she went off to America she was on a high. Just before her departure she went to have tea with Georgina Ward, daughter of a former Cabinet Minister, a girl she had taken to and had found parts on the stage. When Vivien arrived she refused to take her mink coat off, and Miss Ward knew that meant she had nothing on underneath. She often did that. After tea she got up to go, seemed highly pleased with herself, and said goodbye in the manner of a great star.'[19]

In America she was wretched and wrote to Merivale that she had never been so unhappy, so ill, or so full of misery. Olivier wrote to her in Boston and she replied eagerly to 'My darling, darling Larry', saying her spirits had been low but had taken a leap at the sight of his dear letter; she ended: 'Gooo byhh darling dearest Baba.' She suffered another breakdown in New York, clawed and slapped her leading man on stage at a Saturday matinée, had more shock treatment, and was brought home to her new country house at Tickerage, near Uckfield, twelve miles from Brighton. She had night and day nurses. One day in late 1963 Olivier drove over to see her. Hester, who had married the doctor who had treated Dickie and become Mrs St John-Ives, happened to be staying with her and saw the two of them together. He was there all day. They sat on a sofa and walked endlessly round the garden. Vivien was so delighted to see him. He was in tears as he drove away.[20]

Devoted to his new family as he plainly was, Olivier had begun an on-and-off affair with Sarah Miles, whom he had met during the filming of *Term of Trial* in late 1961 and early 1962. He played the part of a schoolmaster and she that of a schoolgirl whom he was falsely accused of seducing on a trip to Paris. The first ten weeks of shooting were in studios near Dublin, and then there were two weeks in Paris during which Olivier asked her, 'Will you lie with me?' She would. She was eighteen. Later they used to meet in a bedsit he had taken near the Old Vic, which she recalled as a grim pad with no hot water. He asked her to call him Lionel Kerr, a variation on the old Andrew Kerr he had used with Vivien. He said the Lionel was for Lionheart. She later said she thought of him as a *grand amour*, but never planned to break up his marriage.[21] Joan, for her part, remembers that Sarah used to write offering herself to Olivier 'tied to bedposts or whatever', and that they read her letters over breakfast. Sarah Miles denies making any such offers, saying that she, like Olivier, was not kinky but romantic.[22] She was in the National Theatre company in 1963 but left suddenly in March 1965, after Noel Coward breezed into Olivier's dressing room one day and found her sitting on his lap.[23] She married the playwright Robert Bolt in 1967, and later wrote three books of memoirs, one of which she dedicated to Lionel Kerr.[24]

By the autumn of 1964, after only a year at the National, the burden kept on increasing. Olivier had taken Coward's *Hay Fever* into the repertory, with Coward himself directing. It was trying out in Manchester when an urgent summons came from Coward: would Olivier come up and fire Edith Evans? She did not know her lines and was fluffing around quite lost. He did go and was dismayed, but then had to return to London when Joan had a miscarriage.[25] She was distraught, and so was he. In Manchester Dame Edith had recovered herself, just. It was, as Joan remembers, a nightmare time,

not only because of the lost baby but also because Olivier – who
had taken over from Michael Redgrave as Solness in Ibsen's *The
Master Builder* – was for the first time struck down by stage fright.
He, with his talent for guilt, thought this some punishment for the
sin of pride; however that might be, he was too tired to remember
his lines. On the first night he went on stage in the grim certainty
that he would not be able to remain there for more than five minutes.
He began to watch for the instant at which his knowledge of the
next line would vanish. His voice faded; the audience began to go
giddily round anti-clockwise; he feared he would be written off –
and then he got on with the play. That should have been that but
for the next five years, in *The Master Builder* and particularly in
Othello, but also in any other role, the fear remained.[26]

It was no wonder that Chichester got short shrift. Evershed-
Martin, wanting Olivier's presence at another royal night, begged
him to hire a helicopter to get there. He telegraphed in reply: 'The
theatre is serious work and not a hobby. I feel sure the Palace would
be first to realise such work must come before social pleasures. . . I
don't think while Chichester is relentlessly pursuing the public for
funds it can afford to go round in helicopters. To tell truth I can't
really afford to send this telegram.' Evershed-Martin was reduced
to asking for a fifteen-minute interview, and was then forced to give
up the chairmanship. Then Olivier resigned too, saying he felt badly
about it but that Chichester prevented him from doing for the
National that which it was 'the right of the board, the Treasury,
and even the nation to expect'. To Lord Bessborough, another
member of the Chichester board, he wrote, 'I just can't cope, my
dear. I just can't cope any longer.' To which Bessborough replied,
'I think the National Theatre job alone must be more arduous than
that of the prime minister. . . Please don't kill yourself by overworking.'[27]

At the Old Vic Olivier was directing *The Crucible*. He wrote to
Arthur Miller saying he was delighted, felt like a young chap in
love for the first time, and was determined to get the seventeenth-
century New England accent right. Should it be a countrified lilt?
And as for Abigail's line to Proctor, about her clutching his back,
could a line be substituted 'meaning more definitely that he's fucked

her'? To which Miller replied, 'You delighted? Not half as much as
I am to think that at last the play will be done by a man who actually is concerned with its language.' He said it should be almost a
brogue. He had found a few old men whose speech reflected if not
the word usage then at least the temperament behind the older
speech. It was gnarled, terse, with a stiff-lipped humour delivered
with hardly the flicker of a smile, and with an imminent cruelty.
The *Crucible* people would always have sounded honest, and would
have found it difficult to distinguish between religion and fanati-
cism. He said he must have written the 'clutched my back' line when
he was a more delicate creature and would 'try for a new Abigail
screw line'.[28] No one could have taken more trouble than Olivier:
Miller's plays had always been better received in England than in
America, and his faithful production did well.

The Crucible opened in January 1965, which was a month of two
ceremonies. On 30 January, Olivier was proud to speak the commen-
tary for the ITV coverage of Churchill's funeral, which was as grand
as any coronation. Three weeks earlier Tarquin had married. He
was twenty-eight, had been working abroad for the Commonwealth
Development Corporation and was about to take his bride, Riddelle,
out to Kenya. She was only nineteen and wept as she took her vows.
Olivier was at the church with Jill. Vivien sat three rows behind
with Jack Merivale. Olivier had been apprehensive about being seen
in church with three wives, so Joan stayed at home in Brighton with
the children.[29] Not everything went smoothly. Tarquin says that
his father had not met the bride's parents before the wedding. They
had invited him for lunch, and for drinks, but he hadn't come. On
the way to the reception the bride's mother rounded on him, saying
he had the worst manners of any man she'd known. If he had been
prime minister he would have been able to find the time. Olivier
protested, 'My dear,' at which she cut him off, reducing him, says
Tarquin, to a shred of himself.[30]

Soon after that Vivien wrote to Joan suggesting they should
meet. A psychiatrist firmly advised Olivier against any such visits,
saying that once started they would be difficult to stop, and in her
manic phases Vivien would certainly never take no for an answer.
It would be the kindest thing for her if Olivier 'side-stepped any

contact'.[31] Vivien continued to call herself Lady Olivier, which of course did remain her proper style. If she had married Jack Merivale she would have become plain Mrs Merivale, but she did not. In 1964 she had made her last film, *Ship of Fools*. In Hollywood she gave candle-lit dinners at which she played the theme music from *Gone With the Wind*.[32] She continued to send occasional notes to Olivier addressed to 'My darling love' and 'Beloved heart', and he wrote affectionately and briefly thanking her for gifts of cyclamen, lilies of the valley, and a crocodile notebook.[33]

At the National, Tynan continued his barrage of memos to Olivier. One at that time takes the cake for outrageousness: 'I asked the director of the Prague National Theatre why his theatre worked so smoothly. He said, "It's simple. I decide on the repertoire with the dramaturge, and then we tell the other directors what they are going to do. Is there any other way?" Perhaps there's a lesson for us all here.'[34] Tynan had already inquired whether three directors at the National were not too many, and had already fallen out with Dexter. He soon attracted the hostility of Gaskill as well. Olivier and his two associates were at Brighton discussing the new season's plans. Tynan said more stars were needed, at which Gaskill objected, saying that he could understand why Olivier might wish to rely on Tynan's advice about the choice of plays, but that it was not his business as literary manager to dictate the choice of actors. It developed into a row. Gaskill became angry and Olivier left the room and went upstairs, reappearing half an hour later to say he must have Tynan involved in all decisions. At that point Gaskill decided there was no point in going on.[35] That summer a big Hollywood proposal was made to Olivier, not for a feature film but for a series of thirty television plays, in colour, for an American network. He would present all thirty and act in nine. The series would take eighty-three days of his time, for which he would be paid $855,000. And, said the proposer – Edward Dukoff of Beverly Hills – if the show were picked up for a second season then his earnings would begin to resemble the annual budget of one of the newly created ex-colonial states. Dukoff continued with his persuasive case: 'I'm completely aware of Larry's dedication to his art, and if he had desired he could have become a money machine rather than the

Olivier he is. On the other hand, this activity and what it represents culturally, and the discovery of Olivier and what he represents performance-wise to countless millions of people who but for TV would still be living in the Dark Ages, could very well turn out to be his single most important contribution to the performance arts.' Dukoff had a point. But Olivier, who had in a quite calculated way gone for what was new in the theatre, and had never minded making money in films, had always been sceptical about television. This was so in spite of a performance in *The Power and the Glory* which compared with anything he had done in any medium. But as far back as 1951 he had declined to make television films out of the two *Cleopatras*, and he had loathed the television presentation of his *Richard III* film. He declined Dukoff's proposal. Cecil Tennant pointed out to him that he might not be able to accept while he was director of the National Theatre, but that after that it would be a good way of making a lot of money quickly.[36]

But the National was never-ending. That summer Olivier did take six weeks off to play a police inspector in an Otto Preminger psycho-mystery, *Bunny Lake is Missing*. He and Noel Coward played only supporting roles, but it was agreeable to them; it was the first time they had acted together since *Private Lives* in 1930. Olivier also took three weeks to film his stage production of *Othello*. Then he contracted another viral infection but bounced back again. He had stamina – 'a gift,' he said, 'not affected by disease, unless worn down by constant onslaughts.' Then he and the National Theatre company were off to Moscow with *Othello* and two other plays from the repertoire.

A tour to Moscow, in those cold-war days, was infinitely more important than it would be now. There was no way into Russia, except for a theatre or ballet company, and the trials of socialist hotels and oppressive hospitality only added a perverse glamour. Olivier, since his reading of Stanislavski's *My Life in Art* while he was with the Birmingham Repertory Company in the late 1920s, had thought of Moscow as some sort of mecca of the theatre arts. He was himself known in Russia for his wartime films, particularly for *Lady Hamilton*, which had been Stalin's favourite; and *Othello* was to Russians what *Hamlet* is to the rest of the world, the best known of Shakespeare's plays. Olivier, getting into the Russian spirit, wore a cloth cap throughout the visit. The performances were given at a theatre inside the Kremlin itself. The ovation after the first night of *Othello* lasted a full ten minutes and so delighted Olivier that by the time he came to write his memoirs his memory had lengthened it to thirty-five. At any rate, the audience surged forward en masse in its enthusiasm. Hundreds from the circle came down to the stalls to add to the crush. When he was finally able to begin his curtain speech the first word he uttered, 'Tovarichi' [Comrades], brought a new storm of applause and then he delivered, in Russian, an address he had learned phonetically, word for word. Parties followed. Vodka and champagne flowed so plentifully that by the small hours, staggering back down the corridor of his hotel, guided by Joan, he broke free from her and victoriously entered a linen cupboard. She somehow got him to their room, where she undressed him and he crawled on all fours to the bed. The Russian audience knew its Shakespeare so well that it had been able to follow *Othello* in English. The other two plays presented difficulties. An eighteenth-century comedy of manners, Congreve's *Love for Love*, and an early twentieth-century Manchester comedy, Harold Brighouse's *Hobson's Choice*, were both at first listened to in respectful silence, in spite of simultaneous translations. Both were strange choices. It did not matter. *Othello* was a triumph. As to the other plays, the visit of the National Theatre of Great Britain playing anything was wildly celebrated and the reception throughout was rapturous.[37] After Moscow Olivier and the company travelled home by way of West Berlin and then returned to the treadmill of the National's London repertory.

While the company was away the Berliner Ensemble, led by Brecht's widow, Helene Weigel, had filled in at the Old Vic and had arrived in London some weeks before, to rehearse. Olivier, who was filming *Othello*, did not appear at a party to welcome her, and Tynan told Olivier she suspected he'd stayed away for political reasons. Olivier wrote, in a memo from Shepperton studios, 'Please do all you can to disabuse Helli. . .and give her my love and tell her not to be such a silly old politically-minded cow.' He did meet her later, but she felt he had behaved a little badly, and knew it, and that this knowledge hurt him.[38]

In January 1966 George Devine, Olivier's friend and Joan's mentor, died, quite worn out from running a theatre company. In his last days he told her, 'It's done for me, and I'm not sure it's worth it. Don't let it happen to him. Get him out before it does.'[39] But Olivier's frantic state of busyness continued. He had taken six days off for a cameo role as the Mahdi, an Arab fanatic, in the epic film of *Khartoum*, which required more hours of make-up each day. But he was at first too busy to accept the offer of $25,000 for one day's work speaking a commentary to Saint-Saëns' *Carnival of the Animals*, and did it only when his agent protested.[40] He hesitated when he was asked to go to Copenhagen to accept the Sonning prize of 125,000 Danish crowns for an outstanding contribution to European culture. Previous winners included Churchill, Albert Schweizer, Bertrand Russell, and Niels Bohr. The organisers first wanted him to take *Othello* to Copenhagen and then asked for a solo act from Olivier. He declined, saying he had no 'parlour tricks' of his own. He did accept the prize, but insisted on flying back the same night.[41]

In July Joan's third baby was born and it nearly killed child and mother. The first signs of pregnancy had been atypical; the doctors had joked about an immaculate conception, and Olivier went jovially about asking his friends to cast him in their minds as the First Member of the Trinity rather than as St Joseph. After a difficult labour of three days the doctors did a Caesarian section. It was then a long five minutes before the newborn baby gave a cry. She weighed only four and a half pounds and was placed in an incubator. 'Thank God from my full heart,' Olivier wrote. 'I didn't imagine I would ever witness such a will to live. Alright, I thought, if that's what you want (personally I think you're crazy) that's what you will get if I can give it to you. . . My love for the little thing will always be of a strange strength, as in some ridiculous way I feel I was in her fight with her.' He wrote these words to Tarquin, and added much surgical detail which he excused by saying it always fascinated him. He had hankered after the name of Henry if the child had been a boy; she was a girl and was named Julie-Kate.[42]

Olivier by then was acting most nights, returning to Brighton at midnight, and after *Othello* not until one. He would then go to the children's hospital and watch Julie-Kate in her incubator.[43] It was three weeks before she began to flourish, and longer before Joan was home and well again. When Olivier acted or directed at the National all was happy. But the Board, and particularly its drama panel, was uneasy about some of the other plays proposed. Tynan had wanted to do Wedekind's *Spring Awakening*, a German impressionist piece of the 1890s, but was headed off by the panel whose members included Kenneth Clark and Binkie Beaumont. In June 1966 a production of *The Architect and the Emperor of Assyria* by the Spanish playwright Arrabal was proposed. Clark thought it 'pretentious nonsense and inexpressibly tedious. . .a mixture of Beckett, Ionescu, and Anouilh; gimmicks from all three'. Tynan said there was no hurry for a decision, but Clark feared this would only mean it would be presented later as a fait accompli. In this he was right. The Arrabal was done several years later, complete with a fork-lift truck on stage. By August 1966 Clark was more alarmed and wrote a strong letter to Chandos, saying three quarters of the plays the executive presented to him seemed to be fashionable nonsense. 'I often try to analyse why the National Theatre has taken a direction so very different from what most of us had anticipated. Apart from our director's obsessive fear of being thought old-fashioned, there are two factors I had not reckoned on: first that producers would feel themselves incapable of putting on straightforward productions, and secondly that famous actors would refuse to repeat their great performances of the past. This last seems a peculiarity of the English stage, and would be perfectly incomprehensible to all the great actors of France, Italy, and Germany, who repeated their parts exactly as the great singers do. I confess that I had never realised that contemporary English actors would take this point of view, and had looked forward to seeing Richardson as Falstaff etc. I am chiefly worried that Larry has got so far out of touch with the Board and with us, and I am going to try to force him to lunch with me as soon as possible.'[44]

The difficulty was not going to lie with Olivier's ideas for the new season. He wanted to do a Molière, and there was talk with Gielgud of their doing *Tartuffe* together. But who should play the name part, and who Orgon? Gielgud inclined towards playing

Orgon.[45] Olivier also intended to direct *The Three Sisters*, and this was more than another play to him. Next to Shakespeare he revered Checkhov as an acute observer of human nature and its depths. He had played the name part in *Uncle Vanya* with the Birmingam Rep in 1927, and the doctor Astrov in the same play at Chichester and at the National in 1962–3. The ending of *The Three Sisters*, with the sisters left bereft in their garrison town – with the lover of one of them just killed in a duel and the regiment commanded by the lover of another setting off for Siberia – was as exact an illustration as there could have been of Olivier's own sense that sometimes one must do without hope. 'Oh,' he said of Checkhov, 'he sees the end of the world. There's no question. All the soldiers are going to Siberia. They'll never meet again. Chekhov was always writing plays about the end of the world. That's what makes them so bloody marvellous.'[46] Olivier not only directed *The Three Sisters*. Later in its run he also played Chebutikin, the old army doctor who had known the sisters since their childhood but is also off to Siberia, and who sits at the end singing 'Ta-ra-ra-boom-de-ay' and saying, 'It doesn't matter. It doesn't matter.' With this production of *The Three Sisters* there also arose the first professional difference between Olivier and his wife. Gaskill, who had left the National to take Devine's place at the Royal Court, was further advanced with plans to do the same play at the Court and wanted Joan as Masha. He asked Olivier if he would drop his proposal of doing it at the National. Olivier would not. As to Joan, he said she had been seriously ill and needed more time to recover than Gaskill's production would allow. This was true in part, but really he wanted his wife as his Masha in his own *Three Sisters*.

Joan was disappointed. She would love to have gone back to the Court for a while. It would also have taken from her some of the burden of being the director's wife at the National. She could not escape the fact that she was, as she put it, in a position to exchange pillow-talk with the boss, and she was sensitive to the resentment that caused. She wanted and needed some independence. But Olivier was adamant.[47]

A difficulty of the kind Clark had foreseen – of Olivier's being out of touch with his Board – would certainly come with Tynan's grand new proposal. The play was by Rolf Hochhuth, a German dramatist who had had a success with a piece that accused Pope Pius XII of collaborating with the Nazis, and now had a play which accused Churchill of cremating German cities and of a convenient political assassination. Tynan wanted to present this play and he wanted Olivier as Churchill. He wrote to him: 'We can try [Patrick] Wymark. We can tempt Burton. We can look for a Lunt. But the P.M. is you. . . This is the man in action, the minute-by-minute making of history. And my God how like you the old bastard is! The passionate maddening love of detail; the concentration that can wither other people by simply ignoring their presence; the sudden changes of subject; the sudden focusing on apparent irrelevancies; the love of anecdote and quotation. . .the brutally realistic assessment of human motives; the impatience; and the patience. Nobody knows the part as you know it, and it is the kind of history you ought to be making.'[48]

Tynan had observed Olivier well. But in asking Olivier just to be himself – as he was in effect doing – he was making the same mistake William Wyler had made in his first attempts to direct Olivier in *Wuthering Heights*. But he persisted, and his stubborn infatuation with Hochhuth would cause no end of trouble.

26

The Concrete Never-Neverland

THE NEW NATIONAL THEATRE remained to be built. There was a site, on the South Bank of the Thames, and even a foundation stone which had been laid by the Queen in 1951, the year of the Festival of Britain. This was the festival which was intended as a Tonic to the Nation after the war. The Royal Festival Hall was built, but as to the National Theatre, the foundation stone was all there was money for. The Queen laid it and Sybil Thorndike read some lines by John Masefield, the Poet Laureate:[1]

> Here lay we stone, that at a future time
> May bear a house, wherein, in days to be,
> Tier above tier, delighted crowds may see
> Man's passions made a plaything and sublime.

The theatre had been long planned, at first on another site in South Kensington. The architect was to be Sir Edwin Lutyens, who had built the vice-regal palace in New Delhi and the British embassy in Washington. Any design of his would have had a neo-classical grandeur. He died in 1944, and his successor, appointed to build the theatre on the new South Bank site, was Brian O'Rorke. He proposed a combined theatre and opera house, to be faced with Portland stone with marble and green-granite panels. Some grandeur remained. These two buildings, facing each other and built in that style, would have had something of the presence of the

Metropolitan Opera at Lincoln Center in New York, with its flanking City Opera and concert halls. The Met was also being built in the 1960s. But in truth the National's plans were never as grand as that, and could not have been. The trouble was always the site. The Met is just off Broadway, in central Manhattan, on a splendid site created by clearing acres of tenements. The LCC did not have the power of a mayor of New York, or the money of those who built the Met on the site he cleared for them. The South Bank happened to be already cleared or already derelict, but it was always the wrong side of the river, away from the theatres of the West End. It happened to be near the Old Vic, but then Olivier did not love the Old Vic.

By 1960 the building committee, which had been meeting for years before there was the prospect of any money to build with, had decided it wanted two auditoriums, an arena or amphitheatre seating 1,300, and a proscenium theatre for 800–900.[2] Olivier himself thought two auditoriums were unnecessary. 'With two theatres,' he told the commitee in January 1963, 'we will get confusion. Let us have one perfect theatre, its capacity not exceeding 1,000.' He would not, however, oppose an adaptable theatre if it could be designed – a theatre to be an arena one day, and somehow a proscenium the next. Peter Hall, who was also a member of the panel though he knew by then that Olivier would be director, agreed that an ideal theatre would be adaptable. It would, he thought, be 'aesthetically dire' for them to limit themselves to producing one type of play in a proscenium and another in an arena. This is of course what has often happened. He went on to say that no member of the audience should be distracted by seeing other members of the audience beyond the actors; this too became commonplace, and is now reckoned by some directors to be a virtue. Kenneth Rae, thinking he was being pessimistic, told Olivier his bet was that they might get one theatre, with an arena stage, by 1964. Olivier repeated the conviction, which was much in his mind at the time, that since television had brought a proscenium into every home, a different kind of experience had to be offered to the public when it went out to the theatre.[3] He firmly believed this, although every London theatre of the day had a proscenium arch, and impresarios like his friend Binkie Beamont were not going bankrupt. Then, with his mind on what would appear on the stage, he said the National would present not so much Shakespeare as 'talent'.

George Devine, also a member of the building committee, had no faith in architects. He was just back from Brazil where, he said, architecture was the current thing. In every case the hospitals were superb but the theatres hopeless.[4] But there had to be an architect. Who should he be? O'Rorke was no longer in favour. Proposals were invited, twenty were selected by the Royal Institute of British Architects, and representatives of the firms who submitted them were interviewed by Olivier, Peter Brook, George Devine, and two others. Most firms sent large entourages of architects to present their designs. One architect who came on his own was Denys Lasdun, who seemed to Olivier to carry within him a quiet conviction. He said things like, 'I imagine the supremely vital element in such a building to be the spiritual content of it.' 'Of course,' said Olivier, 'we all fell like a hod of bricks for that one.'[5] So they did. Lasdun had designed the headquarters of the Royal College of Physicians in Regents Park and the new University of East Anglia, both essays in the new concrete brutalism. It was the fashion. He was appointed architect in November 1963.

By then there was a National Theatre Board, with Lord Chandos as its chairman, and a newly created South Bank Board chaired by Lord Cottesloe, who as John Fremantle had been a close friend of Vivien Leigh in the 1930s. The NT's building committee and its architect met monthly. At the sixteenth meeting Olivier felt the need to spell out who was responsible for what. The NT was the customer. The SBB was responsible to the Treasury for building the theatre and paying the bills. The consensus, he said, seemed to be in favour of an open stage, which had not only a social but a ritualistic significance.

'I agree,' said Lasdun. 'The Church is now also going in the round.'

At which Olivier, champion of the arena, suddenly seemed to change his mind and to speak as a practical showman. 'It was not,' he said, 'entirely a sociological instinct that made the actors [in the Elizabethan theatre] go back from the public. . . Comedy is very difficult in the round. In the seventeenth century, growing use of the aside made it imperative to put the audience in one direction. The inn yard was a useful form, and the theatre could always be converted to a bear pit if it fell on evil days; but I think the actors wanted their backs against the wall from time to time. . . I like movement. When I did *Vanya* at Chichester I thought I added fifteen per cent to what I would have done in a picture frame. Now I find I have cut out very few moves in transferring it to the proscenium at the Old Vic.'[6]

The monthly meetings continued. Lasdun, always ready with spirituality, produced his famous diagram of a 'room' with a stage in the corner. 'This diagram,' he said, 'has no ancestry. The ground that is being broken has nothing to do with shape but with human relationships.'[7] Whatever that may have meant, by early 1964 the honeymoon between him and the committee was coming to an end. Sean Kenny, the designer who had done the sets for the National's opening *Hamlet* and engineered the unrevolving revolve at the Old Vic, became angry. 'It seems to me that once again the theatre is put back into the old formula of having to explain to an outside designer-of-buildings what it wants. One always hopes that Mr Designer won't go off and design another monument to himself or to architecture. . . Speaking as simply as I can without going into a blind rage, I do know that the answer to our future does not lie in architecture.'[8]

By October the committee was agreed on two auditoriums. Even Lasdun had at last, with reluctance, admitted that a proscenium theatre was practicable. Then, at that month's committee meeting, this snatch of conversation ensued:

Gaskill: 'It would be proper proscenium theatre.'

Olivier [changing his mind again]: 'I'm not interested in a proscenium theatre. Do we all feel strongly enough to throw it out?'

Devine: 'A bit late to say that now.'

Gaskill: 'To create a link with tradition we need the two. I am now convinced that the actors of Shakespeare's day played directionally. If there were spectators at the side they had a tough time.'[9]

Olivier notwithstanding, the consensus was firmly for a proscenium as well as an amphitheatre. At the end of that year a third, small auditorium was also added, for experimental plays.

In 1965 four building meetings were cancelled at Lasdun's request and then, instead of attending the June meeting, he invited members to inspect a model at his offices. He was acting high-handedly, sticking stubbornly to his own first proposals and not giving the committee the choice of plans it wanted to see. And the government was again hesitating about money. All in all, nothing much was being achieved. Olivier wrote to Cottesloe telling him the inspiration of his company's work at the Old Vic had been that the company would be rewarded by the building of a proper home. 'This was, in fact, the promise that made us undertake it. May we hope, therefore, that every effort is made to see that Denys Lasdun's inspired "Fairyland" does not become a "Never-Neverland."'[10] At that time the National was, as Chandos warned the board, 'basically insolvent'. Board members had before them an accountant's report reminding them that the theatre had no working capital, only an overdraft of £100,847 which the banks would be fully justified in refusing to increase, and if that happened it would bring their operations to an abrupt halt.[11] This was true, and it was humiliating, but the reality was that the Labour government was not going to be seen to desert one of its favourite projects. Jenny Lee, minister for the arts, was not a member of the Cabinet, but she was the widow of Aneurin Bevan and a friend of the prime minister, Harold Wilson; she had a political clout altogether more powerful than her rank suggested.

By 1966 the shape of the auditoriums was broadly agreed, but Lasdun still did not produce plans to satisfy the committee. In August Tynan, who attended the building meetings by invitation, wrote a memo to Olivier: '[Lasdun] doesn't give a damn about the proscenium theatre. He has designed the Denys Lasdun Memorial Theatre. . . He's a fanatic defending an abstract vision. Already he's insulted you and the committee in a way that you would have thought insufferable if he were your solicitor or your doctor. For your servant, he is acting remarkably like a master – and in a field where you are the expert, not he. . . We are not building a monument to anyone. We are not called upon to create anything utterly new and undreamt-of. Our task is to enable 2,000 people every night to see and hear good plays of all periods in maximum comfort. . . We are paying a

man to decorate our house; and if he succumbs to the illusion that
the house belongs to him, we must – however regretfully – escort
him to the door and engage someone else.'[12] Olivier conveyed much
the same feelings to Cottesloe, though more circumspectly, saying
he was beginning to feel a bit frustrated at the intractability of their
architect. He wanted to see more plans, and hoped that Cottesloe's
board would not be swept off its feet by what he now recognised as
Lasdun's superb salesmanship and accept his designs as they stood.[13]
Cottesloe supported Olivier but remarked that how Olivier could
get it into Lasdun's head that the wishes of the ultimate user were
dominant, as in all buildings, was quite beyond him.[14] It was not
beyond Olivier. He silkily asked Lasdun to stay away from committee
meetings, telling him, 'The august presence of our architect seems
to put a check on the members of the committee from uttering their
true opinions. . . When we meet by ourselves, you see, we can
squabble all we like but it does not take nearly as long as you might
think to come to an amicable conclusion.'[15] The committee proceeded
to meet without Lasdun, submitted a list of requirements to him in
April 1966, and by the end of the year he produced detailed designs
of a proscenium theatre.

By 1967 the idea of the opera house had been abandoned. The
National Theatre proceeded alone. Since Lasdun had at last produced
plans which satisfied both the building committee and the South
Bank Board the interiors were settled, but then the site itself was
changed. The theatre remained on the South Bank, but whereas it
had previously been in a more or less central position between
Westminster and Waterloo Bridge, to the west of the Festival Hall,
it was now moved east of Waterloo Bridge into a wasteland. In the
new position, the views across the Thames to the noble façade of
Somerset House and east to St Paul's Cathedral were magnificent,
but the design of the building was such that these views were seen
not by theatre-goers in the foyers, or by the actors from their green
room, but by the administrators from their offices. Lasdun built his
concrete theatre facing the river, from which direction no one ever
approached it. Nobody came by boat. He built a theatre which had
no easily discernible entrance, and still has not. There was and is
no portico, not even a sign saying National Theatre over the door.

Twenty years after the theatre was finished, as if he had a copyright on his memorial, Lasdun was still obstructing all efforts to make a proper entrance or to remove concrete walkways which no one ever used but which took away light from the foyers. His great gifts to the National were nothing to do with spirituality. They were a spacious underground car park, spacious foyers, and air-conditioning throughout. He was knighted and made a Companion of Honour.

The planning, then, was complete by 1967. All that remained was to build the theatre. It was originally to have been finished in 1964. By 1967 not a spadeful of earth had been shifted. In May that year Harold Wilson offered Olivier a peerage. With the usual formal letter saying that the prime minister 'had it in mind' to confer on him the dignity of baron of the United Kingdom, for life, Wilson sent a second, informal letter saying this was 'nothing political', and not an honour conferred for services rendered. It was a job of work; he thought that Olivier had something important to say and hoped he might like the House of Lords to say it in.[16] Olivier liked honours, and this was the first peerage ever to be offered to a man of the theatre. But he declined, and did so in a convoluted letter of five hundred words, which said in part: 'Please understand that my life and its interests are entirely wrapped up in the National Theatre and it is the thoughts proceeding from this fact which have guided and must continue to guide my every footstep; and it is only after gruelling heart-searching that I feel I should, however reluctantly, decline this great honour.

'I am a workman, certainly; an artist, hopefully; but I should be a Lord, only very uneasily. Only from one of your gargantuan output could I hope it might be understood and not be dismissed as an impertinence, if I said, I honestly feel I have not got the *time* for it.

'You refer to "a job of work" and of course I entirely appreciate the point, but consequent to it, I must reckon with the new burdens that that involves. The extra feeling of responsibility to my new Peers; the endorsed free-for-all of distractions from my real work; social obligations and expectations stepped up a hundred fold. I really don't think I can manage, Sir. I would have to give up acting altogether, with no time to learn or give due study to my roles – (an increasing worry at my time of life) and I don't think, perhaps,

I ought to do that quite yet, or take from my growing company that companionship, or rob myself of it.'

Paradoxically, he said, he felt that if he accepted this enviable step-up he would fear some strange loss of face with his fellow artists and with the man in the street, and it was to these that he felt most sense of responsibility for the conduct of 'their National Theatre'. Saying he was aware of the weakness and naïveté of his arguments, excusing his 'poor reasonings', admitting he might regret his decision and deeply sensible of the honour done him, he declined.[17]

Olivier told Chandos that he had declined, said it had been a struggle making what he called an 'awkward 51% decision', and added, 'Always seem to be having to tear myself in two these days. Oh dear Oh dear – Ah'm getting a bit tired of it.'[18]

Busy prime ministers don't usually have time for heart-searching letters, particularly of this length, and it was nonsense for Olivier to say that he would have to give up acting, but Wilson replied within days saying he was frankly disappointed. If Olivier accepted he would only have to appear in the Lords once or twice a year. He hoped that on reflection he would be able to accept. Olivier did not find himself able. At a Downing Street reception Wilson said to Joan Plowright, 'You'll persuade him, won't you?' She thought Wilson smug and complacent, and she would not.

Why did Olivier refuse? Partly no doubt because of his stated reasons. He was always afraid of social engagements which took him from his real work, and he regularly offended hostesses who could not understand his refusal to 'say a few words'. But Joan Plowright says he refused because there had been delay after delay in building the new National, and he considered the honour a sop to keep him quiet. 'He thought they were giving him a peerage in compensation, and it might never go up. That he was being put out to grass and would be brought out on occasions with all those decorations, but the building would not go up. That's why.'[19]

27

Listening to that Man Breathing

THE FIRST MONTHS OF 1967 were as taxing as any in Olivier's life. He was still appearing in the last performances of *Othello*. He was rehearsing the part of Edgar, the passed-over Captain in Strindberg's *Dance of Death*, a story of love and hate in a marriage, which was as he said nine tenths hate. It became one of his greatest and most memorable parts, and he played it with a demanding athleticism which only he could have brought to it. He was planning the production of *The Three Sisters* in which he had insisted Joan should remain with the company to play Masha. He had a tour of Canada arranged for the autumn. And he lost John Dexter, his only remaining associate director, in a quarrel over an all-male *As You Like It*. It was a pet project of Dexter's and was in rehearsal when Olivier dropped it from the repertory, fearing it might be seen as a drag show. Dexter was outraged, could earn much more elsewhere, and went his own way, eventually becoming director of productions at the Metropolitan Opera, New York.

Olivier enjoyed playing the Captain, though he wrote to Chandos that both Strindberg and Ibsen, whose *Master Builder* he had done, seemed to know an uncomfortable amount about him. 'There's hardly a thing I haven't been guilty of saying or feeling towards some or other marriage partner; I think he was a passionate young man, as I was. . .and sometimes when the nature of passion is changed by [fate's?] cruel hand, it has to find for itself another medium, as it were, like the desire to hurt, and the power to wound becomes the obsession.'[1] *Svenska Dagbladet* of Stockholm, reviewing Olivier's performance in this masterpiece by Sweden's most celebrated playwright, said, 'Apart from dying and being born, this is one of the most remarkable things that ever happened to Strindberg. Only a giant is equal to the self-immolation demanded by Edgar's role. [Olivier's] uninhibited physical performance takes the spectator's breath away every bit as much as his sovereign command of the balance between shattering tragedy and wild farce – exactly as it must be in this dance of death.'[2]

Olivier as the captain in Dance of Death. *Sketch by Claude Marks.*

The old stage fright still remained. Peter Hall one night saw Olivier in the wings, waiting to make his entrance, with the stage manager holding him. 'Just before his cue Larry said, "Right, push, push, push," and the stage manager pushed Larry on stage, and one saw Larry walk on stage and become Olivier. I remember saying to him, "Can anyone help you?" He said, "It's the curse of being me. Some nights I walk on stage and I think the audience is saying, 'And *that's* Olivier?'"[3]

Throughout all this time Tynan was picking a public quarrel with the National Theatre Board and embroiling Olivier in what he was beguiled into seeing as a matter of principle and artistic freedom. Tynan should have been Olivier's support and ally. If he had set out to damage him he could hardly have done worse.

The occasion for all this was Hochhuth's play *The Soldiers*, which damned Churchill's saturation bombing of German cities and accused him of complicity in the assassination of the Polish leader Sikorski. Tynan wanted a political play. It was the fashion. The RSC had presented *US*, which vilified the Americans in Vietnam; Jean Louis Barrault had presented a play in Paris which reviled the French army for its Algerian atrocities; and the Royal Dramatic theatre in Stockholm was playing to full houses with a play which arraigned its politicians for remaining neutral in World War II. Tynan cited these examples in a memo to Olivier, asserting that the theatre was 'a sleeping tiger that can and should be roused whenever the national (or international) conscience needs nudging'.[4] It did not seem to concern him that there was no evidence Olivier ever held such a view. Tynan no doubt felt he was speaking up for freedom, but given his record he may just as well have been influenced by his taste for the sensational and the outrageous. In November 1965 he had been the first man to say 'fuck' on English television.[5] At the same time as the Hochhuth affair dragged on he was inviting writers to contribute sketches to *Oh! Calcutta!*, the sex revue he later put on in the West End and New York, and was himself offering to *Playboy* magazine articles on hard-core pornography and on 'the Social History of Underwear – from Queen Victoria to the miniskirt'.[6] Whatever the virtues of these things, they did not fit Tynan for his job of advising and supporting the director of the National.

He wanted *Soldiers* at all costs. When he had read only the prologue and first act he told Hochhuth he was 'overwhelmingly in favour' and 'tremendously convinced of the play's power and stature', and was already talking about producing it in May or June of 1967. Before he had seen a finished translation he was confident the National would put it on.[7] By late December 1966 he was writing to Olivier: 'I don't know whether this is a great play, but I think it's one of the most extraordinary things that has happened to the British theatre in my lifetime.' To Dexter, who was to direct – this was before the quarrel over *As You Like It* – he first embarked on his mysterious shaggy dog story that Hochhuth had locked up the sworn statements of his secret informants in three bank deposit boxes, witnessed by three eminent Swiss scholars, with the proviso that they were not to be opened for fifty years. To Olivier again, at the beginning of 1967, Tynan wrote that Hochhuth might not be Euripides and *Soldiers* might not be *The Trojan Women*, but it was in the same tradition and in Britain that tradition was in their hands. He thought the Hochhuth play was a test of the NT's maturity – 'the test of our willingness to take a central position in the limelight of public affairs.'[8]

The choice of plays was normally the director's, sometimes with the advice of the drama panel, but in the last resort the Board had the legal responsibility. In a matter of such controversy the Board was bound to decide. The chairman of the Board, Lord Chandos, had been a member of Churchill's war cabinet. Tynan was picking a fight, on his and Olivier's behalf, which he must have known they could not win. Everything he did made this more certain. The Board was to meet on 9 January 1967 to decide. Before it did so Tynan addressed to its members a memo which was downright insolent and self-defeating. 'To suppress a serious work on a subject of national (and international) concern is an act that the Board should not lightly undertake. In totalitarian countries, such suppression in the arts is easy and frequent. . .' And then: 'A theatre can survive without even a first-rate chairman; but it cannot survive without playwrights.' Chandos, in his copy, underscored these words in red and wrote 'impudent' in the margin. Tynan went on to write that he had consulted a large number of historians and legal experts and that the result was 'very much an open verdict'. 'Ludicrous,' wrote Chandos in the margin.[9] In response to another letter from the persistent Tynan, Chandos mocked the supposedly sealed bank boxes, saying, 'When this frayed con-man's device was trotted out, it seemed to be an argument for not producing the play for fifty years.' He wrote to the historian Robert Blake that it was a funny world, and that he would have supposed that anyone with the slightest common sense, common loyalty, or even good manners, would have refrained from putting up such a play to a Board whose chairman had been a friend of Churchill's and who knew the 'so-called facts were phoney'. 'Many of the people in the theatre today,' he told Blake, 'if they cannot find some thin ice to put their feet through, go out and refrigerate a puddle, and then put their feet in it.'[10]

The Board acted moderately and postponed judgment until it had seen a complete playscript. This did not arrive until 15 March. Meantime Tynan had written to Hochhuth describing Chandos as 'our major enemy'.[11] He also set about making an enemy of the Lord Chamberlain's office, which was still responsible for the licensing and censorship of plays. He had previously submitted the play, and the Lord Chamberlain's response had been to seek a private word with the chairman. Tynan then wrote, 'Will you kindly fulfil the function laid down for your office in law – namely, that of informing us whether or not you will grant a licence for the public performance of the play in question? To drive the point home more clearly: whether or not the National Theatre subsequently decides to present the play is – quite obviously – none of the Lord Chamberlain's business.' The Lord Chamberlain's office, which was prepared to give Tynan shorter shrift than the Board, replied that it was obliged to give a decision only when the play was submitted by 'the Master or Manager of the theatre'.[12]

The matter was to be decided at a Board meeting on 24 April. Before then, Chandos tried to settle things personally with Olivier and came to his office for a quiet chat, during which he repeated that he had been a member of the war cabinet that sanctioned the bombing of Dresden. Olivier replied that he could see that made things awkward for him. Chandos said it wasn't for himself so much as for his friends and partners in those times of such special responsibility. 'Then,' said Olivier, 'I went further and asked if the National was really to ignore a matter that could be explored by every other theatre, merely to spare the feelings and save the faces of his old cronies from more than twenty years ago. He shrugged apologetically. I said, "I'm sorry, Olivier, you've lost me now. I must be against you on this.". . . I just knew which side I was on and it was not on the side of authority. I had chosen golden youth.'[13] It was a strange choice of words. There was nothing golden about Hochhoth's play.

So the formal Board meeting was held. Olivier spoke of conflicts within his soul. He said he had been torn between his prejudices as an Englishman and his wishes for the National Theatre as its director. He said, and this is astonishing, that *Soldiers* was a far finer and more important piece of work than Miller's *Crucible*. He asked the Board to give him back his play. Tynan then spoke. Chandos as good as accused him of lying, which he had, when he told the Board that the historians he consulted had delivered an open verdict on the theses of the play. Tynan had told the Board he had consulted Hugh Trevor-Roper, Regis Professor of Modern History at Oxford; Trevor-Roper had since written to Chandos saying Tynan had ascribed to him an opinion diametrically opposed to that he clearly gave him.[14]

The Board, which included Binkie Beaumont and Kenneth Clark, both old friends of Olivier's, unanimously decided not to do the play. Tynan said he wondered whether to resign. He then decided not to, and wrote copious letters instead. To Hochhuth he wrote that he was 'sickened by the behaviour of Chandos and his henchmen'.[15] When Lord Chandos told the *Sunday Times* in an interview that he thought it odd that Tynan should conduct a campaign against his chairman and Board while retaining his salary, Tynan wrote grandly to that newspaper: 'My first loyalty is to the National Theatre, not to its Board.'[16] To *The Times* he wrote that, unlike Lord Chandos, he did not subscribe to the patronising myth that men of the theatre were unqualified to make responsible judgments on matters of serious consequence. 'In course of time the director may lose the confidence of the public and the critics. If so, the State can always give him the sack.' To the editor of *Playboy* in New York he wrote offering an article on 'a study of the faggot influence on the arts'.[17]

Soldiers, as was seen when it was eventually put on by private managements in Berlin, Toronto, New York, and London, was a poor piece of theatre. Its only importance is that it wounded Olivier and wrecked his long relationship with Chandos. As Olivier said, 'I was deeply distressed and torn about, and by this play as well as

by the various effects it had upon other people and their conduct.'
In his autobiography he devoted twenty-one pages to the episode.[18]

It is obvious, from Olivier's papers and from those of Tynan's which were later printed, that Tynan used Olivier for his own purposes. Olivier, having been seduced into the whole mess, believed himself to be defending a matter of principle – that of the artistic independence of the director. It was Tynan who summoned reporters to the huts and held forth about resignations while Olivier sat silently and unhappily at his side.[19] Tynan could blithely write at the time that the State could give the director the sack. The Board could have done, but did not consider it. The Board could profitably have sacked Tynan, and Chandos did draft a letter asking him to undertake no more attacks on the Board. Olivier, when he saw it, objected that this would lead to Tynan's resignation, which he could not face. Chandos agreed not to send the letter and to leave Tynan alone, but did say, 'You should, however, realise what this means to me in particular. He is a man completely lacking in probity and loyalty, and is unscrupulous and untruthful. . . This is the man we are to keep, temporarily, at your request, and for your sake, dear Larry, I am willing to do it, out of friendship and out of gratitude to you. . . In the meantime, I am horrified to think of the extra strains which are put upon you. For myself, any annoyance that I have is due to the ineffable tedium of dealing with people like Tynan.'[20]

It was not only Chandos who could not stand Tynan. Dexter and Gaskill had distrusted him. John Osborne denounced his 'intellectual spivvery', saying that Olivier mistook it for up-to-date awareness. Peter Hall would not have him at any price.[21] There has been no convincing explanation of Tynan's hold over Olivier. Joan Plowright, who had at first been Tynan's ally, now says, 'He did stir it up a lot. He did. He'd got too big for his boots by then.'[22]

It was at this bad time that Olivier was offered the life peerage which he declined. He did agree to lend his portrait by Harold Knight to his widow, Dame Laura Knight, for a retrospective exhibition. It was of him as Romeo in 1935, his first Shakespearean lead. It was always the portrait he most liked, and galleries often asked to borrow it. He wrote back to Dame Laura: 'When it came back from its last journey I embraced it, hanging it up once more, and saying, "There you are, my beauty, this time I'm going to keep you." But how can I resist this sweet request from you? Of course, my dear, you shall have it.'[23] And he wrote his last known letter to Vivien. She was back in London, living with the devoted Jack Merivale. She had been preparing to play in Edward Albee's *A Delicate Balance*, but this had been postponed when she developed a cough that hurt and her doctors diagnosed a return of her old tuberculosis. Olivier had gone to see an Italian company do Goldoni and wrote to her that it was the purest delight. 'You know I would rather be an acrobat and/or juggler than anything – look there it all was, fed right through the production with delicious and rapturous result – I was so moved by it I could hardly find words for the cast afterwards – "Les Jongleurs." Oh God what a beautiful craft.'[24]

That was near the end of May and he was ill and in pain. Joan noticed that he was more worried and preoccupied than usual. She was woken three or four times a night when he rose to change wringing-wet nightshirts. She saw that he knew something was wrong but was reluctant to go and find out.[25] He knew exactly what was wrong and how serious it might be. In his diary for 25 May, three days after his sixtieth birthday, he wrote: 'Prostate pain'. He carried on playing *The Dance of Death*, sometimes twice daily, and before he saw a doctor he wrote to Ralph Richardson saying, 'If you really do feel you could bear to see me in *Dance of Death* (not exactly light entertainment for you and me) I should love it.'[26] He also continued to rehearse *The Three Sisters* and then, ten days after he first wrote 'pain' in his diary, he did at last consult a surgeon. During a week of examinations by three doctors he continued to play in *Dance of Death*; he then entered St Thomas' Hospital, London, under the name of Lionel Kerr. He had cancer of the prostate, which he elected to have treated not by surgery but, as an outpatient, by hyperbaric radiation. He often described this treatment in detail, how he was slid into a cylinder, how he was surrounded by oxygen under high pressure, and how the site of the disease was bombarded with radium-soaked cobalt. 'Torpedo tube', he wrote in his diary, after each treatment. Even he admitted that he felt dreadfully ill.

While this went on he continued, although much weakened, to rehearse *The Three Sisters*, and to commute between London and Brighton. On 18 June, the week before the play opened, he took the children for a walk on the beach; that night he found he could breathe only with great difficulty. 'Fitz 2am' says his diary.[27] Dr W.F. Frazer was his Brighton general practitioner. He had pneumonia. In the early morning he and Joan began the drive to London and St Thomas'. She says: 'It was a journey I shall never forget. He would suddenly gasp instructions to the driver to take a certain turning and drive through a small village or past a church or the windmills we had visited with children. I realised he was envisaging it as a possible last journey and I wanted to take him into my arms and tell him to stop it; but I knew I must respect his need to do it, and just smile and keep saying, "Yes, darling, I remember."'

When they got near the hospital he told the driver to go to the Old Vic instead, about a mile away. By then it was early morning, 9.30. There were few people at the theatre but he wanted to see whoever was there. Harry the caretaker rounded up carpenters, electricians and someone from the props department, and Olivier shook hands with them all. They were frightened. Harry kept whispering, 'You must get him out of here', and at last they got him back into the car and to the hospital, and then Joan cried. 'I shall never forget it. Driving out of our way, and around, and listening to this man breathing.' Then she had to go back to the theatre for a dress rehearsal.[28]

This time Olivier was kept in hospital. *The Three Sisters* opened triumphantly on 4 July and afterwards the cast went to his room with champagne. When one critic said of Joan's performance as Masha that it was well beyond anything she had done so far, she felt it was to do with life imitating art, or art imitating life, or simply that she had grown up with a vengeance in the previous three years.[29] Two days later Olivier, who even in his weakened state retained his fascination with the body and its workings, wrote in his diary: 'View Heart Operation'. He had persuaded the surgeons to let him come into the operating theatre and watch, as he had in New York back in 1931. On 7 July he wrote to Peggy Ashcroft that he would have his last treatment that afternoon, would take two quiet weeks and a holiday, and be all right.[30]

That night Vivien Leigh died in the flat at Eaton Square. Jack Merivale had returned late, after his show. He looked in on Vivien and saw she was asleep with her Siamese curled up beside her. He went to the kitchen to make himself some soup out of a tin and when he returned found her lying on the floor.[31] She had haemorrhaged on the carpet and was dead. He telephoned the doctor, two friends, and Peter Hiley, in the country, who was there by the next morning. Then they telephoned Olivier in hospital. 'I must come,' he said. He discharged himself and came to the flat.

This is Peter Hiley's recollection of that day: 'He appeared at about eleven or twelve o'clock, and wouldn't go. He stayed and stayed. He hung about. He went round the rooms – after all, he'd lived at Eaton Square for quite a long time. "Oh that," he'd say, "that was my father's. I remember that." He had quite an eye to what belonged to whom. It was absolutely typical. He felt great grief and great responsibility, but it didn't stop him going round and being himself, and wondering about the pictures on the wall. "Is that mine or is it Vivien's?" We were shocked by Vivien's death, all of us, and he added a touch of almost hilarity.' When the undertakers came to take Vivien's body away they suggested that everyone should stay in the sitting room while they went past. 'But I want to be there,' said Olivier. 'I should be there.' 'He wanted,' says Hiley, 'to be in on everything. And also there was his passion for the macabre.' Reporters were outside and arrangements were made to get Olivier out quietly. But when he looked out of the window, at about five in the afternoon, there were no reporters there. 'He was,' says Hiley, 'frightfully disappointed. It was a typical Larry situation, quite comic really. But he engendered that sort of thing.'[32]

Olivier's own account, in his autobiography, is that after he arrived at the flat, evading reporters by entering through a side entrance to the basement. Merivale left him alone with Vivien, 'alone with the one with whom I had shared a life that resembled nothing so much as an express lift skying you upwards and throwing you downwards in insanely non-stop fashion. I stood and prayed for forgiveness for all the evils that had sprung up between us'. He went on to say, getting as he put it 'to the heart of the ulcer', that it had always been impossible for him not to believe that he was

The real interpreter of Shakespeare

39 ON AN AMERICAN tour in 1946 Olivier received his first honorary degree, from Tufts University, Mass., where he was praised as the 'real interpreter of Shakespeare of our age.' He received five such degrees, one from Oxford, but could not find time to collect one offered by Yale

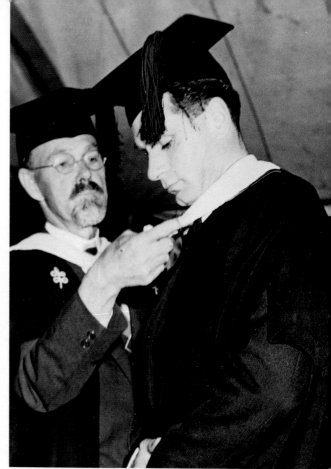

Roles of 1945-46

40 AS ASTROV (top left) in *Uncle Vanya*, his favourite in Chekhov

41 OEDIPUS blinded (left), and

42 MR PUFF in *The Critic* (above), parts he played in a double bill

The baronial period

OLIVIER MADE Hamlet in 1947, was knighted in 1948, and lived extravagantly at Notley Abbey, with constant house parties. He called these his baronial days

43 ON THE SET of Hamlet (above), where Olivier was star, director, and producer, and won an Oscar. To limit the running time to two and a half hours he cut almost half of Shakespeare's text

44 IN THE GROUNDS of Notley (right) about 1950, with Vivien, Danny Kaye (sitting) and Bobby Helpmann

Living like royals

45 OLIVIER AND VIVIEN LEIGH, at the height of their popularity and fame, were the royal family of the English stage. Here they are photographed on their return to England after the 1948 tour of Australia and New Zealand. Olivier is leaning on a stick after his recent cartilage operation

'Not hungry at all, just dying'

46 Olivier as Hurstwood in William Wyler's film of Theodore Dreiser's great novel, *Sister Carrie*. In this story of a man who ruins himself for a girl Olivier gave one of his finest film performances

Olivier by Dalí

47 THIS PORTRAIT by Salvador Dalí of
Olivier as Richard III was painted in 1954
after his film of that name, and was given
to Olivier by Alex Korda. This, with a
much earlier painting of him as Romeo,
remained his favourite until he had to sell
it to pay his children's school fees

48 OLIVIER'S FIRST CAMEO role, in *The
Magic Box*, 1951, a film about the invention
of moving film, starring Robert Donat.
Olivier played a bewildered policeman
brought in from the street to be given a
demonstration of a flickering film projected
on to a wall

49 OLIVIER AND Marilyn Monroe (right), whom he came to loathe, in *The Prince and the Showgirl*, 1956

50 OLIVIER CIGARETTES earned him twopence for every thousand sold. In 1956, 415 million were bought

OLIVIER
Tipped Cigarettes

Specially
blended for

Laurence Olivier

OLIVIER

51 WITH THE QUEEN and Edith Evans at the film premiere of *Richard III* in December 1955

The dropping of the legend

1957 was a year of radical change for Olivier. He was determined to break with Vivien and, in search of things new, left the commercial theatre and went to the Royal Court to play the lead in *The Entertainer* by John Osborne

52 IN APRIL 1957 he opened at the Royal Court in *The Entertainer*, with Dorothy Tutin (above). By the time of the West End transfer that autumn, Miss Tutin was replaced by Joan Plowright, whose very name, he said, was enough to make him think thoughts of love

53 BETWEEN the two runs of *The Entertainer*, Olivier was committed to a five-week tour of Europe with the Stratford company in *Titus Andronicus*, with Vivien Leigh. They are pictured here at the Paris opening (right), which was an artistic triumph for Olivier. But Vivien was exhausted and on the verge of another manic high, and the rest of the tour was an ordeal for her husband

A Taste of Honey, and children

54 OLIVIER AND JOAN were married in March 1961. Here (above) they are seen on the evening of their wedding day, in New York, walking past a poster for *A Taste of Honey*, which the Royal Court had taken to Broadway. For her performance she won a Tony award for Best Actress

55 IN 1962 OLIVIER was named as first Director of the National Theatre. He and Joan settled in Brighton. Here he is seen (right) in 1964, with Richard, aged two, and Tamsin, aged one. On the wall is the 1935 portrait of him as Romeo

National Theatre at the Old Vic

Among the most memorable plays in the National's years at the Old Vic were Chekhov's *Three Sisters*, which Olivier directed, and his celebrated black *Othello*

56 OLIVIER directs Joan (left) as Masha in *Three Sisters*, 1967. He was already ill, and was in hospital for the first performance

57 BLACKED UP (below) as Othello, 1964-66, with Maggie Smith as Desdemona

Last great stage roles at the National

58 IN 1967, after his first grave illness, Olivier continued to play Edgar in Strindberg's *Dance of Death* (right), a play of love and hate in marriage. His dancing was as athletic as ever

59 AS JAMES TYRONE (below) with Constance Cummings, in Eugene O'Neill's *Long Day's Journey Into Night*, 1971-72, his last big role on any stage

60 SING-SONG (below right) in November 1971 in a rehearsal room at the Old Vic after his last day as Director of the National, with Dennis Quilley at the piano

Darling, I'm too old and I can't learn my fucking lines your eternally worshipping L (You can cut this off, you see.)

Back into films

61 ON THE SET of *Sleuth*, which he filmed in 1973 with Michael Caine. The inscription to Joan reads: 'Darling, I'm too old and I can't learn my fucking lines, your eternally worshipping L. (You can cut this off, you see.)' The moustache recalls the Ronald Colman look he cultivated in 1930s Hollywood

62 WITH SARAH MILES (right) in *Lady Caroline Lamb*, filmed 1972

63 WITH HIS SON Richard (right),1978, on the set of *A Little Romance*, in Paris

64 AS BIG DADDY (below) in *Cat on a Hot Tin Roof* with Natalie Wood, 1975

65 BRIDESHEAD REVISITED,1980. As Lord Marchmain in the deathbed scene with Stephane Audran

The last portrait

66 EMMA SERGEANT, then a student at the Slade, made this fine oil portrait of Olivier in 1982. He gave her two sittings. She sensed his power and energy, and found him hypnotic and the most excellent company. But at the second sitting he was so exhausted that he asked if he could lie down, and fell asleep on her bed. When he woke he walked up to the canvas, observed the nose, eyes, and mouth, and told her it made him look the 'mean bastard' that he was

67 A SKETCH of Olivier in New York in 1980 by the American Claude Marks, who had previously drawn Olivier in his roles in *The Dance of Death* and *Long Day's Journey into Night*. Olivier liked the sketches and signed several of them

King Lear at last

68 OLIVIER HAD performed *King Lear* at the Old Vic in 1946 but had declined to play the part at the National Theatre, in spite of Peter Hall's frequent requests. In 1982, wondering if he had not himself become a little like Lear, he decided to play the part for Granada TV. 'I wear,' he said, 'an invisible theatrical crown which I am very attached to and will not give up.'

69 Olivier and Joan with President Reagan and his wife Nancy at the White House in April 1983 (below). After a showing of *King Lear*, the president gave a small dinner party for them

Happy Birthday, Sir Larry

70 OLIVIER'S EIGHTIETH BIRTHDAY in 1987 was celebrated by a gala performance in the Olivier auditorium at the National Theatre. Here (above) he acknowledges the applause, which rolled on and on. Richard Eyre, later his successor as Director, said Olivier seemed to be crying, unwilling to leave, and certain that this was the last time he would hear such applause, 'his life's music'. With Olivier are (r to l) Joan, David Plowright, Tamsin, and Richard Olivier's wife Shelley.

71 EARLIER the same day (left) at home in Steyning, Sussex, with Tamsin, Joan, and Julie-Kate

Olivier in his theatre

72 OLIVIER SELDOM visited the auditorium named after him at the new National Theatre on the South Bank. But the American photographer Arnold Newman persuaded him to pose there in June 1978, between the matinee and evening performances. He wrote: 'Because of the technical difficulty in lighting the huge space and keeping the atmosphere, long exposures had to be used. When we had finished, Olivier, obviously exhausted, shook hands with all those who had waited to say goodbye to him. We watched him walk across the stage, hesitate, and take one last look at the auditorium before vanishing into the wings.'

somehow the cause of her disturbances, and that they were due to some fault in him. Then he came to the description of the dead Vivien. This has offended many of those who knew her, but it is part of the man. He saw what he saw and wrote what he wrote: 'Looking for the last time at that beautiful dead face, I discerned a drawn look in her expression that I knew to be of faint disgust. . . I had noticed that between the bed and the bathroom was a stain, and connecting this with the expression on her face which had caused me to wonder, I now realised what must have happened. What a cruel stroke of fate to deliver that particular little death-blow to one as scrupulously dainty in all such matters as she was.'[33]

A post mortem established that she had died from natural causes and no inquest was held. *The Times'* obituary was full of hints, saying that Somerset Maugham had encouraged her to play the charming, promiscuous Rosie Driffield in his own *Cakes and Ale*, and Bathsheba Everdene, the innocently vain and unstable heroine of Hardy's *Far from the Madding Crowd*, but that she had done neither. 'It might almost be said that the roles she did not play and the opportunities that now lay behind her gathered about her lately to form an aura peculiarly her own.'[34]

Letters of condolence flooded in to Olivier and to Jack Merivale, who had stood by Vivien for the last seven difficult years. Ginette Spanier wrote to Olivier: 'Poor lovely pathetic Vivien. Vivien with the one bad fairy at her christening who ruined everything. . . So many lovely times to remember. So many horrible times. Thank Heavens you got away and made a real life for yourself. But you must be very unhappy now with it all crowding back on you.' Peggy Ashcroft wrote: 'Dear darling you are certainly getting some hammer blows . . . I thank God more and more for my children, as you must – and I'm sure you feel the same – *and* for work, though I think you have too much of that. So much love darling, REST.'[35] Katharine Hepburn, who had been at Vivien's wedding to Olivier, wrote to Jack: 'I knew that you would stick. You were the one that delivered the goods. . . It is a ghastly business this thing of dying – so final and I don't know how one goes about facing it, but one must, so one does.'[36]

The funeral was on 12 July. Driving back from it Cecil Tennant, Olivier's agent and close friend of many years, was killed in a car crash. Olivier, who between 7 and 8 July had written in his diary 'Vivien†', now wrote 'Cecil†'. To Peter Hiley, who gave him the news of Tennant's death, he said, 'Oh, what *have* we done?'

Chandos had written to congratulate Olivier on *The Three Sisters*, and then to offer his condolences for Vivien's death. On the morning he learned of Tennant's death Olivier wrote a long and intimate letter in reply.

'Oh God – and now my old Cecil Tennant – last night. He wasn't supposed to die, you know, he was supposed to live forever and look after me. He's been looking after me for thirty years. When we used to meet on leave in the war – he in the Coldstream, me in the Fleet Air Arm – I *knew* that nothing could happen to him, that I need never fear for it was ordained that he would always be *there*, that without question he would by many years outlive me, so that he could sort my children out; and look after my widow; and find some secretly hidden *estate, somewhere*, and then, last night, he killed himself in his motor car. . . It's a shock because he was going to outlive me by many years – the only thing I've ever been *absolutely sure of* – and now he's not "there" to sort out Vivien's estate. Sorry to howl, but the boys upstairs have been throwing things about a bit. There should have been a *comet* or *some*thing. . .

'I was writing to Katharine Hepburn the other day about Spencer Tracy, to whom she was partner for many years, and I was saying that I thought he and I felt a special kin-ship whenever we met, which was all too seldom; as people might, who felt instinctively that their destinies were spun of a bewildering mixture of incredibly good and incredibly bad fortune.

'And so you see when I get one lovely letter from you about *Three Sisters* and another about Vivien, almost by the next mail, I suddenly think of Richard II gazing into that old mirror – or something like that. Anyway, it's time I counted up to achieve some modicum of proportion. Had Vivien lived – incidentally it was a very virulent type of TB – and outlived me by some ten years – she would not have died in a comfortable flat in Eaton Square. So *that's* alright. Cecil is a shock and we ought to be prepared for that, for God's sake, at my age.

'My disease is at its worst just now – "they" told me the convalescent period was the worst, and "they" are bloody well right. But I shall get over all that and get a whole chapter written on "the things I've done for England" theme, by getting to Canada *and* (what is more) coming back.

'Now your first letter comes up again. In spite of all heart-searchings, I really believe (even including our first not entirely respectable *Hamlet*) that I have never prayed for success with the fervour that I did for *Three Sisters*. Of course I wanted to prove that *Uncle Vanya* was not a fluke, but that is really nothing, but nothing.

'I wanted to show that the company was alright without me – well that has been done before. But above all, we needed the success didn't we?. . . And so, it comes back to the recurring thought, that maybe GOD wants the National Theatre *almost* as much as you and I do. – Always gratefully, Larry.'[37]

The reference to Richard II is to the deposed king demanding a mirror, looking in it, and saying, 'No deeper wrinkles yet? Hath sorrow struck/ So many blows upon this face of mine/ And made no deeper wounds?'

Five weeks after Vivien's death a memorial service was held at St Martin-in-the-Fields. Jill Esmond went, sitting at the side and at the back of the church. At the end when she turned to leave she found Olivier standing right behind her. She put her hand on his and he put his other hand on top of hers. She thought his face looked grey all through.[38]

The Hochhuth business dragged on. On the same day that *The Times* reported Vivien's memorial service it carried on the front page, with a picture of Olivier, the news that the script of *Soldiers* was with the Lord Chamberlain. The National would not be doing the play but Tynan had assured Hochhuth that he, Olivier, Peter Hall, and Gaskill would present it under the auspices of a subsidiary company of LOP. Tynan, having given up the idea of Olivier playing Churchill himself, was now putting up to him the names of Orson Welles and Albert Finney.[39] In August Olivier flew to Zurich to discuss the play with Hochhuth and the translator. Only after that did he withdraw. Tynan continued with it, and the play had its premiere in Berlin in October, where it was booed.

There was no longer any question of Olivier's resignation. While he was in St Thomas' Joan Plowright had received a letter from Chandos saying he was obviously loath to bother Larry at the moment, but his contract ran out the following summer and the Board would like to renew it, with any get-out clause he liked. The Board on its side wanted no powers to terminate.[40] A new contract was negotiated, at the same salary, but this time the National would pay for a London flat – to save him having to commute every day – and would pay half the cost of his chauffered Daimler.[41]

In his weakened state Olivier then embarked at the end of September on a six-week National Theatre tour of Canada. The day before he left he received a letter which can hardly have cheered him. It was from Sir Malcolm Sargent, the conductor, who in 1947 had been knighted on the same day as him and had been a frequent visitor at Notley. He wrote, 'I am more fortunate than you as I have been given a definite date (a week or two more) and it is wonderful to know what one need bother about in the affairs of this untidy world, and what one can just pass by as being of no consequence to one's own life. I am really not well informed with regard to your illness but I do hope that either you get completely well or will come to a comfortable end.' Sargent signed himself, 'Your devoted friend for many years and always'. He died four days later.[42]

Olivier's doctors were not happy that he should tour and neither, for once, was he. He did drop the promised performances of *Othello*, not feeling up to the strain of them, but he travelled from Vancouver to Edmonton to Winnipeg to Montreal and to Toronto, and appeared in the scarcely less demanding *Dance of Death*. On top of everything, his stage fright continued.

Back in England he arranged for Gielgud to play Orgon in Molière's *Tartuffe* and Oedipus in the Seneca play of that name. At Brighton he marked out a rose-bed in the garden.[43] He declined MGM's offer of $200,000 to play the Soviet prime minister in Maurice West's *Shoes of the Fisherman*, with Anthony Quinn as the Pope. Laurence Evans, who had succeeded Tennant as his agent, talked MGM up to $240,000 and protested to Olivier that it seemed dreadful to let that amount of money go begging. He did then find three weeks to film in Rome but refused to be referred to as 'Sir Laurence' in the billing, saying archly that it made him feel like

Cedric Hardwicke or Aubrey Smith. He also insisted that his name should appear at the end of the cast list, telling Evans, 'In the music hall that used to be the top billing, but I don't think Quinn will twig this'.[44]

He was still seeing his doctors, and still feeling the effects of the radiation treatment, but his stubborn exertions continued. Giving another unnecessary performance of Edgar in *Dance of Death* in Edinburgh, at a time when no one could reasonably have expected him to tour, he was stricken with abdominal pains which were diagnosed as appendicitis. Not wanting to be kept away from his work in London, he dangerously insisted on being taken back to St Thomas' for the operation, which was just in time. As he said later, the appendix was about to explode and make a horrible mess. The surgeon took the opportunity to check the prostate and found the cancer had gone. Olivier's consultant in Brighton wrote saying he had much admired his courage in submitting to the oxygen radiotherapy, and that it should raise his morale no end to know that all was now well down below.[45] The appendicitis was followed by gout, which had plagued him for years. His understudy, a young actor of exceptional promise called Anthony Hopkins, took over with great success, but within a month Olivier was back, flogging himself again, doing *Dance of Death* at Leeds and Oxford. Then came a blow at the Old Vic.

He had brought in Peter Brook to direct *Oedipus*. Gielgud found the rehearsals exhausting, like being in the army, and dreaded them. Brook was enjoying his authority, being curt with the actors and too clever by half. After Gielgud's last exit he wanted to end the tragedy on a note of jollificiation, and to have his actors dash up and down the aisles to what Olivier called 'a hideously jazzed up version of God Save the Queen'. To bargain him out of this, the patriotic Olivier agreed that if Brook would cut these antics, he would in return undertake that the national anthem should not be played again at any performance at the National.[46] It had been a theatrical custom for years to play it at each performance, but this offended a new generation of directors who were happy to take the State's money but unhappy to play the national anthem. Brook made this bargain and then put one over on Olivier. At a dress rehearsal a monolith six feet high and draped in a cloth appeared on stage. After the blinded Oedipus was led off the cloth was torn from this object, which was seen to be a huge golden phallus. Olivier was adamant that it should not remain. Brook was adamant that it should. Tynan supported Brook. The dispute went on all night and was resumed the next morning.

'I felt weak;' said Olivier, 'I was weak; and weakly I gave in. Peter [Brook] came back in and I told him the decision. Almost with a crow Peter said, "Well, I'm going for a drink, anyone join me?" The others said goodnight and left, and I was alone, naked in my misery. Peter had, in fact, dealt a shrewder blow to my *amour propre* than he could have known. . .like a defeated boxer I knew I should remember it as the punch that started my undoing; that little inner voice squeaked, "You're only allowed three like that, you know." Well, there were two more to come then.'[47]

When *Oedipus* opened the actors invited the audience to join them in a fertility dance round the phallus. Gielgud refused to take part. The whole charade was derided by the critics and disappeared after a few performances.[48] But the damage had been done. Olivier – after cancer, pneumonia, the death of Vivien, and appendicitis – regarded not those things, but rather his giving in to that piece of Brook's puerility, as the blow that started his undoing. He then retreated for nine days to his friends the Waltons on Ischia, and while he was there wrote a note in his diary quoting his son: 'Dick: "Daddy doesn't know he does these things, because he does have a busy life you know (stepping on people etc.)."' His son Richard was six years old. Whatever he meant, it was a pity his father had not stepped on Brook.

Back in England he had his portrait painted by Bernard Hailstone. In it he wears a loosened Garrick Club tie and sits looking quizzically at the artist. It is meant to be informal but is a portrait of an uneasy man.[49] That summer he made three films. First, over a week at Brighton and Pinewood studios, he played Field Marshal Lord Haig in *Oh! What a Lovely War*, an adaptation of Joan Littlewood's musical of World War I. Then, out of patriotism and for a nominal fee, he spent another week playing Dowding, head of Fighter Command, in a spectacular epic of *The Battle of Britain*. It was a small part but greatly moving, particularly in one underplayed line of Dowding's: 'Our young men will just have to shoot down their young men at the rate of five to one.' Then, for a month in June and July, he filmed the National Theatre's production of *Dance of Death*.

In August he took an untypically long holiday of four weeks in Spain and then returned to the National, where his long-running dispute with the chairman over Tynan was resumed. It had been settled for more than a year that *Soldiers* would not be done. Tynan, however, had other projects. John Osborne's *A Patriot for Me*, a play with a homosexual theme, had been refused a licence at the Royal Court, and that theatre had been obliged to turn itself into a club in order to show it. In May 1968 Tynan suggested that if it were announced that the play would transfer to the National, with Olivier in the leading role, then the Lord Chamberlain might be compelled to give ground. 'At the very least it would bring the whole Lord Chamberlain controversy on to the front pages. . . As you will see, your part is exactly the sort of rip-roaring camp you have always been looking for.'[50] Olivier did not want controversy for its own sake. Tynan did. He persisted in his projects and by October Olivier was telling him, 'Please understand that. . .short of the power of choice of plays being put into my hands – which [it] has not been and is not likely to be in my generation – I cannot put on plays without the understanding, cognizance, and blessing of the chairman. When the present list of scripts get back I will shove one right under his nose and tell him that I want to do it more than I want to do anything in my life and make it near impossible for him to turn it down.'[51]

It is not clear what script he had in mind but he did talk to Chandos and then, the next day, wrote to him. It was a letter he regarded as of the greatest importance. His diary entry read, 'My Letter to Chandos', and he underlined these words with a wavy line. His letter said that one aspect of their talk had taken a little bit of sleep away from him, and that was the thing about Tynan. 'Your conviction that he is dishonest goes back a long way to circumstances which, to put it mildly, were not in my opinion ones out of which any of us emerged with any great credit. . . I do not regard the conduct of any of us as being immaculate, and I can never do so.' He then went over the National's repertory since its beginnings, almost play by play, saying there had been twenty-two hits out of thirty-eight, and that a great many things which had given the National an aura of success had come from Tynan. He particularly mentioned *Othello* and Tom Stoppard's *Rosencrantz and Guildenstern Are Dead*, which could be their 'greatest money-spinner'. He wrote that he did not wish to give Chandos an ultimatum, but that if Tynan were got rid of he would be stricken.[52] He regarded this as a 'final plea' to the Board to lay off what he saw as its attacks on a man he considered his 'lieutenant'.[53]

Chandos replied that this letter had angered him beyond measure. He objected to the implications of the phrase 'any of us'. 'The suggestion,' he wrote, 'that my conduct and truthfulness are to be rated no higher than his [Tynan's] has overstepped the limits of my forbearance.' He asked Olivier to withdraw the letter, saying that if he did not it might damage their relationship irreparably. He did not want to see Tynan go immediately, but did not want his appointment to be sustained beyond its usefulness. Olivier wrote an angry reply, then drafted a more tactful one, and then did withdraw his original letter, 'for the good of the National'.[54]

In December Tynan's own production of *Soldiers* opened in the West End. He wrote asking Olivier to come. He added, fatuously, that one Irish critic had compared the play favourably with Shakespeare's histories. He said in one breath that Olivier could lurk at the back of a box and be smuggled out, and in the next that his absence would cause undesirable comment. It was a deeply disingenuous letter. 'Listen, love, please listen do,' replied Olivier: he had rehearsals, he hated first nights, and he had given up interest in *Soldiers* when, eighteen months before, it was obviously going to interfere with his work at the National. He said the assurance that he needn't be seen was inconsistent with Tynan's real reason, which was that he (Olivier) should be a centre of interest. He would not come.[55]

But he continued to defend Tynan against all representations, however well meant, from Chandos. Both Olivier and his chairman recited the old arguments about *Soldiers* in letters to *The Times*.

In January 1969 Chandos wrote, 'My dear Larry, I have done my best, as your devoted friend, to keep you out of the Sikorski turmoil . . . I beg you to be careful, because Tynan as a controversialist is a piece of cake to his enemies and a disaster to his friends. He is both dishonest and untruthful, and if you recognise this fact it will save you a lot of tears in the future.'[56]

There was a lightening of mood when in the spring of 1969 the National Theatre was awarded a Tony for achievement in the theatre arts. This is an American award, named after the distinguished theatre manager Antoinette Perry. Olivier was flattered that his company's reputation had spread so far, and went off to New York dreaming that this trophy might be the first of many silver cups to display in the foyer of the Old Vic's dress circle foyer. He was not a fit man, but his visit to collect it was typically frenzied. He flew the Atlantic, got to the Algonquin just in time for a shower and a sandwich, threw on his tuxedo, and dived into a waiting car which took him to the Mark Hellinger theatre. There he uttered the 'deeply moving, completely spontaneous lines' he had thought up on the plane; then, clutching his Tony, he was given a police escort to Kennedy Airport where he caught the 11 p.m. plane back to London. It has the air of a boyish escapade.[57]

Then it was back to controversy. Olivier took no notice of his Board's advice. In June Chandos lost patience, abolished the post of literary manager and made Tynan literary consultant at the same salary. Olivier at the time was ill again, and undergoing an operation for piles. When he came out of hospital he demanded to know why the Board had acted as it had. 'The reason for this change,' said Chandos, 'is that he will no longer be able to speak as an "officer" of the National Theatre, and pontificate on theatrical matters as if he were speaking with our voice. If he wishes to act as an impresario, he will be free to do so. It was, and is, completely improper for him to act as an impresario when holding the position of literary manager. This is a fundamental change from the present conditions, which I find intolerable, and the decision of the Board on this is final. The Board did not consult you specifically on these points because, as always, they wished to keep you out of controversy. . . Tynan was a member, although a junior one, of the "establishment", and if he disagreed on a major matter with the Board, he should have resigned. [He has] carried on a prolonged campaign, some of it in the Press, some of it in conversation, against his employers.'[58]

In two years, from 1967 to 1969, Olivier had been harried by recurrent serious illnesses, by the death of Vivien Leigh, and by the fear of his own death. He had been humiliated by Peter Brook and exploited by a self-interested Tynan. He was at a low ebb, and his long friendship and partnership with Chandos was irretrievably at an end.

28

The College of Cardinals,
and Surprise

AT ABOUT THIS TIME Noel Coward wrote to Olivier from Switzerland with a sensible and impossible suggestion. 'Darling Larry-boy, Don't administer the National Theatre. You have already made it and given in it several of the greatest performances of this century. Administration is more frustrating and tiring than prancing about and shouting "Ho there," or "In fair Verona's lofty cunt." What you need is a full year off duty. Please listen carefully. Take Joanie and the tots – never mind about disrupting their education – fly from here to Los Angeles, from Los Angeles to Tahiti. . . then fly overnight to Bora Bora and sit down for a long time. The hotel is oddly luxurious, you will have a private bungalow on the lagoon and it is Paradise. . . Don't dismiss this as impossible. Everything is possible if you put your mind to it.'[1]

Olivier did dismiss the idea, though he was much concerned with his family. He recorded Dickie's sports day in his diary, his walks on the beach with his children, and the day his son attained the height of four-feet six and a half inches. And he wrote down, one day in July 1969, 'Joanie. I had forgot to tell her about LA.' This was serious. He thought of it as body-blow number two, more severe than the first, which was the time Brook made a fool of him with that golden phallus. He had arranged for a company from the National to visit Los Angeles in the spring of 1970, taking two plays, one of which would be *The Three Sisters*, with Joan. Then he had second thoughts and cast her in *Tartuffe* at the Old Vic instead.

She would not be going on tour. Someone from the National rang up and told her and she was furious, first at the change – since she had already booked a house at Malibu for herself, Olivier, and the children – and secondly because he had not even told her himself. He first insisted he *had* told her, then flailed around about the cost of air fares and beach houses, but then realised that he was beginning to lose his grip and slipped into his familiar remorse, reflecting that he had allowed the demands of his job to outweigh the importance of his family. Joan was angry and remembers they had an awful row, though she does not remember it as quite the body blow he does. 'I suppose I was just taken for granted as a member of the family, which I had begun to feel a bit. Then I began to think I'd like to get away from the National a bit. He couldn't treat Maggie Smith like that, or Geraldine McEwan, because their agents would be up in arms, but his wife he could. Finally I had to put up with it. Life went on, [but] he recognised that he had pushed me beyond my limits.'[2]

This realisation that he had taken her for granted, and could no longer do so, was indeed a body blow to him. But she also knew she was still the only one he really trusted and that he needed a confidante. She was afraid that his threat to resign if she left cloaked a fear that he had lost his passion for the job.[3] If he had, he soon recovered it. By the spring of 1970 he was playing Shylock to her Portia in *The Merchant of Venice*, which turned out to be one of his last two great roles. Joan had agreed to play Portia when the Shylock was to be either Paul Scofield or Alec Guinness. It was only when both these actors pulled out that Olivier stepped in, not altogether reluctantly. The new director, Jonathan Miller, was setting the play in the nineteenth century and Olivier had been surreptitiously looking at portraits of Disraeli and the Rothschilds. Joan had always been mindful of Devine's advice to her of a few years before: 'Marry him if you must, but don't act with him too often, or it will destroy you.' She put this admonition aside and went on with the play.[4] It turned out to be one of their most successful partnerships.

Olivier had bounced back again and was taking control of everything. He decreed that the colour of stage wine should be improved:

the magenta pink of the Ribena they used would not do at all. And he sent a sharp memo to Frank Dunlop, his new associate director, to Tynan, and to six others saying that acrimony, edginess, tantrums, and bitchiness were to be avoided at all costs. 'And I beg and request, in fact I bloody well command, that this advice be most carefully taken from now on and for ever. Any infringement of this in the future will cause trouble, big, big, trouble, I do most faithfully promise.'[5] He had a little trouble with a persistent fan called Zena who inveigled her way into his dressing room, shouted from the gallery, and made much of her grand connections. It was eventually discovered that she was claiming to be the fiancée not of David Merrick, the New York impresario, but of the Messiah.[6]

In the later spring of 1970 he gave a long and jolly interview to a *Guardian* reporter. It started at the huts in the afternoon and continued in his car to Victoria, and then on the train home to Brighton. Olivier, who had just come from a rehearsal of Shylock, was in a high old mood. On the wall of his office he had a framed poster for 7 May 1814 which advertised a double bill at Drury Lane: *Othello* and a piece called *The Woodman's Hut*. 'It's all right,' he said, looking round at his own wooden walls, 'but seven years in a Nissen hut?' He volunteered that he was playing Shylock as a last resort, the others having dropped out, and said, 'I'm reaching an age when I have to be cajoled, caressed, persuaded, stroked, before doing anything on the stage.' He named the trees he had planted – limes, oaks, willows, walnuts, poplars, apple trees, umbrella pines. He spoke of the thorn he had given to Thornton Wilder, and of medlars with the fruit of which girls pleasured themselves. He agreed he had just subjected himself to two of the busiest years of his life, with films as well as plays, but said, 'I haven't got much money; I worry about my children and the future, dying and leaving nothing, and my wife with three hulking kids.' Then into his vast car, through heavy traffic to the station. 'Only a Daimler,' he said – half the price of a Rolls-Royce and he could get nine people in it. Having caught the train by two minutes he talked about his petition to restore kippers to the breakfast menu of the Brighton Belle. A famous boxing promoter had signed with him.

British Rail gave way. The day kippers reappeared the waiter asked: 'Kippers, sir?' 'No thank you,' he said. 'Scrambled eggs this morning.' That evening on the train with the reporter he was unrecognised and looked the most unactorly of men, but his sense of the sound of words was there. About his early days in Hollywood he said, 'I needed the lick of luxury of those lush valleys.' About the National: 'It is the chief labour of my life.' And: 'What is life about? Strife, torment, disappointment, love, sacrifice, golden sunsets, and black storms.' Had he been near resigning over the Hochhuth affair? 'I was bitter. But resigning? No, that would have been an hysterical thing to do. Actors are not the most theatrical people.' As the train pulled into Brighton he was asked what he planned next: 'I've got a wonderful wife, angelic children, a company to run, what the hell more do I want?'[7]

That March Joan had been made a CBE, which delighted Olivier. Then, confident that the new National on the South Bank would after all be completed, he accepted a renewed offer of the life peerage he had been offered three years before. This time he made no objection that it would be a distraction from his real work. There then occurred an incident that gives an insight into the nature of the man. He told a few intimates, in confidence, that he was accepting the peerage. One of them was Laurence Harbottle, who had acted as his solicitor for ten years. One day, about three weeks before the formal announcement was due to be made, Harbottle returned to his London office after lunch to be told that Olivier had arrived and had been waiting for about twenty minutes. He was sitting in a mucky raincoat, looking worried, and said, 'I'm in terrible trouble'. He took from his pocket what looked like a writ but turned out to be a summons for parking on a double yellow line. 'Do you think it will stop my peerage?' he asked. Harbottle told him not to be so silly, found out from him that it was anyway his chauffeur who had parked the car, and arranged to pay the small fine. 'Larry was a chameleon,' says Harbottle. 'It could be quite frightening. Was he playing games? He had scared the girls in reception, sitting there acting trouble. Did he know he was acting? One never knew.'[8] Olivier was fined £3 by the Brighton parking office. He wrote to Harbottle expressing great gratitude for his brilliant handling of the affair, and in the Queen's birthday honours of June 1970 he was made a peer.

Newspaper cartoon of Olivier, with Archie Rice's hat and cane, waving his coronet during his maiden speech in the House of Lord's, 1971.

'Baron, Baroness & Hons!' he wrote in his diary. Joan did become a baroness, but that is a title which the wife of a peer never commonly uses. Though her rank was now higher her usual style remained Lady Olivier, as it had been when she was the wife of a knight. All Olivier's children, starting with Tarquin, were invested with the courtesy title of 'The Honourable' before their names. Kenneth Clark, by then himself Lord Clark, congratulated Olivier, saying no one called you My Lord except the policemen in the House of Lords, but that they ought to have lunch there one day since the food was good and cheap. Terence Rattigan sent a telegram saying, 'I shall lift up mine eyes unto the Lord.' Peggy Ashcroft called him 'the lordly one'. Richard Burton cabled: 'By the Lord Harry, Larry.'[9]

Olivier's elevation was not achieved without some proper drama. He wanted, naturally, to keep his own family name and become Lord Olivier rather than, say, Lord Dorking, after the place he was born.

He also wanted to become *simply* Lord Olivier, but the custom of the time did prefer a peer to annex some territory to his title and to make him Lord Someone of Somewhere. These two matters were discussed in a long and involved correspondence between Olivier and Sir Anthony Wagner, Garter King of Arms – the principal officer of the ancient College of Heralds which governed the forms and show of ennoblement, chivalry, coats of arms, and suchlike. First there was the matter of the name itself to be settled. Garter explained that since the previous Lord Olivier, Laurence's uncle Sydney, had not been dead for a hundred years, the ordinary rule would not allow a new peerage of that name to be created. Olivier replied that he was distressed and asked if an exception could not be made. No one he had spoken to could, in these 'ungrateful times', remember ever to have heard of his uncle and, as he pointed out, though there might be quite a few barons Brown, Smith, or Robinson, there was only a 'slender likelihood of there being a great run on the name of Olivier'. In any case he infinitely preferred the simple title to what he called the more pompous 'of Somewhere'. Would Garter mind if he approached the Lord Chancellor to ask if the hundred-year rule could be changed? Garter replied that the Lord Chancellor had nothing to do with it: 'My route to the sovereign in this matter lies through the prime minister.' A compromise was reached. Although Sydney's title had become extinct when he died without a male heir, he had had four daughters – Margery, Brynhild, Daphne, and Noel. Garter agreed that the title of Olivier could be revived if these daughters or their representatives agreed. Brynhild and Noel were dead. Margery, according to Angela, daughter of Noel, had been 'in the bin since her twenties', and though she used to follow Olivier's films could now not even remember whether she ever had any sisters; there was as much chance of getting sense out of her as out of a tree struck by lightning half a century ago. Angela gave her own consent and so did a son of Brynhild; so did another cousin from Toronto. Garter at last appeared to be satisfied. Then, at a party, an irritated Olivier unknowingly talked to the writer of an upmarket gossip column in the *Sunday Telegraph*, who ran a story about the protracted dispute and about the concession wrung from Garter. The reporter added that there might be further wary exchanges between Garter and Olivier, since the white swan Olivier wanted on his crest was the same as Henry V's. The day after this report appeared Olivier wrote to Garter, 'fearfully disturbed', apologetic, and hoping that his 'armorial ambitions' would not be condemned. Garter was magnanimous. He replied that he had suffered a slight shock but was used to being represented as an ogre, and had passed Olivier's petition on to Bluemantle Pursuivant of Arms. Everything, it seemed, would be all right.

But Olivier was now nervous that his choice of crest, with its white swan, might indeed be presumptuously like Henry V's, and wrote asking Garter if it would drive him mad if it were changed to a black swan. Garter replied that it would not drive him mad, but that the white swan was different enough from Henry V's badge 'to be clearly, for Heralds, an allusive reference or mark of devotion, and not a presumption'. It was settled at last, the whole business having taken fourteen months, a very good run for any show. Olivier sent his helpful cousin Angela two bottles of best champagne and gave a lunch at the House of Lords for friends and family, including the most distant cousins, at which he served steak and kidney pie. Garter, though, had prevailed in the matter of territory. The ennobled Olivier kept his family name but was gazetted as 'Baron Olivier, of Brighton in the County of Sussex' though he signed himself plain 'Olivier'.[10] He kept the white swan.

As a newly created peer he was invited to a garden party at Buckingham Palace, and two weeks later wrote the Queen a letter of thanks even longer and more fulsome than that he had sent three years before to the prime minister. He described himself as blushing in shame, and blenching with fear of her displeasure, for writing so late. He felicitated her on having recovered so gallantly from a very bad cold and then apologised for having failed, through cowardice, to congratulate her on the installation of Prince Charles as Prince of Wales, which happened to have taken place three years earlier. So he was, he wrote, 'slinging two sins into one confession'. Perhaps, he said, it might be better to say nothing about that, so long after the event, 'but just in case it might just possibly give to Your Majesty the briefest of pleasures, the slimmest of smiles, or the most momentary lightening of the burden of your mighty responsibilities' he dared to risk saying that her sublime and simple dignity had lent more lustre to her subjects' beloved monarchy than, probably, fortune had ever afforded in his lifetime, and that it had filled his heart with pride and homage. He ended by assuring her that in case she might imagine he thought his recent and most gracious elevation gave him the licence to write her chatty letters, he would, no doubt to her intense relief, finish his letter there and then and had the honour to be Her Majesty's most humble and obedient servant. It is a letter which bears out Peter Hiley's remark that in the presence of royalty he sometimes feared Olivier might break into a bow.[11]

He had decided to do the musical *Guys and Dolls* at the National, himself playing the gambler Nathan Detroit and with the American Garson Kanin as director. He was emboldened to be sharp with Tynan, telling him not to take an option on the French musical *Operette* and saying, 'I never feel the least flicker of joy at the sight of a nude person on the stage. . . As a showman I feel bound to listen to my voices when they tell me that *Oh! Calcutta!* may well provide its own surfeit of this side of show business.'[12]

He was elated. On stage he was a greatly praised Shylock, and during its run he had lost the stage fright which had plagued him for five years; he was ennobled; and the showman in him was delighted with the prospect of *Guys and Dolls*. Then he fell ill again. At the end of July there was pleurisy and then, on 1 August, he was taken to hospital with a right leg ten pounds heavier than his left. It was a thrombosis extending from mid-thigh up to the vena cava.[13] He was planning *Guys and Dolls* but was in no shape to move let alone dance. Garson Kanin suggested postponement. Olivier wanted to continue but then had to agree. At the end of September 1970 it was announced that he would not perform for a year. He remained director but there immediately followed a period of great confusion about his eventual successor.[14]

Above all, Olivier wanted an actor to succeed him. 'Well,' he said later, 'it should have been Albert Finney, of course. He was the right one – at the time. If he'd been chosen at the right time, in the right breeze of wind, I'm sure he'd have come out on top.'[15] He had strongly recommended Finney, saying he was 'a person of the right sort of age, with the right sort of following, the right sort of promise, the right sort of generosity and natural trust with his colleagues'.[16] But Finney did not want it. When Olivier knew he had to rest, as far as he ever could rest, he wrote to Chandos saying Joan should become an associate director since she had been acting as such. So she had, and Olivier, in putting her name forward, had in mind the role played by Helen Wiegel, Brecht's widow, at the Berliner Ensemble. In his letter Olivier said he had been to see Lord Goodman, chairman of the Arts Council – which was broadly responsible for distributing government money to the arts – and had suggested to him that 'a kind of College of Cardinals' should be established at the National – if that is not placing me in too sanctified a position'. He said he knew people might feel that the next director of the National should be a director rather than an actor, but he opposed this because he thought an intendant at the head of a theatre, a man who wagged his finger from behind a desk, had never made for a happy or efficient company. In proposing this college of cardinals, of which Joan would be a member, Olivier was certainly seeing himself as pope, and he had chosen to address himself to Goodman, who, though he was the prime minister's solicitor and friend and had a great reputation as a fixer, had no responsibility for the running of the National. Chandos was angry that Olivier had gone behind his back and said so in his reply. He also thought that to make Joan an associate would be a mistake and called Olivier's College of Cardinals a 'Soviet'. He said he had no intention of continuing with things as they were: the executive was in turmoil, the Board apprehensive, and he himself was 'unable to command the slightest loyalty'. Olivier called this reply a threat and said communication between him and Chandos had ceased to exist. 'I just cannot talk to you any more. . . I can talk to Arnold [Goodman] and so I have done so.'[17]

While all this was going on Olivier had been canvassing Richard Burton. Burton and his wife Elizabeth Taylor, having read in the newspapers that Olivier had to take a year off, had written offering Olivier and Joan their yacht and their houses in Mexico and Switzerland, with servants.[18] They then went down to Brighton to see Olivier. Joan arrived home late one night from a performance in

London to find that the three of them had dined too well, and that after much wine had been drunk Olivier had as good as offered Burton the succession as director of the National. The following evening they dined together again, this time with Joan present, and between the soup and the fish Burton asked her if she would stay on to help him if he took over the National. A silence fell on the table. Olivier looked startled, aware he might have gone too far the previous night, further than he had intended or could even remember, and Joan then explained that the directorship was a Board appointment and not Olivier's to give away. Elizabeth Taylor was quite put out that this had not been explained before, saying Burton had a fragile ego and that she could not allow him to face the possibility of rejection, but they all parted as good friends. Burton later wrote asking Olivier to drop any idea of his doing the job. He wrote from his yacht on the coast of Dalmatia saying he hadn't the ability or experience, and that anyway Olivier would be a hard man to follow.[19]

Olivier then went back to Goodman to say, 'God knows how reluctantly', that it was impossible for him to continue with things as they were between him and Chandos. Olivier's account of the meeting is that Goodman murmured a few words of sympathy and told him Jenny Lee, minister for the arts, would be along for dinner in a few minutes. When she arrived Goodman said, 'Larry says he can't work any more with Oliver Chandos,' to which she replied, 'Well, no one'll blame him for that.' Olivier said he was stroked and patted and asked what he would think about Max Rayne, who had just been elected to the Board.[20] Rayne was a merchant banker and property man. Goodman doubted if he 'knew Ibsen from a boiled egg', but saw him as a very able administrator. Olivier believed Chandos was quietly got rid of, and that he had played his part in getting rid of him, but it was not quite like that. Chandos' term of office, which had already been extended for a year, came naturally to an end in July 1971.[21] Olivier says that at the last meeting he chaired no questions were asked and no announcements made, but in fact Chandos made a robust farewell speech. He did describe himself, for form's sake, as an extinct volcano, but then made some telling points. He said educated people should be allowed to recognise fustian – and pretentious fustian – for what it was, and that public interest and public taste were not necessarily ridiculous. He asked for more Shakespeare, saying that in his time no *Julius Caesar*, *King Lear*, *Macbeth*, *Antony and Cleopatra*, *Twelfth Night*, or *Midsummer Night's Dream* had been done. He warned the National against hubris and against pronouncements on statecraft. And then, as loyal as he had always been to Olivier, he said that the directors generally — and he made the point that he was *not* speaking of Laurence Olivier — should repeat to themselves, 'Nemo sapis ominbus horis', which he said he might translate as, 'Nobody need be clever all the time', It was the dignified farewell of a civilised man.[22]

When Rayne took over, in August 1971, Olivier offered his formal resignation as director, which was declined; Rayne said he expected him to stay on and lead the National into its new building when that was finished.

Olivier may have been stroked and patted, and may have believed he had got rid of Chandos, but his dealings with Goodman had not been so fortunate as he thought. Goodman saw Olivier, rather sardonically, as the National's patron saint and hero. As he later recalled, 'He directed the plays, he acted in the plays, he installed his wife Joan Plowright in the few parts he could not play himself, and he turned it into a family romp of remarkable quality and charm. Some of the productions were outstanding.' Nothing, thought Goodman, could go wrong, but it did. Actors became disaffected. Olivier fell into ill health. 'Once things took to sliding, they slid.' Olivier was indecisive about the succession. 'He had notions of a triumvirate to succeed him, including his lady wife. None of his notions was realistic. A great theatre cannot be run by a committee and least of all by a nepotistic committee.' That is Goodman's account. It is entertaining, but Joan Plowright now dismisses it as rubbish. It is certainly factually inaccurate. Olivier directed only nine plays out of seventy produced while he was director, and acted in only thirteen. And she is particularly scathing about Goodman's implication that Olivier was running an Olivier-Plowright actor-managership. That, she says, is exactly what she would not have. When in 1968 the Board proposed that she and Olivier should appear together on Broadway in *The Dance of Death* she refused, because it might have given that impression.[23]

Then Olivier suffered the third of what he thought of as body-blows, and he had told himself he was allowed only three. It was to do with the plans for his beloved *Guys and Dolls*, which the Board cancelled in June 1971. He was manifestly unfit to do it. Without him its appeal would have been much diminished, and without him the National could not afford to put on so costly a musical, but what riled him was that the decision was taken in his absence. 'As usual,' he wrote later, 'the hurt I do to myself is worse than that intended by the one who delivered the blow; the tap on the jaw can be quite light, it is the heavy weight with which I fall that does me the injury.' He felt drained, exhausted, gutless, and hopeless. 'I gave up, opted out, I allowed myself to be cut adrift from my will. If one finds that one's colleagues and friends are content to take actions that they must know are acts of treachery, then it is more than hard, and in my case impossible, to continue the grotesquely unequal struggle any further.' In his diary he wrote, 'G's and D's cancelled after being twice laid on – decided not to stay much longer – 9th year.'[24] Olivier felt betrayed and showed it. Some around him speculated that the traitor was Binkie Beaumont, a commercial impresario who was also a member of the NT Board and who had been his friend for twenty-five years. It was not Beaumont, and Olivier never believed that it was. But the Board, however it was persuaded, was being no more than practical. Without Olivier the National could not take the financial gamble of doing so costly a show as *Guys and Dolls*, and Olivier could no longer have played a part so physically demanding. Olivier probably knew this. He was not betrayed. What mattered was his bitter belief that he had been.[25]

But, exhausted as he was, he was preparing for his last great part with the National and indeed his last great part on any stage. This was James Tyrone, the decayed great actor in Eugene O'Neill's darkly autobiographical play, *Long Day's Journey Into Night*. Tynan had been pressing him to do this since 1970. Olivier felt it was 'too clearly' within his compass, but he had always resisted playing an actor; he had seen Frederic March play Tyrone in New York and had recognised it as a part with every trap in it, and not for him. He told Tynan he had 'a cold dislike for the part, the play, and the whole occasion', and dreaded sweating out long performances for

many months.[26] But play it he did. It is a long night's play and
Olivier wondered to Peggy Ashcroft whether he would *ever* learn
the bloody part. But when it opened it was splendid and he played
it – through more illness and through a bitter controversy over his
successor – for one hundred performances. Olivier, a great actor at
the end of his stage-acting life, was playing Tyrone, a celebrated
actor at the end of his. 'For once,' he said, 'when people say, "You
were born to play that part," it isn't all that cheering.'[27]

For persuading Olivier to play that role Tynan deserves credit.
But it was not for this that Olivier relied on him. Years later, still
defending Tynan, he said; 'I found that Tynan was of immense
personal use to me on account of his unique aptitude in suggesting
some clever choices for the repertory. The fruits of his extraordinary general knowledge of anything striking that had, for the past
few years, appeared in any of the theatres of Europe (something of
which I am afraid I never had time to be well-versed in) was to me,
of course, invaluable.'[28] It was just these clever, striking and self-
indulgent European plays – the Arrabal, the Hochhuth, and
Buchner's derided *Danton's Death* – that pleased few and caused a
quite disproportionate amount of trouble. And Tynan's real view
of Olivier was next to contemptuous. He concealed this at the time,
but later on he described how Olivier called him in to discuss the
1971 repertoire. 'He goes through my familiar list of plays, making
remarks he has made a hundred times about each of them. . . The
odd thing is that he should have such a low opinion of me to think
I would be mollified by a few words from the Godhead. I conclude
he is a man of no imagination or sense of contemporary theatre,
sluggish of mind and insensitive to current definitions of talent,
interested only in hanging on to power.'[29]

Such was Tynan's loyalty. And though Olivier continued to respect
his judgment, he did tire of his endless importunings. Since Tynan
had been reduced from literary manager to consultant he had kept
up a stream of discontented memos. He complained about lack of
consultation, saying he found it infinitely depressing. Olivier at last
turned on him and replied, 'If you want to consult with me you
know perfectly well that you may do so at any time and welcome,
but what is getting less and less welcome are these snappy notes

of yours.'[30] Tynan was particularly aggrieved that Derek Granger, from London Weekend Television, had been brought in as a second consultant. 'I am not by temperament a credit-grabber,' he wrote to Olivier, 'but honestly, dear heart, I am getting a tiny bit fed up with sharing equal billing with Derek.' In the same paragraph he went on to claim credit for rescuing Tom Stoppard's *Jumpers* by 'rethinking and reshuffling the text' and attending every rehearsal.[31] He then wrote complaining that he had been 'elected National Theatre spokesman', with the implication that he was being blamed for what he called a crisis at the National, when the truth was that he had done his utmost to push himself forward as spokesman ever since he arrived. He pestered Olivier to intercede with the Board to give him back his title as literary manager. Olivier replied that it was only by insisting that consultancies were within his gift and not the Board's that he had managed to keep him on at all. Tynan finally overstepped himself when he wrote: 'I think the company is at present so weak that it could not succeed in *any* programme of plays. . . What I'm suggesting is a cutback to a figure of about fifteen actors (*at most*) and building from there. . . There may not be another chance like this of rising from the ashes.' To which Olivier, who had always wanted a company of sixty, retorted that this was 'a bit of nonsense'.[32]

Some months before Olivier immersed himself in *Long Day's Journey* the search had begun, quite without his knowledge, for a new director. In a sense this was reasonable enough. Olivier's five-year contract would end in 1973, his health would not allow him to continue, and he himself had put forward no one acceptable to the Board. It was Rayne's business to look for a successor, but in this he was greatly assisted, influenced, and steered by Goodman, who was the most consummate of fixers. Peter Hall had resigned from the Royal Shakespeare Company in 1968 and had freelanced as a theatre, film and opera director. He was due to take over in September 1971 as co-director at the Royal Opera House, Covent Garden, but withdrew in July. Goodman met him at Glyndebourne, sounded him out about the National Theatre, thought that 'the release of Hall's remarkable talents for full theatrical employment' might be for the best and 'in a sense. . .seduced him from opera back to the theatre'.[33] A lunch followed between Goodman, Rayne, and Hall. Hall was as good as offered the job, and said he would be happy to talk further only if Olivier was determined to resign. He was asked to keep quiet about the offer and on the whole did so, though he did tell a few intimates, among them Peggy Ashcroft and Trevor Nunn, his successor at the RSC. Nobody told Olivier. It has to be a miracle that in so gossipy a trade as the theatre no rumour ever reached him, but it did not. Months went by. As late as February 1972 Olivier made two different suggestions for the succession. First he proposed to Rayne the name of Michael Blakemore. Olivier had known him as an actor as far back as the *Titus Andronicus* tour of 1957 and, after he turned to directing, had brought him to the National as associate director, where he had made a great success of directing *Long Day's Journey*. Blakemore did not even know at the time that he had been proposed, and did not learn of it until he read Olivier's autobiography ten years later. Rayne thought him too little known. Olivier then proposed David William, who later went to Stratford, Ontario, but at the time certainly did not have the stature. By this time Olivier had proposed – over the previous two years – Albert Finney, Richard Burton, Richard Attenborough (known almost entirely as a film director), Michael Blakemore, and David William. He then suggested to Rayne a variation of the College of Cardinals, which this time he called a Regency Council, to include Joan Plowright and Tynan.[34]

Rayne rejected this idea – gently, he said – and proposed that they should fix a date for a chat after Olivier had finished the run of *Long Day's Journey* and after he had taken a short holiday. Olivier then had a sense of what was happening, though he still did not know what. The same day he wrote to Tynan, who had asked him again to intercede with the Board on his behalf, to say he could not. He wrote, 'He [Rayne] has refused any discussion. . .until I have a very long, as he calls it, relaxed chat with him. If that sentence does not bear with it the sound of an axe on the grinding stone I don't know what does.'[35]

The axe was on the grinding stone, and this came at a time when the National was about to go through a splendid period. Blakemore directed Hecht and MacArthur's *Front Page*, and then there were

Jonathan Miller's *School For Scandal* and Dexter's production of Molière's *Misanthrope*, in Tony Harrison's verse translation, all of which filled the theatre.

The meeting with Rayne took place on 24 March, at which Olivier believed he was given six months' formal notice and told that Hall would take his place. That is how he remembered it, but it cannot have been like that. First, he cannot have been given notice: his contract ran until 1 August 1973, and when it was entered into the Board had made it clear that that it wanted no power to end it earlier. Furthermore, Rayne had since agreed that the period of the contract should in any case be extended until the new theatre opened, which was then expected to be at the end of 1973. As to Hall, Rayne's recollection of the meeting was that he told Olivier that Hall appeared to be the only candidate of sufficient stature, but that Hall, Rayne, and the Board would proceed 'only on the basis that the proposal was welcome to Larry'. Whether the Board could have given Olivier what amounted to a veto is doubtful. What did happen was that, after he saw Rayne, Olivier sent a long and generous telegram to Hall, welcoming him, and then promptly felt betrayed. 'Why all the secrecy?' he asked himself. 'Why the shoddy treatment?'[36]

Hall and Olivier met and talked for hours. Hall found him clearly upset, wanting to retire and yet not wanting it.[37] Both had promised to keep the matter quiet and both did until someone, probably Lord Goodman, leaked the story to the *Observer* on 10 April. Olivier then held an emotional company meeting, at which he told his actors and technicians that the succession had not yet been decided, which was formally true, and that he would lead them into the new building, something which had also been agreed. Tynan, furious that Olivier had not told him about Hall, went to Rayne. 'I explained,' he said modestly, 'that most of the important decisions of the last few years had been taken by a small group of us, myself being a dominant factor, and that many of the bad ones had been taken on occasions when we had allowed Larry a free rein.' Tynan wanted to meet the Board. Rayne refused this request. Tynan wrote in his diary: 'What emerges from this is that Larry has behaved appallingly. He has sold us all down the river without a single pang – by refusing to nominate a possible successor from his own colleagues he has passed a vote of no confidence in us all. He has hired us, stolen our kudos, and shows no compunction about discarding us.'[38] A Board meeting was arranged for 13 April to settle the succession. Olivier and Hall were to be present. Hall arrived. They waited for Olivier, then after an hour it was discovered that he had gone home to Brighton. 'I have no idea,' Hall wrote in his diary, 'whether he never intended to come, lost heart at the last moment and is using this as an excuse, or if he actually did forget. He is a great actor. But it is part of the schizoid situation . . .'[39] The Board reassembled five days later. 'The last day of the farce' wrote Hall. This time Olivier did come, and a statement was agreed saying that Hall would join as director-designate in 1973 and take over after Olivier had opened the new building. The Board hoped Olivier would accept the title of President of the National, and the biggest auditorium would be named after him.[40]

Tynan, who had several times been saved by Olivier from the wrath of Chandos and the Board, fulminated against him, calling him an Uncle Tom and a traitor. He had the gall to warn Hall, whom he also despised as 'a burnt-out conservative', to keep a sharp eye on the Board and its doings. Hall for his part asked for it to be minuted that a condition of his accepting the job was that Tynan should go.[41]

Olivier was filming *Sleuth* with Michael Caine at Pinewood – something, he said, which severely burdened him – when his resentment over the manner of Hall's appointment came to the surface again. A member of the Greater London Council, which had an interest since it was paying part of the cost of the new theatre, stated in council that Olivier had been fully consulted, was happy with the outcome and had not been treated shabbily. Olivier could not remain silent, and replied that although he had no aversion to Peter Hall he definitely felt the carpet had been pulled from under his feet. He had been informed of a fait accompli. 'It is, I think, pretty good humbug for anyone to say now that if I had had any reservations on the choice I should have voiced them, since I could not possibly have done so without creating an appalling scandal.'[42] He also drafted a note to Rayne: 'The foolishness of my position starts to obsess me, having regurgitated the calm acceptance with which I first received it. . . Perhaps "discourtesy" is not the right word which I should ascribe to this treatment. "Brusque, cavalier, opportunistic, insensitive" come nearer.' He apparently did not send this note, but he did send Rayne a copy of his letter to the council member.[43]

Rayne replied that the sooner they directed their thoughts to the future the better, and that if, at any point, Olivier had expressed reservations about Hall, 'the only embarrassment to the Board would have lain in the problem of finding a comparably suitable alternative'. Olivier replied bluntly: 'You had been negotiating with Peter Hall three months before you told me of it. Most certainly it was too late for me to do anything other than accept the situation as a *fait accompli* as gracefully as I could. . . [Otherwise] an extremely damaging scandal would have been the result. . . I just get sick of evasions and bluster, that's all.'[44]

He had an unanswerable argument. And it had been more than three months before he was told. It was nearer nine. But he had also put the Board in an impossible position with his suggestions of colleges of cardinals and regency councils. And he did have an aversion to Hall. It was not personal, but Hall was young, he was not an actor but a director, and he came from the Royal Shakespeare Company, which was the opposition. There was also the history of Hall's ambitious efforts, from 1959 through to 1962, to establish a de facto national theatre round the RSC, which he had largely achieved, and which Olivier had not forgotten. And to make all this worse, Hall came to him as a real surprise, and nothing is more dangerous than surprise.

Hall's recollections of all this are enlightening. He had directed Olivier's *Coriolanus* at Stratford in 1959 and thought him an obsessed professional, delightful to work with, with an instinctive intelligence that had nothing to do with scholarship or reasoning; it could lead him astray but nine times out of ten it was genius telling him what to do. In 1971 at Gyndebourne he had met Goodman, who asked him to lunch. There he found Rayne, whom he had not expected. They asked him if he would do the job. He asked if Larry knew. They said, 'Well, no, he's not been well', and he said they could take things further once Larry had been told. They asked him to keep it secret, and he didn't even tell his wife, though he did tell Trevor Nunn and Peggy Ashcroft. It didn't go any further for eight or nine months. There were times when he thought nothing was going to happen. It was clear the Board members didn't know what to do. When at last they had the courage to tell Larry, he says, Larry sent him a four-page telegram of purple prose, and he went round to his flat and drank champagne and it was all lovely. Then the next morning Larry was standing in front of the entire National Theatre staff, with Tynan at his side, saying he'd been betrayed. That, Hall thinks, was all Tynan's doing, and of Tynan he had a low opinion: 'Of all the people I met in [theatrical] politics he was probably the worst, and he thought he was the best. He had an extraordinary ability to advance great theories which you could always see through. You could see what he was really at. Larry of course had the horse-sense of genius, which is something else. Ken was really untrustworthy, and he loved being the power behind the throne, but he was not quite as secure as he thought. He had a non-job really. We can all think of plays. He never thought anything through in terms of making it, because that wasn't his role. Flash Harry? Well, he was.'[45]

Throughout 1972 Olivier remained director, but thought himself on sufferance. Joan had gone to Chichester for the season. In July he suffered from tracheitis and bronchitis. In September he went to Paris for two days to make television commercials for Polaroid cameras for $300,000, on the understanding that they should never be shown in Britain. In November he was back briefly back in St Thomas' hospital: 'R[ight] groin scare (Lymphangitis).' He did a recording in London for the Dick Cavett show, on which he agreed that he had resisted becoming a lord because it might make him seem out of touch with his public, and being called 'My Lord' had a slight aura of the New Testament about it. He didn't like the word 'genius'; the theatre was too practical for that. And he was asked, yet again, about his rejection by Garbo in 1933. Did he still find it embarrassing? 'Not now. I just didn't measure up. I wasn't good enough for her. She was a master of her trade.'[46]

In late 1972 Noel Coward came to London. After a party at Claridge's for three hundred friends he was asked to play something. His hands were shaky. He limped to the piano and played 'If Love Were All'. Olivier and others saw him to his car and as he drove off he waved back. Olivier had the sense that they both knew they would never see each other again. In January 1973 Coward died. Chandos, Olivier's old friend and enemy, had died just before.[47]

At Brighton there was trouble. Half the façade of Olivier's house was declared unsafe and had to be rebuilt at great expense. The house was twice burgled and the second time Olivier was coshed. Douglas Fairbanks sent a cable: SORRY MY OLD STUNT MAN NOT THERE TO HELP YOU.[48]

The bare walls of the new National Theatre building had risen and a topping-out ceremony was held in May. Olivier shovelled in the last spadeful of concrete and the builders were fed and danced Irish jigs. The interior was nowhere near completed; the opening was now set for 1975 and Olivier wanted to step down. He suggested – and it was his own suggestion – a 'gentle takeover' by Hall, who from April 1973 became co-director and was to take over in November, with Olivier remaining only an associate. The time had come for Tynan to go. His contract called for three months' notice. Tynan – who apart from his pay at the National had earned more than as much again from *Playboy*, *The New Yorker*, and *Oh! Calcutta!* – turned to the man he had called sluggish of mind, a traitor, and an Uncle Tom and demanded a year's severance pay. 'I never had one in my life,' Olivier retorted, 'and I don't look for one now.' But he still asked to address the Board on Tynan's behalf and got a year's pay for him. Tynan sent Olivier a last memo, this time of thanks, on behalf of his wine merchant, his wife's dressmaker, and the management of 'La Mère Charles's restaurant, Mionnet, near Lyon (trois étoiles)'.[49]

Olivier made an entry in his diary for 1 November 1973, in capitals: FIN DIR N.T. There was no ceremony.[50]

The style of Olivier's and Hall's directorships could hardly have been more different. As Hall put it, Larry progressed up and down the corridor in the huts every morning, putting his head in here and there, greeting, cajoling, flattering. 'He was a fascinator, and most of those working for him would have gone to the South Pole and back if he'd asked them to. He headed a tight-knit little court, and who was in and who was out was always the main news of the day. . . But it couldn't be like that any more. For one thing. . . I hadn't the great actor's extraordinary magic, which was so much a part of Larry's personality. I hoped, however, that my style was more democratic; it was certainly more open.'[51]

Blakemore saw things differently. At first he got on well enough with Hall, who admired his abilities and perhaps reasoned that if he could get Blakemore on board – who had been appointed by Olivier – then the takeover would look more harmonious. Blakemore agrees that Olivier was a monarch, who had a strong sense of territory, and that Hall appeared more democratic. 'But,' he says, 'as long as you acknowledged Larry was king, then as one of his chamberlains you had infinitely more real power than you did with Peter.'[52]

Looking back many years later Olivier made much of his surprise that it was Hall who succeeded him. 'I suppose tragic isn't too big a word really. What was tragic was the futility of what I had been at for the last ten years. Because I had spent that ten years searching for a successor – every single director I invited in – instead of doing half the plays myself which I was *dying* to do. I gave up all these directorial opportunities, I gave up the chance of being an English Stanislavski, in order to find a successor, and that I felt was my mission in life. I knew I couldn't possibly last for ever. I was twice ill, and I knew the Board were worried sick. And whoever I found – of course my favourite was Michael Blakemore – they said, 'Oh, he hasn't got the stature.' They wouldn't understand. I said, "Listen, the job makes the stature." And so rather than have anyone who would have been the slightest risk, and the slightest excitement because they'd be new, Peter Hall it was. I just never thought of it, never thought of it because I was always thinking of somebody new, and exciting, and somebody to push up, and somebody to create the job for themselves. I mean everybody knew perfectly well that Hall could direct the National Theatre. And I was so upset. Not in any sense against Peter Hall. I was only hurt because I had wasted all these opportunities, giving them to other people in case they showed up a likely young master. Out of seventy seven plays I directed seven. I could have directed forty five, and everybody would have said, "Yes, bravo." And I was dreadfully stricken.'[53]

This idea that Olivier should have wanted to be seen as a Stanislavki figure comes as another surprise, but Joan Plowright confirms that it was so. 'He wanted that stature and that reputation. I think he felt people were not all that admiring of him as a director. They thought he should stick to acting. He wanted to be the father figure of the company. He wanted to be the founder of a tradition.' She emphasises the influence upon him of Michel Saint-Denis, the French actor and director who had made his first reputation in France, with his uncle Jacques Copeau, but came to England in 1936. He first directed Olivier in his *Macbeth* of 1937, and again after the war in his famous *Oedipus*, both at the Old Vic. He was also, with George Devine and Glen Byam Shaw, one of the directors of the Old Vic Theatre School, at which Joan was a pupil. Olivier shared and greatly admired Saint-Denis' idea of a multi-talented theatre ensemble, all of whose members could not only act but also sing and dance. This versatility, Joan believes, is what Olivier wanted to demonstrate with the National's proposed production of *Guys and Dolls*, and the frustration of that ambition accounted for the depth of his bitterness when that production was cancelled in his absence and against his wishes. So it was not, as she sees it, that Olivier wanted a sign on the South Bank saying 'The Olivier National Theatre', but he *did* want to be known as the founder of a tradition. In Europe there had been Stanislavski, Brecht, and Jean-Louis Barrault. 'Barrault had formed his own company and it was known as his company. Secretly I think Larry would like the National to have been known as *his* in the same way. In one way it was. When he was there, there was nobody else to touch him.'[54]

29

A Bit Worried about
Time Running Out

WITH PETER HALL, OLIVIER was fickle. His London flat was in a tower block in Victoria. Hall lived in a duplex on the thirty-ninth and fortieth floors of the Barbican, a 1960s concrete monstrosity of apartment blocks in the City, four miles to the east. Olivier, *not* wanting to talk about work, would flick his lights on and off and telephone Hall just to ask if he could see this display, across London. In another mood he would telephone wanting *urgently* to talk about work and appear in Hall's flat, make many remarks about it being higher off the ground than his, and then bring up a dozen matters.[1] And there was work to talk about, for though Olivier had abdicated he was, in 1973 and into 1974, appearing in two plays at the Old Vic and directing another.

In Eduardo de Filippo's *Saturday, Sunday, Monday* he played the eccentric grandfather in a Neapolitan comedy in which Joan played the lead. She had returned to the National at Hall's request. The play was directed by Franco Zeffirelli, and this was her first meeting with a man who later directed her in films like *Tea with Mussolini*. She also played in Priestley's *Eden End*, which Olivier directed. It was the last play he did direct at the National. Here there was some disagreement with Hall, who wanted her to tour in the play. She did not, and neither did Olivier, who said it was 'miz enough for Joanie to be parted from all sight and sound of her nippers for three months on end' in London, without two more months playing 'to empty houses'.[2] And for his last part at the Old Vic he played not Prospero or Lear – Joan having told him she would never speak to him again if he did anything so predictable – but the part of John Tagg, a Glaswegian Trotskyite in a new play by Trevor Griffiths called *The Party*. It was not the lead, but it was a virtuoso performance in which he could demonstrate yet again his mastery of an accent, and it demanded from him one speech twenty minutes long in which Tagg lamented the failure of his beloved communism. Olivier had not long recovered from his stage fright and his fear of drying. That speech took him four months to learn in the summer of 1973, stretched out on a garden seat from six to eight every morning, adding another twelve or fifteen lines a day. Tynan considered it the most inspiring call to revolution ever heard on an English stage and was struck by the irony of its being made by Olivier.[3]

The National, apart from his fee as associate director, paid him £35 a performance. To pay his childrens' school fees Olivier renewed his contract with Polaroid, being paid another $300,000 for four days' shooting in Paris in the spring of 1974. Polaroid, telling him that the commercials had sold one million cameras in America alone – bringing in almost a quarter of all the dollars Americans spent on cameras – congratulated him on his unique artistry and sent him cameras and films to play with. The advertising agency sent him two sterling silver and crystal hurricane lamps, which he said in his thank-you letter would be just the thing for dark days.[4]

All this time Hall was constantly pressing Olivier to say what he might like to do in the future, and in particular in the new theatre when it eventually opened. In a taxi one evening Hall suggested Prospero in *The Tempest*, saying he ought not to be played as a remote old man but as a man of power, as shrewd, cunning, and egocentric as Churchill; Olivier listened. For a whole weekend he appeared to have agreed to do Prospero. A month later they discussed *Lear*, and then *The Tempest* again; Olivier wondered. Then Olivier, having insisted on a meeting, said it had been a pity he could not reach Hall the previous weekend, as he had been going to tell him he had decided on *Lear* but had since decided against. Three months later Hall offered to direct *Lear* himself, or direct it as an associate, or to let someone else direct it, whichever Larry preferred; Olivier appeared to accept. When in January 1974 the National at last embarked on *The Tempest*, not with Olivier but with Gielgud, Olivier was in earnest attendance at rehearsals, making Gielgud uneasy; Hall thought he knew he had that effect. Later that month Hall repeated his suggestion of *Lear*, saying Dexter could direct if Olivier preferred that; again nothing was settled.[5]

Joan Plowright remembers that Olivier just wanted to stay away from the theatre and did everything he could to obstruct Peter Hall. Hall accepts this, saying, 'The man was God in the theatre. He had been asked to leave his Heaven. Although without him there would not have been a National Theatre, he knew he would not actually enjoy it. I just tried to be as forgiving as possible. But he didn't make it easy. No he didn't.'[6] In July 1974 Rayne wrote to Olivier, repeating his suggestion that he should become life president of the National and offering to commission a portrait of him by David Hockney. Olivier, still prevaricating, replied that he was not sure about the presidency. He did not know about Hockney's portraits but he found his still lifes above his head. If the Board felt kindly enough, he would like a portrait of his three children by some more formal artist. But that was not the Board's idea.[7]

Both Hall and Rayne were dealing with a sick man, and it was more than the cancer and thrombosis and other ills he had suffered. As early as that February he had noted: 'Frozen shoulder'. He was regularly taking Valium by day and Mogadon to sleep at night. On holiday in Italy with Zeffirelli, in August, he thought he jarred his back diving. On 31 August he wrote in his diary. 'Aching arms and shoulder starts'. A week later he learned that his first wife Jill had cancer. In the middle of September he went for X-rays. Then, 'Aching arms and thighs and sore fingernails starts', and on 30 September, 'Face blown up'. Both eyes almost disappeared into the swelling. He saw a dermatologist at Brighton who referred him to Dr Joanna Sheldon, whom he found a very handsome woman with whom he had an immediate rapport. He went into the Royal Sussex Hospital for blood tests, and she explained to him that he was suffering from a rare disease called dermato-poly-myositis – dermato for skin, poly for much or general, myo for muscle and sitis for inflammation – and that he should prepare himself to stay in hospital for six or nine months. He took the news, he said, as heroes do in melodramas, cool and unmoved, and she later told him he was a brave chap. He did admit that the disease, once it took hold, turned out to be 'rather scary'.[8] After four days in hospital he wrote a detailed account of his symptoms and treatment to the surgeon who had treated him for cancer at St Thomas', ending, 'My condition feels very weak but the pain seems to be disappearing from my muscle and my face is beginning to subside. I am being treated with steroids. . . I am feeling very low but at the same time beginning to feel I shall live.'[9]

But he got worse. For two weeks he wrote not a word in his diary. Joan was still playing in the West End transfer of *Saturday, Sunday, Monday*, and each night when she returned to Brighton after the performance she sat with her husband. Dr Sheldon told her that the condition was static. There was no improvement. They were not giving up hope but it was serious. He was finding it difficult to swallow and was fed through stomach tubes. Tarquin came to see his father and found him like a mad King Lear.'[10] After he had sat with his father for a while Dr Sheldon beckoned to him and told him Olivier might not last six weeks. Sometimes his voice was so weak on the telephone when Joan called him from London that she feared he might slip away before she got back to Brighton.[11]

At the beginning of December, after eight weeks, the immediate crisis passed. He was still too weak to lift either an arm or a leg. A physiotherapist treated him daily until, as it seemed to him, his limbs began to lift and move themselves. He appeared to gain strength. Within a week he was so much recovered that Joan encouraged him to think of beginning his memoirs. She had successfully hidden the gravity of his condition from the press. She had admitted, after two weeks, that he was in hospital, but by then this had happened so often that it created no special alarm. Her good friend John Dexter, who was by then director of productions at the Metropolitan Opera, New York, happened to be in London. She told him the truth. He suggested that he should ask Olivier to direct Verdi's *Macbeth* for the Met, and that this should be announced. This would deflect the press and give Olivier something to work towards and a reason to fight. Dexter could arrange with his board that if Olivier could not in the event direct, he would take over himself. This was done.[12] To help him with his memoirs, Olivier asked his sister Sybille to come and stay in Brighton so that she could visit him and talk of old times. He dictated a letter to her, saying, 'You see, I am a bit worried about time running out – not for you and me in so many gloomy words, but general time in which I can undertake such an assignment. . . I don't think you probably took in what was wrong with me. In fact I haven't had time to take it in myself, but I am suffering from dermatomyositis which is painful and induces the most appalling lethargy ("lechery, I defy lechery") and tiredness of the most intense kind.'[13] She did come, at the beginning of December. His physical condition was such that at the time he had, as he put it, to be helped across the room by four of the largest nurses in Sussex, and life was 'slow, very, very slow'.[14] But his talks with Sybille were taped and his voice on the one surviving tape is very much Olivier's, not at all weak. Their conversation, however, is sometimes strange. They talked about their parents' early days and their father's parishes. They discussed their parents' intimate life, on which Sybille said their father had consulted the family doctor.

LO: 'He said, "Press in." Father told me. . . He said "Press in. Right to the very base. Be sure that you press good and hard at the base."'

Sybille: 'Oh no. I wasn't told that one.'

LO: 'Father told me.'

Sybille: 'All he told me was that it was necessary to hold back, he said, and Fahv of course with his temperament would have been much too eager and impetuous.'

LO: 'Of course. Yes.'

Sybille: 'But the point was, I think to establish that they were happily married.'

LO: 'They were very happily married.'[15]

They also talked about their mother's grave in Hampshire. Olivier told Sybille he still had a letter from cousin Evelyn, the daughter of his artist uncle, Herbert Olivier. Five or six years before she had written saying the grave was in a disgraceful state. The wooden

cross, with the name barely decipherable on it, had fallen across the
mound. She had asked him if he didn't want to do something about
it. On the tape Sybille said she thought he had done something
about it.

Olivier: 'No, I didn't. I never have done. . . Darling, what should
I do? What should one do about one's mother's grave? I don't know.'

Sybille: 'I understood you had.'

Olivier: 'I haven't. I didn't do a blind thing about it.'[16]

The day after Sybille left he wrote in his diary, in red, STARTED
WRITING. He was determined to do it. To Jill he wrote, 'Mine is a
longish job, I'm afraid – but do you know, the curious thing is I don't
seem to mind it one bit. I think that bloody old National nearly killed
me, and the idea of being looked after while I write a book would be
welcome.'[17] He wrote diligently and plentifully for several days in a
large red leather-bound notebook. There are fifty pages in his quite
firm handwriting about his childhood, his sister's early loves, the
scholarship interview with Elsie Fogerty at the Central School, and
his first recollections of Noel Coward. In the same notebook, and
apparently written at the same time, there is a random mixture of
other entries. On one page there are 'Quelques Crudités et des Oddités.
Unholy Pomes by L.O.', one of which, adapting the traditional first
French lesson about 'La plume de ma tante', reads in part:

La plume de ma tante est dans le jardin
MAIS
Les pantalons de ma tante
Sont dans la poche du jardinier

[My aunt's pen is in the garden
BUT
Her knickers are in the gardener's pocket.]

There is also a separate and lyrical account of Joan bathing their
first two children, Dickie and Tammy, when they were three and
two years old, and trying to teach them the Lord's Prayer.

Then, on a blank page, he wrote this note:

Three great dreads of those embattled with the 70s
Impotence
Incontinence
Incompetence[18]

He was getting on so well with the memoirs that he dictated a long letter to his old friend Hamish Hamilton, the publisher. He said his illness was 'nothing dramatic or heroic, merely a great nuisance for rather a large section of time'. He knew he had for years been 'dillying and dallying, coying and bridling' about his autobiography; the idea had been simmering for years, and he had turned down tempting offers from America, but now that no one promised his release from hospital before June or July he had started writing. Having a crack at his friend David Niven's book *The Moon's a Balloon*, he said he was not thinking of something delicious like *The Moon is Blue*, but of wider shores. The book might stretch to more than one volume. Could he get his agent to talk to Hamilton?[19]

His voice grew stronger. Joan saw that though the body was still weak his mental energy was back – 'almost manic, planning opera, writing books, redecorating our house'. She took the children to see him and they were so cheered to find him lively that it did not matter to them that his conversation veered erratically from one subject to another. Then one night at the hospital she asked how the book was coming on.

'It's done, finished,' he said. 'All seven volumes.'

'Seven?'

'Yes, seven,' he said at the top of his voice. 'O-L-I-V-I-E-R.'

And the opera? 'Done. Next thing is for me to throw myself out of that window.'

Joan remembers that this went on for ten or fifteen minutes. 'It was total mania. I called the sister, who said he had not been himself. I said, "Not himself? He's round the bend."' Next day builders turned up at the Brighton house saying Olivier had ordered iron bars to be erected at every window. She sent them away.[20]

Olivier's own recollection was much the same. 'I actually went out of my mind; poor darling Joan believed that I was to be like it for life. It was an appalling feeling, as if there was something right through my face and head turning at a steady pace round and round, about in a level with my right eye from front to back, churning like a wheel.'[21]

The dosage of steroids was reduced and then, says Joan, 'It took three days for him to come down from wherever he was'. The madness departed.

He had continued to be fed through tubes. Then one morning when Joan rang him up to tell him she had a matinée and so could not go in to see him that day, he said, 'Well, if anyone's interested in me, I had scrambled eggs this morning.' She believed he had turned around.[22]

Then he fell back again. When Joan took the children in one day Dickie said he ought to be getting on with his book, and in front of them all he said, 'I can't write. Look at my hands.' He abandoned the memoirs. One weekend, home from Bedales – the boarding school which all three children attended – Richard, who was thirteen, went to see him and found him struggling to get out of bed, ripping tubes from his body and his face blazing with rage. He turned and ran, 'to wipe the nightmare image of the mad, dying father out of mind'.[23] He appeared to have lost the will to live. Joan told her brother David that she could not take the children in any more. David Plowright had always got on well with Olivier who, he thought, regarded him as a substitute for his lost brother Dickie; he always introduced him as his brother, never as his brother-in-law, and called him 'Dear boy'. He knew Olivier's moodswings and tempers. He knew Olivier had once shown Joan a photograph of David's son Nicholas and told her, 'I want one like that'. Plowright was programme controller at Granada Television. This was then by far the best of the British independent companies and later, when he was managing director, David made the celebrated drama series of *Brideshead Revisited* and *The Jewel in the Crown*. When he visited Olivier in hospital he saw that he was despondent, knew the family thought he was on the way out and, with his sister, came up with the idea of suggesting to him that he should undertake a series of modern plays for television under the title 'Laurence Olivier Presents'. It did not matter if all Larry did was choose the plays. If, God willing, he were well enough, he could direct one or two.

The important thing was that he should be in charge of a project. At first Olivier showed no interest. He never had been much interested in television. But then after two weeks he became suddenly enthusiastic.[24]

'That,' says Joan, 'is *really* when he began to turn around, suddenly back in charge. That was fairly extraordinary. Joanna [Sheldon] had been warning me. And I hadn't come out of my play because if I had people would have thought he was dying. Suddenly his bed was littered with these scripts, and he had his scrambled eggs, and on he went.'[25]

Olivier later admitted he had not thought he would live. Ralph Richardson came to see him and behaved with such calmness, as if there was nothing at all out of the ordinary, that Olivier, knowing him as he did, was confirmed in his suspicion that his condition was critical. To Toby Rowland, the producer of his wife's play, he wrote, 'I daily get more alarmed at the apparent anxiety that, beautiful actress that she is, she cannot help but express'. Kenneth Clark wrote to him at the time, and it was a letter which had something of the obituary about it. He felt sad to think of someone with Olivier's marvellous powers stuck in bed; it was like Benjamin Britten unable to write. He apologised for having opposed the Hochhuth play against Larry's wishes, said that his most thrilling moments in the theatre had been *Othello* and *The Dance of Death*, and he had always considered it the blackest mark against show business that it had never found the money for Olivier to film *Macbeth*, which would have been a masterpiece.[26]

On Christmas Day 1974 he came home for a few hours and was pleased that his Shakespeare films were shown on television. He was not to know they had been planned as a posthumous tribute. He returned to hospital and continued to recover. In January 1975 there are entries in his diary like, 'Walk. 12 minutes' and 'Walk. 17 minutes'. He was three times allowed home for a few hours. On 27 January he wrote to Clark: 'I can see from a couple of visits that I shan't really be able to be in a state to face a more normal life for quite a while . . . I lost two and a half stone in a few days, all muscle (didn't actually boast any fat) so that I had to be carried about with just strength to press a bell – so it's a bit like starting again at two years old. I tried walking with the kids on the beach yesterday on those disappointing stones and sat down after about fifty yards while the kids played around; to my alarm after ten minutes I couldn't get to my feet. Thank God Dickie is phenomenally strong for thirteen.'[27] Weak as he was he still left hospital on 31 January, four months earlier than his doctors had expected. Peggy Ashcroft came to see him at Brighton and was shocked by his appearance and by his high voice. Ginette Spanier wrote from Paris: 'Oh how happy you must be to be in your own home, in your own bed. . . I think of you so much and so lovingly. I think of you as a brother for whom one would have incestuous feelings.'[28]

At home he discussed the Granada series with David Plowright and his colleagues. Joan thought the idea was a life-saver. She remembers reading a newspaper article at the time with the headline, GREAT MEN OUT OF OFFICE HAVE GREAT ILLNESSES. It named prime ministers and presidents of great corporations who had suffered such breakdowns, and she felt it was the same with Larry.

Another of his worries was money. He no longer had even the full salary of director of the National, and could not foresee what other work his health would allow. He remembered the shotgun he had been given in Hamburg in 1945, which had since been on loan to his cousin, Colonel William Olivier. He had heard that such guns were now worth five figures and put it up for sale at Sotheby's. The saleroom told him it would fetch more if he were named in the catalogue as its owner, but he refused, partly because it had been 'a bit of booty' and partly because he did not want the publicity. It was offered anonymously, failed to meet its reserve and eventually went for only £800.[29] He had a summary of his assets made. In investments, property, furniture, jewellery, pictures, theatrical relics, and insurance his estate was worth £224,250. Joan's assets, including the Brighton house, came to £218,300.[30] He went off for four weeks to his old refuge with the Waltons on Ischia. Susana Walton thought he looked at death's door. His fingers were still wound up in plaster bandages and the finger tips were constantly breaking into new sores. She spent hours each morning changing the dressings on his bleeding fingers. He was like a pincushion from injections, but gradually the sores healed and at last he could dress without pain when his clothes touched his skin. Before long he and William Walton were holding hymn-singing contests to see which of them could remember his choirboy days the best.[31] From Ischia he wrote to Joan: 'I am missing you but *dreadfully* and beginning *really* to pine for the kids. I know they can be and probably always will be a difficulty to contend with on hols and that you can cope a great deal better without me because at least you don't have to put right the mistakes I make in my dealings with them, but I miss a great thing in my life without them just the same, tho' I'm fully aware they don't miss me much — that is quite natural. I hear myself making the same mistakes and feel it's somebody else. . . Darling, one bit of really good news, at least for me it is marvellous as it is one of my main sources of nervousness. My hands are actually getting better — the sores have found a terminal point and are retracting and shrinking back. . . It's wonderful to feel that possibly all these aggravating secondary symptoms may have some terminality, the finger ends persist, but who knows?. . . All my love to you, my wonderful pride and joy.'[32]

Back home he suffered relapses, influenza, quinsy, and dreadful trouble with a wisdom tooth. 'One night the whole of the inside of my mouth seemed to burst and the most charming and delightful substance, of course quite delicious-tasting and scented with asphodel itself, filled mouthful after mouthful. It was really too charming! However. . . I was able to open my mouth after many, many days of not being able to.'[33]

By then John Schlesinger had telephoned proposing to Olivier a film called *Marathon Man*, in which, as it happened, the part he offered was that of a Nazi war criminal who specialises in torture by dentistry. 'There is nothing,' said Olivier, 'so revivifying as the bewitching appearance of opportunity, and I have always regarded John as my restorer of life; through him I felt that life, real life was starting again, and I seemed to breathe nothing but oxygen.'[34] He charmed Dr Sheldon into giving him her certificate that his health was unlikely to deteriorate in America. 'Anything to oblige,' she replied, signing herself 'Joanner'.[35] Then he was off to the United States, at first as a warm-up, for a three-day cameo part as the villainous Dr Moriarty in a Sherlock Holmes film called *The Seven-Per-Cent Solution*, which managed also to drag in Sigmund Freud as a character. On the way to Heathrow Airport he dictated a letter: 'At last I begin to feel better. I think it must have been just scraping past the insurance medical for the film.'[36] Moriarty brought him $75,000 and eased his money worries. Back in England he spent much of the summer sitting in his garden, planning his series of plays for Granada. Then in October he was off to New York and Los Angeles again, this time for almost three months, to film *Marathon Man* for $135,000 and a share of the profits, if there were any. He wrote long letters to Joan with his painful fingers, one ending. 'Sleep in my love, My darling dove.' Tamsin, aged twelve, wrote to him from her boarding school: 'Is it nice in Hollywood? Everybody at school says they wish they could go to Hollywood. We have just heard your name mentioned on the radio. I think it was something about the theatre.'[37]

Olivier spent the New Year of 1976 in Los Angeles. Also in Hollywood at the same time was Sarah Miles, his mistress of the early 1960s. Her marriage to Robert Bolt was about to end in divorce. She had appeared as a conspicuous Irish beauty in David Lean's film, *Ryan's Daughter*, and had just had a great success in *The Sailor Who Fell From Grace With the Sea*. She and Olivier had not met since the few days they had spent filming *Lady Caroline Lamb* together almost five years before. She was alone and staying at a borrowed house off Benedict Canyon, Beverly Hills, where Olivier appeared on the afternoon of 14 January. He had just completed *Marathon Man*, and she got the impression that he was more cock-a-hoop at surviving the physical ordeal than with his performance. He took her to a party with Kirk Douglas, Dustin Hoffman, Burt Lancaster, Jean Simmons, and others. Some stood up when Olivier appeared. They looked on him, she said, as more than a great actor and more than a genius even; perhaps more of a god. The party broke up early. He took her home, sent his driver away, and asked himself in. He feared the nights. He told her he was not able to give her what he once had, but she led him to bed and they lay quietly together. He was frail and shrunk. He showed her his sore fingers and explained that was why he could not hold her hand. He left after dawn. She remembers him, waiting for the taxi, as bouncy and youthful, not the stooped creature who had arrived.[38]

He spent three days of March in Tunis, playing the bit part of Nicodemus in Zeffirelli's *Jesus of Nazareth*, and then during six days in May, for $200,000, played a Dutch doctor in *A Bridge Too Far*, an epic of the failed airborne invasion of Arnhem which starred Bogarde, Caine, Hackman, Hopkins, Connery, Redford, Liv Ullmann, and a cast of thousands. One day's filming, in Holland, clashed with an appointment he had at the Granada Studios in Manchester. Ill as he had been, and frail as he still was, he devised a typically Olivier-like solution. He found an 8.30 a.m. plane from Amsterdam which, with any luck, would get him to the Manchester studio by 10 a.m.[39] He was again cramming into a day anything that could be crammed. The taping of his series of plays with Granada was about to begin. And the new National Theatre on the South Bank was at last, after a delay of twelve years, ready to open.

30

A Gesture Somewhere Round Glory

THE NEW NATIONAL THEATRE had risen slowly. It was to open in 1974, then 1975, then 1976. At one point it was even expected to be delayed until 1977. The only consolation then, as Rayne saw it, would have been that the opening would form part of the festivities for the silver jubilee of the Queen's accession.[1] For a year or so there was not even any agreement on which company would perform in the building once it was completed. A proposal to merge the National and the Royal Shakespeare companies was on the cards, or the RSC might regularly put on Shakespeare in one of the three auditoriums. Nothing came of these schemes. Then there was a proposal that Henry Moore should make a sculpture of Shakespeare to stand outside. Moore had after all once been a member of the theatre Board. Recognisable figures were not his style, but he had sculpted a massive reclining object for Lincoln Center in New York. He was taken on a tour of the new building but would not commit himself. Eighteen months later he declined the commission and offered a sculpture from stock, which was in turn declined by the Board.[2] A protocol committee was set up to organise the opening, which was to be by the Queen. Kenneth Rae, company secretary at the National, was a close friend of the Queen's private secretary, Sir Martin Charteris, who, when Hall visited Buckingham Palace to meet him, confided amid much mirth that she didn't much like plays.[3]

From all this Olivier withdrew himself. He was still a consultant director. His name appeared before that of the chairman in the theatre programmes. He could have attended Board meetings. He was a member of the protocol committee, but when a copy of the minutes was sent to him he scrawled across the top, 'Keep Out'.[4] He had withdrawn himself so effectively that, although he did write to tell Peter Hall when he went into hospital with dermatomyositis, saying he would not be able to play Father Christmas for his children that year, it was four months before Hall realised how seriously ill he was. Peggy Ashcroft eventually told him in February 1975. Hall telephoned him, found his voice high and odd, and thought it dreadful that a man who had spent his life getting the last note out of his voice should now find his vocal chords affected.[5] Hall wrote offering to go to Brighton to see him, and said the theatre was really beginning to look something, the Olivier auditorium particularly; it was a fantastic experience to sit in it.

Olivier suffered relapses and said he was too poorly to see Hall. Then in July he wrote: 'What I want to tell you as we can't meet – and really for the easement of any sort of conscience that is left in my rotten character so much nicer it would be if we could meet, but if we can't there is nothing for it but to write like this – when my contract is up at the end of September I would like gently to disappear from view. . . I am enormously appreciative of the Board for providing for me all this time and I shall make these feelings abundantly clear to them. There is one thing that needn't happen now – £25,000 to David Hockney for a portrait. . . You have been very kind to me all this time, and understanding about my situation, and indeed admirably brave in your efforts to look as if you were paying attention to anything I said!. . . If there is anything for which I am really required advicewise or experiencewise or any such thing as that, you have only to call on me, but I shan't be in the tiniest bit surprised if you never do.'[6]

Hall replied that he was sad to contemplate Olivier's 'fading away gently' just when his great work was about to spring to life. Could they come to some compromise? Frankly, he said, he needed him. The two men did meet in August 1975 at Olivier's London flat. Hall found him alert and humorous, but reduced: the physical presence seemed to have gone. He said he knew people would be disappointed if he did not appear in the new theatre, but he would rather that than have them disappointed if he did.[7]

The fencing continued. Olivier insisted on referring to the Olivier auditorium as the 'Upper Theatre', explaining that he was too modest to call it by its new name, but he was too busy to think of doing a production for the National. Hall said the press would love a story which could be slanted to say that he wouldn't have Olivier in the theatre or, worse, that Olivier didn't want to come.[8]

Peter Hall then embarked on his 'foot in the door' policy. The building was not finished but he would move into those parts that were, first into the offices, then into each of the three auditoriums as it was completed. Lord Cottesloe, chairman of the South Bank Board which was responsible for getting the theatre built and handing it over to the National Theatre, invented a little joke: 'We may not be out of the wood, but at least we're in it.' In October Hall wrote again to Olivier: 'Now we're actually in the South Bank, I feel I must press you in the light of all the conversations you and I have had for the last two and a half years. Please can you come and do something as actor or director in your theatre as soon as possible? It may seem stupid to offer you carte blanche. But I hope you know that there is no project that we would not do for you.' He suggested Olivier should direct *Romeo and Juliet*, or a Checkhov, or Ibsen's *Wild Duck*, or a new play by Howard Brenton, or Stravinsky's *Soldier's Tale*. 'It is up to you. If you feel you can do something, tell me. We'll do it.'[9]

Olivier did then come and look round the theatre for the first time. 'It must,' thought Hall, 'have taken great courage on Larry's part to come and see everybody after a year, his appearance so different, feeling so frail, and being the man outside this wonderful place he has created.'[10] Olivier enjoyed his visit, and thought the proscenium theatre, the Lyttelton, a perfect gem, but could not swear that the impression given by the Olivier theatre was 'over-whelmingly one of intimacy'. He had forgotten that the Lyttelton was the auditorium he had not wanted to build. Opinions of the new building varied. Gielgud, when he saw the Lyttelton, found it drab and dreary and the stage proscenium dreadfully wide, like an American stage. Ralph Richardson, on the other hand, thought the building 'stunning in its magnificence'.[11] In spite of all Hall's proposals Olivier still did not feel there was anything he particularly wanted to do, though he wrote, 'I am a thing that belongs utterly to the Board, so it is not really a question of my departing with a careless flick of the cloak to separate myself from any future relationship'.[12]

But he did then separate himself. He declined to go to the gala performance at the last night of the Old Vic, saying he could not face an audience. Albert Finney and Peggy Ashcroft led the rejoicings, assisted by Gielgud and Richardson.[13] Rayne was generous and wrote to Olivier telling him that he had been sorely missed but that his spirit had dominated the occasion. Nor was he there for the public opening of the Lyttelton. The formal royal opening was still to come, and that was the most important. Hall asked if he would take charge of that. Or would he be the centre of it? 'You have,' said Hall, 'to open your own building'.[14]

Olivier replied that he could not by any stretch of the imagination do what Hall asked. He was doing a full-time job with Granada Television, which he thought Hall had realised. He could possibly undertake 'a few ill-chosen words to get the thing going'. As for the other arrangements he had this to suggest: the bars should be kept open, '[and] it might be conceivable to clear the stage during an interval and fill the back of it with an orchestra and ask Her Majesty to dance. . . It would be charming to have Her Majesty's dainty feet treading those boards'.[15]

Olivier was making himself awkward in every way. Joan Plowright saw this and thought that everything he did was coloured by his illness.[16] When he had been made a peer he had pinned up a notice telling members of the company to carry on calling him Larry, or Sir Larry, or Sir Laurence, or just 'Sir', as they always had done. Now he wrote to the secretary of the protocol committee asking that he should be referred to in the minutes as a member of the House of Lords: to refer to him as Sir Laurence Olivier seemed, he feared, to be 'a deliberate flouting of their lordships' company'.[17] He had already fallen out with Rayne over the date for the royal opening. Rayne had stated in a meeting of the protocol committee that October had no special significance for the National. Olivier, who had not attended the meeting, saw the minutes and was 'shocked with amazement and outrage'. He wanted the opening in October, and he wanted it on the twenty-second. That was the date on which the National had opened in 1963 at the Old Vic. He proposed forcefully that the new theatre should open on that date, even if it was a Friday and even if Friday was not a socially popular day with the Palace. He wanted this 'in recognition of the first eleven years of the National Theatre, of what those years achieved, and what all the people concerned achieved in making it possible, not to mention enabling our committee to find itself perched just where they are whenever they meet'. If that date was too unsociable for Her Majesty, he proposed the day before, the twenty-first, which was Trafalgar Day and Agincourt Day; he was unsure whether it was not Bosworth Field Day too. He then finished: 'If the committee still wishes any contribution from me for this occasion – maybe they don't – I most earnestly request that the utmost consideration be given by them to this proposal.' The chairman of the protocol committee produced a tactful reply. He confessed he had not remembered the date of the 1963 opening. An October date would indeed be decided upon. The Palace had suggested the twenty-fifth or the twenty-sixth of that month, but he would see if the twenty-first was possible. 'It is,' he concluded, 'too obviously superfluous to add that the official opening of the National Theatre without a major contribution from you would be like celebrating a birth without a word from a parent, and indeed without any champagne.'[18]

The twenty-fifth was settled upon. Peter Hall proposed that Goldoni's *Il Campiello* or Coward's *Blithe Spirit* should be given. There would be a play in both the Lyttelton and the Olivier. The committee minuted that Lord Olivier might be prepared to speak a prologue in one theatre and an epilogue in the other.[19]

Or he might not. He made it clear again that he thought there should be a ball with an orchestra on stage or, if not, then revivals of single acts from plays of his own regime. Hall remarked that the scenery for such plays did not exist. 'Larry,' he wrote in his diary, 'was at his most Richard III: smiling, charming, constantly saying how generous all of us had been, but obstinately refusing to agree to anything that we wanted him to do.'[20] Olivier was also embroiled in a dispute about tickets for the members of his original company. Three people on his list had not been invited. 'Invite all three,' he wrote. 'I will insist on it or stay away, giving my place to Lord C's chauffeur! Will say we cannot do with less than *sixty*.'[21]

Quite apart from the royal opening, and before it, there was the public opening of the Olivier theatre for Hall to worry about. He was putting on Marlowe's *Tamburlaine* with Albert Finney and asked Olivier to come and speak the prologue. He havered, but was obviously not going to do it. It was all over the papers that he had opened the new Royal Exchange Theatre in Manchester but would not come to the first night of his own theatre. The London *Evening Standard* remarked that opening the Olivier without Olivier was like *Hamlet* without the prince. Rayne was again tactful, was sorry Olivier could not be there, and asked his permission to have a bust of him made by William Redgrave to display in the Olivier foyer.[22] Having declined a portrait Olivier did agree to the bust, and it is still in the foyer. In a last effort Hall wrote asking Olivier, at some future date, to direct a Feydeau farce, *The Lady from Maxim's*. He said he knew Olivier was busy with his marathon television series but it would give everyone in the building a new lease of life if they knew he would come back to direct. *Tamburlaine* opened without Olivier who, two days after it had opened, wrote saying sorry, but he couldn't possibly get to it. 'Thank you too,' he wrote, 'for the very sweet suggestion about the Feydeau. I started to read it and stopped, realising suddenly that it was in fact hopeless for me to consider it, and that I was merely reading to enjoy myself. If I get through this year's work by the end of May, my religion requires that I pray for a motion picture, to pick up my Manchester career again in the summer.' He said he was dearly touched that Hall should keep thinking to put things his way.[23]

Olivier was mischievously playing with Hall, who had troubles enough of his own. The building's air-conditioning was noisy and then broke down, stage-hands and technicians were refusing over-time and threatening to strike, union militants picketed the theatre, and Finney had bronchitis. The play for the royal first night was to be *Il Campiello* and Hall was uneasy with the rehearsals he saw. He did not know for sure whether Olivier would take part in the royal opening until, only four days beforehand, he learned that he had been turning up at 8 a.m. and rehearsing his speech behind the locked doors of the Olivier theatre. He had previously rehearsed it in the bathroom at Brighton. Joan, knowing his memory was going, had begged him to read it. He refused. On those early mornings in the Olivier stage he moved around till he found the acoustically perfect spot from which to command the auditorium.[24]

Michael Birkett, deputy director of the National and in charge of the royal arrangements, sent Olivier the seating plan that he and the Queen's private secretary had worked out for the opening night. Olivier was in E59. 'I hope it's all right with you. Your seat for Act I will be easy to reach after your greeting to the Queen from the stage. . .and the audience at that time will be distracted, indeed completely swivelled round in their seats, because the entire cast comes on from the back of the auditorium (including a dog, a monkey, a band, two large stuffed carnival figures and assorted streamers and conjuring tricks!). In the middle of which the stage staff actually carry the set through the audience and set it up! It takes minutes before it has all died down and the play begins.'[25]

This did at least give fair warning about the play.

On the night it poured with rain. The Queen was welcomed in the foyer, where she unveiled a plaque. She was to see *Il Campiello* in the Olivier, and Tom Stoppard's *Jumpers* was to be performed in the Lyttelton. She took her seat and then Olivier walked on stage and gave one of the great performances of his career. He had his speech typed on cards but did not use them. What follows is the manuscript text of the speech he learned by heart, given as he originally wrote it in a small notebook.[26] The eccentric line arrangement gives some idea of his emphases on the occasion.

Your Majesty, Your RH's, My L's, Ls & G's

It is a nationally characteristic
understatement to say
that I am happy to welcome you,
at this moment, in this place

For this moment
we must be grateful to the
timing
and the durable cladding
of Mr Peter Hall's foot when
he put it in the door

For this place
we must be grateful to many
another besides him.
I do not ask to be forgiven if
I do not mention by name all the
contributors to this achievement
since 1848, as it might be harder
to forgive me were I able to achieve
such a feat of memory.

He then thanked, among others, Lord Chandos, who had 'carried a feisty enthusiasm and a vital persuasiveness into significant quarters' and without whom no one would be present there; Lord Esher (the man who had sacked him from the Old Vic in 1948); Lord Goodman (the fixer who had fixed so much, including Hall's appointment); Lord Cottesloe (who had got the theatre built); and Kenneth Rae (who had faithfully served the idea of the theatre and then Olivier himself for forty years). He thanked 'all boards, councils, committees, departments, Her Majesty's Treasury, and our brother and sister taxpayers'. He thanked Denys Lasdun for the building which 'rewarded their eyes and all happy senses'. He thanked colleagues who had lent their rich talents and selfless devotion to the creation of a standard which justified the creation of these temples to their art, for the benefit of their fellows and their successors. To those who would follow he wished joy of all of it. There was an unkind dictum which declared that a true artist must not expect satisfaction from his work. Let him wish them, then, that blessed sense of dedication such as had been inspired some years before by Lilian Baylis. He then ended:

Yr M, My L's, L's and G'n,

I thank you for your
kind attention
and for the glory
and the lustre
of your attendance.

The performance of *Il Campiello* was a disaster. To choose a bad play for the opening of the National Theatre of Great Britain was one thing; to choose a bad Italian play was another. The cast could not begin to achieve the sleight of hand of Goldoni's *commedia dell'arte*. Hall thought the actors were like men struggling through a nightmare and was deeply ashamed. He had thought something 'light, short, and amusing' might serve, but it did not. The specially commissioned rendering of 'God Save the Queen' was discordant and made worse by the trumpeters of the Household Cavalry playing wrong notes.[27]

This did all have the effect of making Olivier's virtuosity the more singular. Joan Plowright – who was not there on the night because she was filming *Equus* with Richard Burton in Canada – recalled that Olivier was glad the play had gone so badly, because by then he hated Hall.[28] But his noting of Hall's foot in the door was just. Without Hall the theatre could not have opened then.

Tynan, in a last unhappy act before departing to live in California, wrote in his diary: 'Larry makes a typically florid speech on the stage of the theatre that bears his name, singling out a dozen politicians for praise and not one playwright, actor, or director – except of course P. Hall. . . The whole evening was what Noel would have called "sheer sauce". The most significant performance was given by a drinking fountain that played throughout the action – quietly pissing on everything we expect of a National Theatre.'[29] Kenneth Rae thanked Olivier for unexpectedly mentioning his name, at which he had burst into tears, and said, 'Oh! Larry – that play and its performance. . . Well, a great occasion is over and you played your part – not an easy one – magnificently and with no sign of bitterness, which, in your shoes, I would have found hard to suppress.'

Maggie Riley, an actress in the company, remembering Olivier's last words thanking the audience for the glory and lustre of their attendance, wrote congratulating him on a splendid speech: 'As for that beautiful extended gesture somewhere round "glory" – well, all I can say is that it conveyed more than one can put into words – as you intended it to be – and that I would be prepared to sit through *all* of Goldoni's pieces in order to see it again. I spoke to Peter Wood [the director of *Jumpers*] later in the evening, when the veritas was coming out of the vino. . .and he started to talk about the phenomenon that some people, surrounded by mirrors and a myriad reflections, don't count for very much, yet one man, with no mirrors at all, standing on a totally empty stage, can mean everything. "He's got magic, you see," he said. "Magic. And that's what it's all about."'[30]

31

Dracula – the Shame of It

THE THREE YEARS AFTER the opening of the National Theatre were a time of persistent illness and unremitting hard work. Olivier knew very well the precarious state of his health, as he showed when Greer Garson – whom he had given her first chance in the theatre back in 1935 – wrote inviting him to come and rest at her ranch in New Mexico and to inspect her thoroughbred Santa Gertrudis cattle. He replied that he often thought darling and splendid things about her. 'I have,' he wrote, 'been terribly lucky in recovering from the last dermato onslaught – or should I say attack – on my existence. . . I managed to train my legs away from the idea of collapse after three or four attempted running strides. So you see I have reason to feel I may begin to enjoy life again, but I do not fancy yer stage acting for a bit of time yet.' He kissed the noses of her mares and wished he could get to see her.[1] To Tarquin he had been more definite. He had been told that he could never appear on stage again. How, Tarquin wondered, could his father accept that, when he had described the sensation of acting to an audience as 'like coming for a living'?[2]

He could still act to camera, resting between takes, and he did not lack film offers. Ben Benjamin of International Creative Management wrote from Hollywood: 'My burning ambition is to get you back here, and have you do some work under the influence of money.'[3] He filmed *Marathon Man*. But his preoccupation for thirteen months up to the end of June 1977 was with his Granada television series, into which he threw himself with typical abandon, as best demonstrated in a letter he wrote to his cousin Mary after Christmas 1976. She was the daughter of his uncle Herbert, the portrait painter, and was then Lady Sanders – being the widow of Air Chief Marshal Sir Arthur Sanders, who had risen to be Deputy Chief of the Air Staff and aide-de-camp to the Queen. She wrote describing a quiet Olivier family Christmas when they had thought of him. Hadn't he really been doing too much, what with 10 Downing Street one day and Buckingham Palace the next? He wrote back calling her 'Dearest coz (Shakespeare, you know)', saying his Christmas could hardly be described as 'quaht', what with fifteen to sleep at Brighton and seventeen sitting down to dinner, each of Joan's brothers having three children. Then he told her about television. 'I like the work very much indeed. . .but when the work is not in actual flood, it seems to be at almost unbeliev-able pressure. After all, ten weeks' work in four and a half days really simply means that a TV director has to think about twenty times as fast as a movie director. I have got it far from buttoned up yet, but I am enjoying the climb.' He signed himself 'Lord Totteridge', a family joke, Totteridge in Hertfordshire being the place his cousin's mother came from.[4]

For Granada he co-produced six plays and acted in all but one, which he directed. He flew twice to New York to charm NBC into putting up much of the production money. He put on Pinter's *The Collection; Saturday, Sunday, Monday*, which had been such a success at the National and in the West End; and James Bridie's *Daphne Laureola*, which had been one of his few box office hits with LOP twenty-five years before. Joan appeared with him in the second and third of that group. Then there were *Cat on a Hot Tin Roof,* with Natalie Wood, Robert Wagner and himself as Big Daddy; *Come Back Little Sheba*, an American play by Dean Inge, with himself and Joanne Woodward; and *Hindle Wakes*, a gritty piece of Manchester mill-town realism, the only one in which he did not act. None of these plays is now remembered as his later television work with Granada is remembered, but their importance is that they gave him absolute authority in a new medium and, by demanding new things of him, gave him even greater reason to work and to live. The four plays that were shown in the US were among the first British television plays ever to appear on an American network.[5]

The director of *Come Back, Little Sheba* was the American Silvio Narizzano, who was an early riser, always awake at five in the morning. When Olivier discovered this he took to telephoning him at five minutes past five, just to talk and to distract himself from what he called the black monkey on his back. When Narizzano asked where the monkey came from Olivier said he was born with it, and that he had understood, long before experience confirmed it, the tragic condition of being a man. 'I was able to understand anything that people do, good, bad, or foolish.' And had that helped him as an actor? 'Oh yes, I think so. I could sympathise with what life puts into anyone.'[6] That, at least, was what Olivier, driving himself to distract himself from his illness, then remembered.

As soon as his thirteen months with Granada were over he was off to Hollywood again for *The Betsy*. It was not a cameo. He played the leading part of a lustful tycoon, the president of a car manufacturing company who, because of the flashbacks in the film, has in some scenes to grow younger, to go from eighty to forty, and to play one scene of soft-porn. 'I began in the *Betsy* time,' he said, 'to feel real lusty.'[7] He did it for the work, and for the money, $350,000 for eight weeks, then two weeks rest, then any further weeks at $50,000, $1,500 a week expenses for the duration of the filming, and a notional share of the profits.[8] As *Newsweek* said, 'God bless Laurence Olivier. And God only knows what the incomparable actor of the Western world is doing in a piece of hilarious idiocy like *The Betsy*. Taking away a zillion dollars, one hopes. . . Having plumbed the depths of Shakespeare and Chekhov, Olivier has little trouble probing the nooks and crannies of Harold Robbins, from whose best seller this farrago was farragoed.' One who did not think the film worthless was his old and close friend Ginette Spanier who, when she saw it in Paris, wrote, 'You are so beautiful in it. Young and old. So sexy. So atractive. So chic.'[9]

Tarquin, who was working in the Far East, came to Malibu to visit him for a week during the filming. He managed to walk, with pauses, across the sand to the sea. Sometimes he sang to the sea, 'How I love you, how I love you'. Perhaps his allusion was to *Titus*

Andronicus, that apparently unplayable play which, twenty years before, he had made not only comprehensible but moving, and in which he likened himself in his misery to the ocean: 'I am the sea./ Hark how her sighs do blow.'

Over dinner father and son talked and Olivier complained bitterly about his impotence.[10]

During that stay he also returned to Benedict Canyon and Sarah Miles. He went with her to a very public party on Sunset Boulevard, dined publicly with her in a restaurant, and took her to look over the San Fernando Valley at night, where in his early days in Hollywood he remembered Clark Gable and Carole Lombard used to have a ranch. His energy was still more than normal. She thought it miraculous. He would come back to her house full of pain but still say, 'Come on, I want to learn Yoga'. He perched cross-legged on meditation cushions, looking with his skinny legs like Gandhi. His fingertips were painful, but she remembers that he still stroked her more tenderly than anyone else had; but then, she says, no one had ever been so *determined* to get it right. He told her, as he had told Narizzano, about the nights. 'The nights play silly buggers. . . Come six o'clock, rain or shine, I ache with the dread of oncoming night. It's been that way for years now.' 'I solaced him,' she says; 'that's what you do as a mistress. I won't have anyone speak ill of him.' He stayed with her for some days.[11]

A few days after he finished filming his old friend Alfred Lunt died. Lunt and his wife Lynn Fontanne had been his friends since the 1930s. After the flop of *Romeo and Juliet* in 1940 in New York, they were the only people who had asked him and Vivien to dinner and tactfully avoided talk of the disaster. In August 1977 he flew to Detroit and then went to Lynn at Genesee Depot, Wisconsin. He lay on the sofa all day and comforted her. Afterwards she told him that that now *he* was the greatest living actor in the English language.[12]

Sarah Miles had gone to London to make a film. When Olivier returned to England he went straight to her house in west London and spent three days with her. In a scene out of Feydeau, he raided the refrigerator in the middle of one night and was discovered by her agent who, as she had forgotten, was staying in the basement.

One dawn, looking at his head on the pillow, she was uncertain whether he was still breathing, panicked, and called a friend. The friend felt his pulse, smiled, and left. Her parents lived in Brighton, so they also met there. She had to return to Los Angeles, and in their last days she noticed that Olivier became visibly more frail.[13]

The trouble this time was with his left kidney, and again it was serious. Again he survived. As Jonathan Miller, the director who was also a doctor, put it, he had developed 'a curious and startling immortality'.[14] He wrote to his sister Sybille's daughter, who was looking after her, saying, 'I am really quite a bit under the weather, having had two small ops. I hesitate whether to tell Sybille this because I do not want it to get about. Above all I do not want the usual clamour and titifalla as it is of excessive importance that everybody thinks I am absolutely in a first-class state of health.' Sybille herself was in a bad way: her unloved husband, Gerald, had died that March at the age of eighty-two and she was herself suffering, so her daughter thought, from senile dementia, letting the dogs eat from her plate at table.[15]

Olivier wanted to be thought fit in order to be insurable for his most profitable film role yet, in *The Boys from Brazil*. He was to be paid $725,000 for thirteen weeks' work, twelve of them in Hollywood, starting in December 1977. The role was that of a Simon Wiesenthal figure, hunting the evil Josef Mengele who murdered thousands of Jews at Auschwitz.[16] He did play this role and received his eleventh Academy Award nomination for it. He then played a Maurice Chevalier-like character in *A Little Romance*, and that succeeded too. *Time* magazine said, 'One of the consistent joys of '70s moviegoing has been Laurence Olivier's game, witty performances in otherwise terrible films. Even junk like *The Betsy* and *The Boys from Brazil* becomes memorable in his hands . . . Olivier is such a sly devil that he could make his Oscar acceptance speech, a riotous stream of sheer poppyock, sound as if it were a Shakespearean soliloquy. In *A Little Romance*, Olivier has another crusty character: a suave old coot of a Frenchman who plays fairy godfather to a pair of star-crossed lovers . . .' The filming was in Paris and Venice and he even took Sybille with him to the Paris studio. She spoke some French on this visit, a language she had not spoken for years, and was more competent in it than he was. But at times, even speaking the language, she still did not realise where she was.[17]

News of his real state had got out. Douglas Fairbanks wrote to him from Florida, 'Larry, dear Larry, oh Larry, me boy, I hear you are ill again and although there are many things going on in the world I don't like and disapprove of, your sad luck is one of my principal protests against an unfair world.' To which Olivier replied, 'Yes, I am afraid I have been overdoing things for about two and a half years, the last eighteen months of which I have had no break of any kind. And when I started this picture. . . I already felt on my last legs the first day. . . I still go to bed a great deal during the day, but I hope to lead a more normal life in a week or so. I am, unfortunately, in a dreadfully weakened condition by a recent operation on the kidney, which took more out of me than I catered for and, as I leapt straight from my hospital bed on to the set. . . I obviously did not realise what a slender chance I was giving myself.'[18] He still did not accept Fairbanks' offer of a holiday by a Florida lake.

He had entirely separated himself from the National Theatre. It was more than a year since, in June 1977, he had resigned his consultancy. In September 1978 a garden on one of the river terraces of the National was named after Lilian Baylis. Olivier promised to make a speech but then withdrew, saying that Gielgud, Richardson, and Peggy Ashcroft had all had longer associations with Miss Baylis' Old Vic. He did telex a message but it was so convoluted that Richardson, who performed the opening ceremony, could not speak it.[19]

He spent much time at the Malthouse in the Sussex countryside and no longer felt much inclined to come up to London. 'I have such a curious reluctance now,' he told Peggy Ashcroft, 'about the journey, I think – it used to be marvellous in the Nat. Th. days. I could get so much home-work done on it, and there was that lovely Brighton Belle.' This was a Pullman train whose comfort was congenial to passengers but which British Railways had abolished as unprofitable. He told her they were about to move from Brighton where they had lived since 1961. 'The kids are wanting London more and more, and all Joanie's friends are there and mine too –

those I haven't lost in the last seventeen years, eccentrics living down here. We're getting (if nothing goes wrong) a pretty nice job in St Leonard's Terrace, looking across the Guards' cricket ground to Nell Gwyn's old soldiers' home [the Royal Hospital, Chelsea]. It's v. quiet but will feel a bit of a crush after the twin houses here. But it's time everyone moved on.' He said Joan had not been home, since her show [de Filippo's *Filumena* in the West End] was going on in a very big way, and he was worried about her getting exhausted.[20]

He was reluctant to make the fifty-mile journey from Brighton to London, but still ready to travel to five times that distance to Cornwall for another film. '*Dracula*,' he wrote to Tarquin. 'God, the shame of it.'[21] It was at least the fourth remake of that film. Olivier played not the name part but that of a Dutch doctor who drives a stake through the vampire's heart. It earned him another $750,000 for ten weeks' work. By now, it was only on a film set that he had any vigour left. When Lauren Bacall came to London in February 1979, to promote her biography, he did go to London for a literary lunch, where Gielgud was dismayed by his appearance. 'Agony to see him so changed and withered, but he talked gallantly, made a speech – a bit rambling – and even said he might be tempted to try and act in the theatre again. He is really very brave.'[22] He was never going to act on a stage again, though he did not abandon that hope for another three years.

And Cornwall turned out to be no distance at all. During the rest of 1979 he flew as much as he ever had before. In April he was in Los Angeles to receive at the hands of Cary Grant a special Oscar for the body of his work and the achievements of his entire career, to add to those he already had for *Henry V* and *Hamlet*. In his acceptance speech he said he was elated, dazzled and solaced. But he plainly did not consider the body of his work complete, and made it clear he was filled with euphoria 'at the first breath of the majestic glow of a new tomorrow'.[23] The visit was not all elation. He was distressed by the appearance in the *New York Times* magazine of a report of remarks he had made the previous summer in Venice, during the filming of *A Little Romance*. He was reported as saying said he had been afraid of killing Vivien and once nearly

had, and that he had left her because in the end there was room
for only one of them on the life-raft. If he had stayed they would
both have perished. He was only doing what he had often done
before, reminiscing about his life with Vivien. This time a reporter
had been present. The article, which was of course reprinted in
England, made public for the first time many details of his last
years with her.[24]

The film Olivier played in that late summer and autumn was
probably the worst he ever made, and one of the best paid. His role
was that of General Douglas MacArthur in *Inchon*, set during the
Korean war, and it was to be filmed in the terrible climate of Seoul.
'Amazing gallantry,' said Gielgud.[25] Olivier's fee was US $1,000,000
for six weeks filming, $250,000 on signature and the rest in four
weekly instalments. He also received $2,500 a week expenses. He
took it as seriously as anything else he ever did. He visited the
MacArthur museum at Norfolk, Virginia and met Alexander Haig,
later Secretary of State, who at the age of twenty-five had been
MacArthur's aide-de-camp. He then worked in Korea through
intense heat and then through the monsoon. His make-up took two
and a half hours and in the end he didn't think he looked a scrap
like himself or, he feared, a scrap like MacArthur.[26] It later turned
out that there had been trouble raising money from Japanese banks
and that the whole project was financed through the Rev. Sun
Myung Moon and his Unification Church, the Moonies. Mr Moon
then wanted his name on the credits but was told by the director,
Terence Young, that this would be the kiss of death, and that if he
insisted on having his name on it he would have to take Young's
off. The film as shot ended with Olivier, as MacArthur, reciting the
Lord's Prayer. The Moonies then tacked on a black and white news-
reel of MacArthur, which Young told them was the most certain
way of wrecking a great performance and destroying the illusion
that Olivier *was* MacArthur. They wanted to distribute it themselves and he told them that would be a total disaster. So it was.
It was shown briefly in the United States, where *Newsweek* called
it the worst movie ever made, but never in Britain.[27]

One last scene was filmed in Rome in October 1979, and there
Olivier gave an interview to Rex Reed of the *New York Daily News*,

who reported that he wore gloves before each take to protect his raw and bleeding hands from the weather and from too much shaking. 'I must look forward to the future,' said Olivier. 'I can no longer bear the sight of myself as a young man. . . In Korea they showed *Wuthering Heights* one night on TV in the middle of a dinner party, and I wouldn't even get up to walk into the other room to see myself as Heathcliff. I have very little adrenalin left. And I'm fading fast. . . I'm almost used up now and I can feel the end coming. My children are twelve and seventeen [either he or the reporter forgot the middle child], and I've got nothing to leave them but the money which I make from films. . . Nothing is beneath me if it pays well. I've earned the right to damn well grab whatever I can in the time I've got left.'[28]

32

Jobbing Actor, O.M.

HE HAD MORE ADRENALIN left than he thought. The first few months of 1980 could hardly have been busier. He had agreed, for another million dollars, to do a remake of *The Jazz Singer*, which had been the first talkie to be made back in 1929. While he was in Los Angeles he arranged for his son Richard, who was now eighteen, to enter the University of California at Los Angeles to study theatre and film. Olivier had first seen the campus in 1931, from Sunset Boulevard, and both he and his son were thrilled.[1] And between two periods of filming in Hollywood he flew to the East Coast to take over the direction of the American transfer of De Filippo's *Filumena*, in which Joan had enjoyed such a success that it had run for two years in the West End. Olivier had been keen that it should transfer and had spent some time persuading Franco Zeffirelli, the play's director, who was less certain. He had also asked Richardson's opinion, who saw the production and gave the tactful warning that there was 'something odd about translated plays in the US'.[2] The play did transfer and at the beginning of the year Joan was rehearsing in Boston, with Zeffirelli, while Olivier, on the West Coast, was having an unhappy time in *The Jazz Singer*.

Al Jolson's old part, that of the young son who would rather sing for money and fame than at the synagogue, was played by Neil Diamond, who was not so much an actor as a pop singer. Olivier's part was that of Diamond's father, the cantor, who wanted his son to continue the family tradition. He had never been so

disenchanted with a film: he complained that the 'molasses senti-
mentality' of it made him sick and called the direction amateurish
and incompetent. One clause of his contract stipulated that there
should be no substantial changes to the script. In fact there were
changes every day.[3]

After he had suffered two weeks of this he travelled east to knock
Filumena into shape after Zeffirelli had left. He saw the play through
its Boston run and its New York opening, in early February 1980,
and then appeared as a witness in a pre-trial hearing in the United
States Court of Claims, in New York. He and the two counsel who
questioned him had a wonderful time. He gave a splendid performance and happily took the opportunity to review much of his career.
If there had been an Oscar for best witness he would have won it.

How he came to be giving evidence in that case needs some explanation. Broadly, Olivier's business affairs had been managed from
1946 to 1972 by Laurence Olivier Productions. From 1969 these
affairs were largely managed by a company called Wheelshare, a
name chosen by Olivier himself as an agricultural play on the word
Plowright, a mixture of ploughshare and wheelwright.[4] His English
film contracts were made on his behalf by that company. When he
started to play cameo parts in Hollywood films a new company was
set up for tax reasons, known as S & L Entertainment, whose head
office was in Geneva. It was that company which had contracted
to provide his services to the producers of *Inchon*, and the fees had
been payable to a Dutch bank in Rotterdam. This was done to
minimise the taxes due, so far as the law allowed. The American
Internal Revenue Service demanded certain sums from S & L, and
that company then brought an action against the United States of
America, seeking a reduction in the amount demanded. Olivier was
not a party to the action but was called as a witness to explain
what the company did for him and what he did for the company.
He responded to questions asked by counsel for the US Department
of Justice and for S & L.[5]

He started by explaining with some vigour why he found himself
in New York. His wife was acting in *Filumena*. He said he had been
beguiled into taking on the direction of the play because Zeffirelli
– extremely eminent director, infinitely much respected director –

had let the play go hang after three weeks' rehearsal and had gone off to Rio for Christmas and the New Year.

He was then formally asked in what capacity he was employed by S & L.

'I am a jobbing actor. I get employed. If they choose to hire me to MGM they do it, and I answer the call.'

He said he had done *The Betsy, The Boys From Brazil, A Little Romance,* and *Inchon* for S & L. He made no bones that he had relished *The Betsy:* 'It was just the sort of part I really love, thoroughly brash, vulgar, hideously rude, horrible, sexy, dirty old man. I loved it.'

Counsel then said he looked forward to seeing *The Jazz Singer.*

'I think I can safely say, you would be wise to skip it. . . . The script has been entirely rehashed scene by scene by scene by scene . . . One of the reasons I am so acutely unhappy is that my great almighty age is paid no respect at all. I am called at 8.30 every morning. I never work before 4.30. But they have a right to do that. They can look at me if I complain and say, "You're paid, aren't you?" . . . But it is good to get commercially more viable and occasionally I have done something for that reason. My agent and I both agree, say, "That will be a hit," and it never hurts to be in a hit.'

So what had he baulked at in *The Jazz Singer?* 'I think I will be going a bit far in a commercial, rather cheap commercial, sense. . . I took it on and I wish to God I hadn't. I am regretting it very bitterly now, but it is so awful, it makes me feel sick; never felt like that about my work as long as I can remember.'

So his objection was to the purported artistic quality of the film? 'It prompted me to say at the time, "Larry, this is about the last of this sort of shit, excuse me, you should take part in.'

But he had still agreed to do it? 'It is not worth making a stink about, not worth getting so rebellious about that I am going to stamp my foot and cause a tantrum.'

And it had offered front-money of a million dollars? 'I thought it might with the priceless name of Neil Diamond. I think that should be all right. I think it will make anyone with any artistic pretensions feel physically ill, but I think that there are too many people that aren't like that to worry too much about them for just this once. But it has been a pretty horrific job.'

After he had made it clear that he owned no stock in S & L, and had no financial interest in it except his fees, he was asked about the companies he had previously run himself. 'I used to present plays. They used to be billed under the title "Laurence Olivier Presents". That wouldn't be on the cards now, I don't think. Don't mind a bit because I lost a fortune being a manager and having my own theatre in London. I ran it for eight years. I think I lost £65,000 which hurt like anything. . . I have tried to make money all my life because I believe that is in the nature of my business and a highly interesting part of my business it is to me. I am an artist and a dreamer and all that, but I also rather occasionally fancy myself as a businessman, usually disastrously, but it interests me all the same.'

When he came to describe his time at Chichester he was more candid about it than he had been before: 'I would use my National Theatre company, spare members of it, by pushing them down to Chichester for twelve or sixteen weeks every year. . . And that worked very well. I tried out three new productions in case I needed them at the National Theatre. I could pull them into the National. It was a very terribly convenient arrangement, shamefully convenient. I should say it was all right, and a good time was had by all.'

What, counsel wanted to know, was the National Theatre? 'It is the result of many years, in fact since 1824, of various separate and divided efforts to bring about the existence of a theatre to be known as the National Theatre of Great Britain. Possibly they wished it to be modelled according to various fashions of the times, possibly first of all on Molière's company, possibly they wished it to be modelled on Stanislavski's company, whatever it was.' Lord Chandos, and almost anyone who had ever been in the National Theatre company, would have been surprised at those comparisons.

Counsel then established what Olivier's salary had been as director and was evidently astonished. He replied: 'You may question how I was able to live for £5,000 a year in England and have three children and all that. The answer was that I was allowed to do enough parts in films, you could call them bit parts, you could call them small parts, you could call them cameo roles, whatever you fancy. . .'

Then he came to *Sleuth*, the film he had done with Michael Caine in 1972, which had been his first leading part in a feature film for eight years and his first real attempt to get back into films. He said he had got on wonderfully well with his co-star, Michael Caine, of whom he was deeply fond, but had been disappointed by what had not happened afterwards. He had expected all sorts of film offers to come along, but to his chagrin nothing much happened. 'Without bringing out my violin too obviously, if I could, there were times . . .when it wasn't sufficient that I was able to earn, and I did indeed sell two or three bits of property, pictures, sort of things. I had a very nice Purdey shotgun. . . I had to sell that. This is all to pay school bills really, and I needed some help with that.' Asked about his dermatomyositis he said, 'I remember being quite certain at one time in my illness that I was not going to recover.' He had not admitted that before, either.

Was he still taking any medication? 'Christ, yes. I am taking a pharmacy every day, morning and evening.'

Asked about the parts open to an actor of his age, he explained how things worked: 'When you are thirty five you can play Romeo, or King Lear, if you have a mind to. As you get beyond thirty five, the parts thin out. Naturally, because you can no longer get away with being twenty eight or twenty seven. . . You can't be thirty five if you are forty five, and you can't be forty after you're fifty. You have to finally – the years pull together so that finally, if you are seventy two, seventy two is the age of the role you play.'

Counsel found it difficult to believe that there were not always roles for Sir Laurence Olivier. He put them straight: 'Nobody is going to pretend that I am younger than I am. Apart from anything else, it is in the papers all the damn time, every time I have a birthday.'

He had given evidence for two and a half hours. Counsel had offered him a break, but he declined. At the end counsel remarked that he had difficulty getting up.

'Yes.'

And running?

'I can't run a step without falling.'

Witness and counsel evidently enjoyed the show. As Olivier frankly said, the money he earned through S & L had been heaven-sent. And he cheerfully told his two questioners, 'So far, I feel very fortunate compared to several other people of my age. I am very, very fortunate. So far. I don't know how long I can look to be fortunate. . . The worst thing that can happen to them [S & L] is that they should go bankrupt, so once more I would be shuffled on to the beach and be the subject of every wind that blows.'

He was not exactly on the beach, nor would he be, but nor was he as rich as fees of a million dollars might suggest. Ten per cent would go to his agent. Then there were the running costs of the companies which sold his services. He did, through them, avoid paying the top rate of British income tax, which was then eighty-three per cent. In the year up to April 1980 he earned £178,000, with £80,000 of that due in tax, and in the following year £98,000, of which £44,000 was payable in tax.[6]

After his matinée performance in the United States Court of Claims Olivier returned to Hollywood, where *The Jazz Singer* continued on its incompetent way, being virtually reshot. This was tedious for him but profitable, since he earned overage for each extra day and continued to receive $2,500 a week in expenses. As to *Filumena*, Richardson was proved right in his fear that some plays would not transfer, and it closed after six weeks in New York.

Back in Europe Olivier completed the filming of Granada's *Brideshead Revisited*, an eleven-part television miniseries based on Evelyn Waugh's novel. This was later shown on American public television and all over the world. His performance as the Marquess of Marchmain became one of the most widely known that he ever gave and it won him an Emmy. His famous death scenes had been shot in England in late 1979, before he began *The Jazz Singer*. The earlier scenes, of the younger marquess with his mistress in a Venetian palazzo, were filmed in April 1980. His diary for the last days of that month records:

24.   Fly Venice – Brideshead. Up 5 o'c. Car 10.45 Lv 13.55 Ar
      17.00 Hotel Cipriani (No sleep)
25.   Lord Marchmain scenes. Bad day. Good sleep.
26.   Better day.
27.   Lord M. FIN Brideshead.

He then met David Niven in the south of France and had expected to go on to Nice, Cap Ferrat and Paris, but all this had to be cancelled. As he wrote in his diary: '1 May. Infected bladder. Bed. Sleep. Home'.[7]

There is no sign in the Venetian scenes, in which Olivier plays a vigorous man of fifty-something, that he was in so bad a state.

In February 1982 he was given the greatest honour of his career, being made a member of the Order of Merit. This is a distinction which brings no title with it. The holder may simply place the letters O.M. after his name, but it is an honour in the gift of the sovereign, not a piece of political preferment, and no more than twenty-four persons may hold it at any one time. It is worth a dozen life peerages. By the time Olivier was made a life baron in 1970 peerages were already devalued. Superannuated trade union leaders were ennobled as a party political reward, and so were members of the House of Commons whose only remaining use to the government was that when they were made lords they had to resign from the Commons, thus vacating a seat to which a useful placeman could be elected. The Order of Merit was established by Edward VII in 1902 and was given to the most prominent soldiers, sailors, prime ministers, scientists and writers. No actor had ever been made an O.M. When Olivier was so made he joined a select lot which had included Florence Nightingale, Thomas Hardy, and Winston Churchill. Here is the draft of his letter of thanks to the Queen:

'(It says in my book of etiquette) Madam (or) May it please Your Majesty,
It is an honour that I never dreamed of and I think, without doubt, it means more to me than anything else in my life. . .
Madam (or Your Majesty), I am still thrilled beyond words, and will, I think, always be and although I get addressed in several strange fashions – Sir Olivier, Lord Laurence, that sort of thing – I do not mind at all so long as they add O.M. after it. . .
Heaps of love (or I have the honour to remain, Madam, Your Majesty's most humble and obedient subject).'[8]

The faithful Jill, herself ill but not so gravely as her ex-husband, wrote saying she was so very happy and proud for him.[9]

The sign of the Order is a simple red and blue enamel cross bearing the inscription 'For Merit', which he received from the Queen. At a cost of £110 he bought from Spink the jewellers the blue and crimson evening ribbon of the Order to hang round his neck, together with miniatures of his 1939–45 service medal, the Danish Order of the Dannebrog, the medal of an Officer of the French Légion d'Honneur and that of the Italian Ordine al Merito della Repubblica, all mounted on one brooch. Spink was unable to supply the order of the Yugoslav flag with a golden wreath to go with the rest. It was not made.[10]

33

That Damned Book

WHEN IN OCTOBER 1979 Olivier told Rex Reed that he had nothing to leave his children but the money he made in films, he did add this: 'I might also write my autobiography when I'm too lame to walk into a film set. Nine books have been written about me and there's not a word of truth in any of them. . . The real book is the only thing I've got left.'[1] Nine books *had* been written, if those are counted which were really about Vivien Leigh but which of course contained some account of his life. He had been particularly irritated by Anne Edwards' *Vivien Leigh*, published in 1977. She had talked to many of Vivien's friends, to Tarquin Olivier, and to John Merivale; she had not, as the publisher's blurb claimed, been given 'total access to Miss Leigh's personal letters' or anything like it, but she had seen some letters to friends, though none to Olivier. She was, however, the first to reveal publicly that Vivien had been a manic depressive. Books had been written about Olivier as an actor and Olivier as a film star, but there had been only three full biographies. The first, in 1948, was by his sister Sybille, which he had suppressed as too revealing. The second, a joint biography of him and Vivien Leigh by Felix Barker, published in 1953, had been arranged with Olivier and has details of the pre-war years which are found nowhere else, but it had been tactfully written so as not to offend him. A third biography, by John Cottrell, published in 1975, he quite liked. At any rate he took no offence at it. It was as good a biography as could have been written without his help and without any of his papers. Then there were two books about him which he could not stand. One was an apparently innocuous collection of brief reminiscences of him by thirty men and women in the theatre – Alec Guinness, Michael Redgrave, Merle Oberon, and William Gaskill among them – which so irritated him that he threw the book across the room. Gaskill, in his piece, did agree with Osborne that Olivier had been desperate not to be thought old hat, and called the National Theatre under him a 'spurious ensemble', but most of the other contributions are anodyne. Olivier's real objection seemed to be that the book was edited by Logan Gourlay, a columnist for the *Daily Express*, a man whose business it had been for years to report the sad personal details of his collapsing partnership with Vivien. The book Olivier most hated was *Cry God for Larry*, published in 1969 by Virginia Fairweather. She was his press representative at Chichester and briefly at the National, and had seen herself as a close friend. They fell out, he dismissed her, and she wrote a short memoir which is good on his days at Chichester but angered him with its account of his and Joan's domestic life at Brighton.[2]

Publishers and agents had been after him for his life story for years. In 1950 Bertha Klausner, a New York agent, wrote to him brashly saying 'Money talks', that John Barrymore had got $50,000 for his memoirs, and that she had agented books for Jack Dempsey, the world heavyweight champion, and for Theda Bara. Olivier declined. In 1957 he received a proposal from a London agent who had done a book for Douglas Fairbanks. 'Sorry,' he replied. 'It takes an enormous amount of blood, tears and sweat. . .and it's just like living one's life again.' In 1959 Little, Brown of Boston wrote saying it was the oldest publishing house in the United States and made the surprising proposal to buy world rights for £20,000, an offer no one in his right mind would have accepted. The editor said he had discussed this with Moura Budberg, a Russian countess who was an acquaintance and hanger-on of Olivier's, who begged him not to let her down. 'Inconceivable', he told Little, Brown. Early in 1979 the *Punch* critic Sheridan Morley, son of Robert Morley, proposed a biography but withdrew when Olivier told him he was hostile to the idea.[3]

Then there was Tynan. In 1975 he had gone to live in California, where he wrote long profiles of Ralph Richardson and Tom Stoppard for *The New Yorker* and contracted to write another on Olivier. Late in 1978 he wrote to Olivier that he had been slowed down by the lung disease, emphysema, with which he had been diagnosed, and that the piece was turning out to be longer than he had expected. 'So long, in fact, that I intend to publish it – in expanded form, of course – as a book when *The New Yorker* have finished with it. There's nothing I'd rather write, and although it won't be the authorised biography or anything as impressive as that, it might be a nice little monument.'[4] Olivier did not reply, but in January 1979 Tynan nevertheless signed a contract with Simon and Schuster of New York for the biography, receiving $60,000 on signature and another $30,000 for research.[5] There would be another $60,000 on completion and another $60,000 on publication. That April, when Olivier was in Los Angeles to receive his Oscar for a lifetime's achievement, Tynan wrote to him saying that the book he had in mind would be 'a belated act of thanksgiving'. He said a fellow critic, whom he did not name, had told him that Tynan writing on Olivier sounded like a literary marriage made in heaven. He wrote that he knew Olivier looked back with something less than rapture on the ten years at the National, but for him (Tynan) they had been a golden time and he would always be proud of whatever small contribution he might have made to their success. His health had not been exactly radiant, he doubted if he had the stamina left for more than one full-length book, and he had been thrilled when his publishers agreed that Olivier would be the ideal subject for it. He said newspaper reports of the amount paid to him had been much exaggerated; it was in any case payable over five years, and if he did not complete the book or died he or his wife Kathleen would have to repay the entire advance. He asked if he could meet Olivier.[6]

On the day he received this letter, Olivier telephoned Tynan to say he would not co-operate with him in any way, and would recommend his friends not to talk to him. Tynan wrote to Joan Plowright asking her to intercede. He said it was shattering news, that the consequences for him could be highly damaging, that Olivier had given the profile his full blessing and could not have been more helpful, but that he was now faced with 'this sudden and chilling change of heart'. He ended: 'I am writing to you, an old friend, for advice. I gave Larry ten years of my life. What else do I have to do to make him trust me?' Joan does not remember whether she replied.[7]

Olivier no longer trusted Tynan. He did not want Tynan's little monument. He would prefer to write his own. As he told Gore Vidal, 'I owe Ken a lot, but I don't owe him my life.' Sarah Miles, who saw them together, says they had a bitter row over the biography and that Olivier thought Tynan had been 'viciously disloyal' to him.[8]

Tynan struggled and disingenuously protested to Olivier that when he had received no reply to his suggestion of a book he had taken silence for consent. He could not imagine why Olivier seemed to be so anxious to 'avoid being perpetuated in print by a colleague who has written about [him] with greater admiration than any living critic'.[9] Soon afterwards John Cottrell, who had already published his own biography, wrote on the letterhead of Time-Life Books proposing to Olivier that he should write an autobiography in 'at least three volumes', which would be tasteful, distinguished, not gossipy, and 'designed as major literature'. Olivier replied that the Tynan work was 'still waffling in the melting pot of altercation', and that he did not want to write an autobiography.[10] In fact Tynan had been obliged to return the advances he had received and Olivier, as Joan recalls, was already set on writing his own book. It is now the opinion of Tynan's editor at Simon and Schuster, Michael Korda, that a Tynan biography of Olivier would have been fascinating, but would not have contained a word of truth.[11]

That October Dorothy Tutin wrote to Olivier proposing a ghost writer to him, and encouraging him to get down to work. 'It would be generous and helpful,' she wrote. 'Your thoughts and experiences, like ancestry it passes on and then we are not bereft.'[12] The following month he signed a contract with George [later Lord] Weidenfeld of Weidenfeld & Nicolson. Weidenfeld, who proposed the idea to Olivier over dinner, saw the work as a sort of cultural history which would do for the theatre what Kenneth Clark's television series, *Civilisation*, had done for the fine arts. He said he would be honoured to be publish it. Olivier had from the beginning, when he first conceived of the book in the Sussex County Hospital in 1974, determined that the title would be *Confessions of An Actor*, and he stuck to it.[13] Olivier's agent assured him that Weidenfeld wanted him to feel free of any pressure and to write as much or as little as felt inclined. He would receive £100,000 for the British rights, and ninety per cent of all foreign advances negotiated by Weidenfeld.[14]

Hamish Hamilton, when he heard that Olivier had signed with Weidenfeld, felt betrayed and wrote him an anguished letter: 'That it should come to this, after forty years of friendship.' He pointed out, fairly enough, that he had understood that if Olivier should write his life story he should be the publisher; he asked to be allowed to match Weidenfeld's offer; and said that otherwise it would be the worst blow he had suffered in half a century of publishing.[15]

Olivier did not relent. He had certainly asked Hamilton to publish the book when he first thought of it in 1974, but he was now committed to Weidenfeld. It only remained to write the book. Weidenfeld provided a ghost, and an uncommonly good one. Mark Amory had edited the letters of Evelyn Waugh, and later became literary editor of the *Spectator*. At first they met at Olivier's house in Chelsea and then at the Malthouse, Olivier's country cottage in Sussex. Amory would stay the weekend. Olivier would cook sausages for breakfast, and then they got down to work. 'It was very agreeable,' says Amory. 'He was professional. This was work. He worked hard. He was friendly, but demanding.' Olivier talked and Amory taped their conversations. At first he talked about the eighteenth and nineteenth centuries, about Garrick, Kean, and Irving. Amory found Joan Plowright kind and reassuring. 'You mean,' she said, 'that your problem is you can't get Larry to talk about himself? I don't think you need worry.' He did eventually talk about himself, at great length and revealingly. He said one strange thing about his mother which ran clean counter to anything he had said before. She had died when he was twelve, and that, he said, was very bad. But to Amory he added this: 'I often say, perhaps it has become a thing I say rather now, but I think I believed it at one time and sometimes still, that I've really never got over it. But that's a bit of theatrical nonsense. Well, I think I've been looking for her ever since. . .for absolutely pure love.'[16] It was theatrical nonsense that he had never got over it, but it was still pure love. This was a typical Olivier equivocation. And when he was telling a story he recreated the mood. 'Talking of unhappy years with a former wife,' said Amory, 'most people would be deliberately detached, perhaps even humorous – he seemed to relive the moment. Recalling a stormy board meeting at the National he crashed his fist down upon the table and fixed me with such a glare that I could not meet his eyes.'

During these conversations with Amory, Olivier was proud of his control of the pharmacy of pills he took. As Amory recalls, 'He'd say, "You must forgive me this morning if I'm a little deaf, because I've taken three of the pink ones and one green one." He took a mass, and he knew exactly the effects. Once he talked gibberish, non-words. But he'd warned me, otherwise it would have been extremely frightening. He seemed to have lost control and he couldn't say words. So I just waited until all was well.' He could also be mischievous. Amory asked him about his great rivals, who surely had to be Gielgud and Richardson, but he insisted they were Robert Donat and someone else Amory had never heard of. At that time he sometimes called Joan 'Vivien' and must have realised it, because he told Amory that if you married more than once it was a *great* mistake to call one wife by another's name. In all they taped fifty-seven hours. Amory was thinking he could begin the writing, but then Olivier went off to Ischia taking a typewriter with him. When he returned he was determined to write the book himself. 'And he did,' says Amory. 'They're all his words.' Nothing from the tapes was used in the book.

Given the state of Olivier's fingers, which were still tender, it seems at first impossible that he typed his own script. Furthermore, those closest to him could not remember ever having seen him type. But just over two hundred closely typed pages, about 60,000 words, still exist, and there appear to have been more. They are very badly typed, full of errors, with crossings-out, with commas and hyphens at the beginnings of lines, and with amendments in his hand. These pages are undoubtedly his original script. Joan later remembered that he had once typed a letter to her, and had invited her to look and see that with his new toy he could change the words to red if he liked. And a letter to his sister-in-law, Hester, mentions that while he was filming *Spartacus* in 1959 he was trying to learn to type. This first typescript contains passages which were later excised, by Olivier or by Weidenfeld's editors – for instance his description of his brother Dickie's coffin bouncing about on the waters of the Solent, and his rejection of Vivien later that night at Notley when she burst in on him wanting to be made love to.[17] That he should have typed anything with his fingers, let alone a script of that length, is another example of the sheer will of the man.

When he returned from Ischia Amory stayed with him, no longer expecting to ghost the book but reminding Olivier that he ought to say something about *Hamlet*, and trying to protect him from his excesses. He considered that Olivier's idea of good writing was a sub-Churchillian prose and tried to get him to modify expressions like 'preciously valuable'. He suggested that the account of Olivier's first marriage to Jill should be softened and that details of Vivien's death throes should be omitted, but Olivier pleased himself. He continued to write about Jill that, though she was not dazzlingly attractive, he wasn't going to wait for anyone better to come along, and he left in his dismal account of their fumbling wedding night.

He persistently referred to his autobiography as 'that damned book'. He wrote to his childhood friend Fabia Drake that, apart from his being no Thomas Hardy, and apart from getting stuck for a word or a phrase, his 'most anguishing difficulty' was that of faithfully telling a story which contained the most painful parts of his life.[18] He meant the 1950s, which, as he told Weidenfeld, had been a dreadful decade. He twice missed deadlines. When Peter Hall asked him up to London he declined, not only because of his aversion from anything to do with the National but also, he said, because he was locked in his cottage with his nose to the grindstone and found that, what with a haircut, a show, and a drink with someone, 'the damned visit pretty well demolishes two days'.[19]

The typescript was at last submitted in April 1981. Weidenfeld had it cut by 50,000 words and rewritten, as he said, to improve its punctuation, grammar, pace, and interest. 'I hope,' he wrote, 'that

you will agree that we have done nothing to impair your style and
that your authentic voice comes across. The process may be compared
to editing a film or tightening up a play during rehearsal.' He and
his colleagues felt that the edited version was 'comparable to
[Olivier's] many great achievements on the stage'.[20] He did not
know Olivier. Nothing could have been more calculated to arouse
his rage. He wrote a long reply condemning the 'woeful mess'
Weidenfeld had made of his book and said: 'I will simply say that
I am not willing that this. . .should be published over my name.
Your editors are clearly anti-pathetic to me, my life, my career, and
story.' He would re-edit it himself, in effect restore it, with the help
of Mark Amory and that, he said, would be Weidenfeld's only hope
of publishing it that year.[21]

Weidenfeld made a soothing reply, which brought another letter
from Olivier: 'I felt hurt by the opprobrium to my writing suggested
by what I can only describe as the dis-limbing of my efforts.
Whatever criticism my writing may deserve, it is at least mine, and
comes straight from my mind and heart.' He objected to Weidenfeld's
request to eliminate tautology, saying that many poets, Shakespeare
specially, had found that device useful and practical. He defended
his split infinitives by saying Churchill had made a powerful plea
for the emphasis they could impart. He hoped that his version would
now be acceptable.[22]

He worked on it for another three weeks and then on 19 May
1981 wrote in his diary: FIN THAT BOOK. The resulting version was
Olivier's own, though still somewhat cut. His chronology is all over
the place. At one point he writes that the Old Vic's 1945 tour to
Antwerp, Hamburg, and Paris had taken place after an arduous tour
of *Titus Andronicus* behind the Iron Curtain, in Belgrade, Zagreb,
and Warsaw, but that tour of *Titus* was with the Stratford company
and took place twelve years later. He recalls having received the
Order of Merit at the time of his dermatomyositis, seven years
before he did. As a book of reference his memoirs are a trap, but
they are eloquent and in his own unmistakable voice, no more so
than at the end when he begs forgiveness: 'For these and for all my
other sins, which I cannot now remember, I firmly purpose amend-
ment of life and humbly ask pardon of God and of you, Reader,

counsel, penance, and absolution.' The book was, as he had promised in the title, the confessions of an actor.[23]

Weidenfeld had sold the American rights to Simon and Schuster,
the same publishers who had commissioned Tynan's proposed biography, and it was handled by the same editor, Michael Korda. When
he saw the typescript he thought Olivier wrote with the grandilo-
quence of someone who had learned English by reading Churchill's
war memoirs. He sent a list of 105 suggestions for changes. Surely,
he wrote, there was too much about Hochhuth's *Soldiers*. In the
margin Olivier scribbled, 'Disagree'. And Korda felt that Olivier's
dispute with Chandos, which was dealt with in an appendix of letters
quoted verbatim, should be retold as narrative, 'Violently disagree'
wrote Olivier.[24] Korda continued to make suggestions and Olivier
continued to ignore them. Now Michael Korda, who was Alex Korda's
nephew, had known Olivier and met him on his uncle's yacht in the
late 1940s and early 1950s. He had known Vivien much better. They
had gone swimming together off his uncle's yacht, he had taken her
to the movies in Nice, picnicked with her on the islands in the bay
of Cannes, driven her to Monte Carlo to go shopping, and been
enchanted with her ribald sense of humour. She was often alone.
Olivier would cable her saying he would join her on the yacht in
Portofino, then that he would not, then that he hoped to meet her
in Capri, and she would receive the cables eagerly and then in her
disappointment tear the flimsy blue forms into little pieces and throw
them over the side like confetti. He saw them both as gifted, beguiling,
manipulative myth-makers, joined in a myth-making marriage.[25]

About the memoirs he thought that the more you read them the
less they seemed to say, and that this was no doubt Olivier's intention. Seldom, he felt, had a book of memoirs mirrored so exactly
the author's mind. Like Amory, he did not see the purpose of Olivier's
statements that he had suffered from premature ejaculation, or his
insistence that Vivien had often been disappointed by his 'intimate
passionate endeavours' because all *that* had gone into his acting –
and it does have to be said that there is nothing in Olivier's explicit
letters of 1938 and 1939 to Vivien to show that there was much
substance to these confessions.[26] In 1982, with the typescript in
front of him, Korda offered to go to England to meet Olivier, who

declined to receive him. Eventually a meeting was agreed in New York. Olivier insisted on being given dinner in a back room at Gallagher's, a theatre restaurant off Broadway, a steak-bar kind of Sardi's with sawdust on the floor. Korda didn't know it still existed. Olivier, looking small and frail, turned up more than an hour late, protesting he had forgotten the name of the restaurant he had chosen himself and pretending he didn't know the customs of this strange country called America, though he had lived there on and off for years. He gave what struck Korda as a splendid performance of the great actor as a doddering old man. He ordered a cocktail, affected to have forgotten the name of that too, and described what went into it and how it was made until the waiter said, 'Ah, a whiskey sour'. Then he said, 'Vivien and I used to come here often, whenever we were in New York. She always had a whiskey sour. We always sat in this room, perhaps at this very table.' He said he hadn't been there since the war. It became clear to Korda why he had chosen Gallagher's.

Olivier ordered an enormous meal of salad, steak, home fries *and* a baked potato, and then played with it. It appeared this was what Vivien usually ordered, and it came back to Korda that for all her slender figure she had always had a hearty appetite, rather like Scarlett O'Hara, and that he had many times seen her put away huge meals. Olivier then ordered what she apparently used to have, three scoops of vanilla ice cream, covered with crème de menthe, which he did not touch but stared at as they melted.

Korda, making conversation, brought up the film of *Richard III*, at which Olivier began to speak the opening lines – 'Now is the winter of our discontent. . .' – and *became* Richard. The waiters stood still. The other diners put their knives and forks down and listened. A few people applauded timidly; Olivier bowed his head in thanks and ordered an Irish coffee, which he did not touch either. Korda found that he could not, in that place with its memories, raise the question of the stain on the carpet after Vivien's death. He had placed on the table, next to the ruins of the crème de menthe sundae, an envelope full of notes and suggestions. Olivier put it unopened in his pocket and declined to make changes, saying that if Simon and Schuster didn't want to publish the book as it stood, perhaps someone else would. He waved a thin hand at the other diners, as if giving them a blessing. Korda never heard from him again and the book was published unchanged.

When it appeared the *New York Times* said it did not belong with the stories of Lana Turner, Lauren Bacall, and Henry Fonda; once again, Olivier was in another ball park. Tarquin Olivier, offended particularly by the slighting references to his mother, said his father appeared to have written in a blind and bitter rage.[27] *Confessions of an Actor* made Olivier about £320,000, and it does indeed mirror his mind, which is a high achievement in any autobiography.[28]

34

No Longer on an Even Keel

THERE REMAINED ONE MORE million-dollar film. For that million, a car and chauffeur, and five per cent of the profits, Olivier was to film in England for six weeks in a cold-war thriller called *The Jigsaw Man*. He played the head of the British Secret Service. Michael Caine, whom he greatly liked, played an English spy who had defected to the Russians. The film was directed by Terence Young, who had done *Inchon*, and this production also ran into trouble. Olivier collapsed on set. The producers ran out of money, one of their cheques bounced, and in April 1981 filming was postponed.[1]

Olivier had just finished his book, had won his battles with Weidenfeld, and was living for the most part in Sussex, solaced by his garden and his planting. He had some time before – in spite of a warning from the Royal Botanical Gardens at Kew that it was rare and the most sought after tree in the world – succeeded in his search for a specimen of *Acer platanoides maculatum*, the Norway spruce. This bore yellow flowers in the spring. It also happened to be the tree Vivien had set her heart on, single-mindedly pursued, and eventually planted at Notley more than thirty years before. That spring of 1981 he ordered Italian cypress and medlars, and madwort, aubretia, and other rock plants.[2] Joan stayed more often in London. She had been in a succession of long-running plays. *Saturday, Sunday, Monday, Filumena*, and Ben Travers' *The Bed Before Yesterday* all ran for more than a year. She was working more than Olivier. He was ill and distressed and at times became mournful, saying she would be better off if he were dead. They were, she said, no longer on an even keel.[3] He sometimes spoke with a cruel irony. When he was told Tynan had died from his emphysema he said, 'Well, he was no more use to me'. 'It was quite funny,' says Joan, 'in a cruel way. He could be quite dreadfully honest, a candour that was quite terrible, and he was capable of it.'[4]

Things were uneasy between Olivier and Joan. They had drifted apart and some of the trouble was professional. Joan had always been an actress in her own right. When she was about to open in a new play by Alan Bennett, and an interviewer from *The Times* suggested that some of the roles she had played at the National had been more suitable for Lady Olivier than for Joan Plowright, she replied: 'I've never understood who I was supposed to be as Lady Olivier. She is a fictional creature born aged about thirty with all her hair and teeth already in place, whereas I grew up knowing who Joan Plowright was. Being Lady Olivier can't alter any of that; it can't change the way you look, nor the way you think.' She said she had come to like West End runs where there were no rehearsals and she could see more of her two younger children who were still at home, but that she might go back to the National if the parts were right.[5]

A part came along at the National which was right: that of Martha in Albee's *Who's Afraid of Virginia Woolf.* But Olivier was furious that she should act at Peter Hall's National, unless he directed. She knew he was too frail to do this. He said it would be grounds for divorce if she went ahead. She did go ahead. He was for the moment busy with preparations to play John Mortimer's blind father in a television production of his play, *A Voyage Around My Father*, and she thought he had forgotten. He had not. One morning, as both of them were leaving for rehearsals, she received a letter from his solicitor. He wrote that, over lunch, Larry had given him brief details of their unhappy conversations at the weekend. He would like to help if he could. If there was a real difficulty between them which was unlikely to be reconciled, then she would need her own legal advice. Would she let him know? That evening she was angry and received her husband coldly, telling him she would reply to the letter. 'What letter?' he asked. He had forgotten it. Two days later she received a second letter telling her the first was to be ignored and forgotten.[6] Olivier was distraught, telling her once again that she would be better off without him, but his very remorse, together with the strain of the rehearsals, told on her. She opened her play on tour in Bath. At dinner with Albee after the first night she received a telephone call from Olivier asking how one should best commit suicide, head in the gas oven or the river with stones in one's pockets? Albee asked her what had become of her *joie de vivre*. Her voice gave way. She came out of the play and went to stay with Tony Richardson at his villa in St Tropez with Julie-Kate and with Richard, who was on vacation from UCLA. She did not appear in the London production and the reason given was a throat infection. Margaret Tyzack took over the part. Olivier took not Joan but his daughter Tamsin to that year's *Evening Standard* awards ceremony, at which it was announced that Miss Tyzack had won the best actress award for the part Joan had left.[7] Afterwards he wrote his wife a remorseful letter:

'My darling, wonderful girl, There is nothing to say, except that I am sorry, sorry beyond words and deeply beyond any kind of measure. . . A wound as deep as that I have inflicted upon you, my darling love, cannot heal – just like that. Health, strength, and trust has to have a reasonable time to mend a heart that has been so mercilessly hacked about. . . I want you to know I love you as deeply as I am repentant. L.[8]

In the meantime he had finished *The Jigsaw Man*. It was his last big film. His accountants, knowing this was likely and reasoning that if he were paid all at once he would spend it, advised Wheelshare to spread the payments to him over five years.[9] They were too cautious. There never was another million dollars but there would be other films, and profitable ones.

He played a small part in a vast, dull, television miniseries on the life of Wagner, whose only glory was its cast. Wagner was Richard Burton. Olivier did not come in until the last episode, but then appeared in one scene with both Ralph Richardson and John Gielgud. It was the first time they had appeared together since the film of *Richard III* in 1955. 'What an unholy three,' said Gielgud.[10]

Joan had another success in the West End, as Madame Ranevskaya in *The Cherry Orchard*. That same year she met Richard Burton again. Elizabeth Taylor had gone, so had her successor, and he was alone. 'We had a glass of wine,' says Joan, 'and after mutual confessions of certain traumatic events in both our lives, he suggested, half-jokingly, that we might set up house together. . . We laughed about what people would say, and I said, also half-jokingly, that for me it would be like jumping out of the frying pan into the fire. Anyway, I told him, I had a commitment for life, however difficult it might be.'[11]

Olivier began to be oppressed by constant requests for autographs, which were more plentiful than in the days of what he called his 'romantic juvenility'. He found it a grim business and wanted to send out a letter to fans saying he could do no more. His secretary said that he was obviously revered round the world and that if he choked people off like that he would only get just as many letters asking if he was ill. She said there was often an hour or two's signing to do, and he got cramp after five minutes. He compromised by sending out a photograph with a printed signature.[12]

He could not sign autographs but he was about to embark on one of the great works of his life. He had played *King Lear* back in 1946 with the Old Vic company, with Alec Guinness as the Fool. He had acted it then without the slightest hint of senility. Since then he had avoided the play. Peter Hall had pursued him to do it often and again but any suggestion of Hall's infallibly ensured that he would not touch it. Now in 1982 he decided to play it for Granada Television. This time there was senility and Olivier knew it. He wondered if he had not become a little like Lear himself. 'Is it now possible that I have placed a part of his clothing upon me? I wear an invisible theatrical crown, which I like, am very attached to and will not give up.'[13] For the first time a man old and frail enough to be Lear played Lear. Dorothy Tutin, previously his loving mistress, played Goneril. Anna Calder-Marshall, who was his Cordelia, thought at the first reading that it had been worth waiting all her life for a moment like that: he was so frail yet spoke with the strength of a lion.[14]

Trying to make things up to Joan he ordered for £267 three British Empire brooches, one for her and one each for Tamsin and Julie-Kate. He considered giving one to Sybille too but then changed his mind. These brooches, in the shape of a pearl-grey cross with the gold effigy of Britannia in the centre, had just been introduced. It was very much a gift to please Joan. He was a peer and a knight bachelor, that is to say a knight attached to no particular order of chivalry. Joan, with her CBE, was a Commander of the British Empire; it was her rank and not his that qualified her, and the women of her family, to wear the brooch.[15]

Olivier was surrounded by reminders of mortality. On the occasion of his seventy-fifth birthday Fabia Drake, the friend and dancing instructress of his youth, wrote recalling the time she had seen him play Romeo in 1935. She could still hear him in the balcony scene, saying 'My dear' to his Juliet, when it had become the most moving line in the play. She told him he had been right to leave Vivien, to save his own life. 'And what you did with it after. It's all been a miracle – and then thumbing your nose at the slings and arrows of outrageous ill health. And now Joan has given you your precious . . . children.'[16] And he received a sad and gallant letter from David Niven, his friend from pre-war Hollywood days and the man who had played a large part in helping him to get Vivien back from Hollywood after her collapse in 1953. Niven, who was making a Pink Panther film in the south of France, wrote saying he was in splendid health except that he had motor neurone disease. He said Olivier's shining example of blazing courage should have inspired him but, alas, he was a gibbering coward. If his injections didn't help, he would ask Olivier to introduce him to his doctor, Joanna [Sheldon], at Brighton.[17]

In 1982 he sat for his last portrait. It was by Emma Sergeant, a young student at the Slade School of Art. She had won a competition, and part of the prize was a commission from the National Portrait Gallery to paint such a portrait. Olivier gave her two sittings. The first lasted almost two hours. He walked painfully up the stairs to her Kensington studio. It was her first professional portrait. He saw she was nervous and relaxed her with talk about Vivien Leigh and Ralph Richardson, but he also saw when she needed to concentrate and at those moments held his silence. She had a sense that he was unwrapping her and directing her: 'I could see he could be hypnotic. There was a coldness and a ruthlessness about the way he measured you, but he was the most excellent company. The power. The energy. If he had wanted anything from you he could have got it.' Yet she also sensed a vulnerability to women. He told her a typical Olivier tale, that Salvador Dalí, when he had painted the portrait of him as Richard III in the 1950s, had unrolled a sheet of paper, made two little dots on it, and walked away.

At the second sitting with Miss Sergeant he was so exhausted that after half an hour he asked if he could lie down, and lay down on her bed and fell fast asleep. When he woke he looked at her canvas, walked up to it with a deliberately fragile walk, like a winged bird, observed the nose, the eyes, and the mouth, and said, 'If my wife were here to see this she would say you've made me look like the mean bastard that I am.' It is a fine portrait, which catches the strength and frailty of the man.[18]

In April 1983 Olivier was strong enough to fly to New York to receive an award at Lincoln Center, where Douglas Fairbanks described him as 'one hell of an actor'. The next evening he and Joan went to Washington where, after a showing of his television *Lear*, President Reagan gave a small dinner for them at the White House.[19] Back home Olivier earned £100,000 for three days' work as Admiral Hood, playing the president of Captain Bligh's court martial in a remake of *The Bounty*.[20] He sent a message of congratulations to Margaret Thatcher on her victory in the June general election. He must have apologised for worrying her because she thanked him, writing in her own hand: 'We are never worried to a "frazzle" by such kind messages. They cheer us up enormously.' Olivier had always been a natural Tory. Back in 1975, when Sir Keith Joseph, a decent man and one of Thatcher's mentors, had scuppered his own chances of the leadership by unwisely saying in a speech that the balance of the population, 'our human stock', was threatened because a high proportion of children were being born to mothers least fitted to bring them up, Olivier had sent him heart-felt congratulations on his courageous stand, signing himself 'Olivier, Cross Bencher, Lords'.[21] He had in fact never attended the House of Lords again after his maiden speech.

In the summer of 1983 Olivier suffered from pleurisy but recovered enough to go to France to play in an adaptation of John

Fowles' novel, *The Ebony Tower*, where he played an ancient painter happy in a *ménage à trois* with two nubile and frequently naked art students. Then there were more blows. David Niven died, and then Ralph Richardson; he wept at their memorial services. Then he was once again back in St Thomas' hospital for three weeks, this time for the removal of a kidney.[22] He returned to Sussex, but his illness and his increasing absent-mindedness made him seem remote. Adrienne Corri, the actress who had taken some trouble trying to authenticate Olivier's portrait of Garrick, and who also told him she was writing a novel satirising Peter Hall, wrote asking him to spare her five minutes. He wanted to talk about neither Garrick nor Hall and replied through his secretary, asking her to excuse him since he tired easily and felt embarrassed if someone came to see him and he slept throughout the meeting. Even Douglas Fairbanks found him difficult to get hold of and wrote, towards the end of a visit to London, 'Dear Larry, Your equerries and ADCs are making you a male Garbo, and it is difficult to get through to you. As you have been so ill, they are quite right to protect you, but it's frustrating to the likes of me.'[23]

He spent a month's holiday on Ischia. When he returned to Sussex Moira, a health visitor, began to call to start memory treatment. Then in September 1984, against all the odds, he began to shoot his last feature film, *Wild Geese III*. Like his first, *The Temporary Widow*, back in 1929, it was filmed in Berlin. He played the part of Rudolf Hess, Hitler's deputy, serving life imprisonment in Spandau. An old factory was rigged up to look like the jail, with barbed wire and dogs. Olivier, with bushy eyebrows and haggard face, achieved a close likeness to Hess. For six camera days he received $300,000. He flew to Berlin with his secretary, Shirley, and a nurse, Leigh. It was extraordinary that he made the film at all. The terms of the contract made the risk clear. They provided that if Olivier could not complete the part but had done enough to be used in the film he would be paid pro rata. If he could not complete his part and the whole of it had to be shot with another actor he would not be paid at all.[24] Olivier, at the end, was back to the terms of his earliest engagements of the 1920s in tat-repertory – no play, no pay. The producer, of course, still stood to lose if he had to go to the expense of reshooting. Olivier did complete the film, from 22 to 29 September, with two days off for bad weather. 'Shooting Hess' he wrote in his diary. He was at work. Joan had been uneasy that he should continue filming for so long. 'But I couldn't,' she says, 'stop a man who felt work was his life's blood.'[25]

Soon after he had returned to Sussex, when he was no longer at work, his mind turned in upon himself and he made quite another sort of diary entry, in green, with emphasis: 'My Nurse's Name (Asked before.)'[26] It was Leigh, who had been with him in Berlin. He could not remember her name.

35

Uninsurable as God

BUT IN NOVEMBER HE was thinking of yet another film. In his diary he wrote, 'Offered part of "God" in God, Satan & the Devil – Terence Young'. Young was the director of *Inchon* and *The Jigsaw Man*. Six years before, Olivier had played Zeus in *Clash of the Titans*, an MGM extravanganza with a delightful supporting cast of Greek goddesses in Susan Fleetwood, Ursula Andress, Claire Bloom, and Maggie Smith. It was rapidly forgotten, the critics thought deservedly. To attempt a Judaeo-Christian God would be quite another thing, which would however have been congenial to him at the time, for he was again pondering the existence of a God.

He had recently written in *Confessions of an Actor* that after he married Jill, in 1930, he had not pursued his religious practices ever again. But at the funeral of his brother Dickie in 1958 he had described himself, Vivien, Sybille, and Hester as 'believers all'. In the draft of his maiden speech in the House of Lords in 1971 he had first included and then deleted the following passage: 'My Lords, I *think* I believe in God. I *think* I do not believe in an after life. I *think* I sense a glint of outrage among the Rt. Revd. Prelates on my port bow [the bishops] that anyone should have the effron-tery to confess to playing it quite so safe as that.' He certainly believed that acting had a quasi-religious side to it and once, writing to Peter Hall about playing the archbishop in *Becket*, said, 'Spiritual quality upon the stage is so closely related to star quality that it is quite easily grasped by anyone possessing such.' And after his recent operation to remove a kidney his mind had returned to God.[1]

Alec Guinness had gone to see him in hospital four days after the operation, taking a gift of caviare. He had found him sitting up in bed, 'frail and beautiful but as chirpy as could be'. Olivier, knowing Guinness to be a convert to Rome, asked for help in becoming a Catholic. Guinness was cautious, suspecting Olivier thought it was simply a matter of acknowledging the Pope's supremacy, and remembered that he twice said, 'I believe in transubstantiation, you know'.[2] Guinness had a Mass said for Olivier that evening, spent a fortune on candles, and then wrote him a letter suggesting three priests he might see ('no obligation to buy') if he really wished. He named two Jesuits and a friend, Father Sir Hugh Barrett-Lennard at the Brompton Oratory, whom he described as eccentric, wearing filthy clothes and going everywhere on a broken bicycle, but probably a saint. 'I don't,' wrote Guinness, 'believe in proselytising so all I could do would be to give you reassurances or warnings – if need be. You would miss, horribly, the splendour of the Book of Common Prayer. On the other hand, much joy.'[3]

Olivier did not enter the Roman Church and, having made yet another recovery, embarked on a second book, this time not formally an autobiography but to be, as its title suggested, *On Acting*. He did it for the money, £75,000, for the occupation, and because Michael Korda of Simon and Schuster thought it would make a better book than the first. Though his name alone was to appear on the title page he did not this time write a word of it himself. It was the work of Gawn Grainger, a young writer and actor who eleven years before had appeared with him in his last play, *The Party*, and had become a family friend. He felt almost like a son. Once he took Olivier into a pub at Islington, where he lived, and someone said, 'What a lovely man your dad is'.[4]

Grainger went frequently down to Sussex and they swam together, fifty lengths of a forty-foot heated pool every morning. He had transcripts of the many hours of recordings Mark Amory had made for *Confessions* but which had not been used. From these he took Olivier's account of theatrical history, from Burbage to Kean, to Garrick and to Irving. Then he taped his own conversations with Olivier, which were concerned with more recent events. They were amiable talks, as this snatch shows:

LO: It's very nice working with you.

GG: As long as you don't get bored, Larry.

LO: No. I'm talking about myself – what greater pleasure is there in life? Solidly talking about myself. Bored? Are you mad, boy?

[Long pause while drinks are served.]⁵

In December 1984 Shirley Luke, Olivier's secretary, told Grainger the rules of the game. 'You do know that, if anyone asks you how he is, he has a bit of a flu-ey cold at the moment, don't you. . . That is to cover us for the LO awards [formerly the West End Theatre Awards] on Sunday night. If we say he's not well, immediately the world Press has him dying, and if we say he's just fine whoever it is says well why isn't he here? Very difficult.'⁶

As their conversations progressed Olivier confided in Grainger, saying he had driven all his wives mad. He credited Jill with having given him the idea of first doing *Richard III* when he knew nothing about the play himself. But with her in mind he also asked Grainger, 'Have you ever been married to a lesbian?' He recalled how Vivien and he, doing the two *Cleos* in 1951, had been 'sailing, set in the galaxy', and then said, 'We used to fuck three times a day until Peter Finch came along. I'm glad he's dead.' He was enamoured of Joan and adored the children.⁷ He recalled one of the very few occasions on which he had met his uncle Sydney, Governor of Jamaica and Secretary for India. He had come to stay, and Fahv had laid on vintage port and good food. He had a dignified bearing and, with his beard, looked quite Jewish. Olivier remembered this and later found his appearance and demeanour an enormous help in creating his Shylock at the National Theatre. Sydney Olivier and his nephew Laurence had much in common. They were the only two men of uncommon ability in the family. Both lived long – Sydney to the age of eighty-three – but both frequently suffered 'under the weather of old age': that was Sydney's phrase, in a letter to H.G. Wells. George Bernard Shaw knew him well and wrote of him, 'Death has a long struggle with men of his vitality.'⁸ So it was with them both, uncle and nephew. In mid-January 1985 there was bad news. Olivier's secretary, Shirley Luke, took a message and wrote in her diary: 'Mr Evans rang – "God" film off – cannot get insurance. LO told. Another script possibly on its way. LO v. upset.'[9]

Olivier was uninsurable as God and there never was another film script. He had appeared on the stage for the last time as far back as 1973. *Wild Geese*, in 1984, had been his last feature film. In February 1985 he made his last trip to New York, flying on Concorde, lunching at the Algonquin, having dinner with Betty Bacall and buying 'bloomers from Bloomingdales'.[10] So many things were for the last time. In March he made his last working trip to Hollywood, staying at the Beverly Hills Hotel and being guest of honour at a party with Swifty Lazar, Michael Caine, Jacqueline Bisset, and Raquel Welch. He presented the Oscar for best motion picture to *Amadeus*.

Back in Sussex with Grainger he ranged far and wide in his reminiscences, though his memory was fallible. He could not remember whether *Gone With the Wind* was filmed before or after the war. He elaborately invented the shaggy-dog story of Ralph Richardson's attempt to murder him. Speculating that actors in the Greek theatre might have performed naked, he thought that must have been the true test – nothing to cover an actor except his imagination. 'I have done it in front of a mirror – I suppose we all have at some time – and I have seen what I wanted to see beyond the nakedness, the emperor's clothes in reality.' He talked about his fascination with the body, thought all actors should have a copy of Gray's *Anatomy* on their bookshelves, and said that when he had his kidney removed he had asked the doctors if it could be done under a local anaesthetic so that he could watch in a mirror. 'They declined,' he said. 'A pity.' Grainger asked what it was like to know he would end up in Westminster Abbey and he replied, 'The Abbey is as cold as the village churchyard. I don't want to die.'[11]

The state of his health was uncertain from day to day. One day he would be fit enough to travel to Chichester, to the theatre he had opened nearly twenty-five years before, to unveil a bronze plaque commemorating twenty-eight roles he had played. The next he would fall down in the house or slip in the pool. He bled easily and there would be blood all over the place.[12]

The book came to an end and Shirley Luke typed out the prologue as Olivier wanted it. In it he spoke about his dreaded trudge to the typewriter in the morning, his staring at a blank page of paper and his hope that, if he looked the other way, when he turned back the page would by some miracle be full. It was all nonsense. He had typed *Confessions* but had not written a word of *On Acting*. Miss Luke typed his lament and then added, for Gawn Grainger's eyes: 'I typed this about the writing of his book with my teeth clenched . . . However, you and I know, don't we!'[13]

Ross Hutchinson – a cousin who had importuned Olivier since 1938 with proposals for this or that infallibly successful theatrical venture, and who had failed to notice he had not appeared on a stage since 1973 – wrote proposing to him the lead in a musical version of Vanbrugh's *The Relapse*, with two solo numbers which he would do 'superlatively well'.[14] In September Olivier did go to Manchester to play the supporting role of Harry Burrard, a sort of aged Archie Rice, in *Lost Empires*, adapted from the novel by J. B. Priestley. The lost empires were old music halls. It was his last television appearance. Greer Garson wrote from Forked Lightning Ranch in Pecos, New Mexico, saying she had told a university class in Dallas that he knew more by instinct than the rest of them could hope to learn in a lifetime. She still had not forgotten it was he who gave her her first chance in the theatre and signed herself 'Devotedly always, your little invention'.[15] Olivier did attend that year's Olivier awards in London, appearing in a box at the Dominion to huge applause, but did not stay. Gielgud, who received an award, wrote to Olivier marvelling at his 'endless courage and resilience' and praising Joan's performance in *Mrs Warren's Profession* at the National.[16] Joan remembers that at one such awards evening they were in a box when Dennis Quilley and Peter Bowles did a turn from *The Entertainer*. 'The audience applauded and Larry got up and bowed. One had to keep hold of him. If he heard applause he thought he ought to get up and take a bow.'[17]

His friends and colleagues were dying – Simone Signoret, Rock Hudson, Yul Brynner, and Dr Joanna Sheldon, the tall and handsome consultant who had treated him for dermatomyositis. She was fifty-four. She died on New Year's Eve. He went to her funeral on 6 January 1986. Later that month he had more blood tests and the

day after wrote in his diary, in red capitals, TRUTH RE HEALTH
DAWNED. A few days later he wrote AMNESIA.[18]

In his diary he now noted when his nurses changed over, when
Jan was replaced by Ann Marie. His most frequent visitor was
Ginette Spanier, who was at that time living in London. She, who
had once told him she thought of him lovingly as a brother for
whom she would have incestuous feelings, now wrote to him as 'My
poor darling', saying she thought of him constantly and was ready
at a moment's notice to pop into a train and come and see him even
for ten minutes.[19] He went to London himself and took her to lunch
at Wiltons in Jermyn Street. Several times she visited him for lunch.
He went to her again. 'LO out to play with Ginette' wrote Shirley
Luke in her desk diary. He told her to arrange to have Ginette's
kitchen windows double-glazed for her birthday.[20] Joan knew Ginette
was completely at ease and loving with him. She saw that theirs
was the kind of friendship that had nearly but not quite become an
affair, and once it had not, that had passed.[21]

On 1 March he wrote, 'Bed, poorly, tired. . . Joan bed, fighting
off flu. Snow on ground. Jan keeping me company. TV. Barbra
Streisand.' On 13 March he bet on Wayward Lad in the Cheltenham
Gold Cup. The horse came second. On 17 March, St Patrick's Day
and their twenty-fifth wedding anniversary, he gave Joan a pair of
diamond earrings, with this note:

LAURENCE OLIVIER. $. Patrick's Day
                                    1986

Darling .
    Surprise Surprise !
    In loving'st gratitude for so much,
So much , and most dear hopes for
our 26th! and unforgettable memories of
of our three years of rehearsal !

Darling, Surprise Surprise! In lovingest gratitude for so much, so much, and most dear hopes for our 26th! And unforgettable memories of our three years of rehearsal! It's been a long run alright, but you have a very special gift for those. Always your L.'[22]

There was a family gathering at the Malthouse and then they drove to London for a dinner party with, among others, Edna O'Brien, Alan Bates, Claire Bloom and her then husband Philip Roth, Eli Wallach, Ian McKellen, Antonia Fraser, and Harold Pinter, in whose play *The Birthday Party* Joan had just appeared. They feasted on water chestnuts, Russian meatballs, apple charlotte – Olivier's favourite pudding – and champagne.[23]

Olivier was by then living almost entirely at the Malthouse. He rarely went to London. His son Richard, after studying theatre and film at UCLA, was directing in America. Tamsin and Julie-Kate came down to Sussex for family weekends. Both, as children, had seen even less of their father than of their mother, because both parents were so often away working. Both daughters had gone to drama school and on to the stage, in spite of their father's warning – and this was a warning he gave everyone – that ninety-two per cent of actors and actresses were unemployed. Once they made this decision he encouraged them, and wanted Tamsin to play Cordelia to his Lear in the Granada film. Joan thought it would be unwise. Both daughters were close to him, and he would ask, 'Is it Friday? Will they be home tomorrow?' They found him alternately gentle and tempestuous. It is Julie-Kate's recollection, but not Tamsin's, that he would sometimes confuse their names, or call them by the names of his nurses, or even 'Joanie'.[24]

On 1 April Shirley Luke noted that Olivier was whipped off to hospital again, she thought for appendicitis, but that could not have been since his appendix had been removed eighteen years before. That month he made his last, vicarious appearance on a London stage as the all-seeing Akash, when his disembodied voice was heard and his three-dimensional hologram seen in a space-age musical called *Time*, featuring the pop-star Cliff Richard.[25] From the end of April he, Joan, and Jan spent three weeks on holiday in Spain, in a villa near Marbella. He fell and cut his head on the bathroom door. One day they drove forty miles along the winding, precipitous mountain road to Ronda. It was a drive he had made with Vivien thirty years before. The last entry he made in his own hand in that diary is in the middle of the year, for Saturday, 14 June: 'Louise Olivier wedding x Piers Cavendish'. Louise was his niece, the daughter of his brother Dickie and Hester. It was the last diary entry he ever made.[26] Then his diary was quietly removed because he would obsessively ask who was going to be where, and when, note it all down, and sometimes sit absorbed in a study of his entries when one of the family tried to talk to him. Then he made notes on bits of paper.[27]

He had reminded himself, in an entry at the beginning of his 1986 diary, '*My Will.* Must remember.' He had of course made wills before. On the day Vivien left her husband for him in 1937 he had made a handwritten will, enjoining her and Jill to live in friendliness and harmony and quoting *Antony and Cleopatra.* On a chart showing Dickie's burial at sea in 1958 he wrote, 'Please deposit my remains in like place and manner, if it is not too difficult'. In September 1960, while he was living with Joan and three months before his divorce from Vivien, he made a will leaving forty per cent of his estate to Joan, twenty per cent to Vivien, and twenty per cent to Tarquin, together with personal mementos to Ginette Spanier, Dorothy Tutin, John Gielgud, Ralph Richardson and others. In 1967 and 1974 he made other wills, both in a hurry, the first on his way to Heathrow Airport and the second signed on Victoria station.[28] In 1977 he divided his property between Joan, for her lifetime or until her remarriage, and their three children, with nothing to Tarquin. Tarquin protested and in a 1980 will was bequeathed £21,000, plus £9,000 to his children. Olivier changed his will again in November 1985, with specified gifts to Hester, her children, Ginette Spanier, John Gielgud, Peggy Ashcroft, Gawn Grainger and others. Shirley Luke reported to Laurence Harbottle, his solicitor, that he had been uncertain, had looked at the list of those who were to receive gifts and said, 'Well yes, that's fine', 'I don't know about Lady Richardson', and 'Oh, oh, yes', but she said she had not known exactly what he was looking at when he said that.[29]

His last will was made on 18 March 1986. He first asked for his body to be cremated, then crossed that out and substituted 'buried'.

He and Joan had moved to another and bigger house in Chelsea which was in their joint names and would pass to her. The rest was divided among Joan and his three younger children. Joan received the household goods, but pictures or other historic pieces were excluded from this gift and he asked his trustees, after consultation with Joan and Richard, to give 'appropriate' items to public collections. The Harold Knight portrait of him as Romeo should go to the National Theatre, and at least one picture and his collection of Garrick memorabilia to the Garrick Club; the remaining pictures or the proceeds from their sale would then go forty per cent to Joan and sixty per cent to their three children. Tarquin was given £25,000 or one tenth of his estate. Small bequests were made to Hester, her children, Ginette Spanier and to his nurse Jan, and small mementos were to be set aside to be chosen by Laurence Evans and his wife Mary, Peggy Ashcroft, Peter Hiley, Laurence Harbottle and others. John Gielgud was left Olivier's early edition of *Hamlet*, which later could not be found.[30]

In September 1986 there was another disagreement between Olivier and Joan. She and Glenda Jackson appeared together in Lorca's play, *The House of Bernarda Alba*. Trader Faulkner, an acquaintance of Olivier's since the Australian tour of 1948, wrote to Joan saying that a friend of his – who had been the last man to see Lorca alive, in 1936 – had been to her performance and thought it the finest in that role he had ever seen. She gave the letter to Larry, who had been enthusiastic and complimentary after her first night. 'This time,' she said, 'his competitive instincts were aroused immediately. "I must get back on the stage," he said, as he dropped the letter on to the table. And I realised that in future it would be better to share such things with my children or my mother, and not with my husband, to whom it would always seem like one-upmanship.'[31]

Afterwards he sent her a long and penitent letter. The envelope is addressed:

Personal as all get out.

Miss Joan Plowright, C.B.E.

from her erring ungrateful
boy
L.

_____

The letter reads, in part:

'My darling wonderful one, It has been made clear to me that I
have been pretty bloody offensive lately, and as it is known that in
such eccentric fits one is most offensive to the ones one loves the
most, I feel sure that you have most likely endured the most ragged
end of the stick. I am writing you to say how truly sorry I am to
have been hurtful to you, my love, to whom I owe such an incal-
culable amount. . . Please, I beg you, forgive me if you can. Your
adoring and unpayably grateful Larry.'[32]

The remorse was typical. And as Joan sees it – though she was
offended and made wary – he had not meant to snub or discourage
her, nor had he intended the coldness he showed. 'Sometimes he
couldn't contain the emotion he felt. It wasn't that he didn't want
me to work; it was just that there was such pain that *he* wasn't on
the stage. And it was endearing, because it was childlike, coming
out with a feeling he couldn't hide. He had a need for love, and at
the same time a huge anger and fury.'[35] It was all of a piece with
his saying terrible things – that he was glad Peter Finch was dead,
that Tynan's early death didn't matter because he could no longer
be of any use – and yet saying them in an entertaining, funny, wicked
way that made people laugh when they remembered what he said.
He could not help being an entertainer.

36

St Paul's or Westminster Abbey

BUT THERE WAS NO question of his returning to the stage. Peter Hiley, his faithful aide and friend since 1948, continued to visit him in Sussex and found him forlorn. 'He felt unwanted by the profession,' says Hiley. 'He longed to work. He was jealous of Joan getting jobs and him not being asked himself. He usually said, "Have you some business for me, something to sign?" He longed to be involved in life and he wasn't any more. He was getting lame. There was a young world going on round him, his children, and Richard's wife, but he found it hectic. He lost gaiety. "Oh, I've had a miserable life," he'd say. And I'd say, "What about Notley?" And he'd say, "Yes, I was happy at Notley, yes." And I'd say I'd been there a few months before and the lime avenue was doing marvellously well, and he'd say, "Oh, what about the wood? What about the trees?" And he'd become animated.'[1]

Olivier continued to try, as he had done since 1968, to reduce the alimony he still paid to Jill but was advised, as he always had been before, that it would cost more to buy her an annuity, even if she would accept a smaller sum.[2] Then came his eightieth birthday and that, in retrospect, was the beginning of the end. Three days beforehand he formally announced, through his agent Laurence Evans, that he would do no more film or television work, though he would continue to read verse and prose for radio or film performances.[3] He spent the birthday quietly. He received a congratulatory cable from President Reagan, who spelt his name Laurance, with an 'a'.

Mrs Thatcher wrote to him saying he had graced his profession for
sixty-five years, brought pleasure to millions on stage and, through
his films, brought Shakespeare to life for millions more. 'Your work,
in both cinema and theatre, has enhanced our civilisation.'[4]

On 31 May the National Theatre put on a pageant, 'Happy
Birthday Sir Larry', in the Olivier auditorium. Tamsin remembers
that the family was apprehensive that he might appear 'weak and
ill and not all there', so he went surrounded by a protective posse
of Joan, Richard, Tamsin, and Gawn Grainger.[5] He was welcomed
on the South Bank by Peter Hall and by Richard Eyre, who had
just been named as Hall's successor as director. Eyre says there was
a wail from the waiting crowd, almost Iranian in its intensity, and
that Olivier, as he stepped from his car, was 'smaller, almost unrecog-
nisably so, a very, very frail man supported by Joan Plowright'. He
appeared at first not to recognise Hall, and then stared bemusedly
at Eyre as if he were the wrong suspect in a police identity parade.[6]
The evening was celebrated with champagne, balloons, glitter dust,
and bands. In a pageant of theatre history, Olivier was given his
place among Burbage, Garrick, Kean, and Irving. Albert Finney
appeared as a laid-back comic in a cocked hat. Peter Hall in a ruff,
impersonating Shakespeare, looked like the Droeshout engraving
in the frontispiece to the First Folio. Peggy Ashcroft appeared as
Lilian Baylis, bestowing a few mildly encouraging words on
'Laurence' for having given his audiences 'something beyond their
working lives'.[7] Out of a huge birthday cake popped Julie-Kate to
say 'Happy Birthday, Dad'. The audience turned to Olivier, who was
sitting in one of the 'ashtrays' at the side of the auditorium, and
the applause went on and on.

The most eloquent description is Eyre's. 'He smiled, an
enchanting, childlike smile of pure pleasure. He was a man for whom
applause was almost better than life itself. He acknowledged the
applause in a beautiful gesture, raising his right hand and turning
it as if he were cupping butterflies. Joan made several attempts to
lead him out but he was not going to be led. The applause went
on and on. And on. The audience would happily have stayed for an
hour. On his way to the stage door he was lured, without much
protest, at least from him, through the Green Room on to a balcony

above the street, still packed with a mass of fans and photographers. They shouted, whistled, and applauded, and when he left he seemed to be crying, certain that this was the last time he'd hear such a sound, his life's music.'[8]

Joan's thoughts went back to the day, twenty years before, when they had made what he thought was his last journey from Brighton to the Old Vic and he had insisted, early in the morning, on saying goodbye to the few stage-hands at the Old Vic.[9] Gawn Grainger and Joan kept saying, 'I think it's time to go, Larry.' 'And he wouldn't come, he wouldn't come,' says Grainger. 'Eventually I got him and we took him out through the kitchens. He stopped and said hello to the chefs and God knows what.'[10]

As Eyre saw it, it wasn't necessarily that Olivier was the greatest actor of his time. He simply satisfied a desire for actors to be larger than life, and to be able to be seen to be acting at the same time as they were moving an audience to tears or to laughter. 'It's the desire to be knowingly seduced. . . People want greatness, glory, extremes. That's why they want to go to the theatre; they want it to be bigger, more extreme, more daring, more physical than their own lives. . . It's impossible, for a catalogue of reasons to do with finance, the structure of the film industry and the theatre, the spirit of the age and the taste of the times, that we will ever again see a great buccaneering actor-manager, who is also a Hollywood film star, who is equally celebrated in the theatre, and who is capable of remaking his life and art so often and so judiciously as he did. It's said, "Happy the land that needs no heroes." Happier perhaps, but duller, certainly.'[11]

Ginette Spanier had died, which distressed Olivier. They had been the closest of friends who would sit together telling old tales, vigorously correcting each other's accounts. Olivier's old friend William Walton was dead too, but in the summer of 1987 he went again to Ischia and stayed with his widow, Susana, who years before had dressed his tender and suppurating fingers.

That June he went to California for Richard's wedding to a Canadian girl, Shelley, whom he had met three months before. It was held in Glendale, twenty miles north of Los Angeles, at the Church of the Niscients, a New Age sect founded in 1953. Tamsin remembers that the ceremony was bizarre and that her father was frail, bewildered, and appalled at the suddenness of it. She says one of the church's tenets was that bride and groom should not sleep together before marriage, and that her father's advice had always been, 'You bloody *will* do, because you need to know whether they're lesbian or not. You must have sex with people. It's really important. I wouldn't have married her [Jill] if I'd had sex with her before.'[12] Richard also remembers his father's bewilderment at the ceremony, but says that he perked up later when the cameras came out at the reception.[13] It was Olivier's last time in America.

Richard then came with his new wife to live at the Malthouse. Joan was often away working. As a teenager Richard had seen his father only as a frail old man and his example of strength had been his mother, working hard while she supervised three children, two households, and an ill husband. He remembered endless silent dinner tables. Later, when his father was too frail to decide how to spend his time, he and Joan would decide for him. 'She would ask my advice, we would consult together at one end of the dining table, while my father became the child, helplessly looking on from the other. I remembered . . . the flashes of bitter resentment that would pass across his face as he struggled even to hear the plans we were making for him. And I remembered [added Richard, with the same instinct for guilt and remorse which had been such a curse to his father] the sadistic pleasure I had felt in not repeating them louder so he could participate, or dare to refuse. I had revelled in the opportunity to punish him, for being away, for being ill, for taking mother away to work, whatever it was.'[14] Tamsin had seen the same thing. 'He admired my mother as an actress and he loved her, but that was very difficult for her. It meant she went to work and couldn't look after him. He was furious with her about that. There was a sense of Mum taking power, and he loathed that. He could be vitriolic, use vile language, and say we were ganging up against him.'[15]

At the time they came to live in Sussex, Richard and Shelley were believers in holistic medicine and so, up to a point, was Joan. Olivier was then taking forty-eight pills a day and sometimes drinking himself to sleep twice a day. They tried to reduce his intake of steroids and to wean him off alcohol by mixing his wine, behind his back, with a non-alcoholic wine substitute called Jung, which Richard thought was horrible stuff. Sometimes his father went along with it, or seemed to. Sometimes he showed that he knew and that he wasn't happy with it at all.[16] Julie-Kate makes it clear that he wasn't. 'That was one of the decisions that was made for him. He hated that. He tried to go along with it for a while, because it was meant to be healthy. . . I hated it, and I remember thinking, "You're ruining the rest of his life." I don't think that lasted for very long, but there was a sense of everyone taking over from him, and of his being deeply frustrated.'[17] Tamsin thinks Richard was brave to try, but that there came a time when she had to ask, 'Is it fair?' As Joan now remembers it, Olivier was prepared to give the holistic approach a try and at first it did seem to do some good. But he was like a chameleon. With people who believed in it, he also would seem to believe. With people who did not, like Tamsin's husband Simon, he would send the whole thing up. Then it became hilarious. At table he would ask Simon to pick up a bottle of Jung and read the label aloud, with its non-alcoholic mantra, and then say, 'Fuck that. Now open a bottle of decent wine. Or shall we open a bottle of the Old Boy?' The old boy was champagne.[18]

Olivier watched videos of his old films with his nurses, mostly the Shakespeares. 'He was like a frisky old satyr,' says Joan. 'I made sure he had attractive nurses. It was not all doom and gloom. The highs were as memorable as the lows.' She remembers that Richard, who as she saw it had gone to university in America partly to study drama and partly to escape the shadow of Olivier, had returned to direct in England and had then looked after his father with great tenderness and affection. Both she and Richard remember well how Olivier perked up when friends came around for the weekend – Anthony Hopkins, Derek Jacobi, Ronald Pickup, Gawn Grainger, occasionally John Osborne, and Garson Kanin on his visits from America. There was talk of old times with John Mills. Olivier and Ian McKellen argued how best to play Macbeth. Joan remembers how, when the champagne was flowing, Larry would talk and talk and talk, spontaneously holding the master classes he had always declined to give at the National, and she wished they had a tape recorder running, but they never did. 'Then,' says Richard, 'there was lots of laughter. The spirit came back into him for an hour, and then he would collapse.' Olivier could vividly remember this and that play and such and such a performance, but in other ways his memory had quite gone. When there was a party he would ask Gawn Grainger to sit next to him, so that he could lean over and tell him who was there and who was coming over to speak to him. He had forgotten even Peggy Ashcroft's name.[19]

The parish priest, the Rev. Peter Burge, visited him, afraid that he might get a frosty reception. But Olivier was friendly and welcoming and afterwards would get his nurse to telephone Mr Burge about once a month, asking him to come over. Sometimes he took communion. Sometimes he just talked amiably, but rarely about the past. He barely mentioned his clergyman father or his days as a chorister, and never his previously expressed desire to become as Roman Catholic. He once attended the baptism in church of his grandson, Richard's son Troy. The vicar thought that he did return to the faith and receive the comfort of Christian belief.[20]

In May 1988 Sarah Miles, whom he had not seen for years, telephoned to ask him to come and visit Athene Seyler on her ninety-ninth birthday. The two actresses were neighbours. Miss Seyler, who had known him for more than sixty years, longed to see him again. It was she who had awarded him the gold prize when he was at the Central School. Olivier agreed but then did not turn up. Sarah was not too surprised. 'I knew it was going to be tricky. Dying gracefully for one's wife and family is bad enough, but dying well for your mistress too?'[21]

Michael Blakemore visited Olivier and found him very frail. His head had shrunk into his shoulders. They ate poached salmon and peas and talked of old times, and he revived as they recalled his 'I am the sea' speech of the *Titus Andronicus* tour thirty years before, and his reckless dying leap as Coriolanus.[22] Joan, well knowing Olivier's longing for work of any kind, became impatient with Laurence Evans for finding him none. She insisted that he could still do readings and there was a plan, suggested by Gawn Grainger, for him to read passages from the Bible.[23] It came to nothing. In spite of his statement that he would do no more film or television he did make one final appearance in front of a camera, in the autumn of 1988, in a version of Benjamin Britten's *War Requiem*. It is not really a film but a sequence of images with no dialogue and no narrative, set against Britten's music. It was shot in a hospital in Kent and Olivier appeared as an old soldier of World War I, in a wheelchair, tended by a young nurse. His voice was heard only at the beginning, in voice-over, reciting a war poem by Wilfred Owen. He was soon back in hospital again, for tests on his kidney.[24]

He had sold the portrait of him as Richard III by Salvador Dalí. It had been done rapidly, in a few sittings at Claridge's in 1955, after his great success in the film. It shows him both in full face and in profile and is a sensational portrait, not at all subtle, but after that of him as a young Romeo it was his favourite. He had kept it illuminated on the walls of his dining room at Brighton and had always been peculiarly possessive of it. He had earlier not even replied to the Dalí Museum's request for information about it and, in response to an American authority on the painter, had got his secretary to reply merely that he had been much excited to sit for Dalí, who was a genius. What more, he asked, could be said? But early in 1989 the painting was sold at Sotheby's for £396,000. It went to the Dalí Museum in Barcelona.[25]

Laurence Evans did at last find Olivier some reading to do. His last contract was signed on 1 February 1989, with an American company, to do a series of audio-recordings to be called 'Olivier Reads Shakespeare'. The advance, for exclusive world rights, was $25,000.[26] He never completed the work. Early that year David Plowright, who had always been a congenial visitor, found Olivier despondent, saying, 'Time I was gone. Time I was dead.' He did travel thirty-five miles to Leatherhead to see a pre-London production of *Shirley Valentine*, a Liverpudlian monologue by Willy Russell, directed by Richard; it was the last time he was in a theatre.[27] In March he fell heavily and endured his last operation, for a hip replacement. His sister Sybille died in April at the age of eighty-seven. He barely noticed his own eighty-second birthday on 22 May.

Joan had continued to work – because it was her vocation and because the money was needed to pay for Olivier's constant nursing. She believes that her his more rational moments he understood this. In a long-running West End play she could earn ten per cent of

the gross, £1,000 a week. In the summer of 1989 she was in
Hollywood, earning $250,000 filming *I Love You to Death*, a black
comedy with Kevin Kline. Laurence Evans remembered that in
those days he kept asking how Joan was and whether she was all
right. Then in early July Richard telephoned Joan to say that Olivier's
one remaining kidney was in a precarious state. He might last six
weeks or six days. She completed her remaining scenes in one day
and came home. By then he was evidently fading and was unconscious much of the time. A male nurse was now looking after him
and, thinking to ease his thirst, tried to squeeze some orange juice
into his mouth. He stirred, some trickled round to his temple, and
he said, 'This isn't fucking Hamlet, you know.' This is the stuff of
legend. It assumes that the nurse who passed it on had a working
knowledge of the play within the play in *Hamlet*, where the old
king, sleeping in his orchard, is killed by his brother Claudius dropping poison in his ear.[28] They would have been magnificent last
words, but they were not his last. Gawn Grainger and Maggie
Smith came to visit him. 'I sat drinking coffee with Maggie in the
patio bit,' said Grainger. 'I remember saying it was like a Checkhov
play. Eventually we went in to him. The doctor said talk to him
because hearing was the last sense to go. I chattered away and held
his hand and left Maggie with him.' Peter Hiley came to say goodbye
and now says, 'I was never a big part of his life, but he was a big
part of mine.' He was dying in a tiny room the size of a ship's
cabin.[29]

When Olivier briefly regained consciousness he told Richard, 'I
don't want this.' Richard did not know whether he meant the pain,
or death. When Joan arrived back he was just conscious. 'He put a
hand up, just like that, and said, "Dear God, get me out of this."'[30]
They are his last known words. He appeared to be unconscious
when the parish priest gave communion at his bedside to Joan,
Richard, and Shelley. The vicar conducted the ceremony with the
intention of uplifting him as well as the family, and hoped he might
be able to hear.[31]

Tamsin remembers that there had been so many near-death times
that it was as if they had been practising for years.[32] Julie-Kate
came down from London and sat with her father that night. Next

morning she went to his room to see how he was, and as she walked in his terrible breathing stopped.[33] He died just before 11.15 a.m. on 11 July 1989. He had been ill for the last twenty-two years of his life.

Tamsin laid roses on his folded hands. Joan, her two daughters, and Richard and his wife said the twenty-third psalm over his body: 'Yea, though I walk through the valley of the shadow of death. . .' Richard called the undertakers. He followed them as they carried out the body in a fold-over sack – purple, he noticed, his father's favourite colour. It seemed to him as if the body had shrunk when the spirit left it. The body was placed in an old Ford estate car, and when it drove off down the lane he felt some energy left the grounds with it. The funeral was three days later, on a perfect summer's day. The family had chosen the smaller of the two parish churches, the twelfth-century church at Ashurst, two miles away, to which Olivier and Joan had sometimes borrowed the key and visited alone on Sundays, though there were no services. At the funeral Richard and Tarquin read the lessons. Anthony Hopkins, who had over the years become a close friend of Olivier's and Joan's, spoke the last lines of *King Lear*:

> I have a journey, sir, shortly to go:
> My master calls me; I must not say no.
> The weight of this sad time we must obey,
> Speak what we feel, not what we ought to say.
> The oldest hath borne most. We that are young
> Shall never see so much, nor live so long.

In spite of his last will, Olivier had lately asked to be cremated rather than buried. At the crematorium, after the coffin disappeared, David Plowright remarked to Maggie Smith that he half expected the curtains to part and Olivier to reappear as Archie Rice and take a bow.[34] He was not alone in such a vision. At a wake in the Malthouse garden – where Olivier's favourite armchair and a crown of herbs and flowers mentioned by Shakespeare were put out on the lawn – Richard, wandering round the garden remembering other parties in the same place with the same guests, half expected his father to emerge from the house, to be congratulated on yet another marvellous death scene.[35]

It had been a funeral for family and friends, though the friends did include Douglas Fairbanks, Alec Guinness, John Mills, and Franco Zeffirelli. There had to be a more public ceremony. On the same day as the funeral at Steyning *The Times* printed a letter from, of all people, the iconoclastic John Osborne, in which he wrote, 'I do not know what Lord Olivier's later wishes may have been, nor would one want to encroach on those of his family. However, it seems astounding to me that he should not be accorded a funeral, like Garrick's, at Westminster Abbey. This was said to be the most remarkable London had ever seen, with Sheridan in full rig as chief mourner, while Burke and Dr Johnson wept openly. . .'[36]

The abbey had already been approached. The dean, the Very Rev. Michael Mayne, was a passionate lover of the theatre: one of his unforgettable teenage memories was of Olivier's *Oedipus* and his heart-rending off-stage cry before he blinded himself. He immediately agreed to conduct a memorial service. But then the family raised the separate question of the burial of the ashes, and there a complication arose, for there was a long-standing convention that no poet, novelist, or actor should be memorialised in Poet's Corner until at least ten years after his death. So dean and chapter said an enthusiastic 'yes' to the service, and a regretful 'no' to the burial.[37]

Laurence Harbottle, as first-named executor, then approached St Paul's Cathedral. He knew a former dean who had told him, 'We'll put him next to Nelson'. Nelson's funeral at St Paul's, in 1805, must have been even grander than Garrick's had been at Westminster Abbey. The dean of the day was happy both to conduct a memorial service and to inter Olivier's ashes in the crypt. This was congenial to Joan and the family, and so St Paul's was decided upon. Then on one day, 18 July, there was a great to-ing and fro-ing of letters and messages. Harbottle wrote to the Prince of Wales' secretary asking if the prince could come to the ceremony, at St Paul's. On the same day, just after noon, Laurence Evans sent a letter by hand to Westminster Abbey thanking the dean for kindly offering a service only, but saying that since St Paul's would take the ashes too, St Paul's it would be.[38] At which the abbey rapidly changed its mind and came up with a better bid. Evans's letter was the first Dean Mayne had known of any competition from St Paul's, and he admits that it came as a shock to him. He felt that St Paul's was the politicians' and military men's place and quite wrong for an actor. He *knew* that Olivier's wish would have been to be interred beside Garrick and Irving rather than Nelson, even if he had played Nelson on film. The dean rapidly called together his colleagues and they immediately agreed to bend the rules and take the ashes too. So Westminster Abbey sent its counter-bid round by messenger, saying it would both hold the service and inter the ashes in Poets' Corner, where a stone would be unveiled a few months later. Joan Plowright and the family, attracted by the prospect of Olivier lying in the same place and appearing on the same bill as Irving, Garrick, and Henry V, changed their minds and opted for the abbey after all. The Prince of Wales was told, in a second letter on the same day, that the venue had been changed to Westminster.[39]

The prince was at first expected to attend, but did not, and proposed that Kenneth Branagh should act as his representative. As such, Branagh would have taken precedence over everyone else at the ceremony and would have entered the abbey last while everyone else stood. He was an up-and-coming young lion, a contender who might one day lead his profession, but he was only twenty-eight and at the time had done little except contend. The only connection between him and Olivier had been when Branagh was at RADA and had written asking for advice on how to play Chebutikin in *The Three Sisters*, to which Olivier had replied, 'The author has it all there for you. I should have a bash at it and hope for the best.' This is classic Olivier: there is only one way to begin to do a thing and that is to do it. His family and friends were firm that he really could not be upstaged by Branagh at the service. Harbottle thought that the Prince of Wales' nomination showed real poverty of imagination.[40] Richard thought several senior actors would have died on the spot, and knew that the last thing his father would have wanted at his memorial was the apparent crowning of an heir to his throne. Indirect murmurings procured Branagh's replacement by the safe Richard Attenborough.[41] The Queen's representative was Lord Zuckerman, a zoologist and authority on baboons,

whose qualification was probably that he was a fellow member of
the Order of Merit. The Queen Mother was asked, and Westminster
Abbey was prepared to change the date to suit her, but she was in
Scotland. So the date was fixed for 20 October 1989. The senior
member of the Royal Family present was Prince Edward, the Queen's
youngest son, who had shown a dilettante interest in television
production. Joan and the three children were the chief mourners,
along with Tarquin, Hester, and Jill in a wheelchair. Maxine Audley
and Ann Todd were among the congregation.

For the ceremony the Battle Hymn of the Republic had been
suggested, perhaps as an acknowledgment of what Olivier had done
for Hollywood and what Hollywood had done for him, but this idea
was abandoned. Dean Mayne felt that the tune needed to go with
a certain swing but knew from experience that the Battle Hymn
was wordy and that congregations found it frustratingly difficult
to keep up with the choir. The dean's theatrical instincts played a
large part in determining the order and style of the grand memorial service. It was his idea that Olivier's trophies should be carried
in procession, and he was unrepentant when some thought this was
over the top.[42] Douglas Fairbanks carried the insignia of Olivier's
Order of Merit; Michael Caine bore his Oscar for lifetime achievement; Maggie Smith a silver model of the Chichester theatre; Paul
Scofield a silver model of the National; Derek Jacobi the crown
worn in the film of *Richard III*; Peter O'Toole the script used in the
film of *Hamlet*; Ian McKellen the laurel wreath worn in the stage
production of *Coriolanus*; Dorothy Tutin the crown worn for his
television *King Lear*; and Frank Finlay the sword presented to Olivier
by Gielgud, once worn by Kean. Albert Finney read from
Ecclesiastes: 'To everything there is a season. . . A time to be born
and a time to die.' John Mills read from I Corinthians: 'Though I
speak with the tongues of men and of angels. . .' Peggy Ashcroft
read from Milton's 'Lycidas'. John Gielgud read 'Death Be Not
Proud' by John Donne. Alec Guinness gave an address in which he
said that perhaps Olivier's greatness lay in a happy combination of
imagination, physical magnetism, a commanding and appealing voice,
an expressive eye, and danger. 'Larry always carried the threat of
danger with him; primarily as an actor but also, for all his charm,

as a private man. There were times when it was wise to be wary of him.' He reminded the congregation that Olivier had been brought up as a High Anglican, and said he did not think the need for devotion or the mystery of things ever quite left him.[43]

The climax of the show was Olivier's own taped voice echoing round the abbey as he delivered the St Crispin's Day speech from *Henry V*. Its quiet resolution was the choir singing 'Fear no more the heat o' the sun', from *Cymbeline*. The ceremony was more showbiz than sacred. For Sacrarium, Lantern and Quire, wrote one perceptive reporter, you could read Proscenium, Apron, and Flies.[44]

Westminster Abbey and St Paul's, the two principal theatres of the Church of England, had competed to stage Olivier's positively final appearance. Richard thought his father would have been tickled pink.[45] Olivier had given the matter some thought. In the mid-1950s Toby Rowland, the producer, had arrived early for dinner at Durham Cottage and found him taking a nap. When Olivier came downstairs he said, 'You didn't really disturb me. I wasn't sleeping. I was just lying down and thinking about my funeral. I could see the sun shining through the windows of the Abbey and I felt joyous.'[46] But when the time came he knew it was as cold in Westminster Abbey as in any churchyard.

OLIVIER REMEMBERED

JOAN PLOWRIGHT RECEIVED HUNDREDS of letters of condolence after Olivier's death. Here are excerpts from a few.

JOHN GIELGUD, *actor, great contemporary*
It is difficult for me to believe that he is gone – what a rich legacy he leaves behind – not only of his brilliant talents and extraordinary range of achievement, but the memory of his own vital, courageous personality, his determination and power as performer, manager, director and defier of lightning, the originality of his approach to every new and challenging venture, his physical bravery, not only on the stage but in the valiant way in which he faced his few failures and defeats, and above all his refusal to give up when he became so ill.

As you know, we were never intimate friends. . . I was, I confess, always a bit afraid of him, for he had a certain remoteness and spiritual authority which I imagine Irving also had? Perhaps it was a fitting part of his own acting genius and his gift for leadership. . .

His meeting with you and the blessing you brought him in giving him the children he always longed for must, to some extent at least, have given him a great reward, despite all the miseries and complications of the South Bank. . . I am sad not to have seen him these last years, but I hesitated to intrude on the family life he had so richly deserved and I felt it might distress him to find me still lucky and well enough to go on working while he himself was so sadly disabled.

PEGGY ASHCROFT, *actress, great contemporary*
I find it unbelievably difficult to write because I still can't believe Larry has gone – illogical, because, God knows he'd been through enough to make any ordinary mortal accept his end – but then, he 'defied augury'. Certainly, for all his ills, there was a special providence that seemed to look after him.

BERNARD MILES, *director of the Mermaid Theatre, second actor to be created a peer*
Such subtlety, such detail, biting deeper into the role than any actor of my time, or indeed *any time*.

JANET HENFREY, *actress at Chichester, 1962*
I think anyone would have leapt off Beachy Head for him if that was what he wanted – walking into the first day of rehearsal and he knew the names of the humblest of us. I was at the eightieth birthday party and I will always see him arm raised so reluctant to leave his theatre and his friends who adored him and his talent and all he had done for us.

CHOREN ABRAMIAN, *Chairman of Union of People's Artists, USSR*
THE DEATH OF GREAT LOURENCE OLIVYE SHOOK ARMENIA. . . THE SORROW RESOUND IN OUR HARTS.

DOROTHY TUTIN, *actress*
I can understand only too well what you must be going through. My thoughts are with you. As a man and an actor he was an inspiration. I loved him.

MARY SOAMES, *Winston Churchill's daughter, chairman of the National Theatre, 1989–95*
The lustre of his name hung around the newly fledged National Theatre; his guidance and direction and personal participation combined to make those years unique and splendid, and set the theatre on its way.

PATRICK GARLAND, *director*
I truly do feel him to have been 'the great inimitable' as Charles Dickens called himself, from whom a whole gallery of rich and extravagant characterisations poured so vigorously, and with infinite prodigality.

LAUREN BACALL, *film actress*
As we all do he needed work. He needed it perhaps more because there was so much there.

AUTHOR'S NOTE

The Androgynous Actor

NOBODY WHO KNEW OLIVIER could doubt his virility. At the same time, there were evidently both male and female sides to him. He did as a young man worry about the idea of bisexuality, something which seems to have been entangled with his religious doubts. He and Jill Esmond, before their marriage, talked about their 'particular pet devil'. He wrote to his confessor about it. It may very likely have had something to do with his ambiguous sexual feelings for Denys Blakelock, his best man at his first wedding (see Chapter 4). In 1936–37 he did in my opinion have a homosexual fling with Henry Ainley, at a time when he was about to leave Jill Esmond for Vivien Leigh. Ainley's letters are explicit. It is only fair to state here that Joan Plowright says of this matter that Olivier may have experimented as a young man and had such a fling – and that if he did he would have been experimenting in the sense of finding out about himself. But she finds it very strange that, if he did, he never told her about it or, to her knowledge, told anyone else. He had told her about his early affairs with women, but never mentioned Ainley. And she concludes by asserting robustly, 'If he did, so what?' She is firm that nothing about the matter diminishes Olivier in her estimation or her love, or in her memory. Her son Richard believes that the evidence 'seems fairly compelling' and says 'It is possible that if he had resisted earlier temptation in the profession, and especially with his great friend Noel Coward, he may have decided to have a go – or try it out. It is odd that no one has ever said anything about it (theatre folk not being renowned for their discretion) but I could imagine that with his religious background he may have regretted it or even thought his soul in mortal danger – and therefore tried to block the episode from his mind.' Many years later, in his autobiography, *Confessions of an Actor*, Olivier hinted at homosexual 'dalliance', and misdirected the reader to assume that that it might have been with Noel Coward, though the 'one male' he alluded to is more likely to have been Ainley. He also wrote in his autobiography, when he need have written nothing, '[It must be] hard to believe that in truth the homosexual act was darkly destructive to my soul, and that I was firm in my conviction that heterosexuality was romantically beautiful, promoting of justice, dissolving in pleasure, rewarding in content-ment.' Perhaps, he said, he had to admit that he had been thrown off course. 'In the study of humanity,' he wrote, 'I don't believe there can be found anything conclusively definite; there must, I am satisfied there must always be, no matter how faintly drawn, a question mark attached to any found solution regarding human behaviour.' (All this is set out in detail in Chapter 7.)

Olivier himself was the first to air this matter of his bisexuality. After his death others pursued the matter, and what they suggest has to be considered. It is a principal theme of *Laurence Olivier: A Biography* by Donald Spoto, 1991, that Olivier was bisexual, and that by 1950 he 'was deeply involved in a homosexual affair with Danny Kaye'. Spoto states that Olivier wrote a letter to Vivien Leigh in 1961 'weakly describing as merely transitory and unimportant the sexual intimacy between him and Kaye'. Spoto does not quote from this letter and gives no single detail of it.[1] Why should Olivier have written any such a letter to Vivien Leigh a year *after* their divorce? This was the year he married Joan Plowright and in which their first child was born. He had hardened his heart against Vivien and wanted nothing to do with her. Spoto states that this letter came into the possession of Jack Merivale, who lived with Vivien for seven years until her death in 1967, and that it remained with him until his death in 1990. I have read dozens of letters between Merivale and Vivien Leigh, from her daughter Suzanne Farrington's collection, and there is no hint of any such thing. Merivale also gave many long and candid interviews to Hugo Vickers when he was writing his biography of Vivien Leigh in 1986–87. I have seen the transcripts of these interviews and there is no hint there either. Yet Merivale was open in these interviews. In one he said he and Vivien had at one time been lent a house on Long Island by a woman agent. 'Very attractive lady,' he said, 'but lesbian. Looking back on it I think there could very easily have been something between them.'[2] So although Merivale undoubtedly loved Vivien, he was not in his conversations with Vickers trying to protect her by concealing anything. As is plain from the correspondence of Olivier and Vivien Leigh in 1938–9, she was sexually adventurous. She was the pursuer. She was also indiscreet. If she had known Olivier had male partners she would probably, in one of her manic phases, have told the world.

Spoto also writes in his biography that the first draft of Olivier's *Confessions of an Actor* 'frankly admitted the numerous homosexual escapades of his adult life – events his third wife prevailed on him to remove from the book'.[3] Joan Plowright clearly states that she did nothing of the sort. Olivier's part-manuscript and the three typescripts of his book in the British Library at CRIT 1, boxes 1 and 2, bear many amendments but not one of the kind Spoto claims. Spoto also describes a lurid scene between Olivier and Kaye. He writes that when in 1953 Vivien broke down in Hollywood and Olivier went out to her, flying from Italy to Los Angeles via London and New York, Danny Kaye met him at Idlewild Airport, New York. There, according to Spoto, Kaye disguised himself as a customs officer and subjected Olivier to a naked and intimate body search. He writes: 'After submitting to the indignities of an inspection of every inch and crevice of his body, Olivier was astonished to see the customs officer step back and slowly remove a complex disguise (dark wig and heavily powdered latex mask), and there before the naked Olivier stood Danny Kaye. They spent the night at the St Regis before continuing to California next morning.'[4] This is a tale that does not bear examination. First of all it assumes the complicity of the United States customs and immigration officers, who are on the whole not given to such things. Secondly, Olivier's diary entries for Friday 13, Saturday 14, and Sunday 15 March 1953 are precise and make a nonsense of the story. At 6.15 a.m. on Friday he took a boat from Ischia, where he had been on holiday, crossed to Naples, and took a train to Rome, from where he flew to New York via Heathrow, arriving at Idlewild Airport – after a journey of thirty-one hours – at 8.56 a.m. on the Saturday. He was not alone. On the last part of the journey, from London, he was accompanied by Cecil Tennant. Kaye did meet them at the airport but Olivier, who must have been exhausted, then went to the Sherry Netherland Hotel (not the St Regis), where he had a massage and a short sleep. He did not stay the night in New York at that or any other hotel, but left just after midnight on Sunday on the 12.30 a.m. Ambassador flight for Los Angeles.[5]

Spoto's book appears to have a full apparatus of notes and sources, but for none of its mentions of Kaye (on pages 181, 191, 194, 197, 211 and 248) and for none of the matters mentioned above, is any single source or authority given. He offers not one piece of evidence for his speculations. But some idea of how the Danny Kaye story could have originated may be gathered from the recollections of Pieter Rogers, who in 1958 was general manager of the Royal Court and later, from 1962, of the Chichester Festival Theatre. He was a friend of both Olivier and Vivien Leigh and knew them well. In 1959, when their marriage had been over in any real sense for some time, he saw their distress. Vivien was appearing in *Look After Lulu* at the Royal Court and he once saw Olivier coming down from her dressing room in tears, followed by a weeping Vivien. She held on to his coat and would not let go, and he unintentionally dragged her down the stairs. Rogers is himself homosexual but firmly believes Olivier was not. He remembers Vivien Leigh telling him that Danny Kaye was a sweet man, spontaneously funny and witty, but eccentric. She told him that one morning in the early or mid-1950s, when Danny Kaye was one of a house party at Notley, she woke to find him in her bed and kicked him out. Then, two or three days later, when she was in bed with Olivier, she woke to find Danny Kaye there again, this time with the two of them; she said he was lying next to her, not Olivier.[6] It is difficult to know how credible her account is. It was a time when parties sometimes went on all night at Notley and some guests slept where they fell, but it was also a time when Vivien was often deranged.

Spoto's speculations, though unsubstantiated, were picked up by others. In 1991, the same year as his biography appeared, Michael Korda wrote *Curtain*, a novel in which the principal characters are Lord Vane (Olivier), Felicia Lyle (Vivien Leigh), and Randy Brooks (Danny Kaye). There are clear implications of homosexuality. Korda is the nephew of Alexander Korda the film producer, and as a very young man had met Olivier and Vivien aboard his uncle's yacht in the 1950s. By the 1980s he had become editorial director of Simon and

Schuster and published the American edition of Olivier's autobiography. Then in 1994 Martin Gottfried published *Nobody's Fool: The Lives of Danny Kaye*, in which he stated that Olivier had privately told Michael Korda that Vivien's abuse of Olivier at the time of her 1953 breakdown included accusations of homosexuality which 'were in part legitimate'. He also repeated the statement that Olivier had deleted detailed admissions of homosexuality from the manuscript of *Confessions*.

I put all this to Michael Korda. He denied that Olivier had told him about abusive remarks by Vivien in 1953, or that he had told Gottfried anything of the sort. When I asked him about his own book, *Curtain*, he said it was a work of fiction. He had invented the plot. He had done the same in a novel about Marilyn Monroe, which was also fiction. He had very much liked Vivien when he met her aboard his uncle's yacht. She had been kind to him, but was certainly willing to speak woundingly about Olivier. He had heard her. She and Olivier were both very good at hurting each other. As to Olivier's having deleted some passages from the manuscript of *Confessions*, Korda said that he as publisher had wanted to change rather a lot of it. I know this to be true because one letter from Korda in the British Library suggests 105 changes. But he said Olivier had insisted that it should be printed uncut, exactly as he finally presented it, and it was.[7]

We then come to the appendix to *The Dictionary of National Biography* for those who died in the years 1985 to 1990. The article on Olivier states that he had affairs with women and men. The author of this piece was Irving Wardle, formerly drama critic of *The Times*. When I asked Mr Wardle about this he said he had met Olivier only twice, had no personal knowledge, and had taken his information from a source he could not remember, though it might have been Spoto. He said that Oxford University Press, the publishers of the *DNB*, had agreed that that phrase should not appear in future editions.[8] It does not appear in the new edition of the *DNB* published in 2004. But of course the appearance of such allegations in the *DNB* appendix, and the fact that the author of the article had for years been drama critic of *The Times*, did give these allegations some apparent authority.

There has also been talk, and no more than that, about a homosexual relationship between Olivier and Kenneth Tynan. This is implausible. There is no hint that anyone in the National Theatre's huts at Aquinas Street noticed anything of the sort. I knew some of them and they would have. Perhaps this speculation was an attempt, by those whose opinion of Tynan's judgment and probity was low, to find some reason, any reason, for his surprising hold over Olivier. But Tynan conspicuously and constantly presents himself in his published diaries as a heterosexual sado-masochist.[9]

There is no hint in the Olivier archive, or in anything I have seen or learned elsewhere, of anything actively homosexual in Olivier's maturity. There is some evidence to the contrary. The homosexual Terence Rattigan, writing with a proposal for a play about the homosexual Diaghalev, which came to nothing, anticipated Olivier's objections by saying he knew he was 'frightfully normal'.[10] And when Olivier, as director of the National, engaged Dexter, whose sexuality was well known, he told him, 'We do not fuck the help. Get it?' Later, when Dexter did seduce a boy who was trying to get a part in *As You Like It*, he told him, 'I'll fire you right off and I'll give it to the Press why. I'll show you no mercy at all if you ever do that again.'[11]

Against this there is the recollection of Sarah Miles, Olivier's mistress in the 1960s, that he not only named his earlier mistresses to her – fewer, she said, than you might have expected – but also told her he had been bisexual. But she says he might easily have done that to 'turn her on', knowing that she had herself been bisexual as a girl. She did remember that when she was at the National in 1965 in *Hay Fever*, Coward was jealously furious when he came into Olivier's dressing room and found her on his lap, but this is more revealing about Coward than about Olivier, and is hardly surprising.[12]

All this has to be seen against the background that Olivier and some of his circle were habitually camp in their manner and had a natural appetite for the bawdy. In Olivier's later life, when he was ill, his very old friend Douglas Fairbanks several times wrote to him racily to cheer him up. In October 1971, when Olivier was about to undertake the burden, which he feared, of playing James Tyrone in a *Long Day's Journey into Night*, Fairbanks – in the hope that he would 'get a giggle out of them' – sent him xeroxes of a set of sixteen erotic drawings which Milton Goldman, the agent, had shown him. Four were bisexual and two had to do with cross-dressing. In April 1978, when Olivier was ill again, Fairbanks wrote to him about 'the silly twerp who thought cunnilingus was the Irish airline'.[13]

However all this may be, one thing is certain, and it is more important than speculation about Olivier's personal sexual preferences. The fact is that Olivier *the actor* had both male and female sides to him. In 1922 – when he was fourteen and played Katharina in the All Saints, Margaret Street production of *The Taming of the Shrew* for one afternoon at the old Memorial Theatre at Stratford-upon-Avon – *The Times* gave him a wonderful notice which said in part, 'You felt that if an apple were thrown to this Katharina she would instinctively catch it in her lap. . .'[14] The boy Olivier, as Katharina, instinctively adopted this essentially feminine gesture, which is not at all the way a boy would catch an apple. Playing a girl he became a girl (see Chapter 2).

Michael Gambon, who was a young actor in the National Theatre company in the early 1960s, dismisses Spoto's suggestions as gossip and is sure there is nothing to them. But he does remember Olivier's bisexual instincts as an actor. 'He walked with a sort of Western sway,' says Gambon. 'A very hippy walk. I remember him saying once, when we were sitting around, "Every member of the audience, both male and female, should want to fuck you."'[15] Michael Blakemore, whom Olivier wanted to succeed him as director of the National, thinks that this observation catches Olivier exactly. He says, 'There was a mixture of male and female, an extraordinary androgynous quality. It is true of some great performers. Take Garbo.'[16]

THE OLIVIER FAMILY

JOAN PLOWRIGHT has continued a distinguished career in films and television and on the stage. Her films include *The Enchanted April*, which won her a Golden Globe and an Oscar nomination; *Stalin*, for which she won a second Golden Globe; *Tea With Mussolini*; and *101 Dalmatians*. In 2001 she published her memoirs, *And That's Not All*. She returned to the West End stage in 2003 in Pirandello's *Absolutely! (Perhaps)*, directed by Franco Zeffirelli, a director with whom she has worked, in the theatre and films, since 1974. In the New Year Honours of 2004 she was created a Dame.

RICHARD OLIVIER, after studying film and drama at the University of California at Los Angeles, worked as a director at the Edinburgh Festival, in the West End, and at the Globe, where he directed *Henry V* and *The Merchant of Venice*. He worked with Tony Richardson on the film *Shadow of the Sun*. In 1997 he founded Olivier Mythodrama Associates, which runs leadership courses round the world. He has published three books: *Shadow of the Stone Heart*, 1995; *Inspirational Leadership: Henry V and the Muse of Fire*, 2001; and *Peak Performance Presentations: Presenting with Passion and Purpose*, 2004.

TAMSIN OLIVIER trained at the Central School, and in 1990 appeared with her mother and her sister Julie-Kate in J. B. Priestley's *Time and the Conways* at the Old Vic. She played the lead in *Antigone* directed by John Dexter at the Haymarket. She now runs a restaurant, The Engineer, in Primrose Hill, London. She is the proud mother of seven-year-old Wilfred and is in her fourth year of training as a psychotherapist.

JULIE-KATE OLIVIER trained at Lamda and has worked at the Old Vic, the Royal Court and abroad. In 1989 she co-produced the documentary *Safari Strife* for Channel 4's *Cutting Edge* series. In 2000 she was production supervisor on *Peace One Day*, a campaign for peace which travelled the world and documented its progress on film. In 2001 she was co-founder of the Women in Theatre company. In 2005 she produced a Tsunami charity gala, *One Knight Only*, featuring six Dames of the English Theatre – Joan Plowright, Maggie Smith, Judi Dench, Helen Mirren, Diana Rigg, and Eileen Atkins – and Sir Antony Sher. She is a trained yoga teacher.

TARQUIN OLIVIER, after serving as an ensign in the Coldstream Guards and graduating from Oxford, worked in the Far East, Africa and the Caribbean, first with the Commonwealth Development Corporation and then with De La Rue, the banknote printers. He rebuilt the mint at Khartoum. In 1964 he published *The Eye of the Day*, a memoir of his Asian experiences, and in 1992 *My Father Laurence Olivier*. He has been seeking finance in Turkey to make an epic feature film about Kemal Ataturk.

SOURCES

THIS BOOK IS WRITTEN almost entirely from original sources to which no previous biographer has had access. They are:

BL: THE LAURENCE OLIVIER ARCHIVE at the British Library, London. This huge collection, which was bought from the Olivier estate in 1999, contains most of his personal, family, and business papers; his contracts, wills, diaries, notebooks and anything down to florists' and laundry bills. Most of his personal in-letters are arranged alphabetically in seventeen sections. Other in-letters, including many which are personal, are classified with the papers relating to a particular play or film, or to the Old Vic or the National Theatre. From 1944 on, Olivier also kept carbon copies or manuscript drafts of most of his out-letters. The papers are classified in eleven main sections, for instance PERS for personal papers, PROF for professional papers, FILMS by title, CRIT for books and the manuscripts and typescripts of books and articles by and about him, and so on. The papers are loose, and within each file are arranged for the most part chronologically. The file numbers and names cited in the notes reflect the arrangement of the archive in 2002–04. Parts of the archive, however, are still being reclassified, and reference names and numbers many have changed. There is no index yet, but there is a forty-six-page handlist.

SFC: THE SUZANNE FARRINGTON COLLECTION. Mrs Farrington, Vivien Leigh's daughter, has a collection second in scope only to the British Library's, though it ends with VL's death in 1967. In many ways these two principal collections complement each other. In 1943 Olivier was making *Henry V* in Ireland and England and Vivien Leigh was touring with a wartime concert party in North Africa. Her letters to him are in the BL. His letters to her, which describe in great detail the making of *Henry V*, are in SFC. This collection is also much richer than the BL's in Olivier's letters to Vivien Leigh, particularly for 1938–39 when he was making *Wuthering Heights* and she *Gone With the Wind*. In that period he wrote her more than ninety letters, which are here. The collection is not formally classified.

JPC: THE JOAN PLOWRIGHT COLLECTION. Dame Joan Plowright, who married Olivier as his third wife in 1961, has many letters personal to herself and Laurence Olivier – only some of which were used in her memoir, *And That's Not All* (see below) – and other family documents and some early papers not included in the Olivier archive at the BL.

HLC: THE HARBOTTLE & LEWIS COLLECTION. This London firm of solicitors acted for Olivier from 1960. Many of his film contracts are here, as are papers referring to the National Theatre, some fan letters, and a valuable pre-trial deposition of more than one hundred pages made by Olivier in 1980 to the United States Court of Claims in New York, in which he reviewed his stage and film career.

MA: THE MARK AMORY TRANSCRIPTS. Mr Amory, biographer and literary editor of the *Spectator*, London, was commissioned in 1979 to ghost Olivier's autobiography, which was published as *Confessions of An Actor* in 1982. He recorded fifty-seven hours of conversation before Olivier decided to write the book unaided, which he did. None of the recorded material was then used in the book as published but Mr Amory's typed transcriptions, apparently verbatim, were seen by Gawn Grainger, who in 1984–85 edited and substantially wrote Olivier's second book, *On Acting*. Since his book's subject was acting and its techniques, Mr Grainger used, broadly, only the historical material. Almost all of Olivier's personal reminiscences on his early life were unused. About a third of the transcripts have survived. The transcripts are cited by number and then page.

CONFESSIONS MSS. Olivier's own part-manuscript and part-typescript of *Confessions of an Actor*. In 1974, when he first began this book, Olivier wrote seventy-five pages in his own hand in a large red leather-covered notebook. He then abandoned the project. Then in 1980, when he had decided to write the book after all and without Mark Amory's help, he typed 157 pages himself. This manuscript and part-typescript are plainly the first version of the book before it was got at by the English publisher's editors, and they contain revealing passages which were later deleted. They are formally part of the BL archive, in CRIT 1, boxes 1 and 2, but are so important that they are listed separately here.

SYBILLE MEMOIR: In 1948 Sybille Olivier, Laurence Olivier's older sister, wrote a memoir of 59,000 words entitled *He That Plays the King* and dedicated to 'Any future biographers'. It had been commissioned by an English publisher but when Oliver saw the typescript he suppressed it. There is much about Olivier's youth that appears nowhere else. The typescript is in the BL at CRIT 2.

SYBILLE TAPES: In late 1974, when Olivier was in hospital suffering from dermatomyositis, Sybille visited him several times to encourage him to write his autobiography. They talked about very early days in the family. One tape of half an hour survives and so does a transcription of one other tape.

GG TRS: THE GAWN GRAINGER TRANSCRIPTS. In 1984–85, in order to ghost Olivier's second book, *On Acting*, Gawn Grainger, actor, writer, and friend of Olivier, met him on ten occasions and they talked for the most part informally. There are 137 pages of typed transcripts. Olivier's memory was by then very faulty. He could not remember whether *Gone With the Wind* was made before or after the war. But there are many insights into how his mind worked. In one of these conversations he can be observed inventing Ralph Richardson's attempt to murder him in 1945. In the BL archive at CRIT 1, box 2.

Many other letters and documents used in the book come from smaller collections, which are cited in full in the notes.

Printed Books

Four printed books contain original material found nowhere else, and are cited in the notes.

CA: *Confessions of an Actor*, by Laurence Olivier, 1982. Important because, although Olivier's original was much cut by his English publisher, he

insisted on restoring most of the deletions, put right many of the alter-
ations, and refused to make many other suggested changes. The text,
though cut, is therefore almost entirely his own. The American edition
is identical, but differently paginated.

JPB: *And That's Not All: The Memoirs of Joan Plowright*, 2001. This
quotes many personal letters to and from Olivier which are not in the
BL archive. Where I have seen the original letters, as I have in many
cases, I cite them in the notes as from JPC (see above). Where I have
not they are cited as JPB, with a page number.

TARQUIN: *My Father Laurence Olivier* by Tarquin Olivier, 1992. Written
by Olivier's eldest son to vindicate his mother's name from the slighting
references in *Confessions of an Actor*. Mark Amory, who spent many
hours taping Olivier's recollections in 1980, believes that Tarquin's
book accurately catches his father's tone of voice.

BARKER: *The Oliviers*, a biography by Felix Barker, 1953. The first biography, a joint one of Olivier and Vivien Leigh, and the only biography
written with the approval and the help of Olivier, with whom Mr Barker
had several long interviews. He is good on the 1936–37 period at the Old
Vic and early pre-war days, and had seen a few letters which no longer
seem to exist. He wrote tactfully, being careful not to offend his subjects.

Other printed sources
I have used nothing from any previous biography except Mr Barker's.
I have, however, quoted from two books which bring together remi-
niscences of Olivier by his friends and colleagues. They are *Olivier*,
edited by Logan Gourlay, 1973, and *Olivier: In Celebration*, edited by
Garry O'Connor, 1987.

A Note on the Text
Quotations from manuscript and typescript letters by or to Olivier are
verbatim, except where I have silently corrected obvious errors of spelling;
ellipses are indicated by three dots (. . .). Quotations from transcripts of
Olivier's conversation, as with the Amory and Grainger transcripts,

have been treated more freely: the frequent hesitations, repetitions, and excursions of LO's speech have sometimes been silently excised or tidied up, but no words have been changed or interpolated.

PERSONAL ABBREVIATIONS USED IN THE NOTES
LO = Laurence Olivier   JE = Jill Esmond   VL = Vivien Leigh
JP = Joan Plowright

NOTES, CHAPTER BY CHAPTER

The abbreviations used in these notes are explained in the preceding section on SOURCES.

NOTES TO CHAPTER 1 As the Olive Tree Flourishes
1 No room for genius, MA 9 p.13. Garbo, LO on Dick Cavett show, 24 July 1973. *Streetcar*, LO cable to Garson Kanin, 6 Oct 1949, BL PERS 1/10.
2 Essex University website, July 1997.
3 The connection to William of Orange is first mentioned in Barker, 1953. Herbert Olivier, the painter uncle, first mentions the *petite noblesse* of the family in a letter to LO of 20 September [1948], BL PERS 227/2. *Burke's Peerage*, 1940, and *The Complete Peerage*, ed. Doubleday and de Walden, 1940, give simpler versions of Sydney Olivier's lineage.
4 *Sydney Olivier: Letters and Selected Writings*, ed. Margaret Olivier, 1948, p.180. Sydney wrote this in a letter to H.G. Wells, 28 August 1942. He knew politics, and his surmise was not too wild.
5 Barker, p.4.
6 Gentry, *Sydney Olivier* (see note 4 above) p.179. H.A. Olivier, obituaries in *Hants and Berks Gazette*, 14 December 1912, and *Church Times*, 27 December 1912.
7 Merton Wardens' and Tutors' Minutes 1888–90 (MCR 2.28). Durham University archives. Sybille tape, 1974.
8 *Burke's Peerage*, 1940. Sydney Olivier letter to mother, 28 May 1898, BL PERS 27/2. The typescript of Sydney's play, which was presented by the Stage Society on 21 January 1900, was sent to LO on 6 December 1975 by his cousin Angela, grand-daughter of Sydney, and is in BL PERS 27/2. Shaw's description of Sydney is from *Sydney Olivier*, p.9 (see note 4 above).
9 Opera training, *Sydney Olivier* p.45. Heidelberg, Sybille tapes, 1974. Cricket, *History of Hampshire CCC*, by Peter Wynne-Thomas, 1988. Dutch ancestry, LO to Gwen Purchase, 10 March [n.d.]; French ancestry, Aunt Mab Crookenden – LO, 26 June 1953; both BL PERS 27/2.
10 Kerr, *Confessions* mss, p.10 of second series. Kilt, CA p.19. Kerrs not traced, LO to Jeremy Gibson (cousin), 15 February 1954, BL PERS 27/2. Hotel; LO and VL registered as Mr and Mrs Andrew Kerr at a Tewkesbury hotel on 8 August 1939 (the bill is loose in his diary for 1936), and he often used this name in America that year.
11 Sybille tapes, 7 December 1974. Mab Crookenden reported in *Daily Telegraph*, 14 May 1939.
12 Birth, CA p.6.
13 Liar, CA pp.7–8, and *Confessions* mss. *Christian Science Monitor*, Boston, 18 May 1939.

14 Attempted murder, *On Acting*, 1986, pp.144–46. See GG trs, pp.80–82 for the invention of the story. Sybille tapes, 1974.

15 Mother's breasts, Sybille tapes, 6 Dec 1974, also GG trs of 5 December 1984. Beating, CA p.8.

16 Nicknames, Sybille tapes, 1974. Fahv's appointments, *Crockford's Clerical Directory*. Gentleman's life, Sybille tapes. Documents of the Olivier and Crookenden Trusts in the possession of Hester St John-Ives, widow of LO's brother, Dickie Olivier.

NOTES TO CHAPTER 2 Sweet Swinging and 'Whispering'

1 The church: *England's Thousand Best Churches*, by Simon Jenkins, 1999, and *All Saints, Margaret Street*, Pitkin Pictorials, 1990. Choir repertory, CA p.1, and MA 1.5.

2 Reports in BL PERS 2a.

3 *Julius Caesar*, CA p.13, MA 1.9, and *Ellen Terry's Memoirs*, ed. Edith Craig and Christopher St John, 1933, p.318. Commercial for American Film Theatre advertising *Luther* and *Three Sisters*, c.1972.

4 Breaking news, MA 18.10. Funeral, Aunt Mab – LO, 26 June 1953, BL PERS 27/2. Procession, Sybille memoir, p.44. Wooden cross, Sybille tapes, 1974.

5 Jump into Thames, author interview with JP, December 2003. LO on Sybille facing Fahv, *Confessions* mss, red notebook p.27, and CA p.17. Whispering, Sybille memoir pp. 48–9, and LO's handwritten comment in margin.

6 Sybille's account is in her 1948 memoir, p.56; LO's in his 1974 *Confessions* mss, red notebook p.21a.

7 Ellen Terry, see note 3 above. Sweet singing, LO interview with Terry Coleman, the *Guardian*, London, and *Show* magazine, New York, April 1970.

8 Fees, Crookenden Trust papers. St Edward's details, school archives and *Encounters* by Stephan Hopkinson. [A privately printed memoir by a contemporary of LO's at St Edwards. When Hopkinson was Guild Rector in the City of London in the 1950s, LO used to come and read the lesson at lunchtime services.]

9 Reviews of Katharina at Stratford, *The Times* and *Daily Telegraph*, 29 April 1922. See also *The Times* of 6 April. See also Fr. Mackay's article in the All Saints parish paper for May 1922.

10 Empire ports, BL PERS 2a. Bader, MA 18.3.

11 Note from boy, MA 18.7. Homosexuality, Hopkinson memoir, see note 8 above.

12 Bath essay, BL PERS 2a.

13 CA p.20.

14 Boys' careers, St Edward's archives.

15 Sydney Olivier, from Bernard Shaw on p.18 of his introduction to *Sydney Olivier*, ed. Margaret Olivier, 1948. Fahv's marriage, MA 1.15

16 1953 version, Barker p.15. Earlier, *Film Pictorial*, New York, 26 August 1939.

NOTES TO CHAPTER 3 An Unanswered Wish to be Liked

1 CA pp.22–3.

2 CA p.23. Ashcroft's own written reminiscence in *Olivier, in Celebration*, ed. Garry O'Connor, 1987, p.23. Letter of 22 September 1924 from Central School to LO offering bursary, BL PERS 2a.

3 Money, Crookenden Trust papers, Hester St-John Ives. Copeau, Ashcroft and Seyler, CA pp.24–5.

4 Brighton, CA p.24. And Barker p.22. Tour dates and contract, BL EARLY 1.

5 CA pp.31–2. Lena Ashwell, *Oxford Companion to the Theatre*, ed. Phyllis Hartnoll, 1952. Contracts, BL EARLY 1. Ibo, GG trs, tape of 5 December 1984.

6 Appalling prospect, GG trs, no date. Sybille, CA p.16; LO's diary, 1926; MA 18.16–18.

7 CA pp.33–4.

8 CA pp.37–41. St Bernard programme in Mander & Mitchenson Theatre Collection, Greenwich.

9 MA 15.15. Also see CA p.41. Method, *On Acting*, p.232.

10 CA pp.47–8. Contracts in BL EARLY 1. Clare Eames, *Round the Next Corner* by Denys Blakelock, 1967. Sincere, Barker p.33.

11 Ashcroft, see note 2 above.

12 From *Finding My Way: A Spiritual Journey* by Denys Blakelock, 1958. LO's remarks are from the foreword he wrote, Blakelock's from Chapter 5 of the book.

13 *Round the Next Corner* by Denys Blakelock, 1967.

14 *Acting My Way* by Denys Blakelock, 1964, p.20.

15 *Advice to a Player* by Denys Blakelock, 1957.

16 CA p.50.

17 CA pp.50–1. *No Leading Lady: An Autobiography* by R.C. Sherriff, 1968.

18 MA 9.5–7.

19 MA 9.8.

20 Sherriff was wounded at Ypres in 1917. He wrote many plays and the screenplays of *Goodbye Mr Chips*, *The Four Feathers*, *Lady Hamilton*, *Odd Man Out*, and *The Dam Busters*.

21 Barker pp.39–40. Pay, BL EARLY 1.

22 Sex and God, CA p.41. Not dazzling, CA p.50. LO to Jane (Welsh) Ritter, 9 November 1976, BL NT34/1 (7); she had written congratulating him on the opening of the new National Theatre on the South Bank. In the west, CA p.53.

NOTES TO CHAPTER 4 Our Particular Pet Devil, or What?

1 Never so excited, GG trs, 10 January 1985. Also Barker p.31 and CA p.53.

2 English plays, Barker pp.41–2. Jill's letters to LO and to her mother, both 9 April 1929. Fight, letter fragment, JE–LO undated, SFC.

3 Parties and Warwick, MA trs 12.1–2. LO *Lancastria* letter, undated.

4 JE–LO, 20 November 1929, SFC.

5 *Crockford's Clerical Directory*, 1930. See also Tiedemann's letter to LO, 22 May 1930, SFC.

6 JE–LO, undated but November 1929, SFC. Tiedemann was a graduate of the universities of Washington (1912) and Columbia (1914), had taken orders in New Jersey and Pennsylvania, was at Keble College, Oxford, in 1926 and was an assistant priest at St Cyprian, St Marylebone, London, in 1928.

7 Ibo perfect angel, GG trs, 5 December 1984. *Last Enemy*, Barker p.42. LO–JE, 5 December 1929.

8 JE–LO, 23 December 1929, SFC.

9 Sybille wrote to LO, 19 August 1949, saying she was well looked after in Netherne mental hospital, Surrey, which was utterly different from 'that ghastly Green Lanes, Finsbury Park, where they dumped me for an unforgettable three months 20 years ago . . .' BL PERS 25. Details of Sybille's 1929 breakdown are in *Rivers of Damascus*, by H.V.L. Day (her husband), 1939. He wrote the book to be of use to others in the

same state and disguised the names of Sybille, who became Sylvia, and Olivier, who became Edward 'of mixed Scottish [the Kerr connection] and French descent'.

10 JE–LO cable and letter, 23 December 1929, SFC.

11 Same.

12 JE–LO, 1 January 1930, SFC.

13 Film contract, BL FILMS 1, CA p.55. JE–LO, 16 April 1930, SFC.

14 JE–LO, 15 and 16 April 1930 and another undated, SFC.

15 Operas, LO's 1930 diary and CA p.55. JE–LO, 22 April 1930, SFC.

16 JE–LO, 7 May 1930, SFC.

17 Olivier autobiography, CA pp.40-41. Alarmingly loose, Oswald Frewen's diary for 28 June 1937, cited in *Vivien Leigh* by Hugo Vickers, 1988, p. 77. This is an impeccably researched biography. Frewen was a barrister and a close friend of Vivien Leigh who met Olivier frequently. Wherever his diary can be checked it is accurate.

18 Jill bisexual, Tarquin Olivier interview with author, 14 April 2003. And after the war LO often referred to her as a lesbian. Blakelock's books, see notes 12–15 of Chapter 3 above. Letter to LO, 29 September 1968, BL PERS (1/3).

19 Tiedemann–LO, 22 May 1930, SFC.

20 Film, CA p.56. Jill's article, *Daily Herald*, London, 22 May 1930.

21 CA p.56.

22 CA pp.59–60.

23 The colleague to whom Olivier told this story, in December 1963, was Pieter Rogers, general administrator at the Chichester Festival Theatre. Rogers told Olivier's son, Richard, after the publication of Donald Spoto's biography of Olivier in 1991 and substantially repeated his account, with some difference in emphasis, in an interview with the author on 19 October 2004. Richard remembers Rogers saying that, when his father was approached by Blakelock, he 'thought about it for a minute' and then decided he couldn't. In 2004, Rogers' recollection was that Olivier was more shocked. Rogers was Olivier's friend, and one of the few who were left mementos in his will.

24 Ibo–LO, 24 July 1930, BL PERS 23.

25 CA pp.61–62.

26 LO–Eva Moore, 'Wednesday' from West Lulworth.

27 CA p.62.

28 JE–LO, 22 August 1930, and two others, undated, in same envelope.

29 *Manchester Evening Chronicle*, 13 September 1930. The article is signed S.P.

30 *Private Lives*, CA p.63. Film contract, BL FILMS 1.

NOTES TO CHAPTER 5 The Lick of Luxury of Those Lush Valleys

1 JE–Eva Moore, 15 and 21 January 1931.

2 JE–Eva Moore, 21 February 1931.

3 Hahlleewood, CA p.64. LO's offers, JE–Eva, 19 March 1931.

4 LO–Eva Moore, 15 May 1931.

5 The house, JE–Eva Moore, 16 June 1931. Fairbanks on LO, in his introductory speech for LO at Lincoln Center, NYC, 25 April 1983. Giggles, JE–Eva Moore, 30 June 1931. LO on Hollywood parties, CA p.67.

6 LO wants to stay, JE–Eva Moore, 20 June and 25 July 1931.

7 *Private Lives* and *Frankenstein* films, JE–Eva Moore, 11 August 1931.

8 Negri, JE–Eva Moore, 3 and 11 August 1931. LO's jaundice, JE–Eva Moore, 1 September 1931.

9 *Westward Passage*, CA p.66. Anne Harding's hair, GG trs, 5 December 1984.

10 LO bored, GG trs, 9 January 1985. Selznick, *Showman, The Life of David O. Selznick* by David Thomson, New York and London, 1993, p.133.

11 LO on Hepburn contract, CA p.69. RKO's version, see Thomson in note 10 above, p.133.

12 LO in GG trs, 9 January 1985.

13 'Lick of luxury of those lush valleys,' LO interview with Terry Coleman, the *Guardian*, London and Manchester, and *Show* magazine, New York, June 1970. The home movies, about thirty minutes, are now in Tarquin Olivier's possession.

14 Not a line in CA or anywhere else I have seen.

15 Harold Hobson, *Theatre in Britain*, 1948. Helen Spencer's handkerchief letter, dated only 25 September, is in BL PERS 1/15, which includes ten other letters of hers; none states the year, but internal evidence shows they date from c.1933 to at least 1974. She married Tully Grigg, who gave LO advice on farming in the 1950s. They later went to live at Biot, near Antibes, where Olivier and his new wife Joan Plowright visited them. Annie Rooney's letter, at BL PERS 1/14, bears no date at all but is written on Globe Theatre paper and had been filed in a way common to LO's letters of the mid-1930s.

16 Whistler's studio described in Sybille memoir pp.82–3, with LO's marginal handwritten annotation. Also CA p.72.

17 *Rats of Norway* ran from 6 April to 8 July 1933. The first MGM offer was made at the end of May. LO did not sail from Southampton until 15 July. The cables are at BL Box 14 FILMS 1, and most are printed in Barker, pp.53–55.

18 LO–Michael Godfrey, 6 August 1947, BL FILMS 5/2.

19 CA p.71.

20 *Collier's* magazine, 10 June 1939, article by Kyle Chrichton.

21 Cable dated 7 September 1933 in BL BOX 14 FILMS 1, and Barker p.59.

Notes to Chapter 6 Matinée Idol to Roaring Italian Boy

1 Jed Harris, CA p.72, Barker p.61. LO letter to Sybille, Sybille memoir p.90. Play contract, BL EARLY 1.

2 Barker p.60.

3 MA 32.2.

4 MA 32.3.

5 BL EARLY 1.

6 *On Acting* p.36.

7 Telegram Coward–LO, 23 October 1934, BL PERS 1/4.

8 *Mirror*, 1 January 1935. *Sketch*, 3 January 1935. Helen Spencer–LO, 1 January 1935, BL PERS 1/15.

9 *Sofka: The Autobiography of a Princess* by Sofka Skipwith, 1968, pp.12–49, 132–33, 135, 141.

10 *Post* and *Telegraph*, both 13 November 1934.

11 *Country Life*, 23 March 1935. Helen Spencer–LO, 15 February 1935, BL PERS 1/15.

12 Miss Greer as LO's mistress. Tarquin Olivier interview with author, 14 April 2003.

13 Blakelock on Tiedemann and Olivier from *Round the Next Corner*, 1967, p93.

14 *On Acting* p.46.

15 Williams in *In Celebration*, ed. Garry O'Connor, 1987, pp.155–8.

16 *Isis* (the Oxford University newspaper), 15 May 1935.

17 14 March 1936

18 Barker p.67.

19 CA p.75.

20 Contract, 9 September 1935, BL EARLY 1.

21 MA 9.19.

22 *On Acting* p.44.

23 GG trs, pp.33–4.

24 David Frost Show, 11 December 1970.

25 CA p.75.

26 Esmond Knight, interview with Hugo Vickers, 11 February 1987. Others, letters in BL EARLY 1. Diary, 13 November 1935.

27 Fabia Drake–LO, 30 May 1982, BL PERS (1/6); the line is from Act IV Scene 1. Ervine, Barker p.69.

28 Barker p.71.

29 Tarquin Olivier, in an interview of 14 April 2003 with the author, recalled that his mother Jill Esmond had told him this as she had earlier of Greer Garson. Gielgud wrote to Paul Anstee on 29 December 1966 saying LO and Ashcroft had an affair: *Gielgud's Letters*, ed. Richard Mangan, 2004, p.336.

30 CA p.75.

31 Peggy Ashcroft–LO, 25 January 1982. LO–Ashcroft, 17 March 1982. Both in BL PERS (1/1)a.

32 No date, BL PERS (1/1)a.

33 Barker p.71. Greene in *Spectator*, 11 September 1936. Flocks, *On Acting* p.177.

34 Barker p.72.

35 The five sittings for Harold Knight, the flying lessons, dinner with Korda, and so on are recorded in LO's diaries. He stated in his autobiography that he kept no diary for ten years after his wedding in 1930. It is true that no pocket diaries survive for 1931–40 inclusive, but three larger desk diaries are extant for 1935, 1936, and 1937. All contain entries in his hand. That for 1937 is full of intimate entries.

NOTES TO CHAPTER 7 Vivling and Dark Destruction

1 Vickers p.41 and p.43. The first part of this chapter, on the early life of Vivien Leigh, owes a great debt to Hugo Vickers' impeccably researched biography, *Vivien Leigh*, 1988, which is by far the best and most scholarly study of her. He examined in detail VL's letters to her first husband and to her mother, from Suzanne Farrington's collection. He also transcribed large parts of Oswald Frewen's diaries and interviewed colleagues and friends of VL's who have since died. In this chapter I attribute some statements and quotations to his book, citing the page numbers, but this does not fully demonstrate the extent of my debt to him. He is of course not responsible for any errors of understanding or emphasis which I may have made.

2 Vickers p.43.

3 Vickers p.47, quoting from an unpublished ms by John Gliddon.

4 *Film Pictorial*, 8 April 1935.

5 Vickers p.48.

6 *The Times*, 16 May 1935. The *Sunday Times*, Barker p.102. See also Barker pp.99–103.

7 The *Daily Mirror*, 15 May 1935.

8 The *Daily Express*, 17 May 1935.

9 Vickers p.52. Barker p.105.

10 London *Evening Standard*, 12 June 1935.

11 The *Sketch*, 28 August 1935. Buckmaster affair, Vickers p.55: VL said this to John Merivale, the man with whom she spent the last seven years of her life and who was devoted to her, so it has some authority.

12 CA p.77.

13 CA p.78.

14 CA p.78.

15 *Collier's* magazine, 10 June 1939.

16 LO's diary, 11 June 1936.

17 Vickers p.61. The source is John Merivale, in an interview with Vickers.

18 Vickers p.68, quoting letters of VL to Holman, 17 and 19 August 1936.

19 Sybille memoir p.108.

20 *Alexander Korda* by Paul Tabori, 1959.

21 VL–Holman, 31 August 1936. Vickers p.69.

22 Vickers p.69.

23 Vickers p.72.

24 Vickers p.73, quoting Frewen's diary for 3 November 1936.

25 *Rex* by Rex Harrison, 1974, p.52.

26 Scent, Tarquin Olivier interview with author, 14 April 2003. Mr Olivier describes the christening in *My Father Laurence Olivier*, 1992, p.68.

27 CA p.78.

28 Vickers p.74.

29 29 September 1936.

30 CA p.65.

31 *Confessions* mss p.18, in BL CRIT 1/1/2.

32 LO was asked about Coward by Gawn Grainger in 1984–5 when he was recording conversations with LO on which to base *On Acting*. The transcript is in BL CRIT 1 BOX 2.

33 JE–LO, 15 April 1930, SFC.

34 Barker p.72.

35 *Who Was Who in the Theatre*; and *The Oxford Companion to the Theatre*, 1951.

36 The Ainley letters are in BL PERS 1/1. The more explicit passages are not quoted here.

NOTES TO CHAPTER 8 *Hamlet* and Mr and Mrs Andrew Kerr

1 MA 11.2–3.

2 Barker p.117.

3 MA 10.37.

4 MA 11.1 and 11.4–5.

5 MA 11.2.

6 Barker p.117.

7 GG trs p.75.

8 GG trs p.67.

9 Barker pp.118–20. CA p.79. MA 14.2.

10 *Tyrone Guthrie* by James Forsyth, 1976.

11 *Morning Post* and *Daily Telegraph*, 24 February 1937.

12 *Harper's* and *Sketch* from LO's scrapbook, undated. *Bystander*, 24 February 1937.

13 *Observer*, 21 February 1937.

14 Peggy Ashcroft–LO, undated but evidently February or March 1937, BL PERS 1/1.

15 *Memo from David O. Selznick*, ed. Rudy Behlmer, 1972; memo of 3 February 1937.

16 Frewen's diary, 3 March 1937, in Vickers p.76.

17 Frewen diary, 28 June 1937.

18 CA p.78.

19 LO–VL, 4 May 1939, SFC.

20 CA p.79.

21 Consuelo–LO, undated but 1937, BL PERS 1/3.

22 Rev. G. K. Olivier–LO, letters of 9 and 21 May 1937, BL PERS 23.

23 Barker p.126. LO's 1936 diary, BL.

24 CA p.78.

25 MA 14.6.

26 Steinbeck–LO, undated but 1951, when LO and VL were in New York with the two *Cleopatra* plays.

27 LO's 1936 diary, BL.

28 Sybille memoir pp.126–7.

29 CA p.78.

30 Frewen diary, 28 June 1937, in Vickers p.83.

31 Frewen diary, 20 November 1937, in Vickers p.86.

32 *Evening News*, 12 July 1937.

33 *Thank You for Having Me* by C.A. Lejeune, 1964.

34 *Farmer's Weekly*, 3 February 1939; *Picturegoer*, 31 July 1937. Miss Lejeune wrote not only for the *Observer* but for these and other magazines.

35 Will dated 17 July 1937. A photocopy is at BL PERS 17, and the original in JPC.

36 *Sofka: The Autobiography of a Princess*, 1968, pp.149, 153, 158 and 282; and author's conversation with Sofka Zinovieff (Sofka Skipwith's granddaughter), 6 November 2004. Sofka went to Paris in 1939 and was interned by the Germans. Her husband, Grey Skipwith, was the son of Sir Grey Humberton Skipwith, the eleventh holder of a baronetcy created in 1622. The family had come over with the Norman conquest. One Skipwith was knighted by Henry V. The younger Grey never succeeded to the title. He served in the RAF and was killed in action as a flight lieutenant in 1942. Sofka, after three years of internment, was repatriated via Lisbon and returned to England in 1944. She became company secretary of the Old Vic company, which she accompanied on its European tour of 1945. She left in 1946. When later she asked Olivier for a reference he wrote, 'I have known Sofka Skipwith, man and boy, for fifteen years. She has been private secretary, company secretary, play-reader, and present help in time of trouble . . .' In the war she had become a convinced Communist, and later established a travel agency and led groups of tourists to Eastern Europe and Russia. She settled on Bodmin Moor in the 1960s, published her autobiography in 1968, and wrote a book on Russian cooking. She does not seem to have kept in touch with Olivier. She died in 1994 at the age of eighty-six. See obituary in the *Daily Telegraph*, 5 March 1994.

37 Bushell–LO, undated, BL PERS 1/3.

38 Shoes from *Vivien* by Alexander Walker, 1987, pp.95–6. Walker had access to Gliddon's papers and quoted them frequently. VL at Elsinore, Vickers pp.81–2.

39 Make-up, Barker p.133. Baylis, Barker p.132.

40 *Sunday Times*, 5 December 1937.

41 *Night and Day* magazine, BL CA6 (cuttings).

42 The Rev. G.K. Olivier–LO, 24 December 1938, BL PERS 23.

43 Letters Ainley–LO, the first undated, the others 25 November 1937 and 10 January 1938, BL PERS 1/1.

44 Barker p.135.

45 CA p.82.

46 Lejeune in *Farmer's Weekly*, 3 February 1939, after the release of the film.

47 Somersault, *Cavalcade*, 30 April 1938. *John O'London's Weekly* 29 April 1938.

48 CA p.80.

49 Barker p.141. CA p.83.

50 Frewen's diary, 29 September 1938, in Vickers p.95.

51 Ainley letters to LO dated 30 August; 4, 18 and 30 September; 8 and 29 November 1938, BL PERS 1/1.

52 Barker p.141. CA p.83. *Film Weekly*, 22 October 1938.

53 Blind with misery, CA p.83. LO's two letters to VL on the train, 5 November 1938 but postmarked 6 November, and one further letter, written on the *Normandie*, sent back on her from New York, and postmarked 10–11 November.

NOTES TO CHAPTER 9 The Making of *Wuthering Heights*

1 MA 9.5.

2 *On Acting* p.178.

3 Letters LO–VL from *Normandie*, 10–11 November 1938, and on board American Airlines, 13 and 17 November 1938, all SFC.

4 LO–VL dated 17 November 1938 but written over succeeding days afterwards, SFC.

5 MA 10.11–12.

6 MA 10.15.

7 LO–VL, first of two letters dated 17 November 1938, SFC.

8 MA 10.16.

9 Barker p.145.

10 VL–Holman, 2 November 1938, in Vickers p.96.

11 LO–VL, 10–11 November 1938, SFC.

12 LO–VL, 11 November 1938, SFC.

13 LO–VL, 12 November 1938, SFC.

14 Same.

15 Same.

16 LO–VL, 13 November 1938 from plane; and sketch enclosed with letter of 15 November from Los Angeles, SFC.

17 LO–VL, 16 November 1938, SFC.

18 LO–VL, 17 November 1938, SFC.

19 Same.

20 Helen Spencer–LO, 24 November 1938, BL 53c.

21 The reference is to *Genesis* XXXVIII.

22 LO–VL in second letter dated 17 November but which has to have been written later, because in it he mentions that Merle Oberon had invited VL to stay with her, something he cabled to VL on 23 October. SFC.

23 VL–Holman, 25 November 1938, Vickers p.97. SFC.

24 Cable LO–VL, 21 November 1938, SFC.

25 Cable LO–VL, 23 November 1938, SFC.

26 Hamish Hamilton in interview with Hugo Vickers, 19 October 1986, in Vickers p.97.

NOTES TO CHAPTER 10 *Gone with the Wind*

1 Three cables, SFC.
2 CA p.83.
3 Selznick to Ed Sullivan, 20 September 1938, in *Memo from David O. Selznick*, ed. Rudy Behlmer, 1972. This book draws on the Selznick archive at the Harry Ransom Humanities Center, Austin, Texas.
4 *Memo*, as above, 12 December 1938.
5 *Memo*, p.180.
6 Barker p.150.
7 CA p.84.
8 *Showman: The Life of David O. Selznick* by David Thomson, 1993, p.278.
9 VL–Leigh Holman, 16 December 1938, SFC.
10 Barker p.152.
11 SFC.
12 Cable, 5 January 1939, SFC.
13 *Showman*, as note 8 above, p.284.
14 24 January 1939, SFC.
15 26 January 1939, SFC.
16 *Showman*, as note 8 above, p.284.
17 VL–Mrs Hartley, 29 January 1939, SFC.
18 CA p.85.
19 CA p.70.
20 LO–Mrs Hartley, 21 March 1939, and VL–Mrs Hartley 8 March 1939; both SFC.
21 Sunny Alexander–LO, 12 March 1939, BL 53c.
22 Same, 30 March 1939.
23 Parsons in *LA Examiner*, 25 March 1939; *LA News* 28 March 1939; *New York Times*, 16 April 1939.
24 CA p.85.
25 Cables, 24 and 25 March 1939, SFC.
26 Ibo–LO dated 'Good Friday 1939', BL PERS 23.
27 Sybille–LO, 'Sunday', BL PERS 25.
28 Ibo–LO, 30 April 1939, BL PERS 23.
29 3 April 1939, BL PERS 1/1.
30 Jeans–VL, 15 May 1939; Consuelo–VL, 30 April 1939, both BL 53c.
31 LO–VL, 10 April 1939, SFC. Olivier addressed all but one of his letters to VL to 'Mrs V.M. Holman'. Du Maurier from *Chicago American*, 3 April 1939; other cuttings unidentified and undated, from BL CA 7 (cuttings book).
32 *Times, News, Post*, all 18 April 1939.
33 LO–VL undated, 'Friday night'.
34 18 May 1939.
35 17 June 1939.
36 BL CA 7 (cuttings book).
37 Sybille memoir p.153.
38 LO–VL undated, addressed to Mrs Andrew Kerr.
39 Critics' poll in *Variety*, undated, in BL CA 7 (cuttings book).
40 LO–VL, 4 May 1939, SFC.
41 LO–VL, 9 May 1939, SFC.
42 JE–LO, 1 May 1939, BL PERS 21/1.

43 LO–VL, 11 May 1939, SFC.

44 VL–Holman, 14 May 1939, SFC. *Memo*, see note 4 above, p.138.

45 LO–VL, 2, 6 and 7 May 1939, SFC.

46 Sunny Alexander–LO, 19 May 1939, BL 53c.

47 LO–VL, 18 May 1939, SFC.

48 Sunny Alexander–LO, 19 May 1939, BL 53c.

49 LO–VL, 16 and 17 May 1939, SFC.

50 LO–VL, 11 June 1939, SFC.

51 Sunny Alexander–LO, 8 June 1939, BL 53c.

52 *Syracuse Herald*, 27 June 1939, in BL CA1 (cuttings).

53 *New York Journal and American*, 22 June 1939.

54 *Express* and *Sketch*, 29 July 1939.

NOTES TO CHAPTER 11 Not Sceeered, Just Proud

1 Estate, solicitor's letter to LO, 2 November 1939, BL PERS 20.

2 Hotel bill (though it is for August 1939) loose in LO's diary for 1937, BL.

3 LO–VL letter, 4 May 1939, SFC.

4 *Memo from David O. Selznick*, ed. Rudy Behlmer, 1972.

5 CA p.86.

6 VL–Mrs Hartley, 27 November 1939, SFC.

7 Barker p.165.

8 Jill's decree was granted on 29 January and Holman's on 18 February 1940.

9 This letter, of twenty pages, bears no date at the beginning but at one point JE writes 'today March 5' in the body of the letter.

10 Barker p.164.

11 LO–Harry Crookenden, 15 February 1940, BL PERS 20.

12 LO–VL, 8 May 1939, SFC.

13 MA 9.21. CA p.89.

14 CA p.88 and p.90.

15 MA p.22.

16 MA 9.21.

17 *New York Times*, 19 May 1940.

18 Sybille memoir p.162.

19 LO says $96,000 in CA p.90. But JE, in a letter to her mother (cited but undated in Tarquin p.89, and probably of October 1940), quotes LO as saying the production cost $96,000, that his own loss was $40,000 and that he had only a few thousands left. She also wrote that VL had not put a penny of her own money into it.

20 BL, LO's pilot's log and enclosed pilot's licence No. 7178–40, Civil Aeronautics Society.

21 Tarquin pp.89–90.

22 JE–Eva Moore, 22 July 1940.

23 JE–Eva Moore, undated but July–August 1940.

24 CA p.90, and MA 19.5–11.

25 Wedding, Barker pp.180–83 and CA p.92, where LO gets the date wrong. Quarrel, Garson Kanin interview with Hugo Vickers, 22 January 1988. Marriage licence is at BL V53c: VL's name was spelled Vivian, with an 'a', as she had been christened.

26 Barker p.183.

27 MA 22.10.

28 MA 19.10.

29 VL–Holman, 22 October 1940, SFC. Cited in Vickers p.130.
30 LO's pilot's log, BL.
31 MA 10.8.
32 JE–Eva Moore, 26 December 1940, SFC.
33 CA pp.93–4.

Notes to Chapter 12 Not Ever Having Been an Actor

1 Pilot, London *Evening Standard*, 28 December 1940. Nurse, *Daily Telegraph*, 16 December 1940.
2 Barker p.189.
3 Barker p.190.
4 BL PERS 3 (Wartime).
5 Two in Barker p.101 (1953); three in *Olivier* by Antony Holden, 1988. 'Made up', Sir John Mills interview with author, 6 September 2004.
6 LO's pilot's log, BL.
7 LO–Lieut. Commander Norman Gash, 28 June 1944, Theatre Museum, London.
8 Barker p.190. VL–Leigh Holman, 29 December 1941, SFC, in Vickers p.138.
9 *The Noel Coward Diaries*, ed. Payn and Morley, 1982, entry for 12 July 1941.
10 MA 18.21.
11 Richardson in *Theatre '73*, ed. Sheridan Morley.
12 MA 18.22.
13 LO in *In Conversation* with Elliot Norton, drama critic of the *Boston Record*, WNET 1967, in Museum of Television and Radio, New York, B567.
14 Tarquin p.104.
15 LO–Gash, as note 7 above.
16 JE–LO, 16 September and 25 November 1941, BL PERS 21/1.
17 JE–Eva Moore 2 and 21 August 1941, in Tarquin pp.95–6.
18 Vickers p.135. Barker pp.189–90.
19 Beaton's diary for 14 November 1941, in Vickers p.137.
20 Novels, CA p.96. Champagne, BL PERS 3.
21 BL PERS 3.
22 Undated manuscript note by LO, in same envelope as his 1937 will, JPC.
23 JE–LO, 26 April 1942, BL PERS 21/1.
24 LO–JE, 14 May 1942.
25 LO film excerpt in *Larry and Vivien: the Oliviers in Love*, Channel 4, 2001.
26 Barker p.195.
27 Undated, BL PERS 3.
28 Barker p.196.
29 LO's pilot's log, BL.
30 CA p.98.
31 JE–LO, 6 December 1942, BL PERS 21/1.
32 Dickie's account in *The Battle of the Narrow Seas* by Peter Scott, 1945 and 1971.

Notes to Chapter 13 The Walrus and the Sceptred Isle

In this chapter some of the notes refer simply to 'FILMS 3', which is the general file for the film of *Henry V* in the BL archive. As my research continued, this general file was in the process of being separated into parts, such as 'FILMS 3/4/1'. I have given this more accurate notation wherever possible.

1 *On Acting* p.190.

2 LO's pilot's log, BL. CA p.101.

3 Tarquin p.101.

4 MA 19.3.

5 Contract, 12 September 1943, BL FILMS 3/2.

6 Del Giudice to Ministry of Information, 1 January 1943, BL FILMS 3.

7 GG trs, tape 3, side 2.

8 *William Walton: Behind the Façade* by Susana Walton, 1988, p.94. In this biography Lady Walton, who was much younger than her husband and had no personal knowledge, was reporting what he had told her.

9 LO–Young, 11 April 1943, BL PERS 1/17.

10 Young–Del Giudice, 18 August 1943, BL FILMS 3. LO grateful, in LO's manuscript in red notebook, BL CRIT 1, BOX 2. LO wanting the lot, *Walton*, as in note 8 above.

11 LO–VL, 29 May 1943, SFC.

12 VL–LO, 28 May 1943, BL 53.

13 Barker pp.202–3.

14 CA pp.101–3. Barker pp.202–3.

15 VL–LO, 1 August 1943, BL 53.

16 LO–VL, letter of 7–10 June 1943, SFC.

17 *Blessings in Disguise* by Alec Guinness, 1986.

18 LO–VL, 13 June 1943, SFC.

19 LO–VL, 15 June 1943, SFC.

20 VL–LO, 15 June 1943, BL 53.

21 LO–VL, 26 June 1943, SFC.

22 Shooting list, BL FILMS 3.

23 LO–VL, letter started 26 June 1943, SFC.

24 VL–Gertrude Hartley, 1 September 1943, SFC.

25 LO–VL, 30 June 1943, SFC.

26 LO–VL, 8 July 1943, SFC.

27 LO–VL, 14 July 1943, SFC.

28 Barker p.210. CA p.103.

29 LO–VL, 29 July 1943, SFC.

30 CA p.105.

31 *Walton*, as note 8 above, pp.94–5.

32 CA p.105.

33 Del Giudice–LO, 19 June 1943, BL FILMS 3.

34 Letters Del Giudice–LO–Del Giudice, 24 and 26 July 1943, BL FILMS 3.

35 E.T. Carr–LO, 24 July 1944, BL FILMS 3/2.

36 Unsigned typescript but with other papers by LO, BL FILMS 34. Clark's article had appeared in the *Cornhill* magazine.

37 Sybille memoir p.181.

38 Memo to 'Paul', undated, in BL FILMS 3.

39 A letter of Phil Samuel of Two Cities to LO, 8 August 1945, quotes Rank as saying this; BL FILMS 3.

40 LO–Rank, 23 July 1945, BL FILMS 3.

41 Del Giudice memo, saying he is giving LO's thoughts 'roughly speaking', apparently to Phil Samuel, undated but February 1945.

42 Del–LO, 7 September and 29 August 1945; LO–Del 29 August 1945, BL FILMS

3/4/1.

43 LO–Del, undated memo, BL FILMS 3.

44 LO–Del, 1 October 1945, BL FILMS 3/4/1.

45 *Time*, 8 April 1946.

46 Barker p.216.

47 MA 7.7.

48 LO's note to projectionists, 24 June 1946, BL FILMS 3/4/1.

49 Tennant (for LO)–Davis (of Rank's), 12 August 1949, BL FILMS 3.

50 BL FILMS 3.

51 Tennant–Davis, 15 January 1951, and Tennant–LO, 29 April 1965, both BL FILMS 3.

52 Clayton Hutton–LO, 23 March 1945, BL FILMS 3.

53 LO–Hutton, 29 March 1945, BL FILMS 3.

54 Restrictive covenant by LO, 3 March 1945, BL FILMS 3.

55 *The Times*, 13 February 1943.

56 Maiden speech in Lords, 20 July 1971, printed in CA pp.284–6.

57 'Some Impressions' by Bernard Shaw, which appeared as a prologue in *Sydney Olivier: Letters and Selected Writings*, edited and with a memoir by Margaret Olivier [his widow], 1948.

Notes to Chapter 14 Kean's Sword, and the Thrill

1 CA p.107.

2 BL PERS 5/5/1, personal finance 1943–52.

3 Hair-brained, LO–Lewis J. Deak, 27 June 1944, BL PERS 2. Contract, Guthrie–LO, 20 June 1944, BL OV 2/1.

4 Fogerty–LO, 27 May 1944, BL OV 2/1. She died in December 1945, when a friend, Marion Cole, told LO that, though she had felt 'awfully outcast', her last days had been brightened by his loyalty: Cole–LO, 1 January 1946, BL OV 2/1.

5 *A Life in the Theatre* by Tyrone Guthrie, 1960. p.203.

6 CA p.110.

7 GG trs, 12 December 1984.

8 VL–Holman 16 August, 1944, SFC.

9 Tarquin interview with author, 14 April 2003.

10 CA p.110.

11 Author interview with Sir John Mills, 6 September 2004.

12 LO–Alan Dent, BL OV 2/1. Right, MA 8.7. Seaweed, CA p.111. Oysters, *On Acting* p.88.

13 Gielgud to mother, June ? 1939, in *Gielgud's Letters*, ed. Richard Mangan, 2004.

14 Barker p.238. Dent–LO, March 1945, BL OV 2/1. Under bed, GG trs, tape 3.

15 Tarquin pp.115–6.

16 Barker p.224. Selznick memo of 19 February 1945 in *Memo From David O. Selznick* ed. Rudy Behlmer, 1972.

17 Knight, Frank and Rutley (estate agents) description in BL PERS 10 1/6.

18 Barker pp.229–30.

19 CA p.113.

20 MA p.8.26.

21 MA 8.27. Also LO–VL, 18 June 1944, from Hamburg, in which he names the officer as Ralph Barnet [?] SFC.

22 LO–VL, letters of 9, 12, 14, 22 and 25 June 1945, SFC.

23 LO–VL, 25 June 1945, SFC.

24 LO–VL, 27 June 1945, SFC.

25 LO–VL, 28 June 1945, SFC.

26 LO–VL, 11 and 12 July 1945, SFC.

27 *On Acting* pp.144–5.

28 GG trs, dated 26 February 1985, pp.80–82.

29 CA p.115.

30 LO–Anthony Hopkins, musician, 26 October 1945, BL OV 2/1.

31 CA pp.115–9.

32 Kenneth Rae–LO, 12 March 1946, BL OV 2/2.

33 LO's own note of talk with Albery, 31 October 1945, BL OV 1.

34 Obituary, *The Times*, 1 November 1945. Memorial service, *The Times*, 14 November 1945. See also *A Little Love and Good Company* by Cathleen Nesbitt, 1975, p.61 and pp.67–69.

35 £60, account of 27 September 1946, BL OV 2/1. High Court order, 21 June 1946, backdated to 1 January 1945, BL PERS 21/1.

36 Articles of Association, 20 May 1946, BL LOP 1/1/1.

37 LOP board meetings, 5 April and 12 June 1946, BL LOP 1/1/1. Bill for car, 14 June 1946, BL PERS 12.

38 Knight in interview with Hugo Vickers, 12 February 1987.

39 Barker pp.241–3. CA pp.119–21.

40 CA p.121. Barker p.244.

41 Details of degrees accepted and declined in BL PERS 16 (HONOURS): the Yale doctorate in fine arts was declined in 1973. See also Wilder letter to LO 10 December, no year, BL PERS 1/17.

42 Crash landing, *New York Times*, *New York Tribune*, *Hartford Times*, and *Hartford Courant*, 19 June 1946. Inquiry, *New York Times*, 23 and 29 June 1946. The aircraft was NC88858. See also www.aviation-history.com./lockheed.

43 LO's account, *Hartford Times*, 19 June 1946, p.1 and p.14. Fuselage, *Hartford Courant*, 19 June 1946.

44 Barker p.246.

45 VL gave this account to Tarquin, who took her to have been describing the fire on board the plane on which they flew back from Lisbon to Bristol in 1941. He agreed in an interview of 21 April 2003 that she must have meant the 1946 incident. See also postcard of Hamish Hamilton to LO, 21 March 1945, in BL PERS 1/9, in which, having just flown back from America himself, he writes, 'Remember your hair's breadth escape, when V looked at L and L looked at the engine?'

46 The Rev. W. G. de Lara Wilson–LO, 25 September 1946, BL OV2/2.

47 CA p.121.

48 Maugham–LO, 12 October 1946, BL OV2/1.

49 Lehmann–LO, 18 October 1946, BL OV2/2.

50 Michael Denison interview with Hugo Vickers, 2 February 1987.

51 Edmund Choate–LO, 13 November 1946, BL OV 2/2.

52 Del Giudice–LO, 24 October 1946, and LO–Del Giudice, 2 November 1946, BL FILMS 3/4/1.

Notes to Chapter 15 Buckingham Palace, 10.15

1 Barker p.253.

2 CA pp.133–4.

3 *Self-portrait with Friends: Selected Diaries 1926–74* by Cecil Beaton, ed. Richard Buckle, 1979, entries for February 1947.

4 Barker p. 254. Rolls, Newman (garage) to LOP, 26 February 1947, BL PERS 12.

5 Heads of contract, Two Cities–Tennant, 12 May 1947, BL FILMS 5. Profits by 27 January 1951, BL FILMS 5/1/3.

6 MA 14.8.

7 *On Acting* p.198.

8 MA 14.7.

9 *On Acting* p.198.

10 MA 14.

11 *Dramatis Personae* by John Mason Brown, 1963.

12 LO–VL, 10–11 November 1938, SFC.

13 Ernest Irving–LO, 11 July 1947, and LO's reply, 20 July, BL FILMS 5/5.

14 LO to 'Darling Angel', 19 March 1947. The name 'Mrs G. Relph' is pencilled on the top of the carbon.

15 Rank–LO, 2 May 1947, and LO's reply of 9 May, BL FILMS 5/2.

16 CA p.134.

17 Coward, CA p. 134. Gielgud, *Gielgud's Letters*, ed. Richard Mangan, 2004, p.105.

18 Barker pp.260–61.

19 Lucky, Cecil Beaton–Greta Garbo, 15 July 1947, in Vickers p.176. Fee, LOP board meeting, 25 June 1947, BL LOP 1/1/1.

20 *The Other Half* by Kenneth Clark, 1977, p.60.

21 LO–Godfrey, 6 August 1947, BL FILMS 5/2.

22 CA pp.123–5. Barker pp.261–2.

23 Accountants' letter to Two Cities, 21 December 1948, BL FILMS 5/1/2.

24 Bushell–LO, 21 March 1948, BL PERS 1/3.

25 Joseph Breen–Rank Organisation, 9 May 1947, BL FILMS 5/2.

26 Justus Lawrence–LO, 4 February 1950, BL FILMS 5/2/3.

27 *Agee on Film* by James Agee, New York, 1958. *In Search of the Theatre* by Eric Bentley, New York, 1955.

28 Letters of chief projectionist, Philip C. Samuel, and LO, 12 and 16 May and 10 June 1948, BL FILMS 5/2.

29 LO–Lew Grade, 4 June 1973, BL NT54.

30 Rank to LO, undated handwritten note, BL FILMS 5/5, and LO desk diaries of 1948 and 1949.

Notes to Chapter 16 God and the Angel

1 *The History of the National Theatre* by John Elsom and Nicholas Tomalin, 1978, p.91.

2 CA p.126. MA 26.5–6.

3 MA 26.10.

4 *Tyrone Guthrie* by James Forsyth, 1976, p.202.

5 Battersby–Beaton, 25 December 1947, cited in Vickers p.180.

6 Craig–LO, 29 January 1947, BL PERS 1/15.

7 Notebook in BL OV4.

8 God and the Angel: in letter home by Michael Redington, one of the company, 27 March 1948, in Hugo Vickers' papers.

9 Barker p.272. CA p.127.

10 Note in VL's hand, undated, in BL VL53c.

11 LO–Esher, 23 April 1948, and Esher's reply, 10 May 1848, BL PERS 21/3.

12 Trader Faulkner interview with author, 16 September 2003.

13 CA p.128.

14 Peter Hiley, interview with author, 5 June 2003.

15 LO–Richardson, 19 July 1948, BL PERS 21/3.

16 Barker p.280.

17 *A Life in the Theatre* by Tyrone Guthrie, 1959, p.204.

18 Cable from agent to LO, 27 January 1934, BL CRIT 2/1.

19 Typescript in BL CRIT 1.

20 Cable LO–Tennant, 5 August 1948, BL CRIT 2/1. The cable to Sybille is quoted in full in the cable to Tennant.

21 Tennant–LO, 3 January 1949, BL CRIT 2/1.

22 Terence Morgan interview with Hugo Vickers, 16 April 1987.

23 CA p.128, where LO mistakenly says he met Finch in Melbourne and that the play he saw was *Tartuffe*.

24 Out of breath, Vickers p.186. Sunrise, Morgan interview with Hugo Vickers, 16 April 1987.

25 VL–Holman, 10 September 1948, SFC.

26 Barker p.282.

27 LO–Beaton, 15 October 1948, SFC.

28 Barker p.282. CA p.129.

29 CA p.130.

30 Draft cable in BL OV4.

NOTES TO CHAPTER 17 Living Like Royals

1 Royal party, LO's diary, BL.

2 Barker p.286. *The Times* thought she lacked power. Felix Barker himself disagreed, saying she had authority and passion.

3 *Self-portrait with Friends: Selected Diaries 1926–1974* by Cecil Beaton, ed. Richard Buckle, 1979, p.218.

4 Barker p.285.

5 Olivier's story, CA p.130. Garry O'Connor, in *Ralph Richardson: An Actor's Life*, 1982, makes no mention of the story, and notes (p.159) that the files from the triumvirates' period at the Old Vic have been destroyed. John Miller, in *Ralph Richardson: The Authorised Biography*, 1995, has the story but gives his only source as Olivier's autobiography.

6 Walter H. Humphries–LO, 22 March 1949, and LO's reply, 1 April 1949, BL OV 4.

7 LO–JE, 8 April 1949.

8 Finch's contract with LOP, dated 21 March 1949, took him on for fifty-two weeks at £40 a week. If he was let out to other producers, as he was, he would also get 50% of LOP's profit on the deal. BL LOP 2/4.

9 LO and VL's tax affairs, all from BL PERS 5/5/1. Tax rates from *Whitaker's Almanack* for these years.

10 Tennant–VL, 23 February 1951, BL 5/5/1. See also Barker p.296.

11 Tax affairs, BL PERS 5/5/1. Bentley upholstery, BL PERS/12.

12 Drinks, BL PERS 7/2/7. Flowers and petty cash, BL PERS 7/2/5–6–7.

13 Claim, 4 June 1947, BL VL53d.

14 Lloyds policy, 22 December 1949, BL PERS 5/5/1.

15 Olivier interview with Terry Coleman, the *Guardian*, London and *Show* magazine, New York, April 1970.

16 BL PERS 10/7. Willows, Peter Hiley–Gray Nicholls, 13 December 1951, BL PERS 10/9.

17 Notley details, BL PERS 10/1–6.

18 BL PERS 10/7–8.

19 List of VL's pictures, Laurence Harbottle–LO, 12 February 1968, in BL divorce papers. Also BL PERS 7/2/1.

20 Hugo Vickers interview with Anne Norwich, second Viscountess Norwich, 16 March 1987.

21 Hugo Vickers interview with Michael Denison, 2 February 1987. Michael Denison and Dulcie Gray's visit was in 1955, but gives a flavour of the Oliviers' baronial period which lasted about twelve years from 1946 onwards. Olivier preferred Bentleys to Rolls-Royces from 1949 on, when he part-exchanged his Rolls for a Mark VI Bentley costing £3,450. BL PERS 12. VL continued to prefer Rolls-Royces, and later had her own.

22 BL PERS 10/1–6.

23 Series of twelve letters between Gerard Dacres Olivier, Cecil Tennant and LO, 21 January 1949 to 13 September 1950, BL PERS 24.

24 Sybille–LO, 9 and 28 August 1949 and 17 September 1949, BL PERS 25.

25 CA pp.131–2.

26 Hester St John-Ives, who as Hester Capel-Dunn married Dickie as his third wife in 1953 and lived at Notley, heard Olivier tell this story in various versions. Interview with author, 12 October 2003.

27 CA p.133.

28 Fry–LO correspondence, ten letters 21 March to 8 December 1949, BL LOP 13/1. Lunt, CA p.136.

NOTES TO CHAPTER 18 *Streetcar, Carrie* and the Cleos

1 Sunny Alexander, 30 March and 8 June 1939, SFC. See Chapter 10.

2 CA p.132.

3 CA p.135.

4 LO to editor of the *Observer*, 4 January 1950, BL PROF 9.

5 CA p.133.

6 Irene Selznick–Tennant, 7 January 1949; contract 16 August 1949; BL LOP 12.

7 19 April 1949, BL LOP 12.

8 *A Private View* by Irene Mayer Selznick, 1983, pp.323–8. Also Barker pp.287–8.

9 LO–Kazan, 11 September 1949, BL PERS 1/10.

10 LO–Williams, September 1949. The BL has a photocopy in LOP 12a. The original is in the Harry Ransom Humanities Center, Austin, Texas. What Olivier calls act II scene 2 is generally printed as scene 9 in the play text.

11 LO cable to Kanin, 6 October 1949, BL PERS 1/10.

12 *Tennessee Williams* by Ronald Hayman, 1993, p.132.

13 *He That Plays the King* by Kenneth Tynan, 1950, p.123. Gielgud letter of 25 October 1949 in *Gielgud's Letters*, ed. Richard Mangan, 2004, p.127. Fry–LO, 23 November 1949, BL LOP 13. VL–Holman, 15 October 1949, SFC.

14 LO–L.F. Pickin, 18 October 1949, BL LOP 12.

15 LO–Priestley correspondence, 9, 14 and 21 October 1949, BL PERS 1/13.

16 Kitty Black–LO, 5 March 1951, BL LOP 2/4.

17 Barker pp.295–6.

18 Files of offered plays, BL LOP 52/1 and 52/2.

19 Wyler–LO, 20 January and 1 February 1950, BL FILMS 6/1.

20 Korda and VL: Michael Korda interview with author, 1 July 2003.

21 BL FILMS 6/1.

22 Helen Dreiser–LO–Helen Dreiser, letters of 9 and 17 June 1950, BL FILMS 6/1.

23 Cables, 20 June, and 1 and 3 July 1950, BL FILMS 6/1. Earlier measurements, cable of 7 September 1933, BL FILMS 1. D.O. Selznick–LO, 5 July 1950, BL FILMS 6/1.

24 VL–LO, 1 August 1950, BL VL53c.

25 Kanin in interview with Hugo Vickers, 22 January 1988. Olivier in CA p.138.

26 Cable, 21 July 1950, BL FILMS 6/1.

27 *Elia Kazan* (autobiography), 1988, pp.386–7.

28 VL–LO, undated, BL VL53c, notes in green folder.

29 As note 27, p.144.

30 LO–VL, 25 October 1950, SFC.

31 LO–VL, 27 October 1950, SFC.

32 Peter Hiley-Lloyds Bank, 31 March 1952, BL LOP 1/3/1.

33 Helen Dreiser–LO, 15 March 1951, BL FILMS 6/2.

34 Helen Dreiser–LO, 4 April 1951, BL FILMS 6/2.

35 Balaban–LO, 24 January 1952, and LO's reply of 30 January 1952, BL FILMS 6/2.

36 Many letters about redecoration in BL PERS 7/1.

37 CA p.138.

38 CA p.132.

39 Gielgud–LO, 12 December 1950, in *Gielgud's Letters*, ed. Richard Mangan, 2004, p.140.

40 Olivier, CA p.139. Gielgud letter, 28 January 1951, as above.

41 CA p.140.

42 Brown, Barker p.304. Tynan, in his *A View of the English Stage 1944–63*, p.109.

43 Salinger–LO, 1 September 1851, BL PERS 1/15. Churchill, CA pp.142–5.

44 CA pp.145–6.

45 Laurence Irving–LO correspondence, 7 and 21 May and 5 July 1951, BL PERS 1/10.

46 Typescript 'Sept 1951 Sung on the River Boat Party'. BL VL 53.

47 Peter Hiley–Lloyds Bank, 5 October 1951, BL LOP 1/1/1.

48 Rowland–LO correspondence, 6 and 14 September 1951; Lawrence–LO, 15 October 1951; both BL LOP 18. Hamilton–LO, 27 December 1951, BL PERS 1/9.

49 CA pp.140–1.

50 First night list, BL LOP 18. Glitter, CA p.141.

51 *New York Times*, 20 December 1951; Steinbeck–LO undated, BL PERS 1/15; Wilder–LO, undated, BL PERS 1/17.

52 LO–Fry cable, 18 February 1952, BL LOP 13/5.

53 LO–Fry, 29 February 1952, letter of 5,500 words written in intervals of performances; photocopy lent to author by Mr Fry; original in Theatre Museum, London. Fry's cable to LO, BL LOP 13/5.

54 *Venus* losses: a note of 8 June 1953 states that the American backers lost $17,989 of the $65,000 they put up, BL LOP 13/5. *Cleos*, CA p.140.

55 Sylvester L. Weaver Jr, vice-president in charge of television, to LO, BL LOP 18.

56 CA p.140. Finances of *Cleos*, BL LOP 18.

57 CA p.141.

58 The only surviving letter of Dr Kubie to LO (in BL VL 53) was sent from New York on 25 March 1953, after he heard of VL's breakdown in Hollywood. In this letter he described VL's conduct at their meeting of the year before in New York, and expressed 'much sadness at our failure to persuade her of the importance of accepting intensive treatment in time to prevent just such a mishap as this'. He added that he had sent a detailed letter to Dr Edward Glover of 18 Wimpole Street, London, to whom he would refer Miss Leigh. 'I did this because I thought that the situation was so explosive that anyone who was going to take hold of it on her arrival in England would have to be armed with this information to use for her benefit.' There is no trace of any reply by LO. He does not appear to have consulted Dr Glover, and after VL's 1953 breakdown he took her to Dr Freudenberg at Netherne Hospital, Coulsden, where his sister Sybille had been treated.

59 CA p.142.

60 Transport details in BL LOP 18.

61 Coward–LO, 21 March 1952, BL PERS 1/4. CA 142.

62 CA p.148.

63 Kubie–LO, as in note 58 above.

NOTES TO CHAPTER 19 Great God in Heaven, What Now?

1 CA p.147.

2 LO letter to Tarquin, February 1952. LO on JE a lesbian, Peter Hiley interview with author, 28 February 2003. Eton, LO–JE, 15 January 1952; court order, 1 September 1951; Tarquin's future, JE–LO, 1 April 1952; all BL PERS 21/2.

3 JE–LO, undated draft.

4 Tarquin interview with author 14 April 2003.

5 LO–Tarquin, 17 June 1952.

6 CA p.168.

7 Trader Faulkner interview with author, 16 September 2003.

8 CA p.151.

9 John Marshall, editor, to LO, 25 April 1951, BL CRIT 2/1. LO had that February put Marshall off by saying Vivien was far from well and that he was 'in the very thickest and thorniest forest of preparations' for the two *Cleopatras*.

10 Frederic Burgis of Walter Burgis, solicitors, to Tennant, 6 March 1953, BL PERS 10/9.

11 LO–Dickie, 19 December 1952, BL PERS 24.

12 Dickie–LO, letters of 12 May and 14 December 1952, BL PERS 24; and Hester St John-Ives interview with author, 12 October 2003.

13 *Finch, Bloody Finch* by Elaine Dundy, 1980.

14 Finch contract, BL LOP 2/4. VL contract, 22 January 1953, BL VL 53c. VL's diary, SFC.

15 Frewen diary, 7 January 1953, cited in Vickers p.210.

16 CA p.152. Great god, *Confessions* mss p.92, BL CRIT 1 box 1.

17 VL's cables, 28 and 31 January and 14 February 1952, BL VL53. VL's diary, SFC. Blaze, CA pp.152–3.

18 CA 153. Finch's notes, undated, BL VL53. VL's 1953 diary notes, SFC.

19 LO's diary, after 28 March 1953, BL. In CA p.155 he misquotes and wrongly dates this entry.

20 Times and dates from LO's diary, BL. Meeting with VL, CA pp. 154–6.

21 Vickers p.213.

22 Cable LO–Asher, 6 March 1953, BL VL53c. Party from *Finch, Bloody Finch* by Elaine Dundy, 1980, p.186. Dundy got her information from Finch's wife Tamara.

23 *Bring on the Empty Horses* by David Niven, 1975, in the chapter headed 'Our Little Girl (Part 2)'; and *Sparks Fly Upwards* by Stewart Granger, 1982.

24 *New York Times*, 8 February 1952.

25 Dr Fraser McDonald called nine times at VL's house from 11 to 18 March, and went with her to the airport on 18 March: his bill was for $600. Dr Ralph R. Greenson attended VL from 12 to 18 March, spent fifty hours with her or with LO, and sent a bill for $1,500. BL VL 53c.

26 CA p.156.

27 Undated note in VL's hand in BL 53c.

28 Escape, CA pp.157–8. Stop breathing, *Confessions* mss, where LO's account is fuller than in CA, and gives dated excerpts from his diary; BL CRIT 1/1.

29 LO diary, BL. VL's diary, SFC.

30 Sybille–LO, 28 March 1953, BL PERS 25.

31 LO–JE, 25 March 1953.

32 Niven–LO, March 1953, BL PERS 1/13.

33 *William Walton: Behind the Façade* by Susana Walton, 1988, pp.136–8.

34 CA p.159.

35 Frewen diary, 10–11 April 1953, cited in Vickers p.215. Holman's visit to Leigh was on 9 or 10 April, as appears from VL's diary, SFC. Coward's gifts and LO blaming himself, CA pp.159–60.

36 LO and VL diaries, BL and SFC.

37 CA p.142.

38 Peter Hiley interview with author, 5 June 2003.

39 Dr Fraser McDonald–LOP, 7 May 1953, BL VL53c.

40 *The Noel Coward Diaries*, ed. Payn and Morley, 1982, p.211, entry for 22 April 1953.

41 BL PERS 10/9. See Burgis–Tennant correspondence of 6 and 7 March, and 1 April, and lease of 15 April 1953. The lease amounted to a legal fiction. LOP could not assign it without LO's permission, he had the option to break it at seven or fourteen years, and it was understood that if he wished to break it before then there could be 'a rearrangement'. The furniture remained the Oliviers' property.

Notes to Chapter 20 *Richard III* and the Ménage à Trois

1 Ground to halt, CA p.160. Bullied him, Tarquin interview with author, 14 April 2003.

2 Correspondence between LO and Del Giudice, 31 December 1951, 19 January and 18 February 1952 and 20 May 1954 (Milan), in BL PERS 1/16. Film contract, 11 November 1954, BL FILMS 9/2.

3 Casting correspondence in BL FILMS 9/1. 9/2, and 9/3.

4 LO's ms draft in BL FILMS 9/3.

5 Tarquin interview with author, 14 April 2003.

6 CA p.162.

7 LO on Cinemascope, LO–Bob Dowling, US director of LOP, 11 June 1954, BL FILMS 9/1. Korda on VistaVision, Korda–LO, 10 September 1954, BL FILMS 9/3.

8 *Portrait of Walton* by Michael Kennedy, 1989, p.194. Strawberry jam, *William Walton; Behind the Façade* by Susana Walton, 1988, p.143.

9 LO–Bob Dowling, 14 April 1956, BL FILMS 9/1.

10 The television showing was on 11 March 1956. NBC handout and London *Times* report, undated, in BL FILMS 9/5.

11 Contract, 13 September 1954, BL FILMS p.9.

12 In More's contribution to *Vivien Leigh: A Bouquet* by Alan Dent, 1969, p.82.

13 London Film Productions-LOP, 2 and 13 May 1955, BL FILMS 9.

14 Hester St John-Ives, interview with author, 12 October 2003.

15 Susana Walton, as note 8 above, p.143.

16 Stratford offer to LO, 6 October 1954, BL SMT 1.

17 *An Actor in His Time* by John Gielgud, 1979, p.177.

18 Gielgud–Stark Young, 3 April 1955, from *Gielgud's Letters*, ed. Richard Mangan, 2004, p.180.

19 Gielgud–LO, 12 April [1955], BL SMT 1.

20 Rattigan, CA P.165. Tynan, the *Observer*, 12 June 1955. Air hostess, *Spectator*, 22 April 1955. Peggy Ashcroft, author interview with Peter Hiley, 28 February 2003. Bowen, *Night and Day*, BL CA6 (cuttings). Both Joan Plowright and Hester St John-Ives, in interviews with the author, said they believed Maxine Audley to have been LO's mistress. JP said MA was 'a warm-hearted woman'.

21 Bit mad, Maxine Audley, interview with Hugo Vickers, 12 February 1987. Olivier's account in CA pp.166–7.

22 *The Noel Coward Diaries*, ed. Payn and Morley, 1982, entry for 7 August 1955.

23 CA p.167.

24 Hester St John-Ives interview with author, 12 October 2003.

25 Finch's story in *Finch, Bloody Finch*, by Elaine Dundy, 1980, p.205. Esmond Knight: interview with Hugo Vickers, 11 February 1987.

26 Author interview with Joan Plowright, 18 November 2003.

27 *Vivien* by Alexander Walker, 1987, p.222.

28 Coward diary, 19 August 1955, as in note 22 above.

29 Gielgud to Hugh Wheeler, in *Gielgud's Letters*, ed. Richard Mangan, 2004, p.188.

30 The party was on 23 November 1955, LO's diary. Hester, see note 24 above. LO's tests, his diary for 2, 3 and 5 December 1955, BL.

31 LO–Nugent, 10 June 1955, and Nugent's reply, 14 June 1955, BL FILMS 9/4.

32 Ginette Spanier interviews with Hugo Vickers, 4 February 1986 and 16 February 1987.

33 LO letter quoted in Tarquin p.191.

34 Tennant–Korda–Tennant letters, 22 December 1955, BL FILMS 46.

Notes to Chapter 21 The Prince and the Showgirl

1 *Timebends: A Life* by Arthur Miller, 1987, [hereafter in the notes to this chapter referred to as Miller] pp.386–7.

2 CA pp.169–70.

3 Frewen's diary 15 March 1956, cited in Vickers p.235.

4 CA p.181.

5 LO–Tarquin, 18 April 1956.

6 Durham Cottage was sold in July 1955 for £5,750, BL PERS 7/1.

7 LO–Tarquin, 6 March and 18 April 1956.

8 The correspondence between LO, Tennant, and Gallagher's about Olivier cigarettes is in BL PROF 7, Advertising and Sponsorship.

9 LO–Tarquin, 18 April 1956.

10 Frewen's diary, 11 June 1956, cited in Vickers p.236.

11 *The Prince and the Showgirl* by Colin Clark, 1995 [afterwards referred to in the notes to this chapter as Clark] p.57. Clark, the brother of Alan Clark the *bon vivant*, would-be rake, and member of Margaret Thatcher's government, kept a diary from 3 June to 20 November 1956. He later acted as stage manager at the Royal Court, went with Olivier on his Iron Curtain tour of *Titus Andronicus* in 1957, and then produced documentaries for Granada Television.

12 Tarquin p.196.

13 *Daily Sketch, Daily Mail, Daily Express*, London, 13 July 1956.

14 *The Noel Coward Diaries*, ed. Payn and Morley, 1982, p.237, entry for 11 July 1956.

15 Coward letter from Jamaica to 'Dear Larry Boy', 12 January 1957, BL PERS 1/14.

16 LO–Tarquin, 13 July 1956.

17 Miller p.413.

18 CA pp. 171–6. Clark p.193.

19 Clark p.106.

20 Hester St John-Ives interview with author, 12 October 2003. VL's mother, Gertude Hartley, also wrote in her diary for 20 August 1956, which was transcribed by Hugo Vickers, 'Viv lost her baby. Very sad poor little pet.'

21 Coward's diary, see note 14 above, 14 August 1956.

22 Barton-Innes–LO, 20 August 1956, and his reply, BL PROF 7.

23 Miller pp.418–21.

24 Clark p.210. Marmoset, Frewen's diary, 17 October 1956.

25 Maxine Audley: Deborah Granville, her daughter by her third marriage, said in an interview with the author on 15 September 2004 that her mother told her of the affair in the mid-1980s. When she died in 1992 she left her daughter the ring. 'Tender venturings' and 'acts of pure kindness', CA p.168. Joan Plowright knew Maxine, and called her 'warm hearted': interview with author, 25 November 2003. Hester St John-Ives remembered her as Olivier's mistress.

26 Miller p.434.

27 Miller p.416.

28 Miller pp.416–7. Arthur Miller's account is probably accurate, but it differs from LO's (CA p.180) and John Osborne's in *Almost a Gentleman; An Autobiography*, 1955–66 Vol. II, 1991, p.28. Osborne remembered meeting Olivier at the Court after *Cards of Identity* in the same season. He wrote that Olivier complimented him on his acting in that play, saying, 'You're my kind of actor,' and hinting at a part for him in the film of *Macbeth* which he never made. Olivier remembered this same meeting and complimenting Osborne on his acting, but he said he also congratulated him on *Look Back in Anger* and then asked if he might think of writing a play with him in mind. He said Osborne kept asking him if he meant it. All three men were writing years after the event. Probably there were two meetings: one in which Olivier congratulated Osborne on his acting and no more, because we know he did not like *Look Back* when he first saw it; and a second as described by Miller.

29 Clark p.190 and p.196.

30 CA p.180.

31 Holiday events, LO diaries in BL. VL sweet and gay, Gertrude Hartley's diary for 15 January 1957.

NOTES TO CHAPTER 22 The King Comes to the Court

1 Devine–LO, 19 January 1957, and LO's reply of 24 January 1957, BL LOP p.36.

2 Film, letter of 30 January 1957, BL FILMS 9. Bumps, LO's diary for 21, 22 and 23 February 1957, BL.

3 *Almost a Gentleman: An Autobiography, 1955–66* Vol. II, by John Osborne, 1991, p.36. Hereafter referred to, in notes to this chapter, as Osborne. The reader might bear in mind that Osborne was almost as much inclined as Olivier to improving stories. As Joan Plowright put it in an interview with the author on 18 November 2003, both were great liars. So details may have been embellished.

4 Osborne pp.36–7.

5 Osborne p.35. The typescript is in the BL at LOP 58/10. LOP's share of the gross was 10% above £1,500.

6 Osborne p.42.

7 CA p.181.

8 Osborne p.41.

9 This story formed the subject of a sketch, 'Thwarted by Goliath', in *Losing My Marbles*, a one-man show presented by Trader Faulkner at the Jermyn Street Theatre, London, on 31 January 1999; the girl was not named. The text of this show was published, as *Losing My Marbles*, in a polished version by Trader Faulkner with John Goodwin, 2003; the girl in the houseboat was there identified as Dorothy Tutin who had died in August 2001. The story is given here as it was told by Trader Faulkner to the author in an interview of 16 September 2003.

10 LO's diary shows thirty appointments for these injections from 22 March to 17 August 1957, when he notes that there will be no more for six months. There were none during the five-week European tour in May and June. BL.

11 Osborne p.42.

12 Osborne p.42.

13 Olivier's letter is quoted in Osborne p.35. Osborne's is at BL PERS 11/13.

14 Osborne p.48.

15 Ffrangcon-Davies–LO, undated, BL LOP p.36.

16 GG trs, tape 3, side 1.

17 Tarquin interview with author, 14 April 2003.

18 The tour was managed by the SMT and LOP, in association with the British Council; for the services of LO and VL, LOP received £100 a week and 7.5 % of the take; the London seasons made a profit of £11,216, shared equally between SMT and LOP; the European tour lost £7,079, of which £6,700 was paid by the British Council; other cities which were considered for the tour were Zurich, Stockholm, Oslo, Palermo, and Los Angeles; chauffeur etc, SMT–LOP, 1 May 1957; all the correspondence is at BL SMT 2. Cabbage, Donnell interview with Hugo Vickers, 17 March 1987.

19 Michael Blakemore, in *Arguments with England: A Memoir*, 2004, pp. 148–70, gives the most brilliant account of this tour. Whenever he is quoted in this chapter the source is that book, or a conversation with the author of this book on 30 August 2004.

20 Lady (Anne) Norwich interview with Hugo Vickers, 16 March 1987. John Julius Norwich had succeeded to his father's title in 1954, becoming the second Viscount Norwich.

21 David Conville interviewed by Hugo Vickers, 24 November 1986.

22 Hugo Vickers interviews with Maxine Audley, 12 February 1987, and with Colin

Clark, 22 February 1987.

23 LO diary, BL. Gertrude's diary, as transcribed by Hugo Vickers. *The Noel Coward Diaries*, ed. Payn and Morley, entry for 30 June 1957, p.358.

24 CA p.182.

25 Conville, see note 21 above.

26 *Daily Mirror* and other London newspapers, 12 July 1957.

27 Conville, as note 21 above.

28 George Hume, SMT–Tennant, 13 September 1957, BL SMT 2.

29 CA p.183. Gertrude Hartley wrote in her diary for 30 July (as transcribed by Hugo Vickers): 'Called to Viv's at 3 am. Dreadful tragedy – sent for Dr Altmann. Spent the night at Lowndes Cottage, Lowndes Place.'

30 CA p.184.

31 Principally author interview with Joan Plowright, 25 November 2003. Also interview with Trader Faulkner, 16 September 2003.

32 Gallagher–Tennant, 29 October 1957, for sales up to 30 June, BL PROF 7.

33 Tarquin p.214.

34 Davis, managing director of Rank, to Tennant on finance, and LO to Carnegie on castle, both in BL FILMS 46. Birthday, LO's diary, 21 August 1957, BL.

35 *Daily Mirror* and *Daily Express*, 12 July 1957.

36 *Daily Mail*, 13 March 1957.

37 Holman–Gertrude, 25 August 1957, SFC.

38 Colin Clark interview with Hugo Vickers, 22 February 1987.

39 W. Vallance Lodge (accountant)–Tennant, 24 August 1957, and Tennant's reply, 28 August 1957, BL VL53c.

40 BL LOP 36.

41 By instinct, JP letter to her parents, 2 November 1949, BL PERS 22/1/1. LO on her name, CA p.180.

42 *Confessions* mss, p.141, BL.

43 Joan Plowright interview with author, 18 November 2003. Also see JPB (*And That's Not All: The memoirs of Joan Plowright*, 2001), pp.47–8.

44 JPB p.48.

45 Osborne p.67.

46 LO–Janet L. Blair, 10 November 1957, BL LOP 36.

47 Colin Clark interview with Hugo Vickers, 22 February 1987.

48 JP interview with author, 18 November 2003.

49 JPB p.48.

50 CA p.186.

51 LO diary, BL. JP interview with author, 18 November 2003.

52 LOP rented the Lowndes Square house from January until October 1957, at a rent rising from twenty guineas to twenty-five guineas a week; BL PERS 8.

53 *Daily Mirror* and other London newspapers, 7 December 1957. Invitation, SFC.

54 Del Giudice–LO, 14 November 1957, BL FILMS 46. Key, CA p.186.

NOTES TO CHAPTER 23 Dropping the Legend

1 JPB p.89.

2 *Confessions* mss p.137.

3 Wyngarde interview with Hugo Vickers, 3 May 1988.

4 Peter Hiley-Lloyds Bank, 8 November 1958, BL VL53c.

5 *Almost a Gentleman: An Autobiography, 1955–66* by John Osborne, 1991, p.101. Also LO's diary, BL.

6 *Confessions* mss p.141. Compare the cut version in CA p.186.

7 Byam-Shaw–LO, 19 and 25 May 1958, BL SMT3.

8 Correspondence with Del, in BL FILMS 46. LO–Tarquin, 21 May 1958.

9 BL FILMS 46.

10 CA p.187.

11 CA p.187; JPB pp.50–1.

12 This weekend is described by Dundy in *Olivier: In Celebration*, ed. Garry O'Connor, 1987, pp.167–73. She is given to exaggeration and uncertain about dates, which are however established by Gertude Hartley's diary.

13 As transcribed by Vickers.

14 Dr H.M. Segal–LO, 24 October 1958, BL VL53.

15 VL–LO, 2 November 1958, BL VL53c.

16 *Daily Express*, 8 November 1958.

17 LO–JP, 28 October 1958; JPB p.53.

18 Hester interview with author, 12 October 2003.

19 Peter Hiley interview with author, 28 February 2003.

20 LO–Tarquin, 13 December 1958.

21 *Confessions* mss p.144, not in printed version in CA p.188.

22 Chart, with LO's and other annotations, in BL PERS 17.

23 Confessions mss p.144. This is LO's first version. He later deleted 'being made to feel so horribly undignified' and substituted 'humiliation'. In the printed version the whole passage was deleted.

24 Hester interview with author, 12 October 2003.

25 LO–Hester, 7 December 1958, in possession of Hester St John-Ives.

26 Gertrude Hartley's diary, transcribed by Vickers.

27 BL PERS 12.

28 *The Noel Coward Diaries*, ed. Payn and Morley, 1982, entry for 21 December 1958.

29 LO's 1959 diary, BL. CA p.188. JPB p.228.

30 Hester interview with author, 12 October 2003.

31 LO letters to Hester, 16 January and 17 February 1959, in possession of Hester St John-Ives.

32 LO–Hester, 16 March 1959, as in note 27 above.

33 *Finch, Bloody Finch* by Elaine Dundy, 1980, p.215 and p.235.

34 JPB p.55. LO–JP, undated but December 1958, JPC.

35 JP–LO, marked in LO's hand as having been received 13 January 1959.

36 LO–Suzanne Farrington, 18 April 1959, SFC.

37 LO–VL, 22 March 1959, VL 53c. This is LO's draft of his letter.

38 LO–JOP, 18 April 1959, JPC.

39 JP interview with author, 25 November 2003.

40 LO–JP, 'Saturday night 12.45', but undated.

41 CA p.189.

42 Coward diary entry, 5 May 1959, as 28 above.

43 LO–Hester, 26 June 1959, in possession of Hester St John-Ives.

44 Royal Jelly: LO Diary 1959, entries for 13, 21 and 29 July for 'Riché', the London practitioner who gave the injections. Michael Blakemore's account in *Arguments With England: A Memoir*, 2004, pp.222–224.

45 Four letters, Peter Hall–LO, starting 26 September 1959, and six others for 1960, BL SMT 3.

46 In contribution of John Osborne to *Olivier*, ed. Logan Gourlay, 1973, p.149.

47 *Almost a Gentleman: An Autobiography, 1955–66* by John Osborne, 1991, p. 135 and p.147.

48 CA p.190 and Coward diaries p.422, as 28 above.

49 Fan letter from Edwina Burdett, 3 December 1959, BL VL53a.

50 LO–Gertrude Hartley, 22 December 1959, SFC.

51 *Sparks Fly Upwards* by Stewart Granger, 1981, pp.400–1.

52 LO–JP, undated but January 1960, JPC and part-printed in JPB p.64. JP's reply, undated, JPB p.65. LO's second letter, 18 January 1960, JPC.

53 JPB p.71.

54 Rachel Kempson–LO, 30 March 1960, BL VL53c.

55 Cable of 22 May 1960, BL VL 53.

56 Notley sold on 30 June 1960 for £32,529, BL VL53c.

57 Dr Conachy gave this 'short report on her psychiatric condition', dated 20 June 1961, to VL after the divorce. It was apparently for her to carry with her on her travels to show to any doctor she had to consult, and remained in her papers. It described in detail her symptoms and treatment of 1958–60. SFC.

58 Coward diary, 19 June 1960, as 28 above.

59 Osborne p.161, as note 5 above.

60 VL–LO, 20 June 1960, on Pan American writing paper, BL VL 53, grey folder.

61 Allen & Overy to Theodore Goddard & Co. 21 June 1960, BL VL 53, file 'Divorce 1961'.

62 LO–VL, dated at end 18 July, arrived in LA 21 July 1960, SFC.

63 LO–VL, 15 August 1960, SFC.

64 Merivale–LO, received 15 August 1960, JPC; partly printed in JPB p.77. LO's reply, 16 August 1960, SFC.

65 Rolls-Royce colours and Renoir, John Merivale interview with Hugo Vickers, 5 February 1987. Divorce papers, Elspeth March interview with Hugo Vickers, 16 February 1987. Coward diaries, 11 December 1960, as note 28 above.

66 Peter Hiley interview with author, 28 February 2003.

67 Certificate of decree nisi, and VL's affidavit of means, of 6 January 1961, in BL VL 53, file 'Divorce 1961'.

68 LO–VL, 4 December 1960, SFC.

69 Dorothy ('Dottie') Welford–LO, October 1976, BL NT 31/4 (7). LO memo of 31 January 1969 to NT company, in BL NT 30/4. LO wrote two long letters to Shirley Luke from Hollywood, 3 April and 2 June 1979, saying she drank too much and was indiscreet, HLC F6439.

70 Peter Hiley interviews with author, 28 February 2003 and 28 May 2003.

NOTES TO CHAPTER 24 New Wife, New National

1 LO–Hall, 3 July 1960. This letter, together with many others to Peter Hall, was destroyed in a fire at his parents' house. It is quoted here from *Power Play: The Life and Times of Peter Hall* by Stephen Fay, 1995, p.130.

2 CA pp.194–5.

3 LO wrote to Fry on 25 July 1951 about *Curtmantle* saying, 'Do it then, but oh, my darling boy, do it quickly. I always fear ideas that simmer for too long.' The play was

eventually presented by the RSC in 1961. Merrick, on 18 January 1960, asked LO to do Anouilh's *Becket* on Broadway (LO–JP, January 1960, JPC).

4 LO–Tarquin, October 1960. Deposit, BL PERS 2/1/1.

5 CA pp.195–6. JPB p.90.

6 Ashcroft–LO, undated, BL PERS 1/1/a.

7 JPB p.91. JP interview with author, 18 November 2003.

8 LO–JE, 21 April 1961.

9 JP to her parents, 2 May 1961, BL PERS 22/1/1.

10 Mesmerise, *On Acting* p.95. *The Power and the Glory* (black and white) shown on CBS, 19 November 1961. Sleep, CA p.197 and LO's Diary, BL.

11 For detailed accounts of the history see *The History of the National Theatre* by John Elsom and Nicholas Tomalin, 1978; *The Royal Shakespeare Company*, by Sally Beauman, 1982; and *Power Play: the Life and Times of Peter Hall* by Stephen Fay, 1995. The last two see things from the Stratford point of view. There is no recent, comprehensive history, though the Olivier papers at the BL, the National's own archive, and the Chandos Papers at Churchill College, Cambridge could provide important sources for one, and much new material.

12 *Confessions* mss p.384; see also CA p.179.

13 MA 28.17.

14 MA 27.2.

15 Kenneth Rae, in annotations on a memo of 16 April 1973, wrote, 'Would have said 58': BL PROF 9.

16 Clark–LO, 6 December 1960, BL NT 44/3.

17 Hall–LO, 26 September 1959, BL SMT3. This is one of a series of ten letters from Hall to LO.

18 Hall's letters to LO, undated but after 18 January 1960, 22 January 1960 and 21 March 1960. BL SMT3.

19 The date of the meeting is given in Elsom as April 1959, but LO was then in Hollywood. The date is 10 April 1960, as in LO's diary. Hall's letter was dated 11 April 1960.

20 As note 1 above.

21 LO–Hall, 10 October 1961, as in note 1 above.

22 LO's diary, BL.

23 LO–Hall, January 1960, from Fay pp.136–8, see note 1 above.

24 LO letters to Bolt, Pinter and Arden, all 2 August 1962, BL CFT 1/1. He asked Bolt to 'come and examine, ponder, sift, the nature of the work we are trying to do'.

25 MA 26.20.

26 CA p.199. MA 17.

27 MA 17.22.

28 JP interview with author, 27 November 2003.

29 15 July 1962.

30 MA 26.23.

31 Terms of agreement in NT Board papers for 10 October 1962, BL NT1. After the five-year contract was up, LO was to be retained as a consultant for fifteen years at an annual fee of £1,750.

32 Destiny, JP interview with author, 8 December 2003.

33 Rae–LO, 7 February and 22 March, 1961, BL NT18.

34 In notes for an interview with Harold Hobson, corrected in LO's hand, undated but 1962, BL CRIT 1/4.

35 LO–Guthrie, 16 July 1963, BL PERS 1/8.

36 Acoustics, LO–Lady Katharine Farrell, 5 June 1968. Ruined, LO in LWT interview with Melvyn Bragg, 1981.

37 *The Life of Kenneth Tynan* by Kathleen Tynan, 1987, and *Kenneth Tynan: Letters*, ed. Kathleen Tynan, 1994.

38 MA 27.22–5.

39 *Cry God for Larry* by Virginia Fairweather, 1969, p.69 and p.81. LO wrote 'Lunch Tynan' in his diary for 6 September 1961, BL.

40 JP interview with author, 25 November 2003.

41 NT board papers, 11 February and 11 March 1963, BL NT1.

42 Gambon interview with author, 11 May 2004.

43 CA p.207.

44 LO letters to Laurence Irving and to Kenneth Rae, both 10 April 1964, BL NT 30.

45 LO–Guthrie, as in note 35 above.

46 CA p.204.

47 MA 27.5.

48 Fabia Drake–LO, 20 January 1963, BL PERS 1/6.

49 Purchases, BL PERS 5/5/1.

50 NT Board papers, 8 July and 14 October 1963, BL NT1.

51 Names, LO memo 27 May 1963, BL NT30. Presents, Xmas 1963, BL PERS 13. Stove, memo 7 October 1964, BL NT30.

NOTES TO CHAPTER 25 Max Factor 2880 and Love of a Strange Strength

1 MA 12.24

2 Evershed-Martin to LO, 1 February and 28 May 1963, LO's replies of 15 and 30 May, and other correspondence, in BL CFT 1/1.

3 More correspondence in BL CFT 1/1.

4 Try-out, MA 17.22. *Othello*, LO to Pieter Rogers in CFT 1/1.

5 LO–Peggy A. Middleton of the LCC Paul Robeson Committee, 2 August 1957, BL LOP 52.

6 CA p.139.

7 GG trs, tape 2 side 2.

8 MA 12.22–3.

9 MA 12.29–31.

10 *Cry God for Larry* by Virginia Fairweather, 1969, p.97.

11 Tynan–LO, memo dated 'Sunday', BL NT 46/1.

12 CA p.213. JPB p.112.

13 CA p.208.

14 Tynan's memo and LO's reply of 8 May 1963, BL NT 46/1.

15 27 May 1963, BL NT 46/1.

16 Tynan's memo and LO's reply of 9 January 1964. As above.

17 Memos Tynan–LO in NT 46/1. Tour, 1 July 1964; Larry-Warry, 24 April 1964; Dexter, 'Thursday', no date.

18 LO to Italian consulate in London, 27 November 1963, BL PERS 1/6.

19 Georgina Ward in a letter to Hugo Vickers, 28 September 1986. Miss Ward, afterwards the Hon. Mrs Tritton, was the daughter of George Ward, Secretary of State

for Air, who was created Viscount Ward in 1960. She was very much Vivien's protegée and held her in deep affection. She never saw her again after that tea.

20 Six letters VL to Merivale 24 January to 16 March, 1963, SFC. VL–LO, 11 February 1963, SFC. Olivier's visit to Tickerage: Hester St John-Ives interview with author, 12 October 2003.

21 *Serves Me Right* by Sarah Miles, 1994, p.96 and other mentions.

22 JPB p.130, and Joan Plowright interview with author, 25 November 2003. Sarah Miles's denial, conversation with author, 30 July 2004.

23 Memo, 6 March 1965, BL NT 50c.

24 The first book deals with her childhood. The second, *Serves Me Right*, 1994, and the third, *Bolt from the Blue*, 1996, contain many references to LO.

25 JPB p.117. CA pp.215–6.

26 CA pp.217–8.

27 Helicopter, LO telegram, 6 July 1964; LO resigns, 28 December 1964; LO–Bessborough and reply, 15 and 27 January 1965.

28 LO–Miller, 13 August and 25 November 1964; Miller–LO, 17 August and 3 December 1964. All in BL NT 52.

29 *Daily Sketch* and *Daily Express*, 9 January 1965.

30 Tarquin Olivier interview with author, 14 April 2003.

31 Dr S.M. Witteridge–LO, 9 December 1966, BL VL 53.

32 *Nostalgia Isn't What it Used to Be* by Simone Signoret, 1978, p.368. She was also in the cast of *Ship of Fools*.

33 Twelve short letters from LO to VL survive from 1965–6. SFC.

34 Tynan–LO, 24 February 1965, BL NT 46/1.

35 Gaskill's contribution in *Olivier*, ed. Logan Gourlay, 1973, p.116.

36 Dukoff–Tennant, 6 July 1965, and Tennant–LO, 3 August 1965, BL LOP 1/7/1/2.

37 This account of the Moscow visit is pieced together from Olivier's own recollections in CA pp.219–221, and from Joan Plowright's recollections in an interview with the author on 11 December 2004. A few details are taken from Chapter 5 of *Cry God For Larry* by Virginia Fairweather, 1969.

38 LO–Tynan, 11 August 1965, NT 46/1. Meet later, *Cry God for Larry* by Virginia Fairweather, 1969, p.117.

39 In *The Theatres of George Devine* by Irving Wardle, 1978.

40 Proposal from Harold French, 17 January 1966, BL REA 1.

41 LO letter to British ambassador in Copenhagen, 15 March 1966, BL PERS 14.

42 LO–Tarquin, 21 August 1966. CA 222–3. JPB p.132.

43 CA p.223.

44 Clark–Chandos, letters of 16 June 1966 and 3 August 1966, CHAN II 4/13/21 and CHAN II 4/13/23, Chandos papers in the Churchill Archive, Churchill College, Cambridge.

45 Letter of 8 October 1966 in *Gielgud's Letters*, ed. Richard Mangan, 2004, p.224.

46 MA 32.8.

47 JPB pp.133.4. Pillow talk, JPB p.110.

48 Tynan–LO, 14 December 1966, BL NT 46/1.

Notes to Chapter 26 The Concrete Never-Neverland

1 The stone was laid by the George VI's queen, better known now as the late Queen Mother, on 13 July 1951. Also present were Princess Elizabeth, who succeeded her

father and became Elizabeth II in 1952; the prime minister, Clement Attlee; Oliver Lyttelton, later Lord Chandos; and Olivier. The stone is now set into a wall in the foyer of the Lyttelton Theatre at the National.

2 NT building committee, 6 December 1960, BL NT1.

3 Perfect theatre, LO to first meeting of the NT building committee after the formal creation of the NT, 3 January 1963: BL NT 31/1. Prosecenium in every home, and adaptable theatre, LO to NT board, 10 October 1962, the first he attended as director-designate, BL NT 1. Hall, to building committee, 3 January 1963, BL NT 31/1. Theatre by 1964, Rae to LO, 6 February 1961, BL NT18.

4 Devine to building committee, 3 January 1963, BL NT 31/1.

5 CA p.202.

6 LO to building committee, 9 January 1964, NT 31/1. The committee minutes contain long passages which are apparently verbatim reports of what was said.

7 Lasdun to building committee, 7 March 1964, BL NT 31/1.

8 Kenny letter to LO, 7 February 1964, BL NT 31/1.

9 Gaskill, Olivier and Devine at building committee, 7 October 1964, NL NT 31/1.

10 LO letter to Cottesloe, 14 June 1965, BL NT 44/2.

11 Chandos' and accountants' warning to NT board, 8 February 1965, BL NT 3.

12 Tynan memo to LO, 5 August 1966, BL NT 31/2.

13 LO–Cottesloe, 8 August 1966, BL NT44/2.

14 Cottesloe–Olivier, 28 September 1966, BL NT 31/2.

15 LO–Lasdun, 18 October 1966, BL NT 31/2.

16 Two letters of Wilson to LO, 8 May 1967, and a third letter of 18 May 1967. BL PERS 14.

17 LO–Harold Wilson, 14 May 1967, CHAN II 4/13/9, Churchill Archive, Churchill College, Cambridge. LO sent a typed copy of his handwritten letter to Chandos, with a note saying he felt Chandos was largely responsible for the idea of his being honoured. Chandos may have been consulted, but the initiative probably came from Jenny Lee prompted by Lord Goodman.

18 LO–Chandos, undated, CHAN II 4/13/8, Churchill Archive, Churchill College, Cambridge.

19 Joan Plowright interview with author, 8 December 2003.

Notes to Chapter 27 Listening to that Man Breathing

The Hochhuth affair has to be reconstructed from several sources. Olivier, in *Confessions of an Actor*, 1982, devoted Appendix A, pp.262–83, to the matter. In his first version he included more letters in this appendix, but some were left out of the printed book at the request of the British publisher. Copies of these omitted letters can be found in the typescripts of CONFESSIONS MSS in the BL, CRIT 1, boxes 1 and 2. Many of the originals of the letters in CA and in the typescripts are missing. They are not in the BL archive. Perhaps LO gathered the bundle together and it was then lost. Some of Tynan's letters are printed in Tynan Letters (see note 4); where these can be checked against the surviving originals they are accurate. Other originals, and some letters found or referred to nowhere else, are in Lord Chandos's papers (see note 1).

1 LO–Chandos, 23 February 1967. Chandos papers in the Churchill Archive at Churchill College, Cambridge, CHAN II/4/13/6. The word quoted in square brackets is conjecture: the paper at this spot has been punched through for filing.

2 K.R. Gieron in *Svenska Dagbladet*, 24 February 1967.

3 Peter Hall interview with author, 6 February 2004.

4 Tynan–LO, 3 January 1967, in *Kenneth Tynan: Letters*, ed. Kathleen Tynan, 1994, p.376. This book is afterwards in these notes referred to as Tynan Letters. Where the letters appear both in the Olivier collection at the BL and in this book, I have preferred to cite the book, as being easier to refer to.

5 On *BBC3*, 13 November 1965.

6 Tynan–A.C. Spectorsky, 27 June 1967, Tynan Letters p.406.

7 Tynan–R.D. Macdonald (translator of the play), 2 November 1966, and Tynan–Hochhuth, 8 December 1966, Tynan Letters p.366 and p.369.

8 Tynan–LO, 23 December 1966; Tynan–Dexter, 28 December 1966; Tynan–LO, 3 January 1967. Tynan Letters, pp.375–6.

9 Tynan memo to Board, 7 January 1967, is printed in Tynan Letters, p.377. Chandos's annotated copy is in the Churchill Archive (see note 1 above) at CHAN II 4/13/244.

10 Chandos–Tynan, CHAN II 4/13/235, as above. Chandos–Blake, CHAN II 4/13/137.

11 Tynan–Hochhuth, 11 January 1967, Tynan Letters p.381.

12 Tynan letter, 10 April 1967; reply, 14 April 1967. Tynan Letters p.395.

13 CA p.283.

14 In Appendix A of *Confessions of an Actor*, pp.262–83.

15 Tynan–Hochhuth, 28 April 1967, Tynan Letters p.398.

16 *Sunday Times*, 7 May 1967.

17 *The Times*, 4 May 1967. KT–*Playboy*, 27 June 1967, Tynan Letters p.406.

18 Distressed, CA p.277. The pages are CA pp.262–83.

19 The author, as arts correspondent of the *Guardian*, attended such a meeting.

20 Chandos–LO, 10 May 1967, CHAN II 4/13/137, see note 1 above. Part printed in *The Life of Kenneth Tynan* by Kathleen Tynan, 1987, p.343.

21 John Osborne, in his contribution to *Olivier*, ed. Logan Gourlay, 1973, p.152, said: 'And to make matters worse there's the disastrous influence of Kenneth Tynan. . . It's a sort of intellectual spivvery Olivier mistakes for up-to-date awareness. He's so afraid of being thought old hat that he's allowed himself to be sadly misguided by Tynan. At least, thank God, he hasn't allowed Tynan to talk him into a nude Macbeth with "bunny" witches.' In 1972, when Hall went to the National, he made it a condition of his acceptance of the job that Tynan should not stay: *Peter Hall's Diaries*, ed. John Goodwin, 2000 edition, 3 July 1972.

22 Author interview with Joan Plowright, 25 November 2003.

23 LO–Laura Knight, 25 April 1967, BL PERS 11/2.

24 LO–VL, 28 May 1967, SFC.

25 JPB p.134.

26 LO–Richardson, 18 May 1967, BL PERS 1/14.

27 LO's diary, BL.

28 JPB pp.134–5, and author interview with Joan Plowright, 18 November 2003.

29 JPB p.137.

30 LO–Ashcroft, 7 July 1967, in possession of her daughter, Eliza Loizeau-Hutchinson.

31 Merivale interview with Hugo Vickers, 4 May 1987.

32 Author interview with Peter Hiley, 28 February 2003.

33 CA pp.228–30.

34 *The Times*, 10 and 11 July 1967.

35 Spanier–LO, 14 July 1967, BL PERS 1/15. Ashcroft–LO, 'Sunday' [July 1967], BL PERS 11/1a.

36 Hepburn–Merivale, 10 July 1967, SFC.

37 LO–Chandos, Thursday 13 July 1967, CHAN II 4/13/10–12; see note 1 above. The king demands a mirror in *Richard II*, act V scene 1.

38 JE–Tarquin, 15 August 1967.

39 Tynan–Hochhuth, 28 April 1967, Tynan Letters p.398. Tynan–LOP, 17 July 1967, Tynan Letters p.410.

40 Chandos–JP, 7 July 1967, JPB p.137.

41 Laurence Evans–Laurence Harbottle [LO's solicitor], on the proposed heads of contract, 25 September 1967; LO's contract as agreed, 6 November 1968; both HLC B299. The contract was for five years at £5,000 a year, and after that for LO's part-time services for another fifteen years at £3,333. If he died during full-time service his wife or children would receive a pension of £833 a year plus £166 for each year served; if he died during part-time service the pension would be £1,666 for his or his wife's life. The London flat and half the cost of a chauffeur would be provided during full-time service.

42 Sargent–LO, 28 September 1967, BL PERS 1/15.

43 Diary, 18 November 1967, BL.

44 Fee, Evans–LO, 20 and 28 November 1967. Billing, LO–Evans, 30 October 1968. Both BL FILMS 12.

45 K.F. Mackenzie, of Hove–LO, 27 February 1968, BL PERS 16/2.

46 *An Actor in His Time* by John Gielgud, 1989, p.171. CA p.226.

47 CA pp.225–6.

48 *Gielgud: A Theatrical Life* by Jonathan Croall, 2001, p.453.

49 The portrait is now in the Garrick Club, London. It was reproduced on the dust jacket of *My Father Laurence Olivier* by Tarquin Olivier, 1992.

50 Tynan–LO, 7 May 1968, BL NT46/2.

51 LO–Tynan, 18 October 1968, BL 46/2.

52 LO–Chandos, CA pp.272–4.

53 LO–Peter Shaffer, 20 October 1983, HLC J4224. Shaffer had objected, after the publication of *Confessions of an Artist*, that Olivier, in this letter, had given Tynan the credit for Shaffer's play, *Black Comedy*. Olivier apologised, said this was unintentional, and asked Shaffer to consider what he had written in the context of his (Olivier's) 'desperate need' to influence the Board to believe in Tynan's usefulness. He admitted that he might have been over-zealous in Tynan's defence.

54 Chandos–LO, 28 October 1968; LO–Chandos, 3 November (not sent), and undated letter (sent). CA pp.274–6.

55 Tynan–LO, 4 December 1968, and LO–Tynan, 5 December 1968; BL NT46/2.

56 Chandos–LO, 22 January 1969, CA p.279.

57 CA p.232. LO's diary, 20 April 1969, BL.

58 Chandos–LO, 19 June 1969, BL NT46/2. LO's diary shows he was in hospital from 29 May to 10 June, but in a separate red notebook of dates and other memoranda he made an entry for 19 June which reads, 'Haemaroidectomy'.

NOTES TO CHAPTER 28 The College of Cardinals, and Surprise

1 Coward–LO, undated, BL PERS 1/4.

2 Family details from LO's diaries, BL. Brook and body blow, CA pp.233–4. JP's view, interview with author, 8 November 2003.

3 JPB p.158.

4 JPB pp.150–153.

5 LO memos of 10 and 27 April, 1970, BL NT 30/5.

6 Correspondence on Zena Rollnick, 1969–70, in HLC B2555.

7 LO interview with Terry Coleman, the *Guardian*, London, April 1970, and at greater length, including medlar anecdote, in *Show* magazine, New York, for same month.

8 Laurence Harbottle to author, 25 February 2003, and letters in HLC B2555.

9 LO diary, 13 June 1970, BL. Clark–LO, undated, NT 44/3, BL. Rattigan–LO, 15 June 1970, BL PERS 16. Olivier reply to Ashcroft, 18 July 1970, BL PERS 16. *Debrett's Illustrated Peerage*, 1970.

10 All this correspondence is in BL PERS 16, Honours. Five letters of LO to Garter from 31 July 1970 to 16 August 1971, five letters of Garter to LO from 29 July 1970 to 21 August 1971, and letters to and from Angela Harris and other cousins. Albany column in the *Sunday Telegraph*, 7 February 1971. The title was announced in the *London Gazette* of 5 March 1971.

11 LO letter to Queen, 9 April 1971, a handwritten draft, JPC. Bow, Peter Hiley interview with author, 28 February 2003.

12 LO–Tynan, 12 June 1970, BL NT 46/2.

13 Dates, LO diary, BL. Also CA p.239 and p.242.

14 Kanin, LO diary 1970, BL. Year off, JPB p.161. The announcement was made on 29 September 1970.

15 MA 26.27.

16 LO–Lord Goodman, 5 February 1970, BL NT 54/1.

17 LO–Chandos correspondence of 10, 21 and 24 October 1970, *Confessions* mss, BL CRIT 1, box 1.

18 Burton–LO, undated but 1970, BL PERS 1/3.

19 Dinners and offer, JPB pp.162–3. Burton letters of 18 Oct 1970 and November [?] 1970, printed in JPB pp.164–5.

20 CA p.240.

21 Goodman on Rayne, *Tell Them I'm On My Way* by Arnold Goodman, 1993, p.341. Jenny Lee–Chandos, 29 May 1970, Chandos papers CHAN II 4/13 at the Churchill Archive, Churchill College, Cambridge. In this letter she thanked him for excellent work and asked him to serve another year.

22 Olivier in CA p.240. Chandos's typed notes for his speech to the Board meeting of 12 July 1971 are in the Chandos Papers, CHAN II 4/13/xxx/11 and 12. See note 21 above.

23 Goodman pp.338–9, see note 21 above. JP on 'rubbish', interview with author, 10 December 2004.

24 CA pp.245–6. LO's diary for 1971 is not with the others in the BL.

25 See letter from J.D.C. Noble about his friend Beaumont, *Sunday Telegraph*, 3 October 1982.

26 LO–Tynan, 6 March 1970, BL NT 46/2.

27 CA p.243.

28 LO–Peter Shaffer, 20 October 1983, HLC J4224.

29 *Diaries of Kenneth Tynan*, ed. John Lahr, 2001, p.14.

30 LO–Tynan, 24 April 1970, BL NT 46/2.

31 Tynan–LO, 3 February 1972, BL NT 46/2.

32 Tynan–LO, 9 December 1971 and LO's reply, 10 February 1972, BL NT 46/2.

33 *Power Play: The Life and Times of Peter Hall* by Stephen Fay, 1995, p.206.

34 Blakemore proposed, LO–Rayne, 2 February 1972. Blakemore not knowing, his conversation with author, 31 August 2004. Regency Council, Rayne–LO, 10 February

1972, BL NT 44/1. Rayne disagreed with LO's account of these proceedings and others in *Confessions of an Actor*, and after its publication gave his version, which is more accurate, in a long letter to the *Sunday Telegraph*, 3 October 1982.

35 LO–Tynan, 10 February 1972, BL NT46/2.

36 CA p.247.

37 *Peter Hall's Diaries*, ed. John Goodwin, 2000 edition, 27 March 1972.

38 Tynan diaries, 12 April 1972, see note 29 above.

39 Excerpt from Peter Hall's diary for 13 April 1972, transcribed from Hall's tape by John Goodwin but not included in published version.

40 National Theatre statement to Press Association, 18 April 1972. BL NT 43G. *Peter Hall's Diaries* (see note 37 above), same date

41 Tynan's diaries (see note 29 above) 10, 18 and 20 April 1972. Hall's diaries (see note 37 above), 3 July 1972.

42 LO–Harold Sebag-Montefiore of the LCC, 5 May 1972, BL NT 44/1.

43 LO's seven-page pencilled draft, undated, is marked by his secretary: 'LO decided not to send this for the time being . . .' BL NT 44/1.

44 Rayne–LO, 8 May 1972, and LO's reply, 11 May 1972, BL NT 44/1.

45 Peter Hall interview with author, 6 February 2004.

46 Illnesses and Polaroid commercials from LO's diary, BL. The Dick Cavett show was recorded in London on 20 November 1972 and shown in the US on 24 January 1973.

47 CA p.250.

48 Fairbanks cable, 26 September 1973, BL PERS 10b.

49 Severance pay correspondence, 1 and 8 October 1973 and 5 February 1974, BL 46/2.

50 LO's entry in small red leather book marked 'Notes', with personal diaries, BL.

51 *Making an Exhibition of Myself: The Autobiography of Peter Hall*, 2003, p.266.

52 Blakemore conversation with author, 30 August 2004.

53 MA 26.27.

54 JP interview with author, 25 November 2003, and letter of JP to author, 19 December 2004.

NOTES TO CHAPTER 29 A Bit Worried about Time Running Out

1 *Peter Hall's Diaries*, ed. John Goodwin, 2000 edition, 1 May 1973 and 23 November 1973.

2 LO–Peter Hall, 28 November 1973, BL NT 43G.

3 CA p.254. *Diaries of Kenneth Tynan*, ed. John Lahr, 2002, 6 November 1973.

4 Polaroid correspondence, all in BL PROF 7, Advertising and Sponsorship. LO's diary shows he was in Paris for the commercials on 24–27 April and 17 July 1974.

5 *Peter Hall's Diaries* (see note 1 above), 3 July and 24 August 1972, 31 January and 27 April 1973 and 2 January 1974.

6 Peter Hall interview with author, 6 February 2004.

7 LO–Rayne, 6 September 1974, BL NT 44/1.

8 CA p.257. Diary entries from LO diary, BL.

9 LO–K.E.D. Shuttleworth, 17 October 1974, BL PERS 16/2.

10 Tarquin p.245.

11 JPB pp.202–3. JP interview with author, 18 November 2003.

12 JPB p.203.

13 LO–Sybille, 4 November 1974, BL PERS 25.

14 LO–Kenneth Clark, 5 December 1974. Kenneth Clark Papers, Hyman Kreitman

Research Center, Tate Gallery, London, 8812.1.3. 2306–2332.

15 Transcript of LO–Sybille tape, 6 December 1974, BL CRIT 2/1.

16 Untranscribed tape, same date, JPC.

17 LO–JE, 5 December 1975.

18 In large red leather notebook, with stamped coronet on front cover, BL CRIT 1 box 1. Inscribed 'To Larry with affection, Kenneth Carten, November 1974'.

19 LO–Hamish Hamilton, 10 December 1974, HLC B2555. Hamilton had written to LO on 17 April 1974 (BL PERS 1/9) saying he had heard he was taking a sabbatical year and inviting him to write an autobiography. He said: 'I am well aware of all the difficulties, particularly of course Vivien. But I also know, from some fifty years' experience, how easily and tactfully such things can be handled.'

20 JPB pp.203–4 and JP interview with author, 18 November 2003.

21 CA p.257.

22 JP interview with author, 18 November 2003.

23 Richard Olivier interview with author, 16 September 2004.

24 David Plowright interview with author, 17 September 2004.

25 As note 22 above.

26 Richardson, CA p.258. LO–Rowland, 25 November 1974, BL PERS 22/1/2. Kenneth Clark–LO, 20 December 1974, BL NT 44/3.

27 LO–Kenneth Clark, 27 January 1975. Kenneth Clark Papers, Hyman Kreitman Research Centre, Tate Gallery, London, 8812.1.3. 2306–2332.

28 Ginette Spanier–LO, 7 February 1975, BL PERS 1/15.

29 Shotgun correspondence in HLC B2555.

30 Assets valued June 1975, BL PERS 5/5/1.

31 LO was in Ischia 13 March–10 April, LO diary, BL; and *William Walton: Behind the Façade* by Susana Walton, 1988, p.221.

32 LO–JP, 1April 1975, JPC.

33 LO–Peter Hall, 8 July 1975, BL NT 43G.

34 CA p.259.

35 Joanna Sheldon–LO. 16 July 1975, BL PERS 16/2.

36 LO–Hall, 8 July 1975, BL NT43G.

37 LO–JP, 8 December 1975, JPC. Tamsin–LO, 9 December 1975, BL PERS 22/3.

38 This is Sarah Miles' account in *Bolt From the Blue*, 1996, pp.73–6.

39 Laurence Evans–LO, 23 and 29 April 1976, BL FILMS 14.

NOTES TO CHAPTER 30 A Gesture Somewhere Round Glory

1 Protocol committee minutes, 21 January 1976, BL NT 31/5.

2 Protocol committee minutes, 26 March and 4 December 1973, and 9 September 1974, as note 1 above.

3 *Peter Hall's Diaries*, ed. John Goodwin, 2000 edition, 30 July 1974.

4 LO's note on minutes of 9 September 1974.

5 *Peter Hall's Diaries* (see note 3 above), 25 February 1975.

6 Hall–LO, 12 and 21 May 1975, and LO–Hall, 8 July 1975, BL NT 43G.

7 Hall–LO, 16 July 1975, BL NT43G. *Peter Hall's Diaries* (see note 3 above), 1 August 1975.

8 Hall–LO, 3 October 1975, BL NT43G.

9 Hall–LO, 7 October 1975, BL NT43G.

10 *Peter Hall's Diaries* (see note 3 above), 10 October 1975.

11 *Gielgud's Letters*, ed. Richard Mangan, 2004. JG–Irene Worth, 14 March 1976. Richardson–LO, 19 March 1974, BL PERS 1/14.

12 LO–Hall, 17 October 1975, BL NT43G.

13 *Gielgud's Letters* (see note 11 above), 14 March 1976.

14 Hall–LO, 17 May 1976, BL NT43G.

15 Hall–LO, 21 May 1976, BL NT43G.

16 JP interview with author, 25 November 2003.

17 LO–Yolande Bird, BL NT31/5.

18 LO–Rayne, 17 May 1976, and Victor Mishcon (chairman of the committee) to LO, 18 May 1976, BL NY31/5.

19 Protocol committee minutes, 20 May 1976.

20 *Peter Hall's Diaries* (see note 3 above), 13 July 1976.

21 Undated memo in LO's hand, BL NT31/4 (1).

22 *Evening Standard*, 21 September 1976. *Peter Hall's Diaries* (see note 3 above), same date. Bust, Rayne–LO, 17 September 1976, and LO–Rayne, 3 October 1976, BL NT44/1.

23 LO–Hall, 6 October 1976, BL NT43G.

24 *Peter Hall's Diaries* (see note 3 above), 21 October 1976. *Diaries of Kenneth Tynan*, ed. John Lahr, 2001, 3 July 1977.

25 Birkett–LO, 23 October 1976, BL NT 31/4 (1).

26 There are two texts of this speech. The first, cited here, is in LO's handwriting in a small notebook, the size of a pocket diary, bound in soft red leather, with LO's diaries in the BL. It is much corrected and interlined. He had first written, and then crossed out, a sentence which reads: 'It may well be assumed, that the honour of welcoming you at this moment, in this place, must fulfil the wildest ambitions of a lifetime.' The speech was then typed on to three small cards. At the top of the first card Olivier wrote in pencil: 'Opening of Olivier NT 26. 10. 76. Speeches (in Bathroom).' He did not read from these cards, but he did use its adaptation of his first sentence, so that he said: 'It is an outsize pearl of understatement . . .' In 1981 these cards were bought by Richard Mangan, company manager at the National, at a book fair. He sent them to LO, asking him to sign them. LO replied that he wanted to keep them, which he did, sending Mangan a copy which he signed. The cards are now in BL NT31/4 (7).

27 *Peter Hall's Diaries* (see note 3 above), 25 October 1976.

28 JP interview with author, 25 November 2003.

29 *Diaries of Kenneth Tynan*, ed. John Lahr, 2001, 25 October 1976.

30 Kenneth Rae–LO, 26 October 1976; Maggie Riley–LO, undated; both BL NT31/4 (7).

NOTES TO CHAPTER 31 *Dracula* – the Shame of it

1 Greer Garson–LO, 23 October 1976, and his reply of 22 November, BL PERS 1/8.

2 Tarquin interview with author, 14 April 2003. Tarquin p245 gives a more detailed account.

3 Benjamin–LO, 26 March 1976, BL PROF 6.

4 Mary Sanders–LO, 5 January 1977, BL PERS 27/2.

5 See 'The Granada Factor', Derek Granger's contribution to *Olivier: In Celebration*, ed. Garry O'Connor, 1985, pp.131–41. Mr Granger had been joint literary consultant at the National Theatre with Olivier, and co-produced the Granada plays.

6 Narizzano–JP, 1989, BL CONDOLENCES 5.

7 MA 16.19.

8 Contract, 7 February 1977, HLC F2417.

9 Ginette Spanier to 'Darling lovely Larry', 5 April 1978, BL PERS 1/15.

10 Tarquin pp.245–51.

11 *Bolt From the Blue* by Sarah Miles, 1996, pp.79–88, and interviews with author, 24 and 29 July 2004.

12 Lynn Fontanne–LO, undated but 1978, BL PERS 1/11. CA p.90.

13 Interviews as in note 11 above, and *Bolt From the Blue*, pp.95–100. See also the earlier book, *Serves Me Right*, by Sarah Miles, 1994.

14 Miller in O'Connor, p.128, as note 5 above.

15 Dinah Day–LO, 9 October 1977, and other letters in BL PERS 25.

16 Contract, HLC F3082.

17 See note 15 above.

18 Fairbanks–LO–Fairbanks, 26 February 1978, 9 March 1978 and 1 April 1978, BL PERS 1/7.

19 *Peter Hall's Diaries*, ed. John Goodwin, 2000 edition, 8 June 1977, 31 May and 14 September 1978. Also LO–Yolande Bird, 21 June 1978, BL NT 31/5.

20 LO–Ashcroft, 9 June 1978, in possession of her daughter.

21 LO–Tarquin, 22 October 1978.

22 Gielgud to Irene Worth, in *Gielgud's Letters*, ed. Richard Mangan, 2004, 5 February 1979.

23 The Oscar ceremony was on 9 April 1979.

24 'Talking with Olivier' by Curtis Bill Pepper, *New York Times* magazine, 25 March 1979.

25 *Gielgud's Letters*, ed. Richard Mangan, 2004, p.426.

26 Contract, 18 April 1979, HLC F6443 and BL FILMS 14. Olivier on *Inchon*, MA 6.2–3.

27 Letters of Terence Young in BL PERS 1/17, and in HLC F3801.

28 Rex Reed interview in *New York Daily News*, 21 October 1979.

Notes to Chapter 32 Jobbing Actor, O.M.

1 LO–Shirley Luke his secretary, 21 January 1980, from Hollywood. He said they had now 'cut out all thoughts of Oxford'.

2 JPB p.211.

3 Contract, 13 November 1979, BL FILMS 14. Molasses, MA 9.1–2.

4 LO's note on letter from Temple, Gothard, solicitors, January[?], 1968, BL PERS 10b.

5 In the United States Court of Claims: Trial Division, *S & L Entertainment B.V.v The United States*. Defendant No. 312–79T, New York, NY, 7 February 1980. Transcript from the HLC archive. Olivier gave sworn evidence for two and a half hours and the typed transcript runs to 109 pages. Counsel naturally moved from topic to topic, particularly among LO's previous commercial ventures, and did so in no chronological order. They also returned at several points in LO's evidence to *The Jazz Singer*. To give a more coherent nattative I have not preserved the original order in which the questions were asked. Ellipses in the passages cited may indicate a sentence omitted, or several pages, but I believe the sense has been preserved. The words attributed to Olivier are as in the verbatim transcript.

6 Temple Gothard to Laurence Harbottle, 16 June 1981, HLC F3801.

7 LO's Diaries, BL. The entries have been slightly shortened.

8 Undated typed draft in BL PERS 16.

9 JE–LO, 6 February 1981, BL PERS 21/2.

10 Spink and Sons, London–LO, 16 April 1981, BL PERS 14.

NOTES TO CHAPTER 33 That Damned Book

1 *New York Daily News*, 21 October 1979.

2 The books are: *The Oliviers*, by Felix Barker, 1953; *Laurence Olivier*, by John Cottrell, 1975; *Olivier*, ed. Logan Gourlay, 1973; *Cry God for Larry*, by Virginia Fairweather, 1969, published in the US as *Olivier: An Informal Portrait*. Anne Edwards, in her biography of Vivien Leigh, writes of the moment in 1939 when Olivier and Leigh, on Douglas Fairbanks' yacht, hear Neville Chamberlain state on the radio that Britain is at war with Germany: 'There was a yawning, agonised silence. The slap of the water as they rocked gently at anchor sounded like the ticking of a time bomb.' This is a fair example of the book's style and content.

3 Klausner–LO, 26 July 1950; E.P.S. Lewin, London, to LO, 1 October 1957, and LO's reply; Little, Brown–LO, 26 September 1959, and LO's reply of 2 October 1959; all BL CRIT 1, box 2. Morley–LO, 12 March 1979, BL CRIT 2/1.

4 Tynan–LO, 30 November 1978, *Kenneth Tynan: Letters*, ed. Kathleen Tynan, 1994.

5 Tynan Letters, p.624, (see note 4 above).

6 Tynan–LO, Tynan Letters (see note 4 above), 2 April 1979.

7 Tynan–JP, Tynan Letters (see note 4 above), 3 April 1979. Author interview with JP, 25 November 2003.

8 Vidal in 'Reputations' by Anthony Howard, BBC TV, 1982. *Bolt From the Blue*, by Sarah Miles, 1996, p.87.

9 Tynan–LO, 15 June 1979, Tynan Letters (see note 4 above).

10 Cottrell–LO, 24 July 1979, BL CRIT 1, box 2. LO–Cottrell, a draft, July 1979, BL CRIT 2/1.

11 Returned advance, Tynan Letters (see note 4 above), p.632, note 5. Korda interview with author, 1 July 2003.

12 Tutin–LO, dated '12 Oct', BL PERS 1/16. The ghost she suggested was John Miller, who she said had done some interviews with John Gielgud, and who in 1979 published *An Actor and His Times*, with Ralph Richardson.

13 That was the title LO gave Hamish Hamilton when in his letter of 10 December 1974 he proposed the book to him. HLC F7290.

14 Contract, 15 and 30 November 1979; Evans–LO, 28 November 1980; both BL CRIT 1/1/1. Comparison with 'Civilisation', author interview with Mark Amory, 25 April 2003.

15 Hamilton–LO, 25 January 1980, HLC B2555.

16 Author interview with Mark Amory, 25 April 2003. Mr Amory also describes his collaboration with LO in his contribution to *Olivier: In Celebration*, ed. Garry O'Connor, 1987, p.187.

17 Author interview with JP, 18 November 2003. LO–Hester Olivier, 3 May 1959. *Confessions* mss, p.144, BL CRIT 1, box 1.

18 LO–Fabia Drake, 2 April 1981, BL PERS 1/6. LO–Weidenfeld, 20 March 1981, BL CRIT 1, box 2.

19 LO–Hall, 16 March 1981, BL NT57.

20 Weidenfeld–LO, 20 March 1981, BL CRIT 1, box 2.

21 LO–Weidenfeld, 20 April 1982, BL CRIT 1, box 2.

22 LO–Weidenfeld, 30 April 1982, as above. Copies of these two letters are also in the HLC.

23 Olivier's diary, BL. CA p.113 and p.260.

24 Suggested changes, Korda's note, dated '3/10/82', BL CRIT 1.

25 Author interview with Michael Korda, 1 July 2003.

26 CA p.229.

27 *New York Times* review by Mary Cantwell, 20 December 1982. *My Father Laurence Olivier* by Tarquin Olivier, 1992, p.xiv.

28 LO's contract with Weidenfeld & Nicolson, 15 November 1979, BL CRIT 1/1/1, gave him an advance of £100,000 for the British and Commonwealth rights, one third on signature, one third on acceptance, and one third on publication. LO retained 90% of the sums paid for foreign rights, which were $270,000 in the US, DM80,000 in Germany, and $20,000 US in Italy. LO received 90% of £30,000 paid for syndication rights by the *Sunday Telegraph*, London, and 60% of £41,500 for the British paperback rights. The contract gave Mark Amory 10% of the book advances and royalties, and LO's agent took 10% of all earnings.

NOTES TO CHAPTER 34 No Longer on an Even Keel

1 Contract, 25 January 1982, and note of 5 June 1982, both in HLC J818.

2 Letters of 1973 and 1981 to Kew and to nurseries, BL PERS 10a.

3 JPB p.220.

4 Author interview with JP, 25 November 2003.

5 Profile of JP by Sheridan Morley, *The Times*, 15 October 1980.

6 JPB pp.221–2. Letters of Laurence Harbottle to JP, 9 and 12 June 1981, HLC F3801.

7 JPB pp.221–3.

8 LO–JP, 8 December 1981, JPC. Printed, undated and at greater length, in JPB p.223.

9 Note by Brian Chilver of Temple, Gothard, 16 February 1982, HLC J818.

10 Gielgud to Irene Worth, 17 January 1982, from *Gielgud's Letters*, ed. Richard Mangan, 2004.

11 JPB p.219.

12 LO's draft letter, Shirley Luke (secretary) to Laurence Harbottle, and his reply, all July 1982, BL PROF 8c.

13 *On Acting*, p.94.

14 Anna Calder-Marshall–JP, undated but July 1989, BL CONDOLENCE 2.

15 Description of brooches and order sent 3 December 1982, BL PERS 14.

16 Drake–LO, 30 May 1982, BL PERS 1/6.

17 Niven–LO, 12 April and 18 May 1982, BL PERS 1/13.

18 Emma Sergeant conversation with author, 17 November 2004. The portrait was unveiled at the National Portrait Gallery in July 1982; *The Times*, 8 July 1982, picture and caption.

19 Fairbanks' address, 25 April 1983, BL PERS 1/7. White House, JPB p.221.

20 *Bounty* contract, 20 June 1983, HLC J2920.

21 Thatcher–LO, 15 June 1983, BL PERS 1/16. LO–Joseph, draft of telegram, undated, BL PERS 1/10.

22 *The Times*, 6, 8, 9, 17 and 29 December 1983.

23 Corri–LO, undated, and LO's reply, 9 March 1984, BL PERS 11/2. Fairbanks–LO, 28 January 1984, BL PERS 1/7.

24 Laurence Harbottle–Laurence Evans, 7 September 1984, and contract, 27 September 1984, both HLC J4853.
25 LO's diary, BL. Author interview with JP, 18 November 2003.
26 LO's diary, 21 October 1984, BL.

NOTES TO CHAPTER 35 Uninsurable as God

1 Jill, CA p.62. Draft of speech to Lords, undated, BL PERS 14. Spirituality, LO–Hall, 14 October 1960, in Hall's letters, cited in *Power Play: The Life and Times of Peter Hall* by Stephen Fay, 1995, p.132.
2 Guinness' diary, 15 December 1983, in *Alec Guinness*, by Piers Paul Read, 2004, p.567.
3 Guinness–LO, 12 December 1983, BL PERS 1/8. There is some inconsistency in the dating of the diary entry and the letter. In his diary entry Guinness says he wrote the letter on the night of the visit.
4 Book contract with Weidenfeld & Nicolson, 15 October 1984, HLC K6226: LO received royalties of 12.5% to 20,000 copies and 15% thereafter; Grainger received £10,000 and 10% of the royalties. 'Like father', and other details of Grainger's co-operation with Olivier, from Grainger interview with author, 27 May 2003.
5 There are ten transcripts, dating from before 7 December 1984 to 22 March 1985, 36,000 words in all, at BL CRIT 1, box 2. In the book Grainger smoothed and edited LO's words. The passage cited here is from the transcript of 26 February 1985.
6 Shirley Luke–Grainger, 7 December 1984, BL CRIT 1, box 2.
7 Author interview with Grainger, 27 May 2003.
8 Old age, Sydney Olivier to H.G. Wells, 13 December 1939, in *Sydney Olivier: Letters and Selected Writings*, ed. Margaret Olivier, 1948, p.178. Shaw's remarks, in his prologue to the book, p.19.
9 From Shirley Luke's desk diary, 1985, BL.
10 LO's diary, entries for 15–19 February and 22–27 March 1985, in his own hand, BL. LO's diaries for 1985 and 1986 also include some short entries in unknown hands, perhaps his nurses'.
11 *On Acting* pp.18, 217 and 135, BL. Transcripts and author interview with Grainger, 27 May 2003.
12 The Chichester plaque was unveiled 5 May 1985. Luke's desk diary has in her hand, 21 June 1985, 'LO bashed leg – blood all over the place', and LO's diary for 17 August has, in a nurse's hand, 'Split leg open in pool'.
13 Luke's note to Grainger is on the transcript of 12 July 1985, BL CRIT 1, box 2.
14 Hutchinson–LO, 11 October 1985, BL PERS 27/2.
15 Garson–LO, 3 October 1985, BL PERS 1/8.
16 Gielgud–Olivier, 16 December 1985; see also *Gielgud–Irene* Worth, 9 December 1985; both in *Gielgud's Letters*, ed. Richard Mangan, 2004.
17 JP interview with author, 25 November 2003.
18 LO's diary, 21 and 22 January and 1 February 1986, BL.
19 Ginette Spanier–LO, undated, BL PERS 1/15.
20 LO's diaries, 24 January, 13 and 28 February and 7 and 19 March 1986. Shirley Luke's diary, 12 November 1985, 16 January and 5 March 1986: all BL. Other dates from LO's diary.
21 JP interview with author, 25 August 2003.
22 Dates from LO's diary. Letter LO–JP, dated 'St Patrick's Day 1986', JPC.

23 JPB p.238.

24 Author interviews with Julie-Kate Olivier, 13 September 2004, and Tamsin Olivier, 18 September 2004.

25 *The Times*, 4 January 1986.

26 LO's entries stop in the middle of the year. There are no diaries for 1987 and 1988. A diary for 1989 survives, but there are no entries in it. BL.

27 Author interviews with Richard Olivier, 16 September 2004, and with Tamsin, 18 September 2004.

28 Handwritten will of 17 July 1937, JPC, and also a photocopy at BL PERS 17. Chart dated 2 December 1958, with LO's annotation dated 2 February 1976, BL PERS 17. Will of 2 September 1960, HLC B2555.

29 Wills of 30 May 1977 and 1980 (after 5 March), BL PERS 17. Will of 25 May 1985, and note of Shirley Luke to Laurence Harbottle, 15 November 1985, BL PERS 17.

30 Will of 18 March 1986, BL PERS 17.

31 JPB p.226.

32 LO–JP, dated 'Mon. Eve 11th Aug [1986]', JPC.

33 JP interview with author, 11 December 2004.

NOTES TO CHAPTER 36 St Paul's or Westminster Abbey

1 Author interview with Peter Hiley, 28 February 2003.

2 1968 proposal, two letters in HLC B299. Letter from Touche Roche, accountants, to Harbottle and Lewis, 15 April 1987, HLC K273.

3 *The Times*, 19 May 1987.

4 Reagan cable, BL PERS 1/14. Thatcher letter, BL PERS 1/16.

5 Tamsin Olivier interview with author, 18 September 2004.

6 *Utopia and Other Places* by Richard Eyre, 1993, p.118.

7 *The Times*, report by Irving Wardle, 12 June 1987. JPB p.239.

8 Eyre, as in note 6 above, p.118.

9 JPB p.239.

10 Author interview with Gawn Grainger, 27 May 2003.

11 Eyre, as note 6 above, p.120.

12 Tamsin Olivier interview with author, 18 September 2004.

13 Richard Olivier interview with author, 16 September 2004.

14 *Shadow of the Stone Heart*, by Richard Olivier, 1995, p.2, p.151 and p.153.

15 Tamsin Olivier interview with author, 18 September 2004.

16 As note 13.

17 Julie-Kate Olivier interview with author, 13 September 2004.

18 Tamsin Olivier's recollections, interview with author, 18 September 2004. The champagne anecdote is hers. JP on LO as chameleon, interview with author, 11 December 2004.

19 Memory, author interview with Gawn Grainger, 27 May 2003. LO as frisky satyr, JP interview with author, 11 December 2004.

20 Letter from the Rev. Canon Peter Burge, 23 August 2004, and telephone conversation with author, 24 August. Canon Burge was vicar of Steyning with Ashurst, 1985–94.

21 *Bolt From the Blue*, by Sarah Miles, 1996, p.197, and her conversations with author, 24 and 28 July 2004.

22 Blakemore conversation with author, 30 August 2004.

23 Grainger as note 10 above. Harbottle memo of meeting with JP, 23 June 1988, HLC K793. Very late on, LO told Harbottle to dismiss Laurence Evans as his agent but he, knowing there was no point in it, did not.

24 *The Times*, 1 November 1988.

25 Dalí letter, Shirley Luke to Paul R. Chimera, undated, BL PERS 11/2. Sale, *Daily Telegraph*, 13 July 1989. Olivier's remaining paintings were valued for probate at £113,365. A dune landscape and a river scene, both by Boudin and both inherited from Vivien Leigh, accounted for £55,000 of this. Apart from these and a river landscape by Daubigny, Olivier's pictures were said by Agnew of Bond Street to be 'not very distinguished'. A small Lowry, '*Lancashire Landscape, 1952*', had no figures in it and a hole in the sky which had not been well repaired. His two portraits of Garrick were not first rate. That attributed to Zoffany was, according to Agnew, 'absolutely not genuine' and was valued at £600. That believed to be by Sir Joshua Reynolds, though it had come from the Duke of Bedford's collection at Woburn, was judged to be a studio replica and valued at £1,500. The portraits of Olivier by Bernard Hailstone, and that of Garrick attributed to Zoffany, were given by trustees to the Garrick Club. The portrait of Olivier as Romeo, by Harold Knight, was as he had requested given to the National Theatre, where it hangs in the chairman's office. The portrait of Garrick after Reynolds was lent for some years to the Old Vic Theatre, and in 2004 was on loan to the Garrick Theatre. At his death, Olivier's shareholding in his company, Wheelshare, was £322,109. Valuations and correspondence in HLC K7095. His net estate was proved at £1,322,383: *The Times*, 4 November 1989.

26 Contract with Simon and Schuster audio, HLC K6226.

27 David Plowright interview with author, 17 September 2004.

28 JP on plays, filming and her return, interview with author, 11 December 2004, and letter to author, 16 December 2004. Nurse and orange juice: Olivier's words are first reported in Tarquin p.258. Tarquin, remembering how his father had loved recounting the alleged dying words of George V – 'What's on at the Empire?' and 'Bugger Bognor' – sought out the nurse before the funeral. Laurence Evans, his letter to JP, 8 September 1989, JPC. See also JPB p.242, where JP quotes from a letter by Don MacKechnie, who had been staff director at the National and wrote an account of the funeral to a friend, Ben Benjamin.

29 Grainger interview with author, 27 May 2003. Hiley interview with author 28 February 2003.

30 JP interview with author, 25 November 2003.

31 *The Times*, 14 July 1989, and Canon Burge to author, 24 August 2004.

32 Tamsin Oliver interview with author, 18 September 2004.

33 Julie-Kate Olivier interview with author, 13 September 2004.

34 David Plowright interview with author, 17 September 2004.

35 Richard Olivier, as note 13 above, p.7.

36 *The Times*, 14 July 1989.

37 Letter of the Very Rev. Michael Mayne, KCVO, Dean Emeritus of Westminster, to author, 16 November 2004.

38 'Next to Nelson', Harbottle to author, 25 February 2003. Family decided on St Paul's, Harbottle to Evans, fax timed 11.55 a.m., 18 July 1989; Harbottle to Sir John Riddell, secretary to Prince of Wales, 18 July 1989; Evans to Rear Admiral Kenneth Snow, Chapter office, Westminster Abbey, 18 July 1969; all in HLC K7284.

39 Shock and bending rules, Mayne to author, in letter of 16 November 2004 and

conversation of 25 November 2004. Second letter of Harbottle to Prince of Wales' secretary, 18 July 1989, HLC K7284.

40 See minutes of special services committee at Westminster Abbey on 26 July 1989, and letter of Harbottle to Hiley, 28 July 1989, both in BL 'Funeral and Memorial Service' file, unnumbered. Branagh–LO, 15 January 1981 and LO–Branagh, 10 February 1981, BL PROF 10. Poverty of imagination, author interview with Laurence Harbottle, 25 February 2003.

41 Richard Olivier, as note 13 above, p.13.

42 Dean Mayne to author, 25 November 2004.

43 *The Times*, 21 October 1989, the *Sunday Times* and *Sunday Telegraph*, 22 October 1989. The text of Guinness's address is printed, apparently in full, in the London *Evening Standard*, 20 October 1989.

44 John Walsh in the *Sunday Times*, 22 October 1989.

45 Richard Olivier, as note 13 above, p.10.

46 Letter of Toby Rowland to JP, after the memorial service, cited in JPB p.185.

NOTES TO 'THE ANDROGYNOUS ACTOR'

1 *Laurence Olivier: A Biography* by Donald Spoto, 1991, p.197.

2 *Vivien Leigh* by Hugo Vickers, 1988. He conducted the interview with John Merivale cited here on 17 February 1987.

3 Spoto (see note 1 above), p.197.

4 Spoto (see note 1 above), p.211.

5 Olivier's 1953 diary, BL.

6 Author interview with Pieter Rogers, 19 October 2004.

7 Author interview with Michael Korda, 1 July 2003.

8 Author's conversation with Irving Wardle, 5 December 2003.

9 *The Diaries of Kenneth Tynan*, ed. John Lahr, 2001.

10 Rattigan–LO, letter dated 27 Sept (no year), BL PERS 1/14.

11 GG trs, tape 2, side 2, BL CRIT 1, box 1.

12 Author conversations with Sarah Miles, 23 and 28 July 2004.

13 Fairbanks–LO, 26 October 1971, from New York, enclosing xeroxes, and 1 April 1978, from Florida.

14 'The Shrew Played by Boys' from Our Special Correspondent, *The Times*, 29 April 1922.

15 Author interview with Michael Gambon, 11 May 2004.

16 Author interview with Michael Blakemore, 30 August 2004.

A CHRONOLOGY OF
OLIVIER'S STAGE CAREER

This list is published by courtesy of Richard Mangan, administrator of the Mander & Mitchenson Theatre Collection at Greenwich. On the few occasions where Olivier's papers or diaries give dates different from those in the collection's own list, Olivier's dates have been adopted.

All theatres are in London, except where another place is named. Where Olivier acted in a play, both the dates and the number of performances are given where known. All National Theatre figures are taken from his own minutely exact notes in his diaries. When he directed a play but did not appear in it, the only date given (except for NT productions) is generally that of the opening. Only a few of the one-night engagements are important, for instance that as Captain Stanhope in *Journey's End* on Nov. 12, 1934, which was greatly praised, but the others, even the charity galas and Nights of a Hundred Stars at the Palladium, are included for the sake of comprehensiveness.

DATE	THEATRE & COMPANY	PLAY OR EVENT	ROLE
1920	All Saints School	*The Taming of the Shrew*	**Katharina**
1922			
Apr 28	Memorial Theatre, Stratford *All Saints School production*	*The Taming of the Shrew*	**Katharina**
1923			
Dec 10	St Edward's School, Oxford	*A Midsummer Night's Dream*	**Puck**
1924			
Nov 30	Century Theatre	*Byron*	**Suliot Officer**
Dec 14	Regent Theatre (1 perf) *The Fellowship of Players*	*The Merry Wives of Windsor*	**Servant**
Dec.	St Christopher's School, Letchworth	*Through the Crack*	**ASM & Understudy**

1925

Feb 8	Regent Theatre (1 perf)	*Henry IV, Part 2*	**Master Snare & Thomas of Clarence**
Apr?	St Christopher's School, Letchworth	*Macbeth*	**Lennox & ASM**
Aug?	Brighton Hippodrome and Tour	*Unfailing Instinct* and *Ghost Train*	**Armand St Cyr Policeman**
Oct	Century Theatre & London area tour with *Lena Ashwell Players*	*The Tempest*	**Antonio**
Oct	Century Theatre and London tour	*Julius Caesar*	**Flavius**
Dec 23 to Mar 20, 1926	Empire Theatre (127 perfs) *Lewis Casson/Albery production*	*Henry VIII*	**First Serving Man**

1926

Jan 10	New Scala Theatre (1 perf) *The Greek Play Society*	*Oedipus Tyrannus*	**Suppliant/ Guard/ Servant**
Mar 8–19	Empire Theatre (4 perfs)	*The Cenci*	**Servant to Orsino**
Apr 7 to June 12	Kingsway Theatre (76 perfs)	*Marvellous History of St Bernard*	**Minstrel**
Apr 23	Theatre Royal, Haymarket (1 perf) *British Empire Shakespeare Society*	*The Merchant of Venice*	**Gentleman**
May 3	Royal Court Theatre (1 perf)	*The Song*, in a triple bill	**Lucio de Costanza**
Jun?	Clacton	*The Barber and the Cow*	**Small part**
Jul–Nov	Tour	*The Farmer's Wife*	**Richard Coaker**
Dec	Birmingham Repertory Theatre	*The Farmer's Wife*	**Richard Coaker**

1927

Jan 31	Birmingham Repertory Theatre	*Something To Talk About* and *Well of the Saints*	**Guy Sydney Mat Simon**
Feb 12	Birmingham Repertory Theatre	*The Third Finger*	**Tom Hardcastle**

Feb 26	Birmingham Repertory Theatre	*The Mannoch Family*	**Peter Mannoch**
Mar 19	Birmingham Repertory Theatre	*The Comedian*	**Herald/Guard/ Lictor**
Apr 2	Birmingham Repertory Theatre	*Uncle Vanya*	**Vanya**
Apr 16	Birmingham Repertory Theatre	*All's Well That Ends Well*	**Parolles**
Apr 30	Birmingham Repertory Theatre	*The Pleasure Garden*	**A Young Man**
May 14	Birmingham Repertory Theatre	*She Stoops to Conquer*	**Tony Lumpkin**
Jun 4	Birmingham Repertory Theatre	*Quality Street*	**Ensign Blades**
Sep 3	Birmingham Repertory Theatre	*Bird in Hand*	**Gerald Arnwood**
Sep 24	Birmingham Repertory Theatre	*Advertising April*	**Mervyn Jones**
Oct 2	Birmingham Repertory Theatre	*The Adding Machine*	**Young Man**
Oct 8	Birmingham Repertory Theatre	*The Silver Box*	**Jack Barthwick**
Nov 5	Birmingham Repertory Theatre	*The Road to Ruin*	**Mr Milford**

1928

Jan 9 to Feb 4	Royal Court Theatre (32 perfs) *Birmingham Repertory Theatre Company*	*The Adding Machine*	**Young Man**
Mar 6–13	Royal Court Theatre (32 perfs) *Birmingham Repertory Theatre Company*	*Macbeth*	**Malcolm**
Mar 19–31	Royal Court Theatre (11 perfs) *Birmingham Repertory Theatre Company*	*Back To Methuselah*	**Martellus**
Apr 2–24	Royal Court Theatre (25 perfs) *Birmingham Repertory Theatre Company*	*Harold*	**Harold**
Apr 30 to May 26	Royal Court Theatre (32 perfs) *Birmingham Repertory Theatre Company*	*The Taming of the Shrew*	**A Lord**

Jun 1   Royalty Theatre   *Bird In Hand*   **Gerald**
Date approximate – took over the part)   **Arnwood**

Jul 8–9   Prince of Wales   *Paul Among The Jews*   **Chanan**
           Theatre (2 perfs)
           Incorporated Stage Society

Nov 4   Savoy Theatre (1 perf)   *The Dark Path*   **Graham Birley**
           Lyceum Club Stage Society

Dec 9–10   Apollo Theatre (2 perfs) *Journey's End*   **Captain**
           Incorporated Stage Society   **Stanhope**

1929

Jan 30   His Majesty's Theatre   *Beau Geste*   **Beau**
to Mar 4   (39 perfs)

Feb 17   Queen's Theatre   *Sketch: Prize Giving at* **McTavish VI**
           (1 perf)   *Woodside House School*
           Green Room Rag Society

Mar 14   New Theatre (48 perfs)   *The Circle of Chalk*   **Prince Pao**
to Apr 20

Apr 22–27 Golders Green   *Paris Bound*   **Richard Parish**
           Hippodrome
           Pre-London tour (8 perfs)

Apr 30   Lyric Theatre   *Paris Bound*   **Richard Parish**
to May 25 (31 perfs)

Jun 20   Garrick Theatre   *The Stranger Within*   **John Hardy**
to Aug 3   (53 perfs)

Aug 5–10   Golders Green   *The Stranger Within*   **John Hardy**
           Hippodrome (8 perfs)

Sep 11 for Eltinge Theatre,   *Murder on the Second* **Hugh Bromilow**
6 weeks   New York   *Floor*

Dec 19   Fortune Theatre   *The Last Enemy*   **Jerry**
to   (97 perfs)   **Warrender**
Mar 15, 1930

1930

Feb 23   Queen's Theatre   *Sketch: 100 – Not Out* **Helen (the**
           (1 perf)   **nurse)**
           Green Room Rag Society

Mar 30   Arts Theatre (9 perfs)   *After All*   **Ralph**
to Apr 6

Aug 18–23	King's Theatre, Edinburgh *Pre-London tour* (8 perfs)	*Private Lives*	**Victor Prynne**
Sep 1–6	Theatre Royal, Birmingham *Pre-London tour* (8 perfs)	*Private Lives*	**Victor Prynne**
Sep 8–13	Palace Theatre, Manchester *Pre-London tour* (8 perfs)	*Private Lives*	**Victor Prynne**
Sep 15–20	King's Theatre, Southsea *Pre-London tour* (8 perfs)	*Private Lives*	**Victor Prynne**
Sep 24 to Dec 20	Phoenix Theatre (101 perfs)	*Private Lives*	**Victor Prynne**
Dec 8	London Hippodrome (1 perf) (Gala matinée for Denville Hall)	*Sketch: Some Other Private Lives*	**Alf**

1931

Jan 27 for 32 weeks	Times Square Theatre, New York, (150 perfs)	*Private Lives*	**Victor Prynne**

1932   **(Olivier was in Hollywood and made no stage appearances this year)**

1933

Apr 6 to July 8	Playhouse Theatre (107 perfs)	*The Rats of Norway*	**Stevan Beringer**
Oct 20 for 21 weeks	Cort Theatre, New York (116 perfs)	*The Green Bay Tree*	**Julian Dulcimer**

1934

Apr 25 to June 2	Globe Theatre (45 perfs)	*Biography*	**Richard Kurt**
Jun 8 to Sep 8	New Theatre (106 perfs)	*Queen of Scots*	**Earl of Bothwell**
Oct 1–6	King's Theatre, Glasgow *Pre-London tour* (8 perfs)	*Theatre Royal*	**Anthony Cavendish**
Oct 8–13	King's Theatre, Edinburgh *Pre-London tour* (8 perfs)	*Theatre Royal*	**Anthony Cavendish**

| Oct 15–20 | Opera House,
Manchester
Pre-London tour (8 perfs) | *Theatre Royal* | **Anthony
Cavendish** |

| Oct 23 to
Dec 23 | Lyric Theatre | *Theatre Royal* | **Anthony
Cavendish** |

| Nov 12 | Adelphi Theatre | *Journey's End* | **Captain
Stanhope** |

(1 perf only in aid of the 'Not Forgotten' servicemen's association)

| Nov 22 | His Majesty's Theatre | *A Kiss for Cinderella* | **Policeman
Prince** |

(1 perf only: Gerald du Maurier Memorial Fund matinée)

| Dec 2 | Comedy Theatre
(1 perf only)
Green Room Rag Society | *Sketch: November
Afternoon* | **The Man** |

| Dec 17 | Adelphi Theatre
(1 perf only, King George's Pension Fund matinée) | *The Winning Post* | **Philip
Cavanagh** |

1935

| Feb 25
to 22 Mar | New Theatre, Oxford
Pre-London tour (7 perfs) | *Ringmaster* | **Peter
Hammond** |

| Mar 4–9 | Theatre Royal,
Birmingham
Pre-London tour (8 perfs) | *Ringmaster* | **Peter
Hammond** |

| Mar
11–16 | Shaftesbury Theatre
(8 perfs) | *Ringmaster* | **Peter
Hammond** |

| Mar 15 | London Hippodrome | *Sketch: November
Afternoon* | **The Man** |

(1 perf only, special matinée in aid of Ladies Guild of the Royal
Benevolent Fund)

| Apr 7 | Comedy Theatre
(1 perf only, for Green Room Rag Society) | *Sketch: Notices* | **Oswald
Parkinson** |

| Apr 8 | Gaiety Theatre
(1 perf only) | *The Down and Outs
Matinée* | **Recited
Kipling's 'If'** |

| May
13–18 | New Theatre, Oxford
Pre-London tour (7 perfs) | *Golden Arrow* | **Richard Harben
& director** |

| May 30 to
June 15 | Whitehall Theatre
(19 perfs) | *Golden Arrow* | **Richard Harben
& director** |

| Jul 10 | Grosvenor House,
London (1 perf) | *The Massed Chorus* | **Footman** |

(1 perf only, for Charles B. Cochran's Mammoth Cabaret in aid of
the Actors Benevolent Fund)

Oct 17 to Mar 28, 1936	New Theatre (186 perfs)	*Romeo and Juliet*	**Romeo; Mercutio, from Nov 28**

1936

May 5 to June 6	Lyric Theatre (37 perfs)	*Bees On The Boatdeck*	**Robert Patch, and co- director with Richardson**

1937

Jan 5 to Feb 20	Old Vic Theatre (42 perfs)	*Hamlet*	**Hamlet**
Feb 23 to Apr 3	Old Vic Theatre (42 perfs)	*Twelfth Night*	**Sir Toby Belch**
Apr 6 to May 22	Old Vic Theatre (50 perfs)	*Henry V*	**Henry**
Apr 23	Old Vic Theatre (1 perf)	Shakespeare Birthday Festival: *Romeo and Juliet* scene, *Henry V* scene	**Romeo** **Henry**
May 6	Empire Theatre (1 perf only in aid of the Cinematograph Benevolent Fund)	*Midnight with the Stars*	**Personal appearance**
Jun 2–6	Kronborg Castle, Elsinore (5 perfs) *Old Vic production*	*Hamlet*	**Hamlet**
Nov 26 to Dec 18	Old Vic Theatre	*Macbeth*	**Macbeth**
Dec 24 to Jan 15, 1938	New Theatre (total 53 perfs) *Transfer from Old Vic*	*Macbeth*	**Macbeth**

1938

Feb 8 to Mar 12	Old Vic Theatre (35 perfs)	*Othello*	**Iago**
Mar 15 to Apr 16	Old Vic Theatre (34 perfs)	*The King of Nowhere*	**Vivaldi**
Apr 19 to May 21	Old Vic Theatre (35 perfs)	*Coriolanus*	**Coriolanus**
May 23	Lyceum Theatre (1 perf only at Henry Irving Centenary matinée)	*Here's To Our Enterprise*	**Alfred Jingle**

1939
Apr 17   Ethel Barrymore   *No Time For Comedy*   **Gaylord**
              Theatre, (72 perfs)   **Easterbrook**

1940
May 9   51st Street Theatre,   *Romeo and Juliet*   **Romeo &**
              New York (36 perfs)   **director**

1941
Dec 7   Empire Theatre, York   All Star Concert in aid   *Romeo and*
              (1 perf)   of Russian Relief Fund   *Juliet* **scene**

1942
Jan 18   London Palladium   Esmond Knight matinée **Henry**
                                                 Henry V scene
              (1 perf only, Green Room Rags Society)

Nov 30   New Theatre (1 perf)   Elsie Fogerty Jubilee   **Poetry Reader**
                                                 Matinée

1943   **(Olivier was filming Henry V and made no stage appearances
              this year)**

1944
Aug 7–12 Opera House,   *Arms and the Man*   **Sergius**
              Manchester   **Saranoff**
              Old Vic Company
              Pre-London tour (9 perfs)

Aug 31 to New Theatre (83 perfs)   *Peer Gynt*   **Button**
Apr 14,   *Old Vic Company*   **Moulder**
1945

Sep 5 to New Theatre (67 perfs)   *Arms and the Man*   **Sergius**
Apr 13,   *Old Vic Company*   **Saranoff**
1945

Sep 13 to New Theatre (83 perfs)   *Richard III*   **Richard, Duke**
Apr 11,   *Old Vic Company*   **of Gloucester**
1945

1945
Jan 16 to New Theatre (25 perfs)   *Uncle Vanya*   **Astrov**
Apr 12   *Old Vic Company*

May 16   Phoenix Theatre   *The Skin of Our Teeth*   **Director**
              (Transferred to Piccadilly Theatre, 11 Sep)

After *The Skin of Our Teeth* opened, there followed a four-week tour of the regions including Manchester with the Old Vic Company, which then undertook a six-week tour of Europe, including Antwerp (see below), Ghent, Hamburg and Belsen, ending with a week at the Marigny, Paris, and two weeks at the Comédie Française, Paris. The plays were *Arms and the Man*, *Peer Gynt* and *Richard III*.

Jun	ENSA Garrison Theatre, Antwerp	*Arms and the Man*	**Sergius Saranoff**
Jun	ENSA Garrison Theatre, Antwerp	*Richard III*	**Richard III**
Sep 26 to Apr 13, 1946	New Theatre *Old Vic Company* (69 perfs)	*Henry IV Part 1*	**Hotspur**
Oct 3 to Apr 13, 1946	New Theatre (59 perfs) *Old Vic Company*	*Henry IV Part 2*	**Justice Shallow**
Oct 18 to Apr 27, 1946	New Theatre (76 perfs) *Old Vic Company*	*Oedipus* and *The Critic*	**Oedipus** **Mr Puff**

1946

May 1 to Jun 14	Century Theatre, New York *Old Vic Company* (8 perfs)	*Uncle Vanya*	**Astrov**
May 6 to Jun 13	Century Theatre, New York *Old Vic Company* (18 perfs)	*Henry IV Part 1*	**Hotspur**
May 6 to Jun 13	Century Theatre, New York *Old Vic Company* (9 perfs)	*Henry IV Part 2*	**Justice Shallow**
May 20 to Jun 15	Century Theatre, New York *Old Vic Company* (15 perfs)	*Oedipus* and *The Critic*	**Oedipus**
Sep 24 to Jan 4, 1947	New Theatre *Old Vic Company* (42 perfs)	*King Lear*	**Lear**
Nov 25 to Dec 1	Théâtre des Champs -Elysées, Paris *Old Vic Company* (7 perfs)	*King Lear*	**Lear**

1947
Feb 1   Garrick Theatre   *Born Yesterday*   **Director**

1948   Old Vic tour of Australia and New Zealand
Mar   Capitol Theatre, Perth   *The School for*   **Sir Peter**
20–30   Australia   *Scandal*   **Teazle &**
             (Only *School for Scandal* plays in Perth)   **director**

Apr 3–17 Theatre Royal, Adelaide   *Richard III*   **Richard III**

Apr 12–17 Theatre Royal, Adelaide   *The Skin of Our Teeth*   **Mr Antrobus**
             (Only *Richard III* and *Skin of Our Teeth* play in   **& director**
               Adelaide)

Apr 19 to Princess Theatre,   *The School for Scandal*   **Sir Peter**
Jun 12   Melbourne   **Teazle**

                                     Richard III   **Richard III**
                                     The Skin of Our Teeth   **Mr Antrobus**

Jun 15–19 Theatre Royal, Hobart   *The School for Scandal*   **Sir Peter**
             (Only *School for Scandal* plays in Hobart)   **Teazle**

Jun 29   Tivoli Theatre, Sydney   *The School for Scandal*   **Sir Peter**
to Aug?   **Teazle**

                                     Richard III   **Richard III**
                                     The Skin of Our Teeth   **Mr Antrobus**

Aug to   His Majesty's Theatre, *The School for Scandal*   **Sir Peter**
Sep?   Brisbane   **Teazle**
             (Only *School for Scandal* plays in Brisbane)

Sep?   St James' Theatre,
               Auckland

Sep?   St James' Theatre,
               Christchurch

Sep?   His Majesty's Theatre,   *The School for Scandal*   **Sir Peter**
               Dunedin   **Teazle**
             (Only *School for Scandal* plays in Dunedin)

Oct?   St James' Theatre,
               Wellington

1949
Jan 20   New Theatre (74 perfs)   *The School for Scandal*   **Sir Peter**
to Jun 4   *Old Vic Company*   **Teazle &**
                                                                     director

Jan 26   New Theatre (35 perfs)   *Richard III*   **Richard III**
to Jun 2   *Old Vic Company*

Feb 2 to Jun 1	New Theatre (39 perfs) *Old Vic Company*	*The Proposal* and *Antigone*	**Director, and Chorus**
Mar 30	Lyceum Theatre (1 perf)	RADA Cabaret	**Personal appearance**
Oct 1	Aldwych Theatre	*A Streetcar Named Desire*	**Director**

1950

Jan 18 to Aug 5	St James' Theatre (229 perfs)	*Venus Observed*	**Duke of Altair & director**
Mar 13	Theatre Royal, Newcastle and tour	*The Damascus Blade*	**Director**
Jun 12	Royal, Lyceum Theatre, Edinburgh	*Captain Carvallo*	**Director**
Aug 9	Garrick Theatre	*Captain Carvallo*	**Director**

1951

Apr 24–28	Opera House, Manchester *Pre-London tour* (7 perfs)	*Caesar and Cleopatra*	**Caesar**
May 1–6	Opera House, Manchester *Pre-London tour* (7 perfs)	*Antony and Cleopatra*	**Antony**
May 10 to Sep 21	St James' Theatre (77 perfs)	*Caesar and Cleopatra*	**Caesar**
May 11 to Sep 22	St James' Theatre (76 perfs)	*Antony and Cleopatra*	**Antony**
Jun 25	London Palladium (1 perf)	The Sid Field Tribute	**Appeared in 'Sit Round'**
Jul 9	Theatre Royal, Drury Lane (1 perf)	Late Night Theatre	**Introduced scene from School for Scandal**
Nov 13–17	Royal Court, Liverpool (7 perfs)	*Caesar and Cleopatra*	**Caesar**
Nov 20–24	Royal Court, Liverpool (7 perfs)	*Antony and Cleopatra*	**Antony**
Dec 19 to Apr 11, 1952	Ziegfeld Theatre, New York (67 perfs)	*Caesar and Cleopatra*	**Caesar**

Dec 20 to Apr 12, 1952	Ziegfeld Theatre, New York (66 perfs)	*Antony and Cleopatra*	**Antony**

1952

Feb 13	New Century Theatre, New York	*Venus Observed*	**Director**
Oct 27	Empire Theatre Royal Film Performance	Stage version of excerpt from *Lady Hamilton*	**Nelson**

1953

Sep 28 to Oct 3	Opera House, Manchester *Pre-London tour* (8 perfs)	*The Sleeping Prince*	**Grand Duke & director**
Oct 5–10	King's Theatre, Glasgow *Pre-London tour* (8 perfs)	*The Sleeping Prince*	**Grand Duke & director**
Oct 12–17	King's Theatre, Edinburgh *Pre-London tour* (8 perfs)	*The Sleeping Prince*	**Grand Duke & director**
Oct 19–24	Theatre Royal, Newcastle *Pre-London tour* (8 perfs)	*The Sleeping Prince*	**Grand Duke & director**
Nov 5 to to Jul 3, 1954	Phoenix Theatre (274 perfs)	*The Sleeping Prince*	**Grand Duke & director**
Nov 17	Theatre Royal, Drury Lane (1 perf)	Midnight matinée for Greek Earthquake Victims	**Spoke Prologue by Christopher Hassall**

1954

Mar 18	London Palladium (1 perf only)	*Midnight Cavalcade*	**Appeared with Jack Buchanan**
May 31	Her Majesty's Theatre (1 perf)	All Star RADA Jubilee Matinée	**Epilogue to Henry VIII**
Jun 24	London Palladium (1 perf)	Night of a Hundred Stars	**Appeared with Jack Buchanan**

1955

Apr 12 to Nov 26	Shakespeare Memorial Theatre, Stratford-upon-Avon (81 perfs)	*Twelfth Night*	**Malvolio**
Jun 7 to Nov 23	Shakespeare Memorial Theatre, Stratford-upon-Avon (56 perfs)	*Macbeth*	**Macbeth**
Jun 23	London Palladium (1 perf)	Night of A Hundred Stars	**Juvenile Delinquent**
Aug 16 to Nov 25	Shakespeare Memorial Theatre, Stratford-upon-Avon (29 perfs)	*Titus Andronicus*	**Titus Andronicus**

1956

Mar 5	London Coliseum (1 perf)	*Green Room Cavalade*	**Sir Peter Teazle**
Jun 28	London Palladium (1 perf)	Night of a Hundred Stars	**White Tie and Tails**
Nov 25	Saville Theatre (1 perf)	Central School Jubilee	**Edwardian soirée guest**
Dec 18	Royal Festival Hall	Evening for Hungary Relief	**Speaker**

1957

Apr 10 to May 11	Royal Court Theatre (36 perfs)	*The Entertainer*	**Archie Rice**

Tour of Shakespeare Memorial Theatre Company in *Titus Andronicus*, to Paris and behind Iron Curtain

May 15–25	Théâtre des Nations, Paris (10 perfs)	*Titus Andronicus*	**Titus Andronicus**
May 28–30	La Fenice, Venice (3 perfs)	*Titus Andronicus*	**Titus Andronicus**
Jun 2–4	National Theatre, Belgrade (3 perfs)	*Titus Andronicus*	**Titus Andronicus**
Jun 7–8	National Theatre, Zagreb (2 perfs)	*Titus Andronicus*	**Titus Andronicus**
Jun 12–15	Burgtheater, Vienna (4 perfs)	*Titus Andronicus*	**Titus Andronicus**
Jun 18–21	National Theatre, Warsaw (4 perfs)	*Titus Andronicus*	**Titus Andronicus**

Jul 1 to Aug 3	Stoll Theatre, London (35 perfs)	*Titus Andronicus*	**Titus Andronicus**
Aug 6	Greenwich Royal Naval College	*Son et Lumière*	**Duke of Gloucester**
Sep 10 to Jan 18, 1958	Palace Theatre (116 perfs)	*The Entertainer*	**Archie Rice**
Nov 11–16	King's Theatre, Edinburgh (8 perfs)	*The Entertainer*	**Archie Rice**
Nov 18–23	New Theatre, Oxford (8 perfs)	*The Entertainer*	**Archie Rice**
Nov 25–30	Hippodrome, Brighton (8 perfs)	*The Entertainer*	**Archie Rice**

1958

Feb 12 to May 10	Royale Theatre, New York (97 perfs)	*The Entertainer*	**Archie Rice**
Jul 24	London Palladium (1 perf)	Night of A Hundred Stars	**'Be a Clown'**

1959

Jul 7 to Nov 27	Shakespeare Memorial Theatre, Stratford-upon-Avon (48 perfs)	*Coriolanus*	**Coriolanus**
Jul 23	London Palladium (1 perf)	Night of A Hundred Stars	**Archie Rice scene**
Dec 15	Lyric Theatre (1 perf)	Gala for Fréjus disaster victims	**Speaker**

1960

Feb 1	Shubert Theatre, Boston	*The Tumbler*	**Director**
Feb 24	Helen Hayes Theatre, New York	*The Tumbler*	**Director**
Apr 28 to Jun 4	Royal Court Theatre	*Rhinoceros*	**Berenger**
Jun 8 to Jul 30	Strand Theatre (Total 105 perfs)	*Rhinoceros*	**Berenger**
Jul 21	London Palladium (1 perf)	Night of A Hundred Stars	**Grace Hubbard**
Oct 5 to Mar 25, 1961	St James Theatre, New York (193 perfs)	*Becket*	**Becket**

1961

Mar 29	Colonial Theatre, Boston	*Becket*	**Henry II**
Apr 24	O'Keefe Centre, Toronto	*Becket*	**Henry II**
	(On tour ending at Shubert Theatre, Philadelphia on May 6, 1961)		
May 8, for 3 weeks	Hudson Theatre, New York	*Becket*	**Henry II**

1962

Jul 3	Chichester Festival Theatre	*The Chances*	**Director**
Jul 9 to Sep 8	Chichester Festival Theatre (28 perfs)	*The Broken Heart*	**Bassanes & director**
Jul 16 to Sep 8	Chichester Festival Theatre (28 perfs)	*Uncle Vanya*	**Astrov & director**
Nov 19–24	King's Theatre, Edinburgh *Pre-London tour* (8 perfs)	*Semi-Detached*	**Fred Midway**
Nov 26 to Dec 1	New Theatre, Oxford *Pre-London tour* (8 perfs)	*Semi-Detached*	**Fred Midway**
Dec 5 to Mar 30, 1963	Saville Theatre (137 perfs)	*Semi-Detached*	**Fred Midway**

1963

Jul to Aug 31	Chichester Festival Theatre (28 perfs)	*Uncle Vanya*	**Astrov & director**
Jul 18	London Palladium (1 perf)	Night of A Hundred Stars	**Host**
Oct 22 to Dec 4	Old Vic Theatre (First *National Theatre Company* production; 27 perfs)	*Hamlet*	**Director**
Nov 19 to Aug 1, 1964	Old Vic Theatre (61 perfs) *National Theatre Company*	*Uncle Vanya*	**Astrov & director**
Dec 10 to Dec 12, 1964	Old Vic Theatre (69 perfs) *National Theatre Company*	*The Recruiting Officer*	**Captain Brazen**

1964

Feb 4; 1967	(105 perfs) *National Theatre Company*

Mar 23–26	Theatre Royal, Newcastle *National Theatre Company*	*Uncle Vanya*	**Astrov & director**
Mar 30	King's Theatre, Edinburgh *National Theatre Company*	*Uncle Vanya*	**Astrov & director**
Apr 6–8	Alexandra Theatre, Birmingham (3 perfs) *National Theatre Company*	*Othello*	**Othello**
Apr 23 to Jun 2	Old Vic Theatre Kodak House, Kingsway, London	*Othello* *Shakespeare – All The Plays In Pictures*, by Angus McBean	**Othello** **Opened exhibition**
Jul 21 to Aug 29	Chichester Festival Theatre *National Theatre Company*	*Othello*	**Othello**
Jul 23	London Palladium (1 perf)	Night of A Hundred Stars	**Speaker**
Oct 23–24	Opera House, Manchester (3 perfs) *National Theatre Company*	*The Master Builder*	**Halvard Solness**
Oct 26–29	Grand Theatre, Leeds (5 perfs) *National Theatre Company*	*The Master Builder*	**Halvard Solness**
Nov 10–12	New Theatre, Oxford (4 perfs) *National Theatre Company*	*The Master Builder*	**Halvard Solness**
Nov 17 to Jul 9, 1965	Old Vic Theatre (73 perfs) *National Theatre Company*	*The Master Builder*	**Halvard Solness**

1965

Jan 19 to Mar 4, 1966	Old Vic Theatre (53 perfs) *National Theatre Company*	*The Crucible*	**Director**
Feb 13	Royal Albert Hall (1 perf)	*Carnival of the Animals*	**Narrator**
Mar 12–13	King's Theatre, Glasgow (3 perfs) *National Theatre Company*	*The Master Builder*	**Halvard Solness**

Mar 19–20	Coventry Theatre (3 perfs) *National Theatre Company*	*The Master Builder*	**Halvard Solness**
Sep 7	Kremlevsky Theatre, Moscow *National Theatre Company*	*Othello*	**Othello**
Sep 9	Kremlevsky Theatre, Moscow *National Theatre Company*	*Love for Love*	**Tattle**
Sep 25	Freie Volksbühne, Berlin *National Theatre Company*	*Othello*	**Othello**
Sep 27	Freie Volksbühne, Berlin *National Theatre Company*	*Love for Love*	**Tattle**
Oct 20 to Jun 9, 1967	Old Vic Theatre (97 perfs) *National Theatre Company*	*Love for Love*	**Tattle**
Nov 22–23	King's Theatre, Edinburgh *National Theatre Company*	*Othello*	**Othello**
Nov 24–27	King's Theatre, Edinburgh *National Theatre Company*	*Love for Love*	**Tattle**
Nov 29–30	Theatre Royal, Newcastle *National Theatre Company*	*Othello*	**Othello**

1966

Apr 26 to Oct 8	Old Vic Theatre (61 perfs) *National Theatre Company*	*Juno and the Paycock*	**Director**
Jun 13 (1 perf only?)	Old Vic Theatre (1 perf)	Performance in aid of George Devine Award	**Appeared in** *The Kitchen* **and as Archie Rice**
Sep 12 to Oct 3	Queen's Theatre *National Theatre Company*	*Othello*	**Othello**
Dec 2–3	Shakespeare Memorial Theatre, Stratford-upon-Avon *National Theatre Company*	*Love for Love*	**Tattle**

1967

Jan ?	Theatre Royal, Haymarket (1 perf)	*Italy, My Italy*	**Spoke prologue by C. Day Lewis**
Feb 21 to July 25, 1969	Old Vic Theatre (108 perfs in all) *National Theatre Company*	*The Dance of Death*	**Edgar**
Apr 17–20	Theatre Royal, Brighton *National Theatre Company*	*The Dance of Death*	**Edgar**
May 8–11	Royal Court Theatre, Liverpool *National Theatre Company*	*The Dance of Death*	**Edgar**
Jul 4	Old Vic Theatre *National Theatre Company*	*The Three Sisters*	**Director**
Sep 6 to Jul 24, 1969	Old Vic Theatre (30+ perfs) *National Theatre Company*	*A Flea In Her Ear*	**Etienne Plucheux**

October and November: National Theatre Company tour of Canada

Oct 18–26	Théâtre Maisonneuve, Montreal	*The Dance of Death*	**Edgar**
Oct 19–28	Théâtre Maisonneuve, Montreal	*Love for Love*	**Tattle**
Oct 21–27	Théâtre Maisonneuve, Montreal	*A Flea In Her Ear*	**Etienne Plucheux**
Oct 30 to Nov 7	O'Keefe Centre, Toronto	*The Dance of Death*	**Edgar**
Oct 31 to Nov 10	O'Keefe Centre, Toronto	*A Flea In Her Ear*	**Etienne Plucheux**
Nov 3–11	O'Keefe Centre, Toronto	*Love for Love*	**Tattle**

1968

Feb 22–24	King's Theatre, Edinburgh *National Theatre Company* (because of illness was replaced by Lewis Jones)	*The Dance of Death*	**Edgar**
Mar 4–9	New Theatre, Oxford *National Theatre Company* (because of illness was replaced by Lewis Jones)	*The Dance of Death*	**Edgar**
Sep 16 to Mar 21, 1969	Old Vic Theatre (47 perfs) *National Theatre Company*	*The Advertisement*	**Co-director with Donald MacKechnie**

| Dec 19 to May 22, 1970 | Old Vic Theatre (66 perfs) *National Theatre Company* | *Love's Labour's Lost* | **Director** |

1969

Mar 7–8	Theatre Royal, Norwich *National Theatre Company*	*Home and Beauty*	**A.B. Raham**
Mar 14–15	Alhambra Theatre, Bradford	*Home and Beauty*	**A.B. Raham**
Mar 22	Theatre Royal, Nottingham	*Home and Beauty*	**A.B. Raham**
Apr 8 to July 6, 1970	Old Vic Theatre (89 perfs in all)	*Home and Beauty*	**A.B. Raham**

1970

Apr 10	Old Vic Theatre *National Theatre Company*	*The Three Sisters*	**Chebutikin & director**
Sep 29 to Oct 1	Theatre Royal, Brighton *National Theatre Company*	*The Three Sisters*	**Chebutikin & director**
Apr 28 to Jan 8, 1972	Old Vic Theatre (138 perfs in all) *National Theatre Company*	*The Merchant of Venice*	**Shylock**
Jun 8 to Aug 1	Cambridge Theatre *National Theatre Company*	*The Merchant of Venice*	**Shylock**

1971

May 3–8	King's Theatre, Edinburgh *National Theatre Company*	*The Merchant of Venice*	**Shylock**
Jun 25 to Nov 8	New Theatre (54 perfs) *National Theatre Company*	*Amphitryon 38*	**Director**
Sep 27	St Paul's Church, Covent Garden	A celebration in memory of Michel Saint-Denis	**Reader**
Dec 14 to Sep 8, 1972	New Theatre *National Theatre Company*	*Long Day's Journey Into Night*	**James Tyrone**

1972

| Aug 23 | Old Vic Theatre (122 perfs in all) National Theatre Company | *Long Day's Journey Into Night* | **James Tyrone** |

| Oct 29 | Theatre Royal, Haymarket (1 perf) | *Sybil* | **Reader** |

1973

| Jan 3 | Royal Opera House, Covent Garden (1 perf) | Fanfare | **Reader** |

| Jan 6 | Old Vic Theatre National Theatre Company | *Twelfth Night* | **Speaker, Prologue** |

| Mar 4 | Yvonne Arnaud Theatre, Guildford | Gala Performance | **Appearance** |

| Oct 25 to Feb 16, 1974 | Old Vic Theatre (42 perfs) National Theatre Company | *Saturday, Sunday, Monday* | **Antonio** |

| Dec 18 to Mar 21, 1974 | Old Vic Theatre (36 perfs) National Theatre Company | *The Party* | **John Tagg** |

(Olivier's last appearance in a play on any stage.)

1974

| Apr 4 | Old Vic Theatre National Theatre Company | *Eden End* | **Director** |

| May 6 | Old Vic Theatre | *Tribute to the Lady* Gala evening for Lilian Baylis centenary | **Narrator** |

1976

| Oct 25 | Olivier Theatre | Royal Opening by the Queen | **Speech of welcome** |

(Olivier's only appearance on stage in the new National on the South Bank)

1980

| Feb 10 | St James Theatre, New York | *Filumena* | **Director** |

(The last play Olivier directed, and the last stage work he did in America or anywhere)

1982

| Jul 18 | London Coliseum (1 perf) | Gala for South Atlantic Fund | **Salutes Falklands Task Force** |

1983

| Nov 8 | Old Vic | *Blondel* (Gala Performance) | **Spoke Prologue** |

1985

Feb 17	Radio City Music Hall, New York	Night of A Hundred Stars	**Personal appearance**
Mar 25	Dorothy Chandler Pavilion, Los Angeles	57th Annual Academy Awards	**Presents Oscar**
May 14	Lyric Theatre	Bob Hope Birthday Gala	**Personal appearance**

1986

| Apr 9 | Dominion Theatre | *Time* | **Akash (as hologram)** |

CHRONOLOGY OF OLIVIER'S FILMS

THIS IS A COMPLETE list, but makes no attempt at detailed descriptions. The best and most comprehensive account of Olivier's films is in *The Complete Films of Laurence Olivier* by Jerry Vermilye, London and New York, 1992. The dates given are, except where otherwise specified, those of a film's release. Directors, producers, and other actors in a film are named only when they were then, or afterwards became, notable.

1930 *The Temporary Widow.* In US as *Murder for Sale*, in Germany as *Hokuspocus*. LO as a young painter. Shot in Berlin in English and German versions, LO in the English version only.

1930 *Too Many Crooks.* A half-hour quota quickie. LO as a dinner-jacketed playboy impersonating a burglar.

1931 *Potiphar's Wife.* In US as *Her Strange Desire*. LO as chauffeur framed by lustful and titled female employer.

1931 *Friends and Lovers.* LO as Indian army lieutenant in solar topee. His first Hollywood film, for RKO, with Adolphe Menjou and Erich von Stroheim.

1931 *The Yellow Ticket.* Fox. LO as English journalist in Czarist Russia, with Elissa Landi, Lionel Barrymore and Boris Karloff.

1932 *Westward Passage.* RKO. LO as novelist who elopes with Ann Harding. His last Hollywood film until 1938.

1933 *Perfect Understanding.* United Artists. Filmed in England but partly set on the French Riviera. LO as man-about-town who marries Gloria Swanson, who starred and produced.

1933 *No Funny Business.* In US as *Professional Co-Respondents*. United Artists. Filmed in England. More French Riviera, with Gertrude Lawrence and Jill Esmond.

1935 *Moscow Nights.* In US as *I Stand Condemned*. LO's first Korda film. Director Anthony Asquith. LO as Czarist captain, with Penelope Dudley Ward and Athene Seyler.

1935 *Conquest of the Air.* Korda. Hour-long drama-history of flight, with LO in bit-part as the eighteenth-century balloonist Lunardi. Not shown until 1940.

1936 *As You Like It.* LO's first Shakespeare film, as Orlando opposite Elisabeth

Bergner's Rosalind. Her husband Paul Czinner directed and produced. With Henry Ainley.

1937 *Fire Over England.* Korda epic. Spanish Armada drama with Flora Robson as Elizabeth I and Vivien Leigh as lady-in-waiting.

1937 *21 Days.* In US as *21 Days Together.* Korda. Director Basil Dean. With Vivien Leigh. After play by Galsworthy, screenplay by Graham Greene, but dreadful and not released until 1940.

1938 *The Divorce of Lady X.* Korda. LO's first colour film. LO as barrister, with Merle Oberon and Ralph Richardson.

1939 *Q Planes.* In US as *Clouds Over Europe.* Korda. LO as pilot and Richardson as detective in spy drama.

1939 *Wuthering Heights.* Back to Hollywood. United Artists. Sam Goldwyn producer, William Wyler director. LO as Heathcliff, Merle Oberon as Cathie.

1940 *Rebecca.* Producer Selznick, director Hitchcock, after Daphne du Maurier's novel. LO as Maxim de Winter, opposite Joan Fontaine.

1940 *Pride and Prejudice.* MGM. LO as Darcy, Greer Garson as Elizabeth Bennet.

1941 *Lady Hamilton.* In US as *That Hamilton Woman.* Korda produced and directed in Hollywood. LO as Nelson, Vivien Leigh as Emma Hamilton, Gladys Cooper as Fanny Nelson.

1941 *49th Parallel.* In US as *The Invaders.* Filmed mostly in England by Michael Powell. LO as Canadian trapper. With Leslie Howard, Eric Portman.

1943 *The Demi Paradise.* In US as *Adventure for Two.* Director Anthony Asquith. LO as Russian engineer in wartime England.

1944 *Henry V.* Two Cities/Rank. Directed by LO, produced by LO and Filippo del Giudice. Music William Walton. LO as Henry, with Robert Newton, Renee Asherson, Leo Genn, Robert Helpmann, George Robey. LO's first Oscar, for 'outstanding achievement as actor, director, and producer'.

1948. *Hamlet.* Two Cities/Rank. Directed by LO, produced by LO and Filipo del Giudice. Music William Walton. LO as Hamlet, with Eileen Herlie, Jean Simmons, Norman Wooland, Felix Aylmer, Anthony Quayle. LO's second Oscar, for Best Actor. Also Oscar for Best Film.

1951 *The Magic Box.* Director John Boulting. LO has two-minute supporting part as policeman in story of William Friese-Greene, played by Robert Donat.

1952 *Carrie.* Paramount. Director and producer William Wyler. LO, in his postwar return to Holywood, plays Hurstwood in this adaptation of Dreiser's novel. With Jennifer Jones.

1953 *A Queen is Crowned.* Rank. LO spoke Christopher Fry's narration in this documentary of the Queen's coronation.

1953 *The Beggar's Opera.* Director Peter Brook. LO co-produced with Herbert Wilcox and played the highwayman Macheath in this adapatation of Gay's musical of 1728. With Stanley Holloway, Dorothy Tutin, Athene Seyler, George Devine.

1955 *Richard III.* London Films. The third and last of LO's big Shakespeare films, which he directed and, with Korda, co-produced. Music William Walton. LO as Richard, with John Gielgud, Ralph Richardson, Claire Bloom, Norman Wooland.

1956. *The Prince and the Showgirl.* Marilyn Monroe's money, producer and director LO. LO as the regent, Monroe as the showgirl, with Sybil Thorndike, Richard Wattis.

1959 *The Devil's Disciple.* LO as General Burgoyne, with Burt Lancaster and Kirk Douglas, in adaptation of Shaw play on American War of Independence.

1960 *Spartacus.* Universal. Director Stanley Kubrick. LO as Roman General Crassus in Hollywood epic with Kirk Douglas as Spartacus, Jean Simmons, Tony Curtis.

1960 *The Entertainer.* Woodfall. Director Tony Richardson. Adaptation of Osborne's stage play, with LO as Archie Rice, Joan Plowright, Alan Bates, Shirley Ann Field.

1962 *Term of Trial.* Warner Pathe, filmed in Ireland and Paris. Director Peter Glenville. LO as schoolmaster falsely accused by schoolgirl. Simone Signoret, Sarah Miles.

1965 *Bunny Lake is Missing.* Columbia. Filmed in England. Director-producer Otto Preminger. LO as police inspector in case of missing child. Martita Hunt, Adrienne Corri, Noel Coward.

1965 *Othello.* Eagle Lion. Director Stuart Burge. Studio film of National Theatre stage production, with Frank Finlay, Maggie Smith, Derek Jacobi.

1966 *Khartoum.* United Artists. LO as the Mahdi in Sudan war of 1884, with Charlton Heston as General Gordon, Richard Johnson, Ralph Richardson.

1968 *The Shoes of the Fisherman.* MGM. LO as Russian prime minister, with Anthony Quinn as Russian pope.

1968 *Romeo and Juliet.* Paramount. Directed by Franco Zeffirelli. LO speaks prologue and epilogue.

1969 *Oh! What a Lovely War.* Paramount. Director Richard Attenborough. LO as General Sir John French in adaptation of Joan Littlewood's Great War musical, with John Mills, Dirk Bogarde, Jack Hawkins, Maggie Smith and cast of thousands.

1969 *The Battle of Britain.* United Artists. LO as Dowding, head of Fighter Command in 1940, with Trevor Howard, Michael Redgrave, Ralph Richardson, Susannah York, Kenneth More.

1969 *The Dance of Death.* Paramount. LO as Edgar in film version of the National Theatre stage production of Strindberg's play, with Geraldine McEwan.

1970 *The Three Sisters.* LO as director and as Chebutikin in film version of the National Theatre production of Checkhov's play, with Joan Plowright, Louise Purnell, Derek Jacobi, Ronald Pickup, Alan Bates.

1970 *Nicholas and Alexandra.* Columbia. Producer Sam Spiegel. LO as the Czar's first minister, with Michael Redgrave, Jack Hawkins, and Tom Baker as Rasputin.

1972 *Lady Caroline Lamb.* United Artists. Director and screenwriter Robert Bolt. LO as Duke of Wellington, with Sarah Miles, Pamela Brown, Ralph Richardson.

1972 *Sleuth.* 20th Century Fox. Director Joseph I. Mankiewicz. LO's first attempt to return to a leading part in feature films after the National Theatre, with Michael Caine.

1976 *Marathon Man.* Paramount. Director John Schlesinger. LO, in his first film after his 1974 illness, plays a sadistic Nazi, with Dustin Hoffman.

1976 *The Seven Per Cent Solution.* Universal. LO as the villain Moriarty, with Nicol Williamson as Sherlock Holmes, Vanessa Redgrave.

1977 *A Bridge Too Far.* United Artists. Director Richard Attenborough. LO as Dutch doctor in story of failed airborne landing at Arnhem in 1944, with Bogarde, Caine, Connery, Anthony Hopkins and cast of thousands.

1978 *The Gentleman Tramp.* LO as narrator in documentary biography of Charles Chaplin.

1978 *The Betsy.* Allied Artists. LO as car company mogul in adaptation of Harold Robbins novel, with Robert Duvall.

1978 *The Boys From Brazil.* 20th Century Fox. LO as Simon Wiesenthal figure, with Gregory Peck as war criminal Josef Mengele. Special Oscar to LO for 'the unique achievements of his entire career'.

1979 *A Little Romance.* Orion-Warner. LO as Maurice Chevalier figure in charming comedy. Shot in Paris and Venice.

1979 *Dracula.* Universal. Shot in Cornwall. LO as Dutch doctor who drives stake through Dracula's heart.

1980 *The Jazz Singer.* LO as Cantor to Neil Diamond's jazz singer in a remake of the first talkie which started Al Jolson. A film LO loathed.

1981 *Inchon.* Produced with the Moonies' money. Director Terence Young. LO as General MacArthur in Korean war drama. Shown briefly in US, but never in Britain.

1981 *The Clash of the Titans.* MGM. LO as Zeus, surrounded by Claire Bloom, Maggie Smith, Ursula Andress, and Susan Fleetwood as Greek goddesses.

1984 *The Bounty.* Orion, LO as Admiral Lord Hood in second remake of the mutiny story, with Anthony Hopkins as Bligh.

1984 *The Jigsaw Man.* LO as head of MI6 in spy thriller with Michael Caine.

1985 *Wild Geese II.* Thorn-EMI. LO as Rudolf Hess in his last feature film which, like his first, back in 1930, was shot in Berlin.

1989 *War Requiem.* BBC. Not really a film – no dialogue, no plot – but rather a sequence of images set to Benjamin Britten's *War Requiem.*

CHRONOLOGY OF OLIVIER'S
WORK IN TELEVISION

FOR MANY YEARS OLIVIER resisted offers to work in television. In 1952 in New York he declined an offer to record passages from Shakespeare's *Antony and Cleopatra* and Shaw's *Caesar and Cleopatra*, which he was presenting on Broadway, in spite of NBC's assurances that a television revolution was coming and that he would reach an audience of 30 million. He bitterly opposed the first showing of his feature film of *Richard III* on American television rather than in cinemas, even though it did reach an audience of 15–20 million coast to coast on one night in March 1956, and NBC paid a fee of $500,000. His first attempt at a play on English television – Ibsen's *John Gabriel Borkman* – disappointed him, but then in the late 1950s, needing the money, he did two highly successful teleplays for US television: adaptations of Somerset Maugham's novel *The Moon and Sixpence* and of Graham Greene's *The Power and the Glory*. Each won him an Emmy, and his performance as the whisky priest in the second bears comparison with any of his theatre or film roles. Later, after his near-fatal illness of 1974, the series he did for Granada Television, Manchester, gave him something to live for, and in his later work for that company – as Lear and as Lord Marchmain in the miniseries of *Brideshead Revisited* – he gave performances which are among his most famous in any medium. The dates, unless otherwise stated, are those of first showing.

1938 *Macbeth*. Excerpts shown by BBC TV from the 1937 Old Vic production, with LO as Macbeth and the American Judith Anderson as Lady Macbeth. No copy is known to exist of this early broadcast, which is mentioned only by Jerry Vermilye in his *Complete Films of Laurence Olivier*, who says Lilian Baylis was paid £75 for everything – actors, props and costumes.

1958 *John Gabriel Borkman*. ATV adaptation of Ibsen's play. LO in name part, with Irene Worth, Pamela Brown, Maxine Audley.

1959 *The Moon and Sixpence*, after Maugham. NBC, producer David Susskind. LO as Charles Strickland, with Jessica Tandy, Hume Cronyn. LO won an Emmy.

1961 *The Power and the Glory*, after Graham Greene. CBS, producer David Susskind. LO as priest, with George C Scott, Julie Harris, Cyril Cusack. LO won second Emmy.

1963 *Uncle Vanya.* British Home Entertainments, director Stuart Burge. Adapted from Chichester stage production, with LO as Astrov, Michael Redgrave as Vanya, Joan Plowright as Sonya, Rosemary Harris, Sybil Thorndike. Shown as feature film in US.

1969 *Male of the Species.* ATV-NBC. Three short stories, with LO as narrator, Sean Connery, Michael Caine, Anna Calder-Marshall.

1969 *David Copperfield,* after Dickens. NBC. LO as Creakle, with Edith Evans, Ralph Richardson, Susan Hampshire.

1973 *Long Day's Journey into Night.* ABC, directed by Peter Wood. Based on Michael Blakemore's National Theatre production. LO as Tyrone, with Constance Cummings, Denis Quilley, Ronald Pickup.

1973 *The World at War.* Thames, producer Jeremy Isaacs. LO as narrator in twenty-six-part documentary series on World War II.

1973 *The Merchant of Venice.* ABC, director Jonathan Miller. Adaptation of National Theatre production, with LO and Joan Plowright.

1973 *Love Among the Ruins.* ABC (US), director George Cukor. Edwardian romantic comedy, with LO and Katharine Hepburn, who both won an Emmy. This was Olivier's third.

1976–77 Six modern plays for Granada in a series entitled 'Laurence Olivier Presents'. All were produced by LO, and the co-producer in all but one was Derek Granger.

> *The Collection,* Harold Pinter. LO with Alan Bates and Helen Mirren.

> *Cat on a Hot Tin Roof,* Tennessee Williams. LO as Big Daddy, with Natalie Wood.

> *Hindle Wakes,* Stanley Houghton. LO did not appear, but directed.

> *Come Back, Little Sheba,* William Inge. LO with Joanne Woodward.

> *Daphne Laureola,* James Bridie. LO with Joan Plowright.

> *Saturday, Sunday, Monday,* Eduardo de Filipo. LO with Joan Plowright.

1977 *Jesus of Nazareth.* Produced by Lew Grade with RAI (Italy), director Franco Zeffirelli. Eight-hour miniseries with LO as Nicodemus, Robert Powell, Ernest Borgnine, James Mason and cast of thousands.

1981 *Brideshead Revisited.* Granada, WNET, producer Derek Granger. Thirteen-part miniseries, adapted by John Mortimer from Evelyn Waugh's novel. LO as Lord Marchmain, with Jeremy Irons, Anthony Andrews, Diana Quick, Claire Bloom, John Gielgud.

1981 *Wagner.* Anglo-German-Hungarian-produced miniseries. Richard Burton as Wagner, with LO, Gielgud and Richardson in cameo parts.

1982 *A Voyage Around My Father.* Thames, adapted by John Mortimer from his novel. LO as the father, with Alan Bates, Jane Asher.

1983 *King Lear.* Granada, producer David Plowright, director Michael Elliott.

With John Hurt, Anna Calder-Marshall, Diana Rigg, Dorothy Tutin, Colin Blakely, Leo McKern.

1983 *Mr Halpern and Mr Johnson.* HBO. LO and Jackie Gleason.

1983 *A Talent for Murder.* BBC. Comedy-mystery. LO with Angela Lansbury.

1984 *The Ebony Tower.* Granada, adapted by John Mortimer from John Fowles's novella. LO as lustfully ancient artist, with Greta Scacchi, Toyah Wilcox. LO's last full-length role in any medium.

1984 *The Last Days of Pompeii.* Columbia TV-RAI. Miniseries after Bulwer Lytton's novel. LO as Gaius.

1986 *Peter the Great.* NBC miniseries. LO as King William III, with Trevor Howard, Maximilian Schell, Omar Sharif, Vanessa Redgrave.

1986 *Lost Empires.* Granada miniseries, adapted from J.B. Priestley's novel. The lost empires are music halls. LO as Richard Burrard is an older version of Archie Rice.

INDEX

A NOTE ON THE AUTHOR

Terry Coleman is an historian and journalist. As a roving correspondent for the *Guardian* and other papers he reported from seventy countries, interviewed the last eight British prime ministers, and was named Journalist of the Year. He is the author of *Passage to America*, a history of nineteenth-century emigration, and of historical novels set in early Australia, seventeenth-century New England, and the Texas Republic. He has also written biographies of Thomas Hardy and Horatio Nelson.